GW00632308

30130 114878860

Peace with Justice

Peace with Justice

A History of the Israeli–Palestinian
Declaration of Principles on Interim
Self-Government Arrangements

Andrew S. Buchanan

First published in Great Britain 2000 by
MACMILLAN PRESS LTD
Houndmills, Basingstoke, Hampshire RG21 6XS and London
Companies and representatives throughout the world

A catalogue record for this book is available from the British Library.

ISBN 0–333–77501–5

First published in the United States of America 2000 by
ST. MARTIN'S PRESS, LLC,
Scholarly and Reference Division,
175 Fifth Avenue, New York, N.Y. 10010

ISBN 0–312–22953–4

Library of Congress Cataloging-in-Publication Data
Buchanan, Andrew S., 1965–
Peace with justice : a history of the Israeli-Palestinian Declaration of Principles on
Interim Self-Government Arrangements / Andrew S. Buchanan.
p. cm.
Includes bibliographical references and index.
ISBN 0–312–22953–4 (cloth)
1. Israel. Treaties etc. Munaòòamat al-Taòràr al-Filasòànåyah, 1993 Sept. 13. 2.
West Bank—International status. 3. Gaza Strip—International status. 4.
Arab–Israeli conflict—1993——Peace. I. Title.

KMM707 .B83 2000
956.95'3044—dc21
                                          00–030582

This book is printed on paper suitable for recycling and made from fully managed and sustained
forest sources.

10   9   8   7   6   5   4   3   2   1
09   08   07   06   05   04   03   02   01   00

Printed and bound in Great Britain by
Antony Rowe Ltd, Chippenham, Wiltshire

Contents

v

Acknowledgements

This project would not have been possible without the support, assistance and patience of my family and friends, to whom I would like to extend my gratitude and thanks for their understanding, indulgence and endurance. I would like to thank those at the Department of International Relations, University of St Andrews, who provided invaluable advice and encouragement throughout my doctoral research, from which this work stems; a special thank you is due to Dr James Kirk of the University of Glasgow for his advice and encouragement, and to Dr Alan Hooper of the University of Hertfordshire who gave me the opportunity to put my education into practice by allowing me to teach live students.

During my doctoral research I had the opportunity to conduct fieldwork in London at the British Library, the Royal Institute for International Affairs and the United Nations office, and in Brussels at the European Commission; to staff and officials I extend my thanks. I also had the opportunity to make research trips to the United States, Israel, Hungary, Poland, Belgium and France where I was able to interview politicians, special advisers, government officials and academics; many of these interviews provided me with invaluable information and unique insights into the understanding of Middle East peace-making and its progress. To those I can mention, I owe special thanks to: in London, Dr John Levy; in Israel, Alan Baker, Deputy Legal Adviser, Ministry of Foreign Affairs, Ms Tali Semash, Academic Services Bureau, Ministry of Foreign Affairs, Mrs Margaret Crawford, Headmistress, Tabeetha School, Jaffa, Dr Dore Gold, Jaffee Centre for Strategic Studies, Tel Aviv University, Dedi Zucker MK, Dr Asher Susser, Moshe Dayan Centre for Middle Eastern and African Studies, Tel Aviv University, Dr Martin Van Creveld, Faculty of Humanities, Hebrew University, Jerusalem, Rageh Kadhoor, Kol Yisrael, Dr Ahmad Tibi, Special Adviser for President Arafat, Dr Samir Abdallah, economist and PLO adviser, Yana and Sasha Gerber; in Belgium Mr A.V. Flynn; and in the United States particular thanks to Jenny Yamine and Gena Gorospe at the World Bank, Washington DC for all their help and kindness, and Professor Rashid Khalidi of the University of Chicago. To many others unnamed who have assisted me in whatever manner, I offer my thanks.

I would also like to extend my gratitude to Janey Fisher for her indefatigable and astute editing and to Karen Brazier and all at Macmillan for their kind support. Grateful thanks are also due to Robert Douglas and the St Andrews University Access Fund, Aberdeen Endowments Fund, the Sutherland Page Trust at The Royal Bank of Scotland, the Bank of Scotland and to Fiona Risk and the Directors of the Buchanan Society, for their generosity in providing much needed financial assistance and support.

Finally, I would like to acknowledge my indebtedness for all the generous help, support and encouragement given me by my parents Andrew and Catherine, my brother Gregor, and especially my best friend, Patricia. To Patty, whom I met in St Andrews, and to our beautiful daughter, Aimée, a captive audience in her pram during long walks along the West Sands, it is because of you St Andrews will always live in my heart long after this work is complete, to you both I dedicate this work.

Introduction

Theories of international relations, conflict resolution and peace studies encompass not only those inter-state, intra-state, interpersonal, inter-ethnic, substate and state-substate relations which are peaceful, but also those that are violent. Owing to the potential for wreaking massive destruction implicit in the very notion of 'have army, will travel', the problem of violence has become central to those who study the nature of disputatious international relations *vis-à-vis* the closeness or remoteness of the subjects to a shooting war. Thus theories of unipolarity, bipolarity, multipolarity, and so on, as the most conducive structure within which to resolve conflict, are a source of disagreement among writers on the subject; examples of comprehensive frameworks with which to address most conflicts are rather limited. This study will argue that there is no single existing framework which can capture the essence of inter-ethnic conflict, as the changing nature of the political realities forces a constant realignment and reassessment of the structural configurations.[1]

Western theories of international relations, and in particular notions of conflict resolution,[2] over the past 50 years have been primarily dominated and overshadowed by the realities of Cold War logic. Thus new realities and new ways of understanding our complex, changing world since the collapse of the bipolar model or world view have to be adapted, and new ones defined. Such an exercise takes time; in essence old thinking still exists and still dominates the many players on the international scene. Since 1989–91 there has been an almost desperate attempt to make sense of the changing nature of the international system as past certainties are subsumed and overtaken so quickly by events. Old enmities still exist; they will merely reconfigure and burst forth in a different guise. For scholars of the Israeli-Palestinian conflict, the challenge ahead is how we are to understand the peace process, coming as it has in the midst of epochal change, and how we are to view a superpower-inspired and -sponsored conflict management/conflict resolution model charged with multidisciplinary and cross-cultural goals.

According to one geopolitical analysis, the occupation of the West Bank and Gaza Strip, together with Israeli control of the western part of mandatory Palestine, has created a new geopolitical historical reality, with such significant dynamics that there is no way back to the pre-1967 status quo. The State of Israel, according to this analysis, has turned from a Jewish nation-state with a relatively small Arab minority to a bi-ethnic state, and the Arab-Israel conflict has ceased to be an inter-state conflict as it was in the years 1948–67, instead reverting to an inter-community conflict as it had been under the British mandate.[3] Traditionally, in this intercommunal conflict, each of the sides has viewed itself as the sole legitimate collective in Eretz Yisrael/Palestine, seeing the ambition of the rival community as illegitimate.

How do these fundamental beliefs and objectives relate to the modern Palestinian-Israeli conflict? It has been, and will be, painful for each side to accept the consequences of its actions. The idealist is opposed by the heretic, the believer is opposed by the collaborator and the majority are trapped in the grey area between the prevailing winds. For the leaders, there have always been excuses to feed the desires for vengeance, whether for those existing in squalid refugee camps, for those landless and stateless, or for those who suffered oppression at the hands of distant persecutors now living within range of knives and Katayushas. The spiral of rejection and counter-rejection begged the questions: Was it ever thus? What has changed? 'When, for instance, will certain national traits or psychological drives find outlets in war, and when in something more peaceful?'[4]

No study of contemporary political processes can be fully comprehensive; what is excluded is sometimes more illuminating than that which is visible. Yet to have the responsibility to account for all tends to dampen enthusiasm, particularly when so much vital information is held in secret. However, we can still undertake a significant analysis of the Israeli-Palestinian peace process, as much important and relevant information is already in the public domain. In order to circumvent the secretive nature of international diplomacy, this study will focus on the primary written document that binds the parties together, namely the Declaration of Principles on Interim Self-Government Arrangements, or DoP. As the basis for the legal framework developing Israeli-Palestinian peace, this document and subsequent documents stemming from it form the central authority for the peace-making initiative. This document is the foundation stone for the peace-making process and, as such, is the most important reference in the peace-building initiative. By augmenting a thorough analysis of the document itself with the memoirs, autobiographies and biographies of principal figures involved in the political process – and combining these with political commentaries, interviews with key individuals, journal, newspaper articles and editorials – we can construct a full analysis and evaluation of the peace process. When political processes that involve the lives of millions of people are conducted in secret, what is publicly transmitted, either in the form of agreed documentation or in public statements becomes all the more significant, particularly in the subsequent political effort to marshal public support for any such agreements made. Thus, armed with an understanding of the intent behind the peace initiative, we can assess and define the DoP in terms of its success or failure as a vehicle for achieving a definable 'peace' between the Israelis and Palestinians, and its potential in signalling the way forward for any future 'peace processes' within the Arab-Israeli conflict.

How inter-communal events are defined and reacted to, and how ways are found to adapt is the basis of history, and more particularly, of international relations. At the very heart of the current Israeli-Palestinian conflict lie powerful, long-cherished and one-sided perceptions of the nature of the struggle. The process of understanding actions and reactions, fears and transgressions begins with the unravelling and re-evaluation of the prejudices of the past. Acknowledging injustices committed and tortured paths followed is concomitant with being able to measure and understand decisions made, and yet to be made. Any such discourse must present a formidable challenge to the pervasive influence of traditional historiography, and as a consequence evaluate and expose popular myths and common misperceptions.

If we wish to achieve any understanding of the nature of the Arab-Israeli relationship, we must concentrate on the most contentious and yet central issue, which is the Israeli-Palestinian conflict. Although the Middle East peace process launched in Madrid in 1991 is an inter-state affair, in essence,

the crux and the kernel of the Arab-Israeli conflict is the Palestine problem. The crux and the kernel of the Palestine problem is the struggle between two national movements: on the one hand, the Zionist movement (and since 1948, its embodiment, Israel), and on the other, the Palestine national movement. The crux and the kernel of this struggle has been, and continues to this day to be, the issue of the control or sharing of the land of Palestine.[5]

Alternatively,

> we must start with fundamentals – beyond theory, beyond ideology, even beyond faith. In relation to this country we call 'Eretz Israel' and they call 'Palestine', two peoples are in existence, each of them deeply conscious in their mind – and feeling in their bones – that this country is their country. And history cannot be amended or corrected. From this terrible situation, there is one of only two possible results and there is no third . . . One of these two peoples conquers and occupies the other country and deprives the other people of the right of national independence. The Arabs tried to do this in 1948 and they lost. But since 1967 we [Israel] have done this – and this situation has brought about all the contemporary horrors. The domination of the state of Israel over another people can be maintained only by violence. The only alternative is partition. Both parties will have to renounce a claim to the entire country. Partition is technically very difficult, but psychologically it's even more difficult – because both peoples have a very deep consciousness that this country is their country.[6]

However, the conflict to date is more succinctly encapsulated, albeit somewhat cynically, by a former Israeli MK, 'when nations are in dispute they go to the high court of nations, which is war. And they lost all the wars.'[7]

Thus whether the development of history is evolutionary, epochal or merely the propagation of propaganda, the antagonisms of nations or peoples is the life blood of international relations. Therefore the Israeli-Palestinian conflict is not a morality play, not a conflict between good and evil. It is a conflict between competing claims and competing justices, affirmation and denial. Reclamation of ancient archetypes with the intent to create meaning for the living, whether as an attempt to explain and therefore make sense of traumatic events, or to use collective memory as a form of affirmation of racial identity, is a thread which can be traced through the annals of almost all races of the earth. If one perceives human history as a series of calamities linked by islands of blessed but limited peacefulness, the power of collective memory in this sense is a form of active resistance. The histories of the Jews and the Palestinians are not only symbolically but intuitively bound together. The most basic controversy, the epicentre of this unfolding drama, has been the question of legitimacy. The connections both ancient and modern between Israelis and Palestinians are to be found not far from the surface of contemporary power politics. Comparisons revolve around legitimacy and the ennobling of past and present suffering. Primarily, comparisons made in the political arena for purely expedient political purposes seek to promote partisanship on one side and to subvert and delegitimize on the other. The images of suffering, both ancient and modern, represent an intuitive link, locking the two communities, Israeli and Palestinian, together in an intimate bond of suffering. Thus the demand for the achievement of goals, which by their very nature are absolute, tenders the assumption that indivisible fulfilment may be more characteristic of groups of people who regard themselves as injured. The achievement of the absolute goal provides the necessary compensation for those injured.

Radical aims and the dehumanization of one's rival affects the actions taken, so that, 'if we can perceive the opponent as less than human, superego controls do not operate and no guilt is felt over a resort to violence.'[8] Such polarization of views leaves no room for gradation, we are left with 'solutions which betray their totalistic nature in that the totally good may learn to be cruelly stern *ad majorem Dei gloriam*.'[9] Israel/Palestine is a place of causes and desires. It has been a prize over the ages 'as well as a place whose very name (and the endless naming and renaming of the place) has been an issue of doctrinal importance.'[10] Even the use of a certain term, a name, is an act of political will. Israel/Palestine is an interpretation: 'Palestine carries so heavy an imaginative and doctrinal freight – transmuted from a reality into a non-reality, from a presence into an absence.'[11]

Thus we have perceptions which are ideologically motivated, history viewed emotionally, distortion becoming reality. On one hand, there is the assertion that 'despite the turbulent history of the land of Palestine and the frequent foreign occupations, there has been a fundamental, uninterrupted continuity in the original population of the country. Wars and occupations could not drive the descendants of the Canaanites, the Amorites, the Jebusites and the Philistines from the land.'[12] On the other hand is the conviction held by a former Israeli prime minister, that it 'was not as though there were a people in Palestine considering itself as a Palestinian people and we came and threw them out and took their country away from them. They did not exist.'[13]

The reality of the modern conflict, the relationship between the competing participants both past and present, may well be illustrated by means of a parable:

> A man once jumped from the top floor of a burning house in which many members of his family had already perished. He managed to save his life, but as he was falling he hit a person standing below and broke that person's legs and arms. The jumping man had no choice; yet to the man with the broken limbs he was the cause of his misfortune. If both behaved rationally, they would not have become enemies. The man who escaped from the blazing house, having recovered, would have tried to escape and console the other sufferer; and the latter might have realised that he was the victim of circumstances over which neither of them had control. But look what happens when these people behave irrationally. The injured man blames the other for his misery and swears to make him pay for it. The other, afraid of the crippled man's revenge, insults him, kicks him, and beats him up whenever they meet. The kicked man again swears revenge and is again punched and punished. The bitter enmity so fortuitous at first, hardens and comes to overshadow the whole existence of both men and to poison their minds.[14]

Therefore we can establish that 'ideologies differ not only in their doctrines but also in their patterns of thought or mindset.' Thus 'when human beings assess reality, they perceive the possible goals, the available means, and the alternative outcomes. Ideology is a lens through which reality is perceived, and in this way can influence policy and deeds. In other words, an ideology and its dominant mentality generate attitudes that influence how people shape policies.'[15] The root of the Israeli-Palestinian/Arab conflict, and thus the Middle East peace process, is basically psychological.

Many learned articles and individual pronouncements have come forth detailing in almost utopian terms what a peaceful Middle East would be like. The difference between desire and the mysticism which envelops all would-be peace builders, is the lack of one very fundamental ingredient, which must inspire caution to all, and that is reality.

For any Israeli-Palestinian peace process to succeed, implemented

stages, negotiated painstakingly, will have to be concluded and rig-
idly adhered to. This process is one of years and not one of months.
The end result will have to be defined in advance, otherwise the
objectives will be unclear and thus open to misinterpretation and
rejection. For example, the Palestinians see the negotiations as a
state-building process while the Israelis see the process as leading
to inter-state comprehensive peace treaties, with the Palestinian
problem as a sub-state issue and therefore not central to the overall process. Confidence building in this environment is a powerful
concept but a diplomatic chimera nonetheless; each side cannot
build confidence and trust in the other when holding mutually
opposing fundamental beliefs and goals. Unless the parties to the
negotiations can ask themselves two fundamental questions, then
there will be no substantially positive outcome to the present talks.
'Do you want war or peace? Are you for the past with its twin
demons of supremacy and indignity, or for a future of which one
can only say: It will be different?'[16]

The Declaration of Principles on Interim Self-Government Arrangements (DoP), the document signed between the State of Israel and
the Palestine Liberation Organisation (PLO), in Washington DC on
13 September 1993, represents progress in the multinational endeavour to realize a settlement of the wider Arab-Israeli conflict, as
signalled by the Madrid Conference of 31 October 1991. Although
the DoP signed by Israel and the PLO ushered in a new era in
Israeli-Palestinian relations marking the beginning of the process
of implementing Palestinian autonomy, which in itself is an historical achievement, the DoP also represents a climax of many years
of confrontation and hostility. The DoP is part of a process which,
in essence, is the cornerstone of the formal mutual recognition pact
which represents a reciprocal acknowledgement of legitimacy, a crucial
first step toward finding a broad and permanent settlement. The
DoP, like all political documents, represents a compromise which
must be compared, not with what each side would consider ideal,
but with what would exist in the absence of the agreement.

The DoP is a first step toward a new political arrangement no
one can yet fully describe. It is a momentous beginning, offering a
glimpse of the chance to end years of hatred and bloodshed, but it
is still only a start. It is a fairly severe test, for Israelis and Palestinians alike. The Israelis through the DoP have to deal with the PLO
they have demonized for so long. The Palestinians through the DoP
have to prove to the Israelis that they can govern themselves and

maintain order if they hope to receive a payoff from the DoP in the form of more land, powers and responsibilities in the occupied territories. The DoP prescribes a series of incremental steps which are important in themselves because these steps signify that the old enemies are, in effect, conceding that the other has a right to exist. More importantly, Israel is essentially granting the Palestinians the chance to organize politically on parts of what has long been declared the inviolable 'Eretz Yisrael Hashlemah' in return for an agreement to contain, curtail and control any and all violence directed at the Israelis by Palestinian elements.[17] In accepting these opening conditions, the PLO still insists that the process must eventually lead to the creation of an independent Palestinian state, although this point remains open to question. Yet, by the very nature of assuming responsibility for the governing of pieces of land under its control, however small, the PLO has changed its very *raison d'être* dramatically and radically.

This study aims to be the first in the English language to analyse and evaluate the DoP from the point of view of whether or not it measures up to its stated goal, namely the achievement of a 'just, lasting and comprehensive peace settlement'[18] 'leading to a permanent settlement based on Security Council Resolutions 242 and 338.'[19] It will examine the complex nature and dynamics of the attempt at resolving the Israeli-Palestinian conflict. The book will seek to review the DoP, to investigate how it came into being, what it means, how it will be implemented and how far it can be used as a blueprint for future peacemaking. It will also address the wider international ramifications and relationships which will be a prerequisite for the evaluation and analysis of the corresponding policies and responses by the major powers and actors from the international community within the framework of the 1991 Madrid Middle East Peace Conference. Finally, it will offer an analysis of the findings in conclusion.

Chapter 1 examines the definition and context of the Israeli-Palestinian peace process as a case study of the bilateral management of an asymmetrical national-subnational conflict as part of an international conflict resolution framework. It also considers the nature of conflict resolution theories, paradigms, philosophies and principles and incorporates an extensive literature review. It questions asymmetric power relationships and explores the understanding of conflict resolution within the context of the Israeli-Palestinian conflict. Chapter 2 focuses on the establishment, purpose and development of the DoP, incorporating a thorough examination of the development of the secret Oslo backchannel, concluding with an analysis of the Oslo negotiations within the official Madrid framework as an example of conflict resolution. Chapter 3 provides an analysis of the DoP as an example of conflict resolution and critiques the meaning and purpose of the document. Chapter 4 provides an analysis of the implementation process of the initial years of the life of the DoP, incorporating the actual implementation of the DoP up to 31 August 1997, including the Agreement on the Gaza Strip and Jericho Area of May 1994; the World Bank aid programme; influential bilateral agreements by the two with third parties; the Agreement on Preparatory Transfer of Powers and Responsibilities of August 1994; the Protocol on Further Transfer of Powers and Responsibilities of August 1995; the Israeli-Palestinian Interim Agreement on the West Bank and the Gaza Strip of September 1995; and the Protocol Concerning the Redeployment in Hebron of January 1997. The final concluding chapter evaluates the attempt by the two communities to shape a common future with an analysis determining the effectiveness of the DoP both as an instrument for, and as an example of, conflict resolution.

1
Peace with Justice, for a Just Peace

'And I will make them one nation in the land,
upon the mountains of Israel;
and one king shall be king over them all;
and they shall be no longer two nations,
and no longer divided into two kingdoms.'
– Ezekiel (37.22)[1]

1.1 Introduction

In order to evaluate the political process that developed between the Israelis and the Palestinians from October 1991 under the aegis of the Middle East peace process, culminating in the drafting of the Declaration of Principles on Interim Self-Government Arrangements (DoP), it is important that the nature of the Israeli-Palestinian interrelationship is understood, and frames of reference for understanding the process of Israeli-Palestinian conflict resolution are properly contextualized and defined. Thus, rather than subjectively defining who is right or wrong and apportioning blame, we must ask less easily quantifiable and consequently more valuable questions. What is meant by peace? What are the rules of the game? What are the power relationships between participants, mediators, third parties and co-sponsors? What are the criteria for measuring success or failure, and how are they evaluated? What is the parties' understanding of the 'peace process'? What are the basic goals and strategic objectives of the DoP? With, and within, which parameters do we assess and evaluate the success or failure of the DoP? What are the expectations raised by the DoP? What shall be deemed

1

a just, lasting and comprehensive peace settlement? Is the DoP a device to contain, control, limit, manage or resolve the Israeli-Palestinian conflict? In essence, how do we grade the test?

The stated intention of the DoP is to put an end to decades of confrontation and conflict, recognize both Israeli and Palestinian mutually legitimate political rights, and strive to 'live in peaceful coexistence and mutual dignity and security and achieve a just, lasting and comprehensive peace settlement and historic reconciliation through the agreed political process.' The aim of the Israeli-Palestinian negotiations within the Middle East peace process is to establish an autonomous Palestinian authority within a transitional period which will lead to 'a permanent settlement based on Security Council Resolutions 242 and 338', and that the 'negotiations on the permanent status will lead to the implementation of Security Council Resolutions 242 and 338.' Thus we can assume two fundamental conclusions:

1. The principal objective of the DoP is to achieve a 'just, lasting and comprehensive peace settlement' leading to the resolution of the Israeli-Palestinian conflict via 'historic reconciliation through the agreed political process'.

2. The foundation of the agreed political process, the DoP, rests on basing the permanent settlement of the Israeli-Palestinian conflict on UN Security Council Resolutions 242 and 338 and on the premise that negotiations on the permanent status will lead to the 'implementation of Security Council Resolutions 242 and 338'.[2]

To assess the DoP, a preliminary exploration of conflict resolution theories and methods is necessary in order to develop a set of standards so that we may best measure the sucess of the DoP. Using the theoretical knowledge we will gain from an assessment of conflict resolution methodolgy and practices, we will then be in a position to analyse the political process set in motion by the DoP. This set of standards will be covered by what we will call the Riceman Formula. The Riceman Formula covers:

a) resolution;
b) institutionalization;
c) confidence-building;
d) empowerment;
e) mediation;
f) administration; and
g) negotiation.

1.2 Conflict resolution methodology

Before the signing of the DoP, Israel and the PLO were enemies engaged in a mainly low-intensity (though sometimes high-intensity), inter-ethnic, existential conflict. Neither side officially recognized the other, and both sought effectively to delegitimize and destroy the other. If one accepts the premise that the Israeli-Palestinian conflict is the core conflict of the wider inter-state Arab-Israeli conflict, then it has always been assumed in layman's terms that the process of building peace in the Middle East has to begin with the resolution of the Israeli-Palestinian conflict.

The Arab-Israeli conflict as a whole is a protracted conflict with frequent and intense outbreaks of open warfare, which prior to the signing of the DoP was regarded as fundamentally unchanged and unresolvable as long as the Israeli-Palestinian conflict remained unresolved.[3] The Arab-Israeli conflict has three distinguishable phases: a) the military/political phase – 'the unmanageable stage'; b) the conflict management phase – the reduction stage; and c) the conflict resolution phase – the peace stage.[4] Any movement by the parties, particularly as one, between any, or through all of these phases, has been characteristically difficult to achieve, with the success that has been achieved limited to bilateral efforts and agreements. Prior to 1991, there existed a formal peace treaty between Israel and Egypt, formal disengagement agreements between Israel and Syria, and Israel and Jordan, and an informal agreement between Israel and Lebanon. Of the principal Arab-Israeli conflicts, the Israeli-Palestinian conflict remained, prior to 1991, the only non-institutionalized conflict, characterized as a state-substate conflict, unlike the other principal Arab-Israeli conflicts which were all state-state conflicts.

The Israeli-Palestinian conflict, until 1988, was in essence a zero-sum affair. Unilateral action by both sides had failed to attain completely the goal of either side – that is, the destruction of the other side's claim to legitimacy and to exist as a sovereign entity in the land of Israel/Palestine. Whilst the emphasis of Israel's conflict resolution relations with its neighbours in the years up to 1987 was on a state-to-state basis, the Palestinian *intifada*, which erupted in Gaza in December 1987, directed the focus of Israel's attention to the burgeoning inter-ethnic conflict with the Palestinian inhabitants of the occupied territories. The *intifada* represented not only the inability of the Israelis to destroy the PLO and dismiss the

Palestinian people, but also the PLO's inability to achieve its stated goal of the destruction of Israel. The popular uprising by necessity demanded of the Israelis a response, and through the *intifada*'s intensity and more so its longevity, elicited a measured and more thoughtful reaction from Israel than the initial one of force. Israel's immediate resort to violence as a means of suppressing the *intifada* was unsustainable in the medium to long term, and thus the failure to employ the techniques required to contain the conflict meant that the Israelis had to accept more conciliatory and concessionary measures with which to manage the conflict. According to Y. Bar-Siman-Tov, the potential to

> shift this conflict from regulation to institutionalisation depends on definitive, accepted and recognised links between institutionalisation and resolution. The Palestinians are not interested in institutionalisation that will freeze their conflict behaviour without promising them a resolution that will end the Israeli occupation. The Israelis . . . are interested in institutionalisation as a means towards ending the *intifada*, but they refuse to make their withdrawal from the West Bank and Gaza dependent on it.[5]

The Arab-Israeli conflict, which at first had a 'zero-sum, protracted nature, has however changed over time, through effective conflict management that has made conflict reduction and even resolution possible.'[6] However the Arab-Israeli conflict is neither a single nor a static conflict system: the differences between the various parties constantly change, in turn affecting the entire conflict system. The Israeli-Palestinian conflict in its turn has steadfastly refused to transform from the state of regulation to resolution, precisely because the two parties hold such different views on what constitutes resolution, and what constitutes merely management. The Israeli-Palestinian negotiations have constantly been affected by the Israeli perception that what the Palestinians consider to be the necessary minimum position is, for them, the necessary maximum position. Separate, independently concluded negotiated agreements have characterized the Arab-Israeli conflict, either presuming or preventing a comprehensive agreement. Thus in the complexities of the Arab-Israeli conflict, 'many actors and different issues' have 'hindered the development of the same rate and scope . . . in each dyadic conflict.'[7]

Whilst the PLO departed from its longstanding position of negation of the state of Israel in 1988 – with the recognition of Israel, the acceptance of UN Security Council Resolutions (UNSCR) 242 and 338, the renunciation of terrorism and the limiting of Palestinian sovereignty aspirations to the West Bank and Gaza Strip – Israel on the other hand refused to concede to a mutual recognition understanding, preferring to ignore the PLO, continue settling the occupied territories and deny the Palestinians the courtesy of acknowledging their existence as a separate negotiating partner to deal with. The main result of Israel's refusal to deal with the PLO is that without the direct participation of that organization in negotiations there was never likely to be any real prospect of reaching an Israeli-Palestinian accommodation. That said, it would follow that those Israelis who professed a desire for reaching a peaceful settlement with the Palestinians, but would not countenance negotiating with the PLO, were either disingenuous or stupid. Likewise those Palestinians who professed a peaceful outcome to the Israeli-Palestinian conflict, but were unprepared or unwilling to accept the flourishing reality of Israel's existence, were so unreasonable that their logic bordered on the absurd. Such rejection by significant constituencies within both sides conspired until 1993, either through external events or through design, sufficiently to inhibit the forces within both camps that counselled compromise and cooperation.

Three factors were responsible for the readiness of the various parties to the Arab-Israeli conflict to accept the invitation to attend the US-USSR co-sponsored Madrid Middle East Peace Conference in 1991: the international realignment signalled by the second Gulf War, the disintegration of the USSR, and pressure applied by the US administration. Two lessons were underlined by the international realignment signalled by the Second Gulf War. Firstly, that due to the massive capability for destruction by technologically advanced weapons, particularly unconventional ballistic missile systems, the holding of territory was no longer the guarantor of a sound defensive posture. New conventional wisdom dictated that the previously held Israeli defensive reliance on the policy of strategic depth as the necessary basis upon which to construct the Israeli military strategic defensive doctrine no longer held true. Secondly, the international community, led by a US administration more bullish about its perceived international role, 'delegitimised war as a means of managing' the Arab-Israeli conflict, forcing the various protagonists to conclude that the 'political costs of new war could exceed its political benefits.'[8] The disintegration of the USSR led to that superpower temporarily orphaning its client states and organizations, in turn ensuring that in the short term, no Arab state or actor with the desire to wage war against Israel, would have the means, patronage or the tacit approval needed. The pressure applied by the US administration derived from the fact that the US was, as a result of the events of 1990–1, the last superpower remaining. Thus US approval or disapproval came to be of greater importance than previously, giving the implicit threat of incurring the wrath of the US administration inherently more power and authority. By accepting these realities, the various parties to the Arab-Israeli conflict were successfully corralled by a US administration riding high on its self-image and on its perceived dominance of the international scene.

The Arab-Israeli conflict has evolved over many years from its intrinsic character of a long-term zero-sum conflict to a point where effective conflict management has culminated in reducing tensions sufficiently to make resolving the basics of the conflict possible. However, any notions of confidence in such an event happening may be overstated, as the Arab-Israeli conflict remains a multi-faceted situation which continues to evade positive perceptions because progress in any one area does not necessarily mean progress as a whole, thus precluding a comprehensive settlement. Indeed the Arab-Israeli conflict is a series of linked conflicts progressing at different rates, with different emphases and differing needs, thus making analysis and evaluation of such dynamics of each and of the whole increasingly difficult, particularly when assessing and measuring the conflict regime through the various phases of its life, from conflict through regulation and then institutionalization to resolution. Thus it is important to assess and define the DoP in terms of its success or failure as a vehicle for achieving a definable 'peace' between the Israelis and Palestinians and its potential in signalling the way forward for any future 'peace processes' within the Arab-Israeli conflict.

The DoP constitutes a set of mutually agreed general principles regarding the interim period of Palestinian self-rule. As such, the DoP defers those as yet unresolved permanent-status issues to a later schedule of negotiations, excluding them from the interim arrangements but neither prejudging nor pre-empting them from such. The DoP stems from the Middle East peace conference launched in October 1991, and carried out within the structure of the Madrid framework. The 1991 Middle East peace initiative was convened in

Madrid, co-sponsored by the US and USSR, and conceived in order to initiate direct peace talks between various interested parties with the aim of reassessing and reshaping the political order of the Middle East. The Madrid framework is an integrated structure composed of three basic links: the Opening Conference, the Bilateral Track, and the Multilateral Track. The Opening Conference, which inaugurated the two separate parallel negotiating tracks, the bilateral and the multilateral, was intended as a preliminary and preparatory occasion providing a pioneering forum for all the participants, although in itself having no power to impose solutions or veto agreements. The Bilateral Tracks are intended as the vehicle with which to 're-solve the conflicts of the past', by sets of direct negotiations between Israel and her immediate neighbours, the Palestinians, Syria, Jordan and Lebanon. The Multilateral Track is intended as the medium to 'build the Middle East of the future' through confidence-building measures across the region, and as such constitutes an integral element of the peace-making process.[9] Formulated to include interested regional and international parties, the multilateral track focuses negotiations on five key issues of regional concern; water, environment, arms control, refugees and economic development. The multilateral track has two interconnected objectives: to determine regional solutions to important regional problems; and to function as a confidence-building measure by which to promote and therefore extend the notion and practice of normalized contacts and relations among the regional and international parties to the negotiations.

This book is not an empirical, comparative study of conflict resolution case studies in order to test a set of hypotheses; it is, rather, a case study of *one* conflict resolution process, how that conflict resolution framework evolved and how conflict resolution techniques were employed to determine a political solution to the protracted and deep-rooted Israeli-Palestinian conflict. However, some general discussion of conflict resolution theory is necessary as background.

1.3   Theory in conflict resolution

Conflict resolution as an academic discipline was stimulated by various movements, synthesizing the study of industrial relations, mediation and two-track international diplomacy, peace-making, alternative dispute resolution, and interpersonal and intercultural disputes practices, particularly in the US. It has developed since the 1950s, defined as a multi- and inter-disciplinary field grounded in Western culture and socio-economic traditions. Theories of international relations, and in particular Western notions of conflict resolution, over the past 50 years have been primarily dominated and overshadowed by the realities of Cold War logic, so that new realities and new ways of understanding our complex, changing world since the collapse of the bipolar model or world view have to be refined, and new ones defined. Such an exercise takes time; in essence old thinking still exists and still dominates the many players on the international scene. Since 1989–91 there has been an almost desperate attempt to make sense of the changing nature of the international system in the light of past certainties having been subsumed and over-taken so quickly by events. Old enmities still exist, they will merely reconfigurate and burst forth in a different guise. The challenge ahead is how we are to understand the Madrid Peace Conference, coming as it did in the midst of epochal change, and how we are to perceive a superpower-inspired and -sponsored conflict manage-ment/conflict resolution model charged with multi-disciplinary and cross-cultural goals. With this in mind we can now analyse and assess the ongoing operation of international relations whether or not within the context of new international systems and structures.

Conflict as encapsulated in an institutional structure that legiti-mates violence, i.e. occupation + repression = conflict, means that more than just a new architecture of relationships has to be con-structed. The causes, conditions and contexts of conflict must be determined; the parties, their milieu, their culture and ideologies, economic relations, all points of contact and interaction, and the very basis of the nature of the conflict have to be transformed so that historical conflict is not merely postponed only to be repro-duced at a later juncture. Thus intra-party conflict has to be addressed in conjunction with the overall inter-party conflict, by making dis-cord explicit in order that less threatening and violent structures may develop.

Theoreticians and practitioners of conflict resolution function within two mainly independent cultures. However, both relate to each other in important ways – theoreticians because they need practical examples to anchor their theories, and practitioners because they need a focus with which to view their work.

If conflict analysis is a fundamental building-block of conflict resolution, then conflict theory 'requires a mapping of the conflict, including a complete picture of the dynamics of the parties, their relationships and issues, and the processes being used to maintain or resolve their conflict.'[10] Analysis alone, however, 'is insufficient in conflict-resolving situations', the parties themselves 'must play an important role in the process if the benefits are to be realised.'[11]

Both the forums and the processes of conflict resolution are usually 'biased to some degree toward the interests of those who create them.' Therefore conflict resolution theory must meet the needs of all the interested parties in designing the process by which they will try to settle their differences. Through inclusion and participation many objectives are accomplished: 'ownership' of the process is encouraged, greater participation by parties in the process of resolving the problem influences the kind of behaviour that parties will use later in the problem-solving process, positive working relationships are built that help to create 'elegant options and implement the chosen solution effectively, and permit outside facilitators to build sufficient credibility to serve in an impartial role.'[12]

Conflict resolution serves as a governing mechanism to respond to changes in political, social and economic variables within a community to the extent that the process drives parties to consider the deepest levels of individual and group interests, values and needs. The informal processes used to deal with particular conflict issues must therefore be linked closely with the community's existing traditional decision-making processes. However, at some point, the community will need to make a collective decision on what level to accept the results or consequences of the conflict resolution process. The deeper the level of acceptance needed, the more change in the community's governing structure required, the more difficult that acceptance will become for those holding positions of leadership in the establishment, thus 'decisions about how much to accept are for the community and its decision-makers to make, after full recognition and consideration of the elements of the problem and their impact.'[13]

Theory offers the practitioner structure, organization, context, preparation, education, motivation, standardization, and the confidence to develop knowledge and skills; however the downside is in the over-reliance on the theoretical framework, wherein lies the possibility of shaping the parties and their conflict to fit the process, rather than moulding the process to suit the parties and their conflict.

An important distinction regarding conflict theory has to be made when dealing with an inter-ethnic conflict which is part of a wider international conflict. This centres on the need to question the determination and utility of existing theoretical and methodological frameworks. Much of conflict theory literature relates to interpersonal, intergroup and intercommunal conflicts which occur within existing institutional frameworks including the powers of coercion, sanction, reparation and punishment. This makes the prescription of models dealing with conflict resolution much easier, as institutional frameworks therefore do not have to be invented or endowed. The dynamics of international conflict, and the lack of effective international institutions, structures and binding punitive measures are such that the applicability, utility and effectiveness of much of the work in the field is unfortunately debatable.

According to D.J. Sandole, there are 'at least four paradigms relevant to conflict and conflict resolution at *all* levels, from the interpersonal to international: (1) Political Realism (Realpolitik); Political Idealism (Idealpolitik); (3) Marxism; and (4) . . . Non-Marxist Radical Thought.'[14] 'Political realism' and 'political idealism' are basically polar opposites, the difference between 'nature vs. nurture', or constructive vs. destructive forces. 'Political realism' stresses that the world is a battleground, that human nature is negatively flawed, that at the international level there is an absence of appropriate conflict resolution mechanisms, that survival in this inherently unstable world is dependent on the successful, and continued defence of the nation against all threats, foreign and domestic.[15] Conflict resolution within this realist, competitive environment is power-based, adversarial, confrontational, zero-sum and win-lose.[16] 'Political idealism', however, stresses man's triumph over environment, or even the more basic image of man's triumph over self, encouraging cooperative processes of conflict resolution, non-adversarial, non-confrontational, non-zero-sum, and win-win. Marxism and non-Marxist radical thought are an amalgamation of the previous two. Marxism stresses the historical determinism of radical structural change as the way to achieve behavioural change, together with the inevitability of conflict. However, Marxism also stresses that human nature is dependent on environment and thus able to change. Both, however, see '*competitive* processes of conflict resolution . . . characterising the efforts of disenfranchised, disempowered, needs-violated persons and minority groups generally, attempting to redefine their relationships with resistant supporters of a status quo which benefits only the ingroup.'[17] Non-Marxist radical thought emphasizes the 'validity, power and rationality of *cooperative* processes (and constructive outcomes) as the only way to achieve fair, long-lasting, durable solutions to problems underlying manifest conflict.'[18] Thus from four different paradigms of conflict/conflict resolution, there are two methods or perspectives with which to manage conflict, either competitively or cooperatively.

Conflict is 'a dynamic phenomenon, . . . a *manifest conflict process* . . . comprised of phases of initiation, escalation, controlled maintenance, abatement, and termination/resolution.' A manifest conflict process is a 'situation in which at least two actors, or their representatives, try to pursue their perceptions of mutually incompatible goals by undermining, directly or indirectly, the goal-seeking capability of one another.'[19] Aggressive manifest conflict processes are

> situations in which at least two actors, or their representatives, try to pursue their perceptions of mutually incompatible goals by physically damaging or destroying the property and high-value symbols of one another; and/or psychologically or physically injuring, destroying, or otherwise forcibly eliminating one another.[20]

D. Druckman argues that conflict resolution may be viewed as a framework of interconnected issues; the conflict's structure,[21] the conflict's processes,[22] the conflict's behaviour,[23] and the conflict's contexts.[24] J.W. Burton believes that conflict resolution is a 'recent concept'.[25] Conflict resolution is 'still not part of any consensual understanding. Indeed, the terms *disputes* and *conflicts* are used interchangeably, as are *settlement* and *resolution*. In the emerging literature on conflict resolution these terms have distinctive meanings. 'Disputes' involve negotiable interests, while 'conflicts' are concerned with issues that are not negotiable, issues that relate to ontological human needs that cannot be compromised. Accordingly, 'settlement' refers to negotiated or arbitrated outcomes of disputes, while 'resolution' refers to outcomes of a conflict situation that must satisfy the inherent needs of all. Hence we have *dispute settlement* and *conflict resolution.*[26]

Clarifying the meanings of terms and their precise usage allows for a framework of parameters and indicators with which to understand properly and, more importantly, assess, the relationship between theoretical assumptions and real events. Among the problems associated with the notions of 'political realism' and 'political idealism' are difficulties in using thought to trace the development of practice.

Therefore if these two concepts are accepted as opposites, then the absence of a theory of conflict must be reflected in a corresponding absence of a theory based not only on explaining conflict but also on prescribing an alternative system. Lacking theories and explanations of terms must then leave us with subjectivity and meaningless sloganeering. Without an understanding of terms and concepts, words are left empty, being defined for whatever purpose suits, at whatever juncture, by whomsoever.

Problem-solving conflict resolution is a political theory based on individuals as the unit of analysis, rather than institutions. By analysing parties and issues, by facilitating an interactive situation in which relationships are scrutinized, and by defining the essence of the problem, resolution options can then be explored. Contained within this framework is the acknowledgement that a conflict settlement is not necessarily a conflict resolved, in the sense that future conflict is incorporated within the problem-solving analysis by the promotion of conditions which will continue to provide a cooperative and creative relationship.

> In this sense conflict resolution is a fundamentally different exercise from any settlement processes: it is concerned with prediction and with policy formation based on a political philosophy that asserts that the satisfaction of human needs that are universal must be the ultimate goal of survivable societies.

Therefore, conflict resolution 'is part of the field of political philosophy. It is relevant to all systems.'[27]

The issues of conflict prevention, the promotion of conflict resolution, the institutionalization of the means of dealing with conflict, and the processes of problem-solving are all ideological concepts and principles incorporated within the Madrid Peace Conference and the DoP. In this sense, then, we may well ask: Is the Madrid Peace Conference and/or the DoP an attempt to institutionalize a conflict resolution regime, and if so, what constitutes the fundamental philosophy underpinning the entire framework?

According to J.W. Burton, conflict resolution has been a neglected subject, however. While it 'helps to provide insights into the nature of conflict and the conditions that stimulate conflict, by itself it does not deal with the problem of conflict.'[28] Thus any theoretical framework or explanation of conflict resolution must include contextual analysis, a problem-solving network, a prevention regime, mechanisms to isolate sources of conflict, arrangements to remove sources of conflict, and the promotion of creative and cooperative relationships.

According to C.R. Mitchell, it seems to be the case with international attempts at conflict resolution, particularly when concerned with protracted and deep-rooted conflict, that a highly unstructured and/or unrelated format of activities is employed, when viewed from a methodological and theoretical standpoint. Such activities that exist are designed to minimize antagonisms, break down barriers and create trust, before moving on to the actualities of the conflict itself. In this environment, ambiguities remain, and connections between conditions, structures and processes, attitudes and behaviour may continue to be only implied. Much of the existing literature in the field of conflict resolution takes the form of 'how-to' handbooks or manuals with rules and instructions. It may be that when one is dealing with the complexities of real life, real people and real problems within life-and-death situations, theoretical frameworks have little or no practical value. When no two conflicts are the same, even between the same parties, any attempts to construct universally inclusive and applicable theoretical frameworks may be beyond the grasp of practicality as long as the international system remains as it is today. In this sense, either theoretical frameworks will have to be so broad as to be able to encompass all and every eventuality, thereby being so non-specific as to be of limited value, or the international system that exists will have to be reconstructed or become subject to a jurisdiction which is universally adhered to. One of the main limitations of any attempts at theorizing within the discipline of conflict studies is that of not being able to test theories prior to their application. Plausible hypotheses are not enough when contemplating real conflict. Where practitioners have limited time-frames to work within and pressing external pressures bearing down, any and/or all theories, ideas and models may be employed, and/or discarded depending on their practical and constructive utility within any given framework. Practice seems to demand that theoretical frameworks which relate to international conflict are only useful if they are applicable and positive, otherwise their utility is redundant. What seems more certain is being able to define a situation of conflict, and a situation of peace, all points in between being ethereal and altogether less quantifiable, more appropriately being categorized as collections of situation-related 'craft knowledge'.[29]

Theorist and practitioner J.V. Montville stresses the healing function of accepting responsibility, making acts of contrition and practising forgiveness within the conflict resolution process. Conflicts which result in painful losses, in lives, in territory, in justice and in legitimacy are the most resistant to traditional methods of diplomatic or political mediation and negotiation, and even those approaches which are psychologically sensitive often have limited success. Montville believes that reconciliation in ethnic and/or sectarian conflict which does not incorporate a process of contrition and forgiveness as part of a wider process of building new foundations of relationships based on mutual recognition and responsibility will falter if it fails to include an agreed analysis of a shared history, which in turn produces acknowledgements of past injustices, acceptances of moral responsibilities, and promises future acts which respect sensitivities.[30] His experiences have led him to conclude that 'superpowers and lesser states have relied on economic and military coercive power as the ultimate "conflict resolvers"' which absolves them of the painful business of apportioning responsibilities and negates the notion that 'forgiveness' can be 'a key element in peacemaking.'[31] Montville states that the

> three main components of victimhood are a history of violent, traumatic aggression and loss; a conviction that the aggression was unjustified by any standard; and an often unuttered fear on the part of the victim group that the aggressor will strike again at some feasible time in the future. To complicate matters, many nations and groups in conflict have competing, if not entirely symmetrical, psychologies of victimhood.[32]

A main task of constructive communication between representatives of groups in conflict should incorporate the issues of changing political attitudes, or political beliefs, or belief systems, because almost 'always deeply rooted in the belief systems of ethnic and religious groups with a history of violent conflict are dehumanised images of the other side.' Thus an aspect of conflict resolution provides the challenge of delegitimizing negative stereotyping, and discarding beliefs and values that undermine positive positions. 'Dialogue, the engine of relationship, promotes mutual confirmation and thereby serves a fundamental need of parties to a conflict to be recognised as individuals with values and unique (and valued) identities.'[33] Or as Thich Nhat Hanh, a Vietnamese Zen master, would have it, 'Rec-

onciliation is to understand both sides, to go to one side and describe the suffering being endured by the other side, and then to
the other side, and describe the suffering being endured by the
first side.'[34]

According to Montville

the purpose of the walk through history is to elicit specific grievances and wounds of the groups or nations in conflict which
have not been acknowledged by the side responsible for inflict-
ing them. Only the victims know for certain which historic events
sustain the sense of victimhood and these become cumulatively
the agenda for healing. Published histories and official government versions of violent events initiated by aggressors very rarely
convey the unvarnished truth. The almost universal tendency is
not to discuss or to gloss or mythologise an event or military
conquest as a justified defence if not heroic advance for the nation
or perhaps civilisation itself. That nations have used the traditional psychological devices of denial and avoidance to exempt
themselves from the moral consequences of their behaviour has
long been known. And the need for revising and cleaning up
the published historical record of a conflicted intergroup or international relationship has become widely accepted as an essential
part of the reconciliation process.[35]

In an actively facilitated problem-solving workshop organized by
the American Psychiatric Association in 1980, Israelis and Egyptians exchanged historical views, during which in

their often profound and emotional exchanges, the Egyptians
and Israelis revealed the significant cultural gaps between the
European-oriented Israeli elite and Arabs in general. But the Israelis
especially reflected the deep sense of victimisation Jews had
suffered before 1948 and the establishment of Israel and since
in the face of Arab hostility. It became clear that the major psychological means of facilitating negotiations would be through
highly developed sensitivity to the Israeli suspicion of Gentiles
that is based on the Jewish historical experience. The underlying political assumption of most Israelis is that Gentiles, at best,
are indifferent to Israel's survival and, at worst, actively conspire
to destroy the state. This is why unconditional public acceptance
of Israel's right to exist – which Egypt conveyed – must be seen

as *the* minimum Arab and Palestinian move necessary, for non-negotiable psychological reasons, to begin negotiations toward a political settlement.[36]

The purpose and notion of contrition and forgiveness as part of the conflict resolution process has not been widely discussed in the scholarly literature of clinical psychology, psychiatry and psychoanalysis.[37] A senior Israeli psychoanalyst, Rafael Moses, who is conversant with group hurts and group wounds, reported on an American Psychiatric Association Arab-Israeli workshop of the acute disappointment experienced by Palestinians when their need for Israeli acknowledgement of the hurts their community had suffered at the hands of the Israelis was not recognized:[38] Moses wrote

> The tension in the air grew palpably. The third party tried to encourage more direct and mutual interchanges ... The most articulate and vociferous spokesman of the Palestinian group made the following statement: 'If you Israelis would only acknowledge that you have wronged us, that you have taken away our homes and our land – if you did that, we would be able to proceed without insisting, without needing to get them back.' This was said somewhat wistfully. It sounded in the main honest, real, genuine. No such acknowledgement was made. The Israelis were frightened of the consequences, of what it might imply to make such an acknowledgement.[39]

1.4   An Assessment of relevant theoretical conflict resolution literature and the aim of the declaration of principles on Interim Self-Government Arrangements

The study of the concept of conflict resolution has embraced many disciplines, among them causes of belligerency, international economic development, conflict analysis, psychology, behaviourism, stress management, crisis management and distinctions between forms of violence. Theorists in the field emphasize the need to analyse the structure, the protagonists and the substance of a conflict scientifically. Thus armed with a comprehensive analysis, the conflict itself can be tackled. Within such a conceptualization, conflict can be compartmentalized in terms of social organization, structure, patterns of interaction, modes of violence, war aims, changes in leadership during conflict, genesis of conflict, and thus dealt with by tackling issues on a smaller more manageable scale.[40] Such an analysis has generated much discussion on whether or not conflict is subjective or objective, particularly in the difference between zero-sum and non-zero-sum games.[41] Within this framework, mediation takes the form of persuading the parties to reorder their goals albeit without compromise.[42] Goals should be drawn from the parties themselves rather than being imposed, because of the danger of leaving issues unresolved which could flare up subsequently because of the non-participation of all the various levels of internal hierarchy; thus conflict resolution solves problems and does not descend into haggling.[43] However, the method of 'principled negotiation' has been devised to sidestep the dangers of 'position bargaining'. This method evaluates issues separately and on their merits, a process designed to avoid unsatisfactory and short-lived agreements, defined as 'one which meets the legitimate interests of each side to the extent possible, resolves conflicting interests fairly, is durable, and takes community interests into account.'[44] In order to achieve a positive outcome, a working framework, internationally legitimated, within which to structure the peace-making initiative is of great importance. Having designed a suitable framework, the business of further refining the process can proceed, incorporating such points as

- separate the people from the problem
- focus on interests, not positions
- propose several options which will benefit all rather than going for the quick fix
- outline objective criteria to ensure a fair outcome
- build in mechanisms for coping with setbacks and gamesmanship.[45]

According to J.W. McDonald, international conference diplomacy refers to 'international, intergovernmental, multilateral conferences, organised by the secretariats of international organisations, at the behest of member states.'[46] Bilateral and multilateral negotiations are 'each quite different and require different skills.' Diplomatically, 'bilateral negotiations involve representatives from two countries sitting down and talking' whereas multilateral negotiations involve 'diplomatic interaction between official representatives of three or more countries.'[47] The two sides in bilateral negotiation

usually know a great deal about each other's language, customs, background, and history and have had an opportunity to get to know each other, and the issues, over a period of time. Individual strengths and weaknesses have been identified and assessed by both parties. These negotiations are usually handled quietly, informally, behind closed doors, often without an interpreter, usually without a specific time constraint on the negotiation process and usually away from the world's press. The conclusion of the negotiation may be an oral agreement or an exchange of diplomatic notes or even a more formal text signed by the two parties.[48]

The multilateral framework is altogether a very different experience. Apart from the fact that there are hosts of official delegates, interpreters, concerned non-governmental bodies and individuals and the intense attention of the press, the main differences of the multilateral framework relate to a number of key features, namely: multilateral gatherings have specific and short time-frames; trying to negotiate consensual, practical outcomes from such gatherings is virtually impossible, and multilateral negotiations almost never produce binding draft treaties which incorporate stated obligations and commitments backed with legally enforceable sanctions. 'The goal of all multilateral conferences is therefore to achieve a meaningful consensus.'[49]

J.W. McDonald has outlined four principles applicable to the activities of international conferences:

(1) 'There is a direct correlation between the success of an international conference and the amount of preparation needed to make that conference successful.'
(2) 'The size and diplomatic level of a delegation to an international conference is in direct proportion to the amount of *domestic* political interest in the subject matter of the conference.'
(3) 'Using the conference structure wisely can be the key to success.'
(4) 'The level of competence of the conference President or the leader of the US delegation can often make or break a conference.'[50]

It is not easy to synthesize theories of conflict resolution and diplomatic negotiating practices, because most diplomatic practitioners 'abstain from reading about conflict resolution theory', whilst many 'academics seem to have little interest in finding ways to test their theories, in practice.' By developing a 'greater understanding of the needs of the other, then one may well be able to expand the understanding necessary, not only to extend the field of knowledge available to both but also to more effectively resolve international conflict peacefully and eventually bring about a less conflicted world.'[51]

For geopolitical theorists, the concept of diplomacy as a preventative factor in international conflict is a central one. However division exists between the value of 'summit' versus professional diplomacy and in the nature of the framework for problem-solving. Summit diplomacy, a feature of modern international politics, is seen by opponents as being imprecise, driven by agenda(s) other than by the matter(s) at hand, having media driven expectations, and is therefore a vehicle which reduces the flexibility and effectiveness of movement by professional diplomats who are trained in the arts of nuance and complexity. Only through professional diplomacy, it is argued, can nations achieve peaceful resolution to contentious international issues. Such an argument can be taken further in opposition to setting up, or working through actors of an international dimension, that is international agencies and/or a comprehensive and binding international legal framework.

Opposition centres on the contention that

> the function of a system of international relationships is not to inhibit this process of change by imposing a legal straitjacket upon it but rather to facilitate it; to ease its transition; to temper the asperities to which it often leads; to isolate and moderate the conflict to which it gives rise, and to see that these conflicts do not assume forms too unsettling for international life in general.[52]

Thus opponents such as G.F. Kennan contend that to expect the United Nations (UN) to play a major role, particularly in the resolution of bipolar global problems, is to impose an impossible burden, and even to assume that international organizations can cope effectively with transnational problems, is to assign them tasks beyond their political competence.[53] Therefore 'leading industrial and maritime nations – the nations which created the most serious problems, which had the resources to study the problem, and which had it in their power to remedy most of the evils in question' should play the principal role in their resolution.[54] Strength, according to Kennan, can only be mustered by a select few on a global scale, therefore the ability to resolve conflict around the world can be achieved only by power mobilized in 'those regions where a major industrial power, enjoying adequate access to raw materials, is combined with large reserves of educated and technically skilled manpower.'[55]

The Madrid Peace Conference framework, conceived, inspired and empowered by the patronage of a superpower is an exercise of power by statesmen for the development of an international structure that would contribute to a peace to be so determined by either the sponsors, and/or their allies. Thus, the Madrid Peace Conference framework is a fusion of the nature and quality of political leadership, the impact and response of domestic political structures upon foreign policy and the relationship between diplomacy and military policy in a changing international system.

Henry Kissinger developed two models to frame his thinking of international politics: firstly, a stable system, and secondly, a revolutionary one. Kissinger postulated that peace is achieved not as an end in itself, but instead emerges as a result of a stable, as opposed to a revolutionary, international system. He contends that stability has resulted not 'from a quest for peace, but from a general accepted legitimacy',[56] legitimacy meaning 'no more than an international agreement about the nature of workable arrangements and about the permissible aims and methods of foreign policy'. Thus legitimacy implies an acceptance of the framework of the international order by all major powers.[57] Agreement concerning the framework of the international order does not eliminate conflict but it does limit its scope. Kissinger defines diplomacy as 'the adjustment of differences through negotiation,' and is only possible within the international framework where 'legitimacy obtains'.[58] Kissinger's paradigm is that the primary motive of national actors is not the preservation of peace, because 'wherever peace – conceived as the avoidance of war – has been the primary objective of a power or a group of powers, the international system has been at the mercy of the most ruthless member of the international community,'[59] thus 'whenever the international order has acknowledged that certain principles could not be compromised even for the sake of peace, stability based on an equilibrium of forces was at least conceivable.'[60] This means basically that foreign policy cannot be conducted without an awareness of power relationships.[61] Failing an agreed, and thus legitimate, international framework, diplomacy is problematic, if not impractical.[62] Without a structure, foreign policy emphasis is centred around creating such a framework.

> All nations, adversaries and friends alike, must have a stake in preserving the international system. They must feel that their principles are being respected and their national interests secured. They must, in short, see positive incentive for keeping the peace, not just the dangers of breaking it,[63]

and thus provide a 'certain equilibrium between potential adversaries'; after all '[i]f history teaches anything it is that there can be no peace without equilibrium and no justice without restraint.'[64]

Conduct of effective diplomacy (by which is meant negotiated settlement) is understood to be, through the realist perspective, almost impossible. This is due to the dilemma of fusing domestic politics and foreign policy, for if one is subject to the other either in conception and execution, through the constant glare of publicity, then it is argued that one cedes flexibility, and thus loses a key stratagem; however if negotiations are conducted in secret they have a greater potential for success.[65] Whilst diplomacy should 'never condone the suppression of fundamental liberties', and should 'urge humane principles and use ... influence to promote justice,' however, 'the issue comes down to the limits of such efforts'[66] – in short foreign policy should be based on national power and interest, rather than abstract moralistic principles or political crusades.[67] If we accept the premise that '[a]ny attempt to conceptualise the causes of war and the conditions for peace that starts from individual psychology rather than an analysis of the relations between nation-states is of questionable relevance,'[68] we must also accept that governmental behaviour at the international level cannot be subjected to the same moral standards that are applied to ordinary human behaviour:

> Moral principles have their place in the heart of the individual in the shape of his own conduct, whether as a citizen or as a governmental official. ...
>
> When the individual's behaviour passes through the machinery of political organisation and merges with that of millions of other individuals to find its expression in the actions of government, then it undergoes a general transformation, and the same moral concepts are no longer relevant to it. A government is an agent, not a principal; and no more than any other agent may it attempt to be the conscience of its principal.[69]

International relations theorists have been taken to task for their seeming concentration on the field of conflict deterrence whilst neglecting ways of controlling, limiting and terminating war once started.[70] Lacking an understanding of resolution leads to paralysis in planning and preparation for such a circumstance as it unfolds. Thus we are caught in

an atmosphere of polarised immoderation – with one group calling
for early termination by victory, whatever the escalation necessary, however great the cost, and however evil the by-product in
domestic and world political consequences; and a second group
calling for early termination, whatever the sacrifices of war aims
necessary, however humiliating the frustration and failure, and
however disastrous the events which follow abandonment of the
struggle – resolute pursuit of some middle way may command
wholly insufficient domestic political support; it mattes not how
rational the in-between, moderate policy may appear in cost-
benefit terms. Paradoxically, the more urgent the demands for
termination by groups with diametrically opposed programmes
for termination, the less may be the chance of a policy com-
manding sufficient domestic support which would in fact end
the war.[71]

As it takes two, or more, to make peace it is not easy to integrate
the aims of minimizing costs and maximizing gains, thus it

appears in the case of limited war that for the turn toward negotiated peace to lead to peace, enough force must still be applied
to keep the military situation stable. Political control over the
use of that force must be carefully exercised, however, to insure
that the force not be used in ways which destroy the credibility
of the peace overture.[72]

Such a strategy must involve a continuing evaluation and future
casualties must not seem excessive in relation to future progress. It
may be that the least possible force may be required in order to
entice an opponent to the negotiating table.[73]
   The intensification of tensions and the difficulties inherent in
controlling such volatility can be conceptualized in terms of an
action-reaction cycle.[74] Calculated steps taken have to cross a mutually agreed line which will determine whether or not a conflict
will expand or contract. Within these limits, however, there can be
actions of violence which produce responses yet can be mutually
agreed to be acceptable levels of violence which do not lead to an
end to comprehensive resolution negotiations. Within agreed limits, therefore, violence can surround tactical rather than strategic
advantage, pressure coming from internal radicals and external
opponents, as well as from the more conventional tactic of 'upping

the *ante'*. Such manoeuvring is not without risk.[75] The connection between subjective perceptions and objective factors can be most complex in trying to achieve level-headed consistency in the decision-making process. Stresses and strains on the human actors are the indeterminate variables, for 'as escalation continues, decision-makers' subjective universes of perceptions and images become steadily narrower. The range of expectations tightens: fewer and fewer possibilities seem plausible . . . The subjective future closes in faster than one anticipates it should because it is closing in for psychological, not just objective reasons.'[76] Efforts to establish limits, whilst engaged in localized violent action, can be all part of the negotiating process, although in this rather dangerous interplay, much depends on the overall framework within which both negotiation and violence can be contained.[77]

Just as there are many causes of conflict, there are as many panaceas aimed at resolution. Attempts to achieve non-violent paths to conflict resolution have constantly confounded the international community for generations; however, there have increasingly, within the present century, been more recognized forums which aim to settle disputes. It has been a feature of multilateral diplomacy since World War II, specifically emanating from the West, that resolution of conflicts can be best achieved through the establishment of a framework which has at its core multilateral economic negotiations, where dialogue in pursuit of peace is intertwined with an economic panacea.

The very ability to agree on a framework within which even to start a resolution process is fraught with dangers: the lack of consensus on the basis, norms, and procedures plagues embryonic efforts at organizing such a process, and the rules by which to play the game are of special importance. However,

[t]he absolute dichotomy between the presence and absence of worldwide agreement on values is false. In the world community, as in national societies, there is a broad spectrum of values and of degrees of consensus on them. A large measure of agreement on values does, of course, strengthen the cohesiveness of a community and the efficacy of its legal order. But it is not a question of all or nothing. A black-and-white contrast between a world in which common ideological values prevail and in which peace rests securely on one hand, and a world in which lawlessness and naked force rule, on the other, is out of place here.

These are but nonexistent extremes of a continuum in which, as history suggests, international law will play varying roles in different periods.[78]

In the absence of existing universal values and standards in the field of international relations, whether political, ideological, ethical, legal or social, progress in achieving consensus even on the definition of what constitutes violent conflict, or the more loaded term, 'terrorism', it is then hardly surprising that there also exists no agreed principles or structure which would facilitate the ending of such conflict; this lack is highlighted even more acutely when non-state actors are a part of the equation, where the very act of recognition that there is a conflict implies the conferring of legitimacy.[79] The United Nations has attempted since its inception to develop universal values in a range of areas: economic, social, education, welfare, legal, diplomatic and political. However, because of the desire of its many members and in particular the Security Council's permanent five, the UN's role in conflict has tended towards the field of peacekeeping rather than peace enforcement or resolution. This has begun to change, in the late 1980s, with the waning of the Cold War. There have been signs indicating that the UN was developing a more independent and more comprehensive approach with regard to conflicts around the world, for example, between Iran and Iraq, in Cyprus, Angola, Afghanistan and Cambodia.

The causes of conflict may lie within, for example in the structure of the international system, the actions of the states and non-state actors as well as domestic structures. Therefore it is of great importance to determine to what extent the causes of conflict are structural, institutional or environmental. Conflict need not merely be the opposition of hostile forces, it is also a more complex and indeterminate phenomenon in which antagonism and cooperation can interact within an adversary relationship.[80]

1.5   The dynamics of peace-making?

A peace treaty between Israel and Egypt, or Israel and Jordan is not institutionally speaking very difficult to either negotiate or develop. However, the main difference as regards the Israeli-Palestinian conflict is that it is, at its most basic, an existential conflict. The Israel-Egypt, Israel-Jordan conflict resolution processes adopted a scenario of entering into normal inter-state relations, such as tourism, trade, communication link-ups, and so on. The inter-state conflict resolution scenario develops with a presumption of a high level of success because basically border posts merely have to be opened in order for relations to begin. However, the Israeli-Palestinian conflict is about conflicting legitimacy, over claim to the same land, to the same water, to the same air. Arriving at an agreeable interrelationship within the confines of an existential conflict has been, and will continue to be, most difficult.

Research into the basic hypotheses and dynamics of mutual threat perceptions by conflicting parties has tended to concentrate on the issues of partisan and subjective portrayals of enemies, psychological dynamics, distortions and misperceptions, in general presupposing parties playing on a level-power playing field, their balance of power being of minor significance to the overall ability to achieve a positive outcome to a process of conflict resolution.[81] An underlying assumption of many studies is that whatever 'social psychological dynamics apply to one party apply to the other as well,' so that conflicting parties engaged in a protracted dispute must therefore share at least a mutually antagonistic and hostile power profile.[82] However, conflicting parties, especially in an inter-ethnic conflict, rarely, if ever, share an equitable balance of power relationship, and therefore perceive threat and security in very different terms. Evaluating conflict resolution for parties with structural asymmetric power relationships has not received much attention in the literature on inter-ethnic conflict. In inter-ethnic conflicts, particularly those of a state-substate nature like the Israeli-Palestinian one, the examination of the parties' fears, opinions, influences and interpretations of such, is of great importance in determining the extent to which power-asymmetric assumptions define the power relationships between the parties, in other words the way the parties assimilate their collective perceptions regarding their opponent in order to determine their collective responses with regard to their sense of collective threat, or their sense of collective security.

The extent of parties' understanding of their conflict, its existential nature, its intensity, its potential, and how such differences in real and perceived power affect strategy and actions is of great importance in being able to analyse such conflicts in order to determine their disposition to resolution. For example, within the Arab-Israeli context of the Madrid framework, the Israeli perception was one of weakness in relation to the Arab world. Within the context of the same framework, the Palestinian perception was one of weakness in relation to Israel. Thus both parties' perceptions of the same framework was one of weakness, which in turn guided and influenced the decision-making process and the relations between the parties during the negotiations process.

In order to understand the basis of an asymmetric power relationship in an inter-ethnic conflict like the Israeli-Palestinian conflict, not only is the definition of the power relationship important, particularly as defined by the parties themselves, but so also are the criteria by which to measure power relative to the two parties. But how do we define the 'essence of the power concept'? The impact of power on the processes of conflict, on the course of negotiations, on the outcome of resolution, and the concept of power, 'remains one of the most elusive concepts in the social sciences'. Concepts of 'power, threat, and intensity of conflict have profoundly different meanings in conflicts that involve groups' collective well-being, identity, and often collective existence,' which makes it 'difficult to define these variables in a way that refers to collective identity, competing political ideologies, and systemic structures that are usually involved in inter-ethnic conflicts.'[83]

A coalition of definitions of power may be of use when integrated with procedures of conflict resolution and with appropriate political theories.[84] Thus three definitions of power may be employed:

(1) *Power as operation*, which alters the opponents' status or their recourse to, or control over, allies, resources and material.[85]

(2) *Power as potential for social influence* incorporating six bases of power or resources – coercive power, reward power, legitimate power, expert power, referent power and informational power.[86]

(3) *Power as dependence,*[87] – one side's dependence is the other's power, in turn influencing events in the course of the party's interaction, thus the characteristics of interdependence define each side's power. It is a salient point 'whether the perceiver and target have mutual or one-sided power or control over each other's outcomes', which in essence means that the 'symmetry or asymmetry of interdependence essentially predicts who pays attention to and thinks about whom and how much the party does so.'[88]

Conceptually, power as an asymmetric interdependence within a conflict relationship, or as a party's source of asymmetric dependence within an interdependent relationship may best be defined by the 'perceived control over the outcome for the other side' and/or the 'perceived control over allocation of resources'.[89] In this sense, the analysis and evaluation of power-asymmetric situations should become central to the understanding of the dynamics of the Israeli-Palestinian conflict resolution process.

Whilst power is a dynamic factor of inter-ethnic conflict, also of importance is the sense of the nature and extent of threat and of security perceived by the conflicting parties. Sense of threat is defined by N.N. Rouhana and S.T. Fiske as the extent to 'which the party feels danger to (or security in) its physical existence, social and economic well-being, or its identity and values.'[90] Such perceptions can be measured by the way in which the decision-making process is influenced by such senses of threat and of security. Thus the

> strength of interdependence in the power dependence theory is perceived as the proportion of one party's outcomes that depends upon the other. Strength of interdependence is here predicted to contribute to the feeling of intensity of the conflict. In power-asymmetric conflict, the proportion of the outcomes that depends on the other party is larger for the less powerful party. Therefore, it is predicted that intensity of conflict is perceived differently by parties to the same conflict, with the low-power party attributing more intensity to the conflict than the high-power party.[91]

If we consider the dimensions of the Israeli-Palestinian asymmetric power dependence-interdependence relationship, some surprising conclusions can be surmised depending on the factors reviewed. For example, institutional power, such as land ownership, economic power and military capabilities, is viewed by either side in different ways. The Jewish state's executive, governmental, military, resource, judicial and economic apparatus is more powerful than the Palestinian community, despite Israeli fears of the Palestinians' ability to remain steadfast and true to their identity and their struggle for self-determination, and their demographic balance. Whilst the asymmetrical institutional power balance between the Israelis and Palestinians may seem at first enormously in favour of the Israelis, not all 'types of power are asymmetric,' as power asymmetry is 'better measured by referring to types of power than just one type of power.' The 'diagnostic and prognostic value of the perceived power distribution among ethnic groups in multiethnic states is of great importance if one assumes that conflict resolution requires addressing the needs of parties for power sharing, equality and identity.'[92] This is of particular importance when trying to realize the vision that Israel has for the future of the Palestinian occupied territories and the Palestinians themselves, in the sense of a long-term and permanent relationship. Since the *intifada* it has become blatantly obvious that the *status quo ante* for the Palestinians was not conceivable, therefore the Israeli civil/military administration apparatus for the occupied territories was not a viable long-term proposition. If the Israelis steadfastly refuse to countenance a sovereign Palestinian state contiguous to Israel, then some other form of administrative and jurisdictional relationship has to be devised. If national sovereignty for the Palestinians is out, and total Israeli control, involving the political annexation of the occupied territories is also out, then some other form or forms of relationship have to be devised, one that inevitably and radically alters the nature of the Jewish and democratic characters of the state of Israel. It is then, in this context, that the Israeli-Palestinian asymmetric power dependence-interdependence relationship becomes of great importance in influencing the continued and future relations between the two.

For instance, the 'combination of more or less balanced power on the integrational power factor and the gross asymmetry on the institutional power factor' may 'mobilise the minority to seek more institutional power' which from the majority Jewish population's point of view would mean that a diminution of control over the institutions of power would correspond with a diminution of the Jewish identity of the state.[93] Thus, in this sense, while there exists a nominally superior institutional power imbalance in favour of the Israelis, there is not, however, a corresponding sense of security felt by the Jewish community. Israelis perceive threats emanating from several factors both foreign and domestic: from the Arab world, from the *intifada*, from terrorist attacks, from a history of persecution, from being a minority in the region, from international legitimation of the PLO, from the Israeli-Palestinian demographic imbalance, from Arab Israelis joining the *intifada* or demanding more institutional representation and from international acceptance of the Palestinian Authority as an equal member of international fora. The Palestinians perceive threats emanating from such factors as unemployment, lack of sovereignty, expropriations of land, emigration, expulsions, closure of the territories, Israeli bureaucratic hassles, Israeli politicians' talk of 'transfer' of Palestinian population, lack or erosion of democracy in both Israel and the occupied territories, IDF death squads and corruption.

An interesting by-product of the agreements between the Israelis and the Palestinians in the occupied territories are the concomitant effects on the Israeli Arab community. Israel's two populations have coexisted unequally since 1948, with the Jewish majority holding an asymmetrical control over the state's institutions of power, with the minority population effectively excluded from the centres of power, that is, the government and the army. With Israeli-Palestinian rapprochement, and a reduction in the sense of threat from the occupied territories, there is a likelihood that Israel's Arab population will feel energized to be more active, politically, economically, demographically and socially. With a heightened sense of security because of the reduction in tensions with the Palestinians, the Israeli Arabs may feel justified in demanding a greater role as equal participants in their state. As long as the Arab minority feels a sense of collective alienation from belonging to the state, identifying with it, and attachment to it, the sense of collective and shared future so necessary for the good health of any nation is gravely put at risk. Without common goals, a common identity, communal values, common justice and a shared vision of the future, the asymmetric institutional power imbalance in favour of the Jewish majority may become a point of serious conflict. For as long as the majority population in such a volatile multi-ethnic state such as Israel is perceived as having complete control over the state's institutional power, and the minority population perceives itself as being 'excluded from the power centres, including determining the character of the state, distribution of political representation, and economic power' then without a 'genuine power sharing' agreement aimed at developing a 'meaningful shared collective identity' there will be clamour for change, particularly if future Israeli-Palestinian relations are cordial, thus removing the reason for fear in the Jewish majority and the reason for maintaining a low profile on the Arab minority's part.[94] This scenario, however, causes a collective sense of threat to the Jewish majority.

Therefore, if the Israelis' controls of powers are motivated by a perceived sense of threat from the Arab world, of which the Palestinians are part, then management of the Israeli-Palestinian or Arab-Israeli conflicts may reduce the sense of threat. However it is not immediate that such a reduction in threat would lead to a corresponding increase in the feeling of Israeli security because such agreements may not address, or may even exacerbate, the inherent tension between any bilateral Israeli-Palestinian condominion and the Jewish nature of the superstructure of any future entity, thus arguably leading to an actual increase in the sense of internal threat as the external threat is reduced.

In essence, what started as a seemingly incontrovertible power balance in favour of the Israelis is more likely to achieve a collective sense of threat among Israelis, whereas for the Palestinians what is perceived by the Israelis as a threat is a reassuring sense of security, even though in institutional power terms the Palestinians share a collective sense of threat in relation to Israel's military power. Thus, what one side construes as a sense of threat may be construed by the other as a sense of security. However, this does not hold issue by issue; there is no complete threat/security mirror image because what for Palestinians may constitute a sense of threat may not necessarily translate to a sense of security for the Israelis, particularly if the Israelis collectively do not put such a high premium on an issue as the Palestinians do. Therefore, if an 'examination of conflict dynamics is limited to power dynamics, one might miss an essential ingredient in the dynamics of conflict.'[95]

The inclusion of a threat/security perception dimension within any analysis of the Israeli-Palestinian conflict resolution process is of great significance within the confines of the present and future relations between the Israelis and Palestinians. Whilst the two communities may feel reassurance that what for them is a sense of security is a corresponding sense of threat for the other, the two do not share identical threat/security perceptions. When combined with differing senses of motivations, senses of balances of power, and senses of the intensity of certain issues in the conflict, the task of evaluating and analysing decisions and actions in the drafting of a peace treaty becomes all the more formidable.

1.6 Resolving intercultural conflict

Conflict resolution theory has not tackled the importance of culture sufficiently, being reduced to meaning by it either custom or ethnicity. Culture is 'more than custom: it is lens, not label.'[96] Profound cultural differences and misunderstandings can lead to a 'dialogue of the deaf' propounded by the '"symmetrical autism" of mutual and costly noncomprehension'.[97] Whilst 'meaning not only structures validity in human thought patterns but also defines truth', 'syllogisms are structured in the same way from culture to culture.' However, the 'inventory of true categorical statements varies from culture to culture.' Therefore it is 'possible for a valid conclusion to follow from a syllogism in one culture but to be false in another', thus 'premises are a variable of culture in the same way as attributed causes.'[100]

One of the by-products of the Second Gulf War was the pressure applied by both internal and external systemic challenges to the Arab states (both individually and collectively), arising from questions as to how the Arab world had acted in the face of such aggression, in terms of collective peace and security. The prospects for disunity fermented by such lack of success, the effects of the failure of a proposed Arab solution to the crisis and the ceding of authority, both moral and political, to foreign powers, created public disquiet.[99] Undoubtedly, among Arabs on the street, Saddam Hussein may have been wrong in his invasion of Kuwait but his challenge to the regional status quo, based on questioning fundamental issues, resonated powerfully. Those issues were democratic representation, political participation, economic disparity, cultural diversity, environmental degradation, poverty and the redistribution of wealth, control of natural resources, human rights, foreign military presence in the Middle East, the Arab-Israeli conflict, Palestinian self-determination, Western imposition of state borders and Islam.[100]

The domination of political, economic, social and cultural discourse by Western precepts, concepts and paradigms, which endorse and justify the 'free market' and 'democratization', not only ignores as irrelevant – and thereby does a disservice to – indigenous Middle Eastern heritage and values, but also violates the notion of natural justice. The imposition of any foreign paradigms merely reflects Western arrogance, presumption and ignorance of Middle Eastern culture, values, diversity and needs. Such an arrangement will ultimately be folly, as there is a great likelihood of rejection, because, 'any system in which local culture has no faith and with which the people cannot identify can be expected to fail.'[101] Without fundamental changes at local levels, where local people see their standard of living appreciably rise and can participate in a development process which is more focused on people than on statistics of economic growth, continued economic disparity will foster division and resentment. Such developmental structures must therefore also conform to local customs, traditions and culture. Just as any peace process must contain political justice, so too must economic justice be a major part of successful peacemaking.[102] Examples such as the principles or notions of *Hukm* (government),

Majlis es-Shura (parliament), *al-mithaqa* (original covenant), *zakaat* (compulsory alms tax), *ijma* (consensus), *waqf* (charitable trust, plural *Awqaf*), *al-Ta'tatuf* (solidarity), *Al-Rahma* (compassion), *al-Maghfira* (pardon) and *ar-riqa* (tenderness) are universal values widely understood and practised.[103] The concept of redistribution of wealth is advocated by Koranic injunction (LIX:7). These aspects of local custom and spirit can easily be incorporated into socio-economic and political structures which arise as a result of negotiations, whether as part of an inter-communal, inter-national or inter-regional system.[104]

Any notion of 'democracy' in a Middle Eastern context must take great care to understand the political role of Islam. Islamic notions of democracy demand that Westerners fundamentally and culturally reinterpret their understanding of political philosophy, political order, plurality and the interaction between religion and politics. Islam demands a different perspective regarding the political fundamentals of the individual, of collective identity, of group association, their rights, obligations and responsibilities. Any framework or structure that comes about as a result of the Israeli-Palestinian and Arab-Israeli peace negotiations must in some way accommodate such understandings. External concepts, experiments and grand designs cannot really last if they attempt to graft alien hegemonic principles where there is no basis in history and culture.[105]

Islam purports not only to be a comprehensive way of life, but also to encompass all human relations, domains and jurisdictions. However, in attempting to construct a generally accepted Islamic value system conducive to conflict resolution, or peace-making, it is rather difficult to find conformity on the very meaning of 'peace'. *Salaam* is internationally recognized as the Arabic salutation for peace, but there is a certain vagueness about the ability to translate it directly to have the same meaning as the English. *Salaam* can mean: 'a sense of tranquillity', 'an unworldly sense of security and permanence, soundness, preservation/ salvation, salutation, resignation without discontentment, and freedom from jarring elements.'[106] The term *sulh* means 'truce' or 'armistice' and 'denotes the ending of war'. It can also be argued that believers and non-believers exist in a state of latent or open war, which if accepted means that there is no concept of peace or peace-making in Islam between believers and non-believers.[107] However, since the Prophet's *sunnah* (practice) is accepted as the basis for human affairs for all believers, certain values can be ascertained from the Koran which may be applied in the context of peace-making and conflict resolution. Several core values can be identified from the Koran: compassion, patience, for-giveness, humanity, creativity, respect and sharing.[108]

Peace-making is a structural conflict resolution approach which emphasizes 'the importance of attitudes, sentiments, emotions and moral obligations.'[109] If peace stems from the absence of direct and structural violence then peace-making is a transformative act that intervenes in 'violent or potentially violent conflict situations'[110] with the express 'goals of reducing violence and protecting the rights of the various parties to the conflict.'[111] Islam, according to the Koran, has a strong position on structural violence,

> And fight them on
> Until there is no more
> Tumult or oppression
> And there prevail
> Justice and faith in God
> Altogether and everywhere.[112]

What is problematic in the Middle East is the concept of conflict, the concept of *jihad* (holy war). It is not clear from the Koran which has the greater force of commandment, to pursue peace with com-passion and justice, or to pursue non-believers or those perceived as the enemies of Islam with extreme prejudice.

1.7   An assessment of power, diplomacy and the peace process

Conflict resolution diplomacy continues to be perceived in terms of relative bargaining strengths based on power variables, such as ability to be able to control or determine the application of power, being the basis of present practice. Richard Falk argues that, rarely in 'conflict situations are guiding assumptions about world order made explicit', an 'aspect of the realist hold on the political imagination, which applies often as much to academic discourse as to the ebb and flow of diplomacy.'[113] This leads one to the assumption that 'peace' as it is determined by official elites comes from above, that it is imposed, rather than having been determined by popular will, 'peace-from-below', reflecting majoritarian consensus and consciousness, that is, democratically. In the realist perspective, strength and interest, the power to impose one's will, is the measure of negotiations and is the basis of bargaining. Within the terms of the Israeli-Palestinian conflict, the nature of their asymmetrical power relationship is high-lighted both substantively and symbolically in the manipulation of the power imbalance within the character and context of the ne-gotiating process. In essence, 'the structure of current world order establishes the conditions' which enables the higher power to exercise its power with impunity. This not only benefits it in real terms but also reinforces the actual power disparity of the existing power struc-ture. Israel, as an established state actor, has a military and political legitimacy which allows it to take advantage of the existing state-centred world order structure, gaining considerable benefit at the expense of the non-state PLO actor. This model of international relations, termed the 'Westphalian' by Richard Falk, 'enables Israel to shape political discourse largely in its favour, treating its on-going recourse to violence as part of the legitimate security function of the state while stigmatising far lower levels of Palestinian viol-ence (and even non-violent modes of collective resistance) as "terrorism".' Such a manipulation of geopolitical realities has meant that Israel can, as the representative of the Israeli people, utilize more extensive violent tactics and strategies, and be no more mindful of 'civilian innocence, international law, and the authority of the United Nations than the Palestinians, and their representatives, the PLO.[114] Principled moral and legal justifications and considerations therefore cannot be deemed to be the preserve of one side or the other. What the international structure and the geopolitical frame-work enables Israel to achieve is the opportunity to claim plausible deniability for any of its immoral and violent actions, thus allow-ing it to continue virtually without let or hindrance, in much the same way that Palestinian violence is surrounded by self-righteous vituperation.

This control of the terms and nature of the discourse has al-lowed Israel to achieve a 'kind of polemical plausibility' to her 'refusal to deal with most legitimate Palestinian representatives and politi-cal organisation, contending that it will not negotiate with "terrorists",' which not only allows Israel to abdicate itself from any moral responsibility for ensuing violence, but also effectively diminishes the Palestinians to such a level of weakness that, through necessity,[115] Palestinian participation in any negotiating process is dependent on the prior acknowledgement and acceptance of the inherent imbalance between the two as a result of the existing asym-metrical power structure. Such a structure, by its very exclusive nature, compels implicitly or explicitly, from the Palestinians, an admission and an expression of the natural invalidation of their equitable status, and thus a concomitant depreciation of their rights. Such a power play has been a manifestation of Israeli-Palestinian relations since 1948, and has been of decisive importance in determining the nature of Israeli-Palestinian relations during the negotiating phase.

What can be constructed from this 'Westphalian' model of international order is that it is exclusionary, hegemonic, and asymmetrical in nature. The ideas and practices associated with such a model as embodied in the terms and conditions of the Madrid Middle East peace process reveals a geopolitical framework which accords privilege to state actors and associates 'realism' 'primarily with perceived power relations, including the will and interests of ascendant geopolitical elites.'[116] The extent to which this model dominates the Middle East peace process is quite clearly shown by the 'reluctance of most radical critics of geopolitics to approach an ongoing conflict of this sort in other than realist terms . . . because the diplomatic participants on all sides tend to be realists.'[117] Thus the very fact that this 'peace process' does not lay paramount stress on non-violence and reconciliation, does not incorporate alternative negotiating success/failure guidelines based on democratic rather than power assumptions, and abandons morality and legality, lays it open to the charge that unless peoples are treated as equals, 'injustice is generated and perpetuated.' The alternative to the realist orientation, which 'seeks to translate asymmetries of power and influence among states (or their diplomatic equivalent) into a negotiated agreement' is to construct a structure based on dignity, demilitarization, inclusion, legitimacy, morality and democracy, which would be by its very nature symmetrical. Such an alternative would be the construction of 'a global civil society committed to identifying and realising human rights and democracy on behalf of the peoples concerned, and to evolving a practical conception of the human interest capable of addressing wider regional and global concerns.' By removing fear, which seems to be an ever-present, stalking factor of the 'Westphalian' model, the peace process may be able to deliver solutions to the generative issues 'of collective violence, political and religious repression, and human misery.'[118]

The resolution of the Israeli-Palestinian conflict within the confines of a 'realist solution' would probably mean that Israel will deny the Palestinians statehood on all the pre-1967 land, substantive authority and/or control over East Jerusalem, in whole or in part, full diplomatic status and the right to self-determination, and will insist on the retention by Israel of jurisdiction over, settlements, water rights, lands classed as 'state lands', and security zones, and will demand permanent Palestinian demilitarization and neutrality. The conference of devolved, domestic powers and responsibilities to be held over a defined autonomous entity, which will not include the entire pre-1967 land mass of the West Bank and Gaza Strip, will more than likely be the sum total of the Palestinian political entity, wrought through the tortuous process of negotiating – that is unless the Palestinians declare statehood in defiance of Israel and thus pre-empt such a scenario – because of inertia and/or perceived bad faith in the negotiations on final status. Any other realistic orientations of resolving the conflict other than the 'realist' approach are very unlikely to be either tried or thought of. It is not so much that alternatives do not exist; it is more that there is, and will be, no alternative.

As the Cold War era wound down, calls for alternative global systemic relations abounded. Noam Chomsky cites two contending philosophies.[119] The South Commission, chaired by Julius Nyerere, which consisted of economists, government officials, and religious leaders from the Third World, in one of the earliest calls for a 'new world order', proposed a plea for such an order based on 'justice, equity, and democracy in the global society'.[120] World order, such as it was and is, seems to conform still to the notion that the conduct of international relations is little more than 'codified international piracy',[121] with the rich nations having no real desire to correct the 'moral shortcomings of foreign nations'.[122] A 'new world order' is predicated on an assumption that the tenets, both intellectual and structural, of the 'old world order' would have to give way or be done away with, in order that one can pronounce a 'new' world order. If the old order was predicated upon the notion that the 'government of the world must be entrusted to satisfied nations, who wished nothing more for themselves than what they had', where 'peace would be kept by peoples who lived in their own way and were not ambitious', in a system which enabled rich nations to derive their power over the 'hungry nations' because not to do so would result in constant 'danger' – which would not allow rich nations to dwell 'at peace within their habitations',[123] then a 'new world order' would have to be organized along different lines. President George Bush proposed a 'new world order' in which diverse nations would be 'drawn together in common cause, to achieve the universal aspirations of mankind: peace and security, freedom and the rule of law',[124] under the protective benevolence of the USA, in 'a future for which America is both the gatekeeper and the model'.[125] Suffice it to say that the US vision triumphed, reflecting the realities of the interests of power, economic, political and military. The 'new world order' then is very much like the old; there are no real fundamental changes, no 'new paradigms' to make sense of our world; with one notable exception – the extension and internationalization of interdependent capitalism. Privilege and power and the 'basic rules of world order remain as they have always been: the rule of law for the weak, the rule of force for the strong; the principles of "economic rationality" for the weak, state power and intervention for the strong'.[126]

Whether the concept of international leadership relates to an unipolar, dominant and/or hegemonic US world leadership, as expounded either within or outside the US foreign policy establishment or both, or to the elevation of the UN to a dominant and jurisdictional leadership, was much debated during 1990 and 1991. If world leadership is defined as an 'activity that promotes action, a role that promulgates vision and purpose, and a force that maintains stability in the post-Cold War international system', then what faced world power relations in 1990–1, was a debate over whether the US would offer world leadership, supported by a great-power consensus,[127] or whether the UN would assume the role 'envisioned by its founders',[128] which was the maintenance of 'international peace and security, of developing friendly relations among nations, ... of taking other appropriate measures to strengthen universal peace' and to 'achieve international cooperation in solving economic, social, cultural, and humanitarian problems, and to promote respect for human rights and for the fundamental freedoms for all.'[129]

The euphoria which accompanied the Western-inspired and US-dominated victory in the Second Gulf War in 1991[130] ushered in a short period in which the hypothesis was proposed that US global hegemony would protect the world, because the US with 'its unique combination of military and economic power, its political culture, and experience in realpolitik'[131] was 'bound to lead'.[132] The period of 1989–91 was in global terms one of structural and ideological upheaval and transformation. New definitions abounded of political goals, national aspirations, concepts of national and international security, the understanding of national security and national interest, international and inter-regional cooperation, and economic interdependency. Thus the concept of cooperative regional security based on a new global system of collective security led by the USA was seen by many as just the redefinition of world power relations needed in the phase of uncertainty which accompanied the era from the collapse of the Berlin Wall to the collapse of the USSR. However this phase of optimism over the perceived triumph of both capitalism and liberal democracy, defined by Fukayama as the 'end of history', was soon replaced, not only by the 'gloom of early 1992'[133] but also by the disinclination, both in terms of political and resource commitment, on the part of the US to lead, their preference being instead to define the US foreign policy agenda in terms of 'assertive multilateralism', which proved 'not to be very assertive' at all. With political inertia over Bosnia, withdrawal from Somalia, and a slow, uncoordinated response to the tragedy of Rwanda, the US's much vaunted 'new world order' disintegrated into 'new world disorder' from 1992 onwards, mocking the moral triumphalism of the recent past, exposing the US-inspired 'New World Order' for the 'circumstantial politically expedient rhetoric that it was', and revealing a leadership characterized by 'a lack of vision and direction' combined with the 'seeming primacy of interests over morality'.[134]

However, while it is easy to mock, it is just as difficult to define what we mean by such terms as 'international leadership', 'international order', and 'new world order', US inspired or otherwise.[135] International relations theory seems to lack agreed, definitive theories of leadership, whether paradigmatic, analytical, structural or functional. Jarrod Weiner has presented a 'classification of leadership theories/definitions according to two levels of analysis, 'macro-unilateral' and 'micro-multilateral'.[136]

Macro-unilateral analyses deal with three main processes:
- provision of principles and an intellectual framework on which to base 'international order'
- creation of authoritative structures emanating from agreed principles
- provision of 'common weal' through a protective security system.[137]

Within the parameters of this theoretical notion, the US has 'emerged with a military ascendancy of a monopoly character' harnessing its 'power and willingness' in favouring a system which stabilizes the status quo and projects 'its own vision of order onto the international system.' Through the institutionalization of US order, the UN is thus founded in order to make the 'rules that govern the manner in which states relate to the dominant power'. Within this explanation, US global leadership is concerned about the 'maintenance of a rule-oriented and norm-governed system' in which 'leadership relates to a political activity in shaping international structures to suit the ascendant state's interests.'[138]

Micro-leadership on the other hand 'refers to a relationship between leaders and followers within a well-defined normative order ... whereby a leader gains a followership behind its agenda through persuasion, negotiation, and brokering the concerns of others to induce them to follow.'[139] Thus leadership is based on a cooperative relationship acquired as a result of communicative proficiency rather than the crude application of cajolery. In this sense, leadership can be defined as 'inducing followers to act for certain goals that represent the values and the motivations – the wants and the needs, the aspirations and the expectations – of both leaders and followers'[140] in order to 'fashion acceptable deals' having brought 'willing parties together.'[141]

The theory of hegemonic leadership incorporates the two analyses above, defining the bases of hegemony as the synthesis and control of 'raw materials, sources of capital, markets, competitive advantage in the production of highly valued goods, finance capital, technologies, natural resources'.[142] It is in this context that Charles Kindleberger argues, 'for the world economy to be stabilised, there has to be a stabiliser, one stabiliser ... a country which is prepared ... to set standards of conduct for other countries and ... to take on an undue share of the burdens'.[143] Such a notion of world regime stability, with its neoliberal/neorealist pretensions of 'the white man's burden', does not distinguish between 'beneficent hegemony' and malevolent, exploitative, coercive hegemony.[144] The theory of hegemonic leadership remains ambiguous in its understanding of the nature of international leadership, 'confusing governance, or management, with leadership', and does not clarify the crucial distinction between 'the normative or ideological underpinnings of a regime' and 'the legitimation of a leadership role'.[145] Whilst the substantive norms of regimes constitute the 'structure of the internationalization of political authority'[146] which rest, not on the conception of legitimacy as authorized coercion and compulsion, but on mutuality of shared benefits or on 'moral coercion'.[147] Legitimacy in this sense confers moral and political obligations, both of the leader and the followers, based on previously accepted principles.

Therefore, whilst we can attempt to accept various understandings of the concept of leadership, deficiencies persist, which means that we cannot neatly pigeonhole US power and its application in the context of global order. It is easy to write off rhetoric, political expediency, moral turpitude and confusion, (Second Gulf War, Somalia, Bosnia, Rwanda) as significant of a greater malaise, as the proof required to disprove the assumption of moral authority required by the US to speak on behalf of all the world's citizens. However, we must remember that there is no globally agreed set of authoritative principles or moral criteria by which to judge the US, be it on the level of state interest, international interest, popularity or morality. In this sense it is instructive and illuminating that theories of, and the understanding of, such international leadership may well be dysfunctional and unrealistic. What then can we salvage from such a discussion?

The post-Cold War international system did not begin afresh, with a blank page. Having inherited the existing imperfect international order, system and functions, we can see that there existed a common thread dating back to President Woodrow Wilson and his 14 points, which not only established the tone for US moral leadership with their insistence that the Covenant of the League of Nations be incorporated into the post-World War I peace treaties, but also set the standard by reflecting 'US political culture' in the promotion of 'order through legislation'.[148] President Bush merely followed an established trend in US foreign policy in espousing a framework of principles that maintained stability, order and security through great-power cooperation. What was new, however, was the explicit notion that, although the US had been deeply disillusioned by what had become of the UN in its Cold War state,[149] the US was willing to re-engage the UN on the understanding that the US would provide systemic leadership for the UN – in other words, in order for the UN to function properly, the US would provide political leadership by activating the collective security apparatus of the UN so as to uphold the new power realities, in the form of an international system of law, order and US hegemonic leadership defined, led and motivated by US 'enlightened self-interest'.[150]

This theory of hegemonic leadership does not define accurately enough whether global leadership is to be based on moral, altruistic, political, resource, economic, military or other uses of power. Each individually and collectively encompass assumptions of superpower status; however, we are left unclear as to how this leadership relates to US power, particularly as it affects the Middle East. Certainly, in the US debate is sometimes fierce over whether the US should be involved in foreign affairs,[151] has overstretched its abilities through overcommitment, is alternatively shaking a 'begging bowl' or run-ning an international protection racket,[152] has the resources to achieve what it and its allies want,[153] or indeed whether Americans have the desire to lead the 'free world'.[154]

What seems evident in the years since the Second Gulf War is that, despite the cosmetic public relations exercise aimed at con-vincing public opinion that the world was protected by a system of collectively managed international security, the US has effectively harnessed the UN in order to control it. This means that, for example, if the US defines an issue to be in its national interests then the UN offers a legitimacy which can be utilized in a way that super-sedes US commitments to the UN and its supposedly subordinate position within the UN; which effectively means the UN becomes 'the tool of vested interests'.[155] Conversely, when American national interests are not directly affected, the UN appears as a convenient 'scapegoat on which to blame inertia' – in fact some American politicians have criticized the US government for 'deferring to the UN, instead of taking a lead'[156] describing such action as an 'abdi-cation of American leadership'[157] and that pursuing multilateralism 'has become a cover for US retrenchment and abandonment of lead-ership to the vagaries of international events.'[158] However, we must still be mindful of the rather schizophrenic nature of chauvinistic elements within some sectors of the US foreign policy debate, who believe that the US should use the UN, not be used by it,[159] whilst at the same time feeling that 'it is time for our friends to bear more of the burden.'[160]

Thus we can see that the US is more concerned with creating an international order and maintaining such an order's stability and security than with asserting a system which sets standards of jus-tice and moral criteria as its defining functions, such as would involve the prevention of genocide, human rights abuses, humanitarian disasters, famines, and so on. In terms of international leadership, the US motivation to undertake global leadership merely follows from perceived national interest, particularly as it is the biggest benefactor in the maintenance of the status quo. At its most basic, what any theory of international leadership should understand is the difference between what is practicable (collective security under US leadership and patronage), and what is improbable (the preven-tion of human tragedy). Thus, self-serving and self-righteous rhetoric apart, the US merely follows a long and established practice of the pragmatic application of power in the pursuit of its own interests.

The principle of non-alignment used to be a cornerstone of Labour Zionism, the argument being that too great a dependency on the US not only creates a dependency culture in Israel, but also leaves Israel both vulnerable to US policy shifts and unable to act independently and pursue a contradictory agenda. The effects of US largesse by successive administrations in their aid policy towards Israel has been mixed. Enormous sums of capital have neither led to real economic growth and stability, nor been concentrated in productive sectors of the economy. Rather, US aid finances non-productive and politically/ideologically motivated sectors of the Israeli economy, such as settlements in the occupied territories, the Israeli military, and loan repayments to US institutions. Stephen Zunes argues that 'annual military aid is in fact simply a credit line to US arms manufacturers, and actually ends up costing Israel two to three times that amount to train operators, to staff and maintain, to procure spare parts, and other related costs' with the overall impact being the increase in 'Israeli economic and military dependency on the US' thus draining 'Israel's fragile economy.'[161] According to Matti Peled, the sum of US aid is arrived at 'out of thin air' and is not directly related either to specific economic or military requirements. The fact that US aid has remained at a constant figure over a number of years does little to diminish the 'impression that it is little more than a US government subsidy for US arms manufacturers' with the resulting bonanza for US defence contractors from Arab demands following every significant arms transfer to Israel.[162]

In an evaluation of US Middle East policy, Zunes argues that in some aspects US policy toward Israel closely 'corresponds with historic anti-Jewish oppression.' By this he is referring to the way that in Europe in past centuries the ruling elites would grant the minority Jewish community limited rights, privileges and cultural autonomy in return for being commissioned as the 'visible agents of the oppressive social order, such as tax collectors and money lenders'. This would result, in times of social disorder when the population rose against the ruling class, in the rulers having a convenient scapegoat in the Jews against whom the ire of the exploited could be turned.[163] Pogroms, repression and exploitation were the structure and nature of diaspora that Zionism was created in order to break free from. In a direct corollary to the present US-Israel relationship, Israel, as the embodiment of US power in the region, finds itself at the centre of a self-perpetuating cycle of Western self-interest, and as the convenient expedient to deflect anti-US criticism from angry Arab governments and peoples. Zionism and the existence of the state of Israel, and not the US superpower, thus becomes for Arab popular perception the root of all Arab evils, in a neat side-step by the US. It can be argued that this aspect of US foreign policy is a by-product of domestic US politics and/or anti-semitism, in that overt US government subsidies are unpopular with the US public and therefore the Jewish lobby becomes a convenient domestic scapegoat for the typical executive distaste for taking responsibility and giving explanations, and for pursuing unpopular policies, particularly those involving the misappropriation of public resources.[164] In a rather ironic twist of the propaganda perpetuated by anti-semites, such as the Protocols of the Elders of Zion regarding the all-pervasive nature of Jewish influence in world affairs, A.F.K. Organski notes that the

> belief that the Jewish lobby ... is very powerful has permitted top US policymakers to use 'Jewish influence' or 'domestic politics' to explain the policies ... that US leaders see as working to US advantage, policies they would pursue regardless of Jewish opinion on the matter. When Arab leaders or officials of allies protest, US officials need give only a helpless shrug, a regretful sigh, and explain how it is not the administration's fault, but that policy makers must operate within the constraints imposed by powerful domestic pressures moulding congressional decisions. Presidents, and those who speak in their names, have followed this strategy time and time again. Congressmen employ this same device.[165]

In questioning the character, function and significance of US pro-Israel groups as a 'major factor in US foreign policy', Peled argues that if it wasn't for the Jewish lobby, 'the US government would have to invent them.'[166] I. Leibowitz goes further, arguing that the

> existence of the Jewish people of 60 to 80 generations ... was an heroic situation. We never got from the goyish world a cent. We supported ourselves. We maintained our own institutions. Now we have taken three million Jews, gathered from here and turned them over to be parasites – parasites of America. And in some sense we are even the mercenaries of America to fight the wars of American interests, or what the ruling persons in America consider to be American interests.[167]

This critique of US foreign policy revolves around the installation of Israel as a regional scapegoat and target for regional ills rather than the 'broader exploitative global economic system and their own elites who benefit from and help perpetuate such a system.'[168] This attitude can be corroborated by ex-PM Shamir in his autobiography, when he recounts a meeting with Japanese leaders:

> 'Your people' a ranking minister said to me (and there were others who echoed his sentiments) 'are so fortunate with your unlimited access and boundless influence everywhere. You are all-powerful. See how you hold the United States in the palms of your hands.' Never mind how strongly I protested that, unfortunately this was not precisely the case, my hosts smiled, nodded and clearly disbelieved me.[169]

The US has for many years been obsessed with policies which dictate military solutions to political problems, not only through misperceiving or being dismissive of popular movements, but also through viewing problems in terms of containment which in turn lead to policies driven by unilateral initiatives and actions. This dominant thinking within the US establishment has led over the years to the encouragement of the more 'chauvinistic and militaristic elements in the Israeli government, undermining the last vestiges of Labour Zionism's commitment to socialism, non-alignment, and cooperation with the Third World.'[170] The US for many years refused to support a two-state solution to the Israeli-Palestine problem, refused to acknowledge publicly and negotiate with the PLO, and refused to make its enormous economic and military assistance programmes to Israel conditional on the latter honouring its international commitments to human rights, international law and UN Security Council Resolutions. Israel's part in the relationship is in supporting the US military-industrial complex, in providing assistance to US agencies attempting to subvert Congress, and in playing the role of regional policeman (in intelligence gathering, in proactive covert raids, in maintaining a semblance of stability, as the enforcer of unpopular policies, and in non-attributable prejudicial actions). In short, according to none other than Henry Kissinger, Israel 'serves the purposes of both our countries best.'[171] Thus Israeli actions must be understood within the context of the US-Israel relationship, and Middle East actions must be understood within the context of Arab-Arab, Arab-Israeli and US-Arab relations. However, whilst this argument does not imply a simplistic and sinister 'grand conspiracy by Western capitalists to divide and rule the Middle East', one must be aware that the policies pursued by the US and her Western allies have indeed 'resulted in a regional system that greatly benefits Western oil companies, arms manufacturers, and national security elites at the expense of the region's population.'[172] If we are to understand why acts of terrorism take place, why some people are driven to extreme reactions to Western policies, and what effects economic, military and diplomatic policies have on indigenous peoples, then it is incumbent upon any assessment of the Israeli-Palestinian peace process to understand the shadows cast upon it by the US, and how far US rhetoric regarding its support for democracy, international law, justice, self-determination, demilitarization, economic development and Arab-Israeli and Israeli-Palestinian peace, measures up to the practical application of US policies and actions. In such a way we can determine whether the particular structure of the Madrid Peace Conference was calculated specifically as a form of partisan domination aimed at imposing a *pax americana* intended to perpetuate Western 'strategic, economic and ideological imperatives' through a 'divide-and-rule tactic designed to further weaken Arab unity and to create increased dependency on the US' or whether it is a process of creative peace building aimed at achieving a just, lasting and comprehensive peace order.[173]

Since 1945, US policy towards the Middle East has been fundamentally contradictory. The two main strategic objectives of successive US administrations have been the securing of reliable and cheap oil supplies, and the institution of Israel as *primus inter pares* in regional terms.[174] For US administrations and policy-makers this 'headache, sometimes a nightmare' has ensured contradictions in US actions, practices and tactics.[175] Given the widely held perception in the Arab world of a strong pro-Israel bias shown by the US, evidence since the Second Gulf War suggests the result has been that not only has the US's image in the Islamic world suffered but so also has the image of those moderate pro-US regimes who support the military, political and economic presence of the US in the Middle East.[176] The growth of US dependence on Middle East oil 'comes at a time when the US military presence' in the 'region is facing a critical phase' because not only is the US in the difficult position of supporting conservative Arab regimes who face domestic challenges from radical elements and externally from radical Iran, but also the US military presence itself fuels radical resentment because of her support for such conservative regimes and of course Israel.[177] Justification for a US military presence in the Middle East, particularly in the Persian Gulf, is predicated on 'the international importance of oil and the fact that half of the world's seaborne crude exports must pass through the Strait of Hormuz.' However, US support for Israel has not only antagonized militants but also undermined conservative pro-US elements keen to distance themselves from being too closely associated with the US.[178] Popular Arab antipathy toward the US for its support for Israel, combined with neglectful and inconsistent US policies towards Arab states, has meant that US actions are in a sense undermining and threatening her twin strategic goals in the Middle East. Furthermore US espousal of commitments to independence, freedom and democracy are at odds with US actions and alliances in the Middle East; thus the growth of a hostile Islamic constituency opposed to the US presence in the Middle East across the region stems, in part, from the lack of respect for such principles in practice.[179] US policy-makers and decision-makers have been unable to grasp that the essence of radical Islam's anti-Americanism stems from widespread resentment at the performance of the ruling elites and governments which are supported by the US, and from the US's unqualified and uncritical support of Israel. Thus anti-Americanism is a 'potent instrument of mobilisation and legitimation' in political movements throughout the Middle East, generated further by US fears, misunderstanding, misperceptions and denials of the legitimacy of popular Islamic public opinion.[180] Such US fears have created the stereotype of the 'Islamic fundamentalist' and the 'Islamic extremist' demonized by the Western media, 'rendering them unworthy of being taken seriously in their criticism of US policies',[181] and thereby creating the impression of an evil international terrorist network out to destroy the US. The conclusion to be drawn therefore is that US resolve must be strong enough and sufficiently aggressive to withstand this new terrorist threat to US interests in the Middle East. Thus instead of being as responsive to public opinion and interest groups in the Middle East polity as they are domestically, successive US administrations have not only been neglectful and ignorant of Islamic public opinion, they have persistently ignored it as unimportant or as of no consequence to US policy-making. The continuation of injudicious actions merely opens up the US to further problems in the Middle East, highlighting both ignorance of, and lack of concern for, ordinary peoples' plights, which will only further emphasize

the limitations of US military power should allies or clients en-
counter political upheaval and overthrow. The failure of the US to
respond to real social and political problems, or at the least, publicly criticize their allies or encourage them to pursue reforms, opens
up the possibility of more scenarios as happened in Iran, or is happening in Algeria.

1.8   Interdependence *versus* asymmetry

Immanuel Kant believed that international conflict became less likely
the more important economic relations between states were, the
more states' executives were limited by constitutional constraint,
and the more international relations were governed by a system of
non-violent relations.[182] Kant argued that peace among democratic
nations would be the consequence of complementary influences.
Republican constitutions would eliminate 'autocratic caprice in waging
war' and the spread of democracy would ensure a universal understanding and acknowledgement of the legitimate rights of all citizens
and of all republics.[183] This creates a

> moral foundation for the liberal peace, upon which eventually
> an edifice of international law can be built. Lastly, economic
> interdependence reinforces constitutional constraints and liberal
> norms by creating transnational ties that encourage accommo-
> dation rather than conflict. Thus, material incentives add their
> force to law and morality.[184]

Classical liberal philosophy contends that the mantra which com-
bines laissez-faire 'free trade' and the institution of 'democracy' is
the best weapon with which to fight the incidence of war.[185] Economic interdependence and similar, suitable regime types organized
within an international structure offer the best solution to an otherwise anarchical system of contending ideologies, regime types and
economic systems. The hypothesis that conflict may be reduced or
resolved via the institution of an economic interdependence between rivals and the sharing of regime types rests on the notion
that trade brings individuals into relationships of common interest,
at the same time increasing prosperity and employment and thus
reducing the vagaries of fortune which might compel the decision
of a ruling elite to wage war.

According to the Kantian theory, democratic governments have structural and normative constraints built in to hinder the initiation of conflict. Collective decision-making and institutional arrangements of checks and balances restrict the ability and willingness to become embroiled in conflict.[186] Thus normatively, 'democracies value negotiation and compromise, respect the rights of others, and eschew violence as a result of the externalisation of domestic norms of conflict.'[187] Benefits accruing from economic and institutional interdependence are central to the hypotheses proclaimed by functionalist and pluralist theoreticians,[188] and of course central to the tenets of Marxist ideology, and the more liberal alternative of socialistic internationalism.[189]

The theoretical challenge to such views comes from those who emphasize that economic ties not only offer the prospect of mutual gain but also may transmit economic ills and create rivalry over the division of benefits. Criticism in this context contends that interdependence, particularly when relations between conflicting parties are asymmetrical, can breed not only accommodation and harmony, but suspicion and incompatibility. Thus in an unequal relationship, economic interdependence can be an agent of influence,[190] even of coercion, which 'may lead to dependency, exploitation, and conflict.'[191]

Whether analysts favour the benefits of interdependence, believe them to be of lesser importance than other issues, or are critical of such liberal hypotheses, is a theoretically moot point. What is of importance and interest to this analysis of the Israeli-Palestinian peace process is how far economic relations are both an aid and a hindrance to the success of the process, and to what extent the Israeli-Palestinian economic relationship is viewed as an integral foundation of the entire conflict resolution process.[192]

The liberal hypothesis that trade is a facilitator of conflict resolution, that economic prosperity can be the basis, or at least a major foundation, of a peace process is rooted in the proposition that the involvement by conflicting parties in an integrated trading network, within an interlocking and interdependent bilateral, multilateral, regional and international economic structure, is such a positive influence in the inhibition of conflict as to have the power to reorder, renew and transform in a constructive manner previously disputatious relationships into favourable and optimistic associations.[193] For liberals, economic interdependence does not have to be equal to be positive. 'Liberals, functionalists, and neo-functionalists argue that the expansion of interstate linkages in one area stimulates further cooperation in other areas',[194] in the sense that trade facilitates and promotes deeper relations, cooperation, convergence of interests and media that cope with conflicts of interest, and, the deterrence on leaders from initiating conflict.[195]

This is however a proposition not without its critics.[196] The latter contend that the ability of commercialism and mercantilism to promote an environment conducive to peace is qualified by the structure and extent of the trading relations between conflicting parties, particularly if the existing and proposed relations contain structural imbalances in favour of one side at the expense of the other. Whilst liberals champion the notion that trade fosters peace, no matter what structural inequities exist, critics contend that simple trade relations may aid a peace process only in so far as such commercialism is part of a symmetrically dependent relationship, and that a trading relationship alone cannot overcome manifest inequalities inherent within an asymmetrically dependent relationship, which further implies an inability or freedom by weaker parties to 'break free from undesirable trade relations.'[197] Liberals assume that trade can foster only positive benefits for furthering relations; however, if the negative/positive impacts of economic interdependency are evaluated in a cost-benefit analysis and it is found that costs outweigh benefits then it follows that trading relations may further tension rather than lessen it. This is particularly true of asymmetrical relationships where the negative costs may well be greater and more marked. The counter-proposition made by dependency theorists and neo-Marxists that asymmetrical dependence-interdependence relations may not necessarily be improved by trade, but may result in the impoverishment of the weaker party, is pursued to highlight a critical response to liberal claims of the universality of benefits accruing from trade. Thus the counter-proposition claims that

> gains from trade are enjoyed exclusively by developed states; trading relations between developed and developing nations retard the development process of the latter; trade destroys traditional political, economic, and social institutions; trade exacerbates inequalities in the wealth of nations; and trade relegates powerless states to a position of dependence.[198]

In an asymmetrical relationship, interdependence may, through a more traditional patron-client relationship, stimulate negative political consequences, foster political and economic exploitation, and force concessions. In such an environment, when 'extensive economic dependence threatens national autonomy and poses problems for domestic . . . policy-makers, tensions may arise among trade partners' and especially more pronounced in asymmetrical relationships.[199]

Although most analysts would contend that asymmetrical dependence serves as a 'source of leverage' in a number of policy areas, it is however 'unclear that the use of power arising from trading relationships is sufficient to create tensions that will manifest themselves in violent conflicts'. Bilateral relations that do not provide mutual benefits or 'impose disproportionate costs on one actor may be viewed as hostile relations.' Such hostilities may be suppressed when relations are of a subservient and/or dominant nature or when 'states perceive some aspect of the relationship as beneficial, and thus seek to preserve a sense of harmony.' However it would seem 'plausible to argue that the existence and abuse of unequal power within asymmetrical relations creates a predisposition for conflict that is greater than that found in symmetrical trade relations' and that the 'absence of net benefits in a trading relationship neutralises the pacifying influence of trade, assumed to exist by liberals', so that relations of unequal exchange may in fact 'heighten tensions in inter-state relations, making conflict more likely in such relationships.'[200]

The history of colonialism and imperialism serves to illustrate just how military force may be used in conjunction with trading strategies to establish and maintain inequitable economic relationships; therefore, the expansion of trade may not just promote peace, but 'may involve increased interstate conflict, as powerful states vie with one another for control over finite resources and markets and use force to subjugate developing states to a position of dependence.'[201]

Neo-liberal triumphalism as a result of the former USSR's ideological and strategic disengagement from global involvement, and subsequent dissolution, rose to heights of 'universalistic pretension' heralding a new world order in which conflict would be successfully and completely concluded. The development of the twin virtues of peace and democracy, with a rejuvenated role for the UN, were predicted as a result of the demise of the 'evil empire' whose world mission was supposedly to foster systemic international violence and radicalism and subordinate democracy and mercantilism with totalitarianism and command economies. Existing and continuing conflict, systemic and otherwise, around the world is still a characteristic of international relations and points to a rather different appraisal which somewhat mocks earlier optimistic neo-liberal pretensions. According to Alejandro Bendana neo-liberalism is an

> ideological attempt to explain in global terms the supposedly common forces, justifications, and objectives sustaining political change not simply with regard to economic policy making but also in terms of the new norms which are to govern the discourse and behaviour of socio-political actors.[202]

Extending market logic to the field of political behaviour 'presupposes peaceful competition and attainable civic harmony', thus conflict resolution and conflict management techniques become, in effect, 'social accords which constitute the containment of societal contradictions within a framework upholding neoliberal dogmas with regard to the role of the state, the central place of the market, fiscal responsibility, and the primacy of the private sector.'[203]

A strategic intellectual vacuum exists as a result of disillusionment with leftist ideology around the world. Nothing in life exists without an opposite, no positive without a negative, no right without left.[204] Neo-liberalism needs a counterbalancing radical, critical and coherent ideology whether it is to develop naturally and reinvent itself, or if it is to avoid confrontation from more obtuse and providential sources. Whilst this is not the place to reinvent leftist ideology, the purpose of this point is to highlight the inherent paradoxes which beset the unstoppable success of Western ideology and Western ways in permeating cultures. How, what, which and why Western ideology, motivations and practices are applied by Israel within the context of the Israeli-Palestinian conflict resolution process are of importance since not only do they determine Israeli policies and strategic planning and define Israeli goals, they also elicit responses from the Palestinians, which is vital in understanding the nature, success or failure, and future of the conflict resolution process.

For two societies attempting to transform their fundamental interaction from deep-rooted and protracted conflict within an asymmetrical power relationship, the concept of peace with justice is paramount in the alleviation of the basis of the conflict and also for protecting the proceedings with goodwill. The attempted transformation of the Israeli-Palestinian conflict framed within a transitional period will undoubtedly incur difficulties. Within this context, it is important to be aware of the anomalies which will be highlighted by the changing nature of power relationships between the two communities, from the individual to the governmental. In a process of change, iniquitous power relations, political privileges and power elites will fight for their survival and control, at the same time as the agents of change, those who have defied and confronted the status quo, will be asked to curtail the intensity of popular agitation. In any transformation of a struggle which attempts to retain much of the status quo at the expense of a liberation movement, new complexities and new relationships will undoubtedly arise meaning that any such process will fall short of the total demands of those pursuing change, and with it will bring new complexities as processes of promoting accountability, democracy and stability reveal their shortcomings, in turn creating new realities and problems. The Israeli-Palestinian conflict resolution process as a mechanism initiated and underwritten by the United States may be seen by cynics as an attempt to preserve, at the very least, a system of relations which may be seen to perpetuate economic and political injustice, and deny access to power, resources and opportunities, by the status quo powers and elites. Within the course of this study, this analysis will evaluate and identify attempts to address such complaints of the Israeli-Palestinian conflict resolution framework, both from an ethical and diagnostic/prognostic perspective. Strategic, tactical and organizational considerations which act as obstacles or as agents of empowerment will be taken into account and explored. 'Techniques are not separable from politics,' meaning that the gamut of Israeli-Palestinian interrelations is inseparable from politics and the political framework within which they operate, as any political analysis 'would necessarily take into account the stage of struggle, the balance of forces, the nature and extent of the transition, and the real or imaginary space that becomes available for negotiated engagement.' 'Conflict resolution, and the negotiations in particular, are a field of struggle. Battles are not won or lost on the basis of the cerebral use of techniques but rather on the amount of power brought to bear in a negotiating forum.' Thus, conflict resolution may be a process either of reform, or of radical restructuring and reordering principal and systemic relations, in which each 'nation and each period will determine its own dynamic.'[205]

Bendana believes that modern 'mediation-centred dispute resolution techniques are underpinned by allegiance to the basic workings of the system, including such cultural premises as the age-old Western historical claim to universalism.' The premise that 'those who imposed war can now bring peace,' allied to the enticement that the Palestinian corporate body can participate as an equal member of the nation-state system, undermines a process of Palestinian self-determination to define its future institutional form and its relations. The prospect is very real for the Palestinians of an economically and politically tied entity, authoritarian, unaccountable and oppressive, unable to afford the costs of cooperation and compromise, and constrained in its actions by the acceptance and thus legitimization of an imposed and external value-system. Conflict resolution techniques, 'like most management or technical aspects of capitalism, cannot be assimilated or copied neutrally', simply to 'transmit them mechanically under the guise of neutrality would be to fall into a partisan trap, to devise another mechanism employed by an unjust system to better reproduce the ideological, cultural, political, and productive relations which sustain it.' Thus in the eyes of those who oppose this particular process of Israeli-Palestinian rapprochement, such 'classic conflict resolution techniques, or indeed many of the models developed and drawn from the indus-trialised world . . . become means of disempowerment, neutralising conflict and coalition-building that could avoid violence and weaken the political culture of domination.'[206] The existence of such processes and procedures in an hostile environment stimulates and activates dissent and opposition. How that opposition takes form and what form it takes will be analysed within the body of this work.

Conflict resolution and peace-building can therefore be regarded as the means to 'attack tensions and contradictions among all those affected by the unjust and arbitrary application of power.'[207] Whether this process of conflict resolution acts as an instrument which promotes the 'pursuit of peace with justice', whether this process can incorporate constant reform and correction 'utilising productive and conceptual structures' which address the fundamentals of the transformation of the nature of the conflict and asymmetrical power relations between the Israelis and the Palestinians, rather than merely being an exercise in the immediate transfer of power, or certain powers, will be the essence of this study. A thorough analysis of the dynamics of the process will thus reveal whether it is truly a conflict resolution process which results in a just and comprehensive peace or whether it is a conflict management exercise by the powerful to anaesthetize a minor irritant, which occasionally becomes a problem.[208]

When assessing the Arab-Israeli and Israeli-Palestinian conflicts utilizing contemporary conflict resolution thinking, it is most important to remember that such analysis of conflict resolution practice must take account of the differing cultural assumptions and mores that the Arab parties bring to the negotiating table. When resolving conflict with Arab parties, the Western analyst must recognize the role that Islam bears, and the beliefs, attitudes, customs and tradition that Arab participants understand and live by. That is to say, any analysis of a conflict resolution process between the Israelis and Palestinians must be mindful of the framework and cultural anchors regarding the biases which pre-exist in the Islamic context and thus, if not directly determining, certainly influence the behaviour and thinking of the Palestinian participants. Cultural difference exists to the extent that misperceptions of one side's desires or prioritizations may be regarded incredulously by the other; however, the root cause may have more to do with inherent inabilities on the part of the Palestinians to engage neatly in a Western-style conflict resolution process when some concepts and techniques are unable to be understood or utilized within a society with its basis in Islam.

Western conflict resolution encompasses defined levels, models and methods within certain boundaries, including the processes of conciliation, facilitation, mediation, negotiation, arbitration and problem-solving. In the West, such principles and procedures are practised in more facets of life than in the Middle East. Basic assumptions and procedures are not only very different as practised in either region, but they are also very different in their definition and implementation. Conflict resolution is practised in the West as a professional discipline within agreed legal and jurisdictional frameworks; in the Middle East traditional norms and community standing provide legitimacy for the conduct of resolving disputes. Middle Eastern conflict resolution processes are neither defined nor constructed as an academic discipline in the strictest Western sense. Traditional Middle Eastern methods of negotiation, mediation and arbitration are practised from the most basic levels of society, within clans, villages, towns and cities, on an interpersonal, inter-community and inter-religious level. Middle Eastern conflict resolution techniques are so much a part of everyday life that they are practised and honed as a skill as an integral part of an individual's life, at work, at play and in the market.[209]

Western and Middle Eastern approaches to conflict resolution, and the performance and application of such, are so different that ap-

plying one within the culture of the other would necessitate redefinition and alteration to suit local conditions to make it of any
worth. Basic contradictions highlight the differences between the
two cultures. In the West, conflict is seen as positive, normal, competitive, confrontational and creative, from which conflict resolution
can foster collaboration, resolve, rationality, mutuality of interest
and understanding, legal formality and goal-oriented frameworks.
In the Middle East, conflict is seen as negative, dangerous, destructive and disorderly. Techniques which resolve conflict are based on
honour codes, emotion, the protection of collective identity and
units of association, arbitration and mediation, social and cultural
values rather than legal formulae, individual senses of dignity/shame,
hierarchical and authoritarian structures, the desire for unity, and
relationship-oriented frameworks.[210]

Cultural and historical differences explain why the two societies
have problems in effecting mutual understanding, mutual respect,
dialogue and progress in their interactions within the region. Western
strategies, involvement, ideas and values, particularly those associated with power relations, are viewed by many in the Middle East
with suspicion, distrust, humiliation, rejection, antagonism and
scepticism.[211] This comes as a direct result of past experience of
Western-Middle Eastern interaction and forms one of the most fundamental differences in attitude between the two societies. Western
political strategy has seen conflict resolution acting as a means with
which to restore order to the existing status quo which not only
benefits the asymmetry of the Western-Middle Eastern power relationship in favour of the West, but also means the preservation of
repressive, brutal, and despotic regimes. The levels of conflict resolution in which Western powers involve themselves in the Middle
East obstruct societal and political reform, and indeed do little to
advance the justice, human rights and economic expectations that
citizens in Western societies not only expect, but take for granted.[212]

1.9   Conflict resolution *versus* adversarial paradigms

According to S.E. Ibrahim, the Middle East is contested by four
competing, adversarial and divergent geopolitical paradigmatic ideologies; a Middle Eastern, a Mediterranean, an Arab, and an Islamic,
within which the policies of 'peace, development, democratisation,
and integration' vie with the states of 'despotism, extremism, violence, and disintegration.'[213]

The Middle Eastern paradigm, dating from World War I, is a strategic geopolitical policy aimed at Western (ostensibly British/French and latterly American) domination and exploitation, through military and economic power, coercion and co-optation of the Middle East, North Africa and the Persian Gulf.[214] Whether as part of the policy of containment of the USSR during the Cold War, as a preventative policy aimed at neutralizing indigenous regimes and/or political movements, or as a device to ensure a cheap, steady flow of oil, the Middle East paradigm is at heart a geopolitical arrangement for the benefit of, primarily, the USA, but also the USA's principal allies (namely Israel) and those deemed friendly by the USA such as Saudi Arabia, the Gulf States and Egypt. The Second Gulf War and the end of the Cold War weakened those Arab indigenous forces committed to the ideal of a pan-Arabist future caused by another Arab-Arab war coming so closely on the heels of the 1980–8 Gulf War. This was not only because oil-based power had been eroded by falling prices during the 1980s and the estimated $500bn costs associated with the Second Gulf War were economically and politically crippling, but also because internal division and wrangling resulted in the disintegration of any popular, cohesive and cooperative vision for the common Arab future. For those critics of the Middle East paradigm, the Madrid Peace Conference and the associated peace process is the embodiment of the articulation of a *pax americana*, which is the culmination of a US-Israeli geopolitical strategy to engage Arab and non-Arab states of the region in a mutual management arrangement which combines bilateral and multilateral economic and security cooperation. At present this paradigmatic scenario dominates the international relations of the Middle East. The determination of peace, security and stability is underwritten financially and militarily by the US, with the aid of the World Bank and other important global NGOs, as well as by co-opted Arab regimes, particularly the oil-producing Gulf States. For most of the region's regimes, implicit or explicit consent to this paradigm depends not only on individual regimes' relations with the US, but also on the willingness of those regimes to deal with the effective realities of power as they presently exist. Needless to say, as a paradigm associated with an external power determined to see its military and economic power accorded tribute, this particular paradigmatic vision is opposed broadly by the mass of Middle Eastern peoples, wherein may lie the ultimate seeds of its destruction.[215]

The Mediterranean paradigm is arguably the oldest of the four, with its roots in the (albeit religious) crusading European attempts at hegemony.[216] Given the inherently imbalanced nature of the Middle East paradigm, with its economic, political and military power distribution perceived as overwhelmingly favouring the US and Israel, in the modern era what propels the Mediterranean scenario is not only the geographic proximity of Europe to the Middle East and North Africa, but also a rediscovery and articulation of mutual interest: economic prosperity, common security and common regional developmental and environmental interests. The Mediterranean initiative stems from northern Mediterranean countries believing that their security and domestic stability can be better achieved through the sustainable economic development of the southern Mediterranean countries, which also allows for greater European participation and influence in regional political and economic frameworks, and in institutional and non-governmental forums. The *quid pro quo* for the Middle East and North Africa is in having a more balanced and agreeable relationship with the outside world. The World Bank claims that by

> 2010 the countries of the Middle East and North Africa have the potential to double their income, increase life expectancy by close to ten years, and cut illiteracy and infant mortality by almost half. They could also become full partners in the global economy, using integration with Europe and within the region as a stepping stone to international competitiveness. Peace, macro-economic stability, and an attractive investment environment could attract billions of dollars of capital from national and foreign investors. The faster economic growth would reduce poverty and bring down unemployment, restoring hope to millions.[217]

The Mediterranean scenario is one which will develop, with its objectives of enhanced 'dialogue and interaction among governmental and non-governmental actors in search for problem-solving and maximizing cooperation between Europe and the Middle East.'[218] Its particular appeal is in the development of a partnership between the Europeans, the people of the Middle East and the North Africans, based on mutual concerns and benefits, with no one region dominating the other in a partner-client relationship. Another implied benefit for the Mediterranean scenario is the absence of the USA as a principal part of the equation, with the concomitant lessening of the dominating impact of Israel, and Israel's presence, on inter-regional relations. The Mediterranean paradigm has been gaining momentum through the mid-1990s, mainly because it is the least hated of the visions of inter-regional relations.[219]

The Arab paradigm reflects the 'pan-Arab cultural-nationalist-strategic project,' responding to the indigenous Arab demands of independence, unification and anti-colonialism which has characterized the political, intellectual and historical consciousness of Arab actions since the nineteenth century.[220] The Second Gulf War and the end of the Cold War have been the two principal events which have reordered geopolitical strategic planning and policy in the Middle East in the 1990s. Whilst even though the pan-Arab institutional, governmental and non-governmental levels remain the most developed indigenous transnational network, the outcomes of these two events have conspired to undermine those Arab intellectuals and policy-makers who still adhere to this paradigm. Within this context, then, it can be argued that although pan-Arabism is presently a dormant force unable to force through its primacy as a paradigmatic alternative, it still retains sufficient latent emotional and political appeal seriously to undermine and constrain any of the other paradigms.[221]

The Islamic paradigm is the only wholly indigenous political and strategic scenario.[222] It is also the least favoured by the status quo actors and agents because it has as its basis the partisan, particular-istic and xenophobic nature which contends that Islam is a target of annihilation, exploitation and humiliation by Christian powers and Jewish Zionism, and that the cause of contemporary Muslim weakness and vulnerability in the face of such a challenge of civilizations is due in part to 'corrupt secular leaders, who have strayed far from the straight and virtuous path of the greatest of all religions.' Islam has the power to mobilize popular support all across the Middle East, with its message of raising religious consciousness, and of the perfidy of corrupt rulers and their acceptance of Western-Zionist hegemonic designs. Thus Muslims will become powerful and virtuous only by returning to a path of righteousness through revolutionary struggle. The Islamic paradigm neatly supersedes the older pan-Arabist paradigm, by realizing the yearning for a strong, culturally homogeneous, and united Islamic Middle East. Whilst few of the states of the Middle East have embraced the Islamic vision, there are signs that Islam represents more than just a latent power, or a symbolic, spiritual and ideological commitment. Islamists from Algeria to Turkey to Iran are either in power, working in coalition, or undermining current secular elites. However, the notion of an Islamic arc of influence or power bloc stretching from the Persian Gulf through the Fertile Crescent to the Atlantic is as yet 'more a promise than a reality; it can break but does not make.' This is because of a number of factors:

- There is a tendency for factionalism and infighting over religio-temporal issues
- Islamist movements inspire fear and determined resistance from secular elites
- Islamist movements collaborate well with an agreed enemy, but not so well without one
- Many non-state Islamic groups are manipulated and managed by Islamic states with partisan agendas
- Islamist regimes have not been able to deal with their socio-economic problems
- Islamic societies are inherently conservative and rhetorical and therefore rather unimaginative and not very innovative
- Islam and Islamist movements have no overall coherent and cohesive geopolitical and socio-economic strategies which will translate into a sustainable political agenda.[223]

1.10 Conclusion

The intention of this study is not to be an empirical, comparative study of conflict resolution case studies in order to test a set of hypotheses; instead it is a case study of one conflict resolution process and the way in which theoretical frameworks and techniques of conflict resolution have been employed to determine a political solution to the protracted and deep-rooted Israeli-Palestinian conflict. The peace process is not a textbook case of conflict resolution principles being applied, but a very fluid political process. In this first chapter we have explored a number of issues which affect the process:

(1) An exploration of conflict resolution diplomacy and of the widely held perception that relative bargaining strengths based on power variables, such as the ability to control or determine the application of power, are the basis of present international practice and experience;

(2) An examination of the relevant literature in the field of conflict resolution by theoreticians and practitioners, and how they both

relate to each other and their work relates to the case study. This includes an explanation as to why the Israeli-Palestinian conflict has not been resolved, by examining why conflict resolution techniques previously employed or adopted to deal with it, such as mediation, shuttle diplomacy, arbitration, power bargaining, and so on have been inadequate and have tended to institutionalize the conflict, leading to temporary settlements without tackling the root causes;

(3) An investigation of the domination of political, social and cultural discourse by Western conflict precepts, concepts and paradigms over Middle Eastern conflict resolution value-systems in an attempt to explore philosophical differences and common ground in the pursuit of a negotiated peace process;

(4) An examination of the conceptualization of the causes of belligerency, international economic development, conflict analysis, psychology, behaviourism, stress management, crisis management and distinctions between forms of violence, through scientifically analysing the structure, the protagonists and the substance of a conflict in order to define a working framework, internationally legitimated, within which to structure the peace-making initiative;

(5) An examination of conflicting parties' balance of power relationships, and the threat/security perceptions in inter-ethnic conflict. Evaluating conflict resolution for parties with structural asymmetric power relationships has not received much attention in the literature on inter-ethnic conflict. In such conflicts, particularly those of a state-substate nature like the Israeli-Palestinian, the examination of the parties' fears, opinions, influences and their interpretations of these is of great importance in determining the extent to which power-asymmetric assumptions define the power relationships between the parties (i.e. the way the parties assimilate their collective perceptions regarding their opponent in order to determine their collective responses with regard to their sense of collective threat, or their sense of collective security). The extent of parties' understanding of their conflict, its existential nature, its intensity, its potential, and how such differences in real and perceived power affect strategy and actions is of great importance for analysing such conflicts in order to determine their disposition to resolution;

(6) An investigation of divergent geopolitical ideologies – Middle Eastern, Mediterranean, Arab and Islamic – and their ability to

incorporate or accommodate accepted Western conflict resolution principles.

From the evidence analysed above we can draw two principal conclusions. Firstly, the foundation of the Israeli-Palestinian Declaration of Principles on Interim Self-Government Arrangements (DoP), that is a 'permanent settlement' to the Israeli-Palestinian conflict, is based primarily on UN Security Council Resolution 242 and is designed to lead to the implementation of that Resolution. In a practical sense the reality of achieving this is open to widely differing interpretations and therefore an agreed compromise will be difficult to determine. Secondly, and following from the first conclusion, the principal objective of the DoP, a 'just, lasting and comprehensive peace settlement' leading to the resolution of the Israeli-Palestinian conflict via 'historic reconciliation through the agreed political process', will be that much harder to accomplish.[224]

Drawn from the above evidence it is important to have a usable, comprehensive and realistic definition of what we mean by conflict resolution within the current international system, in order that we may use it not only to measure the effectiveness of the DoP at achieving a state of resolved conflict, but also to measure the DoP against its own stated goals. Thus for the purposes of evaluating the DoP as a 'peace process', conflict resolution shall be understood to be a state in which conflicting parties agree to cease all politically motivated and national-goal oriented hostile acts toward one another, and contract to coexist benignly, with mutual respect, refrain from malevolent acts aimed at the disruption of internal affairs to the detriment of the other party in pursuit of national goals, and allow for the free movement of peoples, goods, services and ideas within an agreed institutional framework based on justice and respect for human rights.

Armed with the tools to measure the intention of producing a 'just, lasting and comprehensive peace settlement', that is using those covered by the Riceman Formula of resolution, institutionalization, confidence-building, empowerment, mediation, administration and negotiation, we can evaluate the outcomes produced by the DoP. The principals in the Israeli-Palestinian peace process only seek to utilize those conflict resolution ideas, notions, models and principles which are effective and politically expedient and advance their partisan notion of the process. It is because there are no accepted models and/or conflict resolution practices, structures and theoretical models being applied, only a loose amalgamation of practices being tried or discarded, that I have tried to outline in this initial chapter an explanation of the theoretical construction underlying the task of finding a workable peace process. Thus my intention in Chapter 1 has been briefly to illustrate the limitations of theory in this case study and the inadequacy of Western conflict resolution principles being applied because of geopolitical, cultural and power limitations.

2
Madrid – Oslo – Washington DC: the Oslo Backchannel

'Who is the bravest hero?
He who turns his enemy into a friend.'
– Avot d'R Nathan[1]

2.1 Introduction

This chapter assesses how the secretly concluded Declaration of Principles on Interim Self-Government Arrangements (DoP) transpired. It provides an analysis of the secret deal-making process that intended to develop a sustainable preventative security regime with a view to implementing an internationally recognized, binding and agreed legal framework setting out specific commitments and obligations, within an enforceable conflict prevention regime. By employing the Riceman Formula, specifically items 3 and 7, covering confidence-building and negotiation, this chapter analyses the evolution of the DoP through its stages of conception and gestation. Confidence-building covers the provision of channels for dispute resolution, crisis prevention, reconciliation, conflict deterrence and reduction, the foundation of political institutions to defuse political instability, human rights abuses and economic uncertainty and ensure compliance and verification of a mutual security environment. Negotiation covers systems employed to facilitate the deal-making process.

2.2 Establishment and purpose of the Madrid Conference

Prior to the convening of a Middle East peace conference all international peace initiatives since the 1973–4 Yom Kippur War

63

disengagement negotiations were of a bilateral or trilateral nature, all attempts at convening multilateral negotiations having failed. Bilateral initiatives were pursued for a number of reasons, depending on circumstances and political desire. An example of conscience-driven diplomacy was the Shulz Plan, devised in February 1988, three months after the outbreak of the Palestinian *intifada*. The plan called for the convening of an international 'event' in April 1988, with the participation of the parties to the conflict and the five permanent members of the UN Security Council. The opening event would be followed by direct negotiations between Israel, Jordan and the Palestinians on an interim settlement involving autonomy for the West Bank and Gaza Strip, to be implemented for a period of three years. Two months after the establishment of such an implementation, talks on the permanent solution would take place with the participation of the autonomy administration within the Jordanian-Palestinian delegation. The permanent solution would be based on the land for peace formula and the PLO would be able to participate on condition they accepted UN SCRs 242 and 338 as the basis for negotiations. Shamir rejected the proposal because it included principles rejected by the Likud – it did not pre-condition the ending of the *intifada* on the start of negotiations and it ignored the Camp David Accords. Shulz gave up in despair in April 1988.[2]

Alternative examples of the initiation of a negotiation system employed to facilitate the deal-making process have emanated from some of the protagonists. The Shamir-Rabin peace initiative, presented in Washington DC by PM Shamir in April 1989, was backed by the National Unity Government on 14 May 1989 and dealt with four issues:

(1) Strengthening the peace between Israel and Egypt on the basis of the Camp David Accords;
(2) Establishing peace relations with other Arab states;
(3) Resolving the refugee problem;
(4) Holding elections in the territories for nominating a representation that would conduct negotiations for a transitional period of self-rule and later for a permanent settlement.

The proposal stipulated that the political process would be by means of direct negotiations with the Arab representatives, that Israel opposed the establishment of 'an additional Palestinian state in the Gaza district and in the area between Israel and Jordan', that Israel would not negotiate with the PLO and that there would be no change in the status of Judea, Samaria and Gaza other than in accordance with the basic guidelines of the government, which meant no Israeli withdrawal from the territories.

President Mubarak of Egypt published his own ten-point programme in September 1989 for the implementation of the Israeli initiative, proposing that the Israeli and Palestinian delegations meet in Cairo. The Likud objected to the Egyptian mention of the participation of East Jerusalemite Palestinians in the elections and to the need for Israel to accept the principle of land for peace. Rabin, however stated that the Egyptian proposals accounted for Israeli sensitivities in that they did not mention the PLO, the Palestinian right to self-determination or a Palestinian state in the West Bank and Gaza Strip.

The Mubarak ten points were followed by a five-point document from US Secretary of State Baker published on 6 December 1989 which dealt with the technicalities for the opening of the Israeli-Palestinian dialogue to be held in Cairo. In March 1990, after little progress Baker addressed the question to the Israeli government: 'Will the government of Israel be ready to agree to sit with Palestinians on a name-by-name basis who are residents of the West Bank and Gaza?' Though Foreign Minister Arens was in favour of a positive reply, PM Shamir objected. The failure of this initiative was the background for the decision by the Labour Party to put forward a motion of no confidence in the government, the resultant fall of the government being the first ever by motion of no confidence.[3]

Thus we can see some of the pitfalls on the way to achieving even an agreed forum for discussion, let alone actual resolution. The traditional Israeli position regarding an international conference has always been that bilateral negotiations with the Arab states, or talks through an intermediary, are preferable to negotiations within the framework of an international conference. Israel believes that in such an atmosphere it would be in an inferior position strategically, tactically and numerically. However, the 1973 Geneva Conference proved that with proper coordination with the US and with the appropriate terms of reference such a conference could be useful. In the 1975 Memorandum of Understanding signed between the US and Israel, Israel received assurances regarding the conditions for reconvening the Geneva Conference: Israel would be consulted about the timing; the PLO would not be invited unless it recognized Israel and UN SCRs 242 and 338; the US would coordinate strategy regarding the conference with Israel; the US would make every effort to ensure that the talks on substance would be held on a bilateral basis; the US would oppose any attempt by the Security Council to change the powers of the conference to Israel's detriment; and the US would act together with Israel to ensure progress to attain peace between Israel and its neighbours on the basis of negotiations.

In September 1977 Menachem Begin expressed his agreement to an international conference, but the peace process with Egypt followed the 'bilateral talks with the help of a mediator' model. The conference idea remained dormant until 1985, when King Hussein of Jordan raised the possibility of an international conference to act as an umbrella for direct talks with Israel. Then PM Peres mentioned this idea in his speech to the UN in October 1985 and expressed Israel's agreement that Palestinian representatives who were not members of the PLO be included in the Jordanian delegation. The London Agreement of 11 April 1987, reached between King Hussein and Peres, concerned the convention of such a conference, but incoming PM Yitzhak Shamir rejected the idea as being disadvantageous to Israel. The international conference was the basis of both the 1988 Shultz Plan and the 1991 Baker Initiative. On Israel's insistence, the Madrid Conference of October 1991 was merely a ceremonial opening to direct bilateral and multilateral negotiations which were to follow immediately. Although the Madrid Conference was not a continuation of the Geneva Conference, the US abided by its assurances given to Israel in the 1975 Memorandum of Understanding.[4]

By 1991, the climate in global international relations had radically changed, whilst attempts at the reconciliation of long-term local and regional conflicts had had limited successes in many areas previously thought of as intractable, such as Angola, Afghanistan, Cambodia, Eritrea, Namibia, Nicaragua and South Africa. Three major factors can be discerned in producing the fortuitous circumstances necessary to bring together the enemies of the Middle East to discuss issues of mutual concern. Firstly, the USSR's power and interest in the Middle East declined. Whilst by 1991 it would still be too early to talk of the end of the Cold War, certainly by the end of 1991, the USSR was no longer the monolithic superpower it had previously appeared to the outside world, for the minds of the peoples of the USSR were focused on internal turmoil. This allowed the US unrivalled breadth of action in the Middle East – towards ally and foe alike. Secondly, the aftermath of the Second Gulf War of 1990–1 ensured respect for US power in the region, which although destroying Iraq militarily, meant that two important points emerged:

1. American power, weaponry and the desire to use it had been dominant in a fight with a former Soviet client using Soviet weaponry, which meant that the anti-Israeli forces could now no longer view a military solution against Israel as viable.

2. Although Israel became one of the most powerful military forces in the region, the US was still obliged both politically and morally to the Arab states that had agreed to produce the aura of internationalism and respectability, in the US-led coalition of Western states' vendetta against Iraq. Western war-fever rhetoric had to be thus backed up by some example of moral justification for waging war for national strategic interests.

Thirdly, and more debatably, is the proposition that the PLO had adopted a strategic strategy of 'open-mindedness and unilateral concessions. . . . in line with the realistic objectives of the intifada'.[5]

What is new about the Madrid concept? asked PM Rabin in 1993 prior to the public announcement of the DoP. He answered that prior to 1993 only limited agreements, and certainly not comprehensive peace treaties were achieved through negotiations with one Arab state at a time. From the armistice deliberations in 1949 agreements were signed with Egypt, Jordan, and later with Syria and Lebanon. The period between 1949 and 1974 Rabin considered a long drought with regard to agreements between Israel and her neighbours. Neither the Sinai Campaign of 1956 nor the Six-Day War of 1967, nor even the War of Attrition of 1968–70, concluded with a bilateral agreement, however limited. Although these wars ended with a United Nations Security Council resolution accepted by the countries involved, it was only after the Yom Kippur War of 1974 that the path of negotiations was used again, and only then to achieve limited agreements. In 1974–5, separate separation-of-forces agreement were concluded with Egypt and Syria. Although the Camp David Accords were signed with Egypt in September 1978, and the peace treaty was concluded in March 1979, before Madrid, Rabin argued, no negotiations between Israel and Arab countries were ever conducted according to the principle that all participants would gather at one location at one time to negotiate accords of any kind. According to Rabin, what was new was that the Madrid concept was two-tiered. At the bilateral level, the Israeli delegation was to meet with the Jordanian-Palestinian delegation (each track separately), the Syrian delegation, and the Lebanese delegation. At the multilateral level, five committees were dedicated to various subjects the main object of discussions being to create mutual expectations and to illustrate, mainly to the Arab world, what could be accomplished for the good of the region, and for each individual state and nation with the achievement of peace.[6] Commenting on Syrian and Lebanese non-participation in the multilateral negotiations, Rabin believed only time would bear out whether the Madrid concept facilitated or debilitated the peace process. Noting that his own past experiences indicated to him that peace could only be achieved by negotiations with one Arab partner at a time, he asked himself whether the present concept should be altered. His conclusion was that,

> any change in the present concept, irrespective of its efficacy, would be a mistake because it would draw attention from substance to procedure. The present concept should be kept as it is, but we should search for ways to change the substance, at least insofar as this depends on us. A simple analysis allows us to differentiate between two types of partners in the present negotiations: 'key partners', Syria and the Palestinians, and 'secondary partners', Jordan and Lebanon. Obviously, Jordan cannot conclude an agreement with us on the basis of bilateral relations alone, ignoring negotiations between Israel and the Palestinians in the territories and preceding any arrangement regarding the latter, whether it be called autonomy or anything else. It is clear that no agreement can be made with Lebanon without a prior understanding with Syria. Therefore, the altering of substance that I mentioned must focus on achieving a peace agreement with Syria and an interim agreement with the Palestinians for a transitional period.[7]

Undoubtedly the most significant aspect of the Madrid Middle East Peace Conference was that the psychological barrier of mutual recognition was broken. Israel, in Madrid, created the first essential stage towards diplomatic recognition by sitting down with its neighbours. The Palestinians, 'in the eyes of international public opinion, established the legitimacy of Palestinian national aspirations and demands'.[8] The location of the venue was no accident, indeed the very historical symbolism and the emotional legacy projected was enormous. Spain represented the ground on which Catholicism confronted Islam and persecuted Judaism. With a positive outcome at Madrid it could also represent the beginning of an historic reconciliation between modern Islam and Judaism. However, Madrid was not the most obvious choice; the decision that Madrid would host the conference in the presence of US President Bush and the USSR's President Gorbachev was announced by Secretary Baker and USSR Foreign Minister Pankin at a press conference on 18 October 1991 in Jerusalem. The co-sponsors wished to present a *fait accompli* to the various invitees, in that none of them would feel able to reject the co-sponsors, in terms of either their relationships with the superpowers, their domestic public opinion or international public opinion.

The US administration, in order not to damage its credibility domestically, because of President Bush's re-election prospects, and internationally, in terms of superpower dynamics, pressed ahead with the Madrid Conference which tended to rely more heavily on form than substance. Secretary Baker concentrated on finding a procedural formula which would be acceptable to avowed enemies. Such a formula would have to be insubstantial and vague on points of significance in order to ensure the initial participation of the primary parties, as the very absence of agreement on any point of substance would be the very reason that they could justify attendance both domestically and diplomatically. However, the major drawback of such an approach meant that issues concerning procedure took on much greater importance than they would otherwise be expected to.

Syria, Jordan and Lebanon all agreed to participate at Madrid with the proviso that actual, as opposed to *de facto*, recognition of Israel would be withheld, this point to be included in the negotiations to be undertaken at Madrid. According to Massalha, the Palestinians, 'by accepting 'autonomy' as a transitional stage, placed themselves in a minimalist negotiating position, thus restricting their room for manoeuvre; they therefore chose a strategy which contrasted with Israel's maximalist stance of denying that the Palestinians had any right to their own land.'[9]

As far as the other parties to the Madrid Conference were concerned, the USSR and the EU for their own reasons decided to follow the US strategy. The EU agreed to 'do nothing which might impede US diplomacy' and supported US efforts.[10] Egyptian, Saudi and Gulf Cooperation Council (GCC) countries' participation was assured through the US carrot-and-stick diplomatic approach, a mixture of cajolery, bribes and obligation. Debt restructuring and massive arms trans-shipments ensured these countries had over the previous number of years fallen well within the US sphere of influence. The UN, the EU and the Arab Maghreb Union participated as observers.

In accepting the US formula, all the parties concerned allowed the US and the USSR as co-sponsors to dictate the terms of Madrid. Israeli demands for a series of regional conferences and the European-Soviet-Arab demand for an international conference under the auspices of the UN, were sidestepped by Secretary Baker, thus ensuring that the conference was convened. This compromise formula was envisaged to enable the UN Security Council to be drawn into endorsing future agreements and peace settlements.

Attempts have often been made to resolve the issues surrounding the Israeli-Palestinian/Arab-Israeli conflict through forms of international arbitration, such as conferences of arbitration, unilateral superpower promises, secret agreements, Commissions of Enquiry, White Papers, national and international congresses, petitions, strikes, riots and wars. Basically, to paraphrase Churchill, the Madrid Conference was convened because there had been too much 'war-war',[11] so because of US supremacy following the Persian Gulf War, the US attempted to fashion, and for some impose, 'jaw-jaw' on the states of the Middle East. The Second Persian Gulf War has left several legacies, not least the suspicion that apart from altruism or opportunism, the convening of the Madrid Conference was an attempt by the US to facilitate its hegemony over the Middle East by trying to marry its competing allies, in order to secure its access to cheap oil resources. For many, the Madrid Conference signalled a break-through which broke an important psychological barrier – just getting the parties into the same room in order to talk peace. Real progress in the Middle East usually follows a war, which shakes things up and shatters previous rigidities. Conferences had been set up before, after Yom Kippur in 1974, and within the framework of Camp David in 1977–8, where there were provisions to discuss Palestinian issues. These proved fruitless as they failed to stimulate sufficient backing or political momentum.[12]

After seven months of intensive shuttle diplomacy in the Middle East which began in March 1991, Secretary Baker obtained the agreement of all the parties involved in the Arab-Israeli conflict to participate in an international conference, which at Israel's insistence would serve as a preamble to direct bilateral and multilateral talks between Israel and her neighbours. This was to expose an inherent problem: how to gain agreement, between and with, states which were still technically at war and in some cases did not even recognize the existence of two of the main protagonists. Israeli demands that there should not be any pre-conditions to the talks, and that the PLO should not be a party to the negotiations, that Palestinians from the occupied territories, approved by Israel, should form part of the Jordanian delegation, were also accepted. While the Bush administration worked to convene the peace conference in Madrid, Israeli PM Shamir continued with the policy of building more housing units and settlements in the occupied territories. Shamir insisted that the root cause of the conflict was not territory but the Arab refusal to recognize the legitimacy of the State of Israel; hence he was not prepared to trade territory for peace. All he would offer was peace for peace. Shamir's position was basic and unchangeable. Palestinian autonomy, for a transitional period of five years, was intended to foreclose all other options, not to be the foundation for further negotiations and concessions.[13] The invitations to the conference were sent jointly by Baker and Soviet Foreign Minister Boris Pankin on 18 October 1991, and whilst none of the opening speeches were conciliatory, the importance of the conference was that the parties directly involved in the Arab-Israeli conflict were present. Furthermore, all the other Arab states (except Iraq) were represented by observers.

The political decision for Palestinian participation at Madrid was founded on economic hardship. During the period December 1987 to January 1991, encompassing the *intifada* and the Second Gulf War, the Palestinian economy suffered significant stresses placed on it, internally by the Unified National Leadership of the Uprising (UNLU), and externally by the Israelis and through international pressures. The GNP of the West Bank and Gaza Strip fell by 30–5 per cent in this period. Palestinian workers were increasingly restricted in their access to Israel for employment. For example, the unofficial number of Gazans employed in Israel declined from 80 000 to 56 000, this meant a fall in pre-*intifada* income from working in Israel of approximately 35 per cent of GNP and 70 per cent of GDP. This represented a dramatic loss of income estimated at $300m, having consequent effects on consumption, investment and living standards.[14]

The *intifada* significantly damaged the occupied territories' economies. Israeli-imposed actions severely restricted the economic capacity of the territories by depleting financial resources, reducing employment opportunities and undermining the economic and physical infrastructure. UNLU-imposed strike actions were designed to break the economic dependency of the occupied territories on Israel, but in practice only increased dependency, particularly in Gaza, where Israel represented economic survival because there was no real alternative employment. The economies of the occupied territories suffered significant decline during the first two and a half years of the *intifada*. Sanctions imposed by Israel, such as curfews, magnetic identity cards and closure of the territories; the taxation campaign; regulation through permits and licences; levies and fines, and measures imposed by the UNLU such as strikes and boycotts of Israeli products all created extreme hardship for most Palestinians.[15] During this period per capita GNP fell by 41 per cent in Gaza – a fall of $700 to $1000 – a sum well below the corresponding Israeli poverty line. The effects of this fall were multiplied because Gazan families are traditionally much larger than those of West Bankers. The level of GNP fell because

- output in all economic sectors (except agriculture) was reduced 20–30 per cent
- remittances from Israel dwindled
- Israeli-occupied territories' trade reduced as tensions increased
- Gulf remittances were eroded by some 70 per cent.[16]

In the beginning of the *intifada*, such losses were offset by individuals' savings, however this respite was of only limited duration since before long these were depleted, and net real income compared to pre-*intifada* income levels fell by some 40–50 per cent for most Palestinians.[17] The depletion of private savings, either in the occupied territories or abroad, together with the acute drop in private income, had a profound impact on the local economies of the West Bank and Gaza Strip, radically affecting consumption, savings and investments, economic activity and living standards.[18] Israeli restrictions forced Palestinians to adopt austerity measures and find alternative capital sources. Israeli policies at the beginning of the *intifada* aimed to highlight and strengthen Palestinian economic dependency on the Israeli economy, and to defeat the *intifada* through intense and ultimately unbearable economic hardship. Defence Minister Rabin revealed Israeli thinking: 'We have to strike a balance between actions that could bring on terrible economic distress and a situation in which [the Palestinians] have nothing to lose, and measures which bind them to the Israeli administration and prevent civil disobedience.'[19] Such economic hardships, whether self-imposed or Israeli-inspired over time began to adversely affect the population's ability to stand fast and threatened to undermine the *intifada*'s inspiration, namely the communal spirit engendered and the attitudinal change effected in respect of rejecting the Israeli occupation.[20] The *intifada* represented not just a political realignment in the occupied territories, which could be determined in the occupied Palestinians' favour, but it also represented an economic situation, which has been termed de-development,[21] where the Palestinian economy had deteriorated to such an extent as to affect the political gains made and the political strategy of the Palestinian leadership directly. The economic effects of the *intifada* laid the foundations for the future political accommodation with Israel, while the political and economic fall-out from the Second Gulf War markedly accelerated this process.[22]

The disastrous effects of the Second Gulf War on the Palestinian economies caused severe and immediate economic hardship. Gaza was most affected as its economy was almost totally reliant on Gulf remittances, direct aid and Israeli employment. Israel imposed a general and sustained closure of the West Bank and Gaza, effectively closing down the territories' economy on 16 January 1991. The closure lasted seven weeks in some places with an estimated cost of $84m as a result of a total work stoppage and the limitation of workers allowed into Israel.[23] Whilst by May, one in three Gazans was unemployed, of those who were employed personal income fell sharply, savings were eaten into, many Palestinian workers were fired by Israeli employers without appeal, recourse or severance, and others were unable to collect monies owed, with the result that for ordinary Palestinians income fell as prices rose. Of a 1990 Gaza workforce of 120 000, by the end of the war: 28 000 worked in Israel, down from 56 000 (80 000 before the *intifada*); 12 000 worked for UNRWA, the civil administration and local municipalities; and 40 000 worked in other sectors. High employment levels in other sectors was assumed, but this is likely to have been wrong, with unemployment rates probably at 35–40 per cent. The loss in wages was estimated at $11m per month.[24] The closure coincided with the citrus harvest, summer planting season, and the end of a severe drought, causing irrigation and insecticide spraying to halt and the loss of principal Gulf markets (Gaza's main buyers of citrus – Iraq, Kuwait, Saudi Arabia and the UAE – closed their markets) meaning much of the fruit rotted on the trees. The resulting domestic glut, rising production costs and diminishing returns meant that citrus prices slumped, for example, lemons fell from $100 to $20 a ton, grapefruits from $100 to $50 a ton, and oranges from $150 to $50 a ton. This resulted in a cash liquidity crisis as people drew on savings and bought only necessities, as evidenced by the 80 per cent fall in red meat consumption, and 70 per cent in vegetables.[25]

In economic terms the most important aspect of the Gulf crisis was the loss of Palestinian remittances from the Gulf, the termination of direct aid from the Gulf states, such as Saudi Arabia and Kuwait, and the decline in PLO transfers. Some 800 000 Palestinians sent home money from the Gulf. In 1987 total remittances from the Gulf amounted to $250m; in 1989 Gulf remittances were $170m, of which direct aid was $140m; in 1988–90 money from Kuwait alone amounted to $140m. Direct aid from the Gulf also terminated so that by April 1991 losses from remittances, exports and direct aid amounted to $350m.[26] Aid from the Gulf states to local institutions, such as financing health and educational facilities and development projects, also terminated, so that when combined with either decline or losses from those employed in Israel and losses of Gulf remittances, the Palestinian economy was dealt a severe blow. The PLO also lost important remittances, money that was sent in part to the occupied territories. According to the PLO, its annual support consisted of $72m from Saudi Arabia, $48m from Iraq, $24m from Kuwait, not including the PLO tax on Palestinians in Kuwait amounting to some $50m.[27] The PLO lost some $480m from Gulf sources, and an additional $62.5m in PLO taxes and donations from Palestinians living in Kuwait and other Arab states. Saudi Arabian funds to the PLO amounted to 10 per cent of the total GDP of the West Bank and Gaza, indeed between 1980 and 1990 the PLO is estimated to have received $10bn from Kuwait, Saudi Arabia, UAE and others which terminated with the Gulf War.[28] The decline in PLO revenue had a devastating effect in the occupied territories as PLO monies funded local infrastructures, cared for the elderly and infirm and contained a strong social welfare element.[29] At this rate, by 1993 the PLO would be bankrupt.

Loss of financial standing in turn affected the PLO's political standing in the community. The inability of the Palestinian economies to withstand repeated closures on top of the Gulf War, with the *intifada* continuing, meant that economic gloom deepened. Gaza was closed for five weeks between May and July 1992, UNRWA estimated losses at $500 000 per day from wages alone based on figures from 24 May–5 July, when workers were allowed into Israel.[30] With a series of closures, curfews, export restrictions for Gazan farmers and commercial strikes called by UNLU, a major indicator of the economic situation during this period was the number of Palestinian families by June 1991 who became dependent on UNRWA food assistance to stave off hunger; some 120 000 refugee and non-refugee families in Gaza and some 165 000 families in the West Bank. This situation continued into 1992 as UNRWA distributed 430 000 family food parcels in Gaza and 119 000 in the West Bank.[31]

An immediate effect on Israeli society of the Soviet Jewish immigration wave was the consequent reduction of Israeli dependence on Palestinian labour. The Second Gulf War merely exacerbated the tensions between the Israeli and Palestinian populations, already running high due to the effects of the immigrant tidal wave. The Second Gulf War meant that the occupied territories were shut off from Israel from mid-January to March 1991, on the one hand creating meaningful hardship for the large percentage of Palestinians who depended on their livelihood from employment in Israel, whilst on the other hand creating opportunities for the immigrant job seekers which would mean the permanent replacement of the Palestinians' jobs. However, the structural realignment of the Israeli economy in such rapid terms had rather an immediate effect on the political scene. Government plans for the construction of 100 000 new housing units by the end of the year had to be postponed as some four-fifths of existing housing construction was idled.[32] Israeli agriculture suffered heavily as the fruit and flower export sector had been so heavily dependent on Palestinian labour, and losses of up to 50 per cent in sales were reported by a number of high-tech sector companies. Foreign anxieties, uncertainty caused by the war and the failure of foreign suppliers to renew orders all caused problems for the economy.[33] Even as immigration resumed after the end of the war, and whilst more jobs were made available by the closure of the territories, unemployment rose to over 10 per cent by mid-1991. The new immigrants rejected the types of jobs available, menial employment traditionally fulfilled by Palestinians, therefore many employers even went so far as to request permission to import foreign labour. This lead to MKs questioning the advisability of paying unemployment insurance to immigrants whilst the agriculture and construction sectors were so short of labour. However these problems in the Israeli economy were temporary and short-lived. Of more significance for the future of Israeli-Palestinian relations was the effect of the war on the Palestinian economy, with the consequent political fall-out. The curfew imposed on the occupied territories for the duration of the war was the longest known in the occupation. Most business was seriously curtailed, currency transfers from Palestinians working in Israel and the Gulf dried up, money was so scarce that even internal trade was restricted by the fact that most people just did not have the means to purchase goods. By the end of the war and the curfew, estimates suggested that the territories were operating at roughly 25 per cent of pre-war activity, the cost of the curfew alone was estimated to be between $150–200 million.[34]

The Second Persian Gulf War was politically and financially ruinous for the PLO. Although the pro-Iraq stance taken was almost universally popular with Palestinians, especially those living in the occupied territories, the backlash suffered by the PLO, however, made such support particularly expensive.[35] Saudi Arabia and the Gulf States withdrew financial aid and the Kuwaitis pursued a repressive vendetta against the some 400 000 Palestinians living in Kuwait. Some 300 000 Palestinians were expelled and thus added not only to the population in Jordan where they sought refuge, but also added to the instability in the kingdom which was also suffering for its somewhat reluctant support of Iraq.[36] From the very start of the crisis many PLO leaders, including Arafat, declared their support for the Iraqi regime.[37] While the Palestinian leaders were undoubtedly concerned about the fate of the some 400 000 Palestinian community in Kuwait, Israeli public opinion believed that this support proved that the Palestinians were disingenuous in their desire for an accommodation with Israel. Rather it convinced many Israelis that the Palestinians would revert to following the first Arab strongman who emerged threatening to destroy Israel.[38]

It was no secret that the PLO's image was suffering among many Palestinians, perturbed by financial corruption within the organization and alienated by the ineffective institutional structures which failed to provide avenues for adequate participation. The PLO's support for Iraq in the Second Gulf War drew severe criticism from most quarters, including the influential Palestinian Gulf community. This led to a decline in revenue from Gulf states where the community retaliated by severing financial aid. However, it is also the case that Arafat could well have irreparably lost his domestic constituency in the territories, in the refugee camps and in the diaspora, major bedrocks of PLO support, if his position had not coincided with public support for Iraq. Thus the rather sardonic observation, 'Our masses are not up to the level of the revolution. When the revolution surrenders to them it betrays itself, when it abandons them it dies.'[39]

The decline of the role of Palestinian institutions, and consequently of adequate representation and participation, had been particularly rapid since the departure of the PLO from Beirut to Tunis in 1982, following the Israeli Operation Peace for Galilee. Demands for power-sharing and for the eradication of corruption, which threatened to fragment the PLO during the 1980s, prompted a centralization of power and financial control in the hands of the leadership in Tunis under Arafat. Consequently, negotiations over reform were, more often than not, reduced to deals cut by Arafat and the factions over the distribution of seats in various organizations and money, rather than on reforming the decision-making processes and their accountability. Consensus at Palestine National Council was attained through the division of quotas of representation and of money to the factions. Arafat however was not solely responsible for such a state of affairs, the various factions acted more out of regard for financial gain and power than for participating in substantive political debate. This situation resulted in the role of the institutions and the departments being overshadowed as real power lay in an ever-decreasing cabal. The decline of the institutions resulted in turn in the alienation of many Palestinian intellectuals and activists who feared for the purity of the struggle.[40] According to Samir Huleileh, who sits on the multilateral committee for economic development, no more than $40 million flowed into the territories in 1992, compared with $120 million in 1990, and the 1990 figure was a sharp decline after the Iraqi invasion of Kuwait. The PLO budget dropped from $245 million to $85 million in 1991–3.[41] The consequences of the decline in economic and political fortunes combined to force the Palestinians to accept the invitation to attend the Madrid Conference.

Many Israelis discerned a major turn in domestic and foreign affairs as a result of the significant events which occurred in the Middle East and in Europe between 1989 and 1991. The exodus of Soviet Jews to Israel, the introspection of the USSR thus undermining its influence in Middle East affairs, the impact of the Second Gulf War and the subsequent supremacy of American influence, conspired to raise hopes that the Arab-Israeli conflict, particularly the Israeli-Palestinian conflict, might finally be settled. However, the fear of an internationally imposed political solution at odds with the more ideologically motivated principles guiding the centre-right nationalist agenda existed with many in Israel, typically those like PM Shamir. Thus Israel accepted the invitation to Madrid with a mixture of institutional suspicion and public anticipation.

According to some, the Madrid framework of 1991 is based on that envisaged by the Camp David Accords of 1978.[42] However in 1991 the demographic map of the occupied territories reflected a Likud settlement strategy which was a corollary to its negotiating policy: spreading large numbers of Israelis throughout the territories in an attempt to prevent any sort of compromise territorial/political arrangement with the Palestinians. The Madrid/Camp David formula insists that autonomy be instituted throughout the West Bank and Gaza Strip. The autonomy plan debate had reopened following the outbreak of the *intifada*. Whilst the Labour Party viewed it as an interim arrangement involving a territorially based autonomy (of which the Palestinians of East Jerusalem could be a part on a personal basis), Likud viewed it as a permanent arrangement involving a personally based autonomy (of which the Arabs of East Jerusalem would not be part). The idea of an autonomy plan came up in the bilateral talks between Israel and the Palestinian delegation following the Madrid Conference and was the background to the decision of Tzomet and Moledet to leave the Shamir government in January 1992.[43] This formula postponed issues of border rectification and Israeli annexation of vital territories to the final stage, when, presumably after a successful autonomy, they would be far more difficult to discuss.

Following from the end of the Cold War, the important developments which emerged in the Middle East are discernible as the Iraqi invasion of Kuwait; the immigration of Soviet Jews to Israel; and a workable, if not friendly, détente between Syria and the West. The decline of Soviet interest in global politics in favour of introspection and domestic turmoil led to a US-USSR reconciliation which in turn signalled the end of the Arab rejectionist states playing the superpowers off against each other in order to avoid outright domination of the region by one or other superpower. The outcome of the Second Persian Gulf War was seen by many as facilitating the likelihood of a Middle East *pax americana*. The Madrid process was tangible evidence of this new US domination, and of US aspirations in the region, namely the protection of its oil resources, strategic interests, and the desire to provide Israel with regional security in the form of a peace settlement and the normalization of Israeli-Arab relations. The political climate in the Middle East following the Second Persian Gulf War was exploited by the US in order to press ahead with its own version of a Middle East settlement, the Madrid process. Each of the main Middle Eastern protagonists had their own agendas as to what they saw as the most pressing issues, each obviously concerned with advancing their own partisan although mutually incompatible causes.

For example:

- The Syrians wanted to reoccupy the Golan within the context of an overall peace settlement
- The Jordanians wanted stability, both in financial and security terms
- The Palestinians wanted independence and statehood
- The Lebanese wanted the restoration of their sovereignty over their territory occupied by its neighbours
- The Israelis wanted peace with their neighbours albeit with the provisions that they did not want to relinquish the Golan in its entirety prior to a peace treaty with Syria, withdraw from southern Lebanon whilst the threat of attack from this border remained, or, see the establishment of a Palestinian state.

Operating with mutual suspicion, these mutually exclusive common interests did not however hinder the attempts of all sides to manoeuvre and negotiate for partisan benefits, even though the supposed referee in this 'game', the US, was intent on pursuing its own national interests in tandem with trying to create the right environment for a freely consented, rather than an imposed, peace.

The perception by the Palestinians was that the possible conclusion of separate Israeli-Arab deals which did not involve the Palestinians might disadvantage the latter to the extent that they would no longer be able to command a central role in the process, thereby undermining, relegating and alienating the Palestinians at a stroke. The Palestinians therefore feared that unless any involvement by other Arab parties in the Israeli-Palestinian negotiations was contingent upon a commitment to the furtherance of Palestinian aspirations, any such involvement would be deemed to undermine Palestinian national objectives. For example, the Palestinians viewed the concept of transitional autonomy in the negotiations with Israel as laying the foundations for statehood, thus Jordanian involvement in the talks was seen by the Palestinians as working towards such a goal, otherwise Jordanian involvement would have been blocked. Conversely, the Israelis saw Jordanian involvement in the talks as a useful and powerful weight to counterbalance the Palestinian nationalist aspirations, viewing Jordanian involvement in the talks as recognition of Jordanian interests and rights over the Palestinians, with the possibility of seeing transitional autonomy as leading to Palestinian integration or confederation with Jordan, or some other such arrangement whereby Israel, the Palestinians and Jordan shared joint competencies. This latter scenario has powerful historic roots in Israeli strategic thinking, from the likes of Dayan, Allon and Begin. The central issue is the containment of Palestinian aspirations, in other words autonomy viewed through continued Israeli military domination. However, Israeli thinking and practice on this vexed issue has shown rather a schizophrenic character. Jordanian domination of the Palestinians is an option which many Israelis do not relish, whilst Israeli annexation of the occupied territories would create a bi-national state thereby diluting significantly the Jewish characteristic of Israel. It seems that what the Israelis want is to control the occupied territories without absorbing them, in peace, cheaply, and without sovereign responsibilities whilst not being prejudicial to Israeli military control and the establishment and maintenance of Israeli settlements. The main reason why the Israelis were unwilling to submit to an international conference under the auspices of the UN, is because to do so would be to submit Israel to the authority of the UN as final arbiter. To do this would logically entail Israel then being subject to enforcing, or at least acknowledging in some form, the legitimacy and authority of the resolutions of the UN passed regarding the issues involved in the Middle East, especially as they relate to Israel in particular.

Those who envisage a Palestinian state

> seek a solution which would enable it to acquire regional and international credibility while avoiding a position of dependence on any other country. As a parliamentary, neutral democracy, such a state would be a model of moderation, stability, pluralism, tolerance and coexistence between the followers of the three monotheistic faiths. It would also be a haven for Christians fleeing persecution elsewhere in the region.[44]

Such a future is one to work towards no doubt, but taking a brief look at history one would have to be very imprudent to view the future in such glaringly optimistic terms. Even a policy of studied neutrality brings with it a concern for and about one's neighbours.

2.3   The US as agent of change

US Secretary of State, James Baker acted as principal advocate of the Bush administration's Middle East policy and architect of the Madrid Peace Conference. President Bush and Baker worked very closely on foreign policy objectives, both were believed to have no more interest in substantive issues than the other, preferring process and face to face deals than geopolitical theorizing. Little difference between the two was noticeable on Middle East policy, both reacted similarly to issues so that Baker effectively had a free hand. Baker's Palestinian-Israeli policy reflected the administration's instincts for caution, inaction, nothing revolutionary or imaginative with a tendency to focus on the status quo.[45] It could be argued that each new administration or set of officials coming new to a problem seek out new ways to define existing situations and problems. However, the maintenance of the status quo seems to have not only fitted Baker's personality but also his style in office so that rather than search for new policy concepts, emphases, goals and action plans with which to define US policy *vis-à-vis* the Middle East, Baker sought the very ideas and personnel which would reinforce his own perceptions, interpretations and prejudices rather than redirect or shatter them. Baker was reported to have embraced a pre-1988 presidential report by the pro-Israeli Washington Institute for Near East Policy, entitled *Building for Peace: an American Strategy for the Middle East.*[46] This report argued for a slow process involving confidence-building measures which would prepare Palestinians and Israelis for direct negotiations rather than advocating dramatic gestures and breakthroughs. What is even more interesting is that not only did this report gain credence but several of its authors gained high-level appointments in the Bush administration: Dennis Ross (the report's principal author, and a Bush campaign aide) was appointed director of the Department of State's Policy Planning Staff, becoming Secretary Baker's principal aide on the USSR and the Middle East; Aaron David Miller and Daniel Kurtzer were appointed Ross's principal Middle East advisers.[47]

Baker may have chosen to view the Middle East with fear, distrust, suspicion, as an ideological battleground or as holy soil. More likely he viewed it with apathy and disinterest. In order to determine policy trends and objectives and thus to explain US Middle East policy, one must try to discern from the policy-makers identifiable rationales for their activities. In order to explain for the

behaviour of the US administration in adopting the Madrid formula it is important to understand the speculative frameworks which
served them as rough guides for their actions, working hypotheses
for the control of international problems, even when the accepted
world order was shaken by dramatic events. In this way it can be
understood how the policy-makers believed they made better sense
of complex issues than their rivals or enemies, and how they anticipated and responded to threats and opportunities as they were
presented. Because the failure rate in imaginative anticipation is
naturally high, international politics as practised and conducted
seems irrational and unprincipled rather than a coherent and logical
evolutionary process. In spite of this, conventional wisdom regarding US policy is that it is guided by protecting its national interests.
In the Middle East those are:

- containment and opposition to Russian dominance in the region
- control of oil resources
- Israel's security.[48]

Analyses of US post-Cold War options observed that with the USSR
disabled, it would be possible to 'liberate American foreign policy
from the straight jacket imposed by superpower hostility'.[49] Thus
emboldened the US would be able to shift NATO costs on to European competitors, take a harsher line with Third World debt and
demands for assistance, and more importantly, the decline in Russia's
ability to project its power would make 'military power more useful as a United States foreign policy instrument', permitting the US
'greater reliance on military force in a crisis'.[50] The first edition of
the post-Cold War White House report to Congress on threat perception and foreign policy, in March 1990, stated that US military power
must focus on the Third World, the prime target being the Middle
East, where the 'threats to our interests . . . could not be laid at the
Kremlin's door'. With US paranoia of the perceived Russian threat
acknowledged, the report therefore believed the US should strengthen
its 'defense industrial base' and develop additional forward bases,
counterinsurgency and low intensity conflict capabilities.[51]

　President Eisenhower had described the Middle East as the most
'strategically important area in the world', the central policy goal
being to establish US control over what the US State Department
described as 'a stupendous source of strategic power, and one of
the greatest material prizes in world history', being 'probably the
richest economic prize in the world in the field of foreign invest-

ment'.[52] For the US, the problem was not one of access to Middle East oil, but rather

> that some form of US control over world oil reserves was necessary . . . the idea that the United States had a pre-emptive right to the world's oil resources [having been] well entrenched by World War II . . . Thus to maintain an international environment in which private companies could operate with security and profit, the US government became actively involved in maintaining the stability of the Middle East, in containing economic nationalism, and in sanctioning and supporting private arrangements for controlling the world's oil.[53]

Furthermore, it had been a US reflex since 1947 to state that 'America's own greatest interest' in any negotiations in the Middle East should result in 'enhanced security for Israel and a durable regional peace', basically meaning the acceptance of Israel into the regional fold under US hegemony, but without too many questions raised about the welfare and rights of the peoples of the region, particularly the Palestinians.[54]

Baker preferred to make Middle East and Arab-Israeli policy himself together with a small group of advisers, effectively excluding the mainstream State Department staffers, as he was more influenced by US political implications and repercussions, than any overwhelming desire to achieve Middle East rapprochement.[55] Baker was cool and businesslike towards both Israel and the Arabs. He was neither willing to risk confrontations with Congress by exerting pressure on Israel, nor keen to make any real efforts to improve relations with the Arabs by expanding the low-level US-PLO dialogue started at the end of the Reagan administration.[56]

In December 1989, Baker had produced a five-point plan, which was a synthesis of Shamir's April 1989 five-point plan, and Mubarak's ten-point plan. The plan's main points were:

(1) A dialogue between an Israeli and Palestinian delegation would be held in Cairo.

(2) Egypt was to act as intermediary not an interlocutor.

(3) Membership in the Palestinian delegation would have to be approved by the Israelis.

(4) Israel would participate in the discussions on the basis of the Shamir plan and the Palestinians would be free to express their views on the negotiations and on Shamir's draft election plan.

(5) A tripartite meeting of the Israeli, Egyptian and US Foreign

Ministers would be held in Washington DC in order to create the right conditions for a constructive Israeli-Palestinian dialogue in Cairo.[57]

On 9 March 1990, the Likud partner in the Israeli national unity government replied by accepting only part of the Baker Plan, only agreeing to begin talks if the Palestinians of East Jerusalem and the PLO would be excluded. Peres, leader of the Labour Party confirmed that he would agree to the Plan without changes. This issue led directly to the dissolution of the national unity government and on 11 June, Shamir formed a new government coalition of the centre-right and nationalist right with Likud as the major partner. The new government thus prescribed its new position for the talks with the Palestinians in Cairo:

(1) Negotiations were to be limited to autonomy plans as described in the Camp David Accords.

(2) Arab countries should make a gesture to Israel before Israel would agree to negotiations with the Palestinians.

(3) Arab-Israeli relations should precede any discussions of the Palestinian problem.[58]

Irritated by such a stance, Baker undiplomatically gave his telephone number to Shamir telling him to call him whenever Shamir became serious about pursuing peace. In a letter dated 27 June 1990 to President Bush, Shamir restated his position regarding the establishment of Israeli settlements on the occupied territories, his continued refusal to deal with the PLO, and his opposition to the inclusion of Palestinians from East Jerusalem or from the Palestinian diaspora in any talks with the Israelis.

The year 1990 was one of many turning points in the Arab-Israeli conflict, and in particular the Israeli-Palestinian conflict. Increased repression in the occupied territories, the failure of the 'iron fist' policy, the threats by extreme right elements in the Knesset to transfer the Palestinians *en masse* to Jordan, the arrival in Israel of significant numbers of Soviet Jews with the inherent possibility of their being settled in the occupied territories, all these factors combined to be viewed by politicians on both sides of the Israeli-Palestinian divide as a harbinger of more committed efforts to achieve national goals. Israeli-Palestinian relations were in stalemate during the summer of 1990, as the Palestinian leadership reviewed their options, when into the equation stepped Saddam Hussein. The serious situation regarding the deterioration in Israeli-Palestinian relations was merely exacerbated by the threats of war coming from Iraq at the start of the summer. For example, at the Baghdad Arab Summit of 28–30 May 1990, Saddam Hussein denounced the economic threats which he believed were directed at Iraq by Kuwait and called on all the Arab countries to take the military option against Israel in order to liberate holy Al-Quds in the name of Allah. As Hussein was not known for his religious observance, having cynically manipulated the appeal of a call to *jihad* in order to deflect hostility towards him, the Palestinian leadership, especially the secular PLO leadership based in Tunis, were caught in a Catch-22 position. There emerged an explosive situation in the occupied territories where ordinary Palestinians were fully behind Hussein's call to the green colours, totally uncaring about what would happen to their own people if Saddam did make good his promise to send his missiles in the direction of Jerusalem.[59] The PLO leadership in particular, fighting for supremacy over the United Command Leadership since the beginning of the *intifada*, were now faced with the desperate policy choices of either having to commit to Iraq's fortunes and risk the opprobrium of the international community especially the Western powers, or conversely remaining neutral, or support Kuwait and risk the opprobrium of the Palestinian masses. On 10 August 1990, eight days after Iraq had invaded Kuwait, an Extraordinary Arab Summit was held in Cairo. Yasser Arafat put forward a plan to settle the dispute peacefully by creating a Good Offices Committee, which would comprise five Arab heads of state to ensure Iraq's withdrawal from Kuwait and that the issues that had heightened tensions between the two could be solved by peaceful means. The plan failed because of the opposition of the majority of Arab states. It was demanded by the anti-Iraq regimes that the Palestinians take an unequivocal stance, as the Palestinian desire to put their faith in a mediated compromise displeased both sides. The PLO rejected the Iraqi demand to form a Palestinian militia in Kuwait, to open a second front against Israel in southern Lebanon and to organize terrorist attacks around the world. However, the PLO refusal to join the anti-Iraq coalition ensured that the PLO was consequently deemed hostile. In Egypt in particular, ordinary Egyptians were in a warlike mood, in the sense that many of them felt the need to deal with Iraqi aggression against a fellow Arab state, yet were very conscious of the many millions of Egyptians who had been in Iraq since the early days of the Iran-Iraq War helping in the Iraqi war effort and who, albeit in lesser numbers by 1990, continued to be in Iraq.[60] The Egyptian press spoke of the need for an all-Arab resolution to this problem, but the call for external aid divided many ordinary populations from their leaders.[61] In the midst of this war-fever, Arafat decided that the PLO would abstain from supporting the involvement of foreign forces in the resolution of the Iraq-Kuwait problem. Unfortunately for him, whilst it was logical for a politician to play to his peoples' overwhelming desire, the PLO stance was overwhelmingly construed by the other Arab states as PLO approval of the invasion of Kuwait by Iraq, and therefore by implication indicative that the PLO would approve of further moves by Iraq, which in the immediate hysteria following Kuwait's invasion many took to be the invasion of Saudi Arabia.[62] The Palestinian response was entirely understandable in light of the years of occupation under which they suffered; however the Palestinian refusal to join or support the anti-Iraq coalition caused a major rift between the PLO and the coalition members, many of whom had been major financial contributors to the PLO.[63] In the wake of Iraq's defeat in Kuwait, the PLO faced a great deal of hostility in the region, especially from the various governments who had stood to lose the most from an Iraqi victory, namely Kuwait itself, Turkey, Saudi Arabia and Syria. Such hostility had the effect of undermining efforts to seek a solution to the Palestinian problem, in the sense that previous sponsors of the Palestinians were now no longer quite so well disposed to the Palestinian cause. The PLO were roundly accused of taking the Iraqi side – indeed the Western response was encapsulated in the annual global economic and strategic report of the French Institute of International Relations thus:

> The PLO leadership, by choosing to side with Iraq – the Arab power which was going to revive the military option vis-a-vis Israel – thus suggested that it renounced its peace strategy. The PLO's resultant loss of credibility in Western eyes and in those of a number of Arab countries is a serious setback which the Palestinian authorities are anxious to put right, as a priority, so that they can recover their previous international diplomatic position.[64]

Re-ingratiating themselves into the international diplomatic mainstream proved to be an overriding concern for the PLO leadership following the Second Gulf War. This would be achieved by agreeing to attend the Madrid Conference. Agreeing to the American terms was the price to be paid for acceptance back into the fold, while refusal would have meant being locked out of subsequent negotiations. The Palestinian leadership was well aware that compromise agreements may well have been worked out by Israel and her neighbours without due regard for Palestinian aspirations.

President Bush, viewing the new circumstances in the Middle East in terms of the realignment of the balance of power in the region which enabled the US administration to press ahead with a new diplomatic process, sought resolution of outstanding regional problems in the wake of the new realities in the region.[65] Bush sought what some commentators have described as a *pax universalis*, but in reality was more the imposition of a *pax americana*.[66] President Bush outlined his new ideas in what he described in somewhat grand terms as the 'new world order'. In an address to the US Congress on 6 March 1991, President Bush declared a Middle East peace initiative in which he stated:

> The time has come to put an end to the Arab-Israeli conflict . . . A comprehensive peace must be grounded in UN Security Council Resolutions 242 and 338 and the principle of territory for peace . . . elaborated to provide for Israel's security and recognition, and at the same time for legitimate Palestinian political rights.[67]

Entrusting his Secretary of State to work for the implementation of the US initiative in order to resolve the Israeli-Palestinian/Arab-Israeli conflict, Baker toured the Middle East from 8 March 1991. On 12 March, Baker met ten Palestinian leaders, authorized by the PLO, at the US Consul-General's office in Jerusalem, the first official meeting between a US Secretary of State and a Palestinian delegation.

Baker embarked on his second tour on 8 April, securing Israeli agreement to the convening of a regional conference; however Shamir attached a number of conditions and guarantees. IDF Radio reported that Shamir presented for approval to his cabinet on 11 April a series of nine points agreed upon by Shamir and Baker. These were:

(1) The two countries accepted the principle of a regional conference, under the auspices of the US and the USSR, leading to direct negotiations between Israel and the Arab states.
(2) The two countries accepted that the final aim of the peace process could not be the creation of a Palestinian state.
(3) The composition of the delegation of Palestinian personalities from the West Bank and the Gaza Strip should be determined in agreement with Israel.

(4) The US did not demand the presence in this delegation of Palestinians from East Jerusalem or of Palestinians previously expelled by Israel.

(5) Israel refused any dialogue with the PLO and the US would not resume its dialogue with it.

(6) The two countries agreed that there was no single interpretation of UN SCR 242, with the US recognizing Israel's right to have its own interpretation.

(7) UN SCR 242 would be the subject of negotiations between Israel and its Arab counterparts in the final phase of the process.

(8) The first phase of negotiations would deal with the status of self-government in the West Bank and the Gaza Strip, and, at the end of three years of such a regime, negotiations should begin on the final status of these two regions.

(9) The USSR should re-establish diplomatic relations with Israel and accept the principles of the peace process in order to be a party to the regional conference.[68]

These preconditions for the holding of a regional conference which the US apparently accepted are strikingly similar to the terms Israel outlined to US Secretary of State Kissinger in 1975 in return for its withdrawal from Sinai. On 14 April, Arafat rejected the convening of a regional conference on the basis that such a conference would reflect the new balance of power in the region, which he perceived to be in Israel's favour, and that such a formula was driven to the attainment of rapprochement between Israel and her Arab counterparts and not between Israel and the PLO. Arafat re-stipulated the PLO's desire for an international conference, to no avail. During Baker's fifth trip to the region, 18–22 July 1991, President Mubarak proposed a lifting of the Arab economic boycott of Israel in exchange for a freeze on Israeli settlements in the occupied territories, a proposal already made by the G-7 at their London summit. On 31 July a joint communiqué, approved of by Presidents Bush and Gorbachev at the US-USSR summit, declared that

> President Bush and President Gorbachev reaffirm their commitment to promote peace and genuine reconciliation among the Arab states, Israel and the Palestinians. They believe there is an historic opportunity now to launch a process that can lead to a just and enduring peace and to a comprehensive settlement in the Middle East. They share the strong conviction that this historic opportunity must not be lost.[69]

Baker began his sixth tour of the Middle East on 1 August and found the Israelis amenable to the US-USSR communiqué, whilst the Palestinians, afraid of being seen to spurn the US initiative, agreed in principle but couched their reply in terms which incorporated many reservations, seeking further conditions and guarantees. Particulars regarding the modalities of the conference, in the form of 'letters of assurance', were delivered to the parties concerned during Baker's seventh tour of the region between 16 and 20 September. These letters pledged the US to agreements with each of the various parties which did not however contradict individual promises. In order not to endanger the whole process from continuing, these commitments and guarantees had to be sufficiently vague, thus avoiding the confusion and conflict which would undoubtedly arise from contradictory positions and promises.

In the letter of assurance to Israel, Baker promised Israel that the US did not wish to see the creation of a Palestinian state; however the US stated that it did not consent to Israeli occupation in the Golan and in the occupied territories, nor the Israeli division of Jerusalem, and that UN Security Council Resolution 242 was open to interpretation. The US letter of assurance to the Palestinians contained a reinforcement of President Bush's speech of 6 March 1991 and of the Baker Plan proposing a limited interim self-government along the lines of that envisaged in the Camp David Accords, yet what was omitted was of more importance to the Palestinians. For example, the letter did not contain a US commitment to Palestinian self-determination nor did it include references to Israeli settlements. The letter did however consent to the Palestinians' right to choose their own delegates and to raise any matter of interest for discussion. The US letters to the Syrians and the Jordanians merely included a restatement of the US policy positions regarding these two countries, namely for Syria that the US did not recognize the Israeli annexation of the Golan Heights in 1981, and for Jordan that the conference would be convened on the basis of UN SCRs 242 (1967) and 338 (1973).

2.4 The bilateral negotiating rounds of the Madrid peace talks

US President Bush in welcoming the delegations to the Madrid Conference attempted to inspire confidence among all parties in the US administration's good intentions, good offices and balanced approach to the Arab-Israeli conflict. He thus specified his parameters for the forthcoming negotiations.

> We believe territorial compromise is essential for peace . . . what we envision is a process of direct negotiations proceeding along two tracks: one between Israel and the Arab states, the other between Israel and the Palestinians. Negotiations are to be conducted on the basis of UN Security Council Resolutions 242 and 338.

Concerning Israeli-Palestinian negotiations, President Bush continued that these negotiations would be conducted over several phases and that autonomy discussions would be based on the Camp David Accords. These talks would initially cover interim self-government, so that 'Once agreed, interim self-government arrangements will last for five years; beginning the third year, negotiations will commence on permanent status.'[70] President Bush indicated that, whilst he did not know where the negotiations would lead, he hoped that the end result would entail the development of a situation whereby Israel and its security concerns were recognized, and that the Palestinians would exercise control over their future. Whilst the bilateral negotiations were of great political importance, the Madrid Conference also included important multilateral issues of common regional interest, such as arms control, refugees, water and economic development.

The first five rounds of the Washington talks were held while the Likud was still in power in Israel. This meant that the talks dealt almost exclusively with procedural issues as Israel rejected any talk of territorial compromise, only willing to discuss a limited autonomy plan for the Palestinians. PM Shamir would not accept explicitly either the Resolution (242) or the principle of land for peace as a basis for negotiation even though the letter of invitation stated that the negotiations would proceed on the basis of UN SCR 242 incorporating the principle of trading land for peace. Observers believed that this was merely an opening gambit in a protracted bargaining process which would produce concessions once the substantive negotiations got under way. The reality however, was that Shamir would 'not bargain about the land of Israel or about any interim agreement that would involve the least risk of losing control over the occupied territories.'[71]

Although the nature of the talks improved in 1992 with the advent of the Labour government in Jerusalem, the only material change in the Israeli negotiating teams was the replacement of the head of the team negotiating with Syria, Yossi Ben-Aharon, with Professor Ittamar Rabinowitz. The new government's policy was to agree in principle to the territorial compromise formula. The new Israeli goal was to reach interim agreements with the Syrians (involving a phased withdrawal from the Golan Heights annexed by Israel on 14 December 1981) and the Palestinians (involving interim self-governing arrangements). The problem with Lebanon was that as far as the Israelis were concerned, it did not have a government capable of ensuring security along Israel's northern border in return for an Israeli withdrawal from southern Lebanon, because the Lebanese government was seen to be too dependent on Syria for its decision-making. As far as Jordan was concerned, King Hussein did not want to reach an agreement with Israel before the others as Jordan was still very much suffering from the repercussions of having been seen to ally itself too closely with Iraq during the Second Gulf War of 1991.

Thus the framework for peace negotiations between Israel and the Arab states, under the auspices of the US and the USSR, took shape, with two negotiating tracks being established: a bilateral one with the participation of Syria, Lebanon, Jordan, the Palestinians and Israel; and a multilateral one with the participation of Middle Eastern states and extra-regional actors. However, after the ceremonial part of the conference, the talks quickly became embroiled in a public impasse, characterized by futile wrangling over procedural matters of dubious substance. The negotiating process merely mirrored external events which overshadowed and undermined the possibility of progress in the process itself.

2.5 Neither Washington nor Moscow, but international facilitation

In April 1992, Terje Larsen from the Oslo-based Institute for Applied Social Sciences (FAFO) met Yossi Beilin MK to discuss a FAFO economic study on Palestinian living conditions in the West Bank and Gaza Strip. In discussion the two agreed that the Madrid process had stalemated, and that for meaningful progress to be achieved, direct talks between Israel and the PLO was the only realistic way forward. Larsen suggested talking with Faisal Husseini. However, unknown to Larsen, Yair Hirschfeld of Haifa University and Beilin had been meeting Husseini since 1989: Hirschfeld met Husseini at least once a week, Beilin met him every few months and Shimon Peres met Husseini eight to ten times.[72] Although they had discussed the idea of backchannel contacts with the PLO following a Labour victory in the elections, designed to circumvent the Israeli ban on contacts with PLO officials and to provide a forum for discussing problems arising from the Israeli-Jordanian/Palestinian bilateral talks, the Norwegian backchannel was only officially mooted with Deputy Foreign Minister Egeland's offer of Norway's good offices on 9 September 1992 during an official visit to Israel.[73] Egelund's doctoral dissertation had focused on Norway's potential role as an intermediary in the resolution of bilateral disputes. Although the Norwegians tried to schedule substantive meetings either in Jerusalem or Oslo, none materialized. Beilin feared conducting backchannel negotiations as opposed to private conversations and thus courting controversy, as Rabin had vetoed Peres having private meetings with Husseini.[74]

For the Norwegians, who did not have major political interests in the region and lacked the strategic scheming that superpowers traditionally use to change the equation of a negotiation, they offered a more modest role as facilitators rather than mediators[75] and in the process 'invoked the experience of the European Community in transforming political relations by institutionalizing shared economic endeavor'.[76] The PLO saw in the Norwegian offer an opportunity for mediation on the Swedish model of the 1980s, when Swedish Foreign Minister (FM) Andersson had been instrumental in persuading the Palestine National Council (PNC) to declare its support for a two-state solution in 1988, and had initiated a dialogue between American Jewish peace activists and Arafat in Stockholm. Ahmad Qurai, in January 1992, and Bassam Abu Sharif, in April 1993, informally requested Norwegian involvement on the Swedish precedent.[77] However the Norwegians were not alone in attempting third-party mediation and establishing plausibly deniable conduits between the Israelis and PLO. For example, over four rounds, a period of nine months, and under the guise of an academic conference hosted by the American Academy of Arts and Sciences, unofficial meetings in London and Rome on the security aspects of peace were being conducted between former PLO and Israeli security officials. Participants included: Nizar Amar, ex-Force 17; Ahmed Khalidi and Yazid Sayegh, academics; Shlomo Gazit, ex-head of Israeli military intelligence; Joseph Alpher and Aryeh Shalev of the Jaffee Centre for Strategic Studies; and Ha'aretz's Ze'ev Schiff. The meetings' purpose was to familiarize the two sides with each other's security thinking, to distribute the findings to 'thirty top members of the security and political establishment', and 'to engage the leadership of both sides to begin thinking about and planning security arrangements and security arrangements within the framework of an interim settlement.'[78] Such informal dialogues, contacts and conduits were maintained in order to solicit and elicit information in various contexts, to gauge and probe each other's views and positions to be used at later dates in other fora. Through such contacts the PLO was able to establish not only its *bona fides* as a negotiating partner which could be trusted but also underline its determination that the PLO could not be dismissed from an active and central role in Israeli-Palestinian negotiations. However the essence of creating backchannels was, for those who believed in them, that they would be useful in either aiding or circumventing the official bilateral negotiations. Neither the Norwegians nor Beilin, although credited with establishing the Oslo channel, were in fact its initiators. Hanan Ashrawi urged Hirschfeld to meet Qurai on 4 December 1992, in London, where he was coordinating Palestinian participation in the multilateral steering committees. Hirschfeld agreed and asked Larsen, who happened to be in London, to organize the meeting. At the meeting in the Cavendish Hotel, Hirschfeld suggested holding quiet talks in Norway. Hirshfeld then consulted Beilin, who consented to further talks in Norway. In a subsequent meeting at the Ritz Hotel, Hirshfeld and Qurai agreed to meet in Norway.[79] On the strength of these meetings, Beilin consulted US officials on their views of Israel-PLO talks. Assistant Secretary of State for Near East Affairs Edward Djerejian and his deputy, Daniel Kurtzer, believed talks to be premature, feeling uneasy about getting involved in something they felt was not sanctioned by Rabin. Hirschfeld informed Kurtzer on 5 December that he had met Qurai who had agreed to hold talks in Norway.[80] Egeland informed Kurtzer in November 1992, but Kurtzer said the US would not oppose Oslo as long as it did not involve the PLO directly.[81] However, Beilin saw potential in the FAFO-disguised talks: participation by private Israeli citizens in an academic context would circumvent the Israeli ban on contacts with the PLO; academic talks could reconnoitre PLO positions without obligation or commitment; by conducting talks under FAFO auspices and funding, the Israeli government avoided official sanction maintaining full official and credible deniability.

The initiation of Israeli contacts with the PLO seems to have been driven by Beilin, in spite of the law forbidding such contacts. Beilin's Mashov faction organized in 1991 for the adoption of a party commitment to repeal the Knesset ban on private contacts with the PLO. Peres, then party leader, overrode opposition from Rabin and others, and ensured that the resolution was included in the party platform. After the 1992 elections Peres, acting on Beilin's request, called on Rabin to implement the party resolution. Rabin waited for the result of the US election before acting, worried about the return of a Bush administration willing to reopen a US-PLO dialogue. On 1 December 1992 the Knesset gave preliminary approval to lift the ban. The Norwegians, asked by Hirschfeld, organized the first Oslo session for 20 January 1993, the law being repealed the day before. Interestingly, Rabin did not attend the vote, and despite the outcome pledged there would be no government-PLO contacts, which may be perceived as an indication that Rabin had no strategic policy to initiate negotiations with the PLO. Despite the bill's passage Rabin pledged there would be no governmental contacts.[82]

Borregard estate

There were five rounds of secret, exploratory 'pre-negotiations' held under the guise of an academic conference at Borregard estate in Sarpsborg, on 20–22 January, 11–12 February, 20–21 March, 30 April–1 May and 8–9 May. Hirschfeld and Ron Pundik represented the Israelis, and Qurai, Maher al-Kurd, and Hassan Asfour represented the Palestinians. If Deputy Foreign Minister Beilin was considered the Israeli patron, then the Palestinian participants considered Mahmoud Abbas their Palestinian patron. The respective parties were tasked initially with exploring each other's positions and their seriousness, and possibly identifying areas of compromise, agreement and flexibility which could be used in the bilateral talks. It was intended that any such proposals be introduced into the bilateral talks as US-inspired.

At the outset, because Beilin believed Rabin was not willing to countenance direct Israel-PLO negotiations, the two Israelis were not to engage in negotiations; they were to identify common ground, determine sensitive issues and work out 'the mobiles and immobiles of negotiations'.[83] The Oslo ground rules were total secrecy, no dwelling on the past, and retractibility of all positions; and the Norwegians would fill the role of facilitator not mediator. The uniqueness of the Oslo talks was that the Norwegian facilitation differed from the US mediation which continued simultaneously in the bilateral talks. The Norwegians were able to foster a harmonious atmosphere, were trusted by both sides to be impartial, unbiased and discreet, which ensured the talks continued even when there were serious disagreements. Larsen and his wife Mona Juul together formed a formidable backchannel facilitation team. Larsen kept in daily contact with Jerusalem and Tunis between sessions, and Juul served as the Norwegian government's liaison, informing officials in Oslo of progress or requesting official intervention to provide pressure when necessary.

The first round of talks resulted in the Sarpsborg document, an agreement on three main points:

(1) Israeli withdrawal from Gaza;
(2) Scaled economic devolution based on proven cooperation, leading to economic institution-building;
(3) An international economic assistance plan for the Palestinian entity in Gaza.[84]

Referral to higher authorities

Whilst Beilin received regular briefings and detailed minutes of the Oslo talks, he needed the sponsorship of a senior party figure with the stature and desire to promote and foster the continuation of the Oslo backchannel. Beilin went to Peres, the Foreign Minister, who agreed to approach Rabin. Peres persuaded Rabin in early February to continue the backchannel without obligations. Part of the reluctance to continue with Oslo, for Rabin, was that Qurai was relatively unknown, therefore Rabin was doubtful of his authority and connections.[85] Peres, as Foreign Minister, had been sidelined by Rabin from being a central figure within the Israeli peace policy-making structure and saw in the Oslo talks an opportunity to become involved in the policy-making process. Rabin had appointed himself Defence Minister giving himself key institutional authority over the occupied territories and excluded Peres from the bilateral negotiations and much of US-Israeli relations that were the centrepiece of the peace process, relegating Peres to the multilateral talks on regional issues. Rabin disagreed with Peres on tactics and the strategic principles underpinning Israel's negotiating positions, therefore he determined that Peres would not influence, interfere or have competence in the negotiations process.[86]

The Palestinians, who reported to Abbas, desired to find out to whom their Israeli counterparts reported. They suspected Beilin, who in turn was close to Peres. This suspicion was tempered by the well-known animosity between the two senior Labour party figures.

Peres returned to the policy-making and decision-making fold owing to Rabin's miscalculation over the deportation of 415 alleged Islamic militants in December 1992, not on the strength of the Oslo case. Rabin needed Peres's political support through a difficult time. Rabin had calculated that mollifying Israeli public opinion at the same time as bolstering moderate Palestinian elements within the occupied territories would 'allow Palestinian negotiators in Washington to be more flexible'.[87] Rabin dismissed warnings of an Arab negotiations boycott from Israeli Civil Administration (ICA) chief, Major-General D. Rothschild, and Elyakim Rubinstein, chief negotiator with the Jordanians/Palestinians. Peres, in Japan in December, later said that the deportations would never have happened if he had been in Israel.[88] Despite the PLO's rivalry with the Islamists, the PLO was compelled to support the deportees, and boycotted the Washington talks. The interesting aspect of the boycott was that the Palestinians showed they had the clout to ensure a total Arab boycott lasting until April 1993. Rabin told a cabinet meeting in early January that the Syrians would not boycott. Syrian FM al-Shar'a had called on the Palestinians to boycott the multilaterals instead. However, the Syrians respected the boycott rather than isolate the Palestinians.

Rabin reversed his earlier refusal and allowed Peres to meet Husseini. Although no agreement could be reached over four secret meetings, Husseini reported to Tunis the presence of Hirschfeld and Pundik with Peres, thus establishing their bona fides as regards Oslo. Increasing violence in the occupied territories led Peres to appeal to Rabin on 9 February 1993 to conduct direct Israel-PLO negotiations, stating that

> as long as Arafat remained in Tunis ... he represented the 'outsiders', the Palestinian Diaspora, and would do his best to slow down the peace talks. I suggested that we propose to Arafat and his staff that they move to Gaza. Once there, they would have the right to vote and to stand in elections; and if elected, they would represent the Palestinians directly in the negotiations with Israel. My criticism of the Washington talks was that we were

trying to reach a declaration of principles without any reference to specific territorial issues.[89]

Whilst Rabin rebuffed Peres's appeal he did however sanction the continuation of the Oslo backchannel, thus allowing Peres a foothold in the policy-making process. Peres thus embarked on his own schedule, indulging in subterfuge and insubordination in his efforts to circumvent Rabin. Rabin requested that Peres delay recommencing the Oslo talks by several weeks because of an imminent visit to Israel by Secretary Christopher. Peres instead approved their immediate resumption. Peres believed if East Jerusalemite Faisal Husseini joined the Palestinian delegation in Washington it would break the boycott – it would privately indicate Peres's power to the Palestinians in Tunis and would publicly signal a shift in the Israeli attitude towards the inclusion of such a high-profile PLO figure from the occupied territories. Therefore Peres manoeuvred Rabin into adopting his negotiating strategy by raising the idea with Christopher in Washington on 16 February. Peres suggested that Rabin would be more likely to accept Husseini's participation if the US proposed the idea. During Rabin's first trip to the US in early March, Rabin assented to the US proposal to include Husseini in the talks.

The referral of information regarding the Oslo meetings to the US brought limited responses. Kurtzer told the Norwegians that Arafat was unreliable and that the Oslo talks were of little value without Rabin's approval; Rabin had stated that US envoys should conduct peace process business only with him. Kurtzer impressed upon the Norwegians that whilst he did not mind some intrusion by Israeli academics, he did mind a foreign government intruding on the US-led peace process.[90] Norwegian FM Stoltenberg briefed Christopher on Oslo at NATO talks in Brussels in February 1993, saying that Oslo was not competing with the Washington track but was supplementary, aimed at resolving deadlocked issues. Receiving no further US response, Egeland and Juul contacted Kurtzer again, going to the US embassy in Oslo to speak to him on a secure phone several times. The Norwegians sent Kurtzer a draft declaration of principles at the end of March.[91] New Norwegian FM Holst informed Christopher at the end of May that Israel had upgraded the talks to the official level. Beilin asked Holst only to tell Christopher that the talks had been upgraded, but not to provide names or indicate the seniority of the officials involved. In early July, prior to the arrival in Israel of US Special Middle East Coordinator Dennis Ross, Peres told US *chargé d'affaires* Brown that Israel was going to reach a deal with the PLO.

In US-Palestinian talks with Christopher in East Jerusalem during early August 1993, the Palestinian delegates to the Washington talks took the unusual step of rejecting the US-proposed 'bridging' language for a declaration of principles within minutes of receiving it. In a meeting of State Department officials in the East Jerusalem consulate in East Jerusalem following the discouraging session with the Palestinians, Kurtzer remarked to his colleagues that the Oslo channel must be delivering substantive progress because Arafat would have never instructed his delegates to dismiss a US draft without offering an alternative. Although the Palestinians subsequently gave Christopher a counter-proposal originating in Tunis that imprecisely mentioned Gaza and Jericho, the US peace team went ahead with a scheduled vacation apparently unaware of the counter-proposal's significance.[92] Even as late as the end of August, Christopher paid only a courtesy call to the Foreign Ministry while visiting Rabin. Former Secretary Baker said that 'The [Clinton] administration just did not take Shimon [Peres] seriously during Oslo.'[93] The Clinton administration believed Rabin to be the principal decision-maker on the peace process, even though Rabin had not consulted with or informed US officials of several unilateral security actions or foreign policy decisions, like the deportations, the closure of the occupied territories and 'Operation Accountability'. US officials therefore dismissed the Oslo backchannel as a Peres vision.

To be fair to the Americans, they heard of a number of secret contacts, such as the AAAS meetings, those of Ephraim Sneh MK and the PLO's Nabil Sha'ath in Washington, and at several international symposia. Just as Holst visited the US, State Department Policy Planning chief and former Ambassador to Israel, Samuel Lewis, was convening a meeting of top US policy-makers and former senior officials on 27 May 1993, to discuss the impasse in the Washington negotiations. Edward Djerejian, the leading US policy-maker in charge of the Middle East peace process, recalled the scene.

> I said, 'Given the Norwegian Foreign Ministry channel and the two to three other channels that we are aware of with the PLO, wouldn't it be ironic if the talks in Washington were a facade and Israel and the PLO are dealing [directly] with one another?' There was nervous laughter in the room.'[94]

The US had organized and founded the Madrid peace process, thus believing themselves to be indispensable to it. One participant was led to remark that 'When you invent the wheel, you believe nobody else can have a car.'[95] Thus, despite American officials receiving regular briefings and information regarding Oslo, they refused to believe that progress would result from Oslo.

Drafting a Declaration of Principles

In order that each side could understand the thinking of the other without setting precedents and produce an outcome from the Oslo channel to whet the appetite of their patrons, Sarpsborg III, a six-page document, was drafted at the second round of Oslo, on 11–12 February, and concluded at the third round on 20–21 March. The document contained 15 articles, with annexes on:

- the status of Jerusalem and Palestinian elections (it was agreed that Palestinian residents of East Jerusalem could both vote and stand as candidates in elections for a council to administer self-rule) (Annex I),
- the establishment of Palestinian economic institutions and economic development (Annex II),
- for aid from the G7 and the Organization for Economic Cooperation and Development to fund infrastructure and other regional projects and regional economic development (Annex III).

This accord served as the basis for the final version of the Oslo agreement. Included in this document were a number of exceptions from existing Israeli policies.

(1) There was to be a complete but graduated Israeli withdrawal from Gaza within two years under the auspices of an interim UN trusteeship, essentially consenting to the eventuality of Palestinian sovereignty. After the initial phase an undefined 'trusteeship' would be established to govern the territory. This provoked a furious response from Israeli policy-makers, particularly FM Peres, who feared it would serve as a precedent for UN involvement in Israeli administration of the occupied territories. The Palestinians agreed to forget the idea, fearing that adherence would slow an Israeli withdrawal from Gaza.[96]

(2) An explicit undertaking was given to negotiate a settlement on Jerusalem, which was a crucial departure from existing Israeli policy and practice. Nabil Sha'ath said on 9 September 1993, that until the Sarpsborg document, Israel had

never accepted that the final status of Jerusalem be on the agenda of the permanent status negotiations. At best they were willing to accept the fact that it is a question to be raised – not an issue to be settled by negotiations. In a way, this calls into question the legality and finality of their annexation. They are admitting that their annexation is not final, that it still needs to be negotiated.[97]

The Labour position before Oslo was that Palestinians in Jerusalem could vote in the elections at polling stations outside the city, but could not stand for election, as that implied a Palestinian jurisdiction in the city. Sarpsborg III allowed Palestinians to vote at polling stations within Jerusalem (Muslims at al-Aqsa Mosque, Christians at the Church of the Holy Sepulchre). Hirshfeld and Pundik believed that having polling booths at religious sites would set elections in the context of Palestinian religious rather than political rights to the city.[98]

(3) An undertaking was given to negotiate on Israeli settlements, and Palestinian sovereignty and borders, within the aegis of final status negotiations on the occupied territories; however sovereignty and borders were removed from later drafts.

(4) There was no delineation of powers of Palestinian jurisdiction, or constraints upon it in the West Bank including East Jerusalem, implying that jurisdiction would be comprehensive and inclusive. Whilst the Palestinians wanted the city to be their administrative headquarters, to ensure its eventual status as a Palestinian capital, the document left the issue of Palestinian jurisdiction in Jerusalem vague. Self-rule would be administered by existing Palestinian institutions, a cryptic reference to Orient House, the headquarters for Palestinian political activity since the 1991 Madrid Peace Conference. This issue would remain the last major sticking point in the Oslo negotiations.

(5) Departing from Camp David, the timetable for an interim period would be altered to commence final status negotiations as soon as the DoP was concluded, rather than having final status talks conditional on elections to a self-rule authority – as opposed to having elections take place within three months. By this flexibility, it was hoped to determine final status issues, or at least minimize the risk to these, before the Israeli elections of 1996, in case a Likud-led coalition was elected.

(6) A willingness was expressed to be bound by arbitration in the case of unresolvable disputes when negotiation and mediation had failed, which represented an extraordinary departure from accepted policy by implying that Israel would be bound by decisions which could cede Israeli territory and/or Israeli sovereignty; for example Article 15 proposed an arbitration panel of Israel, the Palestinians, Russia and the US.

Israeli criticism of Sarpsborg III centres around the fact that what was included was significantly at odds with existing Israeli policy, which meant that official Israeli negotiators had to make concessions when the talks were upgraded in order to withdraw from positions put forward by this document. Although both sides had agreed to the retractibility of positions, once the process was deemed worthy by its senior patrons, a momentum evolved which proved difficult to negate. The reason for this state of affairs lay with the vacuum at the top of Israeli policy-making and the in-fighting between the two most senior Israeli politicians. Political in-fighting allowed the original negotiators a broad latitude because being identified with Peres meant that few took the backchannel seriously enough to consider that it might prove successful. Rabin had no discernible strategic policy for dealing with the PLO other than in terms of security. His acceptance of the Oslo backchannel and its subsequent incorporation into mainstream policy highlight that despite election promises to pursue peace, there exists little concrete evidence of a separate, positive and identifiably Rabin-inspired political policy process *vis-à-vis* the PLO.

Gaza, what am I bid?

A central tenet for Beilin and Peres was that they wanted to relinquish control over, and responsibility for, Gaza. By doing so, they not only hoped to unburden themselves from a repressive occupation but also to entice the PLO into negotiations without having to compromise over the more politically sensitive and volatile issue of the future status of the West Bank. The driving force for the Israelis behind the notion for 'Gaza First', seems to be political expediency. Whilst a harsh judgement in retrospect, particularly as this new proposal included transferring territorial and functional authorities to the local Palestinians, this was the inference the PLO made, fearing 'Gaza First' to be 'Gaza Only' or 'Gaza Last', or 'Gaza without the PLO'. The PLO had previously rejected a Gaza scenario, its existence as a seething slum also being politically expedient, and thus Rabin concluded that the PLO would not be interested in Gaza, which led him to believe the Oslo channel had little to offer. Peres's conclusions concurred. However, acting without Rabin's explicit approval, his proposal of 'Gaza Plus' to 'sweeten the deal', incorporated the idea of ceding Jenin or Jericho to the PLO as a 'downpayment' on future Israeli intentions regarding the West Bank.[99] Peres hoped Rabin would agree to Jericho on the basis that withdrawal from Jericho had been part of Labour Party planning (Jericho Plan) since the Allon Plan of 1968.[100] The PLO rejected this proposal in November 1992, partly because they suspected an Israeli divide-and-rule tactic to separate the insiders from the outsiders, but more significantly because Arafat refused to agree to a solution which did not offer him actual, personal, tangible control and authority. This was confirmed by Israelis at the third AAAS meeting, on 26–27 March 1993, in Rome. There Nizar Amar told Israelis that Arafat wanted to administer self-government personally. During the last AAAS session, from 17 to 19 June in Rome, Amar told the Israelis that their focus on security would be meaningless if Arafat were not included in the deal.[101]

Without Rabin's knowledge or approval, Peres approached the Egyptian Ambassador to Israel, Mohammed Bassiouny, offering territorial jurisdiction to Arafat and the PLO over Gaza and Jericho. Bassiouny reported to President Mubarak, who approached Arafat. Arafat informed Mubarak on 12 April that he would accept Peres's proposal, thus reversing his earlier rejection of the 'Gaza Plus' proposal, because this revised proposal accepted his return to Gaza and implied Israeli recognition of the PLO. Two days later at the Rabin-Mubarak summit at Ismailiya, Osama el-Baz, Mubarak's adviser, showed Rabin a document indicating Arafat's apparent readiness to assume control of Gaza as part of a package deal including Jericho and the control of 'key arteries'. A surprised Rabin claimed this was the first time he had heard of the 'Gaza-Jericho' idea.[102] Peres claimed he had informed Rabin of the idea of ceding Jericho (minus the bridges) to the PLO, but Rabin had no idea that Peres had contacted the Egyptians or the PLO.[103] Rabin was reportedly 'intrigued', 'depressed' and made so furious by the PLO document that he 'jumped to high heaven'.[104] Rabin was intrigued by the PLO's commitment to control Gaza, but he was depressed at the security implications of PLO control over key bridges which was included in the Jericho proposals. Arafat proffered a map which outlined PLO control over the West Bank-Jordan bridges, the Rafah border crossing, and an 'extra-territorial' road across the Negev linking Gaza with the West Bank. Rabin feared loss of Israeli control over the flow of weapons and Palestinians into the territories, and he was furious at Peres's unilateral policy-making.

Peres spent months trying to convince Rabin of the need to reach a deal with the PLO. It was in 'late June or early July', having confirmed the *bona fides* of PLO's Oslo negotiators, that Rabin agreed. Rabin worried that Oslo had not ascertained the PLO's true position, which led him, uninformed of Peres's role, to test the PLO negotiators in Oslo to find out if they were acting under the full authority of the PLO leadership.[105] Rabin determined that Jericho was to be excluded from the negotiations. However, Rabin finally agreed in mid-July to include Jericho, when he became convinced that unless the PLO secured a presence in the West Bank they would reject an accord. Rabin's acceptance of Jericho was conditional on the PLO's abandonment of their proposals for the bridges and the extra-territorial road between Gaza and Jericho.[106]

From Washington to Oslo

Whilst the bilateral talks in Washington resumed in April after the US brokered a series of deals over the deportees issue, for the Israelis frustration with Washington centred on the fact that they had begun to realize the fiction of their hope that Faisal Husseini would assume the mantle of Palestinian spokesman for those in the occupied territories, thus defying and excluding the PLO in Tunis and therefore splitting the Palestinian national movement. For progress on the bilateral front between the Israelis and Palestinians, Arafat and the PLO was the only option. Rabin became convinced in April and May that Israel needed to talk to the PLO after Faisal Husseini did not offer an alternative leadership. The fact that he sat out part of the round in Tunis symbolized that the people in the territories were subordinate to Tunis.[107] A turn to Oslo was a welcome relief to the stalemate in Washington; however Oslo only appeared more productive because of the stalemate in Washington. In Washington, the talks did not put aside past injustices; agree to disagree; allow for new concessions; provide a wide negotiating latitude; or remain insulated from events in the Middle East. According to an Israeli delegate in Washington, 'Many if not all of the Palestinian delegates had either been deported or jailed' by Israel. 'The PLO people sitting in Tunis did not have the trauma of someone such as Haider Abd al-Shafi, whom we deported in 1967. Every day he would bring up Jewish settlements and human rights. Those talks hardly moved.'[108] Arafat instructed the Palestinian delegation to sustain the Washington talks without moving them forward. Thus, progress was procedural rather than substantive. One Israeli delegate said that progress occurred when the Palestinians agreed to hold a committee session with them, though no substantive changes were actually made.[109] At Bir Zeit University in Ramallah in June 1993, Saeb Erekat said that Palestinian strategy was to block progress in Washington in order to prompt Rabin to deal directly with Arafat.[110] The dynamic of Oslo was what aided progress, for it was everything that Washington was not. The main differences between Washington and Oslo were:

(1) The Israeli position in Washington was that there were to be no direct negotiations or recognition of the PLO, self-rule was defined in functionalist terms as 'personal autonomy' including a quasi-territorial dimension which offered Palestinian authority within but not beyond municipal boundaries.

(2) At Oslo the Israelis offered direct PLO-Israel negotiations, recognition of the PLO, the return of Arafat and the outsiders to Gaza, real territorial as well as functional authority on a gradual scale.

For Rabin, his electoral pledge of territorial compromise for peace would have to go beyond what was on offer in Washington to include and encompass defined territory, devolved authority, acceptance of the PLO and commitments to a common but separate future, or there would be no deal. In March 1993, military intelligence chief Major-General Uri Saguy reportedly told a closed session of the Conference of Presidents of Major American Jewish Organizations that attempts to promote an independent Palestinian authority within the territories had failed.[111] More important, Rabin gave a similar assessment to Christopher during a visit to Washington that same month. Rabin admitted that only Arafat could make a deal for the Palestinians because the Palestinians living in the territories were not willing to defy him. What the Palestinians were being offered in Washington was limited devolution, not sovereignty, nor recognition of their right to self-determination, which they naturally dismissed. Where Oslo broke from Washington was in the promise from the Israelis to the Palestinians that territorial compromise meant a state was a real probability, in the intermediate as opposed to immediate future.

However, before committing fully to Oslo, Rabin wished to survey his options, keep them open, and use Oslo as it had been originally intended, to supplement Washington. Washington remained officially an Israeli-Jordanian/Palestinian dialogue, excluding recognition and inclusion of the PLO. Before renouncing Washington for Oslo, Rabin wanted to ensure that no progress nor compromise was possible and also to test the *bona fides* of the Palestinians in Oslo. At the end of fourth round of talks, 30 April–3 May, the PLO agreed to exclude Jerusalem from interim self-rule and agreed to the vague idea of Palestinian Jerusalemites' 'participation' in elections, as opposed to defining whether Palestinians from Jerusalem could be candidates and voters in elections for the interim self-rule authority. Rabin insisted that the continuation of Oslo was contingent upon resumption of the Washington talks, Husseini's return to Washington as head of delegation, the end of posturing in the multilateral talks, and the removal of Yusef Sayigh from one of the plenary meetings.[112] Unaware of Oslo, strained relations between Arafat and his Washington negotiators resulted in a challenge to Arafat's tactics with threats of resignation at a meeting in Tunis in August, but despite friction with Husseini and other Palestinian delegates, Arafat complied.[113]

By conceding to Rabin these points, the PLO were able to manoeuvre him into pursuing Oslo more seriously. Whilst the Palestinians conceded on Jerusalem in Oslo, Arafat instructed the Washington delegation to demand the inclusion of East Jerusalem as integral to an interim agreement. This 'diplomatic masterstroke' whereby Arafat pursued contradictory negotiating positions, 'achieved two objectives simultaneously': the Washington talks halted, as the Israeli public feared for the status of Jerusalem, which in turn further promoted the Oslo negotiations as an agreeable alternative.[114] In return for PLO compliance respecting Rabin's wariness, Arafat in turn demanded Israeli concessions regarding Oslo's status. Arafat wanted Israeli negotiators of equal stature with official status, otherwise Oslo would cease.[115]

Although possibly motivated more by fear that the PLO would halt Oslo rather than stemming from a unilateral desire to upgrade the Oslo backchannel willingly, Peres and Rabin agreed on 15 May on a *modus operandi* which suited, namely that Rabin retained political distance whilst Peres nominated suitable officials. Peres offered himself as delegation head but Rabin rejected this as too high a level of political involvement. Peres named Uri Savir, director-general of the Foreign Ministry, as delegation head.[116] The choice of Savir signalled to the PLO that Rabin's *imprimatur* was not just benign, it represented direct decision-making involvement. This development was important for the PLO, knowing as they did the animosity the two Israelis held for each other, since it represented a level of seriousness and intent hitherto only hinted at in Oslo, significantly registering official sanction and recognition of the PLO. Oslo in transforming to official status converted from backchannel to main channel, making an 'Israeli decision to publicly recognize the PLO more a matter of "when" than "if."'[117] However, at this early stage, agreement in Oslo was still intended by the Israelis to supplement Washington, and any agreement in Oslo was to be presented in Washington as a US proposal, to be concluded with Palestinians from inside the occupied territories, and as yet would not officially confer mutual recognition.[118]

Red lines

Both sides approached official negotiations from different viewpoints. The PLO thought that 'official status' meant ironing out the details of the Sarpsborg III document. Savir was mandated only to ascertain whether or not Israel could conclude a deal, he was not to negotiate a deal. Savir was instructed to:

- ensure the PLO continued the Washington talks
- maintain total secrecy regarding Oslo
- ensure Jerusalem was not part of an interim agreement
- temporarily waive Jericho
- ensure Israel's veto on referring disputes to arbitration.

For the Palestinians, Ahmad Qurai proposed that the US and Russia sign any agreement so that the Palestinians would have leave to appeal during disputes. However the personal chemistry between Savir and Qurai allowed them to 'cut to the chase'. For Savir this meant that the Palestinians needed to know that autonomy could lead to a state, while the Israelis needed to know it would bring security, because once the 'red lines' were understood, everything else could be negotiated. But if these were not understood, negotiations could have continued for years without results. For Qurai this meant an Israeli indication that agreement would lead to statehood and to acceptance by the Israelis that a Palestinian state was an 'eventuality rather than a distinct possibility'. Qurai needed to know the Israeli view on whether the interim agreement [would determine the scope of] final status, which was 'the most key point.'[119]

Although the Israelis did not guarantee a state, their conditional inference that if an interim agreement was concluded which ensured Israeli security, maintained stability, established Palestinian institutions and elements of Palestinians sovereignty, linked Tunis with the occupied territories and resulted in economic cooperation, then the impetus would exist to go beyond an interim stage to a final status which would inevitably include negotiating statehood. Thus Savir and Qurai established a negotiating *modus vivendi* based on implied mutual recognition and respect for each other's aspirations, namely, security and a state, bolstered by economic interdependence. Agreement was reached on a security annex, calling for a demilitarized Gaza, a Palestinian police force which would maintain security over the Palestinian population under its control, and an IDF redeployment outside Palestinian population centres. Such mutual confidence and respect energized the negotiators to continue talks in a convivial atmosphere and in turn ensured their enthusiasm in evangelizing wider support for their negotiations. After initial talks Savir reported to Rabin that a deal was possible.[120] Whilst Qurai and Asfour reported back to Abbas in Tunis that Savir was serious about pursuing a deal, Beilin acted on Savir's recommendation for a legal expert, bringing in lawyer Joel Singer. Singer's immediate impression of the Sarpsborg document was that it lacked legal precision and created some very bad precedents, for example the UN trusteeship idea for Gaza. However his initial professional disdain aside, his assessment of the spirit of the backchannel was that Oslo indicated that the PLO was willing to compromise, despite the insistence of the Palestinian negotiators in Washington that during the transitional interim period to Palestinian autonomy the Palestinians should have jurisdiction over Israeli settlements and East Jerusalem and that a declaration of independence should be made. Singer produced a one-page analysis and legal opinion which, whilst critical of the document, believed that there were intriguing possibilities about some of the proposed ideas.[121] Before continuing, however, Rabin wanted Singer to travel to Oslo to determine if the PLO offer was real. Rabin trusted Singer's objectivity, preparation, attention to detail, legal expertise, critical temperament and ability to provide him with analytical assessments that reflected his concerns. Singer provided a perfect balance to the rest of the Israeli team, who were too closely identified with Peres. Singer's attention to legal detail and concerns over security ensured Rabin had a kindred spirit on board.[122] With Singer's appointment, Rabin became more actively involved in guiding the negotiating team in Oslo.

Singer's role in Oslo from 11 June was to interrogate the Palestinians, bring analytic clarity to the document drafting process, and confront previously avoided problematic issues. Singer brought not only his legalistic and adversarial traits to Oslo, but also Rabin's personal authority which convinced Qurai, Abbas and ultimately Arafat of the changed status of the backchannel.[123]

Israel's negotiating strategy was developed by an informal steering group of Savir, Singer, Hirschfeld, Pundik, Beilin, Gur and Gil, who formulated option papers for Peres, who in turn submitted them to Rabin.[124] Rabin for his part did not develop or divine independent military advice or intelligence assessments and during the course of the Oslo negotiations excluded his usual circle of advisers, senior IDF officers, intelligence officials and Arab affairs experts. Rabin apparently informed IDF Chief of Staff Lieutenant General Ehud Barak about the secret backchannel. Barak said that 'The prime minister showed me all the papers coming out of Oslo,' and added that the PM was 'waiting to see which channel would deliver results, either Oslo or' Rubinstein in Washington. According to Barak, Rabin made the final decision to proceed with Oslo on his own personal responsibility in order to avoid politicizing the IDF.[125] Rabin vetted every line of the draft DoP personally.[126] Though he became increasingly involved in the substance of the talks, he remained sceptical about whether Oslo would produce success.[127]

The group dynamics that evolved in Oslo saw both teams negotiating back and forth to their superiors, using the threat of domestic intransigence as a bargaining ploy to extract concessions. Internally the dynamics that developed saw Singer confront issues, Savir reassure Qurai, Qurai and Asfour grow closer as equals, whilst the others took less central roles, as analysts engaging in strategy sessions. Qurai requested of Abbas that Maher al-Kurd be replaced. Muhammed al-Koush, an accountant but lawyer by training, serving on the PLO delegation at the UN in Geneva dealing with social and economic affairs, replaced him.[128] When the two delegations broke to brief their respective leaders, it was Singer's role which proved crucial and pivotal. Not only did Singer's assessment provide Rabin with the relevant evidence as to whether to proceed or not, Singer's presence underlined to Abbas in Tunis that Rabin was centrally involved, and that if Singer's analysis was positive, then the negotiations would continue until an agreement was concluded. Singer told Rabin that he favoured negotiating mutual recognition because it would probably be inevitable and therefore could be used to extract important concessions. However Peres disagreed, instead favouring mutual recognition as a final resort in order to extract last-minute concessions. Thus whilst Singer briefed Rabin that a deal could be done, he reportedly told Peres in Vienna, 'If we don't make peace with these people, we are idiots.'[129] Rabin instructed Singer to draft a new DoP incorporating the responses he had elicited from his in-depth questioning of Qurai, ironically in Washington DC. From the PLO, the promise of Arafat controlling Islamist terrorism and ensuring that Israeli security fears were allayed proved to be too great a temptation for the Israelis, who may have believed what they wanted to hear on the issue of security. Qurai said that only Arafat had both the capability and will to end terror against Israel, that PLO police would enforce Arafat's will, and Arafat's return to Gaza would turn the public against Hamas. Singer said that the Palestinians 'kept saying all the time that Arafat could and would stop terrorism. We heard this from May 1993 to May 1994, that Arafat would make the difference.' Taking it at face value, Rabin hoped the PLO would handle Hamas without libertarian constraints. However, Rabin had information to the contrary: in January, Nablus academic Khalid Shikaki (brother of Islamic Jihad leader Fathi Shikaki) quoted Hamas leaders as vowing to continue violence against the IDF and Israeli settlers after a peace agreement. The PLO did not incorporate into the agreement any promise to end the *intifada* nor bear any responsibility for groups outwith PLO control.[130]

Thus following the 25–27 June session the Israelis presented the Palestinians with the first formal written draft Israeli-PLO document on 4 July at the Gressheim session. The Gressheim DoP superseded Sarpsborg III. The Gressheim document contained provisions for the following:

- an Israeli withdrawal from Gaza and Jericho (except settlements) within three months of the DoP being signed
- Israeli settlers, settlements, visitors to the territories, and military locations to be exempt from PLO jurisdiction, which was important to Rabin as he wanted deliberately vague language so that he could claim jurisdictional exemptions during final status negotiations for 'security zones'. (At the implementation talks of May 1994, Rabin attained a definition of clusters of settlements as contiguous areas or 'blocs' as opposed to individual 'islands' of Israeli authority isolated from one another in a sea of Palestinian jurisdiction.[131])
- the PLO to have functional jurisdiction, early empowerment, over

health, education, welfare, taxation and tourism – any further Palestinian administrative responsibilities would require mutual agreement

- Israel to retain responsibility for external security, Israelis in the occupied territories, and internal security in the Palestinian entity
- an Israeli military redeployment from Palestinian population centres in the West Bank on withdrawal from Gaza.

Rabin insisted at a 10 June meeting that redeployment be made a matter for Israel's sole discretion. The Declaration could include a requirement for 'consultation' with the Palestinians, the Prime Minister said, but not for 'agreement' with them. The detailed deployment of Israeli troops for strategic defence or for the protection of Israeli settlements and Israeli civilians would not be conditional on the other party's agreement.[132] However the Gressheim document was intentionally vague about redeployment proposing an initial IDF redeployment on the eve of Palestinian elections (without specifying from which population centres) linking further redeployment to Palestinian performance on security. Article XIII(3) of the final DoP states: 'Further redeployments to specified locations will be gradually implemented commensurate with the assumption of responsibility for public order and internal security by the Palestinian police force.' Peres declared that there 'were various hints during the Oslo process that the elections might be deferred or might not be held at all,' as some senior Israeli officials hoped that cancelling the elections would be an indirect way of effectively cancelling the second phase of the Oslo accord because Article XIII(1) of the DoP specifically relates interim redeployment to the holding of elections.[133]

Where the Gressheim document differed from Sarpsborg was on the issue of Jerusalem. The PLO proposed that a definition of Palestinian jurisdiction over defined institutions in East Jerusalem be incorporated. However, not only was this rejected by Rabin, through the absence of permitting East Jerusalemites to stand for election, but the Israelis also attempted to simply abandon their previous agreement to negotiate Jerusalem in final status talks. At Palestinian insistence the Israelis 'eventually reaffirmed their previous commitment'.[134] Whilst the Gressheim document did not explicitly commit Israel to negotiate on 1948 refugees in final status talks as Sarpsborg had, it echoed Camp David with the requirement in the interim phase for liaison and cooperation arrangements between Israel, the

Palestinians, Jordan and Egypt to discuss persons displaced from the West Bank and Gaza Strip in 1967 (Article XII of the final DoP). Thus the Gressheim document represented for the Israelis an arrangement to cohabit rather than a plan to divorce. The Palestinian negotiators were initially furious with this draft; however after working through the draft point by point, initialling and incorporating their own positions next to every point, disagreement was narrowed to five points:

- the inclusion of UN SCRs 242 and 338
- the permanent status negotiations
- the 'Gaza/Jericho first' approach
- elections and Jerusalem
- the issue of Palestinian displaced persons from 1967.

The Israelis carried the authority to sign a declaration at this point in July, then to pass the agreement on to the Washington track, thus ending the need for the Oslo backchannel. However, as far as Qurai was concerned, whilst the PLO wanted a deal, the real hard bargaining had just begun.[135]

Although the political patrons were keen to continue the momentum generated by negotiations in Norway, from 10 July the backchannel began to test the participants' nerves, as diplomatic games threatened to collapse the initiative a number of times in an orchestrated scenario of brinkmanship, of proposal and counter-proposal, manoeuvre and counter-manoeuvre, of halting or threatening to halt negotiations. Whilst the Israelis were preparing to negotiate on the sticking points of the previous rounds,[136] at Halvorsbole on 10 July the Palestinians demanded more than 20 revisions of the Gressheim document.[137] In the same way that Rabin had been behind the revisions incorporated within the Gressheim document, Arafat was clearly behind the new Palestinian proposals being put forward, having now concentrated on all the details put before him. Qurai, Abbas and Arafat had spent time working on their revised draft in Tunis. Arafat found Singer's version 'not acceptable'. The PLO asked Egyptian lawyer Taher Shash, the legal adviser to the Washington delegation, who had worked on Camp David, to help draft a revised document.[138] Qurai confirmed Arafat's involvement through Arafat's first direct message to the Israelis. Whilst Arafat wanted a deal, he also wanted the replacement of the word 'Palestinian' with 'PLO' in respect of the political body with whom the agreement was to be made and with whom the Israelis would be partners; control of the Allenby Bridge, extraterritorial roads between Gaza and Jericho (including an air corridor), with Gaza/Jericho crossing points 'under the responsibility of the Palestinian authorities, with international supervision and in cooperation with Israel'; and Palestinians from East Jerusalem to be eligible as candidates in elections for an autonomous authority.[139] An air of crisis thus enveloped the Oslo channel over a number of subsequent weeks with both sides toughening their positions from the initial cordiality of the opening academic atmosphere.[140]

The Israelis grumbled that the PLO negotiating strategy was an 'inversion' of the standard model, in which both sides start from maximalist positions and gradually move toward a compromise somewhere in the middle. Singer described the PLO strategy as beginning with a 'relatively centrist position' then moving 'backward' as the opposing party moved toward them. Thus they put forward their opening position but instead of then moving toward agreement, as in any other negotiation, they moved *beyond* their opening position, so that the Israelis were almost at the Palestinian opening position as the negotiations moved on.[141]

The Norwegians had to work hard to rescue the talks from crisis. Through the tireless efforts of Larsen, Juul and Holst, they tried to resolve the issues which threatened deadlock. Much of the Norwegian effort revolved around the human dimension, that is on convincing both sides as to the real and genuine desire of the other to reach an agreement, rather than concentrating on purely technical and substantive points of disagreement. On 11 July FM Holst, under cover of an official visit to President Ben Ali in Tunis, met with Arafat. Accompanied by Larsen and Juul, Holst tried to resolve the deadlock by assuring him that Israel was committed to reaching an agreement in Oslo. The Israelis also sought assurances from the Norwegians regarding the PLO's commitment to Oslo. They wanted to know whether Arafat was fully cognisant of the negotiations and committed to their success. More importantly, the Israelis wanted an authoritative judgement on whether the previous round's deadlock was negotiable. 'The Israelis asked us to come [to Jerusalem] because they were about to end the [Oslo] channel,' recalled Juul. Holst sent Juul and Larsen to Israel on 12 July with a letter assuring Peres that the negotiations were worth pursuing. 'The letter was partly substance, ... But it was also psychological. Holst stressed his impression that Arafat was very much behind the Norway talks. He was involved in the details and dedicated to the talks' success. This made an impression on the Israelis.' In addition, Larsen and

Juul briefed the Israelis about their meeting with Arafat. On 13 July at the Laromme Hotel in Jerusalem, Peres and the Norwegians discussed the details of a deal. After insisting on confidentiality, Peres said that Israel would allow Arafat to come to Gaza and Jericho 'as long as he does not call himself "president".' Juul and Larsen returned to Tunis with a letter from Peres to Holst seeking clarification of the Arafat's intentions. Holst passed it to Arafat, who conceded on issues of extraterritoriality and Rabin permitted talks to continue. 'I think [our assurances] helped keep the talks going,' Juul said. Peres's statement at the Laromme marked the first known occasion on which any Israeli involved in Oslo confided to a third party that Israel would allow Arafat to return to Gaza.[142]

Progress thus continued warily. By mid-July, whilst 16 substantive points remained unresolved, the central issue of contention was that of the official link between an agreed DoP and mutual recognition, that is, recognition of Israel's right to exist in peace and security by the PLO, and of the PLO as the official, legitimate representative of the Palestinian people by Israel. The Israelis did not want to link the DoP with official mutual recognition, however both Peres and Rabin knew realistically that the former would not happen without the latter. Rabin and Peres repeatedly rejected proposals for mutual recognition for tactical reasons, 'Rabin wanted the DoP to stand independently of mutual recognition, and Peres worried that by pursuing both objectives simultaneously, they would "overload the wagon" and achieve neither.'[143] However, it was clear from Oslo that the PLO wanted a 'package deal', the DoP for mutual recognition. Arafat's approval was a *sine qua non* for any agreement, as he believed that return to Gaza not only symbolized the embodiment of Palestinian nationalism, it was also important for his and the PLO's existence, the importance of which to Arafat was not lost on the Israelis when considering extracting concessions.[144]

Rabin and Peres accepted that mutual recognition was crucial to Arafat and the PLO, and that if they wanted to do a deal with Arafat and the PLO, they would have to recognize officially whom they were dealing with. Rabin and Peres preferred the tactic of negotiating the DoP and mutual recognition sequentially rather than simultaneously. However, whilst Rabin authorized Savir to mention the issue of mutual recognition in passing at the 11 July session, then offering more specific terms at the 25–26 July session as an unofficial personal initiative, by agreeing to offer terms Rabin was merely engaging in a tactical rather than strategic ploy. The acceptance of the concept of mutual recognition meant Rabin had already accepted, in principle, the PLO and Arafat as partners.[145] More significantly, mutual recognition brought with it implicit Israeli recognition of the PLO's political agenda, that is the Palestinians' right to self-determination and thus a state.[146]

During the 25–26 July session, the PLO forced the issue of mutual recognition by determinedly sticking to their range of demands stemming from their objections to the Gressheim document. The furious refusal by the Israelis in response to these PLO demands resulted in Qurai stating his intention to resign. With Qurai preparing to depart, Savir privately negotiated with him a 'combination of a package deal and a swap arrangement' outlining seven pre-conditions for mutual recognition linked to 'eight for eight' concessions, whereby if the PLO agreed to the seven pre-conditions and yielded on eight areas of dispute, the PLO would receive eight Israeli substantive concessions in return. The points of contention related to security, and Gaza/Jericho. For the Israelis there was a strong reluctance to compromise on the issue of security, knowing that on such issues as the security of settlers, settlements, borders, redeployment, and IDF control over internal and external security, there would be no concessions from Jerusalem. For the PLO, there was just as strong a reluctance to concede on such issues as the powers and responsibilities of a Palestinian autonomous authority, where the council should be, the timetable of transfer of powers and responsibilities, the competencies being transferred and physical connections between Palestinian entities.[147] Thus the negotiations focused on an agreement which incorporated mutual recognition covering:

- PLO recognition of Israel's right to exist in peace and security
- PLO commitment to resolve the Israeli-Palestinian conflict on the basis of UN SCRs 242 and 338
- repeal of the PLO covenant's provisions calling for the destruction of Israel
- PLO renunciation of terrorism and cooperation with Israel in countering violence
- PLO call to stop the *intifada*
- PLO commitment to resolve all outstanding issues with Israel peacefully
- Arafat's agreement to represent himself as chairman of the PLO and not as the president of Palestine.

The draft list of seven points that Savir handed to Qurai omitted acknowledgement that Arafat would lead a PLO-administered Palestinian authority in the autonomous areas. Israeli officials apparently wanted to retain such a concession for later bargaining. Nonetheless, senior Israeli officials were concerned about Israeli public opinion and a deal with the PLO, preferring the Palestinian negotiators in Washington to sign the final deal, despite the fact that PLO officials would be in charge of the new Palestinian entity. However Rabin believed the public would support a peace deal with Arafat. Pollster Kalman Geyer conducted a poll for Rabin indicating that the public was willing to support a deal with the PLO. Rabin had sufficient enough information at that time to tell him that the public would back him up. The Israelis were so desperate to get out of Gaza that they were willing to accept Arafat as long as he agreed to end the state of war and amend the PNC charter.[148]

Syrian versus Palestinian tracks

In attempts to outmanoeuvre each other, both sides indulged in endgame strategies that obviously would incur the least concessions whilst maximizing their gains. The PLO made a number of concessions in the first week of August, precipitated by a strong concern that Israel was possibly in the process of shifting its focus and emphasis in negotiations from the Palestinian to the Syrian track. Israeli officials admitted later that they talked up the prospects of progress with Syria to give the impression that Israel was pursuing such an option.[149]

Rabin's peace strategy, such as it was, whilst having a tendency to appear reactive as opposed to proactive, had to fuse two realities: Israeli public opinion and what it could cope with, and what was pragmatic and practical in the international arena. Neither Israeli public opinion, nor the immediate neighbourhood, could withstand the political fallout from a comprehensive peace agreement incorporating, in one fell swoop, agreement between Israel, Syria, Jordan and the Palestinians, particularly one conducted, negotiated and concluded in secret. Rabin therefore sought to gain agreement bi-laterally, individually and sequentially by operating a 'push-pull' diplomatic tactic in which progress on one track promoted progress on another by instilling fear of exclusion in each party, thus maximizing his gains, minimizing his concessions, dividing and ruling his enemies, and ensuring that the Israeli public would not have to digest too much change and deal with too many concessions on several fronts concurrently. Rabin believed his primary, principal negotiating partners were either the Palestinians or the Syrians, Lebanon having no independent political authority, and Jordan being unable to conclude a peace treaty before a Palestinian or Syrian deal, because of its large Palestinian population and out of concern for Syrian reaction.

On the international level, Syria presented a far greater real and potential threat to Israel's security than the Palestinians. Syria could present an existential threat, therefore resolution of conflict with Syria would constitute a major breakthrough in the Arab-Israeli conflict, and would allow Israel to reassess strategic priorities and reconfigure resources and allocations aimed at meeting the perceived future threat from Iran and Iraq. Rabin told Israel TV in January 1993 that not only would an Israeli-Syrian agreement change the strategic equation of the region and end the war of attrition against the Iranian-backed Hezbollah Islamic militants in the security zone along Israel's northern border but also that Syria's leader could be trusted to implement any accord. Alternatively, a deal with the Palestinians would merely be 'public relations'.[150]

However, Syria's demands – full withdrawal from the Golan Heights without a formal peace treaty including recognition and full diplomatic relations leading to normalization – were not only too unacceptable politically, but also complete withdrawal from the Golan was less easily reversed militarily. A paper giving the Syrian position presented at Washington in July 1992 offered only the prospect of non-belligerency, essentially codifying the existing Israeli-Syrian truce. Important politically was the extremely sensitive issue within Israel of ceding control of the strategic Golan Heights. Full withdrawal required the dismantling of all Golan settlements, politically difficult to implement due to previous Labour party policy urging settlement on the Golan. Peres said 'We did not have the [political] strength to dismantle the Golan settlements.'[151] Thus, whilst Rabin may have preferred dealing with Syria for long-term strategic advantages, Israeli public opinion regarded the Palestinian issue as a more immediate problem. In response to public demand, Rabin publicly committed himself during the 1992 election to concluding an interim agreement with the Palestinians within six to nine months. According to Peres, 'Rabin promised the public... there would be a deal and nothing happened.'[152] Deaths of Israelis in Gaza, perceived as a political and strategic burden on Israel, where

Israel's citizen army had to deal daily in repression and occupation, were not popular with the Israeli public. Also influencing Rabin's
negotiating strategy was the domestic political scandal surrounding
Shas which threatened to bring down the coalition. The effects of
the drawn-out *intifada* and the steadfastness of the Palestinian population, 'had focused the Israeli public on the need to address the
Palestinian issue'; indeed, Rabin's coalition believed the Palestinian
issue more important than Syria, with both Labour and Meretz
ministers feeling the Palestinian issue to be the 'heart of the Arab-
Israeli conflict.'[153]

Thus, the immediacy of the Palestinian problem allied to the
minimalist nature of immediate territorial and jurisdictional concessions necessary to conclude an interim agreement with the
Palestinians convinced Rabin for political and strategic reasons that
a deal with the Palestinians represented a better bet than negotiating with Syria. However, this did not preclude Rabin from pressuring
the Palestinians by appearing to favour the Syrian track for tactical
reasons. At least twice Rabin prospected a deal with Syria prior to
the final Oslo breakthrough. Rabin had believed the Palestinian
boycott at Washington over the deportations had been a bluff; therefore he put pressure on the Palestinians by playing up prospects
for a deal with Syria. However Israeli-Syrian prospects dimmed when
Damascus tied resumption at Washington to the PLO's return. Thus,
the Palestinians demonstrated that they had a *de facto* veto over
Syrian unilateral movement. In recognition of this, the US quietly
nudged Rabin back to the Palestinians. At US urging, Israel tempted
the Palestinians back to Washington in April. Thereafter Rabin's
attention remained focused on the Palestinians, officially upgrading
the Oslo channel in May. In early August the US, disappointed by
the lack of progress with the Palestinians in Washington, began to
favour shifting focus to Syria. However, Secretary Christopher's visit
to Damascus in August achieved nothing, therefore the lack of
movement from Syria factored into Rabin's decision to finalize Oslo.
Rabin recounted that he had decided to go all the way with the
Palestinians because the Syrians still demanded a total withdrawal
from the Golan Heights, the uprooting of Israeli settlements there,
whilst they were not even ready for a fully-fledged peace.[154] Peres
confirmed that a major factor in Rabin's decision to deal with the
PLO was the realization after Christopher's trip in August that there
was no 'Syrian option'.[155]

Getting to an agreement

Israel's launching of 'Operation Accountability' on 26 July, a major IDF-Hezballah border skirmish which entailed the heavy bombardment of southern Lebanon, brought Secretary Christopher to the Middle East in early August intending to broker an IDF-Hezballah cease-fire, resuscitate the Washington talks and initiate an indirect dialogue between Rabin and Assad. 'Operation Accountability' fulfilled two objectives for Rabin: he gained great 'security' kudos from public opinion for his massive action directed at Hezballah, and Christopher's visit to the region provided the Palestinians with the illusion that Rabin was serious about dealing with Syria, thus providing Rabin with an opportunity to pressure the PLO into reigniting the stalling Oslo process. To put pressure on Arafat, Dennis Ross suggested Christopher return to Damascus from Jerusalem, to create the impression of 'shuttle diplomacy' and thus of movement on the Israel-Syria track. Peres wrote a letter to Holst to be shared with the PLO, saying that if the negotiations were not completed, 'the vacuum may be filled by opposing forces, or with other initiatives, including the possibility of desired progress between Israel and Syria. Secretary Christopher is at this very moment visiting our region.'[156] Arafat apparently understood the significance of what was happening, continuing negotiations under cover of the Washington process in order to keep the US involved in the wider process but not involved with Oslo. Arafat promised Mubarak in Cairo that the Palestinian delegation to Washington would give Christopher a counter-proposal to a previous US proposal presented in Jerusalem. Mubarak passed this information to Christopher. Arafat's counter-proposal included a vague reference to Palestinian self-rule in Gaza/Jericho but did not mention the PLO or other vital issues. Arafat insisted they transmit the proposal to Christopher, saying he would explain later in Tunis. Neither the delegates nor the US officials understood the significance of the Tunis proposal. The delegation handed Christopher Arafat's authorized draft; Ashrawi, Erekat and Husseini then flew to Tunis to submit their resignations, which Arafat refused to accept. Ashrawi said she asked him if there was another channel besides the Washington talks, and that Arafat explained how he would build a Palestinian state from a Gaza-Jericho deal.[157]

Rabin dismissed Secretary Christopher's enquiries about the Oslo channel, giving him a letter for Clinton requesting more US involvement on the Syrian track, because not only did he not want US involvement in Oslo, he claimed that he genuinely was not sure whether Oslo would produce success until at least mid-August. Singer stated that Rabin deliberately played down the viability of Oslo when talking to Christopher.[158] Rabin in his turn stated that by mid-August he was surprised by the growing list of PLO concessions. On some four or five major issues, the Palestinians agreed to things he had doubted they would agree to, primarily keeping all of Jerusalem under Israeli control and outside the jurisdiction of the Palestinians for the entire interim period. In addition, they agreed to retain all Israeli settlements, conceded overall Israeli responsibility for the security of Israelis and external security, and kept all options open for negotiation on a permanent solution.[159]

In the end, the stalemate in Oslo was broken with a secret exchange of letters between Rabin and Arafat, creating ironically a 'backchannel within a backchannel', in which deadlocked issues on substantive positions were clarified. Without disclosing Oslo, Arafat asked Ahmed Tibi to open an independent line of communication to Rabin. Tibi met Haim Ramon on 17 July urging him to ask Rabin to correspond with the PLO. Tibi travelled to Tunis on 19 July with Rabin's letter, returning on 4 August with a letter from Arafat to Rabin passed via Ramon. Neither letter was addressed directly to the other party or signed by its author. Rabin thought he was writing to Abbas. This correspondence marked the only known exchange between the two leaders during the Oslo process, and one that Israeli negotiators knew nothing of.[160] Rabin's letter was dedicated to eliciting from the PLO a definition of the PLO's understanding of functional and territorial jurisdiction, getting clarification of the status of Jerusalem during the interim period, and signalling that agreement to mutual recognition would not be dependent on being formally linked to the DoP. Rabin sought for Israel 'final authority on all security issues in Gaza and Jericho and total freedom of movement for the IDF in the territories, so that it could intervene either pre-emptively or in retaliation as well as maintain "hot pursuit" of suspects', whilst he opposed giving the PLO unqualified jurisdiction over settlements and military locations in the territories beyond Gaza and Jericho, because it would have allowed the PLO to claim *de facto* sovereignty over the entire West Bank in final status talks.[161] Meanwhile at the Washington talks, the US produced a compromise on the issue of territorial jurisdiction, proposing 'early empowerment', meaning the immediate transferral of non-controversial civil responsibilities, like taxation, education, and so on.

In reply, Arafat agreed to Israeli control over settlements, settlers, and Israelis travelling in the territories, but qualified Israeli jurisdiction as being responsible for 'external' rather than (as Israel had insisted) 'overall' or 'comprehensive' security; he also agreed to exclude Jerusalem from the Palestinian self-rule area, and linked these concessions to the Israeli acceptance of mutual recognition.[162] As a result, between the two leaders, Rabin later hailed this first correspondence as 'the turning point' that led to breakthrough.

However, Rabin sought to discover through the same channels from the PLO, whether or not they would modify their position on assuming responsibility for 'comprehensive security' and demands for control of territory which included military areas. Rabin authorized Ramon to ask Tibi to contact Abbas, however on 7 August the PLO replied it would not change its position. According to Tibi, the PLO favoured 'flexible phrasing' but would not give in on those two issues.[163] Whilst in the background for the PLO there existed the threat of Israel's turning to a Syrian option, the Israelis found that the domestic political corruption scandal enveloping their junior coalition partner threatened the future of the government. Therefore both sides felt convinced of a sense of urgency. When the Norwegians proposed an unofficial 'non-meeting' in Paris to provide fresh impetus to the backchannel, not only did the PLO exhibit a new flexibility and agree to restart the talks,[164] but also a concerned Rabin and Peres decided to formally raise the issue of mutual recognition. Rabin instructed that mutual recognition be formally included at the 13–15 August round of Oslo talks. The Paris meeting produced the desired result of resuming talks, but substantive disagreement over important interim issues remained. What the negotiations concluded was an agreement to disagree whilst pressing on with reaching an agreement. At this point, it seems that the negotiators were intent on concluding an historic deal, with finer points of interim period disagreement, let alone final status issues disagreement, to be left to future, post-deal negotiations. Evidence for this conclusion comes from various discrepancies over aspects of jurisdiction, security, Jerusalem, the size of the intended Jericho entity, and control of Jordan-West Bank passage points. Israel defined Jericho by its existing municipal boundaries, while the PLO referred to a 'Jericho District', an area ten times larger than that demarcated by Jordan. The compromise agreed was to use the term

'Jericho area' leaving precise borders to be negotiated during im-plementation talks. The two were unable to agree on control mechanisms for Jordan-West Bank or Egypt-Gaza passage points, because Israel feared unrestricted arms smuggling and Palestinian immigration; as Israel would not yield on the issue the compro-mise agreed was therefore to 'coordinate' arrangements.[165] These issues were only finally resolved through intense and intensive negotiations in Stockholm, involving Singer, Gil, Peres and Larsen, through the medium of FM Holst to Arafat, Abbas, Qurai, Asfour, Yasir Abed Rabbu and Muhsen Ibrahim in Tunis. During a previ-ously scheduled official visit, Peres met with Holst on 17 August under cover of a pretext to assuage the Swedish authorities. Holst's presence allowed him to mediate the final issues by telephone with the PLO leadership in Tunis. During the evening of 18 August, Holst engaged in a seven-hour phone call with Arafat and Qurai in Tunis from Peres's guest house. Gil and Singer negotiated with the PLO via Holst, whilst Peres remained in the background being woken for consultations on various Israeli positions three times during the night. There were precarious moments when Peres threatened to shift Israel to the Syrian track, or when Holst read parts of the DoP over an unsecured link, substituting 'blurp' for 'Israel'.[166]

Jerusalem was the last major issue to be resolved. Every scenario during negotiations envisioned postponing the symbolic issue of Jerusalem to the end to prevent the talks from collapsing prema-turely. The PLO compromised by dropping their initial demand that Jerusalem be included in the self-rule area, but during the Stock-holm negotiations they insisted that the draft DoP allow for the administration of self-rule in Gaza and Jericho from Jerusalem. Annex II(5) states that the 'offices responsible for carrying out the powers and responsibilities of the Palestinian authority under this Annex and Article VI of the Declaration of Principles will be located in the Gaza Strip and Jericho area pending the inauguration of the Council.' The PLO wanted to add 'or other places in the West Bank' after 'Jericho area'. The 5 July Gressheim document had allowed the PA to administer institutions in Jerusalem, grouped together in a special quarter.[167] Rabin and Peres knew that Israeli public opinion would have difficulty in accepting PLO headquarters in Jerusalem, fearing that Israelis would perceive that Jerusalem's sovereign status had either been provisionally negotiated or compromised, creating a precedent leading to Jerusalem's sovereign and jurisdictional di-vision. Peres told Holst that the domestic political situation involving

Shas had become so acute that not only would the talks need to be concluded as soon as possible if a deal was to be done prior to any prospective domestic upheaval, but also that given the domestic political climate it was imperative that to reach such an agreement Jerusalem's status must remain unaltered, that is as the indivisible sovereign capital of Israel. Peres believed that if the PLO had insisted on maintaining a presence in Jerusalem, there might not have been either a government or an agreement. The Palestinians gave in, but in return Peres, with Rabin's approval, agreed to a letter confirming that 'Palestinian institutions of East Jerusalem . . . [were] of great importance and would be preserved'. Indeed, Peres stated that Israel would not 'hamper' their activity, but on the contrary, the fulfilment of 'this important mission' was to be encouraged.[168] Peres was extremely aware of the political sensitivity of the issue; therefore he insisted that the letter be written and dated after Knesset confirmation of the agreement was obtained so that he could state categorically that there were no secret written agreements outstanding. Peres wrote the letter on 11 October 1993 addressing it to Holst rather than Arafat, so that no inference could be interpreted that Arafat, otherwise as recipient, would have some form of jurisdictional representation regarding Jerusalem's future status, or that Jerusalem's current status was in any way compromised. The letter remained secret until Arafat divulged its existence in Johannesburg in May 1994, whereupon Likud MKs Binyamin Begin and Dan Meridor pressed Peres to release the letter, following a denial of its existence in the Knesset by Police Minister Moshe Shahal. Peres was slated for publicly denying there were any secret deals with the PLO in the Knesset debate on the Oslo accords, then covering up the letter's existence until June 1994.

The final compromise formula was based on the understandings arrived at by Rabin and Arafat through their secret correspondence. Rabin agreed to moderate his demands for comprehensive Israeli responsibility for external security after an Israeli withdrawal or redeployment, and conceded to PLO pressure on the issue of jurisdiction.[169] Arafat agreed that Israel's powers and responsibilities would remain over the settlements and for all Israeli citizens, either permanently resident or not, anywhere in the occupied territories including the proposed self-rule entities. Israel wanted it made clear in the accompanying agreed minutes to the DoP that 'Jurisdiction of the Council will cover West Bank and Gaza Strip territory, except for issues that will be negotiated in the permanent status negotiations: Jerusalem, settlements, military locations, and Israelis' (Article IV.1). Furthermore, 'The Council's jurisdiction will apply with regard to the agreed powers, responsibilities, spheres and authorities transferred to it (Article IV [2])' contingent with Article VII.5 that the 'withdrawal of the military government will not prevent Israel from exercising the powers and responsibilities not transferred to the Council.' The PLO wanted to keep the minutes secret, but at Israeli insistence they were published as part of the DoP.[170] Thus the Stockholm negotiations clinched the deal on 19 August, so that despite minor modifications made later that day, the DoP with the agreed minutes was initialled in a ceremony in Oslo on 20 August. The pre-dawn ceremony at 44 Parkveirenin included all the Oslo negotiators plus Holst, Peres, Larsen, Juul, Heilberg, Gil and Geir Pedersen. In the first known meeting between Peres and a PLO official, Savir, Qurai, Singer and Asfour initialled the DoP, and then Savir, Qurai, Holst and Larsen gave speeches extolling its virtue. Peres watched but did not sign the DoP, since negotiations with the PLO had not received cabinet approval. In a touching moment of historical significance the desk used to sign the DoP was brought in especially for the occasion, the same desk used by Christen Michelson to sign Norway's secession in 1905 from Swedish rule. Aware of Israeli sensitivities, the Norwegians asked Peres if he would mind using the desk, and he agreed.[171] This however did not mean that negotiations were concluded; the negotiators reconvened the next day to conclude a mutual recognition agreement between the PLO and Israel.

Thus the outcome of indulging in brinkmanship was the attainment of agreement to negotiate on mutual recognition, which was politically and psychologically, the most significant outcome of the Oslo backchannel. Mutual recognition was regarded as being 'more important' than the DoP, because it was the 'centre' of the conflict, turning the Israeli-Palestinian conflict from an 'existential' to a 'political' conflict.[172] Mutual recognition was a *sine qua non* for cooperation between Israel and the PLO, vital for Arafat 'organizationally', and, for Rabin, it meant letting go of Israel's historic rejection of the PLO and abandoning efforts to separate Palestinians inside the territories from those outside.[173]

Surprising the United States and finessing the deal

With the DoP initialled, it became imperative not only to assuage feelings but to garner support for the Oslo DoP, to inform various interested parties not only before media reports leaked too much detail, but also before it became too obvious that Oslo was the principal Israeli-PLO channel, and not a supplementary backchannel. The US had invested much political and financial power and prestige in convening the high-profile international Madrid initiative in order to broker a settlement in the Middle East, by which the US not only sought to shape the future of the Middle East, but also by which it sought to confirm its paramount status in the world. Surprise was the overwhelmingly constant emotion felt by most interested parties. Rabin had deliberately misled Elyakim Rubinstein, head of the Washington delegation, saying 'Leave it alone, it's all multilateral,' when Rubinstein asked him about rumours of a secret backchannel with the PLO. Rubinstein spent three hours with Rabin, furiously refusing to return to Washington and saying that he would resign.[174] Jacques Neriah was taking notes at a previously scheduled meeting between Rabin and Lester Pollack and Malcolm Hoenlein, officials of the Conference of Presidents of Major American Jewish Organizations when 'The prime minister said he had reached an accord with the PLO and that Arafat would be coming to Gaza and Jericho. I almost fell off my chair.'[175] During May and June, the Clinton administration had pursued its 'equal partnership' policy, paying little regard to events in Oslo. Thus even though the US had been briefed of the Oslo channel's existence, information about, and knowledge of, the substantive details of the Oslo backchannel had been highly restricted. Therefore the reaction of the US to the specifics of a deal conducted without their imprint would be crucial and would need sensitive handling in order to present a credible public-relations selling exercise to Israeli-Palestinian and international opinion, provide immediate political support for the deal, and marshal financial assistance to underpin the future success of the deal.

On 26 August Arafat and Abbas convened a meeting of the Executive Committee of the PLO to break the news of the DoP to the Palestinians. Among Palestinians, many rumours had circulated that Arafat was to make humiliating concessions in order to do a deal with the Israelis. Two days of stormy meetings of the Executive Committee began the process of placating Palestinian public opinion.[176] The terms of Oslo were unpopular with those involved in the Washington talks. Hanan Ashrawi said to Abbas that it was 'clear that the [Palestinians] who initialed this agreement have not lived under occupation.' Ashrawi argued that the agreement 'postponed the settlement issue and Jerusalem without even getting guarantees that Israel would not continue to create facts on the ground that would preempt and prejudge the final outcome.' Concerned about domestic Palestinian opinion, she demanded of Abbas,

> And what about human rights? There's a constituency at home, a people in captivity, whose rights must be protected and whose suffering must be alleviated. What about all our red lines? Territorial jurisdiction and integrity are negated in substance and the transfer of authority is purely functional.

Abbas replied 'All these [things] will be negotiated', revealing PLO thinking about Oslo. Abbas said,

> We got strategic political gains, particularly the fact that this agreement is with the PLO and not just a Palestinian delegation and the recognition of the Palestinians as a people with political rights. We got ... a commitment to discuss the refugee issue and Jerusalem in [subsequent negotiations on] permanent status. We're going to discuss boundaries and that means statehood. Could you have gotten more?

Ashrawi replied

> It's not who makes the agreement, but what's in it ... My main concern is about substance. I think this agreement has many potentially explosive areas and could be to our disadvantage ... Strategic issues are fine, but we know the Israelis and we know that they will exploit their power as occupiers to the hilt and by the time you get to permanent status [negotiations], Israel will have permanently altered realities on the ground.[177]

Meanwhile Peres consulted with Rabin in Israel, and on receiving Rabin's approval on 27 August, Peres, Holst and their top aides flew to southern California to brief Secretary Christopher and Dennis Ross about the terms of the DoP and its ramifications on US policy. Ross asked Peres whether the DoP was linked to mutual recognition, whilst Peres replied it was not, the Rabin/Arafat correspondence made clear that there could be no DoP without mutual recognition. Christopher enquired about the implications for US policy toward the PLO. Peres told him that a letter from Arafat renouncing terrorism was forthcoming, and therefore Israel hoped the PLO Commitments Compliance Act of 1989 (known as the Mack-Lieberman Act) would be repealed. Christopher responded that the administration would work with congressional leaders to repeal the ban. He indicated that support from the American Jewish community would be important. In reviewing the text of the Mack-Lieberman Act, Ross noted that the law required the PLO not only to renounce terrorism but also 'evict or otherwise discipline the individuals or groups taking acts in contravention of the Geneva commitments.' Therefore, he suggested that the PLO letter include a phrase that the PLO not only renounced violence but would 'discipline its vio-lators'.[178] Although the Egyptians had also informed Christopher and Ross about the accord, the Americans' response was favour-able. They indicated they would back the deal, importantly and significantly agreeing to ensure the success of the agreement, through the convening of an international donors' conference to secure sufficient funding for the Palestinian entity (conceived afterwards), by exerting US influence in urging a 'peace dividend' in the form of Arab recognition of Israel, with the establishment of Arab-Israeli diplomatic relations, and by ending the Arab boycott of Israel. On receiving US assurances, Rabin called a cabinet meeting on 30 August to inform his colleagues of the agreement, who after discussions voted in favour. Rabin made clear that no amendments could be made. Rubinstein presented 21 objections to Oslo, mainly that Israel could not enter final status talks with all options open. Barak objected to the security provisions of the deal. As IDF Chief of Staff, although he neither liked the continuous police duties in the occupied territories nor favoured their annexation, he warned that, despite its political advantages, the interim arrangement forced the IDF to protect settlers and other Israelis while relinquishing juris-diction over the Palestinians. He further argued that the IDF would have to rely on Palestinian police to hand over armed fugitives, and that Shin Bet would lose significant intelligence-gathering assets and the coercive leverage of administrative authority to elicit Palestinian cooperation and compliance. He complained the IDF could not guarantee the security of the occupied territories' main roads nor provide military escorts to settlers beyond their settle-ments. On how Israel would handle the chaos of a potential collapse of the Oslo agreement, Barak warned cabinet ministers who esti-mated that the IDF could retake control of Gaza in a day not to disregard international reaction to such a move. Finally however,

Rabin received almost total approval for the accord. Economics Minister Shimon Shetreet of Labour and Deri of Shas both abstained.[179]

The Israelis and the PLO then faced a public relations dilemma – how to present such an historic breakthrough which had been negotiated at the very highest level as a *fait accompli*, whilst officially not recognizing each other. The conventional wisdom of those negotiating in Oslo had been that once agreement had been reached, the deal would be presented through the forum of the Washington talks. However in light of the comprehensiveness of the agreement, there was little realistic hope that the Washington delegations could be plausibly used in such a way. The Israelis were particularly sensitive to the issue of officially recognizing the PLO whilst appearing not to have kept the Americans abreast with developments. However suggestions that presenting the DoP as a US-brokered, or as an Egyptian-US sponsored, document not only unfairly undermined the central and unselfish role the Norwegians had played, but stretched credibility too greatly, as the truth would out eventually. Thus, the idea for a dramatic public presentation of the agreement at a signing ceremony in Washington DC was conceived, to lend international credibility and demonstrate US support for the DoP. However this was only possible and plausible as long as the two adversaries publicly recognized each other, which in turn would allow for the repeal of the US law barring PLO officials from the US. Christopher had said the US would not object to having a PLO official come to Washington to sign the accord as long as each side recognized the other. If mutual recognition were not concluded before then, PLO officials had assured the Israelis that they would instruct Faisal Husseini to sign the Oslo accord without making any changes.[180] Thus, the issue of mutual recognition became the cornerstone in selling the grand conceptual design conceived within the DoP, that is 'to strive to live in peaceful coexistence and mutual dignity and security and achieve a just, lasting and comprehensive peace settlement and historic reconciliation'.[181]

Domestic political considerations dominated the run-up to the signing ceremony, as both sides sought to sell their own constituencies the accord. The settling of mutual recognition continued through intensive and delicate negotiations in Oslo as the specifics of an agreement on mutual recognition had to be worked out before any formal signing of the DoP. Both sides realized that mutual recognition 'meant more in fundamental terms' than even the DoP, as it resolved the nature of the relationship between the two adversaries for ever, no matter the future of the DoP.[182] Mutual recognition represented the crossing of an existential barrier, which could not be renegotiated or renounced. In Oslo, FM Holst again mediated in finding mutually acceptable language. His intervention changed the previous nature of Norwegian facilitation from one of non-active participation to one of involved problem-solving through personal intervention, but with unsuccessful results. Inconclusive talks in Norway led to another telephone negotiating session over 3–4 September between Paris and Tunis, with Arafat and Peres communicating once again through FM Holst. Arafat was asked to make

- an explicit renunciation of all violence and terror
- an explicit call to all Palestinians to put an end to armed struggle and the *intifada*
- an explicit affirmation that Israel had the right to exist in peace and security, and
- an explicit promise to change the relevant articles of the PLO Charter which called for the destruction of Israel.[183]

Peres played 'hardball', not being in any hurry to compromise. Agreement was reached on only two points. Arafat agreed to the PLO acceptance of the US-inspired requirement that the PLO accept responsibility for all PLO factions. Arafat had been concerned about being made responsible for those outside his control, like Hamas. Arafat's preferred phrase, 'We recognise the right of Israel to live in secure and recognised boundaries', suggestive of merely acknowledging Israel's presence, was reworded to 'The PLO recognises the right of the State of Israel to exist in peace and security' which confirmed Israel's legitimacy.[184] The respective teams returned home, having failed to complete the necessary agreements. On 6 September FM Holst engaged in telephone negotiations with Arafat, who was in Cairo in an effort to stimulate regional support for the agreement. On 7 September the Israelis returned to Paris ready for face to face talks. Qurai arrived in Paris the next day to begin negotiations as the two prepared for the endgame. Throughout the night of 8 September proposals for acceptable texts for the letters which would be exchanged forming the mutual recognition pact were forwarded and rejected.

Whilst Rabin's letter to Arafat was to be a straightforward statement of recognition, contention surrounded Arafat's letter to Rabin.[185] Two main issues of dispute remained: the wording of the changes to the PLO Charter and the question of how to reject violence and terror. The PLO wanted both sides to declare an end to terrorism and violence, but Israel rejected this. The PLO then offered to re-state Arafat's 1988 renunciation of terrorism and violence; however that was also rejected. The Israelis 'wanted a one-way letter that was clear and not shrouded by other statements'.[186] Arafat there-fore agreed to 'renounce the use of terrorism and other acts of violence' and 'assume responsibility over all PLO elements and personnel in order to assure their compliance, prevent violations and discipline violators.'[187] Israel had originally wanted Arafat to assume responsibility for the acts of all Palestinians, including those not affiliated with the PLO. Regarding the PLO Charter, the Israelis demanded that the PLO declare the relevant provisions calling for the destruction of Israel 'non-operative and non-valid', whereas the PLO preferred 'not in effect'. Arafat consulted with the PLO Execu-tive Committee, whose approval he needed for committing to a promise to change the PLO Charter, eventually affirming 'that those articles of the Palestinian Covenant which deny Israel's right to exist, and the provisions of the Covenant which are inconsistent with the commitments of this letter are now inoperative and no longer valid'. Arafat committed himself to submitting the necess-ary changes to the PNC for formal approval. However, no timetable was stipulated as amendments to the Charter required a two-thirds majority which Arafat claimed he could not arrange immediately.[188] Regarding the *intifada*, it was agreed that an additional letter, from Arafat to Holst, would suffice to encompass the PLO commitments for the people in the West Bank and Gaza Strip. However, whilst Qurai was prepared to accept that the people on the West Bank should renounce violence, expecting them to renounce terror im-plied they were all terrorists, therefore Qurai preferred 'rejecting violence and terrorism'.[189] Agreement was finally believed to have been concluded in the small hours of 9 September. However, Arafat called from Tunis to say that he did not agree to the wording on the clause committing the people of the occupied territories to 're-ject violence and terror'.[190] With the Israeli cabinet due to meet within the hour to approve the text, Arafat was piling on the pres-sure. With everyone in Paris believing the deal had been done, Arafat was ready to have the Israeli cabinet postpone its meeting in order to achieve final concessions. Israel settled for a letter from Arafat to Holst saying that the PLO would 'take part in the steps leading to the normalization of life, rejecting violence and terror-ism, contributing to peace and stability, and participating actively

in shaping reconstruction, economic development, and cooperation.'[191] Qurai telephoned Arafat, and having received his assent to
complete negotiations, informed the Israelis, allowing the letters of
mutual recognition to begin their journeys.

FM Holst flew to Tunis to pick up Arafat's letter for Rabin, then
continued on to Jerusalem, delivering it to Rabin on 10 September.
Rabin's reply was faxed to Tunis with FM Holst returning to Tunis
delivering the actual letter in person. With the exchange of correspondence, President Clinton announced on 10 September that the
US was resuming its dialogue with the PLO.

With the DoP initialled, and with mutual recognition approved
and signed, the official signing ceremony remained. Agreement about
the nature of the event was still unresolved. The Clinton administration seemed keen to preside over, and be associated with, a
high-profile ceremony, a glamorous foreign policy achievement, and
an act of choreographed political theatre, particularly since as a
new administration its record in Bosnia and Somalia and on domestic issues left a lot to be desired. Arafat signalled his willingness
to attend if Rabin were to be there also; however Rabin fretted
over obliging the US on the one hand and being seen to accord
Arafat the status of a head of state or government. Clinton himself
urged both leaders to attend, phoning Rabin personally on 9 September. The issue was resolved when Arafat let it be known that
he wanted to attend anyway, prompting Secretary Christopher to
phone Israel to reiterate Clinton's invitation to the PM.[192] The US
decision to resume dialogue with the PLO swayed Rabin into confirming his attendance.

With the participants in place, all was set for the culmination of
the negotiated process. However, with four hours to go Arafat, through
Ahmed Tibi, indicated his refusal to sign unless the agreement to
be signed included direct references to the PLO in the text. Peres
and Rabin consulted, agreeing to the change since they had recognized the PLO; however, Peres intimated to Tibi that as the Israeli
cabinet had approved each word of the DoP, there was no way
changes could be authorized. Tibi announced to Peres that Arafat
was getting ready to leave, and with 20 minutes to the signing
ceremony, Peres agreed to the inclusion of 'PLO' in typescript, but
in one place only, in the preamble, to read 'The Government of
the State of Israel and the PLO team (in the Jordanian-Palestinian
delegation to the Middle East Peace Conference) (the 'Palestinian
delegation'), representing the Palestinian people agree . . .'[193] In the

heat of the sunshine in Washington, the Norwegians privately calculated that whilst the US had spent billions of dollars and many years in efforts in the Middle East, Norway had spent roughly $500 000 in less than one year and achieved an historical agreement.[194]

One of the most remarkable aspects of the Oslo DoP was that despite the existence of extensive, highly organized social and political institutions, both Israeli and Palestinian, the decision-making process, and the decision-making itself, depended on, and involved, only a very small, highly personalized political elite. In a sense, either it is testament to the cohesiveness of both Israeli and Palestinian polities that they could digest such political upheaval, or the DoP highlights the inherent potential for its destruction, in that as it was not popularly conceived, divined and acclaimed, its birth and continued existence may reveal deeper schisms within both societies, not so immediately apparent within the first instance of its publication. Indeed, the proof of the DoP's historic achievement and its place as a revolutionary event, will be in its longevity and the trust it engenders in providing for, and overcoming the mutual exclusivity of, both communities national interests, be they for security or self-determination.

2.6 Turn to peace: the evolution of the negotiations for peace

A key factor in 1992, a year of significant events, was undoubtedly the inertia and the uncertainty generated by the Israeli general election and the US presidential election. Both these elections were to have a considerable impact on the outcome of the negotiating process, although as far as 1992 was concerned little actual progress was achieved in the negotiations themselves, as attentions were focused elsewhere.

The 1992 Israeli election has been called many things, including a referendum on peace – between territorial expansionism and territorial compromise. This is too simplistic an analysis of the election. There seem to be several reasons why the 1992 Knesset elections marked the second time in Israel's political history that there has been a significant transfer of power from one side of the political spectrum to the other, a second *hamahapach hamedini*[195] and, as in 1977, a reordering of the country's national priorities.[196] One such analysis suggests that this new era is based on 'a new coalition of the traditional Ashkenazic voters, secular Russian immigrants, and disgruntled Sephardic voters committed to a more accommodative national consensus.' Hence the conclusion that in 1992, Israeli voters 'chose the Westernized, secular, and progressive vision of Zionism' that such a government would reflect.[197]

Israeli voters' dissatisfaction with the Likud government's mismanagement of the economy was as important a factor in Labour's victory as the promise to end the violence and hatred which had defined relations with Israel's neighbours, principally the Palestinians. Unemployment stood at a record 11.6 per cent, with unemployment among Russian immigrants, many of whom were voting for the first time, running as high as 40 per cent. To a large extent the 1992 election 'represented more a vote against the Likud than a resounding vote for Labour.'[198] Economic factors fuelled anti-incumbency. Labour's internal party reforms, its primary election system, its organization of a popular party conference, developed a rejuvenated public image as a more self-confident party, with a renewed sense of direction, purpose and hope. Labour was identified on the official electoral list and ballot as 'Labour, headed by Rabin.' Focusing on Rabin was a successful electoral strategy. Rabin made it clear that he intended to be a strong PM.[199] Many *sabras* felt that the Likud government's commitment to its ideology – be it encouraging *aliya* from Russia, spending too high a percentage of the national budget on building settlements in the territories, or attempting to defeat the *intifada* by enforcing the occupation through the IDF, which meant having to do riot-control reserve duty in the territories – was misplaced when confronted with economic hardship behind the Green Line.[200] Jobs and new houses in Israel were more important to the majority of voters than the dream of Greater Israel. Israeli newspaper *Ma'ariv* quoted Shamir in a post-election telephone interview as saying, 'moderation should relate to the tactics but not the goal . . . In my political activity I know how to display the tactics of moderation, without conceding anything of the goal, the integrity of the Land of Israel.' Shamir continued, 'I would have conducted negotiations on autonomy for ten years, and in the meantime we would have reached half a million people in Judea and Samaria.' He also stated, 'it's very painful to me that in the next four years I will not be able to increase settlement in Judea, Samaria and Gaza, and complete the demographic revolution.'[201]

The Likud government's poor relationship with the US was emblematic of an administration bereft of new ideas that could no longer provide for its ideological programme. Shamir's failure to gain $10bn in US loan guarantees illustrated to the Israeli public the depths to which Israel's relationship with the US had fallen. Voters were acutely aware that Ariel Sharon's over-zealous housing programme had forced the government to buy back thousands of units of empty new homes built for Russian immigrants who never arrived (there were enough unsold units to provide for another 35 000 settlers in the West Bank and Gaza Strip, with a reserve of 10 000 housing units). The Likud government could not provide for those Russians who had already emigrated, the majority of whom chose to live within the Green Line, at a time when the government was spending over $1bn on West Bank settlers, most of whom were Ashkenazim from America and Europe. The 1992 election result was primarily a domestic fight over the economy and the prioritization and allocation of national resources. Sephardic voters, traditional supporters of Likud, turned to the Labour platform which argued for state money to be better spent in the poor neighbourhoods of greater Tel Aviv where so many Sephardim live than on low-cost mortgage settlers who commuted to work in Israel from the territories. The mood of high expectation for change, especially in employment, education and housing undoubtedly incorporated the desire for positive progress in the stalled peace process.[202]

During the hiatus provided by the Israeli election, a period of stocktaking was inevitable. For the Palestinians it was a time when the link between the PLO in Tunis and the Palestinian delegation became more explicit. A week after his plane crash in Libya, on 15 April 1992, Arafat welcomed to Cairo the whole delegation including its advisory committee. The institutionalizing of this bond took place at the PLO Central Council, the 103-member decision-making body of the PNC, which convened in Tunis between 7 and 10 May 1992 to discuss, among other things, the peace process. The Council endorsed, by 57 votes to 16 against, the continued participation of the Palestinians in the multilateral and bilateral negotiations. The Central Council sought to emphasize the issues concerning it. These were:

- the establishment of a Palestinian state with Jerusalem as its capital
- Palestinian attachment to the principle of land for peace
- international protection for Palestinian civilians and the holy places
- the seizure of land and the stopping of settlement construction
- international pressure on aid to Israel
- rejection of Israeli annexation of Jerusalem

- the transitional period
- Israeli intransigence
- elections – both municipal and general
- the confirmation of the PLO to form the Palestinian delegation
- national unity, and
- strengthening the *intifada*.[203]

What made this meeting important, was not only that a Palestinian delegation, comprised of Palestinians from outside the territories, would participate in the multilateral working groups on refugees and economic development but also, more symbolically, that it demonstrated the link between the PLO in Tunis and the Palestinian delegation, in that this was the first open and public PLO session attended by Madrid delegates. In order that a *fait accompli* be presented to the incoming Israeli government, Arafat and other PLO officials publicly and formally received the Palestinian delegation in Amman on 18 June, five days before the Israeli election.[204]

Rabin's election implied a change in the Israeli philosophy and tactics regarding the Palestinian delegation, particularly with reference to negotiating with the Palestinians directly rather than through the joint delegation. The obvious inference in this stance as far as the Palestinians were concerned would be the opening up of the negotiating process leading to direct talks between the PLO and the Israeli government, the inclusion of East Jerusalemites in the delegations, and with it the possibility of resolving outstanding issues such as the interim period, linkage between interim period and final status, and the extent of Palestinian central authority. New texts were drafted for presentation which would, it was hoped, lead to a basis for agreement in order to meet the target date of 31 October, the objective for reaching agreement on interim self-government arrangements as proposed in the US-USSR letter of invitation.[205] Expectations of progress surrounded the delegations as they prepared for renewed negotiations. This was particularly true for the Palestinians, who desired either to negotiate an interim agreement, or at least reach consensus on a framework which would facilitate this process, in advance of the uncertainty of the November US presidential elections. However, nothing substantive was achieved.

Whilst it is obvious that 1992 did not represent an epochal political realignment, yet the trends undercurrent in Israeli domestic politics from early 1992 identify a strong shift in favour of practical as opposed to overt ideological politics. Since the *intifada* began, until 30 April 1994, there had been 219 Israeli deaths (151 civilians) and 17 872 Israeli wounded (2810 civilians), a fact which did not instil confidence in the Likud government's policies. In the same period there were 1114 Palestinian deaths (plus 922 killed by Palestinians) and 18 967 wounded.[206] The status quo led many on both sides to the conclusion that the level of violence in the current situation was no longer acceptable.[207] Thus when discussing the impact of the 1992 Israeli election, it does seem that the differences between Likud and Labour were, 'quite significant, both in the realm of ideology and in the realm of practical policy' to the extent that as far as Israeli-Palestinian relations were concerned, 'the Labour victory of June 1992, which ended a decade and a half of Likud hegemony, constitutes another watershed in Israel's relations with the Palestinians.'[208]

The new PM, Rabin, had coined the phrase, 'marching with two feet', to reflect the military and the political after the realization that the *intifada* was a political problem.[209] In a speech to the Knesset on 13 July 1992, Rabin spelled out his government's departure with the past, saying 'we inherited the framework of the Madrid conference from the previous government. But there is one significant change: the previous government created the tools, but they never intended to use them in order to achieve peace.'[210] After winning the 1992 election, Rabin promised to divert resources to the absorption of immigrants, to social and economic reforms, to the war against unemployment and to better education.

Labour's victory in the Israeli elections had allowed pro-Madrid Palestinians to believe that there would be progress in the peace talks, because of Labour's promised peace policies, and the hope that the PLO would be included in the official diplomacy of the Madrid framework. However, the Palestinians were presented early on with a number of changes that did much to dispel their premature confidence in the new Rabin administration. On 13 August 1992 James Baker was named as White House Chief of Staff in order to organize and improve President Bush's re-election chances. Dennis Ross, Baker's key assistant, was also removed from direct personal supervision of the negotiations, making the Palestinians fear that the US administration was concentrating on domestic political concerns rather than trying to maintain the image of honest broker in the process, balancing up Palestinian weakness relative to Israeli strength. When negotiations resumed in Washington DC on 24 August for round six of the bilaterals, Elaykim Rubenstein, nominated by Shamir, remained as Israeli delegation head for the Israeli-Jordanian/Palestinian bilateral talks. The Syrians presented at the sixth round their own declaration of principles for the Israeli-Syrian talks, provoking Rabin's interest in the Syrian track, a development which the Palestinians viewed as an additional concern for its potential in signalling a separate Israeli-Syrian deal at Palestinian expense. Rabin pursued a 'Syria first' position having started the talks from a 'Syria last' position. Having planned to concentrate on Palestinian autonomy first, he relegated the autonomy talks to lesser status.[211] During this period, all Israel offered was the delegation of tasks to the administration council, while the Palestinians maintained their insistence on a transfer of authority. The Palestinians' chief complaint was the definition of territoriality, as geographical boundaries clearly delineated the limits of authority. Such a complaint has much justification and much precedence, such as 'wherever the king's writ runs, there is the king's power!' The real problem for the Palestinians was that while the negotiations between Israel and the Arab states were intended to lead to final peace settlements, their talks were designed to produce only an interim solution. To get over this hurdle they called for a direct link between the interim self-government phase and the final status of the occupied territories.[212] Rabin retained the Defence Minister's portfolio, prompting memories of his previous 'iron-fist' tenure in 1984–90, indeed he resumed the policy of deportation, and various other repressive measures in the occupied territories, which in turn escalated radical opposition leading to an increase in violent attacks on Israelis, which in turn led to Rabin's decision to deport 415 Palestinians on 17 December from the West Bank and Gaza Strip.

On 18 December 1992 the UN Security Council adopted Resolution 799, which condemned and opposed the Israeli action of deporting 415 Islamists to southern Lebanon, and which further demanded that Israel ensure the immediate and safe return of all those deported. This resolution did not however lay down a timetable for the return of the deportees, nor did it outline any sanctions to be imposed on Israel for non-compliance. In an attempt to secure compliance with the resolution, UN Secretary-General Boutros Ghali sent two special envoys, James Jonah and Chinmaya Gharekhan, to Israel at the end of December and the beginning of January respectively. However, both returned unsuccessful. In his report to the Security Council on 25 January 1993, the Secretary-General recommended that 'all necessary measures' be taken to ensure Israeli compliance with Resolution 799, with a further proposal to establish a UN mechanism to monitor the situation in the occupied territories. The next day Ismat Abdel-Meguid, Secretary-General of the Arab League, responded to Israel's non-compliance with UN SCR 799, saying that it was high time that 'the Security Council understood that the policy of double standards can no longer be pursued.'[213] On 28 January Israel's Supreme Court unanimously rejected the appeal made on behalf of the deportees, continuing to rule that, whilst collective expulsion orders were illegal (thus allowing each of the deportees to be heard individually), the individual expulsion orders issued on 17 December were valid, thus creating a legal precedent.[214] On New Year's Day a US-Israeli deal was brokered. Israel agreed that 101 deportees would be returned immediately with the rest having their period of exile halved to one year, and humanitarian aid might be provided by air. In return the US guaranteed to veto any binding resolutions against Israel in international forums, to refrain from demanding any Israeli concessions, regardless of other interested parties or of US obligations *vis-à-vis* the peace process. Whilst the deal was rejected by the deportees, the PLO and other Arab countries who demanded compliance with UN SCR 799, Israel thus avoided a confrontation with the Security Council at the same time as avoiding complying with the above resolution. Warren Christopher deemed further UN action unnecessary, the EU followed the US lead and on 12 February the Security Council even endorsed the US policy as a 'step in the right direction'.[215] The Arab countries were determined to prevent Hamas having a veto over the peace process. They did not believe that an immediate settlement was a precondition for a resumption of the talks. However, this issue highlighted the fragility of the PLO's assumption of automatic political leadership. The PLO, as the principal Palestinian political force, was concerned not to lose all credibility with Palestinians in the occupied territories by not being seen to support the deportees, although they were engaged in a political battle for the hearts and minds of the Palestinian population with the Islamists, so they indicated that they might accept a phased return of the deportees over a period of six months, or alternatively an Israeli assurance that there would be an end to the policy of expulsions.

Bill Clinton's election as US President ensured a dramatic change in the priorities of the new US administration. The new Clinton Administration appeared as one of the most openly pro-Israeli in some years.[216] Clinton's campaign had focused on the domestic issues of the US economy, the budget deficit and health care reform. In so far as Clinton expressed interest in foreign policy goals, this was limited to how far international issues impacted on domestic affairs, in particular on the domestic economy. The impact of the North American Free Trade Agreement (NAFTA), the prospects of a trade war with Europe and Japan due to disagreements in the Uruguay Round of the GATT talks, the potential crisis of thousands of Haitian refugees arriving in the US following the military coup deposing President Aristide, and the slaughter in Bosnia, were seen as the major issues to be addressed by the incoming administration. As far as the Madrid peace process was concerned, the new administration tended to mouth the typical stock phrases of support and hope for the process to continue and bring prospects for peace in the future.

Sections of the pro-Israel lobby in the US had in the course of the election campaign tried to tar President Bush and Secretary Baker with an anti-Israeli, or even an anti-semitic brush in the wake of their stance over the $10bn loan guarantees. Clinton and his Vice-President Gore did not hide their support for Israel, either pre- or post-election. Securing a high percentage of Jewish voters whilst polling one of the lowest percentages of votes cast for a winning candidate in decades, Clinton would be unlikely to change his pro-Israel stance regarding the peace process, especially in light of the fact that leading Palestinian negotiators had openly supported Bush's re-election. The Arab participants in the peace process and the Palestinians in particular had expected a Republican triumph, expecting Secretary Baker to be back at the forefront of US foreign policy, especially returning to active duty in the peace process.

Clinton's nominations for the vacated posts at the State Department and the National Security Council (NSC) reflected his intentions, if not his debts. Warren Christopher was nominated to State. He was a former senior Carter administration official who had been closely involved in the Camp David Accords and was co-chairman of Clinton's transition team. Senior ranks at State and the NSC were staffed with people known for their admiration for Israel. For example, Samuel Lewis, a former US ambassador to Israel, replaced Dennis Ross, and National Security Adviser Anthony Lake, his deputy Sandy Berger, and the principal analyst on the Middle East, Martin Indyk, were all known for their sympathies towards Jerusalem. By these nominations, Clinton, who expressed his desire to focus on domestic issues, delegated US foreign policy in the Middle East to people whose impartiality was somewhat circumspect. Relations between Washington and Jerusalem improved markedly. A visit by PM Rabin to the new president was particularly warm, with the inference that future US-Israeli relations would not be soured in the same way as the previous administration's attempts both to exert pressure on Israel and to appear impartial with regard to the Madrid process. US-Israeli strategic security cooperation agreements were renewed, and to all intents and purposes the US did not publicly oppose Israel's defiance of UN SCR 799 regarding the Palestinian deportees. Repeated statements aimed at ending the Arab boycott of Israel and commending the new Israeli administration, together with a lack of pressure on Israel regarding the deportees and settlements, all combined to give the Palestinians the impression that the new US administration had repudiated even the tenuous attempt of the previous administration at impartiality as an honest broker.

During Christopher's Middle East tour he stressed the US's desire to be a full partner in the peace process, and he reiterated that the US would continue Bush's policy of peace talks, promoting democracy and non-conventional arms control. US policy was however deemed to be somewhat hypocritical particularly in light of events in the former Yugoslavia where Bosnia's Muslim population was left to suffer at the hands of homicidal Serbs, a point not lost on the Arab populations. The perception therefore in the Arab world was at that time one of US disingenuousness, especially when viewed in relation to the alacrity and extent of the US response in aiding Kuwait. This issue pitted the PLO's continued involvement in the peace process at odds with general popular feeling within the occupied territories, which feared resuming discussions with an Israeli government that evoked Palestinian fears of a repeat of 1948 and 1967.

In Washington the ninth round of bilateral talks opened on 27 April 1993 after a hiatus of nearly five months due to the expulsion of Palestinian activists to Lebanon. The newly elected Clinton administration stepped up its involvement in the process. Reversing a 26-year-old American policy, a paper presented by the US accepted the Israeli claim that East Jerusalem and the rest of the West Bank and Gaza were disputed and not occupied territories. For the Palestinians, this represented a new and alarming change in direction of the talks, something in all conscience they just could not countenance. The American model was a non-starter for the Palestinians:

it signified and exemplified to large extent the total impasse we were in – the strictures of Madrid actually threw up a wall. I think one of the problems is that once the American team devised their model, they developed what could be called a 'Pygmalion complex' and couldn't let go of their Madrid formula.[217]

Thus at the end of 20 months and 10 rounds of talks the Madrid process was not producing results. At this stage Rabin could be said to be faced with two alternatives: (a) deal with Syria, which would entail full withdrawal and the dismantling of Israeli settlements on the Golan Heights (to be preceded by a referendum on the Golan because of annexation in 1981 – never an easy option for an incumbent government) or (b) deal with the Palestinians (not necessarily the PLO) on interim self-government which did not entail an immediate commitment to withdraw from the West Bank, to territorial compromise, to a referendum, or to dismantle Jewish settlements.[218]

The Oslo backchannel represented for the first time, albeit unofficially, the direct participation of the PLO, at the highest level, in the Madrid peace process. The difference in the secret Oslo channel negotiations was that they succeeded in accomplishing Israeli-PLO dialogue and agreement. The Madrid framework incorporated Israeli-Palestinian dialogue within the formula of a split-bilateral process, which in essence was an offshoot of the formal Israeli-Jordanian bilateral negotiations, the Palestinians being incorporated into the Jordanian delegation in order to sidestep the issue of a separate and official PLO-Palestinian representation which the Israelis initially refused to recognize.

The evolution of Israeli-Palestinian mutual recognition and political negotiation, for Israel, stems from coming to terms with three hard facts. Firstly, Israel is, and must be, 'part of the Middle East' and must either 'gain acceptance and legitimacy in the region or be faced with an unresolved situation'.[219] For David Ben-Gurion, 'Levantinization' was as 'great a danger to Israel's society as was Arab hostility.' Ben-Gurion acted on the

premise that Israel must be a modern society, Western in its parliamentary pluralist politics and in its orientation on science and technology. He saw the surrounding countries as a morass of backwardness and rejected their culture en bloc. This was the root of the rift between the Labour party leaders, who envisioned a modern socialist society, and the traditional Jews of the Sephardi communities, who were seen and treated by the ruling Labour party as backward children, to be tutored and encouraged, but not consulted.

This emphasis on a secular, scientific and technologically based state formed the basis of Israel's dominant socialist politics and policies since statehood. This policy concentration has caused great divisions in Israeli society between Ashkenazim, Sephardim and Mizrachim, between a European and a Levantine outlook. The emergence of respect for the important role that the Sephardic community plays in Israeli society and politics has played its part in educating Israelis about Palestinians. Common cause among Sephardic Jews has been important in understanding Palestinian grievances.[220]

Secondly, demography demands that if Israel wishes to retain control over the occupied territories, with its growing Arab population, Israel's democratic character or its Jewish identity will suffer, because

> The proposition that in holding the West Bank and Gaza, Israel doomed itself to giving up either its democratic or its Jewish character was first enunciated only a few weeks after the Six Day War. At a symposium at the Hebrew University, Nissan Oren explained to an overflow audience of students, almost all recently returned from the battlefronts, that maintaining control over the Arabs of the West Bank and Gaza would inevitably involve Israel in acts of repression and in depriving the Palestinians of civil rights, which would erode the democratic nature of Israel's regime and society. If Israel annexed the territories and conferred citizenship on the Palestinians, the high birthrate of the latter would quickly bring about the loss of the Jewish majority in Israel, and though the state might be democratic, Israel would cease to be a Jewish and Zionist state.[221]

Rabin, speaking as Defence Minister in the mid-1980s, said that Israel needed the 'goodwill of friends like the US, which requires our being seen as morally in the right', and that Israeli repression of the *intifada* was causing many to 'view us as no different than our enemies', a catastrophe, both 'for our soul and for the support we need'. Rabin believed that nothing good would come from the blunt application of force, 'real peace here will come only when the Arabs move' from their grudging acceptance of 'the fact of our existence' to an appreciation of Israel's 'right to exist. Our power can guarantee us as a fact probably forever, but who wants to live like that?'[222]

Thirdly, Israel should not fear negotiations with any Palestinian political representative body that will recognize Israel's right to exist in agreed and secure boundaries as specified by UN SCRs 242 and 338, and will renounce politically motivated terrorism and violence. Thus Israeli public acceptance can be assured given that Israel should negotiate with any Palestinian faction which would recognize respect for and acknowledgement of the sovereignty, territorial integrity and political independence of Israel and its right to live in peace within secure and recognized boundaries free from threats or acts of force, as stipulated in UN SCRs 242 and 338.

The Labour-alignment victory in the 1992 elections brought these three principles into the centre ground in Israeli politics. However, these points by themselves were not enough to form the basis of the secret Israeli-Palestinian dialogue, but merely reflected a growing acceptance by a significant proportion of the Israeli electorate and political establishment that the *status quo ante* was unsustainable.[223] The step towards mutual recognition depended on a number of factors which only when combined led to the Israeli-Palestinian breakthrough, factors which had the timings been different may never have influenced the willingness to negotiate. These factors included:

(1) The reconfiguration of the international structure from a bipolar to a unipolar one. This meant that the Israelis and Palestinians had to reassess their positions. The Palestinians lost the political backing and logistical support of their superpower advocate, the USSR. The Israelis feared that they were no longer such an important strategic ally of the US, uncertain of their future relationship with the US, and the US's Middle Eastern strategic policies and economic commitments.[224]

(2) A realignment of the political relations within the Middle East. The Second Gulf War and the resurgence of radical Islamist movements forced a re-evaluation of their priorities by many of the wealthier, conservative Arab states. The steady rise of contemporary radical Islam in Iran, Sudan, Algeria and Lebanon, and political violence in Egypt, forced many states to be more sensitive to their vulnerabilities and weaknesses, and to consider the containment of such radicalism as their most im-

portant priority rather than continuing opposition to Israel. Israel and the PLO shared similar concerns with regard to radical Islamic opponents. Israel had encouraged the initial efforts of Hamas in Gaza as a counter to PLO influence, however the Hamas movement provided the ideological and physical backbone to the *intifada*, being the most violent and inflexible movement unwilling to consider accommodation with Israel. The PLO found themselves fearing a haemorrhage in popular support to the Islamists which in turn would diminish their position and power as leader of the Palestinian national movement in the occupied territories.[225]

(3) The demonstrable will and investiture of authority by the Israeli and Palestinian leaderships in the pursuit of peace. The cut in financial aid and receipts to the PLO following the Gulf conflict meant that Arafat's ability to employ the politics of patronage within the Palestinian national movement was curtailed severely. Compounding this was the wane of PLO external support from the USSR. Arafat therefore had to reassess his options. The Madrid framework provided a positive, albeit limited, opportunity for the PLO. The framework initially only offered the PLO semi-legitimacy, but when the talks bogged down Arafat sought new channels of communication to the Israeli leadership. To upgrade the PLO's status Arafat would have to accept the conditions of recognition of Israel and the renunciation of terrorism and violence against Israel. Arafat was influenced and pressured from a number of directions:

- by Hamas, particularly in Gaza
- by the emergence of a West Bank PLO leadership whose direct influence in determining the policies of the *intifada* brought them frequently into conflict with PLO Tunis
- by mortality, when he was in a plane crash at the age of 65.[226]

On assuming office, Rabin set about redefining and reordering Israel's priorities, stating to the Knesset that as he had once led Israel's forces to victory in 1967, he regarded making peace as the culmination of his work.[227] Rabin stated his government's priorities: the exploitation of the opportunities arising from the collapse of the USSR, the end of the Cold War, the military action against Iraq, and mass immigration from Russia, giving rise to the advancement of Israeli life in the areas of national and personal security, peace, the prevention of war, unemployment, prevention of emigration, economic growth, fortification of the foundations of democracy, the rule of law, equality and human rights. The government would work towards the creation of a new Middle East devoted to development, grounded in economic, cultural and scientific cooperation. Peace would be based on recognition, by the Arab states and the Palestinians, of Israel as a sovereign state in the region and of its right to live in peace and security. The government would advance the peace process with the Palestinians without preconditions, within the Madrid formula, by proposing as an interim arrangement, a programme for the implementation of self-administration for the Palestinians in Judea, Samaria and Gaza, and refrain from courses of action that would obstruct the proper conduct of negotiations.[228]

The turn towards peace by Rabin was possible because of the acknowledgement of a number of factors. Israel was militarily strong with powerful friends and not isolated and weak. In bringing the DoP to the Knesset for ratification, PM Rabin said that Israelis 'must overcome the sense of isolation that has held us in thrall for almost half a century.' Israel 'must join the international movement toward peace, reconciliation, and cooperation that is sweeping the entire globe ... lest we be the last ones to remain, all alone'.[229] The establishment of a Palestinian state, or 'state-let' would not be a mortal threat to Israel's existence. Without the PLO, any deal with the Palestinians would neither have the legitimacy nor the support of the majority of the Palestinian people thus giving greater credence to Palestinian radical elements, both temporal and secular. Rabin argued that his military credentials meant that he was the only man who could be trusted by the Israeli public to deliver a peace that was in Israel's best interests. The Likud's fictitious stance at Madrid where the Israeli government negotiated with a Palestinian delegation, albeit formally part of the Jordanian delegation, made up of representatives of the West Bank and Gaza and not members of the PLO, highlighted to the Israeli public the absurdity of the situation and prepared them for the more pragmatic inevitability of negotiating publicly with the PLO. Whilst both Palestinians and Israelis may have agreed that a political solution would be logical, bringing people toward peace would mean overcoming years of distrust and fear. The choice of Rabin as the Labour candidate for PM therefore incorporated a hard-line image of a tough, soldier-politician and respected negotiator, coupled with the constant mantra of 'peace with security' in the election message of the Labour party.[230] Rabin's election meant both the Palestinians and the Israelis had leaders who possessed the personal authority to negotiate a political solution that could be trusted by the majority of their respective peoples. The Palestinian community had enjoyed enthusiasm and energy from the outbreak of the *intifada*; however, five-and-a-half years on weariness, economic malaise and the feeling that there was no end in sight combined to depress the population. A combination of factors manoeuvred Palestinian consciousness away from confrontation to conciliation with Israel. Palestinians worried over their childrens' futures, curfews, closures, taxes and deprivation, the realization that the *intifada* had resulted in an increased Israeli presence in the form of soldiers, settlers, and Soviet immigrants, and the spread of inter-Palestinian violence – from December 1987–22 December 1993, 964 Palestinians were killed by Palestinians as opposed to 1067 killed by Israelis.[231] Additionally secular nationalists such as those who supported the PLO feared being marginalized by the rise of the militant, radical and violent Islamic opposition to Israel, which was a departure from the earlier collaborative mass non-violent civil protest which characterized the *intifada*. These factors proved conducive to a popular willingness to consider a negotiated Israeli-Palestinian settlement. However, these conditions were, whilst necessary factors, not enough to guarantee successful negotiations. The final factor was that both Israeli and Palestinian public opinion coincided and aligned in their desire and readiness to achieve political accommodation, an element hitherto missing from previous attempts. Israeli and Palestinian public opinion although reserving final judgement on the purity of the peace, had to invest enough goodwill for the peace to be nurtured in order to grow. Public consent would also confer the requisite legitimacy to the process.

The *intifada* was just as important an historical event for the Israelis as for the Palestinians. Coming so soon after the morass of Lebanon, the *intifada* stripped Israelis of the illusion that they were benevolent occupiers, bringing civilization and prosperity to the Palestinians. Critical self-examination found that force could not make the Palestinian problem disappear. The generational change in Israel fostered a more relaxed and self-confident Jewish population, so allied with the pride of the recent massive Soviet and Ethiopian Jewish immigration, the realization that Israel's destiny was not best served enslaving Palestinians but building the Jewish state encouraged many Israelis to withdraw their support from Likud in 1992. The feeling was that massive immigration provided an economic opportunity for businesses, in increased demand for housing, consumer goods, and the like. Beyond the immediate boom, many Israelis began to sense that economic prosperity could be deepened, widened and prolonged through the opening up of markets in Africa, Asia and the Middle East. Occupation was not only a drain on human and material resources but also a political millstone that denied Israelis access to economic progress.

'Greater Land of Israel' advocates have hoped for two demographic outcomes. Firstly, they wished for Jewish *aliya* in significant numbers. However, demographers have outlined that immigration, even in massive proportions, would only delay a Palestinian Arab majority by only a few years on the basis of approximately one year for every hundred thousand new immigrants.[232] Secondly, they sought Arab emigration and a natural reduction in Arab birth-rates. Ironically, Likud's settlement-building programme from 1977 onwards created an economic boom which not only attracted Palestinians seeking work elsewhere but also enabled them to eschew emigration.[233] F. Gottheil shows the out-migration balance of the West Bank dropping steadily from a high of 23.7 per 1000 population in 1980 to 6.1 per 1000 in 1986. Although Gottheil attempted to make a case against the 'demographic argument', he noted that the drop in out-migration and the very young composition of the population presage a major and rapid growth of the Palestinian population.[234] With the *intifada*, came the concept of forced 'transfer' of the Palestinian population into Israeli politics, embraced by Rehavam Zeevi's Moledet party, which won three seats in the 1992 Knesset. Among the general Israeli population was not only a distaste for such a policy of 'transfer', there was also the realization that the occupied territories' chronic problems, and the political extremism which arose as a result would not disappear, that Israel would have to deal with the Palestinians in some form or other. The 1992 election characterized the swing from a Greater Israel policy with the emphasis on territory to parties which addressed the broader issues of social, economic and political well-being, concentrating on reordering social, economic and security priorities. The 1992 election highlighted Israeli willingness to listen to the promoters of coexistence and mutually profitable cooperation, reflecting the Israeli mixture of empathy and scepticism of the Palestinians that characterizes volatile Israeli public opinions.[235] Thus it could be argued that the public debate in both communities moved, albeit slowly and not uniformly, from a question of survival to a question of quality of life, from whether security considerations were more important than finding common cause for bettering their childrens' futures.

The DoP did not occur in a political vacuum. Necessary changes to previously held personal, political, and strategic visions were critical in producing the environment conducive to revolutionary and historic understandings. Between 1991 and 1993 the Israelis and Palestinians discovered some fundamental truths about one another.[236] Palestinians who favoured a negotiated settlement with Israel realized that such a settlement would not be reached through improving relations with the US; rather they concluded that a settlement, negotiated directly with the Israelis, would lead to improved relations with the US. Israeli public opinion, phlegmatic at the best of times, concluded pragmatically (and hopefully) in 1992 that negotiating a deal with the Palestinians, including the PLO, would not only materially affect their daily lives in removing an element of uncertainty and fear of random violence, it would also preclude more politically divisive settlements such as with Syria. Moreover PM Rabin became increasingly convinced of President Ezer Weizman's argument, that unless Israel dealt with the PLO, only Hamas would remain.[237] Many Israelis also concluded that trying to circumvent the PLO in any negotiated settlement with the Palestinians was merely wishful thinking – the reality was that the PLO was the only credible partner. Both sides also concluded that establishing cooperation and trust through the negotiation of an interim settlement could dramatically affect the possibility of ever being able to determine emotionally charged final status issues. By defusing tensions on the streets by means of an interim agreement in order to establish goodwill and build confidence, a more conducive environment to construct new arrangements could be created, a task which would be almost impossible otherwise.

Rabin's return to political power coincided with a general trend in Israeli society towards pragmatism. Two months before the election, Shamir was asked if he considered himself an ideologue or merely a hard bargainer. Shamir said, 'Without ideology, you can't achieve anything serious.' 'Tacticians [who lack] ideology will not achieve anything. Someone with ideology has the possibility of getting help from tacticians, but the top priority is ideology.' Shamir expressed admiration for V.I. Lenin, saying:

> Lenin succeeded in getting events under control and directing their course as he desired, Lenin was a genius . . . He orchestrated

everything theoretically in his brain and he acted according to his theoretical model . . . [T]he ideals were inflated and unjustified – it's a fact where they led to. But Russia is still waiting for [another] man like this.[238]

Whilst Rabin did not explicitly campaign on a 'land-for-peace' policy, even though Labour party policy explicitly proposed territorial compromise, he campaigned for increasing Palestinian self-rule in, but not over, the West Bank, insisting that responsibility for security would remain with Israel. Rabin did not confuse Israelis' desire for their government to explore genuine peace initiatives, either unilaterally or in response to overtures, with their concern for campaign commitments to wholesale territorial concessions. Rabin campaigned on his strength that he was the only politician with both the will and the credibility to pursue peace. Rabin's departure from previous conventional wisdom was in his belief that Palestinian terror was not an existential threat to Israel, rather it was an issue of personal security, which would be resolved not by more conflict but through negotiations with the Palestinians. Autonomy for the Palestinians therefore meant personal security for Israelis, that is, no terrorism within the Green Line. Coexistence would be achieved by a separation of the two peoples, religions and political entities. In a rare TV address on 24 January 1995 following a double suicide bombing near Netanya claiming 21 Israelis – all but one young soldiers – Rabin returned to the theme of separation. He said Israel must continue negotiating 'to bring about a separation between Israelis and Palestinians, but not [along] the pre-1967 borders. Jerusalem must remain united forever, and the security border of Israel must be the Jordan River.'[239]

With Rabin's well known distaste for conventional politics, his political standing derived more directly from the electorate than from his party, therefore public opinion played a greater role in influencing his policy-making, particularly with regard to politically motivated violence stemming from the unresolved Israeli-Palestinian conflict. Thus the action-reaction cycle figured more prominently within the decision-making process. The deportation of 415 Islamists in December 1992 followed the killings of eight IDF officers in a 12-day period, culminating with the kidnap and murder of Sergeant Nissim Toledano in central Israel. Chief of Staff Barak advocated the deportations to fight terrorism. Rubinstein warned that deportations would prompt an Arab boycott of the negotiations. Rothschild anticipated international condemnation and that the UN would impose sanctions, advising Rabin that newly appointed Lebanese PM Rafik Hariri's actions could not be predicted and could potentially embarrass Israel. No high-level official anticipated events, as Hariri refused to accept the deportees leaving them stranded in no-man's-land, thus providing the Israelis with an international public relations disaster. Some lower-level IDF officers reportedly anticipated events, one source claiming that Barak received their analysis but did not pass it to the PM. Rabin later admitted that he thought Lebanon would accept the 415, and he blamed the IDF for poor execution of the operation.[240] The deportations did not put an end to violence. In March, a wave of spontaneous, unorganized fatal stabbings by Palestinian day labourers, largely within the Green Line, alarmed the Israeli public who were fed hysterical headlines during a vicious newspaper war between *Ma'ariv* and *Yediot Aharonot*. Such violence could not be easily interdicted by the GSS, therefore in order to be seen to act Rabin, who had previously rejected calls for sealing the occupied territories in response to attacks, implemented a total closure despite almost universal opposition from the defence establishment. In order to offset the loss of work to 120 000 Palestinian day labourers, Rabin initiated a large-scale public works programme increasing employment from 8000 to 40 000. Unintentionally closure reinforced the notion that the reimposition of the Green Line, in other words separation, would bring safety. Separation proved very popular in Israel: 'The public just doesn't want to be knifed, ... It cares less about where the border is than the fact that it exists and the Arabs are on the other side.' Likud opposed closure and the resurrection of the Green Line, because it physically, and dramatically, reinforced political and ideological distance between the settlers and the rest of Israel through the feeling of separation whilst undermining the Greater Land of Israel ideology, and encouraged the notion of an independent Palestinian entity. Labour seized the political opportunity to attack Likud: 'The difference between Likud and Labour, is that the Likud wants the Arabs over here, and we want them over there.'[241]

Events on Israel's northern border also helped play a part in the peace programme, albeit in a convoluted sense. The IDF-Hezballah cycle of retaliation escalated into a major border clash on 25 July 1993. Hezballah fired Katyushas into northern Israel in retaliation for civilian casualties from IDF bombings of guerrilla installations in villages beyond Israel's self-declared security zone in southern

Lebanon. Rabin warned Assad that Israel would take decisive action to end the attacks. Assad, however, insisted through US officials
that Hezballah had the right to resist the IDF in southern Lebanon
and liberate their country. Under public pressure for a response,
Barak laid out a complex plan to bomb the south and create a
mass exodus of Lebanese refugees, thus forcing PM Hariri and President Elias Hrawi to plead with Assad to call off Hezballah, in turn
forcing Syria to turn to the US to broker a ceasefire. The cabinet
approved the plan on 26 July. The US brokered a compromise, remi-
niscent of the deportations issue. A ceasefire was worked out within
five days. Under the ceasefire, Hezballah committed to refraining
from hitting Israeli towns, as long as Israel did not bomb villages
outside the security zone unless it could determine the exact location of attacks. Thus Rabin scored points with Israeli public opinion.
Several US officials privately held that the US had 'bailed out' Rabin
and Barak.[242] All these actions were taken in response to public
unrest following violent episodes directed at Israelis. Taking such
decisions to inflict great pain and suffering was predicated on providing an image of a leader not scared to take extreme measures
on behalf of Israeli public opinion. What was important in these
acts was not the acts *per se*, but the portrayal of an image of willingness to engage in violence either to assuage crude Israeli desires
for vengeance or to offset the impression that being interested in
pursuing accommodation with one's enemies meant being weak *in
extremis*, thus ensuring the political survival of the government and
founding credibility for any future negotiated agreements.

Rabin well knew that whilst he and the Labour-led coalition had
been elected, Israeli public opinion's knee-jerk response to Palestinian violence and general security matters was more akin to the
Likud's. Therefore Eitan Haber, Rabin's speech writer, told him: 'If
you want to make drastic concessions on peace, you must show
the public you can take drastic measures for security.' Thus Rabin
announced that Israel would 'pursue peace as if there were no terrorism, and fight terrorism as if there were no peace process'.[243]

One of the striking features of conducting Israeli-Palestinian secret
diplomacy is the relatively similar, highly personalized nature, of
the two sides' decision-making apparatus. Within the confines of
such strictures, the power of personality is of great importance.
Whilst the PLO reflects a structure which is highly representative
of guerrilla/quasi-military national liberation movement, the Israeli
decision-making process is not institutionalized nor is the notion

of collective cabinet responsibility highly developed. Rabin as PM and Defence Minister held enormous power, with wide-ranging authority. As most Israeli PMs are highly aware of and experienced in Israel's main foreign and defence issues, professional, civilian inter-agency staffs and task forces would probably only serve to complicate and obstruct the decision-making process. The IDF plays such a central and dominant role in Israeli policy-making, that its remit and its competencies with regard to security surpass that of any other governmental agency, particularly in regard to intelligence-gathering capabilities. No other agency is deemed sufficiently informed to offer alternative views. What makes Oslo remarkable is the central role the Foreign Ministry played in the initiation, formulation and definition of strategy and policy-making. Whilst a ministerial committee for national security exists (consisting of the PM, a dozen senior ministers and military advisers), convening weekly, its authority extends to approving military operations, having no more actual influence or authority than the cabinet. On the occasions of the deportations, closures and Operation Accountability, Rabin merely sought formal approval from the inner cabinet and the full cabinet for decisions already taken. Neither debated nor influenced the final outcome. With the DoP, both inner and full cabinets neither knew of the existence of nor were kept abreast of developments at the Oslo channel. They were both asked to ratify the DoP after its conclusion, being neither allowed to demand substantive changes nor given sufficient time to study the document minutely. There were two exceptions to this trend, however, both of which related to the peace process. In October 1992, the cabinet vetoed plans to stage deep-penetration bombing raids into Lebanon, fearing it could lead to a repeat of the 1982 Lebanon War, and in March 1994, the cabinet voted for a commission of inquiry into the Hebron massacre against the wishes of Rabin, who feared it could only sully the IDF's morale.

For the Israelis, the ability of legendary rivals Peres and Rabin to cooperate so closely on such a politically sensitive undertaking as an Israeli-Palestinian peace was of great importance, particularly given their past animosity and their 'differing strategic visions of Israel's future, contrasting management styles and sharply distinctive personalities'.[244] Though in the 1990s Peres was considered the dove to Rabin's hawk, it was not always thus. Peres had been previously associated with Dayan and the hawkish Rafi faction, whereas Rabin had been associated with the Ahdut Ha'avoda faction of his mentor, Yigal Allon, who favoured withdrawal from parts of the occupied territories in a condominion arrangement with Jordan. During the Peres-Rabin power struggle in 1974, Dayan backed Peres, Allon backed Rabin. Peres's lack of combat experience in a country full of old soldiers has always counted against him, despite numerous highly important appointments within the defence establishment throughout his career. A senior Peres adviser described a key difference between their approaches: 'Rabin takes the public position of the other side as being final, while Peres sees public pronouncements as an opening position to be modified in backroom negotiations.'[245] However, Peres and Rabin found common cause in pragmatism as neither was ideologically committed to retaining the West Bank, nor motivated to view Israel's security in ideological terms. Rabin believed that whilst there are obviously limits to the practical application of military force to achieve political objectives, strategically speaking, diplomacy which was not backed with the implied threat of military force was not productive. Rabin also believed in the supremacy of a conventional military force. Peres believed security was relative, that security was not only a state of mind, but whilst dependent on military power was equally dependent on economic strength and well-being. Thus in strategic terms, particularly in relation to their attitudes to the Palestinian question, the two envisioned Israel's future well-being in relatively similar terms. Peres dreamed of a Middle East economic and political regional interrelationship similar to the EU which worked to bury past animosities, whereas Rabin remained a sceptic rather than an enthusiast. To persuade Rabin to pursue Oslo, Peres focused on security issues, used third-party assessments to back his views, playing down the significance of controversial proposals. A Peres aide confirmed that Peres did not say that the result of the negotiations in due course would be a Palestinian state. He would leave Rabin to come to those conclusions himself. Peres played down the significance of talking with the PLO; instead of talking about it as a 'revolutionary' step, he would tell Rabin that it was something to try, and if it did not work, it did not work.'[246] Peres claimed Rabin usually instinctively rejected his ideas, however some believed Rabin involved Peres in negotiations to distance himself from them. Rabin ally and Agriculture Minister Yaacov Tsur recalled that Rabin told him, 'I have given Peres some slack, under certain conditions.'[247]

However, despite their differences, the two managed to cooperate, conceptually, politically, secretly and personally over the Oslo backchannel, particularly from March/April 1993 onwards, when Rabin needed Peres's political backing in light of the deportations and closure issues. Peres was the only other senior member of Rabin's cabinet with the political clout and he had the most experience with regard to international and security issues. Peres also realized that the survival of the Rabin administration depended on breaking ground on the peace processes. Thus Rabin drew Peres into his confidence, over the course of many private meetings and sessions, where the two covered broad principles regarding the direction of the Israeli negotiating team's strategy for the Oslo channel. Unfortunately much of the content of these meetings remains unknown.

Regarding Oslo, Rabin eschewed civilian and military analytical advice and policy conceptualization in favour of his personal experience, his own analytical focus and his decision-making abilities. Rabin preferred to receive raw IDF intelligence without conclusions so he could determine his own, so that his policy formulation regarding Oslo had no alternative intellectual counterweight to that being collectively formulated in great detail at the Foreign Ministry under the talents of Yossi Beilin. Without Rabin's goodwill and authority, the DoP would have been stillborn. However without Beilin, the DoP would never have been initiated. Peres subsequently put his political weight to the backchannel in March before Rabin became deeply involved. Beilin formulated position papers, conceived the ideas that developed the process to the highest political level, and played a central role in decision-making throughout the process.[248] Rabin excluded the military, therefore the Foreign Ministry over which he had no direct responsibility dominated policy-making, an astonishing denouement, particularly when Rabin was well known for his military background and preference for military people and their advice. Peres felt that Rabin did not involve the IDF in decision-making because he regarded Oslo as a futile exercise. A senior Peres aide thought that initially Rabin did not confide in Barak and others because he did not think the Oslo backchannel was a serious option. When matters developed, he did not consult them because he did not want them to slow him down. A senior Rabin aide said the generals would have requested delays in order to clarify details, such as the level of security arrangements, control of bridges, and the size of Jericho. Rabin believed military people would merely slow things down, and that such details could be dealt with in the implementation process. He did not believe that negotiations could go on too long in Oslo without leaking.[249] Whilst senior IDF officers later criticized the security 'holes' in the DoP, no evidence suggests that any of the top three generals would have opposed a PLO take-over of Gaza and Jericho. Yossi Ben-Aharon, director-general of the PM's bureau during the Shamir government, said that, together with GSS head, Yaacov Peri, 'there is not a Likudnik among them.' The three senior IDF officers were known to favour progress with Syria to alter the region's strategic equation. Saguy was a 'Syria First' advocate.[250] However Shahak's views on the Palestinians were moderate. As head of military intelligence in 1987, he reported to the Knesset Foreign Affairs and Defence committee that the PLO was the only representative of the Palestinians, repeating this assertion during a verbal presentation of the March 1989 annual intelligence assessment to Shamir, Rabin, Peres and Moshe Arens. Peri, who had operational responsibility for dealing with Palestinian violence, was known to favour accommodation over ideology. Though appointed by Shamir in April 1988, around October 1991 Peri issued an internal directive ordering Shin Bet to prepare for the prospect of protecting Israelis' security during Palestinian autonomy. Although there is no evidence that Rabin consulted Peri about Oslo, it seems clear that Peri supported the general thrust. Barak also favoured accommodation in return for security and peace, believing that Israel 'must limit friction with the Arabs' to mitigate longer-term regional threats. Making peace with Israel's immediate neighbours fits into a broader regional strategy. Barak has said 'We have no control over whether Iran will have non conventional nuclear capabilities in another ten years,' but 'Given this long-term uncertainty, it is not an exaggerated risk to attempt to relax the conflict in our immediate circle, including with Lebanon and Syria . . . as long as we do not waive our vital security interests.' Whilst 'On one hand, the Palestinians are weak,' Barak said,

> On the other hand, they are perceived by [Israeli] citizens to be the source of terror and day-to-day frictions, and they legitimise pan-Arab hostility toward Israel. As long as we reduce [Palestinian] terror without damaging any of Israel's vital interests by smoothing relations with them, it will be more difficult to motivate hostile acts against us from Benghazi to Teheran.[251]

Other members of the IDF General Staff favoured Rabin's strategy of promoting secure and peaceful accommodation with neighbouring Arabs to allow Israel to face future threats from Iran and Iraq. Rothschild, ex-deputy head of military intelligence, believed negotiations with the Palestinians should be based on pragmatism rather than ideology. However precisely because of the politically sensitive nature of the Oslo negotiations Rabin decided not to consult the IDF, neither demanding strategy formulation, nor seeking IDF advice on the finer points of the document being negotiated. Barak defended Rabin's exclusion of the military from Oslo as justifiable since the real decision was not to involve the military, even at the highest levels, in shaping the political decision that had to be made, namely whether to enter a deal with the Palestinians or not.[252] By excluding the military, Rabin avoided any stigma of the politicization of the Israeli defence forces. Whilst Rabin informed Barak, it is not known how far Rabin consulted him, or even sought his advice, or even having sought his advice, took it. Thus the IDF merely provided Rabin with a number of option scenarios on the approach to political and security issues within negotiations, allowing Rabin to know where the IDF stood on various issues without having to ask for specific action-reaction policy responses to ongoing negotiations. According to Barak, Rabin knew exactly what the army felt were the consequences and the significance of every alternative.[253]

If Rabin's initial reluctance to believe that Oslo would produce any real rewards was tempered by the incompatibility of his stated desire to force the Palestinians in the occupied territories to deny their compatriots in the PLO in Tunis in order to promote an independent Palestinian authority and leadership in the occupied territories, then at least Rabin, by March 1993, had the common sense to realize that such an outcome was highly unlikely. Rabin had stated 'that he who stands at the head of the PLO fears, maybe justifiably from his personal perspective, that if [interim self-rule] is created, . . . such a body will become the source of Palestinian identity, and then what will the organization sitting in Tunis do?' Rabin had hoped that the PLO's political and financial predicament would enable a deal with Palestinians in the territories rather than with PLO in Tunis.

Rabin initially rejected the PLO as a negotiating partner because of the PLO commitment to a state in the West Bank and Gaza, encompassing Jerusalem, settlements, refugees, security arrangements, borders and external relations. Rabin hoped that a debilitated PLO could be forced to agree to a deal made by local Palestinians to ease the occupation. The election of the Clinton administration confirmed the feeling that less pressure would be applied on Israel to make concessions to the Palestinians which would offer Israel a great opportunity to take advantage of a seriously weakened PLO. Rabin believed that among the Palestinian leadership in the territories and outside, and even in PLO headquarters in Tunisia, there were Palestinian leaders who had 'wised up', and who understood that they could not repeat the mistakes of the past, who understood that it was better to establish the 'nucleus of a Palestinian entity', even only an administrative one.[254] This 'wising up' however had to be mutual. Rabin had to admit the inevitable, that there would be no meaningful and substantive progress in the Washington talks as long as Arafat and the PLO were not full negoatiating partners and officially recognized as such.

Thus it was Rabin's reading of the international situation, both short-term opportunities, intermediate possibilities and long-term considerations, which offered the diagnosis-prognosis that the resolution of the conflict with Israel's immediate neighbours was both possible and imperative due to:

(1) The loss of superpower conflict by proxy – compromise was more attainable than strategic parity.

(2) The radicalization of the *intifada* since 1991 which if not confronted politically would continue to spiral from a popular outpouring of Palestinian frustration and anger within the confines of civil disobedience to a more extreme form of struggle involving armed confrontation, and indiscriminate suicidal terror. This implacable foe eschewed accommodation and assumed the mantle of existential confrontation. For all the talk of rising Islamic fundamentalism sweeping across the Middle East and North Africa and influencing Palestinian fundamentalism in the occupied territories, the inescapable truth was that the appalling poverty, hopelessness, anger and discontent that was spreading like a malignant cancer through Gaza only highlighted that Israeli policy in Gaza provided sustenance to Islamist radicalism. Thus whilst the secular/nationalist PLO haemorrhaged financially and politically, a leadership vacuum was being created in the territories which was being rapidly filled by Islamists such as Hamas.

(3) Israel's most obvious confrontational Arab foe with the previously perceived ability to unite the Arab world in pursuit of an existential threat to Israel, Iraq, was no longer a threat. The

US, Israel's ally, through its intervention in Kuwait had demonstrated its willingness to militarily intervene in the region
in protection of its interests, to which Israel regarded itself as a
special US ally. Rabin stated,

> I am convinced our deterrent capability has increased as a
> result of the crisis in the Gulf, if only indirectly and because
> the United States demonstrated its readiness to act resolutely.
> I am not saying that Washington will automatically do the
> same for Israel; nor has Israel ever asked the United States
> to do so. But the fact that this time the United States stood
> firm and was ready to become involved against an aggres-
> sion in the Middle East adds somewhat to Israel's overall
> deterrence. It discourages initiation of war in the region,
> though I do not know for how long.[255]

(4) The analysis that the PLO's financial and political weakness
    could encourage flexibility and could lead to the conclusion
    that their willingness to moderate their positions in order to
    negotiate a deal would be greater than ever before. This was
    particularly with regard to the PLO's continuation of violent
    actions and to its strength to negotiate on such issues as a
    Palestinian state, refugees, and Jerusalem. Furthermore Israeli
    concessions were in essence pre-ordained, in that a blueprint
    for Israeli-Palestinian negotiations already existed in the form
    of the Camp David accords, whereas none existed for an Israeli-
    Syrian accommodation.

(5) That a 'Syria first' option involved territorial concessions which
    carried too great a political sacrifice, unlikely to be borne by
    Israeli public opinion without a great struggle, for debatable
    reward.

(6) The realization that whilst PLO violence was decidedly low-
    intensity and non-threatening in existential terms, the Palestinian
    ability repeatedly to enter regional centre stage, whether being
    unscrupulously highjacked by a venal Iraq, or being able to
    force a boycott at the Washington talks, meant that the Pales-
    tinian issue was not one which could be left unresolved.

(7) International and regional circumstances offered Israel a 'window
    of opportunity' to resolve the immediacy of the Israeli-Palestinian
    conflict, which in turn could lessen intermediate frictions with
    the Arab world. Thus Israel, by resolving immediate dangers,

would be able to prepare for long-term strategic existential threats, from Iran and a resurgent Iraq. Rabin argued that Israel had a seven-year 'window of opportunity' to resolve the core conflict and make peace with its neighbours before the Iranian threat became real. Rabin believed that Iran was the main source of fundamentalist Islam in the region, and that it had replaced Iraq in what he called its 'megalomaniacal ambitions in empire-building'. Within seven years, he warned, Iran would be the main threat in the Middle East. 'We have this time to resolve problems. I believe we will succeed.'[256]

2.7   Conclusion

Yitzhak Rabin stated in his inaugural speech to the Knesset as PM on 13 June 1992, that an ill-considered peace agreement which ultimately initiated future conflict was unacceptable. He said that 'When it comes to security, we will concede nothing. From our standpoint, security takes preference even over peace.' However he continued,

> It is our duty, to ourselves and to our children, to see the new world as it is now – to discern its dangers, explore its prospects and to do everything possible so the State of Israel will fit into this world whose face is changing. No longer are we necessarily a 'people that dwells alone,' and no longer is it true that 'the whole world is against us.' We must overcome the sense of isolation that has held us in its thrall for almost half a century. We must join the international movement towards peace, reconciliation and cooperation that is spreading all over the entire globe these days – lest we be the last to remain, all alone, in the station . . . A number of countries in our region have recently stepped up their efforts to develop and produce nuclear arms . . . The possibility that nuclear weapons will be introduced in the Middle East in the coming years is a very grave and negative development from Israel's standpoint . . . [T]his situation requires us to give further thought to the urgent need to end the Arab-Israeli conflict and live in peace with our Arab neighbours.[257]

On 16 November 1992 at a speech at Tel Aviv University, Rabin stated that 'I believe that we are on a path of no return . . . to reach peace, even if it takes another year or two years, . . . I think that the reality of the international situation, the regional situation, the genuine need of nations and countries, is to arrive at a resolution of the dispute.'[258]

By building confidence between the PLO and Israel that a deal could be negotiated, Rabin sought to provide a framework which formalized channels for reconciliation, for conflict deterrence, to ensure a mutual security environment and to build a mutual future. From realizing that political compromise with the Palestinians was not possible without dealing with the PLO, it was a short journey to seeing that by not dealing with the PLO in the immediate future, the rise of absolutist, Islamic fundamentalism would result. Compromise was possible with the PLO by building confidence through negotiating a mutually perceived future via the Oslo backchannel. However, compromise was not an option to be considered with Hamas and Islamic Jihad. Rabin believed that

> Our struggle against murderous Islamic terror is also meant to awaken the world which is lying [in] slumber. We call on all nations and all people to devote their attention to the great danger inherent in Islamic fundamentalism. That is the real and serious danger which threatens the peace of the world in the forthcoming years. The danger of death is at our doorstep. And just as the state of Israel was the first to perceive the Iraqi nuclear threat, so today we stand in the line of fire against the danger of fundamentalist Islam.[259]

Israeli and PLO concern about the potential threat of extremist Islam provided both sides with a mutual enemy. The DoP was conceived, developed, negotiated and concluded with such a threat in mind, from both sets of negotiators. The Oslo backchannel provided the necessary environment in which to conceive a working arrangement upon which to build. The facilitation of the process was nurtured by sensitive intermediaries – the Norwegians. In an atmosphere of cordiality, confidence in one another could be fostered and developed. The negotiating system employed, although secret, aimed to reach a deal that could be built on and improved. Contentious issues which could not be agreed upon were sidestepped to be dealt with in the future. The DoP was meant as a first important step – to break the barrier of past conflict.

Before the DoP neither side officially recognized each other. The DoP established a nominal agreement for a ceasefire of hostilities, instituted a mutual recognition pact, transferred specified territorial enclaves of Gaza and Jericho to Palestinian authority, provided for the inauguration of an autonomous self-governing Palestinian entity with the prospect of elections to such an autonomous legislative body combined with the devolution of additional civil powers and responsibilities, arranged for the withdrawal and redeployment of Israeli military forces from specified locations and population centres, founded a framework for the resolution of disputes and Israeli-Palestinian public order and security cooperation and offered a plan for Israeli-Palestinian cooperation in bilateral and regional economic and development programmes. It also prepared for further negotiations on unresolvable issues within the framework of a permanent status arrangement covering Jerusalem, refugees, settlements, security arrangements, borders and foreign relations. A rolling process of considerable substantive negotiations would have to follow from the initial DoP because of the inherent contradictions, ambiguities and material differences in interpretation contained within the limitations of the original document. Subsequent sequential documents had to be negotiated to formulate further interim arrangements ready for implementation in order that the process begun by the DoP could proceed. The DoP as a document represents an agreement to pursue a living legacy, to undertake a process whose final outcome is not determined in advance. The DoP is not a symmetrical agreement outlining mutual obligations on a *quid pro quo* basis, rather it is an agreement to further the basic interests of both sides. For the Israelis, the DoP provides a reliable, legitimate interlocutor and the ability to transfer responsibility for a large proportion of the Palestinian population, if not of the territory they inhabit. For the Palestinians, the DoP provides for the establishment of a legitimated political and moral authority with the mandate to negotiate on behalf of the Palestinian people to pursue Palestinian national interests.

3
The Declaration of Principles on Interim Self-Government Arrangements: an Analysis

'Dat veniam corvis, vexat censura columbas'

– Juvenal[1]

3.1 Introduction

This chapter analyses the specific terms of the Declaration of Principles on Interim Self-Government Arrangements (DoP) within the conflict resolution parameters of items 2, 5 and 6 of the Riceman Formula, which pertain to institutionalization, mediation and administration. To achieve the goal of an agreed, recognized and legally binding conflict resolution framework, which sets out specific commitments and obligations within an enforceable conflict prevention regime, a bureaucratic regime must be initiated to institutionalize the conduct, management, regulation and supervision of such a framework. This chapter analyses how the terms of the DoP conform to such a conflict resolution framework, how they anticipate and monitor potential areas of future conflict and how they allow for sustained support and political direction from interested third parties which aim to nurture and advance the peace process. This chapter will also assess the DoP's provision for procedures which enable peaceful change, mechanisms which allow for the review of settlement terms and the raising of grievances and adjustments to the settlement as new realities are created.

The DoP is regarded by some as an interpreter's nightmare, a patchwork of old Israeli and US drafts, incomplete procedural suggestions, deliberate ambiguities and obfuscations.[2] However the 17 articles and four annexes of the DoP indicate that they are firmly intended to lead to some final political settlement. The document was painstakingly drafted and covers, at least in outline, the most sensitive concerns of both sides. The DoP is a bilateral agreement which is historic in the sense that the Palestinians became full partners, with the Israelis, in the regional quest for peace. The destiny for both sides is to deal with the DoP realistically, to overcome its limitations and by inference overcome the weaknesses and flaws that continue to divide them. The dilemma for the participants is how they will move forward constrained by the limits of the DoP and by their own histories.

The DoP does include somewhat soaring rhetoric. The two sides have pledged to 'strive to live in peaceful co-existence and mutual dignity and security and achieve a just, lasting and comprehensive peace settlement and historic reconciliation.'[3] However the most striking aspect of the DoP is that it deals with procedures and timetables for the implementation of Israeli military redeployment and Palestinian self-government. It is a living document which seeks to maximize developing confidence-building measures. It is a studied example of a carrot-and-stick approach to diplomacy, that is, the more that is achieved the more that can be achieved. Yitzhak Rabin described it thus when making his annual speech to the Daily Newspaper Editors' Committee in Jerusalem on 8 December 1993, the 'Declaration of Principles is not a peace agreement. It is a huge step in the direction of peace; it is an agreement on establishing an arrangement for an interim period.'[4] Therefore just what exactly is being agreed?

3.2 *La cohabitation*: a textual analysis of the Declaration of Principles

The DoP comprises the following documents:
(1) The text of the Declaration itself.
(2) Four annexes dealing with elections, early withdrawal from the Gaza Strip and Jericho Area, Israeli-Palestinian economic cooperation and Israeli-Palestinian cooperation at the regional level.
(3) A series of Agreed Minutes amplifying various articles in the Declaration. These Agreed Minutes were separately signed by the parties, and, according to Article XVII of the DoP, they constitute an 'integral part' thereof. The DoP is supplemented by an exchange of correspondence dated on the 9th and 10th of September 1993.[5]

Between them these documents set out a framework for the arrangements to apply in the West Bank and Gaza Strip during a transitional period of five years until the implementation of permanent status arrangements.[6] The texts themselves will not alone determine the nature of self-rule, but they do constitute a contractual treaty between the two parties.[7]

The letters, taken together, constitute the agreement on mutual recognition between the PLO and the State of Israel. The first one is from PLO Chairman Arafat to Israeli Prime Minister Rabin, the second is from Arafat to Norwegian Foreign Minister Johan Jorgen Holst, and the third is from Rabin to Arafat. The letters are all dated 9 September 1993, although the third was actually signed and dated personally by Rabin, on 10 September.[8] Whilst the letters of mutual recognition have great clarity regarding Israeli demands, they are full of obscurity concerning the rights of the Palestinian people.[9] For example, if we consider the PLO's recognition of Israel, the central phrase reads 'The PLO recognises the right of the State of Israel to exist in peace and security.'[10] The wording of the mutual recognition statements was very important especially the phrasing of the recognition of Israel. Arafat had wanted the statement to read,

> 'We recognise the right of Israel to live in secure and recognised boundaries', but agreed to change the phrase 'live in secure and recognised boundaries' to 'exist in peace and security'. The difference between the two expressions is very significant; the former suggests the right of Jews to live in the area simply because they are already there, the word 'exists' in the latter confirms the legitimacy of the Israeli state.[11]

What does this recognition mean in terms of substance and consequences? It endows a legitimacy on Israel hitherto lacking as many states withheld recognition contingent on a positive resolution of the Palestinian-Israeli conflict. The letter fails to define which Israel is being recognized as the only borders so far defined are the Egypt-Israel borders. The act of recognizing the State of Israel is tantamount to recognizing Israeli law, in spite of the fact that Palestinians used to describe these laws as 'occupier's law' and therefore devoid of any legitimacy. The recognition of Israeli sovereignty over territory implicit in the letter entails recognition that any legislation passed by a territorially sovereign state is thus legitimate. It has been argued by many who oppose the DoP that the prominence in the letter of the phrase 'right to exist in peace and security' implies a special obligation on the part of the Palestinians in relation to this right and that Israel has the right to remedy any situation it deems threatening. Since the terms 'peace' and 'security' are undefined, they could be argued to extend to concepts such as economic security (the boycott, normalization, administrative restrictions), societal security (demographic composition) and technological security (industry, science, education).[12]

What is also rather significant in the letter is that Israel's right 'to exist in peace and security' is prominently mentioned yet there is no mention of Palestinian rights to peace and security, in fact there are no mentions of any reciprocal Palestinian rights to those being recognized for Israel. There is even the implied undertaking to take certain actions against the members of the PLO for any transgression against Israel and the peace. It seems clear from the wording that there is an undertaking by the PLO to police and enforce transgressions. By using this phrase the PLO has accepted the American requirement to assume, morally if not specifically, responsibility for all PLO factions, including those of the rejectionist front who disavow the entire agreement. The letter renounces terrorism and other acts of violence, going as far as to undertake to 'discipline violators'. The affirmation that 'those articles of the Palestinian Covenant which deny Israel's right to exist and the provisions of the Covenant which are inconsistent with the commitments of this letter are now inoperative and no longer valid' is seen by some to imply a renunciation of the Palestinian armed struggle in particular, and the Palestinian struggle in general. In fact, Article 33 of the Palestine National Charter stipulates that any amendment must receive a two-thirds majority within the Palestine National Council (PNC) *before* action is taken, whereas Arafat declares that the offending articles '*are*' no longer valid as opposed to 'will become'. This is all the more confusing when Arafat states that he thus 'undertakes to submit to the Palestine National Council for formal approval the necessary changes in regard to the Palestinian Covenant.'[13] By these commitments, Arafat has exceeded his authority as PLO Chairman.

What is implicit in Arafat's letter to Rabin is explicit in Arafat's letter to Holst, which Israel considers to be an integral part of the letters of mutual recognition, when Arafat calls upon the 'Palestinian population in the West Bank and the Gaza Strip to take part in the steps leading to the normalisation of life, rejecting violence and terrorism, contributing to peace and stability and participating actively in shaping reconstruction, economic development and co-operation.'[14] Many Palestinian critics of the DoP feel that Arafat by this letter not only unilaterally signalled an end to the *intifada* without consultation and as if it was within his power unilaterally to command, but also that it seems that potential economic gains are more important than the struggle for self-determination.[15]

In return for these undertakings, what are the Palestinians to receive? In 56 words to Arafat's 256, Israel undertakes to 'recognise the PLO as the representative of the Palestinian people and commence negotiation with the PLO within the Middle East peace process.'[16] How the two leaders express themselves in the three letters is of some interest, when trying to gauge their thinking. Rabin writes that the Government of Israel has 'decided to recognise the PLO' because 'of the PLO commitments included' in Arafat's letter to Rabin, thus Rabin makes very clear that he relies on a firm written text containing clear commitments for his understanding of the process.[17] On the other hand Arafat considers 'the signing of the Declaration Of Principles marks a new era in the history of the Middle East', and he continues in the same vein when he declares: 'The PLO considers that the signing of the Declaration of Principles constitutes a historic event, inaugurating a new epoch of peaceful coexistence, free from violence and all other acts which endanger peace and stability.'[18] There is however a curious aspect to Rabin's letter where he decides to 'commence negotiations with the PLO'[19] when the documents were the result of many months of discussions and negotiations between Israel and the PLO. The PLO's commitment is clearly defined, its own role in further negotiations is determined by the PLO declaration 'that all outstanding issues relating to permanent status will be resolved through negotiations.'[20] Such a declaration locks in the PLO to the peace process as determined by the Madrid Conference.

The PLO has by these letters recognized a sovereign, territorial state with a recognized status, albeit with borders still to be negotiated. Israel, on the other hand has recognized the PLO as an organization and negotiating partner, as the 'representative of the Palestinian people' and will 'commence negotiations with the PLO within the Middle East peace process.'[21] An obvious discrepancy in the letters is Arafat's linkage of the letters, which have more legal weight than a declaration of principles especially as the DoP had not been signed by the date of the letters, with the DoP. The DoP is more forthcoming on matters relating to Palestinian rights, legitimacy (for example, preamble of the DoP and Article III.3) and territory (for example, Article IV). Rabin made no mention of any of this in his letter.[22]

The two references in Arafat's letter to Rabin of UN Resolutions 242 and 338 are significant more for their absence from Rabin's letter. It seems these were added for a reason. The US has always stipulated, for instance, that their acknowledgement of the PLO as a partner for peace must be predicated by the PLO's acceptance of these resolutions prior to opening a dialogue. The letter is unclear whether the acceptance of the UN resolutions is a condition for negotiations, or a basis for them.[23] However, senior PLO official, Nabil Sha'ath believes that what is new in the DoP is that

> the model we have now differs in many aspects. It addresses itself to the Palestinians as a people – not to Palestinian residents in the territories. It names the territories as those of the West Bank and Gaza. It addresses the issue of [UN Security Council Resolution] 242 very clearly as the basis of the entire negotiations, but to be implemented in the permanent status stage of negotiations, with which there is a very clear linkage. The entire non-prejudice issue has been removed ... The model includes accelerated withdrawal, so it has a physical basis on the ground. A rapid withdrawal that would leave the Palestinian government with a territorial base – territorial jurisdiction – with exceptions that are not defined as political or administrative, but as temporal, or time-related. In other words, if Jerusalem and the settlements and the return of the refugees are not dealt with now, and are not within the jurisdiction of the Palestinian government now, it is not because of any exceptions to territoriality but because of the temporal requirements of the division between interim and final.[24]

The fact that the letters of mutual recognition preceded the DoP by some four days must be significant. Dajani argues that it means that they must be the 'ultimate reference, it makes them the root to the DoP's branch'. Dajani continues that

> more important, perhaps the time lapse allowed the government of Israel to bring the DoP under its wing of sovereignty. For the

'State of Israel', which considers itself to be the 'sole legitimate' authority, any agreement it concludes with the PLO, whose status lies beneath that of a state, is an exercise of its sovereignty.

Thus, Dajani concludes that the DoP, 'suggests a "declaration"' that has been made by the Israeli state and agreed to or endorsed by the Palestinians, thus focusing attention from the outset on the qualitative discrepancy between the two sides . . . such a declaration could have been issued unilaterally.'[25] There is also another angle, that

> reaching the agreement with the PLO really strikes against Zionist ideology: the reconciliation is made with the official representative of the Palestinian people, with an organisation that was created to fight the State of Israel and to fight its occupation and to fight its dominance. So the deal was struck with the organisation of struggle, the liberation movement that fought the Israelis, rather than with 'Palestinian elements that live in the occupied territories.'[26]

However, Henry Kissinger believes that the Palestinians' major achievement with the signing of the accord is the *de facto* recognition of the PLO as the governing authority in the autonomous areas and the establishment of a distinct Palestinian entity. Under the terms of the accord, if final status negotiations do indeed lead to the establishment of a Palestinian state, the accord will be the document which ensures such an establishment *de jure*.[27]

There are also many questions from Israeli doubters, such as, when the Palestinians recognized Israel, did they mean that they have become genuinely reconciled to its existence, or is it merely a stage in a continuing struggle? Is it endgame or tactical ceasefire? Although coming eight months later, Arafat's speech in South Africa caused consternation and controversy in Israel when he quoted the principle of *solh al-hodaibiya* which meant that 'an agreement can be made with the enemy and then broken as soon as possible.'[28] As the PLO leader's weakness compelled him to seek a compromise with Israel, his weakness will now burden the peace. Chairman Arafat is as constrained by internal Palestinian politics as he is by Israeli politics. Just as PM Rabin showed, and continued to show strength in action, the Israelis will have to be mindful that Chairman Arafat would need to protect himself, through words and deeds to maintain his credibility within his constituency. Indeed he had to be careful to be seen to incorporate Palestinian consensus in his pronouncements lest he be removed or become irrelevant, thus ambiguity and obfuscation will no doubt remain a weapon in his arsenal. Therefore, according to Henry Kissinger, the follow-on negotiations must continually strive to remove this ambivalence, on one hand stressing that there is a point beyond which Israel should not be expected to make concessions, and on the other hand seeking to convince the Palestinians that their dignity will not be compromised and that this aspect, which is not at all nebulous, must be incorporated as an essential aspect of a final settlement.[29]

Principal points agreed to in the DoP

The timetable envisaged by the DoP for the transitional period is based on that included in the Camp David Accords and subsequently adopted as a basis for the Madrid peace process. In Article V, the DoP provides that a five year 'interim' or 'transitional' period will commence on the withdrawal of Israeli forces from the Gaza Strip and Jericho area. By the start of the third year of this five-year period, negotiations will commence on the final status of the West Bank and Gaza Strip.[30]

The principles set down in the DoP cover a wide range of issues, which broadly fall into four categories:

(1) Arrangements to apply throughout the West Bank and Gaza Strip during the interim period, including arrangements for the holding of elections for a Palestinian Council.
(2) Arrangements to apply in the Gaza Strip and Jericho Area subsequent to an early withdrawal of Israeli forces implementing the 'Gaza first' plan.
(3) Arrangements for early empowerment, which constitutes a preparatory transfer of powers and responsibilities in agreed spheres to be implemented in the rest of the West Bank, concurrently with the early withdrawal from the Gaza Strip and Jericho Area.
(4) Permanent status arrangements.

As its title suggests, the DoP is not a comprehensive agreement, but rather a statement of agreed principles. In other words, it is not a self-executing document which purports to set out practical arrangements, but rather an 'agreement to reach agreement', which leaves the details to be negotiated between the parties. Thus, the DoP provides that separate agreements are to be negotiated between the parties with respect to the special arrangements for the Gaza

Strip and Jericho Area (Annex II, Article 1), the elections for the Council (Article III and Annex I), and the interim period arrangements (Article VII). In relation to a number of other areas, such as a economic and regional cooperation, the DoP provides that special liaison committees will be established in order to develop joint programmes, such as those intimated in Articles XI and XVI. Although the practical details are left to be negotiated, the DoP nevertheless provides significant guidelines for these arrangements. The following section will consider the main implications of the DoP in each of the areas outlined above.[31]

Implications of the DoP

Regarding the Interim Agreement, the DoP provides in Article VII.1 and VII.2, that the agreement on the interim period to be negotiated by the parties (that is 'the Interim Agreement' [IA]) will 'specify among other things, the structure of the Council, the number of its members . . . the Council's executive authority, legislative authority . . . and the independent Palestinian judicial organs.' The Interim Agreement would outline and determine the powers and responsibilities to be transferred by Israel to the Council.[32]

The DoP covers two stages – an interim stage and a permanent stage. The interim stage is to last five years, with negotiations on permanent status to begin no later than the beginning of the third year of this stage. According to the DoP, two aspects of the transfer of authority have definitely been agreed upon: firstly the authority to assume responsibility for five spheres – education and culture, health, social welfare, direct taxation and tourism – and secondly, the formation of a police force. Beyond this, everything else is subject to negotiations, subject to the structural restraints of the DoP, necessitating constant supervision and revision in all mechanisms. According to James Baker, former US Secretary of State,

> ultimately I think there will probably be different degrees of ownership – sovereignty of various lands in the territories, depending on their nature and location. Even the DoP points toward three different types of status during the interim period: for Gaza and Jericho, for the rest of the West Bank, and for Israeli settlements.[33]

At this point, most commentators believed that at least four separate major agreements would have to be negotiated during the interim phase; an interim agreement, an elections agreement, a withdrawal agreement and an agreement on economic matters. This would have the effect of tightening up all the inadequacies of the DoP, into an overall workable basis for a future peace treaty.[34]

According to Article III and Annex I, the parties will negotiate an agreement on the exact mode and conditions of the elections. While the details of the elections and the Council will be negotiated in these agreements, the DoP sets out a number of principles to apply to these, as well as to other aspects of the interim period. Regarding elections, the DoP sets out the guiding principle that 'direct, free and general political elections will be held for the Council under agreed supervision and international observation' (Article III.1).[35] Among the issues of contention in this regard is the extent to which Palestinians resident in East Jerusalem will be permitted to participate in the elections. During the negotiations, Israel agreed that such Palestinians would have the right to vote, but a Palestinian proposal which would have permitted these Palestinians to stand as candidates in the elections was not adopted. The adopted text, in Annex I, Article 1, provides that: 'Palestinians of Jerusalem who live there will have the right to participate in the election process, according to an agreement between the two sides.' Dajani argues that this right is conditional on the conclusion of an agreement to that effect, and that this phrase may have been inserted in order to pre-empt any early determination of the status of Jerusalem. However, an interesting aside is the wording 'Palestinians of Jerusalem who live there'.[36] This seems to make it obvious that only those Palestinians actually living in Jerusalem at the particular time of future elections will be able to vote, thus denying those Jerusalemites around the world who would be eligible but who are considered refugees. There is also the small matter of not defining to whom this refers, visiting Palestinians from the territories perhaps, as Jerusalem has been united, annexed and is regarded as Israel's eternal capital. There is also no mention of which Jerusalem this refers to. East Jerusalem? Israeli Palestinian citizens? There are more than 100 000 new Jewish inhabitants of what was once East Jerusalem. Will they vote? Or does this mean that Palestinians who live in Jerusalem are entitled to vote in the elections to the Palestinian Council, operating in Gaza Strip and Jericho Area?[37]

Thus the exact extent to which Palestinians from East Jerusalem would be able to participate in the elections was left to be resolved by the parties in the negotiations on the election agreement. In these negotiations Israel continued to oppose any participation of

Palestinians from East Jerusalem as candidates in the elections. Participation in the election process does not require that Palestinians would be able to cast their votes in Jerusalem itself; their votes may be cast at polling stations situated in the territories. Indeed during the negotiations on the DoP, a Palestinian proposal stating that Palestinians of East Jerusalem would cast their votes in East Jerusalem was not adopted.[38]

William Quandt believes that Israelis have shown little interest in the crucial issue about what kind of state may emerge from the carefully controlled transitional period, although the DoP does give the Israeli government room for involvement in the type of political structure to emerge in the autonomous areas. This stems from Israel's primary concern with its own security and widespread scepticism among Israelis regarding the possibility of democracy anywhere in the Arab world. Israeli leaders in some cases have found certain advantages in negotiating with Arab dictators who are not accountable to the vagaries of public opinion, e.g., Sadat's trip to Jerusalem in November 1977.[39]

Edward Said calculates that some 50 per cent of the Palestinian population do not even live in the West Bank and Gaza Strip, thus those refugees from 1948–67 have simply been left out of the DoP, 1967 refugees having been deferred until the final status negotiations. For Said, one of the major aspects of the DoP is that, whilst the Palestinians have been recognized by Israel and the US, there has to be a recognition of what the disabilities of the PLO are. The PLO negotiated the DoP in complete secrecy, in a language neither Arafat nor his emissaries in Oslo knew fluently, and with no recognized legal expert. There is even little knowledge of what constitutes the Palestinian population. A census is seen as a priority, not just as a bureaucratic exercise but as the basis of enfranchisement and thus empowerment. Said argues for a worldwide census of Palestinians, believing such an exercise would give the Palestinians too high a profile in countries where they are supposed to be invisible, thereby constituting not just a nation or a collection of people, but also being an act of historical and political self-realization outside the limitations imposed on them by the absence of sovereignty. Such a move would enhance the need for democratic participation which has been ostensibly curtailed by the Israelis and the PLO within the parameters of the DoP.[40]

However Henry Kissinger, who is positive about the actual commencement of elections, argues that after the elections in the autonomous areas are satisfactorily concluded, Israeli recognition of the Palestinian entity will be irrevocable, and in the eyes of the world community, so will be the redeployment and withdrawal of the IDF. Kissinger believes that 'Israeli politicians who speak blithely of reoccupying vacated areas are deluding themselves'.[41] The international opprobrium with which Israel would be greeted should such a circumstance transpire would prove unsustainable, though cynics may level the charge that some 30 or more years as an occupying power have not unduly hindered Israel on the world stage. Even if Israel were to withdraw its recognition of the Palestinian entity, the rest of the world would not automatically follow. Cooperative patterns between Israeli and Palestinian authorities in the autonomous areas will improve with constant contact and relations will develop in a positive vein as both authorities share many similar concerns. Relations with other Arab countries will improve if Israel becomes a permanent feature at regional forums under the aegis of the multilateral talks, though full recognition of Israel, concomitant peace treaties and the abolition of the Arab boycott will probably be postponed pending a resolution of the final status negotiations.

Regarding the source of authority on the establishment of the Council, in accordance with Article VII.5 the Israeli Civil Administration (ICA) will be dissolved; on the other hand, however, the Israeli Military Government (IMG) will not be dissolved but will simply withdraw from the West Bank and Gaza Strip to Israel. In fact, the headquarters of the Regional Commanders of the West Bank and Gaza Strip are situated within Israel, while only district offices are currently maintained in the occupied territories.[42]

The dissolution of the ICA will have no impact on the status of the West Bank and Gaza Strip. The ICA was created in 1981, as an organ of the IMG, in order to discharge the powers and responsibilities of the military government in civilian matters. This is according to the Israelis. However, Palestinians would have seen the ICA as an important stage on the road to annexation, as military government transforms to civilian, as the territories are perceived as peaceful and therefore no longer a security threat. With the dissolution of the ICA, the IMG will simply resume all powers and responsibilities of the ICA not transferred to the Palestinian Interim Self-Governing Authority (PISGA or 'the Council' as described in the DoP). In this context, the fact that the IMG in the West Bank and Gaza Strip will continue to exist is very significant. It emphasizes that, notwithstanding the transfer of a large portion of the powers and responsibilities currently exercised by Israel to Palestinian control, the status of the West Bank and Gaza Strip will not be changed during the interim period. These areas will continue to be subject to military government. Similarly, this fact suggests that the PISGA will not be independent or sovereign in nature, but rather will be legally subordinate to the authority of the IMG. In other words, operating within Israel, the IMG will continue to be the source of authority for the PISGA and the powers and responsibilities exercised by it in the West Bank and Gaza Strip. This provision resolves one of the ambiguities left open by the Camp David Accords. In these accords, which spoke of the IMG being 'replaced' by the Palestinian self-governing authority, it was left unclear as to where the source of authority lay, and in whom any residual powers would be vested. The provisions of the DoP ensure that Israel, through its military government, shall continue to be the source of authority and to retain any powers and responsibilities not specifically transferred to the Council.[43]

Regarding the jurisdiction of the Council, Article IV of the DoP provides that the jurisdiction of the PISGA to be established 'will cover the West Bank and Gaza Strip territory, except for issues that will be negotiated in the permanent status negotiations. The two sides view the West Bank and Gaza Strip as a single territorial unit.'[44] It may be inferred that 'issues' refers to territories, and thus territories that may eventually be negotiated out of the area over which Palestinian authority will extend. One can conclude this is a reference to Jerusalem, although in Article V.3, Jerusalem is one of the 'remaining issues'[45] to be dealt with; thus cynics may conclude that this signifies that it is not considered a territorial issue, or part of the West Bank.[46] A list of such permanent status issues is provided in the Agreed Minute to Article IV, which lists Jerusalem, settlements, military locations and Israelis. Article IV's formulation for excluding these issues from the Palestinian jurisdiction ('except for issues that will be negotiated in the permanent status negotiations')[47] was adopted because it effectively enabled the Palestinian delegation to agree to put aside their demands in relation to these issues during the transitional period and to claim that discussion of these issues has simply been postponed until a later date. In addition, the Agreed Minute to Article IV states that jurisdiction of the Council 'will apply with regard to the agreed powers, responsibilities, spheres and authorities transferred to it'.[48] In other words, the Palestinian Authority will have no jurisdiction in relation to powers and responsibilities retained by Israel. In this context it should be noted that the wording proposed by the Palestinian side in the DoP negotiations, referring to the transfer to the PISGA of *all* the powers and responsibilities currently exercised by the IMG and ICA, was not adopted in the text. Instead, the DoP provides in Article VII that the PISGA will only have specified powers and responsibilities to be detailed in the Interim Arrangements (IA). This provision represents, from Israel's point of view, an advance on the Camp David arrangements, which left open the question whether or not all of the powers and responsibilities of the IMG and ICA would be transferred to the Palestinians.[49]

This functional limitation is only one of the factors defining the jurisdiction of the PISGA. In fact, as described in the DoP, the jurisdiction of the PISGA is limited by three cumulative criteria: territorial jurisdiction, personal jurisdiction and functional jurisdiction.

Regarding territorial jurisdiction, Article IV provides that 'the jurisdiction of the Council will cover the West Bank and Gaza Strip territory'.[50] Significantly, by declining to adopt Palestinian proposals to include the word 'all' or 'the' before the phrase 'West Bank and Gaza Strip', the parties made it clear that they intended that the territorial jurisdiction of the PISGA will not necessarily cover the entire West Bank and Gaza Strip.[51] The language of Article IV thus follows the wording of UN SCR 242 which deliberately omitted the word '*all*' before the word '*territories*' in the phrase 'withdrawal of Israeli armed forces from territories occupied in the recent conflict'.[52] In both cases, the omission of the word '*the*' or '*all*' was deliberate and meant to leave for negotiation between the parties the extent to which the withdrawal (in the case of UN SCR 242) or the PISGA's jurisdiction (in the case of the DoP) would apply to the West Bank and Gaza Strip. On the basis of this provision, during the IA negotiations Israel may seek to exclude such areas as state lands or land privately owned by Jews which are located outside the settlements. In addition, it is clear that the jurisdiction of the PISGA will not cover Israeli settlements and military locations which, as noted above, are defined by the Agreed Minute to Article IV as permanent status issues. This list of exceptions is not necessarily exhaustive; indeed, the text of the Agreed Minute to Article IV suggests that they come in addition to the requirement that the extent of West Bank and Gaza Strip territory over which the PISGA has jurisdiction be defined through negotiations.[53]

Regarding personal jurisdiction, the PISGA's jurisdiction shall not include Israelis, who are excluded from its jurisdiction in the Agreed

Minute to Article IV. Thus, Israelis will not be subject to laws legislated by the PISGA, to arrest or detention by Palestinian police or to the jurisdiction of the Palestinian courts. In this respect, the DoP makes no distinction between Israeli civilians and soldiers, or between Israeli residents of the West Bank and Gaza Strip and Israelis visiting from Israel. Israelis, without distinction, shall remain under exclusive Israeli jurisdiction whether they are in the settlements or military locations or anywhere else in the West Bank and Gaza Strip.[54]

Regarding functional jurisdiction, the Agreed Minute to Article IV limits the PISGA's spheres and authorities transferred to it. As a result, the Council's jurisdiction shall not cover any powers and responsibilities not transferred to it. The DoP contains a number of specific issues in this category: external and internal security, public order of Israelis and foreign relations. The parties may also agree on other matters to be excluded from the PISGA's jurisdiction. Thus, for example, if the parties agree that powers and responsibilities relating to broadcasting in the West Bank and Gaza Strip shall not be transferred to the PISGA, then the issuing of licences to Palestinians shall continue to be an Israeli responsibility even though the application would relate to broadcasting stations located within the areas under Palestinian territorial jurisdiction. Similarly, if it is agreed that the administration of Jewish Holy Places or of state lands, is not to be transferred even though they may fall within Palestinian territorial jurisdiction, the administration of such lands will continue to be an Israeli responsibility.[55]

The DoP thus resolves one of the key issues left open by the Camp David Accords, the question of whether, as the Palestinians claimed, their jurisdiction would be territorial, covering the entire West Bank and Gaza Strip, or, as Israel claimed, covering only the Palestinian residents of the territory. The DoP resolves this conflict by providing that the jurisdiction of the PISGA shall be limited to a specific territory. Within that territory its jurisdiction shall only extend to non-Israelis, situated outside the Israeli settlements and military locations, and will apply only in spheres which have been specifically transferred to the Council.[56]

Regarding Israeli jurisdiction, on the inauguration of the PISGA, the ICA will be dissolved and the IMG shall be withdrawn (Article VII.5). The Agreed Minute to this Article provides that the 'withdrawal of the military government will not prevent Israel from exercizing the powers and responsibilities not transferred to the

Council'.[57] This provision has three important implications:

(1) It emphasizes the principle that not all of the powers and responsibilities currently exercized by Israel will be transferred to
the Council.

(2) It stresses that powers and responsibilities not transferred to the
Council shall be exercized by Israel. In this context, it renders
untenable the suggestion that powers not transferred to the Council
will not necessarily lie with Israel, but may be suspended for the
duration of the interim period.

(3) It indicates that Israel retains the residual powers in the West
Bank and Gaza Strip. Thus, where no provision has been made
in relation to any specific area of authority, that area shall remain with Israel.[58]

Accordingly, Israel's jurisdiction in the West Bank and Gaza Strip
shall encompass the following: a) Israelis wherever they may be; b)
the Israeli settlements; c) military locations; and d) any functional
issue which has not been transferred to the Palestinian Council.[59]

Regarding legislative powers, the same general principles outlined
above in relation to the jurisdiction of the PISGA will apply in
relation to its legislative powers. Article IX provides that the Council will be empowered to legislate 'within all authorities transferred
to it'. Accordingly, the Council shall not be authorized to legislate
in fields which have not been transferred to its authority. Legislative powers in such areas will remain with Israel. Moreover, even
within the spheres of authority transferred to the Council, the power
to legislate must be exercised 'in accordance with the Interim Agreement'. Thus, the IA may limit the exercise of this power by, for
example, requiring Israeli affirmation for legislation promulgated
by the Council in order to enter into force.[60] It should be noted
that the power to legislate is vested in the Council itself. Israel
rejected the proposal that legislative powers be vested in an independent legislator, to avoid the possibility that such a separation
of powers might be construed as an attribute of independence.[61] As
regards existing legislation, Article IX.2 provides that laws and military
orders in spheres not transferred to the Council, shall be reviewed
jointly by the parties. The provision emphasizes that the legislation
promulgated by the IMG shall remain in force in the territories in
relation to areas of authority that it retains, although Israel is prepared to review such legislation together with the Council and to
consider its suggestions.[62]

Regarding security in the interim period, the security principles contained in the DoP provide more clarity than those included in the Camp David Accords, which provided only that the parties would negotiate an agreement including arrangements for assuring internal and external security and public order, but gave no indication of which party would be responsible for these spheres. Article VIII of the DoP establishes the following principles in relation to security and public order.

First, the PISGA will be responsible, by means of a strong police force, for guaranteeing 'public order and internal security for the Palestinians of the West Bank and Gaza Strip'.[63] From the mandate of the Palestinian police force as expressed in Article VIII it is clear that it is only intended to be responsible for the protection of Palestinians, and not of Israelis, who will remain under Israeli jurisdiction. However, instilling respect for law and order in the autonomous areas will be amongst the toughest tasks the new Palestinian administration will face. Life under Israeli occupation produced a distinct sub-culture with its own *modus vivendi*. Abuses of human rights, particularly in the Gaza Strip, include kidnapping and torture, summary execution, extortion and attacks on women for 'moral collaboration' (meaning licentiousness, prostitution and drug abuse). Many militants regard the PLO autonomous administration as an extension of Israeli occupation, so that the task of maintaining control over the population and respecting individuals' rights in face of such opposition will be a daunting task. The Palestinian police force is envisioned by the DoP to be a 'strong' force and expected to keep control of the areas by the Israelis.[64] Shlomo Gazit, former head of military intelligence, believed that self-administration would take two forms, full authority in Jericho and Gaza and limited authority in the rest of Judea and Samaria. Gazit felt that Israel

> agreed to grant full administrative rights to the Palestinian authority to be established in Gaza and Jericho – rights it obstinately refused to give until now. Even though there's no commitment as regards the next stage, the broad rights indicate Israel's intentions for the rest of Judea and Samaria.... [The] key to success will depend on the ability of the leadership to impose its will on the district... The interim stage is intended to relax tensions and create conditions for coexistence. This process is intended to create a new psychological atmosphere, one that will make it possible to progress to the permanent solution while softening the more extreme positions of both sides.[65]

In principle, Israel is responsible for the free movement and safety of Jewish settlers. How this was to work in practice was problematic, especially concerning the issues of hot pursuit and the harbouring in the autonomous areas of those suspected of violence against Israelis. A major concern for both sides was the ability and the desire of the PISGA's 'strong' police force to apprehend offenders and keep the peace. However, a note of wise caution is sounded by Gazit, when he contended that, 'if they achieve self-government . . . they will not want to lose it because someone wants to knife someone in Jerusalem or open fire on the road.'[66] Furthermore, from the Agreed Minute to Article VIII, which speaks of the transfer of powers and responsibilities to the Palestinian police force being 'accomplished in a phased manner', it is evident that this police force would not receive all of its powers immediately on the implementation of the Interim Agreement, but rather that the transfer of powers to the force would take place in stages. The number of stages, the scope of powers and responsibilities to be transferred at each stage, and the extent of the intervals between the stages, are matters that would have to be negotiated and agreed upon by both parties.[67]

Second, Israel shall remain responsible for defence against external threats. The DoP does not place any restrictions on Israel's responsibility for defence against external threats, nor is the phrase 'external threat' limited in any way. The phrase thus covers both strategic threats and low-intensity threats such as terrorist infiltrations. Israel is entitled to take all necessary measures to prevent and defend against such hostile acts coming from outside the borders of the West Bank and Gaza Strip, as well as from the sea and air. The phrase used in Article VIII that 'Israel will continue to carry . . .' is significant in that it implies a continuation of the current arrangements while the words ' . . . the responsibility' indicate that the responsibility is indivisible and rests with Israel alone.[68]

Third, Israel shall remain responsible for the 'overall security of Israelis for the purpose of safeguarding their internal security and public order'. Again in this context, the phrase 'Israel will continue to carry . . .' indicates a continuation of the current arrangements.[69] Additionally, the word 'overall' underlines the fact that the security of Israelis is to be understood in the widest possible sense.[70] These principles would obviously need significant amplification in the Interim Agreement. Among the most sensitive of the security issues which would need to be addressed in the Interim Agreement is the treatment of criminal offenders, Israeli and Palestinian, from the moment of their arrest until the completion of legal proceedings against them. Broadly there are four main scenarios:

(1) An Israeli commits an offence against an Israeli.
(2) A Palestinian commits an offence against a Palestinian.
(3) An Israeli commits an offence against a Palestinian.
(4) A Palestinian commits an offence against an Israeli.

The DoP indicates that where any criminal or security incident occurs in an Israeli settlement or military location, it will fall within Israeli jurisdiction, even if both offender and victim are Palestinian. Where the above scenarios take place in areas under Palestinian territorial jurisdiction some further thought is required. With regard to the first two scenarios, no particular difficulty arises; it seems clear that where an Israeli commits an offence against an Israeli, the handling of the matter will be exclusively Israeli responsibility. Similarly, where the offence is committed by and against a Palestinian, the responsibility will be exclusively that of the PISGA. The third scenario, where an Israeli commits an offence against a Palestinian, is more complex. The Palestinian police is responsible for the security and public order of Palestinians and it may therefore be argued that the incident should fall within its responsibility. However, the DoP makes it clear that the jurisdiction of the Council does not extend to Israelis, and therefore the handling of the matter – at least as far as the Israeli offender is concerned – remains an Israeli responsibility. It is worth noting however that there is no provision distinguishing between normal civil and criminal activity and political activity of a nature designed to inflame populations against the DoP. The fourth scenario, where a Palestinian commits an offence against an Israeli, raises the question whether Israel has authority, in relation to an event which took place in territory under Palestinian jurisdiction, to arrest a Palestinian offender, or investigate him or her, and bring to trial before an Israeli court.[71] The DoP would seem to indicate that, where the victim of the offence is an Israeli, Israel does have this authority. Israel is entrusted with responsibility in relation to the security of Israelis by Article VIII, which states that Israel will 'continue to carry . . . the responsibility for overall security of Israelis'. The phrase 'continue to carry' implies a continuation of the current arrangements in this regard, while the word 'overall' indicates that the responsibility is to be understood in the broadest sense. Moreover, the Agreed

Minute to Article IV limits the Council's jurisdiction to those powers specifically transferred to it. Since responsibility for internal security and public order of Israelis remains with Israel, the Council therefore has no jurisdiction in the matter.[72]

Regarding the redeployment of Israeli Forces, Article XIII provides that 'after the entry into force of the Declaration of Principles, and not later than the eve of the elections for the Council, a redeployment of Israeli military forces in the West Bank and Gaza Strip will take place'. This redeployment is different in nature from the 'withdrawal' from the Gaza Strip and Jericho area referred to in Article XIV. Rather than requiring a removal of any forces from the territories, redeployment is intended to ensure a redistribution of forces within the territories, having regard to the general principle stated in Article XIII.2 that 'military forces should be redeployed outside populated areas'. That the redeployment is not intended to involve the transfer of forces outside the occupied territories is also underscored by Article XIII.3 which speaks of redeployment 'to specified locations'. Locations within Israel would not need to be specified.[73] While Article XIII provides that a redeployment of forces was due to take place prior to the eve of elections for the Palestinian Council, the DoP did not suggest that the process of redeployment be completed by that date. Rather, Article XIII.3 provides that 'further redeployments to specified locations will be gradually implemented commensurate with the assumption of responsibility for public order and internal security by the Palestinian police.'[74] Thus the process of redeployment is intended to continue through the interim period, its pace being dictated by the extent to which the assumption of security responsibilities by the Palestinian police makes such redeployment possible.[75] Other than Article XIII.1, 2 & 3, Israeli withdrawal and redeployment is dealt with in several parts of the DoP, such as Article XIV and Annex II pertaining to it. Redeployment and withdrawal are emotive words and have been used extensively for propaganda purposes particularly for their psychological impact. Under the terms of the DoP the IDF was intended merely to redeploy to areas within the occupied territories. Yitzhak Rabin asked in a speech in Knesset session,

> what did we insist on? . . . We insisted that Jerusalem would not be included in the framework of the interim agreement . . . Jerusalem remains under Israel's sovereignty and is Israel's unified capital. The settlements remain . . . Every agreement that concerns an

arrangement with the Palestinians on the establishment of the transitional period – the interim arrangement, autonomy – is then subject to change if it is violated significantly . . . I am telling you, at this stage and in the future a partial withdrawal in Gaza is better than the evacuation of the Golan Heights.

Rabin also mentioned that 'I do not want, and I said as much during the election campaign, to annex 1.8 to 2 million Palestinians and turn the State of Israel into a binational state.'[76] While the Labour Party's 1992 election platform categorically rejected the establishment of a Palestinian state west of the Jordan River, however, Arafat is on record as saying that the DoP constitutes 'an initial step that spells out the ground rules governing the interim solution, as well as the basic components of the final solution, which must result in the dismantlement of the occupation and the complete withdrawal of occupation troops from our land, holy places, and holy Jerusalem.' He also said that the most important aspect of the DoP is 'not that the Israelis will withdraw from Gaza and Jericho, but rather the acknowledgement that the jurisdiction of the Palestinian authority covers all occupied Palestinian territories'.[77]

Regarding displaced persons, Article XII, dealing with arrangements for liaison and cooperation between Israel, the Council, Jordan and Egypt, provides that these arrangements would include the constitution of a 'Continuing Committee that will decide by agreement on the modalities of admission of persons displaced from the West Bank and Gaza Strip in 1967, together with necessary measures to prevent disruption and disorder.'[78] This wording, taken directly from the Camp David Accords, is significant in that it indicates that the modalities for the admission of displaced persons can only be implemented along with those measures necessary to prevent disruption and disorder.[79] It should also be noted that the Continuing Committee was only intended to deal with those persons displaced from the West Bank and Gaza Strip in 1967, which in itself would be a contentious point not least concerning the actual number of *bona fide* refugees. For example one Jordanian assessment of the numbers of 1967 refugees was 530 129.[80] The question of the refugees arising in 1948 was not to be considered by this committee, but rather was designated by Article V as an issue to be included in the permanent status negotiations. In this context, it should be noted that Article V does not limit the issue to be discussed to Arab refugees, the permanent status negotiations may equally focus on the large number of Jews who were forced to flee to Israel from neighbouring Arab states. Nor does Article V give any indication as to the manner in which the refugee issue should be resolved. As with all issues to be included in the permanent status negotiations, all options remain open.

Regarding the resolution of disputes, Article XV deals with the procedure to be followed in order to resolve disputes arising out of the application or implementation of agreements during the interim period. Article XV.1 provides that such disputes 'shall be resolved through the Joint Liaison Committee (JLC)'. This committee, established under Article X, was intended to 'deal with issues requiring coordination, other issues of common interest, and disputes'. Where the JLC is unsuccessful at resolving the dispute, there is no mandatory next step. Article XV.2 provides that 'disputes which cannot be settled by negotiation may be resolved by a mechanism of conciliation to be agreed between the parties.' The use of the phrase 'may be resolved' clearly indicates that this is a voluntary proceeding, while the fact that the method of reconciliation is 'to be agreed by the parties' indicates that there must be an agreement between the parties both as to the need for conciliation and as to the appropriate forum and procedures. Where conciliation fails, Article XV provides that 'the parties may agree to submit to arbitration' the outstanding dispute. Once again, the word 'may' indicates a voluntary proceeding. Similarly, from the second part of the sub-article, which provides for the establishment of an Arbitration Committee 'upon the agreement of both parties', it is clear that there must be agreement between the parties both as to the need for arbitration and as to the appropriate forum and procedures.[81] Finally, it should be noted that the mechanisms proposed by Article XV relate only to disputes 'relating to the interim period'. Disputes relating to the permanent status arrangements shall be resolved only through negotiations. This principle is stated in the letter of the PLO Chairman to the Israeli Prime Minister dated 9 September 1993 – ' . . . all outstanding issues relating to permanent status will be resolved through negotiations.'[82] The DoP calls for the establishment of four joint committees for the resolution of disputes: (a) the Joint Israeli-Palestinian Liaison Committee; (b) the Israeli-Palestinian Continuing Committee for Economic Cooperation; (c) Continuing Committee (with Egypt and Jordan to review the refugee problem); and (d) the Joint Israeli-Palestinian Coordination and Cooperation Committee for mutual security purposes.[83]

The most striking thing about these committees is that they seem to operate above the jurisdiction of the Palestinian self-governing authority. It will probably be in the hands of these committees that real power will lie. Important decisions will be channelled through them, highlighting the extent of the democratic nature of the PISGA, and the inability of the Palestinians to operate as equals. The PISGA will be like a municipal council, while real authority rests with the Israeli government. The DoP could be seen as having a pyramidal structure, the apex being the government of Israel, on the next level the joint committees, then the Palestinian authority and at the bottom would be the Palestinian people in the occupied territories.[84]

Regarding the Gaza-Jericho arrangements it appears that the idea that separate arrangements should be instituted in the Gaza Strip and Jericho area was based on the common belief that an agreement in these areas might be easier to reach than one which includes the rest of the West Bank. This was so because problems relating to such issues as security, water resources, Jewish population and holy places in these areas are less complex. The agreement of the Palestinians to discuss a transfer of powers in a specified part of the territories represented a significant change from their previous stance of all or nothing. It seemed that they agreed to such an arrangement because Israel agreed to transfer more powers in these areas and transfer them more quickly, than in the rest of the territories.

Negotiations on the special arrangements to apply in the Gaza Strip and Jericho Area, including the early withdrawal of the IDF from these areas, began immediately on the entry into force of the DoP. As indicated in Annex II, the aim of these negotiations was to conclude and sign an agreement on the Gaza-Jericho arrangement within two months of the entry into force of the DoP (in fact 13 December 1993), with the early withdrawal of the IDF being completed within four months from the signing of this agreement (in other words by 13 April 1994). However, the two-month target for concluding an agreement was not accomplished, and the four-month period for completing the withdrawal therefore did not end on 13 April 1994, but rather was intended for 4 September 1994, four months from the date such an agreement was signed, that is 4 May 1994.[85]

The DoP addressed the Gaza-Jericho agreement in Article XIV and in Annex II, together with the Agreed Minute to that Annex. Among the subjects to be covered in the Gaza-Jericho agreement are the following.

Withdrawal of Israeli forces

Article XIV provides that 'Israel will withdraw from the Gaza Strip and Jericho Area, as detailed in . . . Annex II'. Annex II provides that the withdrawal of the IDF was due to commence immediately with the signing of the Gaza-Jericho agreement. Unlike the 'redeployment' due to take place in the rest of the territories, this withdrawal would involve the removal of forces from these areas, though not all of the IDF forces were to be withdrawn. Indeed, a Palestinian proposal to use the phrase *'withdrawal of all Israeli military forces'* in Annex II.2 was rejected.[86] Moreover, that some Israeli forces would continue to be present in the Gaza Strip and Jericho Area is clear from a number of other provisions of the DoP:

1. The Agreed Minute to Annex II provides that even after the withdrawal of the IDF, 'Israel will continue to be responsible for external security, and for internal security and public order of settlements and Israelis.' It is evident therefore that those Israeli forces required to fulfil this responsibility will remain in the Gaza Strip and Jericho Area.[87]

2. The Agreed Minute to Annex II also provides that 'Israeli military forces . . . may continue to use roads freely within the Gaza Strip and Jericho area.' Clearly, those military forces making use of the roads in these areas will not have been withdrawn.[88]

3. Article XIII, dealing with the redeployment of forces in the West Bank and Gaza Strip on the eve of elections, states that this redeployment was to take place 'in addition to withdrawal of forces carried out in accordance with Article XIV'. Since the withdrawal of the IDF from the Gaza Strip and Jericho Area was due to take place before the elections, it follows that the DoP envisages, that subsequent to the withdrawal, there must be some remaining forces in those areas and it is these which will be redeployed. As noted above, the principle guiding this redeployment was not that military forces be removed from these areas, but rather that they 'should be redeployed outside populated areas' (Article XIII.2).[89]

Jericho area

While there was little difficulty ascertaining the extent of the area known as the Gaza Strip, the size of the Jericho area was the subject of some controversy. In this context it should be noted that in the negotiations leading to the signing of the DoP, Jericho was always regarded by the parties as a limited and symbolic addition to the

'Gaza first' plan. Moreover, the reason why Jericho in particular was found acceptable was precisely because no Jewish settlements were located in the immediate vicinity of the city. In line with the above, a Palestinian suggestion to refer to the former Jordanian province of Jericho was rejected. In the course of the negotiations on the DoP however, Israel agreed to consider the inclusion of two adjacent refugee camps – Aquabat Jabber and Ein El Sultan – which led to the use of the term 'Jericho area' instead of *'Jericho city'*.[90]

Establishment of a Palestinian Authority (PA)

Annex II of the DoP provides that powers and responsibilities transferred by Israel in these areas would be exercised by a Palestinian authority. This would be an appointed body since the early withdrawal from the Gaza Strip and Jericho Area would take place before the elections. The offices of the PA were to be located in the Gaza Strip and Jericho Area (Annex II, Article 5).[91] A number of limitations were placed on the scope of the powers and responsibilities of the PA. In particular, Article VI.1 provides that authority would be transferred to 'authorized Palestinians' preparatory to the 'inauguration of the Council'. It would appear from this that the Palestinians authorized were to be selected by the PLO and then approved by Israel.[92] Annex II, Article 3b provides that the PA would have no powers or responsibilities in relation to 'external security, settlements, Israelis, foreign relations, and mutually agreed matters'. Thus the notion of withdrawal actually amounts to a redeployment outside populated areas. Annex II.3b specifies that these powers and responsibilities should not encompass external security or foreign relations, Israeli settlements or Israelis. These powers were therefore not territorial but personal, relating to Palestinians alone, excluding foreigners and Israelis, which is everyone else in the world except Palestinians.[93] Moreover, unlike the elected Council, there is no reference in the DoP to the PA in the Gaza Strip and Jericho area having legislative powers. In practice however Israel indicated its willingness to transfer legislative powers to the PA within its jurisdiction, in order to enable it to fulfil its functions effectively.[94] In exercizing these functions, the jurisdiction of the PA was also to be subject to the same limitations on territorial, personal and functional jurisdiction as the council, contained in the Agreed Minute to Article IV. This principle is explicitly stated in Section A of the Agreed Minutes, which provides: 'Any powers and responsibilities transferred to the Palestinians . . . prior to the inauguration of the Council will be subject to the same principles pertaining to Article IV, as set out in these Agreed Minutes below.'[95]

Security and public order

In order to fulfil the Palestinian responsibility for internal security and public order, Annex II provides for the establishment of a Palestinian police force. At the same time, Annex II and the Agreed Minute to this Annex make it clear that this police force would have no authority in relation to external security, nor in relation to internal security and public order of settlements and Israelis. All of these were to remain areas of Israeli responsibility. The withdrawal of Israeli forces from the Gaza Strip and Jericho Area cannot derogate from these responsibilities.[96] Moreover, according to Annex II.3f concerning the 'Emergency Fund', it may be deduced that this fund was in fact intended as a security fund to be provided by international donors to pay for the budget of the Palestinian police, its agencies, equipment and its intelligence branch. One of the most worrying aspects concerning the setting up of the police force was its lack of accountability to any Palestinian authority, or other body, in the stage before an elected Palestinian Council emerged. In essence what emerged was that the police force was subordinate only to Arafat's authority and was run independently of any direct collective Palestinian responsibility, a trend that continued after the Council's election. The nature of the nascent Palestinian authority was therefore undemocratic, unaccountable, and ultimately unstable, as this important factor was either overlooked or ignored.[97] The existence of concurrent Israeli and Palestinian responsibilities would give rise to number of practical complexities. Thus, Annex II provides for the establishment of a joint Coordination and Co-operation Committee for mutual security purposes (Annex II, Article 3e). This committee was designed to coordinate the allocation of security responsibilities, and serve as the mechanism for cooperation in matters of mutual security concern.[98]

Safe passage

Annex II, Article 3g provides that the Gaza-Jericho agreement would contain arrangements for 'a safe passage for persons and transportation between the Gaza Strip and Jericho area'. The use of the words 'safe passage', as opposed to the idea of 'free passage', was significant in that it indicated that Israel's obligation was limited to ensuring the security of the passage. There is nothing in the

DoP to support the suggestion that an extra-territorial corridor was envisaged. In fact, the phrase 'safe passage for persons and transportation' indicated that a personal rather than a territorial right was envisaged. In addition, it would be hard to sustain an argument for Palestinian jurisdiction when such jurisdiction, under Article IV only extends to 'West Bank and Gaza territory'.[99] Indeed, Israel proposed that the implementation of its obligation to ensure safe passage be carried out through the use of not one, but a number of roads crossing Israel.[100]

Passages between Gaza and Egypt and between Jericho and Jordan

The Gaza-Jericho agreement would also include arrangements for coordination regarding passages between Gaza and Egypt and between Jericho and Jordan, as provided for in Annex II, Article 4.[101] The arrangements to be agreed in this regard must be consistent with Israel's responsibilities for foreign relations and external security. Such issues as entry of foreign nationals, visas, passports, and so on are essential aspects of foreign relations, while control of the border crossings is an integral part of the control of the borders, which, in turn is an integral part of external security. It would make no sense for Israel to retain control along the length of the borders for security reasons, without at the same time having control over persons passing through the border crossings. Not only was this an issue over the control of persons who may pose a threat to Israel's internal security, but it was also a question of sovereignty. The emotive issue of land dramatically affects the negotiations, as well as affecting the perception of how fair the process has been. Land and borders define status, however it should also be noted that in Article V of the DoP the issue of borders is listed among the issues to be included in the final status negotiations and that the issue was not to be determined in the interim period.[102]

Status of Gaza Strip and Jericho Area

During the interim period, the status of the Gaza Strip and Jericho Area was to be identical to that of the West Bank. This principle is emphasized in Article IV, which states: 'The two sides view the West Bank and the Gaza Strip as a single territorial unit, whose integrity will be preserved during the interim period.'[103] In addition, Annex II, Article 6 provides that the status of the Gaza Strip and Jericho Area will 'continue to be an integral part of the West Bank and Gaza Strip, and will not be changed in the interim period'.[104] It follows that, as in the case of the West Bank, the status of the Gaza Strip and Jericho Area will continue to be that of areas subject to military government, with Israel remaining the source of authority (see page 184 above). Two additional important principles are enshrined in Annex II, Article 6: firstly, that any attempt made by the parties to change the status of the Gaza Strip and Jericho Area during the interim period will have no effect; and secondly, that any such attempt would be a clear breach of the terms of the DoP, which may be considered a material breach and therefore grounds for terminating the DoP.[105]

The principle of early empowerment was to be provided for by the implementation of special arrangements in the Gaza Strip and Jericho Area agreement. Article VI of the DoP provides for a preparatory transfer of powers and responsibilities with regard to five specific spheres in the rest of the West Bank. The transfer of powers and responsibilities was due to commence on the completion of the withdrawal from the Gaza Strip and Jericho Area. In particular, Article VI.2 provides that, immediately after the withdrawal, authority would be transferred to the Palestinians in the spheres of education and culture, health, social welfare, direct taxation and tourism. Other than these transferred areas of authority, the IMG and ICA will continue to fulfil all of their existing functions pending the inauguration of the Council, though as Article VI.2 notes, the transfer of additional powers and responsibilities may be negotiated between the parties.[106]

In the complex transfer of power between the PLO and Israel and the creation of limited Palestinian autonomy in Gaza and Jericho, the focus of attention was mainly on the difficult and often violent issues which surround the issue of security. However, hardly noticed amid the *brouhaha*, there emerged among the supporters of the DoP a shared conventional wisdom which held that the DoP would be the harbinger of a high degree of economic cooperation which would be the panacea for all the region's ills. Close coordination and cooperation, especially between the nascent Palestinian entity and Israel, was universally heralded as the touchstone which would lead to a wider regional structure of economic cooperation, if not integration, using the European Union as the model. This hypothesis assumed that close Israeli-Palestinian economic cooperation was the key not only to regional stability, but also to anchoring the DoP in the realities of economic infrastructures and gaining acceptance from previously sceptical populations. There was widespread use of the analogy of peace-making between France and West Germany, where the past was buried in the rapprochement which led to the eventual formation of the EEC. However, European economic integration started with economies and peoples which were at a comparable stage of industrial and technological development and which enjoyed similar political institutions and traditions. By contrast, Israel and the Palestinians are at very different stages in economic development. Economic standards and infrastructure, political traditions, institutions and civil society are all as widely disparate as those between France and Algeria. Economic integration between Israel's developed economy and the West Bank and Gaza Strip would more likely create a new mode of Palestinian dependency and would be a very unequal partnership. The uneven and unequal relationship which has existed for the past thirty years and more would be perpetuated and thus cause a continuation along the same lines, which would be both detrimental to the Israeli and Palestinian economies and to the emerging relationship between the two which was meant to be based on a desire to redirect the history of conflict which previously existed.[107]

All development for the autonomous entities was to be funnelled through the Palestinian Economic Council for Development and Reconstruction (PECDAR), headed by someone appointed by Arafat, and the joint Palestinian-Israeli Economic Cooperation Committee, even though, according to the DoP, both sides would 'coordinate and cooperate jointly and unilaterally with regional and international parties to support these aims'.[108] A study by Israeli journalist Asher Davidi quoted Dov Lautman, president of the Israeli Manufacturers Association, as saying: 'It's not important whether there will be a Palestinian state, autonomy, or a Palestinian-Jordanian state. The economic borders between Israel and the territories must remain open.'[109] According to Said, Israel, with its well developed institutions, close relations with the US, burgeoning relations with Asia, aggressivity and economic drive, would be in a very good position to dominate the territories economically, maybe as far as keeping them in a state of permanent dependency. Exploiting the new political benefits of the peace process, Israel then could move to exploit and dominate the Arab economies in the region.[110] As evidence of this theory, Dajani cites Annex IV, the 'Protocol on Israeli-Palestinian Cooperation Concerning Regional Development Programmes', which relates to the reference in Article XVI concerning the promoting of a kind of regional Marshall Plan. The relegation of this protocol to an Annex, Dajani feels, was to mask its significance, for this protocol outlines that the entire process of development was contingent on joint action by the two sides and places development funds in a joint framework, which may be seen as subordinating Palestinian development to Israeli control. The same process was evident in the protocol on Israeli-Palestinian economic cooperation of Annex III, subjecting all decisions to a joint economic committee. Many Palestinians feared that either dangerous and/or dirty environmental industries may be located in Gaza as indicated in Annex III.2, 3 and 7, or that the primary beneficiary under joint committees for items such as capital earmarked for building industrial projects would be Israel.[111]

It is a fair statement that 'Economic dependency has political consequences.'[112] Unbridled Israeli economic hype about an '*economy of peace*' has made many Palestinians wary and suspicious that their former enemy was going to perpetuate economic control after a phased redeployment of its armed forces.[113] In an article in the Israeli newspaper *Ha'aretz*, on 19 September 1993, former deputy mayor of Jerusalem Meron Benvenisti wrote that up to that point, Israeli exploitation, discrimination and domination in the Occupied Territories had been justified as necessary for security, nationalistic-political, or even altruistic reasons. Now a new dictionary was being compiled to justify the self-same policies and enrich the same elements [of society], but the arguments would be reversed: it's all for the good of the Palestinians, it's all for the success of peace, it's all so that the Palestinians will finally understand what their fathers refused to understand – that the Zionist enterprise is here to rescue them from the morass of hardship and backwardness – and they must be eternally grateful.[114] Benvenisti argued that the

> best route to a new chapter in Israeli-Palestinian relations would allow the painful process of Palestinian nation-building to proceed with a minimal Israeli presence. The Palestinians should be empowered to develop their economy and society with as few links to Israel as possible . . . Palestinian development and reconstruction should be a joint Arab project.

Thus assistance would mobilize Arab public support for the Israeli-Palestinian accord and legitimize not only the DoP but also the Madrid multilateral process which was ongoing in regional terms.

There is much opposition in the Arab world to the Israeli-Palestinian peace, and the process wholly depends on people being able to see tangible and significant improvements in their living conditions, such as those economic assistance and investment can provide. Continued Israeli economic paramountcy in the territories may well seek to further the cause of those opposed to the DoP by playing on the resentment of a people who know dependence, for manual work in Israel, for produce, for social inequality and for the kind of vulnerability brought by exposure to natural Israeli fears which have security reasons but which result in the closure of the territories and curfews.[115]

Elsewhere, Article VII.4 provides for an admirable list of authorities to be established in order to promote the economic situation of the two entities, especially of Gaza, such as: electricity, a sea port, a bank and export promotion among other things. However, of the five spheres transferred to the PISGA, economic matters fell outside their competency, though these aspects may have been constituted at a later date and placed under the jurisdiction of the joint economic committee as indicated in Annex III.[116] Normalization of revenue-raising structures would have to be done as the authority could not hope to exist as an international charity case for too long, for many and obvious reasons. Questions therefore had to be raised regarding the financing of the self-governing process. Under Article VI.2, direct taxation would be one of the responsibilities transferred to the Palestinians, which would mean in practice primarily income taxes. While income taxes constitute a heavy burden on wage earners and salaried workers, a burden borne almost entirely by this group, the fact is that the most important source of revenue-raising for any government in developing countries is indirect taxation such as customs fees and taxes on consumer goods.[117] There are also two main factors to be mindful of here that would constitute possible areas of friction which may have led to unrest, namely: unemployment was estimated to be running at around 60 per cent in the Gaza Strip, precluding the ability to raise much revenue from those currently working, and secondly, there was the refrain the US would have known only too well, '*No taxation without representation*'.

Keeping indirect taxes outside the jurisdiction of the Council meant that the Israelis would maintain a high profile where such taxes were collected. Moreover, the fact that the authority for direct taxation would be transferred to the Palestinians still does not preclude Israel from levying taxes. According to the Agreed Minutes Article VI.2 and 3:

> Each of the [five] spheres... will continue to enjoy existing budgetary allocations in accordance with arrangements to be mutually agreed upon. These arrangements also will provide for the necessary adjustments required in order to take into account the taxes collected by the direct taxation office.[118]

The 'direct taxation office' referred to is, of course, Israeli; it is from the government budget of Israel that allocations to the five spheres would come. This means that it is the direct taxes levied by the Council that would constitute an additional burden on the Palestinian taxpayer, a possible area of resentment for a burden to be endured.[119]

However it is still too early to conclude that Israelis will be freely wandering Arab capitals setting up deals and dominating the entire Middle Eastern economy. What can be concluded was that it appeared that economic aid for Palestine was being supervized and controlled by the US, bypassing the UN, some of whose agencies, such as UNWRA and UNDP, were better placed to administer aid monies. Also excluded from being formally incorporated in the Israeli-Palestinian peace process was the World Bank. The IRDB, which would demand stringent accountability, is the main source of financial aid for projects in the developing world, and it was hoped by sponsors of the peace process that it would constitute a major investment vehicle for the directing and disbursement of monies to the autonomous areas. However, the bank faced a potentially problematic obstacle to the actual production of assistance, that the bank could only lend monies to projects in the territory of a member state and that such loans had to be guaranteed by a government. The Palestinian autonomous areas were not members of the bank and there was no 'Palestinian government' able to guarantee the repayment of any such loans. A possible solution to this hurdle was the proposal of the creation of a free-trade area comprising Israel, the occupied territories and Jordan, in order to promote economic cooperation as well as promoting stability. Eytan Gilboa, professor of international relations at Hebrew University, said that Israel would be unable to rely simply on the generosity of the US taxpayer forever, and that a greater effort would be 'required to mobilize financial resources from the oil-rich states in the gulf and from Europe and Japan.'[120] Israel's relatively high-tech economy is more attuned to European than to Middle Eastern markets and labour costs in Israel are consequently higher than the majority of Middle Eastern counterparts. Amnon Rubin, senior director of economic-policy issues at the Bank of Israel, pointed out that after 14 years of peace with Egypt, Israel's exports to Egypt were a mere $7m in 1992.[121] Sounding a word of much-needed caution was Shimon Shetreet, Israeli Economic and Planning Minister, who said that 'Hamas thrives on poverty, distress and bad social conditions.'[122] Thus the nature of the Israeli-Palestinian agreement was that Arafat's PLO, in order to maintain a dialogue with the Israeli government would have to be given resources to invest in economic and social projects. Therefore although Europe, the US and Japan all had economic difficulties and other worthy commitments, one mitigating factor in favour of financing the DoP was that the populations and geographic areas were small. There are five million Israelis and 1.5 million Palestinians in the West Bank and Gaza Strip. Economies were therefore on a similarly modest scale, especially when one compared aid to Palestine with the aid necessary to revitalize the former USSR.[123]

Permanent status negotiations

Article V.2 of the DoP provides that permanent status negotiations were to commence 'as soon as possible, but not later than the beginning of the third year of the interim period.'[124] This was with a view to implementing the permanent status arrangements at the conclusion of the of the five year transitional period. This proved a very important point of contention as it meant that final status issues could be raised immediately. Unlike the interim arrangements, for which the DoP gives extensive guidelines, the DoP is conspicuously silent about the form the permanent status negotiations would take. The list of issues provided in Article V.3 to be included in the permanent status negotiations, Jerusalem, refugees, settlements, security arrangements, borders, relations and cooperation with other neighbours, and other issues of common interest is not inclusive. Neither the inclusion of an issue in the list contained in Article V.3, nor its non-inclusion, should be taken as any indication of the outcome of the permanent status negotiations. In fact, the principle that all options should be left open is explicitly stated in Article V.4, 'The two parties agree that the outcome of the permanent status negotiations should not be prejudiced or preempted by

agreements reached for the interim period.'[125] While the permanent status negotiations are not to be influenced by agreements for
the interim period, they will be subject to the principles which
form the basis of the current peace process.[126] Thus, Article I re-
states the fact that the permanent status settlement shall be based
on UN SCRs 242 and 338 (although 242 is subject to differing interpretations), while the preamble reflects the letter of invitation
to the Madrid peace conference in speaking of the attempt to 'achieve
a just, lasting and comprehensive peace settlement.'[127]

It will at this stage be instructive to ask some questions concerning the permanent status negotiations. What are the guarantees
that the series of intracommittee and extracommittee negotiations
will lead to a final agreement, and what happens if they do not?
The five-year time limit, like everything else pertaining to the DoP,
is in principle. Only treaties are binding, and only states can conclude treaties. The DoP is neither a treaty nor an international
resolution supported by international organizations, it is simply a
declaration. Article XV.1 refers to the potentiality of disputes arising, and refers such disputes to the establishment of mechanisms
for conciliation and arbitration, for example the Joint Liaison Committee. Such recourse does not extend however beyond the interim
period into the final status negotiations. If reconciliation cannot
be achieved, according to Article XV.3 'the parties will establish an
Arbitration Committee,' the nature and structure of which will be
decided through negotiations.[128] The inclusion of this provision is
probably as a result of Israeli experience during its negotiations
with Egypt over Taba, where the parties after some eight years of
negotiation finally resolved their dispute over a single square
kilometre. The Israeli lesson learned was that they lost when the
issue spent two years at international arbitration.[129]

There is no word in the DoP about recourse to external arbitration in the event of failure of the negotiations, nor of penalties for
failure. The DoP provides for a series of negotiations during the
interim period, but is silent on the parallel and unilateral process
of Israeli legislation. Article V.4 provides that 'the two parties agree
that the outcome of the permanent status negotiations should not
be prejudiced or preempted by agreements reached for the interim
period.'[130] Only arrangements for the interim period are mentioned,
there is no word about the changes which can be effected through
legislation or by *faits accomplis*. The DoP contains no Israeli commitments on settlements, expropriations, confiscations, new link

roads, demolitions, taxation, movement of individuals, and so on. The DoP therefore makes it difficult from a Palestinian point of view to challenge Israel's future legislation, indeed even to challenge as they did in the past Israeli laws pertaining to the violation of rights and liberties on the basis of the 4th Geneva Convention regarding occupying powers. No safeguard remains against Israeli administrative or legislative measures that can in effect undermine the self-governing process. It seems that the PLO was not aware that through its unconditional recognition of Israel, it can be argued that the PLO actually affirmed Israel's sovereignty beyond the 1949 and 1967 borders. Thus Israel can claim the redefinition of her borders as they are extant, through the provisions of the Rhodes armistice agreement – especially the agreement signed between Israel and Jordan on 3 April 1949, UN Security Council Resolution's 242 and 338, and the 1974 Disengagement Agreement (though Jordan didn't sign an agreement with Israel because of the Rabat decision to recognize the PLO as the sole legitimate representative of the PLO). Regarding UN Resolution 242, in paragraph 1(ii), there is a call to respect the sovereignty, territorial integrity and political independence of every 'state' in the area.[131] This may cause the Palestinians problems from recidivist Jordanian claims on the West Bank which was annexed by her in April 1950. Not constituting a state means that the Israelis could claim that the resolution doesn't apply to the West Bank, and although the PLO may counter citing Article IV of the DoP which provides that the West Bank and Gaza Strip constitute a 'single territorial unit, whose integrity will be preserved during the interim period' this only pertains to the interim negotiations and does not apply to final status talks.[132] The PLO's acceptance of Resolution 242 as the basis for permanent negotiations (DoP Article I) could severely compromise the legal status of the West Bank because since 1988 the territory has ceased to be regarded or claimed as part of an existing state, which means legally it is almost in a kind of limbo status. Therefore it can be concluded that UN Resolution 242's applicability to the occupied territories is equivocal and vague, pertaining to a set of situations as they existed in 1967; indeed it is devoid of even any reference to the Palestinians, their rights, land or status.[133]

3.3   *Genesis – Il sera une progression chaotique*: analysis of the Declaration of Principles as an example of conflict resolution

Whether or not the negotiating process is about breaking the matrix of hate remains to be seen, what is certain is that the fires of enmity cool slowly. The forces of history may cool the passions with bold leadership and decisive diplomacy, but in reality in the case of ingrained historic hatreds, true and lasting change can only come from the volition of the parties involved. When the cost of hatred is deemed too high then peace becomes possible. Haim Ramon, then-Israeli Minister of Health stated he believed that the DoP peace process was irreversible, and that through reaching agreement both sides had crossed the Rubicon.[134] The nature of crossing the Rubicon is that once crossed, the distance that once was deemed too great becomes in retrospect quite small. The demolition of the Berlin Wall, the repealing of apartheid laws in South Africa and the relatively free and fair elections in Cambodia and in Eastern Europe are testament to the will of people to change once perceived certainties.

For many, the DoP represents the culmination of a process of reconciliation based on compromise, namely the acceptance by both sides, of each other and of the principles of political partition and territorial compromise as the basis both for the settlement of the conflict and for peaceful coexistence. Thus the DoP is heralded as the triumph of pragmatism.[135] Such an opinion contends that the abandonment of territorial exclusivity and partisan ideological justification for the claim to the patrimony, as the source of national identity, came more from the dawning realization that both sides could not, for various reasons, expect the other to disappear. However, the question has oft been posed, What is the alternative? To those who suffer misgivings, this is a good question if it were not asked so often in the rhetorical sense. Palestinian objectors demand to know if the Palestinians are to be ruled by predetermined agreements arrived at in secret? To such people alternatives only appear by default, their having been locked out of the political process and therefore denied the courtesy of providing their collective assent. The *intifada* highlighted the drawbacks of division, where distant leaders bereft of ideas and strategies, were only reinvigorated by events 1500 miles away. The principle of the *intifada* for many ordinary Palestinians was that responsibility for the Palestinian polity was to be determined collectively.[136]

Like any 'momentous' historic occasion, the DoP did not come out of the blue. For many it was a surprise, but many events previously had led to the fostering of an atmosphere which was favourable enough to provide for such an agreement. The signposts along the way also allowed the observer of the region to conclude that there was something happening. For example, the closure of the territories in March 1993 by the Israeli government intended to reinforce in the minds of the Israeli public the separateness of the occupied territories and to return Israel to the notion of the Green Line division prior to any announcement regarding changes to the governance of the occupied territories. The DoP resembles in many respects the 'Camp David Frameworks for Peace', of 17 September 1978, signed by Sadat and Begin and witnessed by Carter in Thurmont, Maryland. Much of the timetable and the objectives of the DoP closely follow that which was envisioned by this earlier process.[137]

The genesis of the DoP could be said to have many birth dates, but the international situation which prevailed in 1992–3 was certainly favourable to the DoP being concluded. What transpired from the DoP was not really anything new materially. What was new was the mutual desire of both sides to conclude a political settlement, however imperfect. The reason the DoP was signed in 1993 was because all the variables which had precluded progress in the past had fallen in such a way as to provide an opportunity for compromise. Whilst the more lyrically minded may wax that 'where ever there is a clash between right and right, a value higher than right ought to prevail, and this value is life itself',[138] the reason it never happened before was precisely because the conditions were not ripe for progress. The 'historic' achievement of the DoP has as much to do with the vagaries of fortune as with design. Positive progress was achieved owing to a series of milestones which in a sense dictated policies and stances taken. External and internal events suffused to create the necessary chemistry for success. There are three possible birth dates for the present peace process.

(1) 14 December 1988 – the date of Arafat's renunciation of terrorism and the implicit recognition of the State of Israel, which added to the political pressure on Israel following from the outbreak of the *intifada* and allowed the US administration under Bush to distance the USA from Israel politically.

(2) 2 August 1990 – a date which changed the political landscape of the Middle East and eventually provided the USA with the

unprecedented political ability to exercise pressure over regional protagonists.

(3) 23 June 1992 – the day Rabin formed a new government, changing the Israeli domestic political scene in favour of finding accommodation with the Palestinians. My preference for the third date is due more to it being the final necessary precondition for progress in negotiations.

The DoP was formally begun with the mutual recognition pact symbolized by the signing and exchange of letters. The letter from the leader of the PLO recognized Israel's right to exist, renounced violence and declared 'inoperative and no longer valid' those articles of the Palestinian national covenant which pertained to territory, Jews, armed struggle, renunciation of Israel and the rejection of the compromise of the Charter's aims.[139] The breakthrough in the peace process was the result less of altruism than of simple pragmatism. The Norway Channel produced the required trust to impel PM Rabin and Arafat to take the first and most important step, mutual recognition. This was the *sine qua non* of the agreement.

One must be honest and accept that most inhabitants of Israel and the occupied territories will not have read and studied the full text of the DoP. They will have received their information from many diverse sources, from newspaper synopses, from television reports, from radio commentaries and from word of mouth. Support for the DoP will be based on instinctive reactions and environment, and in this milieu the importance of the politics of last outrage will play a determining factor. Peace has not been achieved with the DoP. The accord is the beginning of a process of negotiation between adversaries who, although they have finally recognized each other's existence, still seize every opportunity to proclaim that they neither like nor trust each other. The accord will follow a long and hard road and success will be determined in the same manner which brought about the DoP itself, that it is believed to be better than the alternatives.

The agreement is based on the principle of finding the lowest common denominator which can be agreed upon, and from there build layer on layer of consensus through negotiation which has as a final destination a settlement which has been arrived at mutually. The Israeli-PLO agreement has the potential to revolutionize politics in the Middle East, but there is a degree of risk proportional to the expected payoff. The basic conflict of interests between Israel and the Palestinians is still far from resolved, thus this is not an historical reconciliation between two peoples, but more a shift to a struggle whose parameters will be defined by the DoP. Therefore the evolution of Gaza/Jericho to statehood via the DoP became a realistic possibility because the recognition of the PLO's role in the peace process gave the Palestinians the credibility needed to make a deal in the eyes of the international community.[140] Just as importantly, recognition gave credence to the Palestinian people's struggle and encouraged their support for any agreement which was made in their name. For the Israelis the issue was not just recognition of the PLO as an organization. It was simply a matter of negotiating with the people who made the decisions, or at the very least with those who were the more palatable. While it is far from certain that there can be a final settlement even if the PLO continues to support the DoP, it is however absolutely unquestionable that there can be no Israeli-Palestinian settlement if the PLO is opposed.[141]

That said, those Palestinians who fought for the struggle, who rose up in the *intifada* and who gave their lives, did not do it for what was achieved at Oslo. Internationally, the Palestinian position had deteriorated rapidly after the Persian Gulf War. The USSR was no longer a major factor in the regional balance of power, Iraq was crushed, the PLO faced hostility from the Gulf States and remittances to the territories dried up. As the PLO faced a budgetary crisis, sympathetic coverage in the Western media declined and the PLO suffered setbacks in the diplomatic arena and in the minds of Western public opinion. Secret talks almost certainly led to a breakthrough precisely because of their secret nature – initially low expectations produced high yields in contrast to the Madrid track which proceeded through the formulaic and ritualized debating process where everything had to be agreed in public and in advance before any announcement of a breakthrough could be made. In such an environment the obvious procedure for negotiators, especially when needing to comfort volatile constituencies at home, was to play safe and continually refer to higher authorities for guidance before taking new and bold lines, thus stagnation occurred and the chances for imaginative steps receded. Thus

> right from the start the Norwegians recognised that secrecy was the number one requirement for the kind of negotiations they were setting up. They knew the failure of the talks in Washington was in large part due to the increase in publicity which

surrounded them. From the moment the Madrid peace process began . . . discussions had been conducted before the cameras of the world. Both sides took great care to choose their spokesmen and women for their media-friendly qualities. Every day the rituals of arrivals and departures at the State Department was broken several times for press conferences and set-piece statements. This had the effect of hardening each side's position. Once Israelis or Palestinians revealed what the hitches were, and defended their stance before a worldwide audience, it was difficult to change it or even to exhibit flexibility, for fear of being seen to back down. So the talks degenerated into sterile posturing and formulaic insults, presented day after day on the television and in the papers. As a result, little or no progress was made.[142]

Arafat is accused of having manoeuvred the Israelis into the Norway channel by deliberately stalling the Washington negotiations so he could force progress with the Israelis in Norway, by creating the impression for the Israelis that the Madrid process was deadlocked and not likely to produce results. However, according to a Palestinian viewpoint,

> up until Oslo, we focused all our thinking on going to the US, which held '99 percent of the cards,' and hoping they would 'deliver' Israel. But this never worked . . . Eventually it became clear that we Palestinians and Israelis would have to create our own dynamic. That's what happened with these 'back channel' negotiations: they began, then stopped, then picked up again – most of the work was actually done in the last month, between 21 July and 19 August.[143]

Mutual recognition was 'something that Arafat, shut out of the Washington process, longed for. By accepting the PLO's right to represent the Palestinian people, Israel would also be implicitly accepting the PLO's political agenda – the Palestinians' right to self-determination and their own state.'[144] During this process, the Palestinians were concerned that there were secret negotiations between Israel and Syria. On 3 August 1993, when Warren Christopher met with Rabin, the Palestinians feared talks were going to bypass them. Arafat's strategy of not wanting the Washington talks to deliver anything because he was excluded from them increased the danger of the PLO being marginalized in the negotiating process because Israel could potentially be forced to seek alternatives through frustration. All such complex negotiations had to be delicately handled. Both sides

> knew that other behind-the-scenes meetings, which might have borne fruit, had been blown apart once the press got to hear about them. Publicity also alerted special interest groups on both sides, groups which often been deliberately kept in the dark to prevent sabotage attempts. The PLO was particularly sensitive to this. It was notoriously faction-ridden and its attempts to establish discreet contacts had often been derisively rejected by the Israelis because of the near impossibility of maintaining secrecy.[145]

Arafat's approval of the secret negotiations in Oslo was done without keeping his Washington negotiating team appraised of developments. Arafat acted as of old – secretively, deviously and for all the protestations that the PLO was a democratic organization, autocratically. Although Arafat made pronouncements of moderation and was becoming more popular, especially amongst the European left, he was still remembered in Israel for allying himself with Saddam Hussein who had vowed to destroy Israel and liberate Jerusalem. In a telephoned speech to a gathering at al-Najah University, Arafat openly declared the DoP was nothing but the first phase of the 'plan of phases', a 1974 PLO blueprint for the destruction of Israel. This was at the same time that many within the PLO, or at least in Arafat's mainstream Fatah faction, had been arguing for a transformation of the PLO, from a revolutionary organization committed to armed struggle, to one espousing diplomacy and negotiation. However, Israelis recognized that the world was changing around them, bringing with it pressure on Israel for the need for a strategic rethink of Israel's national objectives which included a settlement of the Palestinian problem. Israel's leaders realized that the DoP offered terms and opportunities to reach a favourable agreement that Israel may never be able to better.[146] Prior to concluding the DoP, Rabin's government had been unable to determine a new post-Cold War role for Israel, to protect Israeli citizens from the violence of the *intifada*, to co-opt Palestinians from the territories to cut a deal irrespective of the PLO in Tunis and to counter the rise of militant Islamic organizations, like Hamas and Islamic Jihad.[147]

It is instructive to consider some of the assumptions which shaped the negotiating process. During the 1980s the PLO began to take

an active interest in cultivating Israelis who were disposed to reconciliation, always with an eye to the influential ones, such as
potential MKs. These private attempts reflected the exact balance
of power between the two – one weak, the other strong. The balance of power is reflected in the rather sad example where partisan
advocates of the higher power party demanded of the weaker power,
victims of military occupation and dispossession, various moral
acknowledgements of contrition to appease the instigators of their
misfortune. It seems that some in the PLO thought of private en-
counters as a form of negotiation with the Israelis, gradually using
more prominent personalities from the PLO such as Nabil Sha'ath,
and notables from the occupied territories such as Faisal Husseini
and Hanan Ashrawi. There does not seem to have been any attempt by the PLO to coordinate such efforts internationally. A standing
committee of the PLO set up to deal with the US never actually
met and most of its members didn't even know English. Arafat
seemed to be courting patrons in the West who would deliver a
solution of sorts, a quixotic fantasy originating in the notion that
the US was like Syria or Iraq, where getting close to someone who
was close to the leader would open all doors which would get things
done. Even Arafat and his principal lieutenants' knowledge of Israel
was known through contacts and hearsay rather than through
scientific and systematic study.[148] Arafat had never seen an Israeli
settlement. There are now over 200 of them. Expropriation of land
is estimated at 55 per cent of the total land area of the occupied
territories and Israel has tapped into West Bank aquifers, using about
80 per cent of the water there for settlements and for Israel proper.
The Palestinian opposition's argument against the DoP ran therefore that it was negotiated by people who were not in full possession
of all the facts. Opponents contended that information regarding
the changing nature of the territories was intentionally disregarded
by the PLO negotiators. The negotiators were charged with negotiating a 'rental agreement' especially as the DoP is ominously silent
on the question of specific mechanisms of how to get from interim
to final status.[149]

> The struggle over what is Israel/Palestine has been one of terri-
> torial sovereignty. The 'Israelis have asserted sovereignty, built
> settlements and roads, expropriated land and water, and deployed
> armed forces. The tactics of the PLO have been to make general
> assertions, and then hope the concrete details will somehow

miraculously fall into place. The PLO accepted the DoP hoping that Palestinian autonomy would lead to independence if enough rhetorical statements were made. When it came to negotiating the details, the PLO had neither the plans nor the facts, nor the discipline of detail. A general idea like 'limited autonomy' might lead to independence or it might lead to continued domination. In either case, the main task for the Palestinians is to know and understand the overall map of the territories that the Israelis have been creating. The essence of the Israeli territorial domination, both in theory and in detail, is 1. effective control over the land within its pre-1967 boundaries; and 2. the prevention of real Palestinian autonomy of the Palestinian inhabitants of the occupied territories by maintaining an ever-expanding Jerusalem as the core of the web extending into the West Bank. Israeli plans for and practices in Jerusalem are therefore central to the future of how far the Palestinians will reach.[150]

The DoP, concluded in secret, circumnavigated the process of circumspection by the presentation of a fait accompli, negotiated and concluded outwith the normal channels of political and popular approval, thus negating the ability of opponents to seek clarification or register objection. However, those who concluded the DoP will have to implement it as they 'own' it – they are its' architects and sponsors. Such a secret process, even if it does produce initial results, by way of opponents maintaining a low profile during initial phases of euphoria and acceptance, does not necessarily mean it will have a benevolent passage. Many Palestinians are angry with their leaders for bargaining away their legacy, and are also wary of any peace agreement that leaves unresolved so many fundamental and crucial issues, such as the question of statehood, the divisibility of Jerusalem, provision for the right of return for refugees and compensation for those who lost land in 1948 and 1967. Critics of Arafat contend that he cut a deal in order to ensure his own political survival, that he signed away their birthright only to become 'mayor of Jericho' responsible for collecting rubbish.[151] If we now turn to reflect on the various reactions to the DoP, we will find some fascinating insights into those players in this drama, as they justify or oppose, depending on timing, circumstance and their relative closeness to the actual centre of political power.

PM Rabin, in his speech in Washington DC, addressed his life-long external adversaries, 'let me say to you, the Palestinians: We are destined to live together on the same soil in the same land . . . we who have fought against you, the Palestinians, we say to you today in a loud and a clear voice: Enough of blood and tears, Enough!'[152] Similarly Chairman Arafat hit a conciliatory note, when he said

> my people are also hoping that this agreement . . . marks the beginning of the end of a chapter of pain and suffering that has lasted throughout this century and will usher in an age of peace, coexistence and equal rights . . . Now as we stand on the threshold of this new historic era, let me address the people of Israel and their leadership, with which we are meeting today for the first time. Let me assure them that the difficult decision we reached together was one that required great and exceptional courage. We will need more courage and determination to continue the course of building coexistence and peace between us . . . Our people do not believe that exercising the right to self-determination could violate the rights of their neighbours or infringe on their security.[153]

The DoP also meant other things too, even to the two leaders. According to Arafat, 'the Palestinian people have been put on the political map. And whoever is on the political map is there on the geographical map.'[154] Rabin, addressing the Knesset, stated that Israelis owed it to themselves and their 'children to see the new world as it is . . . and do everything so that the State of Israel becomes part of the changing world. We must rid ourselves of the feeling of isolation that gripped us for almost a quarter of a century. We must join the international march of peace, reconciliation and cooperation.'[155]

Alternatively one could believe that Rabin hoped to find a partner to take responsibility for the internal problems of the Palestinians, who would 'deal with Gaza without problems caused by appeals to the High Court of Justice, without problems caused by B'tselem and without problems from all sorts of bleeding hearts and mothers and fathers.'[156] Similarly there is an identical interest among mainstream Palestinian nationalists in their opposition to the rise of Islamic fundamentalism. Palestinian nationalists would only be able to make their case with their own people if they represented achievements and interests worth protecting, even at the price of the indefinite postponement of sovereign independence.

The ceremony at the White House lawn was made possible, according to former Secretary of State Kissinger, by exhaustion, material exhaustion on the part of the PLO and psychological exhaustion on the part of Israel. Kissinger argued this was why all truly contentious issues were set aside – borders, settlements, refugees and Jerusalem, and that even the mutual recognition on which the agreement was based was ambiguous. This gave rise to the illusion that Israel had recognized the PLO but believed that it had not recognized a Palestinian state and that it could continue to choose the representatives with whom it was prepared to deal. Kissinger argued that after Arafat was received on the White House lawn on an equal footing with PM Rabin, and once elections were held in the territories, a Palestinian state was inevitable sooner or later. PM Rabin, interviewed in Cairo declared:

> I stick to my position: no Palestinian state, Jerusalem must remain united under Israeli sovereignty, and be our capital forever ... With all due respect to Kissinger's position, I look at it differently. I believe that in any autonomy there is danger of an independent state ... I believe we can do many things to prevent it from becoming inevitable ... Basically I will judge it by two criteria: First, security for Israelis in Israel, in the territories and in the Gaza Strip. Secondly, how they move in taking over the running of the life of the Palestinians.[157]

However, Rabin was nothing if he was not a pragmatic and practical man. Although as Defence Minister in the National Unity Government in 1988 he vowed to defeat the *intifada* with 'force, might and beatings', he was astute enough to declare after only three months of the *intifada* in February 1988 when he told fellow Labour Party members 'I've learned something in the past two-and-a-half months: you can't rule by force over 1.5 million Palestinians.'[158]

The DoP meant that the Palestinians had to face two choices: to remain in the state of occupation which relegated even the very idea of Palestine to the status of faded memory or to adapt to the offer of what the DoP may yield. One road to dependence, the other to independence. Everything short of independence means a form of devolved power with real power remaining in the hands of the Israelis. Unless the Israelis foresee the eventual outcome of the DoP process as Palestinian sovereignty, in whatever configuration, then the DoP will survive as a local administration charter on structural organization. Thus it will go the way of all previous attempts at resolution of the Israeli-Palestinian conflict which did not include the realization of Palestinian sovereignty. There is an Arab proverb which says that the journey of 1000 miles always starts with the first step. Dr Zehi Wanhaid of UNWRA, felt Arafat had no option but to accept the accord.

> Of course we have had harsh words from Amman and Damascus but we have to go through the neck of the bottle to save Palestinian nationality. If we insist now on nationality with all the land we will finish as a minority inside a bigger Israel, deserted by the world. Let's have the flag and the years can take care of the rest.[159]

Similarly for Sari Nusseibeh, the road to Palestine must begin somewhere, 'we have the choice of continuing to dream of a palace in the sky or building a hut on the ground. From the hut, a palace can be built.'[160] Arafat's supporters tended to agree with an unlikely ally, Chaim Herzog, former President of Israel, when he summarized that 'it is yet to be proved that this is one of the great moments of history. But certainly it is one of the great opportunities.'[161]

It is instructive to consider the reactions of various people who reflect differing shades of opinion. Secretary Warren Christopher hailed the DoP as a 'conceptual breakthrough'.[162] Other US responses also tended to be upbeat, like Zbigniew Brzezinski, who concluded that

> what has happened in my judgement, is a fundamental political and psychological breakthrough that has changed the mutual perceptions of the two parties. They no longer view each other as mortal enemies. This creates the basis for continued progress toward peace, even if that progress is from time to time punctuated by outrageous acts of terrorism or violence or even top-level assassinations. In that sense it's irreversible even though there may be reverses.[163]

Most foreign commentators felt the desire to be confident despite misgivings, particularly in the Western world which hailed the arrival of peace whilst not fully understanding what had actually been achieved. In this respect it may be fitting to give the last word to

Ruslan Khasbulatov, former chairman of the Russian federal parliament, who declared 'I do believe that a wonderful example has been set for settling conflict by peaceful means.'[164]

By far the most important opinions come from the two communities most affected by the agreement, the Israeli and Palestinian. Opinion formers and representatives of organizations considered the DoP through the gamut of prognoses, from the darkest to the most hopeful.

By considering the reactions from the Israeli side of the debate we will be able to determine whether the government had the power to steer its policies through to their conclusion. One must be mindful here that although the Israeli political milieu is robust, there was then no history of actual open insurrection nor of defiance of the supremacy of the parliamentary system, despite rather questionable exhortations by militant individuals. Professor Yeshayahu Leibowitz, whose heartfelt concerns for the soul of Israel viewed the DoP as the vehicle 'to liberate the Israelis from this accursed domination through violence.' Labour MK Yael Dayan also felt that the DoP heralded the end of the conflict in turn meaning that Israelis could be comfortable in their 'own skin'.[165] For Dedi Zucker MK, 'it was a combination of two different people who are both at the end of their careers, and knowing that fighting each other would lead them nowhere. One came with imagination and vision and a belief in a better future. And the other brought a lot of skepticism and pragmatism.'[166] At the time of signing, Arafat was 64, Rabin 71 and Peres 70. All were considered indispensable to the process. Thus there were many fears that, a single assassination, heart attack or parliamentary defeat could derail the process in its most crucial phase, the first two years. However, according to Uri Savir, Director-General at the Foreign Ministry who led the Israeli team in Norway, 'the longer the peace process goes on, the more successful it will be, and the less dependent on individuals.'[167] Savir said that 'We negotiated with the PLO because they were [the only Palestinian group] that could deliver the goods.'[168] Making peace 'will take a lot of patience', Savir believed that 'One finds ambiguous feelings among Israelis. On the one hand, there is extreme distrust – and there are historical reasons for that – and on the other hand, a strong desire for reconciliation. I think the same ambiguities exist on the [Arab] side.'[169] Yossi Beilin, deputy Foreign Minister described the government's goals,

> I hope we have legitimised something that was totally unthink-
> able . . . but for doves in the Labour Party was thinkable for a
> very long time. I hope people will refer to it as a type of fait
> accompli. Even people who are not sure about this agreement or
> think we went too far, believe this is irreversible.[170]
>
> Everyone knows there will be a Palestinian state, [said a Labour
> Party official close to Peres,] this includes Rabin. And they all
> agree that such a possibility is the most realistic one . . . They
> don't admit it publicly for two main reasons. One is Jordan. We
> don't want to frighten or be seen as undermining the regime.
> The other is the Israeli public. They [Rabin and Peres] don't think
> the Israeli public is ready yet.[171]

There is evidence that Israeli negotiators at Oslo aimed at creating
competition between Jordan and the PLO. Officials played down
the machinations at Oslo, saying that the interim agreement was a
step toward the final goal, rather than an aim in itself.

However, Rabbi Yehuda Amital, co-dean of Har Etzion yeshiva in
the Alon Shvut settlement in Gush Etzion and head of the centrist
religious party Meimad, was a cynical opponent of the DoP who
stated that 'if we have reduced the chances of war, and weakened
the *intifada*, then we have achieved something . . . There is no doubt
there will be settlements that will have to be dismantled if we get
to the final agreement. But I have serious doubts we will be able to
come to a final agreement.'[172] Many Israelis feared that the autonomy
accord would only be a first step toward full Palestinian sovereignty.
Ariel Sharon regarded 13 September 1993 as 'the day on which
they have established the Palestinian state.'[173] Benyamin Netanyahu,
then-leader of the largest opposition faction in the Knesset, Likud,
accused the government of 'saving the PLO from breaking apart
and giving it a Palestinian state, which will endanger the very
existence of Israel.'[174] Netanyahu, in his speech to the Knesset during
the special debate on the Israel-PLO agreement demanded, 'what
are the legitimate and political rights of any nation? A state. What
are the legitimate political rights of the Israeli nation? A state.
What are mutual political rights with the Palestinians? A state for
them too.' The Likud opposition leader went on, 'the agreement
lays the foundations for the establishment of the Palestinian state.'[175]
Those on the far right like Eliakim Ha'Etzni, a former Tehiya MK,
believed that the accord was 'an agreement for the destruction of
Israel.' Ha'Etzni of Kiryat Arba and an organizer for The Struggle

Command Against Autonomy stated that 'Arab terrorism and the Jewish reaction will smash this agreement to pieces.'[176] This scare tactic proved a rather self-fulfilling prophesy.

For a more thoughtful summary of opposition, Dore Gold, then director of the US Foreign and Defence Policy Project, Jaffee Centre for Strategic Studies, believed that Rabin 'fed a society thirsting for international normality with the hope that peace' had 'arrived at long last.' Gold believed that Rabin, rather than countering 'war-weariness with solid new leadership,' had 'drawn on the exhaustion of the public to sell it the PLO accord.' Moreover Gold argued that Rabin had 'ignited a new creed of secular messianism that is sweeping wide sectors of Israeli society. He has left the public totally unprepared to face any collapse in the current process, much less to contend with any new military threat that may come later in the decade.'[177] Thus the many Israeli opponents of the accord rail against it revealing more about themselves and their personal or political fears than in promoting cogent arguments rationally analysing the accord, not for what it is, but for what it may become. All will end in tears is the litany of the spoilt child who watches in the wings desperate to scream, 'I told you so', whilst at the same time working to see the prophecy fulfilled. For example, Dore Gold, described as a security hawk, believed that the notion that Israel and Jordan would continue to collaborate in the future against unstable trends in Palestinian politics now appears outdated with the introduction of the DoP. He believed Jordan was being displaced as Israel's main strategic partner as Israel and the PLO hammered out an embryonic form of security collaboration in the implementation of the DoP.[178] President Assad's biographer Patrick Seale, who tends to reflect his subject's stances, asserted that Assad suspected that Israel made peace with an enfeebled PLO in order to isolate Syria, undermine its negotiating position and tilt the regional balance of power still further in Israel's favour. This argument had more to do with Assad's dislike of the PLO's acceptance of a territorial compromise as Assad had always been of the opinion that the Palestinian problem is too crucial to be left entirely in Palestinian hands as it affected wider Arab interests, namely Syrian. Seale also contended that one possible meaning of the accord was that the PLO had chosen Israel rather than Syria as its long-term political and economic partner.[179] Whilst Arafat continued to mollify Assad, addressing Assad from Cairo, saying 'I am confident that our relations will be strengthened in the future',[180] the fact that Damascus offers sanctuary for the dissident Palestinian groups who congregate under the umbrella of rejection, and Arafat's personal experiences of Syrian 'friendship' in Lebanon, will not have been lost on him. Therefore, depending on your point of view there is an alarmist viewpoint which seeks to undermine the rapprochement between the Israelis and the Palestinians. The evidence points to the trend that the Israelis sought to complete bilateral agreements with the Palestinians because there was more that was achievable from an Israeli point of view, as the idea of being able to deal with more than one opponent proved logistically impractical if not impossible. A deal, any deal, with the Palestinians made the process of coaxing other more accommodating Arab governments to the table all the more easy. It would make sense for Israel to make deals with a view to getting the best position slowly and surely rather than be forced by external demands, by what could be termed 'Salami diplomacy' – slice by slice.

However for many, judgement was reserved, either for not wishing to tempt providence or to be seen to be out of step with the initial mood of euphoria. As Foreign Minister Peres told Israeli newspaper Hadashot, 'people prefer remembering, rather than thinking.'[181] The inherent problem Israelis would face would be psychological. Chaim Herzog, former president of Israel, succinctly captured most Israelis approach to the negotiations with the PLO as 'honour him, but suspect him'.[182] This was reflected in the Knesset vote, where approval for the agreement was 61 to 50, with six members from Shas abstaining (Labour 44/ Meretz 12/ small leftist parties 5).[183] A public opinion poll conducted by Israeli newspaper Yediot Ahronot days prior to the signing ceremony showed 53 per cent of Israelis in favour of the peace plan, with 45 per cent opposing. A similar survey carried out in the occupied territories by Al-Nahar, an East-Jerusalem paper, showed that 52.8 per cent backed the Gaza-Jericho plan, though the approval rate was significantly higher in the areas scheduled for early Israeli withdrawal – 70 per cent in Gaza and 75 per cent in Jericho.[184]

If we turn now to the Palestinians, there was a similar pattern to the reaction to the DoP. Those people who were allies of Chairman Arafat, or who at least supported the mainstream Fatah line, tended broadly to favour the DoP, whether because they really thought it was in the Palestinian people's best interests or because they did not wish to appear disloyal. Dr Nabil Sha'ath, a senior political adviser to Chairman Arafat, believed the DoP was 'not a cease-fire', neither 'an administrative arrangement,' nor 'even a purely interim agreement' though it was an 'interim part of a long-term agreement', it was 'much more than an interim agreement.' The DoP allowed that the PLO's 'goal remains, and legitimately remains, the establishment of an independent Palestinian state that will confederate itself with Jordan and that will have peace with Israel.'[185] Thus 'the optimism that swept around the world in the wake of the accord created the illusion that a single peace agreement could be a panacea for all ills in the region, that it could change the reality on the ground forever'.[186] However the reality was more sobering:

> the rosy terms in which the agreement is debated in the West are alien in Gaza, almost surreal. In Gaza, there is no peace, no peace process, no prospect of peace. What there is, is a pervasive sense of loss, of a past diminished and a future marred, of achievements undermined and destroyed, of a society teetering between submission and revolt, a moving backward in time and thought. This regression is characterised by a number of features: the disintegration of political life and purpose, social corrosion and fragmentation, and economic decay.[187]

It is instructive to consider the arguments and the personalities proposing opposition to the DoP, because it is they who will actively work to derail the process.

George Habash, leader of the PFLP, stated that 'our Palestinian programme, that of the PLO, includes the right of return, self-determination and an independent state. The agreement makes no rule on these subjects.'[188] Riyad Malki spokesman for the PFLP in the occupied territories and Professor of Civil Engineering at Bir Zeit University considered the DoP as a defeat, saying that it fell 'short of all Palestinian expectations' and that it presented 'a real betrayal of the struggle of the Palestinian people for the last four decades.' Malki believed that 'The moment you accept autonomy, you compromise yourself. For me, this is nothing but administering the occupation.'[189] More ominous perhaps were the reactions of those like Mohammed Nazzal, Hamas representative in Jordan. When interviewed by Bahraini daily Al-Ayyam he believed that the agreement was the 'worst' that had 'been proposed as a solution to the Palestine Question.'[190] The fundamentalist and rejectionist line was best summed up by a Hamas representative thus: 'la terre de Palestine ne sera jamais une merchandise à brader.'[191]

For Palestinians who fled in 1948 from what became Israel, the DoP effectively signals an end to their dreams to return to Israeli cities like Jaffa, Haifa and Lod. Khaled al-Hasan, a founding member of Fatah when interviewed from Tunis, said, 'how can we accept this text? Where are we going to go, all those who like me are refugees from 1948?'[192] Indeed Arafat himself is a 1948 refugee and although born in Cairo, maintains that his home is Jerusalem where his immediate family were from.[193] Further evidence for this comes from the fact that when the PLO's executive committee voted to support the letter to Rabin by 8 votes to 4, with 6 not voting, all the members voting in favour were refugees from 1967. Among those who grudgingly supported the accord was the feeling that it was the best deal available, not only likely to bear fruit but also one that they themselves would live to see. Haider Abd al-Shafi, head of Palestinian negotiating team at Madrid talks, struck a chord stating that

> our people cling to the threads of hope, no matter how thin. But the despair will be very cruel if their expectations are not met ... I am not belittling the significance of an agreement of principles, but it remains only an agreement of principles, and not a peace accord. Peace will not be attained without achieving our fixed rights.[194]

Prior to the conclusion of the DoP Arafat had often been accused of suffering from non-urgency perception:

> inattention = neglect = lack of urgency = diversion or
> non-deliverance of resources = non-resolution

Palestinian eulogizing about the lost Palestine has the almost mirror image in Judaism's Diaspora lament, 'Next year in Jerusalem', repeated by the head of the household each Pessach incorporating the biblical covenant and the hope of the exiles' return to the land of milk and honey. Arafat was popularly perceived to be neither achieving the PLO's stated goals, nor even being seen to be working towards them. Arafat not only faced a diminution in domestic popular support, but he also faced opprobrium from former state sponsors, like Saudia Arabia. Arafat's problems did not just disappear with the conclusion of the DoP. Saudi Arabia and the Gulf States still harboured a grudge toward the PLO over the Second

Gulf War, and thus only initially provided the bare minimum in investment aid in order to satisfy world opinion and US pressure. Even with money from the oil-producing states, aid would be incremental and dependent on positive progress. Inside the occupied territories Arafat's Fatah had been in many respects replaced by the younger battle-hardened activists, especially in Gaza, where the popular committees formed during the *intifada* had assumed control of much of the social, economic and political activity.[195] However, one positive way of looking at the importance of the secret nature of the Oslo Accord was that Arafat played a clever, directing and central role. He deliberately blocked the main channel and overrode the clamour for internal discussion and ratification of policy stances from the committees and members of the PLO. His strategy was to have PLO delegates in Washington impose conditions to create deadlock at the table and thereby force the Israelis to deal directly with Arafat and the PLO in Tunis, and in doing so, recognize him, the PLO and Palestinian national aspirations.[196]

However it is important to consider the voice of a PLO stalwart, an educated and articulate spokesman well versed in the ways of the Western world – Edward Said. Said is indicative of the type of moderate whose support, if Arafat loses it, will define ordinary Palestinians' levels of commitment to the DoP. According to Said, in a visit in summer 1992, there was a 'magical' expectation in the occupied territories that President Bush would take care of Palestinian problems and was a friend. Hope was also placed in Yitzhak Rabin after the elections of June 1992, that he was the man to deliver Palestine. Said believes this mass amnesia overcoming the population created unreal expectations from dubious quarters, and that concerted efforts by the Palestinians themselves to overcome their own shortcomings was removed from the collective consciousness.[197] Said argues that the PLO in the 1990s acquired an unmistakably eccentric prominence, becoming a quasi-official Arab state organization, resembling far too much the bureaucracies and dictatorships in the region. Said contends that the long battle for the acceptance of a Palestinian national authority was waged so much so that the nature of the organization was neglected.[198] The initiative of 1988 had not yielded very much for very long, Arafat and his inner circle were marooned in Tunis becoming increasingly reclusive and forced to bear the humiliation of endless losses, as well as the opprobrium of its own Palestinian constituencies. The gap between reality and rhetoric widened, as the PLO became more bureaucratic and less determined on the goal of liberation.[199] The PLO became a reactive rather than proactive organization. All proposals and plans aimed at resolution of the Arab-Israeli conflict originated from outside parties. The US vetoed no less than 29 UN Security Council Resolutions censuring Israeli practices which contravened many of the accepted norms of international behaviour. Israel and the US took positions designed in advance to protect their vision of peace – when the PNC recognized Israel (having implicitly done so in 1974), there was never a reciprocal demand for Israel to recognize and deal with the Palestinian nation.[200] Resolution was seen as an inter-state affair as the parties' proposals offering resolution operated at this level. Therefore even though the Palestinian dimension would have to be incorporated within an international framework, the Palestinians rejected any proposals which did not recognize the PLO as their legitimate representative, thus decisions regarding their future were made by those who may not have had the best interests of the Palestinians at heart.[201] Thus critics contend that Arafat fiddled while Palestine burned, in that his personal ambition cost Palestinians dear.

Edward Said attacks the DoP as a Palestinian Versailles treaty with the Palestinians cast in the role of the Germans. He felt that a number of times during the previous 15 years the Palestinians could have negotiated a better deal than a 'modified Allon Plan'. Said contended that previous, similar overtures had been refused by the leadership, such as the 'Gaza-Jericho option' offered by Sadat in 1977.[202] Said believed that the gains of the *intifada* were squandered away, and that the plaintive cries of the DoP supporters that 'we had no alternative' should have been rephrased as, 'we had no alternative because we either lost or threw away a lot of others, leaving us only this one.'[203] Said lambasted Arafat for unilaterally cancelling the *intifada*, for failing to coordinate his moves with the Arab states as he had promised them he would and for provoking appalling disarray within the ranks of the PLO. Said claimed that the PLO had 'transformed itself from a national liberation movement into a kind of small-town government, with the same handful of people still in command.'[204] For the deal itself, Said had nothing but scorn,

> all secret deals between a very strong and a very weak partner necessarily involve concessions hidden in embarrassment by the latter. Yes, there are still lots of details to be negotiated, as there

are imponderables to be made clear, and even some hopes to be fulfilled or dashed. Still, the deal before us smacks of the PLO leadership's exhaustion and of Israel's shrewdness. Many Palestinians are asking themselves why, after years of concessions, we should be conceding once again to Israel and the United States in return for promises and vague improvements in the occupation that won't occur until 'final status' talks tree to five years hence, and perhaps not even then.[205]

Said argued that Arafat's recognition of Israel's right to exist carried it with a whole series of renunciations, of the PLO Charter, of violence and terrorism and of all relevant UN resolutions, except 242 and 338 which do not even mention the Palestinians by name and by implication the PLO had thus deferred or set aside numerous other resolutions that had granted the Palestinians refugee rights since 1948, including compensation or repatriation. The Palestinians had also won many international resolutions from bodies such as the EEC (EU), Non-Aligned Movement, the Islamic Conference, the Arab League as well as the UN, which disallowed or censured Israeli settlements, annexations and actions against the occupied population. The primary consideration of the DoP, in Said's view, was the concern for Israeli security. This was despite that in Palestinian eyes, Israel is the occupying power, continues to control sovereignty and holds the River Jordan, Jerusalem, settlements and roads.[206] Said argued that the intent of this Vichy-like collaboration was to deter Palestinians from denouncing the occupation, and that as the internal security apparatus developed, the PLO would become Israel's enforcer. A contrast was drawn with the South African ANC, which after winning political recognition refused to supply the South African government with police officials until after power was shared, precisely in order not to appear as the white government's enforcer.[207]

Yacov Ben Efrat, writing in *Challenge*, questioned the essential content of the agreement, whether it served as 'a solid foundation for peace between the two peoples', or whether it was 'a reflection of the current balance of forces, world-wide and regional, which leaves the roots of the problem unsolved.' By 'calling an end to the *intifada* and changing its charter, the PLO has cashed in its bargaining chips. It has nothing more to offer. There will be no reason for Israel to make further concessions.' Thus Gaza first is also last. Interim is final. The PLO gets to rule much of the Gaza Strip, but in return it gives up any prospect of really ruling the West Bank. Jericho becomes the 'capital' of autonomy, in exchange for Jerusalem, omitted from the agreement altogether and to remain under Israeli control. Where PLO 'rule' goes into effect, it will mean that Palestinians in authority will be required to control their population by means of a Palestinian police force. The ultimate sovereignty remains Israeli. Israel's security needs will dictate priorities, and the local authorities had better comply if they wish to stay in power. . . . Israel's purpose, however, is clear: to wipe out the Palestinians' national movement and eliminate their claim to sovereignty. If it really wanted a true and lasting peace, Israel would have had to concede much more.[208]

While Israel 'watches from the sidelines, ready to enter in force whenever things get out of hand', Arafat is subject to a test. If 'he succeeds in crushing the opponents of occupation and autonomy in Gaza, including the democratic currents as well as Hamas, then the second phase will come: a cosmetic autonomy in the West Bank.' In concluding, Ben Efrat believed Israel had 'imposed an agreement which makes a deal with a leadership, not peace with a people.'[209]

3.4   Conclusion

When analysing the way in which the DoP was concluded, and the way in which it will ultimately be carried out, one can observe the Middle Eastern method of negotiating – the brinkmanship, the all-or-nothing approach, which all seems somewhat unnerving for those used to consensus bargaining. The DoP was intended as just a stepping stone along the road to peace, graduality being the guiding principle of the agreement which would allow Gaza and Jericho to become the first experiments in peace.

  The DoP recognizes the Palestinians as a people, within a framework of legitimate rights and reciprocal political rights, but there is a clear evasion of anything relating to land, other than that relating to the Gaza Strip and the Jericho Area. The recognition of Israel, by the PLO, also implies shared sovereignty, on any part of the West Bank and Gaza Strip – indeed the DoP assures Israeli sovereignty over the authority of the Palestinian Interim Self-Governing Authority during the interim period.[210]

One of the biggest reservations that has been voiced about the agreement was that it offered no guarantees that the parties would apply it in full or negotiate in good faith when postponed issues were raised. According to the leader of the Palestinian delegation to the Madrid talks, Haider 'Abd Al-Shafi, there were several points he felt were cause for Palestinian concern. The first, and most important, was that the agreement failed to 'address Israel's illegal claim to the occupied territories.'[211] Al-Shafi claimed that Israel had always maintained that it was not an 'occupier', but that it was in the occupied territories by right. According to Al-Shafi, Israel's claim had been expressed from the beginning through its confiscation of land, establishment of settlements, annexation of Jerusalem and adoption of a conduct dedicated to implementing a political programme that considered all of Palestine as Israeli territory.[212] Al-Shafi argued that there was nothing in the DoP that indicated that Israel had renounced any part of its claim over Palestine, indeed rather than confronting the issue, the DoP evaded it. Al-Shafi claimed the major weakness of the DoP was that there was nothing in the agreement that indicated whether settlement activity would stop. By not challenging or objecting to this claim, the Palestinians were in essence condoning it, and through Palestinian silence Israel could spuriously claim Palestinian acquiescence as an abandonment of their right to an independent state over the entirety of the occupied territories. Al-Shafi was horrified that the status of the territories was being blurred from being recognizably 'occupied' to becoming 'disputed'. He claimed that a further flaw of the DoP was the 'tacit acceptance of two separate entities in the Palestinian territories – two separate administrations, two separate judicial systems – indirectly a kind of apartheid'. By allowing or even by deferring to this situation, the Palestinians were conceding something that was illegally established.[213] Al-Shafi argued that Palestinian acceptance of the terms of the DoP meant that Palestinians would have no one to blame for future happenings but themselves, for by agreeing to be bound by the DoP the Palestinians had helped to confer legitimacy on their occupation by Israel. Al-Shafi further complained that while the DoP enumerates such issues as Jerusalem, settlements, borders, to be deferred, there is no mention in the DoP of any withdrawal beyond that of the interim period, indeed a complete withdrawal from the occupied territories was never mentioned for the final status negotiations. While it is claimed that this was implied in the DoP's reference to UN Security Council Resolution 242, which includes withdrawal, Al-Shafi argued that when dealing with state interests there can be no reliance on things implied, especially since Israel had repeatedly made it very clear that it had no intention of withdrawing outside the occupied territories. Al-Shafi draws this conclusion citing that the DoP is phrased in generalities that leave room for wide interpretations, and does not make specific provision for a complete withdrawal from the occupied territories, even as a final status issue. For Al-Shafi, the final confirmation that the agreement was, and would remain, inherently imbalanced and unjust was that Israel would always have the unilateral power of veto.[214]

Despite such constraints, the Palestinians for their part had to come to terms with the cold new realities of Israeli-Palestinian relations. The dream of defeating Israel and the temptation to continue the struggle by inflaming the *intifada* had to be resisted, particularly while negotiating a new relationship with the Israelis. The rhetoric of traditional objectives was, and is, incompatible with the technicalities of brokering an agreement, especially one which is part of a process which relies so heavily on mutual confidence for continued life. The question many Israelis asked was, could the Palestinians with their history of internal schisms, militant factionalism and lack of collective sovereign existence prove their *bona fides* and earn Israeli trust and confidence in a mere five years? The bottom line of the DoP remains that, as the higher power party, Israel can always dispense with the process of negotiations if Israeli doubts about Palestinian intentions persist. As Rabin put it at the opening of the special Knesset debate on the Israel-PLO agreements, 'in any event, the might of the IDF – the best army in the world – is available for our use.'[215]

The ultimate challenge to the accord remains the negotiations which will determine the final status of the two parties' living arrangements. Irredentism will continue to shadow the process but above all, the two sides will have to guard against the psychological barriers which remain as an obstacle and a challenge to be overcome. These barriers for the Israelis will be the two extremes of previously accepted conventional wisdom, namely, a) that military force and its use can solve what is essentially a political problem and b) that the incantation that a peace treaty must be the harbinger and thus the foundation that will guarantee indefinite peace, can in no way guarantee indefinite peace. There has never been a peace agreement in history which takes the form of an unbroken, inviolable, eternal covenant. Wars generally have a habit of occurring

between parties which were legally at peace. However, for the optimistic, the DoP does not underestimate the practical complexities
involved in negotiating and implementing the arrangements it
envisages, as it states in its preamble, it is predicated on the conviction that 'it is time to put an end to decades of confrontation
and conflict'.[216]

This chapter has analysed the terms of the Declaration of Principles on Interim Self-Government Arrangements (DoP) within the
conflict resolution parameters of items 2, 5 and 6 of the Riceman
Formula, in other words institutionalization, mediation and administration. Thus we can conclude that the DoP has achieved the
goal of agreeing a conflict resolution framework, which sets out
specific commitments and obligations within a conflict prevention
regime. However, the inherent structural asymmetrical power imbalance robs the agreement of balance, and the nature of the
state=non-state bilateral agreement ensures that the DoP's international and legal foundations remain dubious, or at least open to
wide interpretation. The DoP does not provide suffiently for an enforceable conflict prevention regime in that such a regime is not
defined and enforcement of what constitutes a conflict prevention
regime is left open to the interpretation of the parties, which, in
an asymmetrical structure, in practical terms means the higher power
party. The DoP as a bilateral agreement does not incorporate third
party mediation to offset the inherent structural asymmetrical power
imbalance, nor does it allow for international assistance which enables
peaceful change, including procedural mechanisms which allow for
the review of settlement terms, the raising of grievances, and adjustments to the settlement as new realities are created, and which
anticipate and monitor potential areas of future conflict. The DoP
does allow for international support and political direction from
third parties aimed at nurturing and advancing the peace process
through economic assistance; however such an international economic assistance programme is based on international goodwill and
the willingness of the United States to provide political, economic
and diplomatic assistance. The international community and particularly the US may be morally bound to offer assistance in the
building of a conflict resolution regime in the Middle East, but
they are not legally bound by the DoP. While the DoP deals with
the provisions for the administration of a conflict resolution framework, such as the procedures and timetables for the implementation
of Israeli military redeployment and Palestinian self-government, it

is a living document which seeks to maximize and develop confidence-building measures, and in that sense is incomplete. The bureaucratic regime that is intended, by the DoP, to develop a conflict resolution framework, to conduct, manage, regulate and supervise the conflict resolution institution, needs further agreements to ensure its progress, evolution and promotion. The peace process provided for by the DoP depends for its continued survival on the fragility of public confidence, on developing and advancing its terms, conditions and provisions, and on building on its foundations. The DoP is akin to a builder's blueprints for developing a new community. The DoP is more than an artist's impression, but the practicalities of making real the plans mean that the dynamic forging the peace process needs much more work before it can be deemed complete.

4
Implementation of the Declaration of Principles, and the Negotiation of Further Transitional Interim Self-Government Arrangements, in Preparation for Permanent Status Negotiations

'The visionary is the only true realist'
–Frederico Fellini[1]

4.1 Introduction

The Declaration of Principles on Interim Self-Government Arrangements (DoP) provided a blueprint for the transfer and exercise of
powers and responsibilities to the Palestinians and the levels of
sovereignty to be attained by the Palestinians. The DoP prepared
the establishment of a nominal cessation of hostilities agreement.
The DoP instituted a mutual recognition pact. The DoP stated the
parties' intent to transfer specified territorial enclaves to Palestinian
authority. The DoP provided for the inauguration of an autonomous
self-governing Palestinian entity with the prospect of elections to
such an autonomous legislative body combined with the devolution
of additional civil powers and responsibilities. The DoP arranged
for the withdrawal and redeployment of Israeli military forces from
specified locations and population centres. The DoP founded a framework for the resolution of disputes and Israeli-Palestinian public
order and security cooperation. The DoP offered a plan for Israeli-
Palestinian cooperation in bilateral and regional economic and
development programmes, and prepared for further negotiations on
unresolvable issues within the framework of a permanent status

arrangement covering Jerusalem, refugees, settlements, security arrangements, borders and foreign relations.

A rolling process of considerable substantive negotiations was intended to follow from the initial agreement because of the inherent contradictions, ambiguities and material differences in interpretation contained within the limitations of the original document. Subsequent, sequential documents had to be negotiated to formulate further interim arrangements ready for implementation in order that the process begun by the DoP could proceed. The DoP as a document, represents an agreement to pursue a living legacy, to undertake a process whose final outcome is not determined in advance. The DoP is not a symmetrical agreement outlining mutual obligations on a *quid pro quo* basis, but rather an agreement to work to further the basic interests of both sides. Further agreements were needed to provide for a sustainable preventative security regime involving reciprocal and cooperative rights and obligations based on shared goals and principles of justice, economic interdependence, collective security and sense of shared community, in order to achieve an equitable and lasting settlement which would master the existing inherent asymmetrical power inequalities.

This chapter analyses and assesses the further negotiated agreements which combine to prepare the foundation of the interim phase of Israeli-Palestinian negotiations envisaged within the terms of the DoP. Incorporating items 1 and 4 of the Riceman Formula, that is resolution and empowerment, this chapter assesses how the further agreements allow for the transfer and exercise of powers and responsibilities to the Palestinians, the levels of sovereignty to be attained by the Palestinians, and how they provide for a sustainable preventative security regime with the goal of achieving an equitable, just and lasting settlement.

4.2 The Agreement on the Gaza Strip and the Jericho Area, 4 May 1994

The Israeli-Palestinian Interim Agreement on the West Bank and Gaza Strip called for in the DoP under Article VII was signed on 28 September 1995 in Washington DC.[2] However, owing to the tardiness in achieving this agreement, the Agreement on the Gaza Strip and Jericho Area, signed in Cairo on 4 May 1994, served as the provisional arrangement, if not as the basis for the wider, subsequent accord. Article VII.1 of the DoP specified that the Israeli and

Palestinian delegations would 'negotiate an agreement on the interim period (the "Interim Agreement").' Article VII.2 further detailed that this interim agreement should 'specify, among other things, the structure of the Council, the number of its members, and the transfer of powers and responsibilities from the Israeli military government and its Civil Administration to the Council.' The interim agreement would 'also specify the council's executive authority, legislative authority in accordance with Article IX below, and the independent Palestinian judicial organs.'[3] Prior to achieving an interim agreement, the Agreement on the Gaza Strip and Jericho Area effectively represented the first empowerment phase of stage 1 of the DoP, the interim self-government arrangements, to apply pending further interim arrangements and the conclusion of a permanent status agreement.

The Agreement on the Gaza Strip and Jericho Area applied to a defined area of some 65 sq km, and in a document of some 300 pages, which included four annexes and six maps, addressed four main issues – security arrangements, civil affairs, legal matters and economic relations. The agreement followed seven months of intensive negotiations and primarily concentrated on the central issue of security arrangements. The agreement covered the withdrawal of the Israeli civil administration and Israeli security forces, the transfer of powers and responsibilities to a Palestinian Interim Self-Governing Authority (PISGA or 'the Council' as referred to in the agreements), the security of Israeli settlements, external security particularly with regard to the boundaries and crossing points of the Palestinian entities, the withdrawal and redeployment of Israeli military forces from Gaza and Jericho, the transfer of authority from the Civil Administration to a PISGA, the structure and composition of a PISGA (powers, responsibilities, jurisdiction), the authority and responsibilities of a Palestinian police force and future Israeli-Palestinian relations.

The security and public order arrangements and the scheduled withdrawal of Israeli forces were negotiated under a security concept to be applied to Gaza and Jericho. These arrangements were regarded as being within an 'Israeli security envelope' which was meant to provide for security from external threats along the boundaries of the designated Palestinian entities. The provision for internal security was to be a shared responsibility, with Israel remaining responsible for Israelis and the settlements, while the Palestinians would assume responsibility for public order and the internal security of Palestinians. Annexe I, 'The Protocol Concerning Withdrawal of Israeli Military Forces and Security Arrangements', covered a range of issues. Article I, 'Arrangements for Withdrawal of Israeli Military Forces', provided for the withdrawal from the designated areas of Gaza and Jericho in coordination with a newly established Joint Israeli-Palestinian Security and Coordination and Cooperation Committee (set up under Article II), designed to deal with-joint security issues, to exchange information, and to provide guidance for the three District Coordination Offices (Khan Yunis, Gaza, Jericho), responsible for Joint Patrols and Joint Mobile Units. Israeli forces were redeployed to specified areas on 18 May 1994, such as to the Military Installation Area along the Egyptian border and to Israeli settlements, in order to fulfil security functions as defined in the agreement. Article III.2–7, which pertained to the 'Palestinian Directorate of Police Force', provided for the operation of the police force's duties and functions, its structure and composition, recruitment, its arms, ammunition and equipment, the introduction of arms and equipment and foreign assistance. Article III.7 provided for the deployment of the police force under the auspices of the PISGA, and outlined the force's responsibilities for the internal security and public order of the Palestinian entities. Article III allowed for some 9000 policemen in an integral force, comprising four branches – civil police (Al Shurta), Public Security, Intelligence and Emergency Services and Rescue (Al Difa'a Al Madani). Articles IV and V, 'Security Arrangements in the Gaza Strip' and 'Security Arrangements in the Jericho Area', provided for the protection of the Israeli settlements and settlement blocs, such as Erez and Gush Katif, the responsibilities regarding the security perimeter and common security fence, the Mawasi area and beach, the Egyptian border, lateral roads to the settlements (Kissufim-Gush Katif, Sufa-Gush Katif, Karni-Netzarim), the central north-south road (Road no. 4), and Joint Mobile Units (located at Nissanit junction, Netzarim junction, Deir el-Ballah junction, and Sufa-Morag junction), clarification concerning the Jericho area, Joint Mobile Units (located at Auja junction, Nahal Elisha junction), coordination and cooperation in the Jericho Area. Article VI, 'Security Arrangements Concerning Planning, Building and Zoning', provided for construction limitations with regard to security requirements. Articles VII, IX, X, XI, and XII, 'The Crossing Points', 'Arrangements for Safe Passage Between the Gaza Strip and the Jericho Area', 'Passages', Security Along the Coastline and in the Sea of Gaza', and 'The Security of the Airspace' provide for:

- passage between Gaza and Israel (crossing points – Erez, Nahal Oz, Sufa, Karni, Kisufim, Kerem Shalom, Elei Sinai)
- passage to and from the Jericho area
- usage of safe passage (permits)
- passage and mode of transit, routes
- control, management, and arrangements for entry and exit from Egypt and Jordan, of passages (border crossings – Allenby Bridge, Rafah)
- maritime activity zones and their extent (zones K,L,M), general rules, maritime coordination and cooperation centre, Gaza port
- operation of aircraft (two VIP transport helicopters, four 20-person fixed wing transport aircraft for travel between Gaza and Jericho, two 50-person fixed wing passenger crafts for travel between Gaza and Cairo). Article VIII, 'Rules of Conduct in Security Matters', provided for the rules of engagement in response to an act or incident constituting a danger to life or property.[4]

The understanding that the provisions agreed upon in the Cairo Agreement[5] were to be a stepping stone to further agreement is borne out by Article I of Annex IV, the Protocol on Economic Relations, signed in Paris on 29 April 1994, whereby the agreement would 'begin in the Gaza Strip and the Jericho Area and at a later stage' would 'also apply to the rest of the West Bank, according to the provisions of the Interim Agreement and to any other agreed arrangements between the two sides.'[6] However, before the interim agreement could be reached, the Cairo Agreement was meant both as a vehicle for progressing the process as well as being a temporary measure prior to a fuller agreement, and as such the Cairo Agreement represented the political achievement of progress. The importance of the Cairo Agreement is in its strengths, and more importantly its weaknesses, as a foundation on which the legal structure of the autonomous areas was to be built. While Article IX.2 of the DoP stated that both parties would 'review jointly laws and military orders presently in force in remaining spheres,' implying that further negotiations would yield more equitable results, the realization of further negotiations resulted in Article VII.9 of the Agreement on the Gaza Strip and the Jericho Area, which stated that '[l]aws and military orders in effect in the Gaza Strip or the Jericho Area prior to the signing of this Agreement shall remain in force, unless amended or abrogated in accordance with this agreement.'[7]

Such a situation represented a continuation of the legal structure in the occupied and autonomous areas, that is a concoction of British-mandate, Jordanian, international and Israeli-military, laws and orders. On 7 June 1967 the military commander of the West Bank announced that 'Every governmental, legislative, appointive and administrative power in respect of the region or its inhabitants shall henceforth be vested in me alone and shall only be exercised by me or by persons appointed by me for that purpose or acting on my behalf.'[8] Israel has always argued that the Hague Regulations and the Fourth Geneva Convention of 1949 do not apply to the West Bank and Gaza Strip because they are not enemy territory, thus those provisions relating to belligerent occupation are not binding on Israel. Such a stance is based on Israel's interpretation that the legal status of the territories is *sui generis*, based on the presupposition that the 'legitimate sovereign' of the occupied territory must have been displaced by the occupant, thus as Egypt and Jordan were not such but there as a result of illegal acts of aggression, therefore Israel is not required to apply the humanitarian law of the Geneva Civilians Convention for the benefit of the inhabitants of the occupied territories.[9] Former Attorney-General Meir Shamgar has stated that

> The territorial position is thus *sui generis* and the Israeli government tried therefore to distinguish between the theoretical, juridical and political problems on the one hand and the observance of the humanitarian provisions of the Fourth Geneva Convention on the other. Accordingly, the government of Israel distinguishes between the legal problem of the applicability of the Fourth Geneva Convention to the territories under consideration, which as stated does not in my opinion apply to these territories, and decided to act *de facto* in accordance with the humanitarian provisions of the Convention.[10]

Israel has declared that it would observe *de facto* the humanitarian rules, Israeli authorities having stated that the relevant articles relating to belligerent occupation were being followed. Since military government results from conflict, the Israeli military occupation has had no time limit 'because it reflected a factual situation, and, pending an alternative political or military solution, this system of government could, from the legal point of view, continue forever.' In addition it expresses 'the intention not to exclude or prejudge any political solution or foreclose any rights.'[11] Thus occupation delivers the occupier territory, but its position is intrinsically temporary pending an alternative solution.

Whether or not occupation is indefinite, the occupant has no right under international law to treat the territories as its own, nor even acquire sovereignty. Indeed the notion of 'belligerent occupant' has been introduced in international law to deligitimize the acquisition of territory (annexation) by force, either through defensive or offensive action. Israel has accepted as binding on its rule of the territories, the IV Convention Respecting the Laws and Customs of War on Land and annexed Regulations.[12] Israel has used laws like the British Mandate Defence (Emergency) Regulations of 1945 to justify extra-judicial punishments such as deportations, house demolitions and administrative detention, and under Military Order 412 the single most influential IDF officer is the one appointed officer in charge of the local judiciary, vested with all the powers and privileges of the Minister of Justice under Jordanian law.[13] Prior to the Cairo Agreement of 4 May 1994, the legal jurisdiction of West Bank civilian courts was clear and was not in dispute, excluding East Jerusalem which had been annexed, but including Israeli settlements. Local West Bank courts had over the years heard cases to which settler and non-settler Israelis had been parties, particularly in civil matters where such courts had jurisdiction, except in cases where the military government had a direct interest, or was a party.

Since the beginning of the occupation, Israeli military courts have shared jurisdiction with the local West Bank Palestinian courts in criminal matters. There have been four legislative phases in the occupation:

(1) During 1967–71 some 200 Military Orders laid the occupation's foundation. The legal system was reorganized soon after occupation began and military courts' jurisdiction was extended to civil matters traditionally in the civilian courts' domain. Military Order 378 created a military justice system with only one level of courts with no provision for appeal.

(2) 1971–9 facilitated Jewish settlement in the West Bank; Military Order 783 established five Jewish Regional Councils covering the entire West Bank.

(3) The period 1979–81 a) extended Israeli law to settlers and excluded settlers from local courts jurisdiction, b) organized settlement administration consistent with local government in Israel and c) reorganized the military government in the West

Bank giving some functions to the new Civil Administration (Military Order 947).

(4) From 1981 to the present, Military Orders covered planning laws for re-zoning land for expropriation, for settlement and for taxation, financial matters controlling the flow into the West Bank.

Shared jurisdiction began with Proclamation 3 and was superseded by Military Order 378 in 1970. Military Order 378 regulates most of the military court process in the West Bank, while an unnumbered Military Order of 1970 is the parallel regulation for the Gaza Strip.[14] Since then a number of further restrictions have been placed on the universality of West Bank Palestinian courts' jurisdiction, particularly since the outbreak of the *intifada*. For example Circular No. 3/1244 of 1 November 1987 advised that West Bank courts could not hear complaints against Israeli identity card holders. The concomitant upheaval wrought on normal court business by occupation and subsequently by the *intifada* has meant that Israeli courts have assumed jurisdiction wherever there was even a tenuous link with the case and Israel, even though the previous formal legal jurisdiction structure remained in place. Israeli military courts have the relevant authority and jurisdiction to try those deemed security cases. Israeli military courts have concurrent authority with local, non-military criminal courts to try all alleged criminal cases. The decision whether or not a case, or class of cases, should be heard by either a local or military court is determined by the military authorities. The military court legal system is based loosely on common law and there is no appeal court in this system. All judges are serving military officers, some of whom have no legal qualifications.[15]

In the Agreed Minutes to the DoP, Article IV stated:

> It is understood that: 1. Jurisdiction of the Council will cover West Bank and Gaza Strip territory, except for issues that will be negotiated in the permanent status negotiations: Jerusalem, settlements, military locations and Israelis. 2. The Council's jurisdiction will apply with regard to the agreed powers, responsibilities, spheres and authorities transferred to it.[16]

The significance of these points was that through defining jurisdiction under the DoP, the Article was an attempt to alter the previous legal set-up, however imperfectly, and in a sense create new legal realities through the negotiations framework. In what amounted to a legal separation of Israelis and Palestinians in terms of juridical authority, the Cairo Agreement reinforced this notion of personal jurisdiction which was superimposed upon territorial jurisdiction. The Annex III Protocol Concerning Legal Matters Article I.1 stated that the 'criminal jurisdiction of the Palestinian Authority' would cover 'all offences committed in the areas under its territorial jurisdiction' subject to the provisions included in this Article. Israel would have 'sole criminal jurisdiction over' offences 'committed in the Settlements and the Military Installation Area', and 'offences committed in the Territory by Israelis'. In exercising their criminal jurisdiction, each side would 'have the power, *inter alia*, to investigate, arrest, bring to trial and punish offenders,' and in addition, 'without derogating from the territorial jurisdiction of the Palestinian Authority', Israel would have 'the power to arrest and to keep in custody individuals suspected of having committed offences which fall within Israeli criminal jurisdiction.' The Article maintained that nothing in it would 'derogate from Israel's criminal jurisdiction in accordance with its domestic laws over offences committed outside Israel (including in the Territory) against Israel or an Israeli', although the exercise of such jurisdiction would 'be subject to the provisions of this Annex and without prejudice to the criminal jurisdiction of the Palestinian Authority.'[17]

What all this means in real terms is that what is internationally recognized as a belligerent and temporary military occupation over a single territorial entity – the West Bank – subject to the Hague Regulations and the Fourth Geneva Convention, has become through negotiations a shared territory.[18] By exercising jurisdiction, whether in criminal or civil matters, and more importantly having this jurisdiction recognized by the various agreements between the Israelis and the PLO, the Israelis have successfully sidestepped continued international and Palestinian refusals to their claims in the occupied territories. This point is further reinforced in the field of civil jurisdiction. Annex III Protocol Concerning Legal Matters Article III.1 states that 'The Palestinian courts and judicial authorities have jurisdiction in all civil matters'; however this is subject to this agreement, exceptions being Article III.2 which states that 'any enforcement of judicial and administrative judgements and orders issued against Israelis and their property shall be effected by Israel.' Although providing exceptions, the main thrust of Article III.3 is that the 'Palestinian courts and judicial authorities have no jurisdiction over civil actions in which an Israeli is a party'. Article III.4 goes on, stating that 'The jurisdiction of the Palestinian courts and judicial

authorities does not cover actions against the State of Israel including its statutory entities, organs and agents.'[19] By exercizing
jurisdiction Israel is in effect exercizing sovereignty. Negotiating the
division of jurisdiction is tantamount to admitting that sovereignty
over the West Bank is not inviolable and that it is thus open to
interpretation, negotiation and by inference change. The Cairo
Agreement in effect removes settlements, Israelis, Israeli security organs
and East Jerusalemites from the legal jurisdiction of the Palestinian
courts. On 19 April 1994, Attorney General Ben-Yair told the Jerusalem Bar Association that Israeli law did not apply in the occupied
territories, 'unless the Knesset expressly states this,' and that settlers are as subject to military law as Palestinians. However, Ben-Yair
stated that in criminal cases 'parallel' authority applied to settlers,
so that they are tried in Israeli courts under Israeli law, not in military courts under military law.[20] Even more important is the fact that
this agreement refers jurisdiction to negotiation, both in terms of
this agreement and also in terms of final status negotiations.

On the issue of land ownership, Annex II Protocol Concerning
Civil Affairs, Article II.B(22) states that 'All powers and responsibilities regarding land registration will be transferred to the Palestinian
Authority, except the Settlements and the Military Installation Area.'
However in respect of planning and zoning, the Cairo Agreement
merely reinforces the status quo in that it neither challenges past
Israeli expropriation of occupied land (such as settlements and military
bases which are illegal under the Fourth Geneva Convention), nor
does it block future expropriation as this issue is still open to negotiation. In respect of land or jurisdiction being transferred to the
PISGA, the Cairo Agreement establishes certain provisos that not
only do not cede full power to the PISGA but also allow for an
Israeli veto over any PISGA legislation.[21] Article II.B(32a) states that
while legislative authorities, powers and responsibilities would be
transferred to the Palestinian Authority, except in the Settlements
and the Military Installation Area, those powers and responsibilities would be subject to a number of restrictions. For example,
planning schemes, bylaws and regulations in effect in the Gaza Strip
and the Jericho Area prior to the signing of the agreement would
remain in force, unless amended or abrogated by the agreement.
The agreement permitted the PISGA to amend, abrogate or promulgate planning schemes, and issue licences and exemptions within
its jurisdiction, provided that such acts were consistent with the
provisions of the agreement. As part of its procedure, the PISGA

would have to publish planning schemes in the form of law, and if Israel considered such a plan to be inconsistent with the terms of the agreement Israel may bring it for consideration by a special subcommittee of the Joint Civil Affairs Coordination and Coordination Committee. The PISGA would then have to respect the recommendation of the subcommittee.[22] Through the definition of jurisdiction within this agreement, the Palestinians are ceding both existing principles of juridical authority and integrity, and also accepting that Israeli jurisdiction, both prior, present and future, is relevant and thus applicable. Article V of the Cairo Agreement stated that the authority of the PISGA encompassed all matters that fell within its territorial, functional and personal jurisdiction. Territorial jurisdiction covered the Gaza Strip and Jericho Area territory, except for Settlements and the Military Installation Area. Territorial jurisdiction included land, subsoil and territorial waters, in accordance with the provisions of the agreement. Functional jurisdiction encompassed all specified powers and responsibilities, but did not include foreign relations, internal security and the public order of Settlements, the Military Installation Area, Israelis and external security. Personal jurisdiction extended to 'all persons within the territorial jurisdiction referred to above, except for Israelis'. The most important point was however, the point that 'The Palestinian Authority has, within its authority, legislative, executive and judicial powers and responsibilities, as provided for in this Agreement,' the relevant point being 'provided for'. Israel would continue to exercize its authority through its military government, which, for that end, would continue to have the necessary legislative, judicial and executive powers and responsibilities, in accordance with international law. This provision would 'not derogate from Israel's applicable legislation over Israelis *in personam.*' However, in keeping with the conciliatory nature of the negotiations process, provision was made that 'Israel and the Palestinian Authority may negotiate further legal arrangements.'[23]

What is remarkable about the legal aspects of the Cairo Agreement is the apparent laxity by the Palestinians in the way which they were negotiated, particularly in terms of future ramifications. Acceptance by Chairman Arafat of these agreements may indeed reflect his tactical and strategic thinking based on political assumptions that these agreements can be cast aside when future conditions are more favourable. Chairman Arafat issued an executive order nullifying some 2000 Israeli military orders enacted since 1967. This decree reinstated pre-1967 laws in the West Bank and Gaza Strip, to take effect from 20 May 1994.[24] However this unilateral action was in contravention of Article VII of the Cairo Agreement, which states that 'Laws and military orders in effect in the Gaza Strip or the Jericho Area prior to the signing of this Agreement shall remain in force, unless amended or abrogated in accordance with this Agreement.'[25]

A very strong warning must be made – the Israelis' assiduity to detail and application of legality is impressive, and it is naïve and unwise to believe otherwise. Chairman Arafat, in a speech delivered in English on Jerusalem to South African Muslims in Johannesburg on 10 May 1994, let slip his cavalier attitude towards the legal status that was being built when he stated

> Now, after this agreement, which is the first step and nothing more than that, believe me – a lot remains to be done. The jihad will continue. Jerusalem is not only of the Palestinian people, but of the entire Islamic nation ... After this agreement you must understand that our main battle is not to get the maximum out of them here and there. The main battle is over Jerusalem ... I regard this agreement as no more than the agreement signed between our prophet Muhammad and the Quraysh in Mecca. We must remember that Caliph Umar refused to accept this agreement and considered it 'an inferior peace agreement'. However, the prophet Muhammad accepted it, and we now accept the peace agreement, but in order to continue on the way to Jerusalem. Together and not alone.'[26]

In a State Department report of 1 June 1994 on PLO compliance with the DoP commitments, Arafat's remarks were interpreted thus,

> In response to a question about this statement in an interview, PLO official Zakaria al-Agha said he believed Arafat meant struggle by other means, such as negotiations. PLO negotiator Nabil Sha'ath said that jihad for Jerusalem meant 'struggle for the sake of insistence on presenting what we demand' ... Arafat himself, in a press conference, said that in speaking of 'jihad' he intended a religious, nonviolent struggle. In the same speech 'Arafat likened the agreement with the Israelis to an agreement Muhammad made with the Quraysh tribe in Mecca.' This agreement, signed in 627AD, called for a ten-year truce between

Muhammad and the Qureish tribe. Two years after the agreement (the 'Hudaybay Suhl' or 'reconciliation') was signed, Muhammad said that the Qureish tribe violated the agreement; Muhammad's followers then conquered Mecca.[27]

In the Palestinians' defence, however, may well be the various provisions they negotiated affording protection toward anticipated final status negotiations in the agreement. Article IV of the DoP states, 'The two sides view the West Bank and the Gaza Strip as a single territorial unit, whose integrity will be preserved during the interim period.'[28] Furthermore, Article XXIII.5 of the Cairo Agreement states that 'Nothing in this Agreement shall prejudice or preempt the outcome of the negotiations on the interim agreement or on the permanent status to be conducted pursuant to the Declaration of Principles. Neither Party shall be deemed, by virtue of having entered into this Agreement, to have renounced or waived any of its existing rights, claims or positions.' Article XXIII.6 states 'The two Parties view the West Bank and the Gaza Strip as a single territorial unit, the integrity of which will be preserved during the interim period', and Article XXIII.7 states 'The Gaza Strip and the Jericho Area shall continue to be an integral part of the West Bank and the Gaza Strip, and their status shall not be changed for the period of this Agreement. Nothing in this Agreement shall be considered to change this status.'[29] Despite these best efforts, we can see that in the key legal and administrative functions, pre-existing arrangements have either been preserved, and/or enhanced. The Palestinians by this second, further agreement have not only conferred legitimacy on their occupation but they have also confirmed that future occupation, over part or whole and in whatever form, is conditional both on Palestinian good behaviour and the strength of Israeli negotiating skills.

In anticipation of a Palestinian transitional authority, the PLO commissioned a draft constitutional document, first made public in December 1993, but amended in January 1994. The new draft was debated at a conference, 'Challenges Facing Palestine Society during the Transition', held in Jerusalem by the Jerusalem Media and Communications Centre on 4–5 February 1994. A third draft incorporating the conference criticisms was then made available in April 1994.[30] The draft constitution was both conditional and temporary. Features of a normal constitution, for example the definition of powers and authorities of the executive, legislature and judiciary were not present, because it was not a document dealing with a sovereign entity. The DoP dictated the character both of the Palestinian entity and the powers and responsibilities any constitution may determine. According to one of the principal architects of the DoP, Joel Singer, the DoP ensured that the status of the West Bank and Gaza Strip would 'not be changed during the interim period'. These areas would 'continue to be subject to military government'. Similarly, this fact suggested that the PISGA would 'not be independent or sovereign in nature', but rather would be 'legally subordinate to the authority of the military government.' In other words, operating within Israel, the military government would 'continue to be the source of authority for the Palestinian Council and the powers and responsibilities exercised by it in the West Bank and Gaza Strip.'[31] In order to exercise sovereignty, land and people are essential ingredients, however whilst the PISGA's Draft Basic Law asserts the rights of the 'Palestinian people', in reality these terms relate directly to those people and lands for whom powers and responsibilities have been ceded by the military government to the PISGA. Chapter One, General Provisions – Article 1 stated that 'The Palestinian people are the source of all authority which shall be exercised, during the transitional period, through the legislative, executive and judicial authorities in the manner provided for in this Basic Law' and termed PISGA territory, 'Palestine' with Article 5 stating that 'Jerusalem shall be the capital of Palestine.' Article 2 stated that the government of Palestine would 'be based on parliamentary democracy', and Article 6 stated that 'Sovereignty over the national resources in Palestine' would be 'vested in the Palestinian people,' and would 'be exploited and disposed of in the interests of the Palestinian people according to law.'[32] It must be conceded that the provisional nature of the draft constitution means that the theory, principles, and practice of constitutional enactment will continue to be evolutionary until such time as final status negotiations are concluded. It is interesting to note the drafting process was carefully controlled, with a limited consultation process, and did not follow from popular participation, deliberation and ratification. The December and January documents were titled, 'Law', not 'Draft Basic Law' implying at least a more serious acceptance of the principle of popular sovereignty through public criticism, thereby effecting significant concessions in the April document.[33] For all its faults and limitations, the Draft Basic Law was an important first step toward a definitive constitution and all that implies, in other words the creation of constitutional and political arrangements, interests and institutions. The relationship between the branches of the PISGA, executive, legislative, judicial were undefined. Article VII.9 of the Cairo Agreement stated that all '[l]aws and military orders in effect in the Gaza Strip or the Jericho Area prior to the signing of this agreement shall remain in force, unless amended or abrogated in accordance with this Agreement.' Therefore everything regarding the legal structure and order would continue to be subject to the overriding authority of the Israelis, meaning that the Israelis retained the power of veto and thus control.[34] Thus it is both an inspiration and an aspiration that the Draft Basic Law reflects, despite the limitations imposed within the transitional phase.

Despite the many praiseworthy features of the Draft Basic Law, it merely reflected the fundamental realities of the day. The draft constitution enabled the PLO to remain as the sole interlocutor, representative and arbiter of the Palestinian people, in effect neutralizing any internal Palestinian dynamic. Article 103 of the Draft Basic Law for the National Authority in the Transitional Period, stated:

> The Basic Law shall apply during the transitional period, but shall not affect the powers and duties of the Palestine Liberation Organisation and its organs including its powers to represent the Palestinian people in foreign and international relations and relations with foreign governments and international organisations.[35]

It must be noted that the entire peace process was not geared specifically to enshrining the fundamental rights and freedoms of the Palestinian people, rather the primary consideration of the Israeli-Palestinian peace process was to end the bloodshed between the parties and to establish a mutually agreed *modus vivendi*. It is within this context that PM Rabin stated

> I prefer the Palestinians to cope with the problem of enforcing order in the Gaza Strip. The Palestinians will be better at it than we were because they will allow no appeals to the Supreme Court and will prevent the Association for Civil Rights from criticising the conditions there by denying it access to the area. They will rule by their own methods, freeing, and this is most important, the Israeli army soldiers from having to do what they will do.[36]

The PLO is recognized in the United Nations as the legitimate representative of the Palestinian people, and as such maintains diplomatic relations with more than 100 countries. The DoP and the Cairo Agreement both prohibit the PISGA from conducting foreign relations, yet the Draft basic Law recognizes that the PLO represents the Palestinian people in foreign relations, and as such places its decisions above those of the PISGA.[37] The dynamism and the potency of the provisional Basic Law were put in question by the DoP and the Cairo Agreement. The DoP and the Cairo Agreement ensured that the PISGA could not enact legislation consistent with the Draft Basic Law's provisions. The PISGA was constrained within its agreed jurisdiction, by its very nature subject both to Israeli limits and to the limits mutually agreed.[38] Indeed the PISGA's independence even within its own jurisdiction was limited by the extra-territoriality of the PLO, a fact which places the PLO above and outside the jurisdiction of the PISGA, and therefore of the Draft Basic Law for the National Authority in the Transitional Period.[39]

4.3 The proceeds of peace will underwrite the process of peace: the Paris Protocol and international aid

In order to market the political dimension of the Israeli-Palestinian accommodation, the main support and guarantee for this political structure was economic prosperity through regional interdependency. Thus the intended thrust of the peace process was to achieve an understanding which mutually reinforced both peace and prosperity. This was the stated intention of the preamble of the Protocol on Economic Relations, the 'two parties view the economic domain as one of the cornerstone in their mutual relations with a view to enhance their interest in the achievement of a just, lasting and comprehensive peace.'[40] The foundation of the Israeli-Palestinian economic accommodation was the Israel-PLO Protocol on Economic Relations, signed in Paris on 29 April 1994. The Paris Protocol provided for the framework which would determine the Palestinian economy and its economic relations in the interim period, and covered the spheres of monetary and financial issues, direct taxation, import taxes and import policy, indirect taxes on local production, labour, agriculture, industry, insurance issues and tourism. The protocol established 'the contractual agreement' that would govern the 'economic relations between the two sides' and would 'cover the West Bank and the Gaza Strip during the interim period.'[41]

The implementation of the protocol was to be followed up by the Joint Economic Committee (JEC) which would decide on related problems and would serve as the continuing committee for economic cooperation as envisaged in Annex III of the DoP.[42]

However, unlike the other developing bilateral relations with the Arab world that Israel had been prospecting as a result of the Madrid process, Israeli-Palestinian economic foundations already existed, having developed under Israeli occupation over a period of 30 years. Following the 1967 war, the previous economic relationships enjoyed by the West Bank and Gaza with adjoining regions were either completely severed or greatly weakened. For example, post-war relationships with Jordan were redefined by Israeli policies and decisions towards the West Bank, and Gaza was isolated from Egypt and administered by the Israeli military government. Both territories gradually developed new economic links with Israel through trade, labour and other economic relationships. Prior to 1967, the Gazan economy was weak and underdeveloped, being highly dependent on external sources of income, while the economic infrastructure was immature and markets were not integrated. In 1966, the West Bank and Gaza's total GNP equalled only 2.6 per cent of Israel's GNP, Gaza's GNP totalled 20 per cent of the West Bank's with a per capita income of less than half the West Bank's. Between 1967 and 1987 the number of Gazans crossing into Israel for work rose from none to 45 per cent of the total labour force.[43] By 1987 the combined GNP of the occupied territories had only reached 6.7 per cent of Israel's GNP, while Gaza's economy equalled only 1.6 per cent of Israel's GNP, dropping to 1 per cent by 1992.[44] Limitations imposed on the occupied territories during these years by Israel precluded any significant economic development, indeed true economic development was not favoured, either for reasons of ensuring no competition for Israeli industries, or because creating a strong Palestinian economic infrastructure would threaten Israeli control.[45] A main element of the *intifada* was the attempt to address the state of underdevelopment and subordination of the Palestinian economy by boycotting Israeli goods, resisting tax payments and encouraging local production and consumption. From 1981 onwards, Israel – which dominated the Palestinian economy – and the Gulf States, which provided employment opportunities and remittances for Palestinians, simultaneously suffered recession. Palestinians unemployed in Israel and the Gulf States could not hope to be incorporated by a West Bank economy which could not generate jobs in industry, agriculture or services. Employment opportunities in the Arab world for educated Palestinians had long been a means of lessening economic and political tensions at home. In 1984, for the first time since the 1950s, numbers entering exceeded those leaving the West Bank: 4000 graduates per annum were now entering a job market that had no hope of accommodating them. Israel required that Palestinians under age 21 remain no less than six months on every trip outside the West Bank, and Jordan required that they return within one month. Young Palestinians were therefore placed in an impossible economic situation, and even more so since the *intifada* and the Gulf War, as Palestinian employment reflected political fortunes. An example of a political rationale for the *intifada* was set out in a 14–point document issued in the name of 'Palestinian nationalist institutions and personalities from the West Bank and Gaza' on 14 January 1988. Among the demands were to cease all settlement and land confiscation, cancel VAT and other direct Israeli taxes, release to Palestinian unions almost $1bn in mandatory deductions made since 1970 from the pay cheques of Palestinian workers in Israel, remove restrictions on building permits and on industrial and agricultural projects, and end trade discrimination in Israel against Palestinian manufacturers and produce.[46] Leaflets of the *intifada* show that it was characterized by decentralized activity that emphasized local action, since a major objective of the various organizations was to erode the Israeli ruling apparatus in the territories. However, economic considerations were not ignored. Financial aid was given to those harmed by Israeli activities, families with dead, wounded, houses demolished, and so on. Steps were taken to reduce economic hardships: for example, commercial strikes were partial, and the boycott of Israeli products and working in Israel was selective. Many leaflets were at pains to ensure that the burden was being shared equally, property owners were called on not to raise rents and to defer rent from those unable to pay, whilst those with means were urged to pay on time, and doctors and lawyers were urged not to increase fees.[47]

Israel's policy regarding the occupied territories in the aftermath of the Second Gulf War aimed at increasing employment and boosting the local economy in an attempt to refocus Palestinian energies away from the *intifada*.[48] This policy was intended to have a two-fold benefit, reduce the economic burden on Israel of policing the occupied territories, and redirect Palestinian violence into economic enterprise thereby further decreasing Israel's security considerations.

Tax incentives and the strengthening of local banking operations were meant to stimulate new investment and production, though the basic subservient and subcontracted role of the Palestinian economy to the Israeli one would remain.[49] Israel's policy aimed at enlarging the Palestinian economy's productive base, especially in Gaza, by encouraging increased consumption capacity, so that Palestinian dependence on Israel for employment would be reduced. This objective was balanced by the desire not to encourage the development of a competitor. In a sense the DoP, at least in the short term, could be seen as a modification of this policy.

The DoP made extensive provision for economic arrangements and relations, either through jointly operated bilateral and multilateral economic and development programmes, or by transferring powers and responsibilities to the PISGA. While the PISGA was intended to assume power and responsibility in certain spheres by the DoP, Israel expected to retain control of strategic resources, such as water, energy and international aid. In such a way, Israel would divest itself of the heavy financial burden of some governing functions without relinquishing overall control of macro-economic development. The DoP could then be used to link Palestinian economic development to the fostering of regional economic development programmes which would involve Israel, and thereby Israel would use Israeli-Palestinian rapprochement to integrate Israel into the surrounding regional economic system and thus sidestep the Arab economic boycott of Israel, without the need for the resolution of a comprehensive regional peace. Thus by transferring certain powers and responsibilities to the PISGA, with the promise of more to come, Israel would not only continue to determine the extent of the occupation but would also receive due recognition of its peacemaking by gaining access to markets and investments long denied to it.

For many Palestinians, the success or failure of the DoP was based on its ability to deliver rapid economic improvements in their lives. While economic development was not the primary impetus for the DoP, in many ways the political success of the DoP and the PISGA would depend on the health of the Palestinian economy, worn down over many years by occupation, the *intifada* and the fall-out from the Second Gulf War. The DoP recognized the importance to its maintenance of economic issues, particularly in warding off political opposition to make it work. Tangible international economic support for the DoP was solicited, in the form of some $2.4bn worth of commitments of loans and grant aid moneys from over 40 countries at a World Bank-sponsored international donors' consultative group meeting in Paris in December 1993. Pledges were initially meant to fund the Emergency Assistance Programme for the Occupied Territories (EAP) worked out between the World Bank and Palestinian representatives, based on the assumption that the PISGA would fund ordinary day-to-day operations from tax revenues. The EAP was designed to channel project aid into the occupied territories, and balance long-term development needs with more immediate employment concerns. Thus the Palestinian Economic Council for Development and Reconstruction (PECDAR) was established to channel funds and cooperate with the bank in both allocation and accountability.

PECDAR was created by PISGA decree on 31 October 1993, to be the central institution for managing the process of reconstruction and development in the occupied territories in the interim period. PECDAR's chairman was Faruq Qaddumi, with Ahmad Qurai appointed as Director General. PECDAR was governed by a 14–member Board of Governors, which appointed a Managing Director, Office Directors, provided overall policy guidance for PECDAR activities, set general programme priorities, established personnel and administrative policies (including procedures for procurement, accounting and auditing), and approved PECDAR's budget and individual EAP projects. PECDAR's basic regulations were laid down by bylaws, developed with donor assistance and approved by the Board of Governors on 11 January 1994 and ratified by the PISGA. The Managing Director formulated proposals, submitted PECDAR's budget to the Board, presented individual projects to the Board, was generally responsible for PECDAR's management, and had an internal auditor, legal adviser and procurement adviser attached to his office. PECDAR, with a staff of about 100, was headquartered in the West Bank with a branch office in Gaza to monitor Gazan operations. PECDAR was set up with an administration office and five functional offices. The office of Economic Policy Formulation and Project Review (EPFPR) was charged with economic analysis and macroeconomic forecasting, formulation of economic policy options, sector strategies, public expenditure programming, and project evaluation and review. EPFPR acts in close cooperation with the Palestinian Development Institute and the Palestinian Bureau of Statistics. The Office of Aid Coordination and Facilitation was the focal point for donor relations regarding programming and monitoring of official aid, except that given directly to NGOs. The Office of Technical Assistance and Funding was given responsibility for managing non-project technical assistance, reviewing training needs, screening proposals and disseminating information. The Office of NGOs and Special Programmes was provisionally charged with developing framework agreements for dealing with NGOs and UN agencies, with additional responsibilities for directing special programmes and activities such as detainee rehabilitation, and formulating policies to encourage private sector development. The Office of Programme Management and Monitoring was responsible for investment programme implementation and monitoring.[50]

The Paris Protocol formally established the new Israeli-Palestinian economic relationship. Taking trade as representative of this new arrangement, Israel demanded that the Palestinians 'harmonise their tax and customs regime with the high levels in force in Israel'.[51] The Palestinians argued that such a policy would make Palestinian products too expensive both for domestic consumption and export, and that any advantages accruing from a cheaper workforce and less regulated business environment would therefore be lost. The Palestinians further argued that they would be unable to act as a conduit for passing third country imports into the Israeli market, which would have the political effect of making further autonomy dependent on Israeli *diktat*, and/or making the Palestinians more dependent on Jordan economically and politically, thereby restricting further independent Palestinian development and/or sovereignty. Palestinian arguments stressed the need for a free-trade agreement between the occupied territories and Israel, with the Palestinians deciding the rates of trade tariffs and customs duties. This represented a major point of disagreement between the two sides. Israel had been undergoing an extensive programme of economic liberalization aimed at dismantling its heavily protectionist and subsidized economy, and as this had not been an easy transformation, the Paris Protocol detailed Israel's desired trade regime.[52] The Israelis wanted the trade regime to follow Israeli import tariffs, trade taxes, import licensing regulations and trading standards. Even though Israel accepted unlimited access for Palestinian products into Israel, Israeli concerns centred on the possibility of the PISGA areas becoming a channel for cheap third country imports into Israel. Due to the underdeveloped nature of the Palestinian economy, Palestinians, however, had little to export to Israel apart from agricultural products, therefore it would only be through low import duties that Palestinians would be able to gain a competitive advantage in the Israeli economy. Political pressure was applied on the Israeli government from concerned sectors of the Israeli economy, fearful of cheaper Palestinian competition. The subsidized Israeli agriculture industry voiced their grave concern and insisted on protection within the terms of the protocol. Under Article VIII.10 of the Gaza-Jericho Agreement, six items were subject to quantitative restrictions on their import to Israel until 1998: poultry, eggs, potatoes, cucumbers, tomatoes and melons. Milk production by each would be for domestic consumption. Israel feared some 5000 Israeli job losses as a result of Palestinian competition, and also that Israeli markets would be swamped by cheap imports from Egypt and Jordan imported via the PISGA areas. The Article VIII.12 Annex IV Protocol on Economic Relations stated that the two sides would 'refrain from importing agricultural products from third parties which may adversely affect the interests of each other's farmers'.[53]

The Paris Protocol allowed for the establishment by the PISGA of its own import policy and tariff structure for certain commodities from Egypt and Jordan, and allowed it to fix customs duties and taxes for imported goods for the Palestinians' own economic development programme on vehicle imports and petroleum products, but this was conditional on petrol prices being no more than 15 per cent less than in Israel. The benefits of the Paris Protocol to the Palestinians were deemed to be: guaranteed access to the Israeli market; and the opportunity to diversify trade, to import some goods at the cheapest price and to raise revenues on imports. The drawbacks were that the PISGA had no independence in making economic decisions, imports from third countries were restricted (imports were determined by the Joint Economic Committee, and even then they could only originate in Egypt or Jordan), and Palestinian competitiveness was hampered by subsidies and protection for some Israeli products and by a PISGA VAT rate 1 per cent lower than Israel's. The PISGA was also denied unrestricted access to critical resources, such as water and land, as Israel had declared 70 per cent of the West Bank state land, though actual appropriation was 60 per cent of the West Bank and 40 per cent of the Gaza Strip.[54]

In order to determine financial development, the Palestinians argued for the establishment of an independent central bank which would issue currency, control commercial bank licences and reserves, and direct monetary policy. However, although this was opposed by Israel as an obvious and therefore unacceptable symbol of sovereignty, Israel did accede to the establishment of a Palestinian Monetary Authority (PMA) which would control, monitor and license the banking system and financial sector.[55] Therefore the protocol provided for the establishment of a central Financial Management Administration to manage fiscal policy with overall responsibility for public expenditure and revenue, a central budget office to supervise the budgets of local authorities and prepare an annual budget in cooperation with UNRWA, NGOs and aid agencies, and a central treasury office which together with other offices and PECDAR would manage taxation and budgeting. Article IV.1 stated that the PISGA would establish a Monetary Authority (PMA) in the Areas, with powers and responsibilities for the regulation and implementation of the monetary policies within the functions.[56] The PMA is an interesting body, empowered in a number of fiscal areas to act as the PISGA's official economic and financial adviser (IV.2), the PISGA's and the public sector's sole financial agent, locally and internationally (IV.3), the manager of all the PISGA's, and all public sector entities' deposited foreign currency reserves (including gold) (IV.4), the lender of last resort for the banking system in the areas (IV.5), the authorizer of foreign exchange dealers, and the regulator and supervisor of foreign exchange transactions (IV.6), the banking supervisory body, responsible for the proper functioning, stability, solvency and liquidity of the banks in the areas (IV.7), and the re-licenser of each of the five branches of Israeli banks operating in the West Bank and Gaza Strip (IV.8). However the protocol did not allow the PISGA to issue its own currency which would assume the obvious symbolism of sovereignty. These institutions would all be subject to the oversight of the Joint Economic Committee as Article IV.10b did allow that both sides would 'continue to discuss, through the JEC, the possibility of introducing mutually agreed Palestinian currency or temporary alternative currency arrangements for the Palestinian Authority.'[57] Israel refused the PISGA's application to issue an ECU-style currency for issuing income-generating bonds, but the official legal tender was to remain the shekel (NIS), although the Jordanian dinar and the US dollar could still be used; thus the Palestinian economy would be linked to prevailing economic conditions in Israel, and to a lesser extent in Jordan, as Article IV.10a stated the NIS would 'legally serve there as a means of payment for all purposes including official transactions'.[58] Although the Palestinian economy could not realistically hope to support a convertible currency, the protocol ensured that the PISGA would be unable to make monetary policy, in particular control interest rates, make strategic interventions, or determine currency values.

The PISGA faced two immediate problems. First, it lacked a trained and experienced administrative corps. The breadth of the tax base was such that it could not cope with financing the PISGA's start-up costs, with the result that the PISGA was forced to use external development assistance to make good budget deficits as there was no capacity for the PISGA to borrow domestically, which in turn proved destabilizing as domestic payments arrears spiralled. However, a positive outcome of the protocol was that foreign and Palestinian banks opened in the occupied territories, giving more generous terms to borrowers than Israeli banks. It was hoped that with Saudi Arabian, Egyptian, Jordanian and Palestinian diaspora capital available for investment credit, public confidence in the financial system could be restored. Israel too, hoped to play a part in developing the financial system through joint ventures and links with foreign, including Arab, capital flows.

One of the major burdens that the nascent financial system would have to cope with was the dreadfully high levels of unemployment in the West Bank and Gaza. The PISGA's inability to create sufficient numbers of jobs meant that, at least for the early life of the DoP, Palestinian jobs in Israel assumed major importance as a vital source of income. Thus the protocol committed Israel to resist the temptation to deny Palestinian access, both physically and institutionally, to employment in Israel. However, closures of the territories preventing workers travelling, and restrictions on the numbers allowed access, to Israel, meant a steady decline in income derived from Israel. This problem was further exacerbated by PM Rabin, who stated that his intention was 'to reduce dramatically the number of Palestinians working in Israel'. From March 1994, 70 000 workers from Eastern Europe, Turkey and the Far East were imported to Israel, and the government subsidized Israeli immigrants at the rate of $13 per day to encourage them to replace Palestinian workers.[59]

Although the Cairo Agreement affirmed the Paris Protocol as an integral part of it, establishing the contractual agreement that would govern the economic relations between the two sides, covering the West Bank and Gaza Strip during the interim period, Israeli redeployment from the occupied territories made slow progress, schedules were broken or postponed, elections did not materialize between September 1993 and January 1996, and constant Israeli closures of the territories seriously undermined a major source of income for the Palestinian population. International and bilateral aid came slowly, causing living standards either to be barely maintained or to drop, resulting in sections of the Palestinian public losing faith in the peace process. Of a total of $760m pledged for FY 1994, only $140m had actually been disbursed by November 1994.[60] Emergency aid, released piecemeal, was used to cover the costs of running the police force but donors were reluctant to releases funds for development funding. Non-security services like health and education were spheres transferred to the PISGA which had to be financed by PISGA tax revenue generated from the population. Tax revenue projections made in early summer 1995 were for a deficit of some $150m, as a direct result of not being able to collect such moneys, either due to the moneys just not being there or through endemic tax evasion fostered under military occupation.[61] The problems inherent in operating in a severe crisis management mode were well demonstrated by two US disbursements in 1994 – one of $5m in May, the second of $4m in October – payments which together were not sufficient to cover the electricity bill owed by the Gaza municipality to the Israel Electric Corporation, which was threatening to cut off supply. In this way, foreign assistance-led development carried a number of risks. Funds did not always appear on the promised dates, were not limitless, and were likely to be reduced as nations reordered their priorities through changing circumstances. In order to use foreign assistance most effectively, the PISGA economy had to be as flexible as possible to be able to cope with the vagaries of financial fortune. This meant that it had to develop its own revenue sources and not become too dependent on foreign assistance for its economy's survival. In essence, aid should have been complementary rather than an integral component of the domestic economy. The trouble with the situation in the Gaza Strip, in particular the high levels of unemployment, was that a politically fluid situation existed regarding the final status, therefore for politically expedient short-term reasons there was undoubtedly an opportunity, if not a desire, for the PISGA's ruling elite to restrict the effects of domestic direct taxation on the community by utilizing aid money for unaccountable political patronage and for limiting the harsh effects of a struggling economy.

In the early stages of the PISGA's life, donor nations were rather worried about the nascent PISGA's ability to resist the temptations of political favours, and they therefore restricted the disbursement levels, being reluctant merely to underwrite the then-unelected Palestinian leadership and provide short-term poverty relief. Arafat alienated many Palestinian economists and politicians by his insistence on taking direct personal control of expenditure at all levels and arbitrarily bypassing PECDAR. However, with typical hypocrisy, foreign donor nations' companies sought contracts in such a system, independently of and in competition with each other.[62] The difficulty for the donor nations lay with the constant delay in announcing elections for a fully accountable PISGA Council, resulting in aid money becoming inseparable from the progress of the Israeli-Palestinian peace process, economically and politically. The election issue became a weapon used by all sides to advance their positions. With high levels of Palestinian unemployment, restricted access to Israel for Palestinian workers, aid discrimination between Israel and the PISGA institutionalized within the negotiated agreements and land expropriation, features of the Israeli-Palestinian economic relationship, no amount of foreign aid could sustain the Palestinian economy for very long or be used to its full potential. The cynical interpretation thus would be that foreign aid was not really intended actually to deliver sustainable economic development, but rather as a bandage to contain the Israeli-Palestinian conflict and merely sustain the political process as determined by the actors involved at the expense of real economic and political development. The spheres which were transferred to the PISGA – health, education, social welfare for example – were not income-generators but rather expenditure-consumers, and other spheres which were later transferred or remained under Israeli authority tended to be of more strategic value, such as resources, which therefore hampered Palestinian economic development.[63]

Article III outlined the PISGA's powers and responsibilities in the sphere of import and customs policy. The PISGA's import policy included independently determining and changing if necessary the rates of customs, purchase tax, levies, excises and other charges, the regulation of licensing requirements and procedures and of standard requirements.[64] Imports from Israel would remain as before under the customs union effectively established by the occupation, but how Israeli economic policy would affect intra-Israeli-Palestinian trade was not covered by this agreement. However the protocol listed 'Goods on List A1', 'Goods on List A2' and 'goods on List B' as determining the types and categories of goods that Palestinians could import from places other than Israel. List A1 covered locally produced items in Jordan and Egypt particularly, and from other agreed Arab countries. List A2 covered Arab, Islamic and other agreed countries. List B covered basic food items and other goods for the Palestinian economic development programme.[65] Lists A1 and A2 included foodstuffs, live animals, agricultural products, construction materials, fertilizers, electrical equipment and household electric appliances.[66] Customs valuations would be based on the 1994 GATT agreement, entering into force as of the date it was introduced in Israel, and until then was based on the Brussels Definition of Valuation (BDV) system, the classification of goods being based on the principles of 'the Harmonized Commodity Description and Coding System'.[67] Items imported from Jordan, Egypt, or other Arab and Islamic countries would have to comply with rules of origin determined by a joint sub-committee. For example locally produced goods will conform if: they have been wholly grown, produced or manufactured in that country; they have been imported directly; and the value of the costs of the materials produced in that country plus the direct processing costs are not less than 30 per cent of the export value.[68] List B included capital equipment for economic development, equipment for the textile industry, industrial equipment, pharmaceutical products, farm machinery and heavy plant machinery. However, List B did not include all capital investment equipment such as computers and pesticides. Capital equipment items subject to the existing customs regime, particularly agricultural items such as pesticides had seen prices fluctuate whilst output had remained constant. The price index of pesticides rose by approximately 50 per cent between 1986 and 1992, while the price of West Bank vegetables rose by 25 per cent, and Gaza's by less than 10 per cent.[69] List B items carried no tariff, origin or quantity restrictions as they were considered essential for Palestinian economic development. Goods and quantities not fixed by the JEC or those not on these lists were subject to the existing customs regime, tariff rates, purchase taxes, levies and any other charges prevailing in Israel, although the PISGA was allowed to levy VAT at one rate for both local products and imports at a level between 15 and 16 per cent – Israel's rate was 17 per cent.[70]

What these powers and responsibilities meant in real terms was that import taxes and customs levies on all goods specifically designated for consumption under PISGA jurisdiction would accrue to the PISGA even if they were imported via an Israeli medium. Revenues accrued in this way were conservatively estimated by the

World Bank at 8 per cent of PISGA GNP.[71] For List B items, the direct saving was 21 per cent, being the value of Israeli tariffs on capital investment goods.[72] However, the ability to collect revenues would be dependent on Israeli goodwill and on how quickly the PISGA would be able to establish an efficient customs control network.

For goods going the opposite way, Article VIII.11 stated that the Palestinians would 'have the right to export their agricultural produce to external markets without restrictions', while Article IX.6 stated that the Palestinians would 'have the right to export their industrial produce to external markets without restrictions', both 'on the basis of certificates of origin issued by the Palestinian Authority.'[73] Any evaluation of the extent to which the protocol was meant as a stimulus for Palestinian agriculture and industry would have to be based on the growth of both the manufacturing base and the agricultural sector. Sectoral growth under the protocol would have to be a policy objective of both sides because of the obvious limitations on the PISGA, so that the Israelis would have to see the growth of the Palestinian economy as an integral aspect of their Israeli-Palestinian peace strategy. However sectoral restrictions placed on production limits, quota limits, one-sided credit and concessionary terms would have the impact of severely affecting Palestinian efficiency and competitiveness. For example, Article VIII.10 listed agricultural restrictions. Israeli quotas imposed on Palestinian agricultural produce virtually negated the advantages of the protocol, with only 25 per cent of Palestinian vegetable produce allowed unrestricted access to Israeli markets. According to some estimates, quotas on some produce were actually below previous levels. For example, cucumber exports 1990–2 averaged 19 000 tons per annum, whereas the protocol imposed a limit of 15 000 tons; potato exports were 17 000 in 1990–2, but the protocol limited this to 15 000 tons per annum. Egg production in the West Bank and Gaza outstripped consumption and quota limits, for example, in 1992 production ran at about 180m eggs whereas the protocol's export quota for 1994 was 30m eggs and the projected quota for 1998 was still only 60m eggs. Switching from egg to poultry (meat) production would not solve the problem as there was a quota system on poultry too. Israel has complex and favoured-trading links and status with international markets, such as those of the EU and US. Israeli imports from the EU and US amounted to 68 per cent and 20.5 per cent of total imports, exports to both amounted to 37.1 per cent and 33.1 per cent of Israel's total exports, and Israel subsidizes its agricultural and industrial sectors in terms of concessionary credit terms, production factors like water and land, export finances and minimum price levels for certain products. Support for Palestinian industry and agriculture in this environment would need heavy investment and protection just to survive let alone compete.[74] Economic integration in regional terms would have met the objective of opening up the Palestinian markets, giving the opportunity to strengthen the Palestinian economy through trade links, however the restrictions imposed through the protocol had both an economic and a political overtone.[75] For example, while Egypt and Jordan would be, for geographical reasons, the most important markets for the Palestinians, the political benefit would be the moderating political influence offered to the PISGA. Thus the Israelis saw the opportunity to constrain the PISGA through the promise of favourable trading concessions with Jordan and Egypt. In this sense inter-Arab trade could not be seen by the Palestinians as a way of counter-balancing the Israelis economic advantages, particularly not in the short and medium term, so that for the foreseeable future the PISGA's economy would inexorably be linked with the Israeli one. Inter-Arab trade amounted to less than 5 per cent of total Arab trade. Jordan, which was well integrated economically in the Arab region, imported 75 per cent of its total imports from non-Arab sources. Inter-Arab trade is not comprehensive, neither is it a major political factor, largely due to the non-complementary nature of the individual markets, the diverse industrial structures and frequent inter-Arab political quarrels.

On 2 May 1994, two days prior to the signing of the Cairo Agreement, donor nations pledged some $1.2bn over three years in financial support and assistance, and the World Bank unveiled a $1.2bn three-year emergency aid programme (prepared by 35 World Bank experts, 150 Palestinian experts, and representatives of 40 donor countries) to create institutions and rebuild infrastructure on territory Israel would turn over to the PISGA. According to the World Bank report, 'Emergency Assistance Programme for the Occupied Territories', a three-year programme was seen as an opportunity to jump-start the Palestinian economy, aimed at bringing social and economic benefits to a large part of the Palestinian population, to focus the international community's attention on the economic and social needs of the Palestinians, and rebuild the infrastructure of the territories in order to stimulate economic growth by attracting private investment. Ciao Koch-Weser, World Bank VP for the Middle

East and North Africa, wanted to see an immediate improvement in living conditions, with $570m being made available for the first year with the rest solidly pledged. The plan hoped to provide what would amount to $200 per person in aid, with project funding and implementation to be administered by the newly organized Palestinian Economic Council for Development and Reconstruction together with some UN and private agencies already operating in the occupied territories. Of the $1.2bn total, $600m would finance public investments ($366m for the West Bank, $234m for Gaza), $225 was earmarked for non-governmental agencies, $111 for water supply and waste water treatment (the World Bank predicted that the beginning of sewer construction and increased solid waste handling would begin by the end of 1994, most sewage in the territories being at present discharged untreated), $300m would support private sector investments in telecommunications, housing, agriculture and industry, $900m would support public sector investments in transportation, water and sewage, electric power, municipal services, education and health, and $300m would provide technical support and help construct a central Palestinian administration. The plan also contained funds for upgrading roads, power and telecommunications systems, building houses and improving agricultural practices. The World Bank, while donating $50m for emergency assistance, said the plan was designed to ensure that the Palestinians manage their own affairs. While the Palestinians fare economically better than most of their neighbours according to per capita GDP comparisons (PISGA=$1275p.a. in 1992, Jordan = $1150p.a., Egypt = $630p.a.), the power, water and telephone systems were comparable with those of the least developed countries (2.9 telephones per 100 inhabitants). The EAP budgeted $100m for the installation of 57 500 new telephones, with another $100m (80 per cent to come from the private sector) to be used for housing (roughly 50 per cent of Gazans, and 10 per cent of West Bankers live in refugee camps), and about $10m over three years would be directed toward upgrading the worst refugee camp housing. The EU, as the largest donor, pledged $600m, one quarter of the $2.4bn pledged as a result of the 1 October 1993 donor conference, the US donated $500m, Japan $200m, Norway $150m, Saudi Arabia $100m, Italy $80m and Israel $75m.[76] The purpose of these funds from the international community was to generate support for the peace process by stimulating Palestinian economic and social development, developing and enhancing the local administrative infrastructure, ensuring political stability through the offices of the PISGA, and creating immediate and real economic benefits in terms of raised living standards for the Palestinian population. The structures that grew from this international effort did not develop smoothly. Promised commitments outweighed actual financial delivery, and the dynamics of the assistance effort, such as multilateral and bilateral economic development, slow and inappropriate donor efforts, ineffective PISGA institutions and the adverse effects of Israeli policies ensured that progress in the aid programme was dependent on progress in the broader negotiating peace process.

The major aid donors were the European Union (EU), the United States, Japan and Saudi Arabia. The bulk of US aid was disbursed through the US Agency for International Development (USAID) with the rest allocated in the form of private sector guarantees administered by the Overseas Private Investment Corporation (OPIC). The breakdown was USAID $375m, OPIC $125m. Likewise, the emphasis of the EU's multilateral assistance was in the form of loans and guarantees to be distributed through the European Investment Bank (EIB). From the signing of the DoP, the EIB had been closely involved in the preparation of the 'Emergency Assistance Programme', developed by the international donor community for Gaza and the West Bank, to supplement the EU's substantial grant aid programme, the EU being one of the most significant donors. The EU Commission's grant assistance programme was providing some 100m ecu per annum by 1995 in grants for housing, education and police, as well as finance for water and sanitation projects. The EIB estimated that the EU (Commission and member states) committed some 400m ecu in grants in 1994, over half the total foreign aid for Gaza and the West Bank committed in 1994. The EIB started its contribution by providing financial assistance and logistical support to the World Bank-based Donors Secretariat, which coordinates the overall international aid effort. The EIB finances, out of its general budget resources, temporary Palestinian staff assistance for the Secretariat. The EIB was requested to make available up to 250m ecu in loans from its own resources for projects in Gaza and the West Bank when satisfactory operational conditions are in place, and sound investment projects capable of bearing loan-servicing charges have been prepared. The EIB maintains close contact with the PISGA, hoping to make its first loan operation in support of small- and medium-sized enterprises in the productive sector in late 1995. Other investment schemes, mainly in the area of infrastructure and private sector development, are being studied for EIB loan finance. Due to the nature of the Palestinian economy, a main priority of the PISGA would be to draw on the substantial concessional funding assistance offered by the international community for the most pressing needs.[77] Japan (initial pledges for 1994 $100m, 1995 $100m) and Saudi Arabia (pledge for 1995 $100m) indicated in late 1995 that they may repeat their annual contributions for the period 1996–8, which would bring the total pledges to date to more than $4bn.[78] Pledges were consistently more forthcoming than actual disbursements, indeed one major complaint made of the aid process concerned the slowness in actual aid delivery; aid pledges were not always committed to specific projects; and actual aid distribution in the West Bank and Gaza was even slower, particularly in 1994, although this seemed to improve in 1995. Roughly one third of pledged aid was made up by grants, the remainder being concessional loans or guarantees, and by the end of 1995 roughly half of all aid was directed at budget support and technical assistance, the remainder at investment projects.

The concept of international financial assistance as an instrument of peace and the process of actual aid delivery within the context of ongoing negotiations which would determine the future shape, scope and limits of a final peace settlement was a challenging one for the donors and the recipient involved. The first year of assistance was fraught with complaints regarding the tardiness and targeting of the aid, so as a result of these complaints the aid structure was modified in order that the targeting, pace, delivery, effectiveness and coordination of the programmes was improved.[79]

The aid structure

Two major structures were established to provide strategic external command, control and direction to the donor aid programme, the Consultative Group (CG) and the Ad-Hoc Liaison Committee (AHLC). The CG was typical of the mechanisms the World Bank uses to coordinate aid programmes, that is incorporating aid officials and technical experts, though in the Palestinian case the CG was generally used to win support and funding for detailed assistance plans. The AHCL consisted of interested out-of-region parties specific to the Madrid peace process, the US, Russia, the EU, Japan, Canada, Saudi Arabia and Norway. The PISGA, Israel, Egypt, Jordan, Tunisia and the UN participated as associate members, as they were either conduits, beneficiaries or recipients of the aid programmes. The AHCL met less frequently although it tended to have a higher level of political representation. It acted as a *de facto* political steering committee, even though technically it reported to the steering committee of the multilateral track of the peace process which was responsible for establishing broad guidelines and policies for the aid process. With Norway as AHLC chair and the World Bank as secretariat, all decisions were reached by consensus. Much of the real work of both structures was done informally at meetings of the major members in between the formal meetings. The US, the EU and the World Bank played the most influential roles, with Israel and the PISGA the most interested parties. Within this framework, to facilitate day-to-day implementation of policies, substructures were created. For example, during the implementation of the Cairo Agreement in May 1994 a Coordinating Committee for Assistance to the Palestinian Police (COPP) was formed to secure and coordinate donor pledges of police funds and equipment. And in November 1994, the AHLC established the Local Aid Coordination Committee (LACC) to facilitate coordination on the ground among the major aid agencies, the PISGA and the Joint Liaison Committee (JLC). The LACC was co-chaired by Norway, the World Bank and the UN. It met at least once a month from January 1995 onwards with roughly 30 local donor representatives attending. The LACC, in turn, established twelve core Sectoral Working Groups, each group with one or more PISGA ministry as gavel holder, a donor as shepherd and a UN agency as secretariat.[80] The JLC consisted of the PISGA (gavel holder), Israel, US, EU, UN and the World Bank (secretariat), and Norway (shepherd) to deal with significant obstacles in the way of the prompt and effective delivery of assistance, as well as to review PISGA budgetary performance, revenue-generation and priorities for technical assistance. The JLC met at least once a month from May 1995.

The JLC was the forum within which implementation of the Tripartite Action Plan for the Palestinian Authority (TAP) was monitored. The AHLC was responsible for a performance review process to oversee the implementation of the TAP. The AHLC asked the International Monetary Fund (IMF) to monitor the Palestinian budget, and appointed the AHLC Secretariat to follow up on donor contributions and the implementation of the public sector investment programme. The AHLC used the LACC and the JLC to oversee on a continuing basis the implementation of the TAP by the PISGA, Israel and the donors. On behalf of and under the instruction of the AHLC, the LACC and the JLC reviewed the quarterly reports prepared by the

PISGA in conjunction with the IMF, together with information provided by the AHLC Secretariat on steps taken to implement the TAP. The JLC was 'the primary forum for working out problems related to the overall assistance effort'. The AHLC met to monitor situations at the request of the chair upon the recommendation of any of its members. For example, on 2 May 1995 in Paris, a meeting was called to discuss the $136m shortfall in the PISGA's start-up and running costs. The AHLC met in Paris on 27–28 May 1995 to consider the new requirements concerning PISGA self-governing financing. Discussion at the meeting focused on how donors could assist the PISGA in financing its budget deficit for the period 1 May–31 December 1995. The discussions which led to the TAP took place in accordance with the existing agreements between the PLO and Israel, that is, the DoP, the Cairo Agreement and the Erez Checkpoint Agreement of 29 August 1994. The discussion also noted the Oslo Declaration of 13 September 1994 and the 'Understanding on Revenues, Expenditures and Donor Funding for the Palestinian Authority 1 October 1994–31 March 1995' signed in Brussels on 30 November 1994. The TAP was between the PISGA, Israel and Norway (as AHLC chair).[81]

The Tripartite Action Plan for the Palestinian Authority contained specific commitments by the parties in the spheres of tax, fiscal expenditure and donor budgetary support.

(1) Palestinian requirements and responsibilities desperately necessitated a functional tax collection system throughout Gaza and the West Bank in order to deal with a number of pressing issues:
- to implement IMF recommendations on improving its tax administrative and expenditure management
- to improve the operation of the tax system
- to freeze salaries and hiring at budgeted levels
- to centralize all fiscal revenues, fiscal expenditures and the payment process within the Ministry of Finance's direct control
- to establish a binding budget forecast for all public expenditure
- to establish a comprehensive taxation plan for financial year (FY) 1995–6
- to make best efforts so that donor support for start-up costs would not be required beyond 31 December 1996
- to prepare for donors a document outlining functional diagrams, policy responsibilities and contacts of PECDAR, Ministries of Economy and Trade, International Planning and Cooperation, Finance and the Palestinian Monetary Authority

- to unify commercial and investment codes and develop import-export procedures for Gaza/Jericho
- to decentralize project implementation, design and execution through PECDAR utilizing municipalities, village councils, NGOs, ministries and UN agencies
- to finalize with Israel a joint concept paper on industrial zones, and
- to work toward the establishment of an appropriate regula–tory framework for the mobilization for private sector investment.

(2) Israeli requirements and responsibilities made cooperation with the PISGA necessary to ensure a functioning tax operation in the West Bank:
- to expedite transfer to the PISGA of all taxes due
- to cooperate with the PISGA in supporting the new tax structure in Gaza/Jericho, re-establish the computer connection for the tax system and ensure the monthly transfers of taxes
- to resolve outstanding May–December 1994 VAT clearances and outstanding issues related to tax clearances
- to cooperate with the PISGA to provide training for Palestinian tax advisers
- to ensure that agreed taxes related to Gaza and the West Bank economic activity would accrue to the PISGA
- to ease the transfer of goods between Israel and Gaza/Jericho, West Bank and Gaza, West Bank and Jordan, Gaza and Egypt and to ensure the swift inspection and passage of goods destined for Gaza and the West Bank development projects
- to take all contingency measures to maintain maximum economic activity whenever security measures were applied.

(3) Donor requirements and responsibilities necessitated their best efforts to address the PISGA financing gap and provide required funds
- to expedite release of outstanding pledges for start-up costs
- to gain agreement to extend, through to 31 December 1995, the operation of the International Bank for Reconstruction and Development's Holst Fund and UN police disbursement mechanisms
- to continue to seek to raise necessary resources for quick disbursing job creation projects, offering preferential trade access to Palestinian goods, incentives and guarantees for private investment in Gaza and the West Bank.

It was stressed that donor efforts would be contingent on Israeli-Palestinian implementation performance.[82]

The World Bank was of central importance in the international aid effort. As secretariat for the AHLC, it facilitated meetings and helped track donor assistance. It also acted as chair for the CG and assumed a major role in assessing economic conditions and in developing packages for projects for donor support in association with the PISGA. The first instrument of aid, the EAP, was presented by the World Bank to the first CG meeting in December 1993. The $1.2bn EAP was based on the earlier World Bank six-volume report, 'Developing the Occupied Territories: an Investment in Peace', published in September 1993. This study was undertaken at the request of the Madrid sponsors. The World Bank supported the work of the Multilateral Working Group on Economic Development by providing analyses of the key economic issues and developmental challenges. At the Working Group's second meeting in Paris in October 1992, the Bank was requested to make an assessment of the development needs and prospects of the economies of the West Bank and Gaza Strip. Officials, comprising five teams, visited the occupied territories between 21 January and 24 February 1993, and focused on Agriculture, Human Resources, Infrastructure, Macroeconomics and Private Sector Development.[83] While the EAP identified sectoral needs and priorities through 1994–6, the World Bank prepared its own aid programme, the $128m Emergency Rehabilitation Programme (ERP), which involved 117 smaller projects throughout the West Bank and Gaza. Initially, $88m was pledged to the ERP, with $30m from the World Bank-associated aid agency the International Development Association, and Saudi Arabia, Switzerland and Denmark provided some of the rest. Other than the ERP, support for private sector investment would come through loans from the World Bank-affiliated International Finance Corporation (IFC). The World Bank was responsible for the Technical Assistance Trust Fund (TATF) which aimed to finance technical assistance, training and feasibility studies over the initial 12–18 months. The TATF, which was part of the overall EAP, consisted of about 100 priority activities for the period 1993–6 and had an estimated aggregate cost of $75m.[84] However, only a portion of these activities were financed by the TATF. Projects were chosen for TATF support only if they helped create a coherent framework of sectoral strategies and policies and institutional development within which other technical assistance activities, funded directly by donors, could be anchored. Due to the mass of work and the urgent need for implementation, it was deemed necessary to tap the existing donor system – UN agencies, NGOs and universities – to help carry out specific technical assistance projects under the umbrella of PECDAR, which prioritized projects and had overall responsibility for the EAP. Due to political and economic uncertainty and the limitation of resources, the technical assistance programme had to develop flexibly as a rolling plan, subject to review and adjustment to accommodate evolving priorities.[85] PECDAR issued a statement to the Palestinian people in response to local and foreign press reports regarding the size of financial assistance from the World Bank and donor countries to the Palestinian economy, because they felt these reports were causing confusion in regard to the possibility of huge commitments to programmes and of amounts allocated. PECDAR released information on all available projects, moneys pledged and actual amounts allocated. For example, the PECDAR-World Bank-supervised Emergency Rehabilitation Programme invested $128m in water, sewage, roads and education – 50 per cent for Gaza, 50 per cent for the West Bank. The PECDAR-donors-administered Emergency Investment Programme invested $150m in infrastructure and manpower sectors – 40 per cent for Gaza, 60 per cent for the West Bank. The PECDAR-World Bank-administered Technical Assistance Trust Fund supported training sectors and implemented technical programmes – $35m was needed, but only $31.6m was committed. The World Bank was also responsible for managing the Johan Jurgen Holst Fund, used to support the PISGA's start-up and recurrent costs. The Holst Fund, valued at $123m with $19m committed as of June 1994, supported the deficit assistance programme, which included supporting the establishment of the Palestinian police force, the rehabilitation of detainees, public works and unemployment.[86] By November 1995, the Holst Fund had disbursed some $157m to the PISGA, the largest contributors being the US, which had provided $40m, and Kuwait ($21m).[87] The Holst Fund played a pivotal role in staving off PISGA administrative collapse, particularly with regard to paying civil service salaries and administrative costs, which had forced the World Bank and Norway into frequent emergency fund-raising. The PISGA's draft budget for FY 1996 projected recurrent expenditure at $629m (civil employees' salaries $250m, 27 000 police officers $147m), with revenues of $554m, leaving a FY 1996 current expenditure shortfall of $75m, which would be made up by the Holst Fund. The budget also expected a capital expenditure of $273m, which was to be entirely financed by donor development assistance.[88]

The UN also played a significant role in providing assistance to the PISGA, channelling upwards of $100m in funds committed in 1994 through several UN agencies, such as the UNDP, UNRWA, UNICEF, WHO, UNESCO and others. The most important of these UN agencies was the UN Development Programme (UNDP), which operated as a channel and implementing agency for a number of aid projects. However the UN agency with the most developed infrastructure and operating history in the occupied territories, particularly in Gaza, was the UN Relief and Works Agency (UNRWA). The International Monetary Fund monitored and fostered PISGA fiscal management and best practices. The United Nations Special Coordinator Office (UNSCO) operated as the coordinator and facilitator for cooperation between the UN, PISGA, Israel and the donors. Norwegian academic Terje Rod Larsen, who had been instrumental in setting up the Oslo process, was appointed to head UNSCO by the Secretary-General in 1994.

The Palestinian equivalent of the World Bank was the Palestinian Economic Council for Development and Reconstruction (PECDAR). PECDAR was set up to be the central institution for managing the process of reconstruction and development in the occupied territories in the interim period. The recipients and managers of PISGA aid moneys via PECDAR were the Ministry of Planning and International Cooperation (headed by Nabil Sha'ath), the Ministry of Finance (headed by Mohammed Zuhdi al-Nashashibi), the Ministry of Economy (headed by Ahmed Qurai), functional ministries depending on the particular aid project, existing municipal government and the office of the president. In October 1995 the World Bank and the UN, in conjunction with the PISGA, presented to the donor community at the CG meeting a seven-volume study entitled 'Putting Peace to Work'. This study presented a list of 16 priority projects totalling $552m, development strategies and $450m in UN project proposals. The study was drawn from lessons learned from the EAP and incorporated the Palestinian Public Investment Programme (PPIP), a $1.3bn investment and development framework for FYs 1995–8. The PPIP proposed a number of major projects, such as water-sewage and drainage, electricity supply and distribution, upgrading roads, a coastal parkway for Gaza, a Gaza harbour, municipal infrastructure improvements, housing development, school improvements, health infrastructure, cross-border industrial estates, private sector regulation assistance, the establishment of a Palestinian Monetary Authority, trust funds for NGOs and for expatriate Palestinian experts as well as some unfunded projects from the EAP.[89] A special ministerial-level donors' conference was scheduled for December 1995, to generate support for the package of project initiatives and to endorse a revised TAP. However the conference had to be postponed due to ministerial obligations arising from the Bosnian peace process.

International aid and the Palestinian Interim Self-Governing Authority

The PISGA and the international donor community viewed donor aid to the occupied territories as an integral element of the peace process. Some $2.5bn was pledged for the financial years 1994–8 as the practical application of building and nurturing the Israeli-Palestinian peace through an international aid effort. A persistent criticism of the donor programme was of the delays in receiving pledged moneys, which in turn resulted in the tardiness on the part of the PISGA in applying such moneys to projects. Throughout 1994, the PISGA complained that the international community was 'moving very, very slowly' and charged that the delays were a form of political pressure. For example, during the first deployment of PISGA security forces in May 1994, Nabil Sha'ath was obliged to arrange private financing to cover the costs.[90]

The major criticism of the donor aid programme surrounded the issue of pledged moneys being actually disbursed. In 1994, $807m was pledged by donors with $773m committed to projects, but only $407m was actually disbursed, with much of it only received in the final quarter of the year.[91] Aid money was slow to find its way to the PISGA for a number of reasons, not least the caution displayed by the donors themselves and their reluctance to become responsible for the day-to-day PISGA administrative costs or make-work programmes. Many donors believed that such a responsibility was the PISGA's, to be funded through taxation, and not through the donor assistance programme, which had altogether different priorities. Donors viewed the PISGA's daily running costs as a drain on finite donor resources, and at odds with the free market philosophy of the assistance programme. Although small amounts of aid did flow quickly through discretionary embassy accounts, larger aid projects were subject to lengthy bureaucratic planning, proposal, assessment and procurement procedures as well as evaluations in terms of donor priorities concerning the environment, gender and private sector development. This inherent disagreement about the envisioned future laid bare the process of delivering international assistance. The PISGA faced politico-economic realities which necessitated rapid delivery of assistance for short-term goals, both to strengthen its own position with the Palestinian population and to appear as a credible alternative to the Israeli military government. Unanticipated heightened Israeli security measures in response to bomb attacks resulted in long-term closures of the occupied territories. Palestinians criticized these Israeli security measures, political expediency and inappropriate Western aid, in the form of funding commitments for long-term development programmes, as unsuitable responses to easing the reality of immediate Palestinian economic conditions.

There is no doubt that initial donor agency assumptions and considerations often underestimated political and economic difficulties. During 1994 strains appeared between Palestinian foreign ministry and international aid officials over the commitment to sustainable development. For example US State Department officials complained about the slow delivery of US Agency for International Development (USAID) programmes. In response USAID officials complained they were being diverted from meaningful development by political pressure to donate to the Holst Fund, which they regarded as an inefficient development mechanism because it supported the unproductive, recurrent costs of PISGA administration. Palestinian foreign ministry officials meanwhile saw receipt of moneys from the Holst Fund as a political imperative.[92] Further complications regarding the delivery of international assistance included in almost all cases some form of domestic legislative restriction binding donors' freedom of action. For example, US legislation required State Department certification of PLO compliance with the Oslo agreement, prohibited direct US assistance to the PISGA and mandated USAID support for the establishment of cross-border industrial parks, despite a pre-existing legislative ban on USAID projects potentially competitive with US manufacturers. This ensured that the USAID budget was a congressional battleground for those critical of foreign aid and the peace process. Senator D'Amato and Representative Forbes introduced draft legislation in June 1995 to place greater restrictions on aid to the Palestinians, and in autumn 1995 aid was hostage to unrelated issues ranging from abortion to State Department reorganization. Japan was bound by domestic legislation that limited its assistance to international organizations and recognized states, thus excluding the PISGA. Despite the peace process's intention of providing for a preventive security regime, domestic legal restrictions prevented almost all donors and most aid agencies from providing direct assistance to the Palestinian police.[93]

As aid programmes expanded from about $200m to about $800m per annum, between 1990 and 1994, further problems arose from international agencies' institutional inability to cope with such rapidly expanding aid programmes and the reordering of economic and employment priorities. Early aid programmes were heavily dependent on small NGO projects and were not easily upgraded or rethought as new priorities and new projects were identified. Pre-Oslo US aid was mainly transmitted through Private Voluntary Organizations (PVOs) rather than administered by US institutions directly. Thus USAID had to expand its infrastructure rapidly in order to effect its mission, which also involved internal bureaucratic and political struggles over issues like staffing levels, location (East Jerusalem or Tel Aviv) and line authority.[94] Political competition between the donors also caused problems. Factors such as individual national priorities, the maximization of national visibility, commercial competition for long-term benefit projects, procurement guidelines mandating supplier preferences, tied aid allocated in the form of loans, risk insurance, or export and investment guarantees, conservative international bank standards and EU-USA geo-political competitiveness, all tended to shape donor assistance through 1993 and 1994. The latter year saw a significant discordance in PISGA/World Bank-EAP-identified sectoral goals and the actual distribution of donor aid funds. The EU allocated half of its assistance through the EIB, and the EU presidency committed itself to accelerating the disbursement of EIB funds. The US allocated $125m to OPIC, although by December 1995 only one project, a Gaza concrete factory, had been financed which led to criticism of OPIC by State Department and USAID officials. The US Trade Development Agency supported six major feasibility and other studies and $70m was allocated through the IFC. By October 1995 only about 10 per cent ($67m) of pledged loan and guarantee funding had been committed.[95] PISGA criticism of the international assistance programme was also influenced by its desire to divert criticism away from its own incompetence and press for further disbursements, as much of 1994's expeditious donor assistance had been rendered through the Holst Fund as the engineering aspects of investment and rehabilitation projects could only be altered to a certain extent.

By the end of 1994, the multilateral and bilateral assistance programmes had to be revised to take account of the serious economic
situation in the occupied territories as a result of repeated Israeli
closures and slow and badly targeted donor assistance. Bilateral donors
adapted their efforts taking account of changing requirements, the
nature of the donor and the restrictions on assistance. UN agencies
were better used, particularly UNRWA because of its well-developed
organization. Japanese assistance went through UN agencies because
of domestic restrictions on direct aid. Germany used commodity
donations to support recurrent administrative costs. However, there
were a number of problems with commodity donations. For example,
the Palestinian police received large numbers of vehicles, but continued donor restrictions prevented handguns and riot-control
equipment being obtained, so that the police had to resort to as-
sault rifles for policing and crowd control. Donated communications
equipment worked on incompatible frequencies not cleared for PISGA
use. Police salaries were funded through UNRWA, while UNSCO
helped coordinate technical assistance and equipment donations.
The EU channelled much of its aid at the PISGA and Palestinian
municipalities to support nascent Palestinian administration. In late
1994, USAID's programme was restructured because of State Department and White House pressure. Previous support for PVOs and
long-term institution-building projects in health and housing were
cut greatly. US support refocused on more rapid job-creation projects
in municipal public works, micro-enterprises and a Gaza waste/storm
water project. USAID assistance refocused on the most politically
effective projects and project processes were speeded up.[96] The World
Bank moved its decision-making authority to its resident representative, Odin Knudsen, to facilitate aid delivery, expedite response times,
facilitate contacts with the PISGA, Israel, and local donor missions
and play a more proactive role in resolving disputes. The UN mandated UNSCO to provide UN coordination and 'good offices'
diplomatic mediation.[97] Recognizing the political importance of
focusing on employment creation and donor coordination, the AHCL
set up a high-level, locally based Joint Liaison Committee (JLC) to
resolve inter-donor differences, endorsed a Local Aid Coordination
Committee (LACC) expediting donor coordination on the ground
in November 1994 and focused local LACC sectoral working groups
on labour-intensive projects.[98] Despite the restructuring of the international aid effort, ironically it was the Holst Fund that continued
to deliver the most effective short-term donor assistance, being mostly

used to bolster and build up the public employment sector – the PISGA employed some 25 000 police and some 45 000 civil servants sustaining roughly 420 000 Palestinians (average household=6).[99]

4.4   The Agreement on Preparatory Transfer of Powers and Responsibilities (early empowerment), 29 August 1994

It is understandable that two sides who have been locked in bitter conflict have to tread a long and tortuous route to achieve trust, understanding and agreement. Israel's cautious and highly legalistic approach to solving the Israeli-Palestinian conflict may be balanced by the Palestinians' desire to speed the empowerment process along with scant regard for legal niceties in order to attend to immediate and pressing problems. However, it is clearly disturbing that the primary co-sponsor, the US, is attempting to determine the course of negotiations for the benefit of one of the protagonists, namely Israel. US Ambassador to the UN Albright wrote to all ambassadors to the UN that, 'the General Assembly's approach to Arab-Israeli issues' should

> accord with today's realities. The UN General Assembly should reinforce the peace process by promoting reconciliation, supporting agreements between the parties, and fostering economic development. Adopting a positive resolution welcoming progress in the peace process, as we did in 1993, will test the UN's new realistic approach. At the same time, contentious resolutions that accentuate political differences without promoting solutions should be consolidated (the various UNRWA resolutions), improved (the Golan resolution) or eliminated (the Israeli nuclear armament resolution and the self-determination resolution). We also believe that resolution language referring to 'final status' issues should be dropped, since these issues are now under negotiation by the parties themselves. These include refugees, settlements, territorial sovereignty and the status of Jerusalem.[100]

By underlining the primacy of the Israeli-Palestinian agreements as the basis for Israeli-Palestinian conflict resolution, the US was in effect emphasizing that these agreements constituted the main legal obligations between the two, at the expense of all others, particularly UN resolutions. Therefore the point that the legal structure being negotiated within the various agreements was most important was all the more resonant.

The 'Preparatory Transfer of Powers and Responsibilities in the West Bank', signed on 24 August 1994, was the fourth principal Israeli-Palestinian agreement. It followed the 4 May 1994 'Agreement on the Gaza Strip and the Jericho Area', and was referred to as the 'early empowerment accord', defining the shape and powers of the spheres to be transferred 'from the Israeli military government and its Civil Administration in the West Bank', pending further agreements, namely education and culture, health, social welfare, tourism, direct taxation, and Value Added Tax on local production.[101] Thus the military government and the civil administration continued to exercise power and responsibility in the West Bank apart from those spheres transferred under the new agreement. The civil administration in the Gaza Strip was dissolved by Military Proclamation No. 4, entitled 'Proclamation Regarding the Implementation of the Gaza-Jericho Agreement', issued by Gaza's IDF Commander Mitan Vilnai after the Cairo Agreement's signing. A similarly numbered military proclamation was issued in the West Bank on 13 May 1994, transferring to the PISGA powers and responsibilities regarding the Jericho Area, signed by 'the commander of the Israeli army in the area of Judea and Samaria'. Clause 3 declared 'the area commander and the head of the Civil Administration have transferred to the Palestinian Authority the powers and responsibilities regarding the Jericho area held by them or by those who were authorized by them or appointed in their stead.' The authority to delegate powers was acquired by Proclamation No. 2 (7 June 1967) and further by Military Order 130, the Interpretation Order. Military Order 130 Article 18 clarified that the IDF commander may delegate any of his powers to individuals or authorities who will exercise powers in his name. By Military Order 947 of 8 November 1981 establishing the civil authority, the military commander's appointee exercised all powers and responsibilities in the West Bank. Clause 5 of Proclamation No. 4 stated that 'the area commander, and all those appointed by him or acting on his behalf, shall continue to be in the Jericho area and shall enjoy all the powers and responsibilities, including legislative, executive and judicial powers, over Israelis and all matters regarding external security, and the security and public order of Israelis as well as any other powers and responsibilities specified in the Agreement. Clause 6 stated that 'all regulations and security legislation in the Jericho area in force at the date of the agreement shall remain in force as long as it has not been annulled or amended or suspended by virtue

of the Agreement.'[102] Indeed in the West Bank, the military government and civil administration's authority in all spheres not
transferred was fully retained, and even in the spheres transferred,
Article VI.5 stated: 'Nothing in this Agreement shall affect the
continued authority of the military government and its Civil Administration to exercise their powers and responsibilities with regard
to security and public order.'[103] The scope of the spheres transferred was in the main, pre-existing 1967 laws, and post-1967 Israeli
military orders.

The importance of security considerations greatly constrains independent Palestinian political development, particularly the freedoms
of assembly, association and Palestinian independent control within
the spheres transferred. The August agreement obligated the PISGA
to 'prevent any activities with a military orientation within each
of the Spheres and will do its utmost to maintain decorum and
discipline and to avoid disruption', notify and coordinate with the
Israelis 'regarding any planned public large-scale events and mass
gatherings within the Spheres', inform the civil administration 'of
births or deaths', inform the Israel Police in the West Bank of 'any
person wounded by any kind of weapon or explosive who is treated
or hospitalized' upon his or her admission, and of 'any death from
unnatural causes', make 'available for transfer the corpse of any
deceased from unnatural causes, for an autopsy in the Institute of
Forensic Medicine, immediately upon request by the military commander' with the PISGA having ensured that 'no prior autopsy of
the corpse so transferred' would be conducted.[104] The importance
of security considerations was further underlined with the provisions that except as specifically provided in the agreement, 'all powers
and responsibilities regarding law enforcement, including investigation, judicial proceedings and imprisonment,' would 'continue
to be under the responsibility of the existing authorities in the
West Bank', and also that the 'transfer of powers and responsibilities to the' PISGA would 'not affect the authority of Israel and of
the Israeli military government in the West Bank to exercise its
powers and responsibilities in criminal matters'.[105]

With regard to powers to legislate under the August 1995 agreement, the PISGA 'may promulgate secondary legislation regarding
the powers and responsibilities transferred to it.' All legislation enacted
by the PISGA has then to be submitted to Israel, which has 30
days to register opposition. In the event of opposition, the PISGA
may 'submit a new draft or request a review by the Legislation

Subcommittee established under the Gaza-Jericho Agreement' If the Legislation Subcommittee is unable to reach a decision within 30 days, then the PISGA is entitled to refer the matter to the Joint Liaison Committee, for consideration and deliberation within 30 days.[106] These stages amounted to an effective Israeli veto over all PISGA legislation in the spheres transferred under the August agreement.

Under the terms of the August agreement, Israel was exempted from 'all related rights, liabilities and obligations arising with regard to acts or omissions' committed prior to the transfer. 'Israel and the Civil Administration' would 'cease to bear any financial responsibility regarding such acts or omissions and the Palestinian Authority will bear all financial responsibility for its own functioning.' Furthermore, any 'financial claim made in this regard against Israel or the Civil Administration will be referred' to the PISGA. In the event that 'an award is made against Israel or the Civil Administration by any court or tribunal in respect of such a claim' the PISGA 'shall, once the award has been paid by Israel, reimburse Israel the full amount of the award.' In addition,

> Israel shall provide [the PISGA] with the information it has regarding pending and anticipated claims brought before any court or tribunal against Israel or the Civil Administration... Israel may, pursuant to agreement within [the Legal Subcommittee of the Joint Civil Affairs Coordination and Cooperation Committee] request an Israeli court or tribunal to dismiss a claim brought before it and, with regard to a pending claim, dismiss the claim and transfer the proceedings to a local court or tribunal.[107]

Whilst denying responsibility for claims against Israel, however, the opposite is not the case; it must be assumed that these provisions cover not only claims made in Israel but also awards made through Israeli courts. It must be remembered that under the various agreements the PISGA has no jurisdiction regarding, among others, Israelis, the military administration area, settlements, Jerusalem and expropriated lands. This rather makes a nonsense of claims made against Israelis, and the Israeli military occupation,[108] and all seemed to amount to Israel denying any responsibility for actions committed by it on the Palestinian population during the years of military occupation, and through this agreement made the Palestinians themselves, embodied in the PISGA, liable for those actions.

The principle of empowering the Palestinian population in either the territories transferred or spheres transferred, to determine the budget for the transferred spheres was not part of the August agreement. This was tantamount to taxation without representation. Schedule 1 outlined a six-month budget for the spheres, but as to expenditure beyond this period, Article XI.8 stated that the PISGA should 'assume full responsibility for any additional expenditures beyond the agreed budget' as well as for 'any shortfall in tax collection' that was 'not covered by the donor countries.' This in effect consigned the PISGA to fiscal insecurity whilst Israel retained effective power over budgetary requirements for the entire West Bank – Israel as the occupying power is responsible for all aspects of the Palestinian population's welfare under international law. Israel was required under Article XI.1 to provide the PISGA with full information concerning the budget of each sphere yet Israel maintained a position of providing limited access to public information from the beginning of negotiations. The Palestinians continually requested full access to information concerning the budgets of the civil administration of the West Bank and Gaza Strip, which the Israelis refused to provide, insisting on releasing only that information which pertains specifically to the spheres to be transferred.[109] The PISGA may assume the 'powers and responsibilities of the Civil Administration in the sphere of direct taxation regarding income accrued or derived in the West Bank', and the PISGA 'will levy and collect income tax on Palestinians in respect of income accrued or derived in the West Bank outside the settlements and the military locations', however, powers and 'responsibilities regarding property tax will continue to be exercised by the Civil Administration', the 'Civil Administration will levy and collect income tax on Israelis in respect of income accrued or derived in the West Bank', and until the 'Interim Agreement enters into force, Israel will transfer to the Palestinian Authority a sum equal to 75 per cent of the income taxes collected by Israel from Palestinians employed in the settlements and military locations and in Israel', all '[w]ithout derogating from the principle of territoriality in taxation, i.e., the right of each tax administration to levy the income tax on income generated by economic activity in its area'.[110] The strength of any direct taxation powers transferred were in the powers of enforcement. Accordingly, the PISGA had no power, 'in relation to criminal offences', were not to 'be authorized to take any enforcement measures against Israelis' and were not to 'have the power to exercise enforcement measures affecting, directly or indirectly, the military government or its Civil Administration.' The two sides were still to agree upon the 'mode and procedures regarding enforcement measures that require the cooperation of the military government and its Civil Administration, with a view to assisting the Palestinian Authority in carrying out its enforcement measures'. The mode and procedures were subject to considerations of security and public order, and the use of force required for the exercise of tax enforcement measures was to be effected only by the Israeli authorities.[111] Whilst the PISGA was entitled to 'establish a tax court in the West Bank for the purpose of hearing appeals with regard to assessments and bookkeeping', the details of this tax court had to be agreed by the Joint Civil Affairs Coordination and Cooperation Committee, and until such was established, appeals would 'continue to be heard by the local courts', which of course had only limited jurisdiction. Article X refers to the Joint Civil Affairs Coordination and Cooperation Committee established in accordance with the Cairo Agreement which was to 'deal with all issues of mutual concern' regarding this agreement.[112] This may be interpreted as amounting to an Israeli veto.

Any imbalance in the early empowerment agreement came more as a result from the Madrid framework/Oslo frame of reference than from complete Palestinian negotiating incompetence. Both sides view the final status outcome in opposite terms, as autonomy versus sovereignty. Thus the path to achieve final status is fraught not just over means but also over ends and means. So many anomalies exist within the early empowerment agreement that one can be forgiven for thinking that empowerment does not mean empowering. When Israeli security considerations subordinate all the transferred competencies without exception, the letter of the agreements becomes more important than the spirit, in fact the importance stressed by Israeli security considerations gives the transfer of powers and responsibilities a hollow ring. As an example of PISGA authority, Annex I of the early empowerment agreement deals with the transfer of Education and Culture. On 10 September 1995 in Hebron, Jewish settlers forced their way into the grounds of Kortoba Elementary girls school, to remove and burn Palestinian flags, legally flown since 13 September 1993, and in the ensuing fracas they beat the headmistress and five little girls, aged between six and ten. The five little girls needed hospitalization and when the IDF allowed two ambulances through their roadblock to them, the settlers tried to steal the ambulances' keys and applauded as the five girls were carried unconscious from the school. Although these attacks occurred one block from an IDF checkpoint, the soldiers did virtually nothing.[113] Under the early empowerment agreement, PISGA restraint of violent settlers is forbidden. In another example, the 350 Gazan students at Bir Zeit University (twinned with Glasgow University) effectively require four permits to study, a magnetic ID card to leave the Gaza Strip, a one/two-day permit to cross to the West Bank, a three-month West Bank residency permit and a month renewal permit for the four-month academic term. Additional stress comes from potential revocation of any of the permits, arbitrary confiscation of permits by soldiers at checkpoints and blanket cancellations of existing permits after security incidents or administrative problems, leaving students vulnerable to arrest.[114] If the transfer of powers and responsibilities to the Palestinians is made in order to 'move decisively on the path of dialogue, understanding and cooperation' to offer 'help in making Gaza prosper and Jericho blossom',[115] 'to build a home, to plant a tree, to love, live side by side with you in dignity, in affinity, as human beings, as free men',[116] to stop the heart of the cancer that afflicts both communities, namely the military occupation, then the question springs to mind whether enshrining the military occupation within the structure of the Israeli-Palestinian agreements does not serve to continue what is the very crux of the conflict between the Israelis and Palestinians, namely occupation versus sovereignty? Articles XIII.4 and XIII.5 of the August agreement, stated that the 'two Parties view the West Bank and the Gaza Strip as a single territorial unit' and that the 'Gaza Strip and the Jericho Area shall continue to be an integral part of the West Bank and the Gaza Strip. The status of the West Bank shall not be changed for the period of this Agreement.'[117] This is a reiteration of Article IV of the DoP and Article XXIII.6 of the Cairo Agreement. This is not the case in practice.

The status of the West Bank is effectively changed – or in a sense consolidated, if not challenged – by the various agreements. Not only is there territorial separation between Gaza and the West Bank, but there is territorial separation between the Jericho Area and the West Bank. IDF General Zohar Gadi, head of the Civil Administration stated that '[w]e are transferring the control of issues but not of territory'.[118] The transfer of powers and responsibilities in the five spheres does not mean that the scope of the PISGA's authority is universal. It is worth noting that Gaza and Jericho do not have the same laws, thereby complicating the consolidation and moni-toring of the legal structure within the PISGA's authority. There is not even a basic understanding about where and when laws apply. Some British Mandate laws apply in both areas, while there are Jordanian laws in the West Bank, Egyptian laws in the Gaza Strip, Israeli military orders in both, Israeli domestic laws for East Jerusa-lem, and even a criminal code brought by the PLO from Lebanon. With no elected Council, there was no clear delineation of authority and responsibility.[119] Not only did separate entities exist but so also did separate legal structures, and within the separate legal struc-tures, there were separate categories. The separate entities were Gaza, Jericho and the West Bank. The separate legal structures were Israeli, Jordanian, British, Egyptian and PISGA. The separate categories were settlements, military administration area, Jerusalem and Israelis.[120] The danger for the Palestinians within this set-up was that as sepa-ration continued, the longer *de facto* control was ceded to the Israelis for land for settlements, military installations, and so on, the more difficult it would be in the future to wrest authority for large tracts of West Bank land from the Israelis. Inevitably the conclusion may be drawn that the PISGA in effect conceded that to manage some territory immediately was better than none at all, and the price to be paid was that the West Bank, as it was occupied in 1967, would not be transferred to PISGA control entirely in that form. After all the West Bank in its 1967 form was merely an arbitrary delinea-tion due to war, demarcation and negotiation.

4.5   Israeli-Palestinian Interim Agreement on the West Bank and the Gaza Strip, 28 September 1995

The Israeli-Palestinian Interim Agreement on the West Bank and Gaza Strip signed on 28 September 1995, also known colloquially as Oslo II, details the mechanisms and limitations of the extension of Palestinian self-rule beyond the Gaza Strip and Jericho areas already dealt with under the Agreement on the Gaza Strip and Jericho Area (the Cairo Agreement) of 4 May 1994. The main text of the In-terim Agreement is 29 pages long and is accompanied by seven annexes with appendices and nine detailed maps, totalling over 300 pages. The Interim Agreement is also accompanied by an ex-change of letters. The Interim Agreement deals with, redeployment and security arrangements, elections, civil affairs, legal matters, econ-omic relations, Israeli-Palestinian cooperation programmes and the release of Palestinian prisoners and detainees.[121] The agreement aimed to establish a Palestinian Interim Self-Government Authority for a transitional period not to exceed five years from 4 May 1994, the date of the Gaza-Jericho agreement. The agreement was intended to settle all the issues of the interim period, none being deferred to the agenda of the permanent status negotiations. The Interim Agreement was the final agreement of the empowerment stage of the conflict management phase aimed at reducing the Israeli-Palestinian conflict to the point where the conflict resolution phase can be prepared for, negotiated and implemented.

The most striking aspects of this agreement are that it effectively marks the beginning of the end of Israel's martial occupation of parts of the West Bank, and that it amounts to a partial rejection of the Greater Israel policy of past governments, whether in religious or strategic-military terms within the framework of military occupation and/or annexation. The Interim Agreement states that the 'two sides view the West Bank and the Gaza Strip as a single territorial unit, the integrity and status of which will be preserved during the interim period.' This point is further emphasized as the

> two sides agree that West Bank and Gaza Strip territory, except for issues that will be negotiated in the permanent status negotiations, will come under the jurisdiction of the Palestinian Council in a phased manner, to be completed within 18 months from the date of the inauguration of the Council.[122]

However, the main feature of the agreement is the provision for the division of the West Bank, excluding East Jerusalem, into three zones or areas, each with a different delineation of Israeli and Palestinian responsibility.

Area A comprises roughly 1 per cent of the West Bank and consists of the seven major Palestinian cities Jenin, Qalqilyeh, Tulkarm, Nablus, Ramallah, Bethlehem and Hebron.[123] In Hebron, a 3.5 sqkm area inhabited by 400 settlers and 20 000 Palestinians, the transfer of authority was to be phased over six months from the signing of the Interim Agreement, although one area would not be redeployed from remaining under Israeli control. Hebron was divided into Areas H-1 and H-2 (see later in this chapter, pp. 277–8). Article VII.2.a, Article VII.2.b and Article VII.2.d stated that the Palestinian Police would 'assume responsibilities in Area H-1 similar to those in other cities in the West Bank', that all civil powers and responsibilities would 'be transferred to the Council in the City of Hebron as in other cities in the West Bank' and that the Palestinian Police would be able to 'operate freely in Area H-1'.[124] However, Israel would 'continue to carry the responsibility for overall security of Israelis for the purpose of safeguarding their internal security and public order' so that in 'the area of the city of Hebron from which Israeli military forces will not redeploy', that is Area H-2, Israel would 'retain all powers and responsibilities for internal security and public order.'[125] In security terms, upon completion of Israeli military redeployment, the Palestinian Council would assume the powers and responsibilities for internal security and public order.[126]

Area B comprises all other main Palestinian population centres, except some refugee camps and totals roughly 27 per cent of the West Bank.[127] The Palestinian Council would assume responsibility during the first phase of redeployment for, land 'in populated areas (Areas A and B), including government land and Al-Waqf land' and all 'civil powers and responsibilities, including planning and zoning, in Areas A and B'.[128] What this means in security terms, is that according to Article XIII.2.a. there would 'be a complete redeployment of Israeli military areas from Area B,' and that in Area B the Palestinian Police would 'assume the responsibility for public order for Palestinians' and would 'be deployed in order to accommodate the Palestinian needs and requirements.' However, whilst the Palestinian Council would 'assume responsibility for public order for Palestinians,' Israeli concerns were protected by the *caveat* that, 'Israel shall have the overriding responsibility for security for the purpose of protecting Israelis and confronting the threat of terrorism.'[129]

Area C comprises 72 per cent of the West Bank and includes all Israeli settlements, military bases and state land. Area C refers to the transfer of 'civil powers and responsibilities not relating to territory.'[130] 'Further redeployments from Area C and transfer of internal security responsibility to the Palestinian Police in Areas B and C will be carried out in three phases' within an 18-month period after the inauguration of the Palestinian Council, 'except for the issues of permanent status negotiations and of Israel's overall responsibility for Israelis and borders.'[131]

Negotiations on the permanent status were to start no later than 4 May 1996, leading to the implementation of UN Resolutions 242 and 338,[132] and would deal with the remaining issues, Jerusalem, refugees, settlements, security arrangements, borders, relations and cooperation with other neighbours and other issues of common interest.[133] The main objective of the Interim Agreement was to set down future Israeli-Palestinian relations prior to final status talks by broadening Palestinian self-government in the West Bank by means of an elected self-governing authority, the Palestinian Council, which was intended for the Palestinians to conduct their own internal affairs, to reduce points of Israeli-Palestinian friction, to usher in a new era based on cooperation, co-existence and common interest and to protect Israel's vital interests, particularly its security concerns both external and personal. All prior Israeli-Palestinian agreements are superseded by the provisions of the Interim Agreement. The Interim Agreement contains five chapters, dealing with the Council, redeployment and security arrangements, legal affairs, cooperation and miscellaneous provisions.

The Palestinian Council and the Ra'ees of the Executive Authority, to be established following elections (directly and simultaneously elected to the 82-member Council, for a transitional period not exceeding five years from 4 May 1994),[134] will assume powers and responsibilities in various spheres, such as: executive, legislative and judicial;[135] security (Article XIII.1; however, Article XIII.2a states that 'Israel shall have the overriding responsibility for security for the purpose of protecting Israelis and confronting the threat of terrorism');[136] and civil affairs (agriculture; archaeology; assessments; banking and monetary issues; civil administration employees; commerce and industry; comptrol; direct taxation; education and culture; electricity; employment; environmental protection; fisheries, forests; gas, fuel and petroleum; government and absentee land and immovables; health; indirect taxation; insurance; interior affairs; labour; land registration; legal administration; local government; nature reserves; parks; planning and zoning; population registry and documentation; postal services; public works and housing; quarries and mines; religious sites; social welfare; statistics; surveying; telecommunications; tourism; transportation; treasury; and water and sewage).[137]

Under the terms of transfer of authority, the new Council would assume specified powers and responsibilities, and all rights, liabilities and obligations from the military government and its civil administration, apart from those powers and responsibilities not transferred. Article XVII.1 states that whilst in 'accordance with the DoP, the jurisdiction of the Council will cover West Bank and Gaza Strip territory as a single territorial unit, except for: a. issues that will be negotiated in the permanent status negotiations: Jerusalem, settlements, specified military locations, Palestinian refugees, borders, foreign relations and Israelis; and b. powers and responsibilities not transferred to the Council.' Furthermore, 2.a states that 'territorial and functional jurisdiction of the Council will apply to all persons, except for Israelis' and 4.a and 4.b states that

> Israel, through its military government, has the authority over areas that are not under the territorial jurisdiction of the Council, powers and responsibilities not transferred to the Council and Israelis. b. To this end, the Israeli military government shall retain the necessary legislative, judicial and executive powers and responsibilities.[138]

With the establishment of the new Council the civil administration was to be dissolved in the West Bank and the military government withdrawn, however the military government would still exercise powers and responsibilities not transferred to the Council according to Article I.1 and I.5.[139] The Palestinian Council and the Ra'ees of the Executive Authority of the Council constitute the Palestinian Interim Self-Government Authority, elected by the Palestinian people of the West Bank, Jerusalem (Article VI of Annex II for Election Arrangements Concerning Jerusalem)[140] and the Gaza Strip (Article III.1).[141] The Council will possess both legislative and executive power, in accordance with Article VII and IX of the DoP and shall carry out and be responsible for all the legislative and executive powers and responsibilities transferred to it under the interim agreement. Legislation 'shall mean any primary and secondary legislation, including basic laws, laws, regulations and other legislative acts.'[142]

The Council was to be a directly elected body, and Article II Elections, and Annex II Protocol Concerning Elections of the Interim Agreement, addressed the modalities of the electoral process. Elections to the Council were to be general, personal and by district, with a separate but simultaneous election for Ra'ees of the Executive Authority. All the stages of the election process were monitored by international observers, and at the request of the parties, the EU agreed to coordinate the electoral observation delegation, comprising representatives from the EU, UN, USA, Russia, Canada, Egypt, Japan, Jordan, Norway, South Africa, Non-Aligned Nations, OAU and ICO.[143]

Regarding security and redeployment, the IDF was to redeploy in the West Bank according to the timetable as set out in Chapter 2, Redeployment and Security Arrangements, Articles X–XVI of the Interim Agreement and in Annex I, Protocol Concerning Redeployment and Security Arrangements. In addition to the redeployments envisaged prior to the elections for the Council, the Interim Agreement provides for a number of further redeployments to take place at six-monthly intervals following the inauguration of the Council. In the course of these redeployments, the Council would assume additional territorial jurisdiction so that by the completion of the redeployment phase, the Council will enjoy territorial jurisdiction over all West Bank territory, except for the areas where jurisdiction is to be determined by the final status negotiations, that is Jerusalem, settlements and military locations according to Annex I, Article I.9.[144] Article II of Annex I, on 'Security Policy for the Prevention of Terrorism and Violence', outlines Palestinian security obligations, and is a powerful indicator of Israeli security thinking, in other words: the 'Palestinian Police is the only Palestinian security authority;' the 'Palestinian Police will act systematically against all expressions of violence and terror;' and the 'Palestinian Police will arrest and prosecute individuals who are suspected of perpetrating acts of violence and terror.' Both sides agreed to carry out the following security functions:[145] 'actively prevent incitement to violence, including violence against the other side or persons under the authority of the other side'; to 'apprehend, investigate and prosecute perpetrators and all other persons directly or indirectly involved in acts of terrorism, violence and incitement'; and to 'prevent and deal with any attempt to cause harm to infrastructure serving the other side'.

In order to develop a renewed programme of development assistance to the occupied territories, following from the signing of the Interim Agreement, representatives of Israel, the World Bank, the PISGA, ten international organizations and 29 donor nations met in Paris between 18 and 19 October 1995.[146] Similar meetings on 1 October 1993 had followed the signing of the DoP, at which donor nations pledged some $2.1bn over five years in financial support and assistance of Palestinian self-government. Delegates from 43 countries met under US and Russian auspices to coordinate economic support for the DoP, pledging $2.1bn. The conference brought together overlapping bodies and agencies: the Multilateral Steering Group; the gavel holders of the Multilateral Working Groups (EU, Japan, Canada, US), G-7 countries; Norway; major donor nations;

Israel; Arab representatives including the GCC; the World Bank; and the UN. The Palestinians sought to organize mechanisms to promote economic development and make effective use of external assistance, and to cooperate with the Israelis in fostering economic development. The participants agreed to support the critical first phase: announcing pledges totalling $600m for the first year; $1bn for the first two years; formal indications of planned support of $5bn for the five-year interim period; future additional pledges were expected. The State Department expected $2.4bn of five-year external assistance would be met. The donor community agreed to support:

- urgent relief efforts;
- short-term needs including rehabilitation of existing infrastructure;
- the establishment of an appropriate PISGA legal framework to enable a smooth implementation of external assistance (UNRWA, non-governmental organizations, the EU, and other bilateral donors are active in these areas);
- efforts to be directed at building the capacity of the PISGA to organize and manage political, economic and social affairs – priority to be given to the development of effective revenue sharing and revenue collection arrangements;
- initiation of an extensive programme of technical assistance to build institutions and to train personnel (the World Bank was to establish and manage a Technical Assistance Trust Fund ($31.6m pledged) to finance technical assistance, training and feasibility studies over the coming 12–18 months while UN agencies including UNDP and other multilateral and bilateral programmes and agencies would provide technical and financial assistance to support institution-building);
- promotion of longer-term goals, public and private investment to lay foundations of sustainable growth of PISGA areas (donors would carry out their assistance projects within the framework of a five-year programme of public investment in physical and social infrastructure and productive capacity while the World Bank was to take a leading role in mobilizing programmes and supporting public development);
- the encouragement of trade and private investment through export financing programmes and investment incentives;
- the need to develop the PISGA areas in regional terms, to identify regional infrastructure projects that could facilitate economic integration of the PISGA areas and its neighbours and to emphasize freer regional trade.[147]

4.6 The final stages of the Interim Phase-Protocol concerning the redeployment in Hebron, 17 January 1997

Although the Interim Agreement of 28 September 1995 set out the arrangements to apply in the West Bank and Gaza Strip throughout the transitional period, pending implementation of permanent status arrangements, the issue of Hebron's status remained unresolved until 15 January 1997. This was despite having reached prior agreement for a redeployment of Israeli military forces in the city and a transfer of civil powers and responsibilities in the city to the Palestinian Council within the terms of the 'Guidelines for Hebron', included as Article VII of Annexe I: Protocol Concerning Redeployment and Security Arrangements of the Interim Agreement. The Interim Agreement, through Article VII, deliniated two areas in Hebron, H-1 and H-2. In H-1, according to Article VII.2 the Palestinian police would operate freely and would assume responsibilities similar to those in other cities in the West Bank, and all civil powers and responsibilities would be transferred to the Council. H-2, according to Article VII.4 was the area of the city of Hebron from which Israeli military forces would not be redeploying and where Israel would retain all powers and responsibilities for internal security and public order. However in H-2 all civil powers and responsibilities would be transferred to the Palestinians except for those relating to Israelis and their property which would continue to be exercised by the Israeli Military Government. Furthermore, Article VII.3 clearly states that, 'According to the DoP, Israel will continue to carry the responsibility for overall security of Israelis for the purpose of safeguarding their internal security and public order', meaning that the interpretation may be drawn not only that Israel retains both powers and responsibilities for Israelis' physical and geographic security within the areas accorded as under Israeli territorial jurisdiction, but also that through this, Israel retains the power to maintain security and public order which may be interpreted to mean that Israel may forestall attacks or react to attacks by any and all necessary means, including re-entering areas previously redeployed from.[148] It is within this context that it re-emphasized that Israeli military forces are being pledged to conduct a redeployment, not a withdrawal. Furthermore, this redeployment is being carried out under the terms of the interim phase, which may or may not be renegotiated in the final status discussions, as nothing in the Interim Agreement 'shall prejudice or preempt the outcome of the negotiations on the permanent status to be conducted pursuant to the DoP. Neither Party shall be deemed, by virtue of having entered into this Agreement, to have renounced or waived any of its existing rights, claims or positions.'[149]

According to the Israeli Foreign Ministry, although Article VII sets out that the Palestinians were to assume municipal and civilian responsibilities throughout the entire city, the original composition of the Article was formulated in such a 'general manner' as to necessitate a clear 'need for further amplification before any actual redeployment could take place'. Postponement and delay was effected not only by the wave of suicide bombings but also by the 'egregious violation of the DoP and the Interim Agreement by elements of the Palestinian police who opened fire, without provocation, on IDF and Border Police units as well as Israeli civilians' following the 24 September tunnel incident. Thus, while the Interim Agreement recognized the presence of Israeli residents in Hebron and stated that Hebron would not become a divided city, it did not specifically outline the modalities for safeguarding these Israelis' security.[150] However, this reasoning must be seen in the context of Israeli domestic political considerations, not only with reference to the suicide bombings of spring 1996 and the responses by former PM Peres in light of the upcoming Israeli general election, but also since the election of Netanyahu as PM bringing with it a concomitant realignment of Israel's national priorities. The new government's priorities put Israel at odds with the stated intentions and commitments of the previously concluded Israeli-Palestinian agreements, for example, the statement declaring its desire to oppose a Palestinian state, ensure the existence, security and development of Jewish settlements in the West Bank and Gaza, and to maintain Jerusalem's status as the eternal and undivided capital of Israel.[151] Therefore Hebron, for the new government, signified an existential *cause célèbre*. Hebron represented a test case to show whether or not the new government would agree to abide by existing, internationally approved agreements, and not only that but also whether it would be seen to be endorsing the land-for-peace principle it had vilified in opposition.

During the election campaign and the interregnum, Netanyahu of Likud outlined the policies and ideology which would form the basis of his negotiating stance, Netanyahu promising that Zionism, as 'the liberation movement of the Jewish people, and its fulfilment' would be 'at the top of the list of priorities of the Government of Israel'. Thus immigration would be increased and settlements 'strengthened', whilst Israel would 'enable the Palestinians to manage their lives freely, within the framework of self-government'. However, 'foreign affairs, defence, and matters which require coordination', would 'remain the responsibility of the State of Israel', and to this end Likud opposed 'the establishment of an independent Palestinian state'. There would 'be no infringement of Israel's use of' the 'vital water resources in Judea and Samaria' and a united and undivided Jerusalem would remain as the capital of Israel. The Jordan River would constitute Israel's 'eastern' and 'permanent border' between Israel and Jordan, allowing Jordan to 'become a partner in the final arrangement between Israel and Palestinians', and the policy of ensuring for seven million Israelis within the decade would be 'a national undertaking'.[152] With Netanyahu's 'victory' address on 2 June, the 16 June publication of the new government's policy guidelines, and the new PM's inaugural address on 18 June, there was delivered a comprehensive outline of Netanyahu's vision of peace with the Palestinians. The new PM stated that his government would 'act on the premise that the right of the Jewish people to the Land of Israel is eternal and indisputable, that the State of Israel is the State of the Jewish people', and 'whose main goal is the ingathering and integration of the Jewish people'. The government would act to 'thwart any attempt to undermine the unity of Jerusalem', would prevent 'any action which is counter to Israel's exclusive sovereignty' and would reinforce the status of Jerusalem 'as the eternal capital of the Jewish people', 'one city, whole and undivided' to 'remain forever under Israel's sovereignty'. The government would 'propose to the Palestinians an arrangement' whereby they would 'be able to conduct their lives freely within the framework of self-government' while simultaneously opposing not only 'the establishment of a Palestinian state or any foreign sovereignty west of the Jordan River' but also 'the right of return of Arab populations to any part of the Land of Israel west of the Jordan River'. The government would 'insist on ensuring the existence and security of Jewish settlements and their affinity with' Israel, would continue to 'bear full responsibility for the Jewish settlements and their residents' and would exercise its right to use the IDF and security forces to act against the threat of terrorism everywhere.'[153] Netanyahu further believed that Israel had fulfilled its land-for-peace requirements and obligations by returning the Sinai to Egypt in

1979. Netanyahu felt that Palestinian autonomy should relate to, and incorporate, most of the Palestinian population, and that while the PISGA should have control over devolved aspects of national life, it should not presume or assume sovereignty. Netanyahu's vision also included the belief that closures should be lifted only when Israel's security was guaranteed, that the self-rule area should not be physically separated from Israel, that peace with Israel's Arab neighbours by the year 2000 was unlikely and that agreement on Jerusalem was impossible.[154] Netanyahu reacted to harsh Arab criticism of his post-election statements, saying he was 'neither impressed nor bothered'. His attitude to conducting continuing negotiations with Arafat and the Palestinians was summed up by his desire that he would only meet Arafat 'when I decide it is vital'.[155]

In keeping with Likud's policy of demonizing the PLO as terrorists, Netanyahu made no reference to Arafat or the PLO/PISGA in his victory speech of June 2nd, referring only to 'the Palestinians'.[156] While Likud's Roni Milo and Faisal Husseini held a get-acquainted meeting on 11 June, prior to the resumption of Israeli-PISGA security contacts on 26 July,[157] Netanyahu officially authorized adviser Dore Gold to initiate contact with the PISGA to confirm Netanyahu's interest in continuing negotiations, and to meet Arafat in Gaza on 27 June.[158] However in response to Netanyahu's indifference to a meeting, Arafat refused to meet Gold on 16 July, having Abbas meet him instead.[159] FM Levy met Arafat on 23 July at Erez, but on 12 August Arafat refused to meet Defence Minister Mordechai until Netanyahu agreed to meet with him.[160] Regarding the continuity of Israel-PISGA relations, Israel announced on 5 August the setting up of negotiating teams for the expected talks on outstanding issues, due to resume in several weeks. With the Higher Joint Israeli-Palestinian Civilian Committee resuming meeting in Jerusalem on 13 August, Israel and the PISGA agreed the next day to reactivate all joint liaison committees which follow-up implementation of the peace accords. This was except for the Palestinian-Israeli Steering and Monitoring Committee, the highest oversight body, which was delayed owing to complaints by FM Levy and DM Mordechai over the use of unofficial advisers and channels by Netanyahu to conduct negotiations with the PISGA. These inter-cabinet power-struggles led Levy to boycott a cabinet meeting on 9 August and to issue a threat to resign unless he received greater control over the negotiations with the PISGA.[161] However, Netanyahu appointed his personal attorney Yitzhak Molho as special envoy to Arafat in charge of ongoing contacts with the PISGA and despatched him to meet the Palestinian leader in Ramallah on 29 August with the remit of holding daily contacts with PISGA officials. Molho travelled to Gaza at least twice a week, but was external to the official Israeli negotiating team.[162]

With Netanyahu's election, instances of settlement expansion and settler provocation in the occupied territories increased dramatically. In Hebron settlers occupied Palestinian-owned properties on 30 May and on 5 June.[163] Near Nablus, settlers illegally confiscated land for the Karyut settlement on 19 July.[164] Settlement expansion plans were submitted, for 50 000 houses in East Jerusalem on 5 June, for four or five United Kibbutz movement pre-settlements on 17 July, for 2000 housing units and 3000 hotel units between Ma'ale Adumim and Pisgat Ze'ev (doubling Ma'ale Adumim's population to 40 000) on 18 July, and for 200 units in Shilo on 4 August.[165] The new government, meanwhile, approved and began a number of building projects. For example, on 10 June construction began on the expansion of Rachel's Tomb near Bethlehem, at Hazayit Hill near Efrat, and on 16 July 6000 units were planned for imminent construction on Har Homa. Plans for infrastructural highways and bridges to tighten Israeli links to the occupied territories were announced by Infrastructure Minister Sharon on 29 July, and in the first official move to expand settlements, approval for 298 mobile homes in Jewish settlements for public and educational use was given on 12 August. On 15 August the IDF presented a review for 300 miles of roads in the West Bank to link settlements with Palestinian lands being confiscated to complete the project.[166] Palestinian homes were bulldozed to make way for bypass roads, near Hebron on 6 August and in Jerusalem and Ramallah on 12 August.[167] Evidence that the new government was taking a more pro-settler line was provided by the unanimous cabinet decision giving approval for the amendment of legislation to facilitate settlement expansion by the lifting of building restrictions on 2 August,[168] and by the permission given the police to escort hundreds of Temple Mount Faithful to pray in the al-Aqsa Mosque courtyard on 25 July.[169] On 12 August, Netanyahu said he did not believe the Interim Agreement prohibited Jews from building settlements on occupied land, and Interior Minister Suissa announced that $5m would be reallocated from local government to settlements to help settlers pay expenses resulting from the agreement.[170]

With Netanyahu meeting IDF and Defence Ministry officials to discuss the issues of Hebron and security on 21 June, DM Mordechai was given the task of designing an alternative plan to the existing one. He presented an initial plan on 15 August, which reclassified the Jewish sections of Hebron as Area B, expanded Jewish settlements in the city by increasing IDF observer points and troops, limited the number of PISGA security forces and their patrol ranges, created a security corridor linking Hebron and Kiryat Arba, provided the IDF with the right to hot pursuit and slowed the redeployment timetable.[171] However, the new administration did not discuss this new plan with the PISGA, as the PISGA had denounced any changes to previous agreements as unacceptable and contrary to the peace process. The IDF recommended fulfilling the original commitments on 24 June, and indeed both the IDF and Shin Bet recommended that Mordechai go further on 2 July, arguing that he should pursue a political settlement because although the closures were a good short-term measure, they would ultimately create serious long-term security problems if continued indefinitely.[172]

According to Article V.3.b[8], further redeployments from Area C and the transfer of internal security responsibility to the Palestinian police in Areas B and C, would commence six months from the inauguration of the PISGA Council, on 7 September 1996. However no progress was reached either in successfully concluding the next stages of redeployment, or in negotiating agreement for further redeployment.[173] This was particularly true of the redeployment concerning Hebron, which according to Article VII.1.b was supposed to have been completed by the end of March 1996.[174] Israel and the PISGA formally asked Norway, on 11 August, to renew the mandate of the Temporary International Presence in the City of Hebron (TIPH) for another month, having already renegotiated the TIPH on 9 May which superseded the guidelines for Hebron outlined in Article VII of the Interim Agreement. There were only 32 TIPH observers in Hebron by August and the full complement of observers from other countries were not due to take up their posts until further IDF redeployment.[175]

The policy of closure of the occupied territories, initiated in late February, was alternately tightened and eased depending on circumstance throughout the summer months. The IDF cited warnings of hundreds of imminent attacks which convinced them they should cancel any measures aimed at easing the imposed closure, and in the first breach of the Interim Agreement's security agreements the IDF entered Dura village near Hebron on 18 May, in Area B under

PISGA control, ordering PISGA police to remain at their bases, and arrested nine Palestinians, including two relatives of Preventive Security Forces (PSF) head Colonel Jibril Rajub.[176] The IDF also increased patrols in Hebron and randomly searched Palestinians. On 3 June the IDF detained several PISGA policemen and searched their vehicles, which resulted in a clash between troops and Palestinian residents.[177] The IDF ignored PISGA Council members' VIP status on 12 June when they prevented 22 Gazan members from entering the West Bank to attend their weekly session in Nablus unless they agreed to be searched. When the PISGA threatened to cancel the session in protest, the IDF relented, letting the Gazans through the next day. When the Civil Affairs Committee met on 14 June to discuss the incident, Israel demanded that Council members submit to security checks. Peres defused the situation by returning VIP status to Sufyan Abu Zayida, Abd al-Rahman Hamad, and Intisar al-Wazir, senior PISGA officials, and on 16 June Peres granted 60 Council members second-class VIP status permitting them to undergo 'less stringent' security checks.[178]

The DoP and subsequent agreements were intended to pursue an Israeli-Palestinian relationship which transcended and reordered their past hostile interaction. The past policies of collective punishment, used aggressively by Israeli security forces during, most recently, the *intifada* were supposed to lead to cooperation and coordination. The corrosive and coercive effect of policies of, closures, curfews, restrictions of a broad and general nature preventing daily activity and individual acts of aggression and humiliation, only served to alienate Palestinians, imbuing them with a sense of rage and hatred for the Israelis. The peace process was meant to reorganize past policies and refocus on cooperative relationships. However, practical reality on the ground during the years following the DoP's signing showed little change. Closures, curfews, house demolitions, economic sanctions, administrative detentions, expulsions and mass arrests continued. *Plus ça change . . .?*

Although neither the 1907 Hague Regulations nor the Fourth Geneva Convention of 1949, the main instruments of international law pertaining to the conduct of occupying powers, specifically mentions instruments of collective punishment such as curfews, house demolitions, economic sanctions, administrative detentions, expulsions and mass arrests, there are clear provisions for what is and is not permitted. The general criterion is that the occupying power has both the right to ensure the security of its own forces and the obligation to respect the interests of the occupied civilian population. These two considerations must be balanced, 'and not determined by one to the exclusion of the other, lest they lose their validity under international law.'[179] Whilst permitting security operations to apprehend those suspected of armed resistance, any actions which are aimed at punishing or deterring an uncooperative civilian population, either to deter future acts of resistance or as an instrument of retribution is specifically and explicitly prohibited. Article 50 of the Hague Regulations states that 'No general penalty, pecuniary or otherwise, shall be inflicted upon the population on account of the acts of individuals for which they cannot be regarded as jointly and severally responsible.' Article 33 of the Fourth Geneva Convention states 'Collective penalties and likewise all measures of intimidation or of terrorism are prohibited. Pillage is prohibited. Reprisals against protected persons and their property are prohibited.' Articles 55–7, and 59–63 cover the mandatory provision of basic necessities to the general population, for example, occupying powers should ensure the normal supply and distribution of foodstuffs, medical supplies and the like.[180] In an official commentary to the Convention, Jean Pictet stated that 'It must be emphasized that under no circumstances may the occupation authorities invoke reasons of security to justify the general suspension of all humanitarian activities in an occupied territory.'[181] The IDF can declare a certain area a 'closed military zone according to Regulation 125 of the Emergency (Defence) Regulations of 1945, and Section 90 of the Order Concerning Defence Regulations (Judea and Samaria) (No. 378), 1970.[182] Therefore any such impositions of collective punishments, despite the rationale of security as a mitigating factor, become less acceptable the longer their intensity and duration hamper and limit the functioning of public life. Whilst curfews and closures are used around the world as exceptional and temporary measures, the continued use of collective punishments throughout the Israeli occupation since 1967 shows no sign of letting up, or even of success. The continued opposition to Israeli occupation has persisted in spite of such, and as a result of them, rather than being extinguished as intended by the Israelis.

An interesting feature of the imposition of collective action against the Palestinian population, particularly that part of it living under PISGA control, was the difference between the reality of everyday life and the relationship that was implied by the various agreements concluded since the DoP. While the security provisions were designed to ensure the safety of Israelis, the Palestinians were expected to assume greater autonomy and control over their lives and territory. For example, Article VIII of the DoP on 'Public Order and Security' stated:

> In order to guarantee public order and internal security for the Palestinians of the West Bank and the Gaza Strip, the Council will establish a strong police force, while Israel will continue to carry the responsibility for defending against external threats, as well as the responsibility for overall security of Israelis for the purpose of safeguarding their internal security and public order.[183]

The Interim Agreement reiterated and developed this article. Article XII set out the 'Arrangements for Security and Public Order', Article XIII provided for 'Security', and Annex I spelt out the 'Protocol Concerning Redeployment and Security Arrangements' (particularly Article I, the 'Redeployment of Israeli Military Forces and Transfer of Responsibilities' and Article II, the 'Security Policy for the Prevention of Terrorism and Violence'). These items provided for the PISGA to assume the powers and responsibilities for 'public order and internal security', that upon the inauguration of the PISGA Council, 'the unity and integrity of the Palestinian people in the West Bank and the Gaza Strip' would 'be maintained and respected', that all 'Palestinian people residing in the West Bank and the Gaza Strip' would 'be accountable to the Palestinian Council only' and that any 'security measures which become effective commensurate with the redeployment of the Israeli military forces' would 'not undermine' nor would 'they prejudice' the 'moral and physical dignity of the Palestinian people in the West Bank and the Gaza Strip.'[184] Therefore, what seems to have been agreed was that the Palestinians would wage security actions against those inside the areas under its jurisdiction whilst the Israelis would ensure the safety of their own citizens and the settlements in the occupied territories. Specifically overt acts to guarantee such security by effectively sealing and confining the Palestinians into separate ghettos does not seem to have been addressed by the Oslo accords.

Despite best intentions, security-related actions by the IDF and the PSF continued to cause disruption, and these affected the chances of an agreement on Hebron being reached. On 1 August, while the Israeli border police arrested the Hebron police chief, thousands of Palestinians protesting in Nablus against the death in PISGA custody of Mahmud Jumayil prompted the IDF to declare Nablus a closed military zone.[185] Since redeploying from Area A the IDF, by declaring a closed military zone, technically put these areas off-limits to Israelis, but in practice the measure resulted in the effective sealing off of the designated area, closing it to everyone. The IDF frequently declared closed military zones citing security purposes, mostly in response to attacks on Israelis. The IDF declared closed military zones in Nablus on 15–16 and 26–31 May, and 1 August,[186] Ramallah on 16 May and 20 July,[187] Janin on 26–31 May,[188] Jericho on 26–27 July,[189] Qalqilyeh on 24 July,[190] and Bethlehem on 10 August.[191] Curfews were imposed on Biddiyya from 16 June to 1 July,[192] Hebron on 10 July,[193] Nablus on 19 July[194] and Sammu' mid-June to 5 July. Israel blocked the entry of $3.5m worth of mutton to the PISGA on 28 June: the 10 500 sheep had been slaughtered during the Hajj and donated by Saudi Arabia to help feed Palestinians under closure, but the meat rotted at the crossing point while awaiting IDF 'security checks' and was destroyed on 14 August.[195] The IDF also closed two West Bank mosques after discovering 'inflammatory leaflets' on their premises and raided al-Ibrahimi Cultural Centre in Hebron on 1 July, confiscating computers, disks and papers, and detained the centre's director, Hijazi al-Shuyukhi, for questioning regarding the distribution of pro-Fatah 'Strike Forces of the Popular Committees for Palestinian National Solidarity' leaflets calling for the renewal of the *intifada*.[196]

In mitigation and in understanding of the Israeli actions, it must be remembered that a heightened state of insecurity caused by ruthless terrorism within Israel's Green Line existed during the summer of 1996. Insecurity was allied with the emotional escalation of political life stimulated and created by the fight for power and the right to determine policy within the near future through the medium of the general election. Israeli sensitivities to Palestinian suffering were therefore more than usually muted or indifferent. However, one must estimate at what cost to the peace process and future negotiations these actions were undertaken, in that the measures of collective punishment may have only exacerbated an already difficult situation, furthering resentment and fostering discord between the extremists in both communities.

Initial pessimism that the change of government would impede the peace process seemed borne out by the perception that the negotiations had entered a period of stalemate, with no breakthrough on substantive issues being made and little or no progress being reported. In order to resume negotiations, Netanyahu suggested on 14 August that UN special coordinator Terje Larsen initiate secret talks the following day. These talks, between Israel, represented by Dore Gold, and the PISGA, represented by Mahmud Abbas, aimed at identifying points of disagreement between the two. Larsen briefed US special envoy Dennis Ross and President Mubarak's adviser Osama al-Baz on their progress.[197] After four days of talks, the PISGA and Israel agreed on 3 September to a vaguely worded statement signed by Larsen, which laid out a framework for continuing negotiations and defining several matters as exceptional to be discussed by the Palestinian-Israeli Steering and Monitoring Committee (PISMC) – these were Hebron, further redeployment, Rafah airport, prisoners, safe passage and economic issues.[198] PISGA Local Government Minister Saeb Erekat and IDF Lieutenant-General Dan Shomron were appointed on 19 August to head the committee. However, it was only on 9 September that the first PISMC meeting was held since the 29 May Israeli elections.[199] At the first Arafat-Netanyahu summit at Erez on 4 September, Netanyahu announced his willingness to negotiate a final peace agreement, improve Palestinian economic conditions and allow 50 000 Palestinians Israeli work permits.[200] However, despite these positive sentiments, on 24 September Netanyahu personally ordered the completion of the excavation of a controversial 500-yard archaeological tunnel spanning the HaKotel and abutting the Temple Mount, to provide access for Israelis to the HaKotel alongside the al-Aqsa compound. Begun in 1984, the tunnel was intended to reinforce the Israeli claim that sole sovereignty over Jerusalem rested with Israel. This act provoked a furious response from Palestinians, who clashed with Israeli security forces in and around the Temple Mount. In response to the Israeli action, Palestinian leaders called for strikes and demonstrations, with Arafat calling the tunnel incident a crime against both Jerusalem's religious status quo and the Oslo accords.[201]

With the PISGA calling for a general strike on 25 September, the issue provoked the most violent Israeli-Palestinian clashes since the height of the *intifada* and especially since the peace process began, with the IDF, PISGA security forces and citizens exchanging rubber bullets, stun grenades, rocks, bottles and live ammunition. The IDF and the PSF engaged in a ferocious firefight in Ramallah, with further clashes in Bethlehem and Jerusalem. With Ramallah declared a closed military zone, the rest of the West Bank and the Gaza Strip were sealed off by the IDF.[202] However with the continuing bloodshed, many worried that not only were Israel-PISGA relations spiralling out of control, but as the violence spread so too did the fear that a wider Middle East conflagration might erupt as a result of the insensitive, arrogant and ill-conceived tunnel decision. As clashes spread throughout the West Bank and Gaza on 26 September, so too did the death toll. Heavy fighting was reported at Erez, Rafah, and Joseph's Tomb in Nablus, with attacks on Jewish settlements in Gaza forcing the brief evacuation of Netzarim. With Netanyahu on a European tour and FM Levy in the US, acting PM Moshe Katzav and DM Mordechai reacted to the crisis by declaring a state of emergency, and by sending Merkava tanks to take up positions on Area A borders, and ordering Cobra helicopters north along the Jerusalem road to Ramallah. The helicopters were reported as having fired on civilians.[203] The death toll rose to 55 by 26 September (44 Palestinians/11 Israelis), with many hundreds wounded. Violent confrontations brought the threat of a renewed *intifada* ever closer. Ma'ariv commentators felt that it 'was not the tunnel-opening alone that led to the outbreak of rioting in the territories, but the accumulation of frustration from what appeared on the surface to be a complete deadlock in the peace process.' One solution suggested to break the impasse, apart from closing the tunnel, which would repair the serious damage done, was to negotiate 'a quick agreement on redeployment in Hebron and rapid removal of Israeli forces from the city, as initial proof that the peace process exists.'[204] Cutting short his European tour, Netanyahu returned to a growing political storm, as the senior members of Shin Bet held an emergency meeting, reportedly furious with Netanyahu, critical of his decision-making performance and of his deliberate ignoring of their warnings and recommendations against the tunnel opening, and his subsequent action carried out without their coordination. IDF Chief of Staff Shahak and DM Mordechai were also reportedly not informed in advance of the opening. Clear divisions of opinion over the issue existed within the inner cabinet, exposing the potential for discord even there, as Agriculture Minister Eitan called for tanks to be moved into Area A, and Tourism Minister (and Deputy PM) Katzav called for an immediate halt to Israel-PISGA negotiations. However DM Mordechai offered the notion of a compromise over the tunnel.[205] Meanwhile Egypt, Israel, the PISGA and the US officials met to discuss the possibilities for a Netanyahu-Arafat summit. Arafat responded to the suggestion by intimating his acceptance would be conditional on Netanyahu making a contrite gesture such as closing the tunnel. Netanyahu refused, saying that to do so would imply that Palestinian protests could be seen to gain benefits.[206]

On 27 September Netanyahu deployed some 6000 police throughout Israel and some 4000 in East Jerusalem, but this did not hinder the continuation of the violence. While Israeli Arabs observed a general strike, PISGA police cordoned off Balata, Erez, Janin and Ramallah to prevent further clashes, and although the offending tunnel was closed for the beginning of Succoth, more fierce clashes erupted throughout the occupied territories, particularly in Rafah and Tulkarm where IDF helicopters fired on the crowds. None were so dramatic as the rioting which caused more deaths in the Old City as Palestinians and Israeli forces clashed within the Al-Aqsa compound.[207] With the death toll rising to 67 (53 Palestinians and 14 Israelis) Netanyahu accused Arafat of deliberately and cynically using the incident to inflame passions and put the blame on him as the sole instigator of the violence, refusing the assessment of senior Israeli security chiefs that the clashes were as a result of Palestinian frustration at the lack of progress in the peace process.[208] Judging by the reaction of interested parties, even including Israel's friends, few agreed with Netanyahu's assessment of the situation. The *Washington Post* commented 'No one even slightly familiar with the immense volatility of the Jerusalem issue could have imagined that Israel would on its own make a significant change on the ground, on the edge of a site sacred to Muslims as well as Jews, without triggering an enraged Palestinian response.'[209] Igor Mann, *La Stampa*'s respected Middle East commentator, wrote that 'Netanyahu has conducted an insensitive, irresponsible policy. He promised the Israeli people "peace and security" and this is the result.'[210]

Intense diplomatic efforts from many sides aimed at both defusing the situation and persuading Netanyahu and Arafat to meet to negotiate a way through the crisis. While Russian and Middle Eastern pronouncements mainly accused Netanyahu of stalling the peace process, and even though Western politicians and media blamed Netanyahu for provoking a new *intifada*, Western diplomatic efforts aimed at mediating a conciliatory Arafat-Netanyahu meeting. However Netanyahu told US special envoy Dennis Ross that any concessions that he would be seen to make would merely encourage the Palestinians to commit further violence, causing his government to fall because of defections from hardline members opposed to accommodation. The United Nations met in a special session to discuss the crisis, with the Security Council beginning a debate on a possible resolution critical of Israel's actions, despite US and Israeli protests. Whilst heads of EU member states, President Chirac, Chancellor Kohl and PM Major all sent messages appealing for calm, the US engaged in a blitz of telephone diplomacy to Jerusalem, Amman, Gaza, and Cairo aimed at rescuing the peace process.[211] Although scattered clashes occurred on 28 September, no deaths nor injuries were reported, as the UN Security Council passed a resolution regarding the tunnel incident and the recent violence. Though not specifically mentioning the tunnel, the resolution called for the 'reversal of all acts which have resulted in the aggravation of the situation.'[212] Although the resolution was passed 14–0, with one last-minute abstention (USA), Israel reopened the tunnel on 29 September, banned Palestinians from travelling between West Bank villages, towns and cities and warned that the IDF would re-enter population centres in Area A to disarm the PSF if they fired on IDF forces. Tanks remained on the Area A borders while more IDF checkpoints were set up along West Bank roads. As the death toll rose to 70, Arafat and Netanyahu agreed to a summit meeting in Washington DC called by President Clinton to discuss the recent violence and the future of the peace process.[213] The arrangement of a summit meeting by Clinton could be interpreted in any or all of a number of ways:

- as a sincere move to resuscitate a dying peace process which had been of special interest to the US since 1991
- as a cynical attempt to sidestep the condemnation of the UN and to sideline both the UN and the EU from becoming more involved in the diplomatic efforts of the peace process
- to be seen to be acting in a statesmanlike fashion five weeks from the US presidential election
- to navigate a path of least resistance for Israel.

In Washington DC on 1 October, the US held separate meetings with PISGA, Israeli and Jordanian delegations, which produced a brief joint meeting and then a three-hour private Netanyahu-Arafat meeting. As EU foreign ministers announced in Luxembourg their strongest condemnation of Israel since 1980 and the death toll rose to 75, Israel refused to set a firm date, either for closing the tunnel or for a withdrawal and redeployment from Hebron.[214] Although Arafat and Netanyahu failed to resolve their acute differences, both agreed the next day to hold non-stop intensive talks until a new understanding on Hebron redeployment was reached, starting on 6 October. Meanwhile in anticipation of possible failure in Washington, the IDF positioned troops, heavy weapons, tanks, helicopters and sniper squads on the Area A border zones. In Jerusalem, 50 000 Israelis marched in support of Netanyahu.[215]

Prior to the round of intensive PISMC talks, Israel's ministerial forum on Hebron security resumed discussions on 18 August, with some members favouring adherence to the Interim Agreement in its entirety and others calling for a civilian partition of the city in addition to the security partition outlined in the agreement. Infrastructure Minister Sharon presented a Hebron redeployment plan on 4 September. The plan called for an expansion of the area to be transferred to PISGA authority which decreased the number of Palestinians left under Israeli control from 17 000 to 3000; the linking of the Jewish enclave to the Tomb of the Patriarchs and Kiryat Arba; the erection of a wall between the Jewish and Arab sections; and the allowance of the PISGA to increase its police presence in Hebron within six months if security was maintained.[216] A month later DM Mordechai presented Arafat with another new Hebron redeployment plan which requested that the Interim Agreement provisions regarding Hebron be reopened. Arafat refused, but agreed to turn the matter over to the PISMC. Netanyahu stated on 4 October that if the PISGA accepted these new security demands, Israel would be more inclined to make concessions elsewhere in the West Bank, but the PISGA refused because it considered such demands an unacceptable precedent, instead insisting that Israel implement the existing Hebron agreements signed by the previous government.[217]

After the Washington summit, the PISMC opened the new round of talks at Erez on 6 October, attended by Secretary Christopher and special envoy Ross. Israel again insisted that the Hebron agreement be renegotiated and demanded more stringent security measures. These included total security control over both Palestinian (H1) and Jewish (H2) areas, new 900-foot-wide IDF-only buffer zones in what is now Area B, IDF control of the hills surrounding the Jewish areas, a ban on Palestinian transportation within 1–2 km of Jewish areas and increased restrictions on the PISGA police, such as limited areas of operation and the carrying of sidearms rather than rifles. Ten days later, Israel added to its demand for a redefinition of the H1 and H2 zones, demanding Israeli control of city zoning and planning, which could be used to expand settlements in and around Hebron.[218] The US attempted to mediate a compromise course, hoping to persuade both sides to achieve progress by making adjustments to the existing accord, rather than attempting to renegotiate a new agreement; however the main sticking points in the talks remained: hot pursuit, a PISGA demand to reopen al-Shuhada Street to Palestinian traffic, movement of joint patrols and the type of arms to be carried by the PISGA police.[219] Talks were divided into three simultaneous subcommittees, regarding Hebron, security (including Rafah airport and closure) and economics.[220] Although according to the Interim Agreement, a further Israeli troop redeployment from Area C and the transfer of internal security to the PISGA police in Areas B and C was scheduled to begin on 7 September 1996, no meetings had been held to identify which areas would be affected. However, on 7 October, Netanyahu suggested to the Knesset that once the Hebron issue was resolved, Israel and the PISGA could move directly to final status talks, skipping clauses of the Oslo accords that had not been implemented, including further redeployment. The PISGA denounced the suggestion.

Security issues continued to impede conciliation. Following from the 24–28 September clashes, the IDF issued on 30 September new 'open-fire' orders for the West Bank and Gaza, allowing soldiers to use concentrated fire with any type of weapon toward any Palestinian – armed or not – who approached within 900 feet. On 7 October the PISGA and Israel decided to set up a hot line between their field commanders to quickly solve conflicts between security forces, and Netanyahu demanded that Arafat punish any policeman who shot at IDF troops during clashes. Arafat issued the next day a 'permanent order' to the PISGA police not to fire at the IDF.[221] Despite such cooperation, Israel's High Court ruled on 14 November that Shin Bet could use physical force while questioning Palestinians suspected of having knowledge of planned anti-Israeli attacks.[222]

Daily PISMC meetings continued until 10 October, without progress, when at that meeting Israel and the PISGA decided to move talks to Taba and Eilat, away from the media. Between 10 and 14 October, continuous 'preparatory talks' took place, with one official security meeting held on 13 October.[223] Resuming in Eilat, Jerusalem and Tel Aviv, on 15 October, PISMC sessions and private high-level meetings took place, involving combinations of Netanyahu, David Levy, Dan Shomron, Dore Gold, Yitzhak Molho, Arafat, Abbas, Saeb Erekat, PISGA Information Minister Yasir Abed Rabbu, Terje Larsen, Dennis Ross, and US ambassador Martin Indyk. Dialogue between Netanyahu and Arafat was indirect and mediated by US special envoy Ross.[224] The sides continued to meet on an almost daily basis, with

Israel and the PISGA claiming, counter-claiming, and denying, that agreement was near. Both sides accused the other of reopening discussions on aspects that had been agreed. For example, on 18 October at Taba, the Israelis announced that progress had been made on the issues of hot pursuit and buffer zone issues between Areas A and B in Hebron. The next day the PISGA claimed that Israel had backed down. On 21 October the PISGA team walked out of the talks on Hebron security arrangements, but Dennis Ross persuaded the sides to resume, saying a few hours later that the talks were 'in the midst of the most promising discussions to date'.[225]

On 23 October, the PISMC issued a formal joint paper, compiling a list of 15 points of contention which had not been able to be resolved during the previous three weeks of negotiations, including hot pursuit, the opening of al-Shuhada Street, the type of weapons PISGA police would be authorized to carry, and the movement of joint patrols.[226] Though the subcommittees continued to meet for several more days, substantive negotiations continued behind the scenes between Arafat and Netanyahu via Ross shuttling between Gaza and Jerusalem. At the 25 October PISMC session, Arafat demanded that Netanyahu include a written commitment to further redeployment and open Rafah airport as part of a revised Hebron deal.[227] The same day the Israelis released a list of ten of the 'most egregious PLO violations of the Oslo accords', which covered such issues as failure to change the PLO Covenant, incitement to violence against Israel, opening fire on Israelis, failure to confiscate illegal arms and disarm and disband militias, failure to extradite suspected terrorists to Israel, opening PISGA offices in Jerusalem, recruiting terrorists to serve in the PISGA police, exceeding the limit on the number of PISGA police, abuse of human rights and the rule of law and conduct of foreign relations.[228] At Ross's request, IDF Chief of Staff Shahak joined the security talks to upgrade the level of talks and to include an Israeli negotiator respected by the PISGA. However on 1 November, Israel removed its chief Hebron negotiator for civilian affairs, Major-General Oren Shahor, for 'improper conduct' in meeting privately with PISGA leaders and passing information to the Labour Party during visits with Peres.

Talks reached an acrimonious impasse on 28 October owing to the reopening of issues previously thought finalized, despite an agreement on the issue of hot pursuit, prompting Ross to return to Washington to consult Secretary Christopher.[229] To break the stalemate, the US submitted on 5 November a document proposing solutions to the remaining security-related disagreements on the Hebron arrangement. The PISGA responded by sending a formal letter to Israel, with copies to the EU, the US, Russia, and Arab states, accusing Israel of deliberately delaying the resumption of committee-level negotiations.[230] Despite this international activity, meaningful negotiations obviously took a less central importance as the US election took place on 5 November, bringing with it Secretary Christopher's resignation two days later.[231]

On 12 November, Israel and the PISGA agreed to raise the level of the Hebron talks in a bid to complete negotiations, with Shahak and Abbas chosen to lead discussions. They held their first meeting the same night at US Ambassador Indyk's home.[232] The next day, Netanyahu cancelled a visit to the US to take charge of the Hebron negotiations personally. He agreed initially to an oral assurance, then subsequently acceded to the PISGA demand that Israel include a written pledge to honour all its agreements with the PISGA. This written pledge would be attached to any subsequent Hebron agreement as long as the PISGA upheld all of its commitments.[233]

Despite the impasse in negotiations, construction of Hebron's joint District Coordination Office began on 4 November. IDF officials said that military preparations for redeployment were virtually complete on 13 November. Additional Israeli police officers were drafted in to deal with any settler resistance, new bunkers were placed at strategic junctions around the Jewish enclave in the centre of the city and the remaining three IDF posts were vacated on 16 November. Although Israel placed Hebron settlement leader and Kach member Noam Federman in administrative detention for two months on 10 November, as part of a plan to round up 20–30 militant settlers before redeployment to reduce the chance of violence during the transfer of powers, a number of worrying events provided evidence that internal divisions existed within senior Israeli echelons regarding both government policy and its personalities. For example, on 3 November Infrastructure Minister Sharon unveiled his plan to build two new settlements in the West Bank that would double the number of existing Jewish settlers,[234] and on 16 November Shin Bet announced that it had earlier ordered troops to appear without weapons when Netanyahu visited an army base because of rising distrust of the PM among top army commanders, upset at being left out of crucial security decisions.[235]

Israeli-PISGA negotiations on Hebron resumed in Jericho on 17 November, although Dore Gold, Mahmoud Abbas and Yasir Abed

Rabbu had met the previous day to discuss a memorandum of under-standing or pledges concerning non-implemented aspects of the Interim Agreement that PM Netanyahu considered extending to Arafat as part of a Hebron deal.[236] However, it appeared that the new government was also repositioning itself for domestic purposes, as former PM Peres, Arafat and the Labour Party were forced to deny rumours on 18 November that Peres had advised Arafat it would be to his advantage to hold up the signing of a Hebron protocol. Peres blamed Netanyahu and his office for promoting the story,[237] and on 20 November Israel released a 14-page report alleging ma-jor violations of the Oslo accords by the PISGA, and accusing PISGA leaders of deliberately stirring up the riots that followed the tunnel opening.[238] On 21 November, Israel and the PISGA held an expanded round of talks on Hebron in Jerusalem, in which the two sides discussed the possibility of another Netanyahu-Arafat summit, but the parties found themselves in a dispute over the Rafah airport project, in which Israel demanded that the PISGA demolish the already completed airport terminal building and build it elsewhere.[239] Following the weekly PISGA, Executive Authority (EA) and PLO Executive Committee meetings on 22 November, Palestinian leaders advocated 'popular confrontation' with Israeli bulldozers every time they appeared on Palestinian land, urged Palestinians to reclaim confiscated land in the West Bank and Gaza, and vowed political and financial support for such Palestinian resistance in the face of the growing political storm over the perceived and revealed Israeli government policy of expanding Israeli settlements. Arafat sent Netanyahu a letter on 25 November urging him to halt Israeli set-tlement expansion, but Netanyahu responded by stating that he would be pressing ahead with settlement plans.[240] Although Hebron talks resumed the next day, the PISGA announced that it would boycott all multilateral talks except those on refugees, in protest at Israel's alleged lack of progress in the bilateral negotiations and its refusal to implement existing agreements.[241]

In what amounted to a dismissal of the new government's insist-ence that any Hebron agreement must include their security demands of 'hot pursuit', Israeli jurists confirmed on 27 November that the existing Oslo accords provided Israel with overriding powers and responsibilities for security in the West Bank and Gaza Strip. This ruling thus permitted and justified any Israeli hot pursuit rights and also guaranteed that Israel had the authority under the agree-ments to re-enter any PISGA area from which they had previously redeployed. Therefore Israel agreed to drop its demand for written guarantees from the PISGA for Israeli hot pursuit rights in Hebron, a controversial issue which had long held up progress in the Hebron negotiations.[242]

Shadowing the Hebron talks was mounting international pressure on Israel over the settlements issue. Former close military partner South Africa called on Israel to withdraw from Hebron, to show that it intended to comply with the existing agreements and to refrain from provocative actions such as the tunnel incident.[243] The EU-Arab Parliamentary Dialogue held an executive meeting on 29 November in advance of its first full session in eight years, on 30 November–1 December. The 14 executive delegates agreed to lobby for the postponement of the ratification of the Euro-Mediterranean agreement between Europe and Israel in order to send a signal to Israel that they were unhappy with its current peace policies, and at the full session in Amman, representatives from 33 nations issued a declaration urging Israel to fulfil its commitments to the Oslo accords.[244] While settlers, Palestinians and the IDF clashed in Hebron, the Arab League held an emergency session on Israeli settlement activity in Cairo on 1 December. The Arab League warned Israel that expanding settlements would endanger peacemaking. However, despite stating that existing settlements should be dismantled, the League stopped short of Syria's demand that Arab states should suspend relations with Israel.[245] While 54 member-states attended the convening of the Organization for Security and Cooperation in Europe on 2 December in Lisbon, Netanyahu not only met US Vice-President Gore and President Chirac, but reiterated his intention that Israel would expand settlement construction in the West Bank. In Damascus Iranian FM Ali Akbar Velayati arrived to discuss bilateral relations, and discussed with FM al-Shara measures to be adopted in case of an Israeli attack on Syria, causing Israel to express concern over the visit.[246] The fallout from the stalled peace process caused IDF deputy chief of staff Matan Vilnai to state on 26 December that the 'working estimate for 1997 is that we can find ourselves in a military confrontation with Syria' with the probability of war no longer low.[247]

Netanyahu announced, on 4 December, that the PISGA and Israeli negotiating teams had exhausted their work, and that he and Arafat should hold a bilateral summit meeting to conclude the details of the outstanding Hebron negotiations. Arafat responded his willingness to conclude the terms of an Israeli redeployment from Hebron.

In the spirit of cooperation, Israel and the PISGA agreed to set up a 'hot line' to improve communications between the Internal Security Ministry and the PSF in case of emergencies,[248] and PISGA negotiators on 6 December declared Arafat and Netanyahu's willingness for a three-way summit between Egypt, Israel and the PISGA to discuss a deal on Hebron, though no date was set.[249] These improvements, however, remained cosmetic, for the next day the PISGA demanded of Israel the provision of dates for further redeployment in the West Bank, the release of prisoners along with a concluded Hebron protocol, and the opening of al-Shuhada Street and the central market in Hebron. The PISGA also demanded Israel eliminate the term 'hot pursuit' from any Hebron deal and allow PISGA police in Hebron Joint Patrols to carry the same weapons as the IDF.[250]

The negotiations remained hostage to the settlement issue and the men of violence. On 11 December as DM Mordechai briefed Jordanian Information Minister Marwan Mu'asher in Tel Aviv on negotiations with the PISGA, receiving in return a warning that Israeli expansion of settlements would raise fears of a military conflict, two settlers were killed in a PFLP drive-by shooting near Ramallah. Although the murders were claimed as a response to Israel's plans to build 132 houses in East Jerusalem and were condemned by the PISGA, the PISGA believed that such murders would only serve as a pretext for the Israelis to delay negotiations further.[251] In response to the murders, EU special envoy Miguel Angel Moratinos met with FM Levy the next day and agreed to set up a 'red phone' between Moratinos, Israel and Arab leaders to discuss misunderstandings in emergencies. While the Arab League issued a statement strongly condemning Israel's settlement activities, PM Netanyahu vowed at the funeral for the two settlers to 'deepen' Jewish settlements on the West Bank, whilst in Kiryat Gat an Israeli settler allegedly shot and killed a Gazan worker to avenge the two settlers.[252] On 13 December the Israeli cabinet reinstated large subsidies, including tax breaks and business grants, for West Bank settlers despite the reaction from the US which described the development as 'troubling', and as one which 'clearly complicates the peace process.'[253] In Gaza, some 15 000 Palestinians attended an anti-settlement demonstration called by Hamas and approved by the PISGA, at which Hamas spokesman Mahmud Zahhar announced that Hamas would soon open political offices in Gaza with West Bank offices planned, with the PISGA's permission, as a transitional step for 'greater participation in public life'.[254]

In an open letter to PM Netanyahu eight high-ranking former US officials wrote about their concern about Israeli settlements. The letter was precipitated by Netanyahu's policies which were deemed by Zbigniew Brzezinski as 'inimical to the peace process and even dangerous'. Architect of the Madrid peace process, James Baker, Brzezinski (ex-National Security Adviser), Frank Carlucci (ex-National Security Adviser), Lawrence Eagleburger (ex-Secretary of State), Richard Fairbanks (ex-Middle East Peace Negotiator), Brent Scowcroft (ex-National Security Adviser), Robert Strauss (ex-Middle East Peace Negotiator), and Cyrus Vance (ex-Secretary of State), wrote expressing their concern 'that unilateral actions, such as the expansion of settlements, would be strongly counterproductive to the goal of a negotiated solution and, if carried forward, could halt progress made by the peace process over the last two decades' and therefore urged Netanyahu 'not to take unilateral actions that would preclude a meaningful negotiated settlement and a comprehensive and lasting peace'.[255] In mounting international pressure over the settlement issue, the EU criticized the decision to reinstate state-subsidized benefits to settlers. The decision also drew criticism from President Clinton who stated his disapproval of both reinstating benefits and plans to expand settlements in the West Bank. British PM Major warned Israel not to inflame tensions by expanding settlements.[256] In response, Netanyahu phoned Arafat to ease tensions over the settlement issue. Arafat and Yitzhak Molho then met on 15 December in the first high level PISGA-Israeli contact in weeks.[257] Israel-PISGA talks on Hebron resumed the next day, and Molho met with Saeb Erekat in Jerusalem in a further effort to defuse tensions over the settler benefits issue. However, the Israeli government publicly rejected President Clinton's comments on settlements, saying that they were unhelpful during a period of Israeli-PISGA impasse, and vowed that government policy would continue to strengthen the settlements.[258] A number of events made 19 December a busy day. Netanyahu held discussions with Levy, Mordechai, Sharon and defence officials regarding a document submitted by US ambassador Indyk, which constituted a compromise on Hebron, incorporating understandings previously reached between Israel and the PISGA, and including clauses relating to the continued implementation of the Interim Agreement and an Israeli commitment to a timetable for a military redeployment.[259] Elsewhere Secretary Christopher announced that US special envoy Dennis Ross would return to the Middle East to 'reenergize' the stalled negotiations, claiming that

Israel had made some unspecified concessions and therefore it was time for the PISGA to reciprocate, a claim which drew denials from the PISGA that Israel had made any concessions.[260] Israel expressed concern that the PISGA would expand the Gaza port beyond the agreed plans to create a commercial, rather than fishing port, in which case Israel would have no control over entering and departing craft.[261] FM Levy met King Hussein and PM Kabariti in Jordan to discuss bilateral relations and the peace process.[262] The YESHA settlers' council ended a three-day convention at which they announced three 'red lines' which, if crossed, would put an end to their support for Netanyahu and would stimulate action on their part against him. Their 'red lines' consisted of calling a halt to construction of housing units in East Jerusalem and Hebron, the implementation of further redeployments from Area C and not allowing for 'extensive and comprehensive' settlement.[263]

As Ross arrived in Israel to meet with Netanyahu and later with Arafat in Gaza on 21 December, a scuffle between settlers and Palestinian children escalated into a melee in Hebron involving hundreds of settlers and Palestinians, which when IDF soldiers intervened led to strong riot control measures being employed.[264] As Ross offered some unspecified ideas for bridging the gaps between the two sides during intensive talks with Israeli and PISGA negotiators on 22 December, DM Mordechai announced that Israel would implement further redeployment immediately after a Hebron deal was reached if Arafat promised to 'wage an uncompromising war against terrorism'.[265] Tensions in Hebron increased when an Israeli military court in Lod sentenced two Palestinians to two consecutive life sentences each for driving suicide bombers to the scenes of the February/March bombings, and when two firebombs were thrown at a Jewish settlement, although these caused no injuries, the IDF imposed a curfew on Hebron, rounded up 100 Palestinians and forced the closure of Palestinian stores, prompting a riot.[266] Attempting to ease the pressure, Ross met again with Netanyahu and Arafat, and arranged for each of them to be briefed separately on the status of the talks by a joint delegation of PISGA and Israeli negotiators which included Abbas and Molho.[267] Intensive diplomatic measures led to the longest face-to-face Arafat-Netanyahu meeting at Erez on 24 December to discuss the problem of final status issues preventing a Hebron deal. Meanwhile DM Mordechai met President Mubarak in Hurghada to discuss the progress of the Israel-PISGA talks, and in Hebron the IDF lifted the curfew on

Hebron and permitted the Islamic University, closed since March, to reopen.[268]

While Ross returned for Washington, Israeli-PISGA negotiations on Hebron continued, and in anticipation of the resumption of final status talks, Netanyahu's inner cabinet began to debate the government's plan for a permanent arrangement with the PISGA. However, in Hebron the IDF and the Israeli police had to arrest 20 settlers as they attempted to seize two vacant houses in the Arab section of town, whilst three firebombs were thrown by Palestinians at an IDF position in the city centre.[269] Israeli-PISGA negotiators continued talks, and announced on 27 December that they hoped to finalize a Hebron deal by New Year's Day and complete the military redeployment by 5 January. However debate continued over the issues of security control of the Tomb of the Patriarchs/al-Ibrahimi Mosque, al-Shuhada Street, the type of weapons to be used by the PISGA police, the buffer zone between H-1 and H-2 areas and restrictions on Jewish construction.[270] Ross returned to the Middle East on 30 December and gave Netanyahu a letter from President Clinton which expressed respect for the former's decision to move forward on an agreement despite his hard-line views, and invited him to visit Washington DC soon. As Amnon Shahak and Mahmoud Abbas held intensive negotiations in Jerusalem,[271] Netanyahu agreed to submit any Hebron deal to the cabinet for approval, under pressure from FM Levy, as seven of the 18 members stated they would veto any agreement or abstain, with a further two unsure as to their intentions.[272]

Israel-PISGA negotiations on Hebron continued on 31 December with the PISGA demanding of Israel a commitment to complete further redeployment by autumn 1998 as set out in the Interim Agreement. This prompted Ross to meet Netanyahu and Arafat separately. For the second time in a week, Jewish settlers broke into the central market area in Hebron to claim it as Jewish property, but the Israeli police arrested 15 and ejected them from the site.[273] Worse was to come. Off-duty IDF soldier Noam Friedman, intending in his own words to kill 'Israel-haters', sat in the middle of the Hebron marketplace and opened fire on innocent passers by, wounding seven. His action precipitated clashes between settlers and Palestinians, with nine Palestinians injured as a result of the IDF attempts to break up the protests, which resulted in a curfew being placed on the city. A planned meeting between Arafat and Netanyahu was postponed, but negotiations resumed at US ambassador Indyk's home with President Clinton personally phoning Arafat to encourage him to conclude an agreement before the situation in Hebron got any worse.[274] In response to the murderous attack by Friedman, the PISGA hardened its position on the Hebron deal, demanding of Israel to withdraw its troops from rural West Bank villages as well. However, Internal Security Minister Kahalani warned that 'the Jews in Hebron must be protected. They are in great danger, despite Noam Friedman's shooting spree', and although Israeli police detained IDF soldier Yuval Jibli on suspicion of complicity with Friedman's plans to attack the Hebron market, the IDF reinforced its presence in the city.[275] On 3 January Netanyahu moved to appease his right-wing cabinet colleagues in advance of a vote on a Hebron deal by saying that he would not give the PISGA a timetable for further redeployment but would rather only give a date on which redeployment would begin, because ten of the 18 cabinet members had announced that they were considering vetoing or abstaining from a vote on a Hebron deal. This drew criticism from the PISGA and the response that it would not sign a deal without a timetable.[276]

After meeting secretly through the night of 4–5 January at Erez, Arafat and Netanyahu announced that they were close to making a firm Hebron deal. A US diplomatic team member stated that the lower level negotiations had reached the end of their utility and that if an agreement was to be attained then the leaders had to conclude an agreement. Netanyahu continued to play up with the Americans his fear of losing his cabinet majority over the Hebron issue in order to stave off PISGA demands.[277] On 6 January Ross spent the day shuttling between Netanyahu in Jerusalem and Arafat in Bethlehem, in an attempt to bridge the gap on the issue of further redeployment, as Israel stated that it wanted to postpone the third and final stage of redeployment from the West Bank until spring 1999. All the parties however cited 10 January, the beginning of Ramadan, as their target date for concluding an agreement on Hebron.[278]

As a deal drew nearer, the endgame manoeuvring intensified. Ben-Elissar, Israeli ambassador to the US, on 7 January accused the Egyptians of encouraging the PISGA to stall on a Hebron deal and of pressing other Arab states not to normalize relations with Israel. Meanwhile Israel eased the closure on the occupied territories by increasing from 3420 to 4520 the number of Palestinian merchants permitted into Israel, by allowing 250 Gazan merchants into the West Bank and vice versa, by increasing from 150 to 200 the number of Gazan PISGA officials allowed into the West Bank, and by admitting 50 Gazan lorries into Israel.[279] As a compromise to Israel's proposal to delay further redeployment to 1999, Netanyahu suggested, on 8 January, delaying completion of further redeployment until May 1998; however this proposal was rejected by Arafat, who stated that under the terms of the Interim Agreement, all three stages of further redeployment were due to be completed by September 1997.[280] Two pipe bombs exploded in Tel Aviv on 9 January wounding 13 Israelis. When no one took responsibility, Netanyahu broke off a meeting with Ross to state that if the bombing proved to have been staged from the PISGA areas, he would not only suspend negotiations, but would also respond with 'great severity'. However Israeli police announced that the bombs were small and unsophisticated and that they had been unable to determine a motive for the attack.[281]

In a round of international diplomacy on 11 January, President Mubarak met with Arafat and Ross separately in Cairo to discuss the Israeli-PISGA talks, Arafat then returning to Gaza to meet with his EA. King Hussein phoned President Mubarak, Netanyahu and Christopher to discuss the Israeli-PISGA negotiations.[282] The next day Hussein travelled to Gaza and Israel to try and break the deadlock in the Israeli-PISGA talks, and as a result Ross, who had planned to return home because no agreement had seemed forthcoming, decided to stay on. After an evening of talks, Arafat and Netanyahu agreed to a compromise on the issue of further redeployment suggested by Hussein, which opened the way for a deal on Hebron to be signed.[283] In Jerusalem the following day, Israeli and PISGA negotiators reviewed drafts of a possible Hebron Protocol in order to work out the final details, although both sides stated that no more substantive differences remained between them. Netanyahu told his cabinet colleagues that the main achievement of the Hebron Protocol draft, as it stood, was that most of the West Bank territory would remain under Israel's control even after further redeployment was completed, as Israel would be able to determine the amount of land that would be returned under the three stages of redeployment.[284] On 14 January, after several hours of talks between Arafat and Netanyahu at Erez, the Hebron Protocol was initialled by Dan Shomron and Saeb Erekat at Erez at 0230 local time, on 15 January, though not officially signed until the 17th in Jerusalem, with an attached US 'Note for the Record' and an 'Agreed Minute'. Letters of Assurance to Arafat and Netanyahu from

Christopher were also exchanged.[285] On the 28th in Jerusalem, Erekat and Molho exchanged lists of their delegations assigned to the eight joint subcommittees which would simultaneously continue discussions on the issues for negotiation. Each subcommittee was to draw up a protocol on the implementation of the Interim Agreement articles specific to its topic. FM Levy was appointed the ceremonial post of head of the Israeli side of the Israeli-Palestinian Steering and Monitoring Committee, while cabinet secretary Dani Nave was to act as chief negotiator opposite Erekat. The Finance Minister Dan Meridor was appointed head of the economic subcommittee opposite PISGA Planning Minister Nabil Sha'ath.[286]

As the Hebron agreement was being resolved, YESHA settlers' council held an emergency session to discuss the Hebron protocol on 14 January, and resolved to start treating Netanyahu's government as a political foe.[287] Also on the same day, in a portent of the future, the IDF began the forced transfer of 3000 Bedouin from their homes near Jahalin in the West Bank in preparation for the expansion of Ma'ale Adumim settlement. Some 45 Bedouin families had lived on the site for 40 years but were being sent to a site outside Jerusalem near the municipal rubbish dump as alternative housing, to live in 29 shipping-freight containers without running water or electricity.[288]

The significance of the Hebron Protocol

What makes the Hebron Protocol of particular interest and significance is the fact that it was the first negotiated agreement concluded between the PLO and a Likud-led coalition government of Israel. Through this agreement, it may be inferred that the Likud-led right wing of the Israel polity accepted both the PLO as a negotiating partner and the peace process. However, before such a conclusion may be drawn, an analysis of the Hebron agreement reveals that it by no means undermines, or means an end to, the revisionist Zionist dreams of 'Greater Israel', with an equivalent assumption that by concluding such an agreement a Palestinian state is more likely than not.

According to Article VII.1.b of Annex I of the Interim Agreement, Israel was to a have completed its redeployment from Hebron by 28 March 1996. However this timetable was suspended by then-PM Peres following the February/March suicide bombings. Negotiations aimed at implementing the 'Guidelines for Hebron' (Article VII of Annexe I of the Interim Agreement) resumed after a ten-month delay caused by the political furore and violence over the suicide bombings of February/March, the Israeli election, and the September tunnel incident. Those involved in the resumed talks at various times included, the PLO's Mahmoud Abbas, PISGA Information Minister Yasir Abed Rabbu, PISGA Local Government Minister Erekat, PM Netanyahu's adviser Dore Gold, PM Netanyahu's personal lawyer Yitzhak Molho, Cabinet Secretary Dani Nave and IDF Chief of Staff Lieutenant General Shomron.[289] The talks centred on the issue of the Israeli redeployment from Hebron, and included other unfulfilled clauses of the Interim Agreement, such as: the reaffirmation of the commitment to implement the Interim Agreement on the basis of reciprocity; Israeli undertakings on the first phase of redeployment, prisoner release issues, outstanding Interim Agreement issues to be negotiated and the resumption of permanent status negotiations; and Palestinian undertakings on revising the PLO Charter, fighting terror and preventing violence, the size of the PISGA police and PISGA activities in Jerusalem.

Talks reconvened in October 1996, reached an impasse on 18 November and stopped altogether at the end of November. Netanyahu and Arafat agreed that the only way to resolve the remaining issues was by bilateral summit meetings at Erez, and despite the fact that Arafat almost walked out of the talks twice in disageement over proposed control of the Tomb of the Patriarchs/al-Ibrahimi Mosque, sufficient progress was made to complete a final draft of the Hebron Protocol by 2 January 1997. At Erez, Arafat had insisted that, owing to the difficulties in securing Netanyahu's pledge to implement the Hebron redeployment, side letters should be included with the Hebron Protocol to provide assurances, not only on the Hebron redeployment, but also on the resumption of final status talks, further redeployment and any outstanding issues from the Interim Agreement. Palestinian insistence on having these letters of assurance tied to the Hebron Protocol, thus linking the Hebron deal with all other outstanding issues, meant that the actual signing of the Hebron Protocol was delayed further. The final differences were overcome by intense shuttle diplomacy led by Ross, who acted as intermediary for Arafat and Netanyahu, and through the good offices of King Hussein, whose special visit to Gaza and Israel on 12 January to offer a crucial compromise proposal on further redeployment enabled the last remaining issue of contention to be overcome.

The Hebron agreement constitutes the technical modalities of implementing the guidelines for the redeployment of Israeli Military Forces in Hebron to be carried out in accordance with the Interim Agreement and the Hebron protocol. The redeployment constitutes the 'full implementation of the provisions of the Interim Agreement with regard to the city of Hebron unless otherwise provided for in Article VII of Annexe I.'[290] The Hebron Protocol was accompanied by the US-drafted Note For the Record, attached Agreed Minute, and Secretary Christopher's letters of assurance to Arafat and Netanyahu, which although not officially part of the deal were considered crucial by both sides.[291]

The Note for the Record

An integral part of the Hebron deal was the attached Note for the Record, an official addendum to the Hebron Protocol, written by Ross, which outlined the reaffirmation by both leaders of their commitment to implement the Interim Agreement on the basis of reciprocity, and within the context of the Note for the Record conveyed their concerns, obligations and undertakings to each other on this matter. The need for the Note stemmed from Palestinian fears that Israel would fail to implement the further provisions of the Interim Agreement once the pressure of Hebron had subsided, making the Palestinians believe it necessary to insist upon a formal linkage between the signing of the Hebron Protocol and other Interim Agreement issues. The Note listed the unfulfilled Interim Agreement requirements either as issues that one or other side was responsible for implementing, or as issues for negotiation, despite having been already addressed within the remit of the Interim Agreement.

On the Israeli side, by reaffirming its commitments to the following measures and principles in accordance with the Interim Agreement, their issues for implementation covered the following.

Further redeployment phases.   The first phase was to be carried out during the first week of March.

Prisoner release issues.   These issues were to be dealt with in accordance with the Interim Agreement's provisions and procedures, including Annexe VII, whereas their issues for negotiation covered

- Outstanding Interim Agreement issues (negotiations on outstanding issues to be conducted in parallel: a) safe passage, b) Gaza Airport, c) Gaza Port, d) passages, e) economic, financial, civilian and security issues, and f) people-to-people)

- Permanent status negotiations (to be implemented within 2 months after implementation of the Hebron Protocol).

The Palestinians for their part committed themselves to implementing immediately measures in parallel and in accordance with those previously agreed within the terms of the Interim Agreement, namely:

(1) Completing the process of revising the Palestinian National Charter.

(2) Fighting terror and preventing violence, by:
   a) strengthening security cooperation;
   b) preventing incitement and hostile propaganda, as specified in Article XXII of the Interim Agreement;
   c) combatting systematically and effectively terrorist organizations and infrastructure;
   d) apprehending, prosecuting and punishing terrorists;
   e) requesting transfer of suspects and defendants, to be acted upon in accordance with Article II.7.f of Annexe IV of the Interim Agreement;
   f) confiscating illegal firearms.

(3) The size of the Palestinian police force to be pursuant with the Interim Agreement.

(4) Exercise of Palestinian governmental activity, and location of government offices, as specified within the Interim Agreement.[292]

The interesting feature of this attached Note is that it commits both sides to a process of reciprocity, meaning that if one or other fails to deliver on its stated intentions, the other can call a halt to its own implementation of the agreement. Thus if one side deems the other to have failed to implement its stated obligations and the other side's interpretation of such, then the agreement becomes hostage to perceived violations of the agreement rather than remaining focused on the issues of implementing and progressing the process.

Though not officially part of the Hebron Protocol, the attached letters of assurances were however necessary to its approval. Secretary Christopher's letters, one to Netanyahu and one to Arafat, were integral to concluding the deal and were carefully negotiated with both sides. The US letter to Netanyahu, the only one made public, was noteworthy particularly for setting the timetable for further withdrawals and for the controversy surrounding its reference to 'US views on Israel's process of redeploying its forces [and] designating specified military locations', widely interpreted to mean US recognition of Israel's right to unilaterally decide the extent of further redeployments.[293] In addition, on behalf of the President of the EU Council of Ministers, Dutch FM Hans van Mierlo presented a 'Letter of Assurances to President Arafat' on 15 January, but it was not made public until 2 February. It was first mentioned by Arafat at a joint press conference held at the Hague with Dutch PM Vim Kok and FM van Mierlo. According to a clarification by van Mierlo, the letter had been requested by Arafat and ultimately agreed to by the Israeli government, which asked that it be kept secret. According to EU Middle East peace coordinator Miguel Moratinos, the letter, drafted after the consultations with the US, helped to convince Arafat to conclude the Hebron Protocol.[294]

Probably the most important provision of both the Note for the Record and the letters of assurances concerned the issue of further redeployment. Linkage of redeployment to a Hebron agreement was raised as a PISGA demand that Israel provide dates for a timetable of redeployment on 7 December, but Netanyahu initially reacted on 19 December by refusing to adhere to any set timetable. On 31 December the PISGA further demanded that redeployment from rural areas be completed by September 1997, as originally envisaged in the Interim Agreement. By 3 January Netanyahu agreed that he would give only the date for the start of the first of the three stages of intended further redeployment, without further commitment on the other dates. Following the Arafat-Netanyahu summit at Erez on 5 January, Israel stated the following day that it wanted to postpone the final stage of redeployment until spring 1999, just before final status talks are scheduled to conclude. On 8 January Netanyahu presented a compromise that would delay the completion of all stages until May 1998, however both options were rejected by the PISGA. In order to break the deadlock, King Hussein presented a proposal on 12 January, accepted by both sides, which set the dates for the start of the first two stages of redeployment as 28 February 1997 and 31 October 1997, but only set 'mid-1998' for the completion of the third stage. Despite King Hussein's initiative, the Note for the Record required Israel only to begin the first stage of further redeployment by the first week of March 1997. Secretary Christopher's letter of assurances stipulated that all three stages should be completed by mid-1998, whereas in Ross' letter to the Israeli cabinet, the US interpretation of mid-1998 is clarified as being by the end of August 1998. The Note also allows for Israel to suspend further redeployment if it deems the PISGA to have not fulfilled its responsibilities and obligations, and since the Note does not include on the list of issues to be negotiated the issue of further redeployment, this amounted to allowing Israel to choose how, where and when it would redeploy.[295]

The main provisions of the Hebron Protocol covered the 'Security Arrangements Regarding Redeployment in Hebron and the Civil Arrangements Regarding Redeployment in Hebron', and also provided for the reduction and prevention of provocation and friction, to ensure free access of peoples, goods and vehicles and the normalization of relations.

The security terms provided for a number of arrangements. Israeli military forces were to redeploy from some 80 per cent of Hebron within ten days of the protocol, as opposed to 85 per cent as agreed within the Interim Agreement. The responsibility for internal security and public order in H-2, the commercial and religious centre of the city which included 400 Israeli settlers and 20 000 Palestinians, would remain with Israel, who would continue to exercise responsibility for the overall security of Israelis throughout Hebron, and was provided with all the powers to take the necessary steps to meet its security responsibilities by enabling Israeli security forces to conduct security activity within areas of Palestinian jurisdiction. Joint Mobile Units and Joint Patrols were to operate in areas of particular sensitivity, with a Joint Coordination Centre headed by a senior officer from both sides to coordinate joint security measures. Access to special areas of particular sensitivity in H-1 located close to H-2 would be limited by the Palestinian police, including restricting the four designated Palestinian police 16-member rapid response teams armed with rifles without prior Israeli approval. The Jewish holy sites in H-1, the Cave of Othniel Ben Knaz, Elonei Mamre, Eshel Avraham and Mayaan Sarah, would be protected by Palestinian police with free, unimpeded and secure access for Israelis ensured, with visits to be accompanied by a Joint Mobile Unit.[296] Both sides reaffirmed their commitment to honour the relevant security provisions of the Interim Agreement, including the provisions regarding the Arrangements for Security and Public Order (Article XII of the Interim Agreement), the Prevention of Hostile Acts (Article XV of the Interim Agreement), the Security Policy for the Prevention of Terrorism and Violence (Article II of Annexe I of the Interim Agreement), the Guidelines for Hebron (Article VII of the Interim Agreement) and the Rules of Conduct in Mutual Security Matters (Article XI of Annexe I of the Interim Agreement).[297]

The terms of the civil arrangements provided for a number understandings. The transfer of the remaining 12 spheres of civil powers and responsibilities not yet completed was to be done concurrently with the beginning of the redeployment. However, those powers and responsibilities not transferred to the Palestinians in H-2, that is those relating to Israelis and their property, would continue to be exercised by the Israeli Military Government. In order to prevent friction resulting from construction activity, agreement was reached with regard to planning, zoning and building, to preserve the historic character of the city including outlining a number of provisions covering proposed construction of buildings over two/three metres, and for non-residential and non-commercial use, to be implemented through prior coordination with the District Civil Liaison Office. The Municipality, responsible for infrastructure and transportation, would provide continued and effective services to the Israelis in H-2, such as traffic management, water, sewage, electricity and communications, agreeing to make required work for Israelis top priority if Israel covered the costs. No more than 50 unarmed plain-clothed municipal inspectors would be allowed access to H-2 to ensure the enforcement of laws and regulations covering the Palestinian population, and they would be able to call upon Israeli police if necessary. Municipal services to all residents of Hebron would be provided regularly and continuously, at the same cost and quality, without discrimination.[298]

In Gaza, the PISGA, EA and the PLO Executive Committee ratified the protocol on 15 January. However, five out of 22 EA members voted against ratification and many PISGA members complained. They were distressed that they had not been asked for their approval prior to its signing, but merely asked for their consent to a *fait accompli*, as they were only initially shown excerpts of the agreements for approval, and that the full text annexes and maps that they eventually received were in English only.[299] After 13 hours of debate, the Israeli cabinet endorsed the protocol by a vote of 11 to 7 on 16 January. The cabinet agreed to 'act to maintain all the conditions and requirements necessary for the existence, security and consolidation of the Jewish community in Hebron', confirmed that 'details of the further stages of the redeployment in Judea and Samaria' would 'be determined by the Government of Israel', and reiterated that a fundamental condition for the continuation of the peace process with the Palestinians was 'the mutual fulfilment of the obligations of both sides'. Those voting against were, Benjamin Begin, Yuli Edelstein, Rafael Eitan, Zevulun Hammer, Yitzhak Levy, Limor Livnat and Ariel Sharon. On the adoption of the decision,

Begin announced his resignation from the government.[300] Halfway through the cabinet debate, Netanyahu had to call a recess amid confusion surrounding US guarantees which resulted from an Israeli TV broadcast which quoted an unidentified US official saying that under the terms of the protocol, the extent of additional redeployments would be negotiated and that Israel could no longer unilaterally decide how much of the West Bank it was going to transfer to the PISGA. At the request of the Israeli cabinet, Ross composed a letter of clarification addressed to Cabinet Secretary Dani Nave, which stated that

> the term 'mid-1998' . . . was originally proposed by King Hussein and is intended to refer to a bridging period between May 1998 and September 1998. In the context of the US proposal, it was proposed to use the term 'the last part of 1998' to indicate the final date for the further redeployments. In the course of the negotiations . . . it was agreed on various occasions that the term 'mid-1998' will cover a time-frame in the middle of the year and will not indicate a precise date. During the negotiations, the speakers specified the months of June, July and August to illustrate how the term will be implemented on the ground.[301]

Netanyahu was also reassured by US ambassador to Israel Martin Indyk , that it was 'clear in the agreement' that Israel would specify the military locations, so that any 'amount Israel hands over' would be 'Israel's decision'.[302] Furthermore State Department spokesman Nicholas Burns issued on 15 January a 'Statement on Further Redeployments' in Washington DC as a result of the confusion. Burns claimed that not only was the reported statement attributed to a State Department spokesman 'erroneous', but that the only relevant US comments on the issue were the Note for the Record, which made clear that 'further redeployment phases are issues for implementation by Israel rather than issues for negotiation with the Palestinians', and the letters of assurance provided to both parties which 'refer to the process of further redeployments as an Israeli responsibility which includes its designating specified military locations'.[303]

With Knesset approval for the Hebron agreement, the IDF began redeploying from Hebron the same day.[304] PISGA police began entering Hebron on 15 January, setting up its rapid response teams by 21 January, with the two Joint Mobile Units and two Joint Patrols commencing operations on 1 February.[305] The IDF began the phased reopening of al-Shuhada Street on 3 February, allowing ambulances and taxis access but not private vehicles, and fully reopened the city's central market in H-2. However, Jewish settlers entered the market and scuffled with Palestinians claiming that the market posed a security risk to the settlers.[306]

What tentative conclusions can we draw from the Hebron Protocol, and of what significance to the final status negotiations are these conclusions? Palestinian critics of the deal contend that it means in effect the PISGA has officially sanctioned and legitimized the extension of Israeli jurisdiction over settlers and their settlements, in return for a partial redeployment, and a commitment to resume negotiations on unresolved Interim Agreement issues and to undertake final status talks. Israel, with US support, thus retains control over the scope and timetable of future redeployment phases. Despite PISGA reassurances that the Hebron Protocol is part of the interim phase of the peace process, and is therefore transitional by definition, the protocol illustrates a powerful vision of the extent to which future, final status negotiations will play out. In essence what is being agreed to under the protocol, is that Israel is not only laying the groundwork for the permanent division of Hebron, but is laying claim to jurisdiction over the settlers and their settlements, and also sovereignty over them, and access to them. In a subtle change of emphasis, the original terms of reference, UN Resolutions 242 and 338, are being superseded by a more pragmatic *modus vivendi* which could well predetermine final status issues by creating precedents whereby Israel will lay claim to large amounts of the occupied territories.[307]

The Hebron Protocol culminated from intense diplomatic efforts by the US to reinvigorate the peace process, which was in danger of collapsing following Rabin's assassination, Netanyahu's election and the tunnel incident. However, the Hebron Protocol does not constitute a new agreement, but is a deal to implement parts of the previously agreed Interim Agreement. It also incorporated, owing to the political atmosphere, a statement of intent to continue to pursue and implement the peace process. What constituted the crux of the disagreement over the Hebron negotiations was Netanyahu's desire to treat Hebron as a separate, interim phase issue, which had previously been articulated within the terms of the Interim Agreement, whereas the PISGA wished to see a deal on Hebron as the linchpin linking interim and final status arrangements, thus providing the peace process with continuity. The Palestinians knew that if the peace process collapsed, autonomy within their uncon-nected *bantustans* would be the most they could achieve. In order to link Hebron, the implementation of other unresolved interim period issues (prisoner release, Gaza airport and seaport, and safe passages between the autonomous areas), an Israeli commitment on a timetable for further redeployment, and final status negotia-tions, the Palestinians sought to achieve a deal over Hebron which would incorporate these issues and thus provide a public statement of intent by the Israeli government that the peace process was still viable. For the Palestinians, a deal on Hebron represented not only an agreement to implement the Interim Agreement, thus linking the new Israeli government with the old peace policy, but also an acceptance by the previously rejectionist Likud of a new approach to the DoP's implicit land-for-peace formula. Despite Likud protes-tations that the Oslo agreements needed modifications and renegotiation to incorporate their positions on settlers/settlements, 'hot pursuit' and their preference for entering into final status talks immediately after redeploying from Hebron whilst controlling some 90 per cent of the West Bank and Gaza, the significance of the eventual deal on Hebron was that it brought the new Likud-led government into the Oslo version of the peace process, the process that had originally begun under Likud at Madrid.

Essentially, both sides have in the past deflected criticism from opponents of the peace process by maintaining that any potential uncertainties would be dealt with through negotiations. 'Uncertainties' referred to the potential establishment of a Palestinian state. For the Israelis, negotiations would ensure this would not happen, whereas the Palestinians sought it as a goal through participation in the negotiating process. The DoP was viewed by both sides as basically an agreement to pre-empt or precede such an outcome, by creating facts 'on the ground'. Thus for the new Likud government the Hebron Protocol represented an opportunity to redefine the trend which linked the entire Israeli negotiating position from Madrid through to Hebron, that is, opposition to a Palestinian state. In this task they were substantially aided by the US administration. Principally, the Likud redefinition amounted to circumventing the basic terms of reference of the entire peace process, namely the implementa-tion of UN Resolution 242. In an intelligent reorientation of the hostility to the peace process which had characterized its period in opposition, the new Likud negotiating strategy deftly chose to close the route to Palestinian sovereignty through the negotiating process rather than through outright repudiation of the entire peace process. By appearing to the international community, and particularly the US administration, as willing to engage with the US-inspired peace process, the Israeli government ensured US cooperation rather than hostility, thus allowing it greater acceptance for its policy of challenging the final creation of a Palestinian state. This reorientation of Likud's strategy meant not only that those policy-makers involved had learned the lessons of past Likud mistakes *vis-à-vis* the Likud, the US and the peace process, but that they had found a way to deflect the Palestinians' dreams effectively whilst retaining US support. In a further twist, the Likud strategy also saw the prospect of a domestic political and ideological reconciliation between the mainstream Zionist parties. Labour leader Peres declared, on 15 January, that the Hebron Protocol signified 'the end of a deep ideological rift that . . . divided the Israeli people from the very day of its creation.' This rift, between those who believed Israel should control all of 'biblical Israel' and those who believed that Israel should control lands with a Jewish majority and for security reasons, had been healed. Peres believed that the 'idea of keeping all of the land [regardless] of its demographic division is over.' In spite of Peres's statements to the contrary, this did not mean that Israeli control over most of the existing occupied territories would not continue, or would not become enshrined through final status negotiations.[308] For Israeli domestic considerations, the internal divisions created by the peace process had, through the Hebron Protocol, been redefined. By engaging with the peace process the Likud found common cause with those domestic opponents who in their large numbers opposed the creation of a Palestinian state, and who believed that Israel should retain sovereignty over settlers, settlements and lands deemed necessary for security purposes. In this way, the Hebron Protocol, by extending *de facto* recognition of the Israeli presence in the occupied territories, not only did much to undermine the authority, legitimacy and acceptance of UN Resolution 242, but also served to reunite Israel and its principal ally, the US, as well as mainstream Israeli Zionism. Whether the coalition of shared interests survives final status negotiations is debatable, it is however nonetheless impressive that the Likud negotiating strategy was able to achieve so much despite domestic political scandals (the Deri-Baron affair) and international concern about Israeli intentions and goodwill.

Following the violence provoked by the tunnel incident, the US was faced with the possibility of a complete collapse of its peace process. President Clinton convened a summit in Washington with Netanyahu, Arafat and King Hussein. Ross was given the task of getting the Israelis and Palestinians to resume negotiations and conclude an agreement on redeployment from Hebron. The initiative to resume Israeli-PISGA negotiations began in October in Taba, with Ross and his deputy Aaron Miller attending. This proved to be an important point in the negotiating process, as it indicated both Likud engagement in negotiations with the Palestinians within the DoP and Interim Agreement framework, and a more direct US role in Israeli-PISGA talks, including discussing details and offering compromise suggestions. The PISGA were keen to open up the negotiating process since Netanyahu's election, either to gain comfort from increasing pressure on Israel from the international community, or to ensure that the US, resistant to widening involvement in the peace process, acted as a more balanced guarantor for further progress. Despite Palestinian desires for greater US involvement in the process, US officials claimed Netanyahu was the first to approach them with the suggestion of their becoming more engaged, and indeed, despite their initial wariness at Netanyahu's election, the US soon realized his pragmatism – to reaffirm the US-Israeli relationship rather than persist in his antagonism to the US-inspired process, to deal with the existing accords, and to 'adopt a new negotiating strategy based on meticulously intricate and legalistic mastery of the terms of the agreement he had' previously 'rejected'. Netanyahu cleverly embraced the US process, which allowed him to gain greater control over it without having to alter his stated intentions of denying Palestinian sovereignty, and maintaining as full suzerainty over the occupied territories as possible.[309] Such manoeuvring allowed the US and the Israelis, close allies at the best of times, to cooperate and coordinate on issues of agreement rather than descend into confrontation and contention. Israel and the US shared the same vision of the peace process generally, and their priorities reflected this, namely integrating Israel into the Middle East, maintaining the primacy of Israeli security concerns, and ensuring that the Hebron deal would provide security arrangements that would outlive the transitional phase. Although the US negotiators agreed with the Palestinians on the principle of linkage, particularly with regard to the Hebron redeployment and the non-implementation of the remaining interim arrangements, Palestinians negotiators and officials from Arafat down believed that the US team members were not only personally biased in Israel's favour, but were using the US pre-election period to manipulate a deal satisfactory to the Israelis. What the Palestinians seemed reluctant to accept was that the US administration, from the highest levels, was not going to attempt an even-handed approach, as US political interests were best served by ensuring an expeditious, pro-Israel agreement, which at the same time appeared to commit Israel to continuing with further negotiations. US insistence and pressure that Arafat accept Israeli proposals which did not include a specified timetable for further redeployment were however offset by Arab, Middle Eastern and international support, encouraged by Egypt, for the PISGA to refuse. Thus the ebb and flow of negotiations passed on to issues of contention regarding the Hebron part of the deal. After having reached agreement on most Hebron issues by the beginning of January, the outstanding issues remained that of the timetable for further redeployments and an Israeli commitment to begin final status negotiations. Agreement was ultimately brokered by King Hussein, who persuaded Netanyahu and Arafat to agree a compromise. King Hussein was able to convince the Palestinians that he was not waiting in the wings to resume his previous responsibilities, and the Israelis that he would not replace the Palestinians as principal interlocutor.

Despite the repeated reaffirmation in each of the Israel-PLO negotiated agreements, 'that the negotiations on the permanent status, . . . will lead to the implementation of Security Council Resolutions 242 and 338' and 'that the aim of the Israeli-Palestinian negotiations within the current Middle East peace process is' to lead 'to a permanent settlement based on Security Council Resolutions 242 And 338', a fundamental flaw of the DoP is its lack of linkage within the terms of reference to define the relationship between the UN resolutions, the applicability of international law and the interim period.[310] Because the interim period deals with a phased, limited and pre-determined transfer of powers and responsibilities for territorial and administrative jurisdictions, the status of the occupied territories during the interim phase is not bound by the same intentions as that of the final status, therefore during the interim phase, the status of the 'occupied' territories becomes that of 'disputed' territories, inferring the inapplicability of international law during the interim phase and allowing for any interpretations of what will constitute 'disputed' territory, and what may be created as a result. Thus despite claims that agreements made during the interim phase are merely transitional, the important point is that by acceding to negotiating demands during the interim phase without clear legal reference on which to press claims, legitimate rights become negotiable, with the possibility of becoming non-redeemable. For example, by accepting Israeli control over Israeli settlers and settlements outside Palestinian jurisdiction during the interim phase, the Palestinians have allowed the Israelis to establish their claims to a division of territorial and administrative jurisdictions, and thus by implication sovereignty, throughout the West Bank and Gaza. Thus whilst the Hebron Protocol may be a transitional agreement, designed to prevent friction between the two sides, in reality it is more likely that it represents an example of Israel's strategic vision to remain in possession of 'occupied' territory.

In his statement to the Knesset on the Hebron Protocol on 16 January, Netanyahu affirmed, 'We are not leaving Hebron, we are not redeploying from Hebron'; 'We do not want to remove the Jewish community from Hebron'; and 'We want to preserve and consolidate it.' Stating that the new government had 'inherited a difficult reality' and 'difficult agreements', which 'comprised written texts' and worse, an accompanying 'oral law', Netanyahu clarified his fundamentals, that he was 'committed to the written agreements' but that he repudiated any verbal understandings and promises reached between the previous government and the PISGA, saying 'We are not committed to the "oral law".' Such agreement was seen by Netanyahu as 'an uncontrolled dash to the "67 lines" whereby he castigated the previous administration for pursuing an agreement which 'would have produced negative results' for Israel, 'withdrawal to the "67 lines," or almost; the establishment of a Palestinian state; and even the division of Jerusalem.' Whilst 'committed, of course to the written agreements' Netanyahu stated that Israel's new 'goals are different', 'to maintain the unity of Jerusalem, to ensure the security depth necessary for the defence of the State, to insist on the right of Jews to settle in their land, and to propose to the Palestinians a suitable arrangement for self-rule but without the sovereign powers which pose a threat to Israel.' Netanyahu outlined three fundamental principles which guided the Israelis through the course of negotiations, 'both on Hebron and on the agreements to follow Hebron', namely, 'reciprocity', 'the implementation of the redeployments will be an Israeli decision', and 'the time frame'.

(1) Reciprocity. Netanyahu's understanding of the 'principle of reciprocity' is that it is 'a basic principle for the continuation of the process of the permanent status negotiations' which formed 'an integral part of the agreement' in which 'both sides agreed on a list of mutual undertakings' which in turn ensured that 'the fulfilment of the understandings of one side will be dependent upon the fulfilment by the other side.' Thus the Hebron agreement, represented '[a]n agreement in which both sides accept the mutual commitment to fulfil obligations.' Such a principle was thus anchored and formalized within the Oslo agreements for the first time, according to Netanyahu. Whilst this principle may seem even handed, in practical terms it represents another example of the Israeli ability to determine the course of the negotiations. As 'peace with security' is the new government's mantra, it does not stretch the imagination to assume that, subjective interpretation notwithstanding, reciprocity can lead to Israel unilaterally determining, on a pretext, that the PISGA has not fulfilled various obligations and thus forfeits further Israeli compliance. Such an interpretation, whilst subjective, may indeed provide Israel with the necessary legitimacy to control the pace and extent of further negotiations, and indeed the ultimate outcome of the final status negotiations.

(2) Implementation of the redeployments – an Israeli decision. The second principle clarified that Israel received agreement that the implementation of further 'redeployments will be an Israeli decision that will not be a matter for negotiation.' Thus, this 'decision must comply with Israel's security considerations, as Israel sees fit.' Israel will also 'define the security zones', and 'will determine the nature and scope of the three redeployments – not only the first and second, but also the third.' Netanyahu reiterated that his interpretation and understanding of the agreement reached with the Palestinians was shared by the US, which he believed was a 'very important distinction'. For Netanyahu this interpretation meant that Israel would 'be able to define, according to its own understanding, the security needs of the State of Israel and to carry out the further redeployments according to this understanding.'

(3) The time-frame. The third principle, Netanyahu stated, does not stand alone, rather it allowed Israel 'room for manoeuvre, room to test reality, room to test reciprocity in the fulfilment of the agreement.' Thus, Netanyahu commended the agreement to the Knesset

because he believed that what had been negotiated allowed Israel, 'the time, the ability and the freedom for political manoeuvre' to 'conduct the negotiations, carefully, responsibly, with discretion' in order to achieve the 'goals of preserving Jerusalem, preserving the security depth, preserving Israel's ability to defend itself' and to negotiate 'a suitable arrangement with the Palestinians.'[311]

However, in analysing the significance of the Hebron Protocol, it seems that the Israeli interpretation of the agreements is borne out by not only a similar understanding stated by US officials, but also the appended US documents, Ross's 'Note for the Record' and Christopher's 'Letter of Assurance to Israel'.[312] US assurances and the agreements made did indeed establish the principle of 'linkage', between the interim agreements done to date, pending interim arrangements, further redeployments and the final status negotiations. Whilst the 'linkage' principle was of great importance to the Palestinians, to ensure the new Likud government's engagement in the peace process, the principle also worked to the Israelis' advantage. Issues which had been previously ignored by the Labour government, such as the expansion of the PISGA police force beyond their agreed limits as set out in the Interim Agreement and the location of PISGA offices in Jerusalem, included in the 'Note for the Record' as items 3 and 4 under Palestinian responsibilities, could now be used to undermine further progress by means of Israeli demands to link past undertakings and present responsibilities with future redeployments by sticking to the letter of the agreements rather than the spirit.[313] Thus the US involvement seemed to underline and endorse the Israeli interpretation that the timing of further redeployments, the determining of Palestinian obligations and commitments, and the definition and extent of military locations, would be unilaterally determined by the Israelis without recourse to further negotiations. In this sense, the Hebron Protocol seemed practically to repudiate the general understanding of UN Resolution 242, with the blessing of the US, and therefore might indeed reinterpret the original principal terms of reference for the peace process, namely the land-for-peace formula, to be replaced by the primary principle of maintaining Israeli security considerations. Thus the importance of the Hebron Protocol within the peace process was that it offered the Israelis the opportunity to determine the future scope, extent and pace of the Israeli-Palestinian endeavour, with US approval and endorsement. The US basically assured Israel that the determination of further redeployments, the implementation of pending interim agreement arrangements, the size of military locations, and the progress of final status negotiations, would be unilaterally decided by Israel without recourse to, or being subject to further negotiations. Despite Palestinian insistence that the Hebron agreement falls within the interim period and therefore that any agreements concluded under this period are of a transitional nature, in reality, the Hebron agreement allows Israel the advantage to reinterpret a new vision of Israeli-Palestinian relations.

The Hebron Protocol may thus be deemed to amount to a repudiation of the original terms of reference for both the Madrid peace process and the Oslo accords and indeed of the basis on which the existing Israeli-Palestinian agreements were concluded, namely UN Resolutions 242 and 338. The appended US assurances to the Hebron Protocol, combined with US official statements, seemed to guarantee Israel's security as the paramount objective of the peace process, and lead one to the conclusion that the US reordered its position on the original terms of reference agreed by the DoP, that is the implementation of UN Resolutions 242 and 338, the land-for-peace formula. Instead, US assurances seemed to be underlining the interpretation that US policy was now motivated to ensuring the recognition of Israeli security considerations as the basis for the Israeli-Palestinian negotiations, whilst undermining the validity and applicability of international law and UN resolutions. Ensuring Israel's security seemed to have become not only the prime motivating factor for the Likud government, but also to have become the principal term of reference for the remaining Israeli-PLO negotiations, and therefore the primary principle by which the negotiations would be measured. Christopher stated in his 'Letter of Assurance' addressed to Netanyahu, that 'I have impressed upon Chairman Arafat the imperative need for the PISGA to make every effort to ensure public order and internal security within the West Bank and Gaza Strip', stressing 'to him that effectively carrying out this major responsibility will be a critical foundation for completing implementation of the Interim Agreement, as well as the peace process as a whole.' Christopher further stated that he had advised Arafat of 'US views on Israel's process of redeploying its forces, designating specified military locations and transferring additional powers and responsibilities' to the PISGA, within the context of the above. Furthermore Christopher stressed to Netanyahu that he could 'be assured the United States' commitment to Israel's security' was 'ironclad and constitutes the fundamental cornerstone of our special relationship', that the 'key element in our approach to peace, including the negotiation and implementation of agreements between Israel and its Arab partners, has always been a recognition of Israel's security requirements', and that the 'hallmark of US policy remains our commitment to work cooperatively to seek to meet the security needs that Israel identifies.'[314]

Reciprocity

As we have seen, the primacy of the principle of Israeli security was further enshrined by the continued US and Israeli usage of the 'principle of reciprocity', referred to by Netanyahu in his speech to the Knesset as 'a basic principle for the continuation of the process of the permanent status negotiations'.[315] This interpretation was further underlined by Dennis Ross's Note for the Record which stated under the heading 'Mutual Understandings', that 'the two leaders reaffirmed their commitment to implement the Interim Agreement on the basis of reciprocity', and by Secretary Christopher's 'Letter of Assurance' in which he assured Netanyahu that 'it remains the policy of the US to support and promote full implementation of the Interim Agreement in all of its parts', and that the US intended to continue its 'efforts to help ensure that all outstanding commitments are carried out by both parties in a cooperative spirit and on the basis of reciprocity.'[316] While the US language sounded benign and even handed, in reality the US effectively underlined the interpretation that Israel's continued commitments and obligations to the peace process were dependent on the PISGA's ability to ensure Israel's, and Israelis', security. Backing up this interpretation was the fact that Israel would be the sole arbiter of the PISGA's performance. Although the break in impasse in the Israeli-Palestinian peace process was essentially brokered by the US, with help from King Hussein, there was no mechanism set up, nor were there any guidelines set out, with which to adjudicate fairly and independently disputatious interpretations of what constituted acceptable conduct by the PISGA in relation to Israel's security considerations. The latter were to be entirely and unilaterally determined by Israel, and therefore the future of the peace process rested with Israel, and its determination of that future. If one accepted that Israel's ability to determine in what areas, and to what extent, to redeploy further within the context of PISGA compliance with Israeli-determined security considerations was valid, then Israel retained the power to determine not only the extent, scope and timing of further redeployments, but also the entire progress of the peace process. This interpretation was publicly posted by the Israeli Foreign Ministry's position paper, 'Further Redeployments: the Next Stage of the Israeli-Palestinian Interim Agreement, Legal Aspects', which stated under the heading 'Conditions for Implementation of Further Redeployment Provisions', that the

> commitment to effect further redeployment is described, in both the Declaration of Principles and the Interim Agreement, as being 'commensurate with the assumption of responsibility for public order and internal security by the Palestinian police'. The intention of this provision is to ensure that, in a situation in which the Palestinian side is incapable or unwilling to enforce its security responsibility, Israel will not be obliged to endanger itself by transferring additional territory to the Palestinian jurisdiction. In other words, the further redeployments are expressly stated to be a mutual obligation: only if the Palestinian side proves itself capable and willing to comply with its security responsibilities is Israel obliged to transfer additional areas of the West Bank to Palestinian jurisdiction.

Furthermore, concerning the nature of 'redeployment', the same source stated that

> Neither the DoP nor the Interim Agreement contains a definition of the terms 'redeployment' or 'further redeployment'. However, the use of the term 'redeployment' must be distinguished from 'withdrawal', as used for example in the context of the withdrawal of Israeli forces from the Gaza Strip and Jericho Area. Unlike 'withdrawal', which required the removal of the majority of forces from the areas in question, 'redeployment' relates only to the location of the forces; it places no restriction on the number of forces and military equipment or the possibility of introducing further forces and equipment if necessary.

Regarding the extent and provisions of further redeployments, both the DoP and Interim Agreement were not specific. In relation to the first two redeployments there was no indication of the areas concerned, merely the fact that Israel was left to determine the extent 'in what areas and to what extent to redeploy.' Regarding the third stage of redeployment, Article XI.2 of the Interim Agreement provided that:

> The two sides agree that West Bank and Gaza Strip territory, except for issues that will be negotiated in the permanent status negotiations, will come under the jurisdiction of the Palestinian Council in a phased manner, to be completed within eighteen months from the inauguration of the Council, as specified below.

Once again it is instructive to point out the Foreign Ministry's interpretation:

> It should be noted that the provision refers to 'West Bank and Gaza Strip territory'; the omission of the definite article (e.g. 'the territory of the West Bank and the Gaza Strip') is deliberate and clearly intended to leave open the possibility that there will be areas of the West Bank, in addition to those connected with the permanent status issues, which will not fall under the jurisdiction of the Council. This is in contrast to the Gaza-Jericho arrangements which referred to 'withdrawal from the Gaza Strip and Jericho Area' (see, for example, DoP Articles V and VI), and so required withdrawal from the entire area except for those areas connected with the permanent status issues.

In conclusion, the position paper stated that the further redeployment provisions of the DoP and Interim Agreement provided that the 'redeployments are to be effected alongside, and are dependent upon, the Palestinian police proving itself capable of exercising its security responsibilities.' Therefore the 'extent of the first two stages of the redeployment is left to be determined by Israel, while at the conclusion of the third and final phase the jurisdiction of the Palestinian Council is to cover some, but not necessarily all, West Bank and Gaza Strip territory.' In those areas in which redeployment takes place, 'permanent status issues – among them settlements, military locations and borders – will remain under Israeli jurisdiction, as will other areas required for the exercise of Israel's overall responsibility for Israelis and borders.' Following the completion of the redeployment process, Israeli forces 'will have redeployed to specified military locations to be determined by Israel'. However, the Interim Agreement 'places no restriction on the number of forces in these areas, or their ability to move outside these areas while fulfilling security responsibilities in accordance with the Agreement.'[317]

Reciprocity in this sense means effectively an Israeli veto over the peace process. The principle, and the inference to be made from it, was however ironically one sided, because the Palestinians had no desire to halt, nor advantage to gain in halting, the peace process as it stood. Mutual security guarantees were not incorporated within the terms of Hebron Protocol, thus whilst 'Palestinian Responsibilities' in the 'Note for the Record' were outlined in Point 2 as 'Fighting terror and preventing violence' (see page 306) similar obligations and commitments are not expected or required of the Israelis. Therefore Israel was neither obligated to halt 'practices that contravene international conventions, such as the expropriation of lands and house demolitions', settlement construction, deportations, imposition of collective punishments, and other human rights violations, nor expected to constrain armed settlers, Jewish terrorists, or hateful propaganda in the Israeli media.[318] The only Palestinian trump card remaining was to refuse to sign a final status agreement, but Israel's determination to create 'facts on the ground' during the negotiations process may well negate the necessity for the Israelis to conclude a final status agreement. The interpretation that Israel retained sole responsibility for determining further redeployments, and thus retained power over the nature of the peace process, was borne out by Joel Singer, who advised Meir Einstein of Kol Israel, that the 'Oslo Agreement and the Interim Agreement determine that all three phases of the redeployment are based on unilateral Israeli decisions.' Israel, having decided to redeploy some of its forces, had therefore at least formally acted in accordance with the agreement; however Singer pointed out that 'as to the extent of the redeployment, that is a political issue, not a legal one', as the 'agreement left it up to Israel to decide on the three phases of redeployment'. Singer outlined that the 'only criterion set down by the agreement is that by the end of the third phase Israel should redeploy into specified locations, into the Israeli settlements and into certain 'yellow areas'' however 'the agreement does not state what the proportion between the three phases should be', despite that during the negotiations the 'Palestinians indeed wanted the agreement to state that redeployment would be carried out in proportional, equally sized phases'. Singer reiterated the point that, ultimately, redeployment 'was left up to a unilateral Israeli decision', and 'the question of percentages – both how much of the territory would ultimately remain under Israel's control, and how much would be transferred to the Palestinians ... remained subject to unilateral Israeli decision' which again meant that the 'extent of the redeployments is of course subject to political considerations'.[319]

Why then did the Palestinians conclude such an agreement, and how does their interpretation fit with the overall peace process? The Palestinian leadership seems to have been driven by the paramount priority to sustain the peace process despite the seeming advantages provided in the Hebron agreement in Israel's favour. In persisting with the peace process, the Palestinian leadership appear to hope that by prolonging their involvement with their peace 'partners', new dynamics would arise in the Palestinians' favour as a result of continued negotiations, leading to the Palestinians' desire to see an end to Israeli occupation and the fulfilment of their ultimate objective of a sovereign Palestine. However, such calculations seem to be based more on hope than on the design of the concluded agreements. Despite PISGA denials to the contrary, and in spite of the validity of Israel's interpretation of the new dynamics of the peace process and its reinterpretation of the terms of reference backed by the US, the Palestinian leadership seems to derive their positive outlook from over-optimistic assumption, rather than a close reading of the agreements and any assessment of evidence of substantive provisions from the agreements concluded, as the authority with which to substantiate their interpretation of the progress of the peace process. In his statement to the Knesset on the Hebron Protocol, Netanyahu stated the Israeli position unequivocally: 'We are committed ... to the written agreements' of the peace process, 'We have demonstrated today that we are fulfilling our commitments'; 'But our goals are different' from the previous government in that

> We are using the time interval in the agreement to achieve our goals, to maintain the unity of Jerusalem, to ensure the security depth necessary for the defence of the state, to insist on the right of Jews to settle in their land, and to propose to the Palestinians a suitable arrangement for self-rule but without the sovereign powers which might pose a threat to the State of Israel.[320]

Palestinian critics of the Hebron deal, such as Edward Said, contend that the Palestinian leadership accepted a formula for

Israeli-Palestinian coexistence, which amounted to the Palestinians having acceded to the Israeli determination of their status as autonomy without sovereignty. Said contends that the Palestinian leadership, even including 'quite a few ... with long histories in progressive politics', has been seduced by 'a few material advantages (a car, an office, a position, a VIP designation)' into accepting 'this appalling situation'. Said asked for an answer to their silence and cooperation with such agreements which deny Palestinians 'specified sovereignty and real self-determination', and which allow Israel to retain control over settlements, settlers, external security, borders, the economy, water, military locations, and maintain effective jurisdictional sovereignty over at least 73 per cent of the West Bank and Gaza Strip during the interim period.[321] Sovereignty denied is sovereignty retained. Said offered 'a series of unflattering rationales' in possible explanation for the continuation of the peace policy:

(1) So 'long as the peace process guarantees the centrality of the PLO and its leader, then more or less anything goes'.

(2) Having been 'so outmanoeuvred, outgunned, and outsmarted by Israel, you feel you have no chance but to go on, trying to brazen it out vis-a-vis your own people with a lot of hopeful but ultimately misleading speeches and promises'.

(3) Following 'the tactic of making more concessions, accepting all the humiliating Israeli conditions in the wishful fantasy that some day either you'll stop having to make concessions or the Israelis will give you a few things back'.

(4) Politics is 'a dirty business', and the Israelis are the Palestinians' 'partners in crime'.[322]

The evidence suggests that the PISGA leadership and its apparatus transformed the PLO 'from a national liberation movement to a police force in the Israeli context', and can be thus deemed to be subcontractors for the Israeli security establishment in its war against militant Palestinian nationalism, without having to contend with the attendant human rights obligations and observance which various Israeli security operatives maintain constrains Israel's freedom and licence to operate punitively without redress.[323]

Said links his disillusionment with the peace process not to the insecurity of what may be achieved by deferring dreams in the hope that they will be realized in the fullness of time, but rather to the daily indignities which are the reality of life facing ordinary Palestinians. For those who support the integrity and stated intentions of the peace process, the dilemma in supporting its continuation is that Arafat's regime is corrupt, abusive of human rights and wholly dependent on Israel for its continued political and economic existence, that Israel's Likud government has imposed collective punishments on the occupied population it controls, and that Israel now seems to have both an asymmetrical structural power imbalance in its favour and an asymmetrical political advantage in the determination of the future status of the Israeli-Palestinian relationship. Azmi Bishara MK has assessed the current dynamic of Israeli-Palestinian relations as 'the imbalance of power and the inequality in the commitments on paper' which means that the future of the peace process 'depends on the intentions of the Israeli government'. The Israeli-Palestinian relationship is one of 'imbalance and dependency', with the objective 'to perpetuate the peace process rather than to arrive at a just peace'.[324] Indeed, Ha'aretz quoted a former legal adviser to the Foreign Ministry effectively stating that the peace process allows Israel to claim that: 'We control electric power, water resources, telecommunications, etc. We control everything. There are a number of natives who serve as middle men. What could suit our purposes better?' The same source advised the Israeli cabinet to read the Oslo agreements carefully adding: 'If you read it, you not only will accept it, you will become its enthusiastic supporters. The power imbalance between us and the Palestinians never served our interests better in the past, not even before the *intifada*.'[325] All this has been achieved with American willingness, connivance and indulgence, and with the 'passivity and collective silence' of those who suffer, and who are yet to suffer because of the indifference to the inequities, injustices, frustrations, desperation and tensions of those whose future is being abandoned.[326]

Final status talks

In anticipation of the resumption of final status talks, a number of senior Israeli officials, including Gold, Meridor, Nave and Netanyahu policy adviser David Bar Ilan, began on 26 November 1997 re-examining the Labour government-PISGA (Beilin-Abbas) talks on a blueprint for a peace accord/final status scenario as a possible basis for continuing negotiations with the PISGA.[327] However on 22 January 1998 in Cairo, Arafat stated that after the interim period the PISGA could unilaterally declare a Palestinian state, without Israeli permission, which prompted Netanyahu to respond the next day that if Arafat were to declare a Palestinian state unilaterally, he would order the retaking of Area B.[328] Through the terms of the Hebron

Protocol, by linking further Israeli military redeployment to PISGA compliance with the terms of the agreements, by the Israelis retaining control over the timing and extent of further redeployment, and by having the completion date of the redeployment phase almost parallel with that of the final date of the permanent status negotiations, the Israelis have effectively negated the likelihood of a Palestinian unilateral declaration of independence. This is because no Palestinian state could be established, prior to a substantial redeployment, because until the agreed further redeployment phases are fully completed, it would not be viable or defensible, and also because the Israelis, knowing world opinion would count against their use of a full-scale military operation to re-enter PISGA areas, have linked redeployment to permanent status discussions in such a way as to shadow the PISGA's future progress rather than be stipulated as either preconditions of such, or binding on good behaviour through already concluded agreements.

A document of understandings intended to map out the common ground between the major Israeli parties in preparation for final status talks with the PISGA was negotiated over three months of discussions by a group of Likud and Labour legislators, led by Michael Eytan MK, head of Likud's parliamentary faction and Yossi Beilin MK, former government minister and principal architect of the Oslo channel.[329] Other signatories included Haim Ramon, Shlomo Ben-Ami of Labour, and Eliezer Zandberg, Zeev Boim, Yehuda Lankri and Meir Sheetrit of Likud. The document, entitled 'National Agreement Regarding the Negotiations on the Permanent Settlement with the Palestinians', was not approved by either party, with the PM's office stating that the document was a private initiative that in no way obligated the government.[330]

Following the Hebron Protocol, Israel remained in direct control of 73 per cent of the West Bank (Area C), and exercised overall security responsibilities for the remaining 27 per cent. In Gaza Israel retained direct control over 40 per cent of the land. It had been Netanyahu's stated intention to cede as little as possible of 'Eretz Yisrael' to 'foreign sovereignty', not only for ideological and existential reasons but particularly with regard to bargaining over final status arrangements, which according to the agreements was to be completed by May 1999. Publication of the Beilin-Eytan agreement helped reinforce the new Israeli negotiating agenda, having been widely interpreted as being somewhat less visionary regarding the Israeli-PISGA final status arrangement than that envisaged in the

Beilin-Abbas agreements just prior to Rabin's assassination. As such, it represented an attempt at repairing the Israeli domestic political consensus so rudely ruptured by Rabin's murder. Having attempted peace with the Palestinians with the resultant costs to the Israeli polity, it was only natural that Israeli politicians would seek to rebuild a more inclusive and hegemonic national consensus which would hold during the final status negotiations. Thus, the Beilin-Eytan document had the potential to become the basis for assuring cross-party support and consensus within the Knesset as Israel entered into talks on the permanent arrangements. However, to conclude that this document was a negotiating blueprint which would reflect the final status outcome, is however to forget that the primary focus of this document had much more to do with healing domestic, political rifts, than with attaining the status of a negotiating text. If viewed in terms of being no more than the latest expression of Zionist/nationalist consensus then the document adhered more to previous policy prescriptions, such as the Allon Plan, than those of the Beilin-Abbas document. Whilst Beilin-Abbas called for the Israeli withdrawal from 94 per cent of the West Bank with a capital in Abu Dis and the Palestinian flag flying over al-Aqsa, the Allon Plan envisaged Israel annexing some 40 per cent of the West Bank, 50 per cent of Gaza, and the establishment of an autonomous framework for the inhabitants of the occupied territories.[331] The document's strong defence of the more than 150 settlements and the 150 000 settlers, and the explicit support of the permanent maintenance of all Israeli settlements under Israeli sovereignty within the terms of the envisaged future, permanent arrangement points to this conclusion. The non-specific descriptive language of the document, referring to 'Jews and Arabs in the Land of Israel' suggests that the Israeli consensus agreed within the document owed more to the desire to heal wounds within Israel than to too much anxiety about Palestinian sensitivities concerning rights to self-determination and statehood. Any deference to the Palestinian hopes is contained in the indeterminate term, 'Palestinian entity', which the Israelis have agreed to disagree over, Beilin referring to a 'state, Eytan to 'enlarged autonomy'. However the main thrust of the document is the agreement on limiting the ceding of Israeli occupation and sovereign powers and retaining strategic and defensive capabilities far beyond those between two normal sovereign entities. Not only does the document expect extra-territorial powers and responsibilities for Israel, but the future of the settlements and the settlers' rights anywhere in the 'Western Land of Israel' must be preserved as one of the basic security requirements regarding any future permanent status talks. The settlers and the settlements are regarded as integral to Israel, which will either have full sovereignty extended over them, or in the case of the settlers will be ensured safe and secure access passages under sovereign Israeli control. The contrast with the Beilin-Abbas document which had envisaged some 100 settlements coming under Palestinian sovereignty could not be more marked. Rather than represent a break from the past, in the form of the Beilin-Abbas document, the Beilin-Eytan document represents a link with the more accepted, traditional Zionist national consensus, and thus has more to do with reconstructing the Zionist, nationalist polity, severely damaged by the peace process.[332] Labour and Likud have few ideological differences on nationalist/Zionist issues, in practice both follow pragmatic and practical approaches with regard to the occupied territories. Both parties are driven by the same ideological nationalist/religious imperative, to conquer the land, to Judaize it, to settle in it, and to prepare it both for further settlement and for the coming of the Chosen One. Secular sensitivities aside, the reason for the whole Zionist enterprise was to establish a Jewish homeland, an idea, which although it was initiated within the ideology of nineteenth-century European nationalism and self-determination, stems from an ancient religious covenant between a people and their God. Thus the parties' main differences really lie in the domestic arena, particularly with regard to the character and extent of synagogue and state relations. Regarding the Zionist/Jewish nature of the State of Israel there is surprising similarity between the actions of one and the commitment of the other. Labour occupied the territory, built and developed the first settlements, deported Palestinians, imposed blanket and selective closures, curfews, collective punishments, detained and tortured Palestinians without due process, and demolished homes. Neither really wants to see a Palestinian state established. The debate between the two has never really centred on the ill effects that the policies of occupation and repression have wrought on the Israeli body politic, although these issues have been raised. However, the real crux of the debate has been on the practical issue of security, whether or not retaining some or all of the occupied territories is in Israel's long-term best interests. Whether arguments are justified by religion or pragmatism, the consensus exists that Israel should retain occupied territory, and what divides the two parties is to what extent territories should be annexed and what to do with the Palestinians as a people. Labour wishes to provide the Palestinians with some of the rights that Israelis demand for themselves, whereas Likud has either wished to ignore the Palestinians or hoped that they would just somehow disappear.

The delay in the further redeployment timetable is not really much of a cause for great concern if seen in the light of the practice of the peace process to date. Originally agreed timetables have gone awry since the first deadline was missed in 1993. As long as Rabin's attitude that no date was sacred is borne in mind, then one way or another, as long as the will and the confidence to achieve an agreement eventually is present, then timetables should be regarded merely as signposts. What is of concern during the further redeployment phases, is the fact that they are not subject to further negotiations. Israel alone is responsible for determining the territorial extent, the timing and the location of the further redeployments. Israel therefore has a wide and unchallenged latitude for interpreting the conclusion of the phases of redeployment. In this sense, the US involvement in aiding the brokerage of the Hebron Protocol was significant. Netanyahu achieved, for the duration of the interim period at least, the ability unilaterally to determine Israel's security needs in the occupied territories, which under Likud have always been expressed territorially. Thus further redeployment from occupied territories will be assessed on a determination that territory provides security, rather than agreement with the Palestinians *per se*. Whilst Christopher reiterated the traditional US view that final status should reflect Israel's needs for secure and defensible borders which should be determined through direct negotiations with Israel's neighbours, however, Ross stated that 'Borders and further redeployment are not necessarily synonymous.' In an attempt to allay international concerns over the settlements issue, Israel received criticism from former high-ranking US officials, the State Department and President Clinton. Christopher's 'Letter of Assurance' to Arafat, whilst not publicly released, is believed to contain a US commitment to the Palestinians that Israel would indeed fulfil its pledges and obligations to redeploy. However Palestinians do not accept the right of the Israelis to unilaterally determine the extent and modalities of their redeployment, insisting that they would not allow Netanyahu to impose the phases and localities of redeployment on them without their influence, as Rabin had previously done. However FM Levy acknowledged this Palestinian fear in an interview with al-Sharq al-Awsat on 22 January, when he stated

> The prime minister said that under the original agreement Israel
> is the one to decide the area of the land needed to protect its
> own security. Security is the main thing. But this does not mean
> that the Palestinians will respond by saying yes to everything
> we tell them. There is give and take. If we succeed together in
> securing suitable conditions for peace, without violence and with
> more trust between the parties and tangible relations of peace,
> everything will be easy, and you will find us all looking for means
> to bring us closer to one another.

The Palestinians believe that Israel should redeploy from all but
some 10 per cent of the West Bank by the end of the third phase
of redeployment, those areas remaining being the settlements, whereas
the US is reported as believing that Israel should cede some 10 per
cent of Area C to the PISGA as part of the first phase. However, in
preparation for these issues, on 10 February the Israeli cabinet
began discussions to determine from which areas of the West Bank
the IDF would redeploy in each of the three agreed stages, with
various security branches making representations of various options.
The IDF Planning Branch submitted to the cabinet for discussion a
'vital interests map' of the West Bank. The maps under review had
been initially prepared at Rabin's request during the Taba talks prior
to the Interim Agreement. According to the IDF map, the PISGA
would control up to 45 per cent of the West Bank by the third
phase. Gaza is not included in this scenario and therefore was presumably excluded from further redeployment phases. The IDF map
outlines three blocs of non-contiguous Palestinian-controlled territory, separated by Jewish settlements and areas to remain under
Israeli control, such as the Jordan Valley. The map includes border
adjustments, meaning annexations, along the Green Line as well
as including additional areas planned for the development and growth
of existing settlements. The IDF plan includes transferring 5 per
cent of Area B to Area A status after the first phase, with remainder
of Area B attaining Area A status following the second phase. This
would give the PISGA powers and responsibilities covering some
30 per cent of the West Bank. It is then in the third and final
phase that Israel would cede territory from Area C.[333] On 10 February,
the IDF presented an analysis of Israel's requirements in the final
status to the cabinet. The IDF outlined these as a permanent presence

of the IDF in settlement blocs in the northern West Bank and the Jerusalem region, the control of major east-west and north-south West Bank arteries, and the control of the Jordan Valley and the border with Jordan. Based on these estimates, Netanyahu's adviser David Bar Ilan interpreted the issue of final redeployment on 15 January to mean that Israel would probably retain 51.8 per cent of West Bank land after final redeployment under a permanent arrangement, whereas Arafat had interpreted on 19 December the further redeployment schedule as laid out under the Interim Agreement to mean that Israel would be obliged to redeploy from no less than 80 per cent of the West Bank.[334] After the meeting FM Levy emphasized that Israel would not hold talks on further redeployment with the PISGA, stating that 'This is a decision that only we will make ... We are not obligated to hold any discussions or negotiations with anyone,' and Netanyahu reportedly urged his ministerial colleagues not to talk in terms of percentages, as doing so would only 'serve the interests of the Palestinians'.[335]

4.7 Conclusion

Having analysed this chapter through the lens of items 1 and 4 of the Riceman Formula, in other words, resolution and empowerment, we can now offer some conclusions as to how successful the further negotiated agreements were in combining to prepare the foundation of the interim phase of the Israeli-Palestinian peace process as laid down within the terms of the DoP. We can conclude that the further agreements allowed for the transfer and exercise of powers and responsibilities to the Palestinians and provided for greater levels of sovereignty to be attained by the Palestinians. The further agreements set out to provide for a sustainable preventative security regime involving reciprocal and cooperative rights and obligations based on shared goals and principles of justice, economic interdependence, collective security and a sense of shared community, in order to achieve an equitable and lasting settlement which mastered existing inherent asymmetrical power inequalities. If we take as an indicative example the issue of economic interdependence, we will be able to assess the relative merits of the negotiated further transitional interim self-government arrangements on the basis of how successful the peace process has been in delivering real and practical benefits to those who are supposed to be the beneficiaries of the entire enterprise, namely the Israeli and Palestinian general publics.

For the proponents of peace, who have argued that economic interdependence and integration between Israel and the Palestinians will provide for an 'economy of peace', events during the period of the negotiations have confounded their optimism.[336] Mass unemployment, extended periods of closure either of parts or of the whole West Bank and Gaza Strip, endemic and systemic structural and infrastructural weaknesses, and a wholly unhealthy dependent economic relationship has countered the notion that economic prosperity could allow difficult political decisions to prosper. In essence, the idea that economic activity would so involve, energize and preoccupy the majority of the Palestinian population, thus buying them off and dissuading them from involvement in political agitation, has not been borne out by the evidence of the past years. Hungry people, whose hope for their and their children's future turns to despair, make for angry people. Many can cope with a denial of their national aspirations and dreams of a perfect world, as long as their personal circumstances are financially ameliorated in compensation. However when externally imposed economic circumstances are so severe as to be oppressive, people tend to view the political system that sustains their straitened lives with eyes that see succour in radical solutions. The tenet that the denial of rights and the legitimacy of a people's struggle could at least be assuaged by a flourishing economy has, despite the infusion of vast amounts of foreign aid, failed, because the Israeli preoccupation with its security fears – with the resultant cost being declining Palestinian living standards – has perversely led to an increase in Israel's vulnerability to further attacks because the economic conditions necessary to contain Palestinian violence have failed to materialize, precisely because Israel's security fears have fuelled actions which have directly led to a worsening of Palestinians' economic conditions.

The Paris Protocol on Economic Relations promised to lay the groundwork for strengthening the Palestinian economic base and extending to the Palestinians autonomy in the economic decision-making process in accordance with their own development plan, and the rights to pursue their own economic priorities.[337] This aspect of the peace process was included because of the acceptance of the principle that 'national sovereignty in economic decision-making is an important prerequisite to political independence.'[338] However the reality has been continued and compounded dominance of the Palestinian economic sector by the Israeli economy, ensuring that Palestinian ability to determine economic policy is severely limited and that the interdependence of the two economies is balanced more favourably for the Israelis.

Israel has severely reduced Palestinian access, in terms of goods and persons, to the Israeli economy, citing security concerns for their actions. The numbers of Palestinians working in Israel have been cut from 116 000 to 29 500 between 1993 and 1996, resulting in severe Palestinian unemployment, as between 33 per cent and 50 per cent of male employment was dependent on employment in the Israeli sector.[339] Estimates of Palestinian unemployment in 1995–6 vary between official and unofficial calculations, ranging between 31 per cent to 74 per cent in Gaza, and between 13 per cent and 50 per cent in the West Bank.[340] These figures also hide the underemployment of the workforce, and the underdevelopment of the economy, brought about by frequent closures, collective punishments, curfews and security actions. The financial costs of closure alone, according to PISGA estimates, run approximately at $6m per day during periods of full closure. These costs far outweigh donor assistance. The costs of closure are generally borne by individuals, families and small businesses, whereas donor assistance is disbursed to the PISGA, its institutions, and earmarked projects. Long-term damage done to personal financial circumstances and small to medium businesses is difficult to assess, however donor assistance is not forthcoming in this area. Closures also ensure structural damage as a result of reduced foreign and expatriate investments and delays to infrastructural development projects. These policies resulted, in September 1996, in a PISGA budget deficit of some 40 per cent of the annual budget, primarily as a result of reduced tax receipts.[341]

Businesses need access to labour and capital, but restrictions in the free movement of labour even within the occupied territories, in raising venture capital, and in business planning capabilities, severely limit the prospects of economic growth. Israel not only limits Palestinian employment in Israel, it also restricts the free movement of goods and persons between the various PISGA-controlled communities, thus isolating local economies, and making the planning and development of an integrated economy almost impossible. This is particularly true with regard to the position of Jerusalem, access to which has been tightly controlled, ensuring that Palestinian labourers, contractors and entrepreneurs are excluded from the Jerusalem market, with the corresponding knock-on effects on small businesses and self-employment opportunities. By restricting employment options, Israel ensures that incomes are reduced overall, meaning that spending power is also curtailed, further hurting local businesses. This 'multiplier effect – a cycle of fewer jobs and less income', threatens the very survival of the Palestinian economy.[342] PISGA policy-makers and the international donor community are unable or unwilling to address this political problem which afflicts the Palestinian economy, and adversely affects fiscal planning and economic development. When skilled and educated Palestinians are forced to accept employment in jobs which do not utilize their skills and training, then support for the continuation of this particular peace process will be set back. Under-utilized ordinary people with no meaningful role in a stalled project of national reconstruction, will increasingly find the process of state-building hollow. The 'feeling of abandonment is palpable'; according to a recent polls, 68.5 per cent of those describing themselves as 'not well-to-do' responded that they were pessimistic about their future, 29.4 per cent responded that they did not trust any political movement, with 20.5 per cent not trusting any of their leaders.[343] Thus the power Israel exerts in unilaterally destabilizing the extremely fragile, nascent Palestinian economy highlights the structural economic asymmetrical power relationship. Therefore, by any indicators, the relative position of the Palestinian economy post-DoP as opposed to pre-DoP, is undoubtedly worse.

5
Conclusion: The Effectiveness of the Declaration of Principles on Interim Self-Government Arrangements as a Means of Conflict Resolution

'God does not change the blessings
He has bestowed on men until they change what is in their
   hearts.
God hears all and knows all...
The basest creatures in the sight of God are the faithless
   who will not believe;
those who time after time violate their treaties with you
   and have no fear of God.
If you capture them in battle discriminate between them
   and those that follow them, so that their followers may
   take warning...
If they incline to peace,
make peace with them,
And put your trust in God.
He hears all and knows all.'
                    – *Qu'ran*: Sura 8, Al-Anfal, verses 53–61[1]

5.1 Introduction

Before the signing of the Declaration of Principles on Interim Self-Government Arrangements (DoP), Israel and the PLO were enemies engaged in a mainly low-intensity, though sometimes high-intensity, inter-ethnic, existential conflict. Neither side officially recognized the other, and both sought effectively to deligitimize and destroy the other. As argued within this thesis, the intention of the DoP was to 'put an end to decades of confrontation and conflict, recognize' each other's 'mutual legitimate and political rights, and strive to live in peaceful coexistence and mutual dignity and security and achieve a just, lasting and comprehensive peace settlement and historic reconciliation through the agreed political process.' The aim of the Israeli-Palestinian negotiations within the Middle East peace process was to establish an autonomous Palestinian authority within a transitional period which will lead to 'a permanent settlement based on Security Council Resolutions 242 and 338', and that the 'negotiations on the permanent status will lead to the implementation of Security Council Resolutions 242 and 338.'[2]

How effective the DoP has been in achieving its stated objectives to date is very much open to interpretation, and dependent on the positive or negative light in which events are viewed. With the negotiation of the Hebron Protocol, the formal agreements covering the transitional interim period, the conflict management stages of institutionalization, empowerment and administration, were concluded. Negotiations for concluding a permanent settlement are still ongoing, so the conflict resolution process is still under construction. Whilst it is important for political purposes to view the DoP in an optimistic spirit, it is also important that the emphasis of any analysis be constructive, concentrating the evaluation of the DoP more closely on the pessimistic and destructive causal elements of the process, as these are the areas which are more likely to produce a deterioration and repudiation of the peace process and a resumption of remorseless conflict.

In Chapter 1, we asked a number of questions relating to the difficulties in achieving durable negotiated settlements. These questions were: What are the critical criteria for measuring the success or failure of an attempt at conflict resolution? What are the dynamic structural processes, and changed systemic/functional power relationships set in train by the DoP to reach a post-conflict settlement? What are the expectations raised by the DoP? How do we define the basic objectives, strategic objectives and prerequisites of the parties to the agreement? Is the DoP a device to contain, control, limit, manage or resolve the Israeli-Palestinian conflict? In essence, how do we grade the test?

The problem with defining success or failure is 'one of infinite regress'. Success is inherently relative because

some processes never manage to get the parties into dialogue,
let alone to agree to a cessation of fighting. Others reach dialogue but fail to find a possible agreement. Still others . . . achieve
agreement only to see it repudiated. Still others break down in
the implementation stage and the process ends in recrimination
and accusation of bad faith.[3]

Linking success/failure indicators to different phases of the peace-
building process 'avoids the problem of defining the concept in
terms of an unrealized, and possibly unattainable, end point.'[4]
However, this does not fully resolve our definitional paradox of
evaluating a peace process which does not result in a peaceful settlement. Do we thus quantify success in minimalist terms as the
establishment of negotiations, the conclusion of a limited formal
agreement, or the maintenance of a cessation of hostilities agreement?
Should more developed and sophisticated criteria be incorporated?
There are no easy answers.

To define and measure the success/failure parameters which will
enable us to understand and evaluate the political process of the
bilateral asymmetrical Israeli-Palestinian national-subnational conflict within the context of the Madrid international multinational
conflict resolution framework, we have to assess the political process in the absence of a definitive system which offers a simple
quantifiable valuation. We shall instead judge the success of the
Israeli-Palestinian peace process using the set of theoretical assumptions as laid out by the Riceman Formula as to whether or not
there has been a marked improvement in the Israeli-Palestinian
relations existing post-Oslo, compared with the environment pre-
Oslo. Improvement will be the qualifying variable by which to
measure relations between the parties as they progress from conflict to definitive peace.

In order to assess and evaluate the DoP, the subsequent agreements made, and the peace process in general against its stated
goals, the intention of the theoretical section of this work was to
apply a set of standards in order to determine the effectiveness of
the DoP as an example of a means of conflict resolution. Thus,
having examined the process in the preceding chapters, we will
now apply the Riceman Formula. To recap, the formula covers:
(1) *Resolution*: development of a sustainable preventative security
     regime involving a reciprocal and cooperative positive peace
     agreement based on shared goals and principles of justice, econ-

omic interdependence, collective security and sense of shared community, and an equitable and lasting settlement which masters inherent asymmetrical power inequalities;

(2) *Institutionalization*: implementation of a recognized, binding and agreed legal framework setting out specific commitments and obligations, within an enforceable conflict prevention regime;

(3) *Confidence-building*: provision of channels for dispute resolution, crisis prevention, reconciliation, conflict deterrence and reduction, foundation of political institutions to defuse political instability and human rights abuses, economic uncertainty, and ensure compliance and verification of a mutual security environment;

(4) *Empowerment*: powers and responsibilities exercised and levels of sovereignty attained;

(5) *Mediation*: sustained support and political direction from third parties which nurture and advance the peace process; procedures which enable peaceful change, including procedural mechanisms which allow for the review of settlement terms, the raising of grievances, for adjustments to the settlement as new realities are created, and which anticipate and monitor potential areas of future conflict;[5]

(6) *Administration*: bureaucratic regime developed to conduct, manage, regulate and supervise conflict resolution institution;

(7) *Negotiation*: systems employed to facilitate deal-making process.

The following sections examine each of these aspects of the formula in the context of the DoP.

5.2 Resolution

From the evidence analysed in the preceding chapters we can draw two principal conclusions. Firstly, the foundation of the Israeli-Palestinian Declaration of Principles on Interim Self-Government Arrangements (DoP), that is a 'permanent settlement' to the Israeli-Palestinian conflict, is based primarily on UN Security Council Resolution 242 and is designed to lead to the implementation of Security Council Resolutions 242 and 338. In a practical sense the reality of achieving such a state is open to widely differing interpretations and therefore an agreed compromise will be difficult to determine. Secondly, because of the first conclusion, the principal objective of the DoP, a 'just, lasting and comprehensive peace settlement' leading to the resolution of the Israeli-Palestinian conflict via 'historic reconciliation through the agreed political process' will be that much harder to accomplish.[6]

Drawn from the evidence provided it is important that we have a usable, comprehensive and realistic definition of what we mean by conflict resolution within the current international system, in order that we may use it not only to measure the effectiveness of the DoP at achieving a state of resolved conflict, but also to measure the DoP against its own stated goals. To evaluate the DoP, resolution shall be understood to be a state in which conflicting parties agree to cease all politically motivated and national-goal-oriented hostile acts toward one another, and contract to coexist benignly, with mutual respect, refrain from malevolent acts aimed at the disruption of the internal affairs to the detriment of the other party in the pursuit of national goals, and allow for the free movement of peoples, goods, services and ideas, within an agreed institutional framework based on justice and respect for human rights. Thus our assessment of the success or failure of the DoP depends on whether or not the DoP produces a peace settlement which, when analysed, conforms to these above criteria providing a just, lasting and comprehensive peace.

Despite the ambiguities contained in the initial arrangements, and the secrecy in concluding the agreement to proceed as partners in a process of peace-building, the DoP has brought about certain irreversible facts, costs and benefits. The political act of mutual recognition cannot be reversed. Both sides conceded to the other the total fulfilment of their national goals, in other words complete victory over the other. Neither can claim to refuse to negotiate further with the other and return to the exclusivity of the military option; it would be too costly politically. For the Palestinians, the DoP allows the PLO a pre-eminent place as Israel's negotiating partner to determine the future of the occupied territories, thus undermining any future role as such for Jordan. The DoP also effectively precludes Israel from denying the most basic of Palestinian rights. It also provides a base to establish an internationally approved PLO presence within the occupied territories, from which to build a new political relationship with the Palestinian people and the Israeli government. The DoP represents for the Israelis an end to the desire to circumvent the PLO as the legitimate representative of the Palestinian people, and the negation of the illusion that there were alternative Palestinian actors who could be dealt with who would not raise the issues of Palestinian statehood and compensation for

1948 and 1967 refugees. It provides for the denial of the assertion that Israel was never really intent on pursuing a meaningful peace with the Palestinians, demonstrating an Israeli willingness to negotiate an alternative to military occupation and repression and regional isolation. By pursuing the goal of peace with the Palestinians in order ultimately to make peace with the Arab world, the DoP accords in the international arena the prospect of the diplomatic benefit of lessening regional tensions, destroying the figment of inter-Arab political solidarity aimed at isolating Israel, and provides for new regional economic and political relationships. The DoP provides an opportunity to build new political relationships, and to establish a new consensus, within both Israeli and Palestinian polities, and between the Israeli and Palestinian political leaderships.

Both sides have to judge the DoP by the politically most important criterion, namely, to what extent the DoP has advanced and achieved the participants' specific national interests, and whether or not the principles laid out in the negotiations still contain the necessary criteria to fulfil such national objectives, and that the DoP remains the most significant and viable vehicle for effecting a mutually acceptable *modus vivendi*.

However, the essential contradiction and inherent flaw of the DoP which separates both sides is what constitutes the objective of the entire enterprise. There is no shared vision, despite the stated intentions outlined in the agreement. The Palestinians see the DoP as the instrument by which Israel would withdraw to its pre-1967 borders, allowing for the establishment of a sovereign Palestinian state on the territories vacated. The Israelis see the DoP as allowing them to legitimate the expansion of their post-1967 borders, including the unilateral unification and annexation of Jerusalem. The DoP has never been able to bridge the inherent contradictions dividing both parties; however, it was an attempt to negotiate a compromise, through a process of confidence-building. For many the spirit of hope in building confidence between enemies outlined in the DoP was as important as the letter of the agreement in trying to stimulate a new relationship between the Israelis and Palestinians. It is this aspect of confidence-building in the future, enshrined in the DoP, which has underlined the basic acceptance by wider public opinion. However such acceptance can only be sustained if those who support it believe that it will bring a just, equitable, and lasting settlement. Without justice and fairness the DoP's promises loses their allure. For Palestinians who have had to endure the abandonment of their dreams of the reunification of historic Palestine incorporating a bi-ethnic political and cultural structure, the failure to compensate their loss with at least a state which includes the West Bank, Gaza and East Jerusalem, heralds 'the end of any viable sense of Palestine'.[7]

Both sides have the option to pursue either a 'full' peace or a 'partial' peace during the final status negotiations. A 'full' peace would be a conflict resolution regime which brought the conflict to an end 'by an agreement in which both sides relinquish all further claims against each other in return for what they get in the agreement.'[8] A 'partial' peace would be 'an agreement to end particular forms of conflict for the time being, even though one or both sides insists that it does not accept the current working arrangements as just or permanent, and reserves the right to make every effort to change them, except for the particular kinds of conflict that they agree to forego in the partial peace agreement.' Either approach is entirely compatible with the terms of the DoP, as the distinction between either 'full' or 'partial' peace 'was not strongly articulated in the discussions related to Oslo'.[9] Indeed there are considerable and contradictory implications concerning negotiating either scenario.

The autonomy negotiations represent a series of significant transitions of Israeli and Palestinian society, political, economic and social. To determine whether the accords have been a success or a failure, it must therefore be determined that Israeli and Palestinian society has been transformed from occupation to autonomy, from war to a just and sustainable peace, from financial instability and external dependency to independent indigenous economic planning and development, from military administration to legislative and judicial accountability, from military orders to pluralistic democracy, from traditional tribal structures and repressive societal controls to individual empowerment through the guarantee of basic rights and freedoms. With Israel controlling some 70 per cent of the occupied territories after concluding all the formal interim agreements, the reality seems to provide for partial autonomy and partial occupation; however, incorporated agreements to disagree are inadequate and not really sufficient to provide for a permanent solution in the longer term.[10]

Has the entire peace process been manipulated for partisan ends? Undoubtedly. Basically, when evaluating the peace process, none of the participants is without reproach by the standards set by their own spokesmen and women, namely the pursuit of peace with justice for a just peace, based on the goal of a just, lasting and comprehensive peace settlement and historic reconciliation through an agreed political process leading to the implementation of Security Council Resolutions 242 and 338. All concerned fall somewhat short of achieving these objectives. However, in defence of all concerned, they all remain engaged, at least technically, within the peace process despite political upheavals which have given grave concern for the continuation of the peace process. On several occasions, the peace process was in pieces, awaiting repair. Before berating the obvious breaches of the spirit, if not the letter of the agreements made to date, one must wonder whether or not the original goals, objectives and dreams were impossibly high and therefore never able to be attained. For despite all the flaws of this peace process, the US, Russia, the European Union, Norway, and many other members of the international community have involved themselves in this undertaking, investing time, money and prestige, in spite of pressing national and domestic considerations. The international community, when pressed for financial contributions, provided several billion US dollars of aid. Would that Bosnia, Angola, East Timor, Somalia and Cambodia had been able to generate such international cooperation, generosity, time, effort and collectiveness of purpose. The international community, and the US in particular, was under no obligation to become involved in a difficult peace process, particularly if they had no intention of having the process succeed. In terms of *realpolitik*, the US had little option but to become engaged as a leading player in determining the future of the Middle East, because of its strategic interests in maintaining close relations with Arab oil-producing states, and because of the domestic political pressure on any US administration from the powerful influence of the Jewish lobby. For example, Warren Christopher flew to the Middle East some 30 times during his tenure of office, whilst in contrast he visited China only once.[11] It is not a perfect world, and the peace process has had to exist within an imperfect world order.

Whilst this in no way absolves the participants for abdicating their responsibilities and falling short of achieving high ideals and goals, what the peace process has managed to achieve is to afford the Palestinians and Israelis the opportunity to negotiate directly their shared futures, in the light of mutual public acknowledgement of each other's existence. Such a process has undermined mutual hostility and repudiation to the extent that the peace process has reached a point of no return, in that the possibility of outright conflict based on zero-sum considerations has been so diminished as to have at least been regarded as having been resolved. As an existential conflict, the DoP through mutual recognition has at least removed the negation of the rival's legitimacy as an integral point of conflict. The DoP provides for the implementation of a recognized, binding and agreed legal framework setting out specific commitments and obligations, within an enforceable conflict prevention regime. What the DoP has not done so far is resolve the conflict on a permanent basis. The DoP has not developed a sustainable preventative security regime involving a reciprocal and cooperative positive peace agreement based on shared goals and principles of justice, economic interdependence, collective security and sense of shared community, and an equitable and lasting settlement which masters inherent asymmetrical power inequalities. There is much still to be determined.

The good intentions stated by the original principals who initiated the Middle East peace process have been diluted by various factors, such as violent events, changes in personnel, and changes in the direction of political imperatives. Such a diminution of original intentions was bound to occur when the process of conflict resolution and political reorientation was intended to be manipulated over a number of years, particularly when such a process is forced to incorporate so many changes to the variables determining a final outcome. Whilst the original, laudable fundamental principles remain as ultimate objectives and guiding policies within the ongoing peace process, the nature of an undetermined and flexible negotiating strategy which is bound to be so obviously influenced by external factors has been transformed by hard-bargaining through a political process beyond that of the initial euphoria which greeted the announcement of Israeli-Palestinian rapprochement, to become a high-stakes political poker game, with land, powers, responsibilities and sovereignty as bargaining chips.

The Israeli government has used, and is using, all its power, intelligence, wit, determination, cunning and friendships to achieve the best possible resolution for Israel. The Israeli government, of whatever shade, is negotiating on behalf of the Israeli public. Their remit and desire is fuelled by their partisan constituency; thus Israeli negotiators are driven by what they believe will be regarded as fair and equitable by the Israeli public, and not by the international community or the Palestinians. Nothing less would be expected by the Israeli electorate. If the Palestinians feel the arrangements are unfair and inequitable, then their grievance is ultimately with their own leaders and negotiators for not achieving better results. Undoubtedly the asymmetrical nature of the Israeli-Palestinian power relationship means that the Palestinians will always be at a disadvantage in terms of institutional power. However, the Palestinian people's representatives are theirs to choose and unmake, and in the final analysis, if the Palestinians feel that the DoP has meant that their desires for sovereignty and statehood have been outmanoeuvred, then the fault lies with those chosen to lead the Palestinian people, and not with those chosen by others to lead others. Naked terrorism such as that employed by the suicide bombers will not sway the Israeli or American publics to sanction the renegotiation of alternatives. After all 'Israel is not, as many Arabs delude themselves into believing, an obsequious monkey whose organ-grinder is the United States. Indeed, to believe that it is an act of political ignorance, wishful thinking and self-deception.'[12] Only a new non-violent *intifada* with a publicly endorsed leadership will have the slightest hope of stimulating pressure on Israel to conclude a settlement viewed as fair, equitable and just by the Palestinian public. It is in this context that Israeli negotiators must be most aware of the obligations that come with enjoying such an asymmetrical power imbalance within the Israeli-Palestinian relationship. Concluding a settlement which is deemed fair and just by one side, and rejected by the majority of the public opinion of the other as unfair, will merely cause the interim phase to persist. For the Israelis, and the right in particular, the prophetic warning is clear, for the future well-being and security of Israel is not so much based on the settlements – on a biblical commandment to settle the land – nor even on a militarily strong Israel. Israel's future security is undermined, not by the establishment of a Palestinian state, but by the emphatic denial of such a state. A permanent settlement has to remove the main injustices and indignities between the two communities despite their power variances, or else the regime installed to negotiate the permanent arrangements will not survive the lifetime of the personalities imposed to conclude such arrangements. Peace is not an indivisible commodity: there are minimum requirements that must be fulfilled in order that both sides may live with the settlement. Peace has its 'objective terms, conditions, and prerequisites, and unless these are recognized and fulfilled, any negotiating process or agreement is not only doomed to fail, but may even produce entirely contrary results.'[13]

It can be tentatively concluded that in a sense Palestine has existed since 13 September 1993. According to international law, there are four basic criteria constituting sovereignty:

(1) A recognized and defined sovereign territory (unlike Israel, through the DoP, effective territorial limits have defined Palestine as the portion of historical Palestine occupied by Israel since 1967 – 'the two sides view the West Bank and the Gaza Strip as a single territorial unit, whose integrity will be preserved during the interim period.'[14] Whilst sovereignty over Jerusalem is explicitly contested within the DoP, sovereignty over the Gaza Strip and the West Bank by the state of Palestine, in the form of a Palestinian body is not. Israel has never formally annexed any occupied territory other than extending the municipal boundaries of Jerusalem, Jordan renounced all administrative and legal claims to the West Bank in July 1988, and Egypt only administered the Gaza Strip. Since November 1988, when Palestine was proclaimed, the only body asserting sovereignty over the occupied territories, discounting the joint claim over Jerusalem, has been the state of Palestine);

(2) A permanent population;

(3) An ability by the political apparatus to discharge international and conventional obligations (as evidenced by the establishment of diplomatic relations between the Palestinian Authority (PA) and many sovereign states and attempts to gain membership in international organizations);

(4) The maintenance of territorial integrity and public order (from 20 January 1996 a democratically elected Palestinian executive and legislature was to exercise effective control over a significant portion of Palestinian territory incorporating the majority of the Palestinian population).[15]

Statehood is not an issue of the 'permanent status' negotiations. According to Article V.3 of the DoP regarding permanent status negotiations, issues shall include: 'Jerusalem, refugees, settlements, security arrangements, borders, relations and cooperation with other neighbors, and other issues of common interest'.[16] The article refers to 'security arrangements', 'borders' and 'relations and cooperation with other neighbors' which would constitute eventual inter-national agreements, thus the acceptance by Israel of Palestinian sovereignty is implicit in the terms of the DoP. Whilst Israel remains the occupying power, the DoP's enshrinement in Article I of UNSCRs 242 and 338, which explicitly preclude the inadmissibility of the acquisition of territory by war and serves as the basis of the permanent status settlement, means that the entire process could be construed as being about the detail of establishing a sovereign entity which can serve mutually inclusive Israeli and Palestinian interests, and not about whether there will be an independent Palestine as this is already implied. In this sense, the signing of the DoP does not imply a Palestinian acceptance of Israeli occupation but an Israeli acceptance of Palestinian sovereignty; however, 'Neither party shall be deemed, by virtue of having entered into this Agreement, to have renounced or waived any of its existing rights, claims or positions.'[17]

Ownership of land is more than just a final status issue to be negotiated without close regard to the emotions of history. To a people without land, whose experience in diaspora was that land – the very basis of power and status – was denied them, forever leaving the mark of the outsider, and to a people who lost or had their land stolen – their land being the very basis of their society, its wealth, power and its identity – the very point of land ownership/ land under occupation is, and will be very central to the resolving of the Israeli-Palestinian conflict. Israeli citizens now own property in East Jerusalem, the West Bank and Gaza Strip, land acquired through war and occupied therefore illegally, in contravention of the Geneva Convention. Zionism is in essence the political determination of a biblical commandment to restore Jews to their ancient homeland, and for many in the modern era, the fulfilment of the Balfour Declaration of 1917 is interpreted by some Zionists to mean the whole of mandatory Palestine.[18] The land of Palestine whether in whole or in part, as understood by either side, has variously been ruled by Ottomans, British, Jordanians and Egyptians as well as Israelis. Thus Palestine has never existed as a political entity ruled solely by Palestinians. Therefore gaining territory to exercise political authority, or the gaining of political sovereignty, is tantamount to the fulfilment not only of Palestinian self-determination but also of Palestinian nationalism.

The entire history of the Palestinian national struggle had, up to the date of 15 November 1988, not accepted the policy or consequences of the abandonment of the pursuit of all of Mandatory Palestine within and under the control of a Palestinian/Arab government. The policy of rejection of the Jewish state, or the hope that it would wither away, has caused the pursuit of Palestinian national self determination over areas of Palestine then under Arab control, namely the West Bank and Gaza prior to 1967, to be stillborn. The

1967 defeat and the subsequent years of serious erosion of Palestinian culture and political identity has had such an effect that the decision to negotiate with the Israelis to form some, or any, Palestinian polity, however imperfect, has been particularly strong, especially taking account of the *intifada* and its outpouring of Palestinian bile at their position. However, it may be argued that making strategic concessions on the very notion of what constitutes Palestine plays into the Israelis' hands tactically in the sense that Israel could never cow the Palestinians inside whilst there remained a significant outside; neither would deal at the other's expense. However, the Oslo accords basically manoeuvre the PLO into the position of being a local leadership that the Israelis can deal with, as they are accepted and endorsed by such a significant constituency of the Palestinians both inside and out – the end result that Israel has been searching for all these years, namely a way to overcome the outside objections and the insiders' determination not to be collaborators.

Despite the success of the peace process in surviving many grave difficulties since 1993, any assessment of the political realities which exist between the two communities since the agreement's signing would have to accept that Israel exercises greater and more far-reaching power and control over the Palestinian people in the occupied territories than at any time since June 1967. The DoP was intended to create a new Israeli-Palestinian dynamic which would be characterized, during the interim phase at least, by tangible improvements in personal and national security and economic prosperity, and by political benefits in the form of an acknowledgement of the aspiration of national rights of existence, self-determination and freedom. Eager populations warmly welcomed and embraced the initial notion that a negotiated settlement would lead to the end of the cycle of violence, repression and occupation. The incremental and transitional nature of the DoP intended to build confidence between old enemies. For the Palestinians, autonomy, however limited, was considered a better option than continued occupation. The inherent asymmetrical power relationship was rationalized as redeemable through a process of cooperation and the accrual of performance-related benefits. Initial difficulties were considered the result of a combination of inexperience, individual impropriety and incompetence, inherited structural and economic inequality, continued Israeli restrictions, and a slow response from the international donor community. For the Israelis, the DoP represented a practical policy which allowed them publicly to embrace the PLO without having to accept the PLO's agenda. The DoP amounted to the practical accordance of a process of devolving local powers and responsibilities without having to sacrifice real power or sovereignty over the occupied territories.

The Palestinian Authority's inability to confront Israeli hegemonic designs over the occupied territories has led the Palestinian public to regard the furtherance of the DoP process with fear if not disdain. Israel's continued policy of closure of the occupied territories has so adversely affected the Palestinian population economically, that the DoP's stated intention of providing economic prosperity and an improvement in the quality of life has proven hollow. The marginalization of the militant Palestinian opposition, through their non-participation in the political process, and the intense PA campaign against them, has highlighted the PA's role within the new Israeli-Palestinian partnership. For the Palestinians, the DoP demonstrates the new balance of power between the PLO and Israel. The establishment of the peace process has led to the institutionalization of the reality that Palestinian fortunes remain hostage to the Israeli-Palestinian imbalance of power relationship. The Palestinians have only full devolved powers and responsibilities for some 3 per cent of the West Bank territory (Area A). Area B covers 27 per cent of the West Bank, where the PA only exercises limited civil and security powers, with Israel retaining powers and responsibilities for security matters, which Israel is free to define. Area C comprises some 70 per cent of the West Bank, covering Israeli settlements, military locations, arterial roads and junctions, water resources, borders and areas surrounding Palestinian-controlled municipal and village boundaries. Area C is a 'contiguous whole that both surrounds Areas A and B in their entirety and parcels them into isolated enclaves'. Restrictions on further settlement building in Area C do not apply. Furthermore, jurisdiction over the settlements has been transferred from the Israeli Civil Administration of the Israeli Military Government (IMG) to Israel's state public administration, integrating the settlements into the existing state machinery. Some 60 per cent of the Gaza Strip is classified as Area A, with most of the remainder classed as Area C. Gaza is surrounded on three sides by an electrified razor-wire fence, with the entry and exit of goods and persons strictly controlled at a series of Israeli and PA checkpoints.[19] Israel is still allowed under the DoP to continue with mass arrests, collective punishments, house demolitions, prolonged curfews and closures, land expropriations, and any other measures deemed necessary in pursuit of Israeli security requirements. Israel still retains administrative responsibility and the power of approval for the registration of Palestinian birth certificates, ID cards, driving licences, passports, and so on through the IMG, although such procedures are conducted by PA officials, rather than directly with the IMG. Closure has ensured that East Jerusalem has been all but separated from the rest of the West Bank. East Jerusalem and its annexed environs comprise roughly some 20 per cent of the West Bank territory, with Palestinians requiring Israeli permits to enter or pass through. With permits hard to come by, and heavy penalties for violators, Palestinian access to Jerusalem is effectively restricted. Senior Israeli military and intelligence officials maintain that no suicide bomber ever applied for an entry permit for Israel, and no Palestinian with a valid work permit has been convicted of a terrorist offence. These officers see the policy of closure as a counterproductive political response to a military problem.[20] The insistence on combating a security problem with a political strategy ensures an economic consequence of endemic unemployment, widespread poverty, PA deficit financing, emergency aid programmes depleting vital employment generation programmes, and the setting back of real economic developmental initiatives. These policies engender the corresponding political desire within the Palestinian community to strike at Israel, ensuring a vicious spiral.

Initial support for the DoP among Palestinians came from the simplistic desire that events would somehow develop dynamically in favour of Palestinian aspirations. The improvements in the quality of life for the majority of the population which are supposed to be an intended feature of the DoP, providing for its continued support, have not materialized. Combined with the perception that the Palestinians' representative is no longer capable of ensuring an equitable outcome, and that the Palestinian opposition offers even less of a viable alternative strategy, pessimism with the peace process and the Palestinian leadership is bound to grow. The PA regime has bolstered its central position domestically as Israel's central partner through autocratic measures. The PA's development as a somewhat corrupt regime, severely restricted by Israeli military orders, without proper democratic checks and balances on the executive by the legislature and judiciary, and with sometimes scant regard for due process, is bound to become more resisted by growing popular frustration and cynicism.[21] The bantustanization of the West Bank and the probable frustration of Palestinian aspirations of self-determination is bound to lead to popular disillusionment, resentment and a 'shaking off' of the construction of such an attempt at benevolent occupation.

Evaluating the Israeli-Palestinian political situation post-DoP, as opposed to pre-DoP, is rather complicated. The Israelis have undoubtedly benefited from the DoP in that their status as occupiers is obscured, and Israel's claims over the occupied territories are internationally legitimated. Israel has contracted out its security undertakings to a relatively pliant Palestinian entity, without compromising jurisdictional and sovereignty prerogatives. The Israelis have conducted a negotiating strategy of incredible dimensions via the DoP, and the peace process produced from it. The litany of past Israeli politicians prior to the DoP was always that the PLO were terrorists, and that no Palestinian interlocutor of sufficient stature existed to negotiate with. The sticking point for the Israelis was always their desire to separate the Palestinians in the occupied territories from the external Palestinians, the PLO and the interested Arab world, because of their greater ability to remain steadfast and resolute on negotiating principles such as Jerusalem, refugees, the right of return and statehood. However, if a negotiating strategy could allow recognition of the PLO and bring a return of the PLO leadership to the occupied territories, without compromising Israel's *vis-à-vis* the above, then Israel could always manage to bring about the one aspect which had always alluded them, negotiating with Palestinian representatives from the occupied territories without preconditions and external interference. By incorporating the PLO into the humdrum of responsibility for daily local government of parts of the West Bank and Gaza Strip, by removing the external focus of Palestinian aspirations, by undermining the purity of the Palestinian national struggle by means of the PA 'getting its hands dirty' having to maintain law and order, the Israelis have managed to achieve their pre-DoP negotiating position, namely, negotiating with Palestinian representatives from the occupied territories whilst having made minimal concessions on such issues as settlements, land expropriations, security, Jerusalem, borders, water and Palestinian statehood. The self-emasculation of the PLO, by negating the PLO Covenant, by ensuring the irrelevance of the PNC, and by sidelining Palestinian opposition within the PLO, means that as the DoP peace process is between Israel and the PLO, Arafat effectively is the PLO. Even were he opposed by the Palestinian legislative council, he retains room to outmanoeuvre all opposition by dint of the fact that technically and legally the DoP ensures only the PLO has the authority to conduct negotiations on behalf of the Palestinian people. A thorough reassessment of the peace process has been avoided to date, despite large segments of both populations registering their opposition to the continuation of the DoP. However, opposition takes many forms, and most is not benign. Palestinian demands for a fundamental reconsideration of the DoP are bound to grow as it slowly emerges that the interim, transitional phase is likely to endure longer than that anticipated within the terms of the agreements made. The Palestinians are in the precarious position in the final status negotiations of more than likely not being able to realize their dreams of a sovereign state, yet fearful of losing what they have achieved to date, the establishment of a Palestinian autonomous entity for the first time in history.

5.3   Institutionalization

The DoP sets out to achieve the goal of an agreed, recognized and legally binding conflict resolution framework, which sets out specific commitments and obligations within an enforceable conflict prevention regime. Therefore, has a bureaucratic regime been initiated by the DoP to institutionalize the conduct, management, regulation and supervision of such a framework?

The DoP is regarded by some as an interpreter's nightmare, a patchwork of old Israeli and US drafts, incomplete procedural suggestions, deliberate ambiguities and obfuscations.[22] The 17 articles and four annexes of the DoP indicate that they are firmly intended to lead to some final political settlement. The document was painstakingly drafted and covers, at least in outline, the most sensitive concerns of both sides. The DoP is a bilateral agreement which is historic in the sense that the Palestinians became full partners, with the Israelis, in the regional quest for peace. The destiny for both sides was to deal with the DoP realistically, to overcome its limitations and by inference overcome the weaknesses and flaws that continue to divide them. The dilemma for the participants is how they will move forward, constrained as they are by the limits of the DoP and by their own histories.

The most striking aspect of the DoP is that it deals with procedures and timetables for the implementation of Israeli military redeployment and Palestinian self-government. It is a living document which seeks to maximize developing confidence-building measures. It is a studied example of a carrot-and-stick approach to diplomacy – the more that is achieved the more can be achieved. Yitzhak Rabin described the DoP not as a peace agreement, but more as a huge step in the direction of peace, an agreement on establishing an arrangement for an interim period.[23] The DoP was intended as just a stepping stone along the road to peace, graduality being the guiding principle of the agreement which would allow Gaza and Jericho to become the first experiments in peace.

The DoP recognizes the Palestinians as a people, within a framework of legitimate rights and reciprocal political rights, but there is a clear evasion of anything relating to land, other than that relating to the Gaza Strip and the Jericho area. The recognition of Israel by the PLO also implies shared sovereignty, on any part of the West Bank and Gaza Strip – indeed the DoP assures Israeli sovereignty over the Palestinian Interim Self-Governing Authority during the interim period.[24]

The ultimate challenge to the accord remains the negotiations which will determine the final status of the two parties' living arrangements. Irredentism will continue to shadow the process but above all, the two sides will have to guard against the psychological barriers which remain as an obstacle and a challenge to be overcome. These barriers for the Israelis will be the two extremes of previously accepted conventional wisdom, namely: a) that military force and its use can solve what is essentially a political problem and b) that the incantation that a peace treaty must be the harbinger and thus the foundation which will guarantee indefinite peace, can in no way guarantee indefinite peace. There has never been a peace agreement in history which takes the form of an unbroken, inviolable, eternal covenant. Wars generally have a habit of being between parties which were legally at peace. However, for the optimistic, the DoP does not underestimate the practical complexities involved in negotiating and implementing the arrangements it envisages: as it states in its preamble, it is predicated on the conviction that 'it is time to put an end to decades of confrontation and conflict.'[25]

Thus we can conclude that the DoP has achieved the goal of agreeing a conflict resolution framework, which sets out specific commitments and obligations within a conflict prevention regime. However, the inherent structural asymmetrical power imbalance robs the agreement of balance and the nature of the state–non-state bilateral agreement ensures that the DoP's international and legal foundations remain dubious, or at least open to wide interpretation. The DoP does not provide sufficiently for an enforceable conflict prevention regime in that such a regime is not defined, and enforcement of what constitutes a conflict prevention regime is left open to the interpretation of the parties, which in an asymmetrical structure, in practical terms, means the higher power party. The DoP, as a bilateral agreement, does not incorporate third party mediation to offset the inherent structural asymmetrical power imbalance, nor does it allow for international assistance which enables peaceful change, including procedural mechanisms which allow for the review of settlement terms, the raising of grievances, and the making of adjustments to the settlement as new realities are created and which anticipate and monitor potential areas of future conflict. The DoP does allow for international support and political direction from third parties aimed at nurturing and advancing the peace process through economic assistance, but such an international economic assistance programme is based on international goodwill and the willingness of the United States to provide political, economic and diplomatic assistance. The international community and particularly the US may be morally bound to offer assistance in the building of a conflict resolution regime in the Middle East, but they are not legally bound by the DoP. The peace process provided for by the DoP depends for its continued survival on the fragility of public confidence, on developing and advancing its terms, conditions and provisions, and on building on its foundations. I have suggested that the DoP is akin to a builder's blueprints for developing a new community. It is more than an artist's impression, but the practicalities of putting the plans into effect mean that the dynamic forging of the peace process needs much more work before it can be deemed complete.

5.4   Confidence-building

Yitzhak Rabin stated in his inaugural speech to the Knesset as Prime Minister that an ill-considered peace agreement which ultimately initiated future conflict was unacceptable. He said that 'When it comes to security, we will concede nothing. From our standpoint, security takes preference even over peace.' However he continued: 'It is our duty, to ourselves and to our children, to see the new world as it is now – to discern its dangers, explore its prospects and to do everything possible so the State of Israel will fit into this world whose face is changing.' Such a situation required Israeli leaders to 'give further thought to the urgent need to end the Arab-Israeli conflict and live in peace with our Arab neighbours'.[26] In a speech at Tel Aviv University, Rabin stated that, 'I believe that we are on a path of no return . . . to reach peace, even if it takes another year or two years, . . . I think that the reality of the international situation, the regional situation, the genuine need of nations and countries, is to arrive at a resolution of the dispute.'[27]

The DoP thus set out to achieve the provision of channels for dispute resolution, crisis prevention, reconciliation, conflict deterrence and reduction, foundation of political institutions to defuse political instability and human rights abuses, economic uncertainty, and ensure compliance and verification of a mutual security environment. By building confidence between the PLO and Israel so that a deal could be negotiated, Rabin sought to provide a framework which formalized channels for reconciliation, for conflict deterrence, to ensure a mutual security environment and to build a mutual future. From realizing that political compromise with the Palestinians was not possible without dealing with the PLO, it was a short journey to realizing that by not dealing with the PLO in the immediate future, the rise of absolutist, Islamic fundamentalism would result. Compromise was possible with the PLO by building confidence through negotiating a mutually perceived future via the Oslo backchannel. However, compromise was not an option to be considered with Hamas and Islamic Jihad. Rabin believed the struggle against Islamic terror to be a real and serious danger which would threaten Israel if not dealt with.[28]

Israeli and PLO concern about the potential threat of extremist Islam provided both sides with a mutual enemy. The DoP was conceived, developed, negotiated and concluded with such a threat in mind, from both sets of negotiators. The Oslo backchannel provided the necessary environment in which to conceive a working arrangement upon which to build. The facilitation of the process was nurtured by sensitive intermediaries – the Norwegians. In an atmosphere of cordiality, confidence in one another could be fostered and developed.

However, one of the biggest reservations voiced about the Israeli-Palestinian agreement was that it offered no guarantees that the parties would apply it in full or negotiate in good faith when postponed issues were raised. There were several points which were cause for Palestinian concern. The first, and most important, was that the agreement failed to 'address Israel's illegal claim to the occupied territories.'[29] Israel had always maintained that it was not an 'occupier,' but that it was in the occupied territories by right, with Israeli's claim expressed from the beginning though its confiscation of land, establishment of settlements, annexation of Jerusalem and adoption of a conduct dedicated to implementing a political programme which considered all of Palestine as Israeli territory'.[30] Palestinian critics have argued that nothing in the DoP indicated that Israel had renounced any part of its claim over Palestine, indeed that rather than confronting the issue, the DoP evaded it. Thus, the major weakness of the DoP was that nothing in the agreement indicated whether settlement activity would stop. By not challenging or objecting to this claim, the Palestinians were in essence condoning it, and through Palestinian silence Israel could spuriously claim Palestinian acquiescence as an abandonment of their right to an independent state over the entirety of the occupied territories. In such a way, the status of the territories was being blurred from being recognizably 'occupied' to becoming 'disputed'. Further flaws of the DoP include the 'tacit acceptance of two separate entities in the Palestinian territories – two separate administrations, two separate judicial systems – indirectly a kind of apartheid', a situation which, by allowing or even by deferring to, the Palestinians were conceding something that was illegally established.[31] Palestinian acceptance of the terms of the DoP meant that Palestinians would have no one to blame for future events but themselves, for by agreeing to be bound by the DoP the Palestinians had helped to confer legitimacy on their territory's occupation of Israel. While the DoP enumerates such issues as Jerusalem, settlements and borders to be deferred, there is no mention in the DoP of any withdrawal beyond that of the interim period, indeed a complete withdrawal from the occupied territories was never mentioned for the final status negotiations. It has been claimed that this was implied in the DoP's reference to UN Security Council Resolution 242, which includes withdrawal, but in reality when dealing with state interests there can be no reliance on things implied, especially since Israel had repeatedly made it very clear that it had no intention of withdrawing outside the occupied territories. Such a conclusion is drawn by citing that the DoP is phrased in generalities which leave room for wide interpretations, and does not make specific provision for a complete withdrawal from the occupied territories, even as a final status issue. For Palestinian critics, the final confirmation that the agreement was, and would remain, inherently imbalanced and unjust was that Israel would always have the unilateral power of veto.[32]

Despite such constraints, the Palestinians have had to come to terms with the cold new realities of Israeli-Palestinian relations. The dream of defeating Israel and the temptation to continue the struggle by inflaming the *intifada* had to be resisted, particularly while negotiating a new relationship with the Israelis. The rhetoric of traditional objectives was, and is, incompatible with the technicalities of brokering an agreement, especially one which is part of a process which relies so heavily on mutual confidence for continued life. The question many Israelis asked was, could the Palestinians with their history of internal schisms, militant factionalism and lack of collective sovereign existence prove their *bona fides* and earn Israeli trust and confidence in a mere five years? The bottom line of the DoP remains, that as the higher power party, Israel can always dispense with the process of negotiations if Israeli doubts about Palestinian intentions persist. As Rabin put it at the opening of the special Knesset debate on the Israel-PLO agreements, 'in any event, the might of the IDF – the best army in the world – is available for our use.'[33] Within such an atmosphere of perceived inequality and questionable political faith, building confidence and mutual trust has always, and will continue to be, a fragile undertaking.

5.5 Empowerment

The DoP
- provided a blueprint for the transfer and exercise of powers and responsibilities to the Palestinians and the levels of sovereignty to be attained by the Palestinians
- prepared the establishment of a nominal cease-fire of hostilities agreement
- instituted a mutual recognition pact
- stated the parties' intent to transfer specified territorial enclaves to Palestinian authority
- provided for the inauguration of an autonomous self-governing Palestinian entity with the prospect of elections to such an autonomous legislative body combined with the devolution of additional civil powers and responsibilities
- arranged for the withdrawal and redeployment of Israeli military forces from specified locations and population centres

- founded a framework for the resolution of disputes and Israeli-Palestinian public order and security cooperation
- offered a plan for Israeli-Palestinian cooperation in bilateral and regional economic and development programmes, and
- prepared for further negotiations on unresolvable issues within the framework of a permanent status arrangement, covering Jerusalem, refugees, settlements, security arrangements, borders and foreign relations.

Fundamentally, the DoP empowers the Palestinians through the transfer and exercise of powers and responsibilities and the levels of sovereignty to be attained. In contrast, the DoP empowers the Israelis in a subtler but more ubiquitous form. The DoP recognizes, enshrines and conforms to the asymmetrical Israeli-Palestinian balance of power relationship in Israel's favour. Israel is thus empowered by the agreement as the superior of the two parties.

A rolling process of considerable substantive negotiations was intended to follow from the initial agreement because of the inherent contradictions, ambiguities and material differences in interpretation contained within the limitations of the original document. Subsequent, sequential documents had to be negotiated to formulate further interim arrangements ready for implementation in order that the process begun by the DoP could proceed. Further agreements were needed to provide for a sustainable preventative security regime involving reciprocal and cooperative rights and obligations based on shared goals and principles of justice, economic interdependence, collective security and sense of shared community, in order to achieve an equitable and lasting settlement which would master the existing inherent asymmetrical power inequalities.

We can now offer some conclusions as to how successful the further negotiated agreements have been in combining to prepare the foundation of the interim phase of the Israeli-Palestinian peace process as laid down within the terms of the DoP. The further agreements have allowed for the transfer and exercise of powers and responsibilities of the Palestinians and provided for greater levels of sovereignty to be attained by the Palestinians. The further agreements set out to provide for a sustainable preventative security regime involving reciprocal and cooperative rights and obligations based on shared goals and principles of justice, economic interdependence, collective security and a sense of shared community, in order to achieve an equitable and lasting settlement which masters existing inherent asymmetrical power inequalities.

Taking the issue of economic interdependence as indicative for our conclusion, we can assess the relative merits of the negotiated further transitional interim self-government arrangements on the basis of how successful the peace process has been in delivering real and practical benefits to those who are supposed to be the beneficiaries of the entire enterprise, namely the Israeli and Palestinian general publics. For the proponents of peace, who have argued that economic interdependence and integration between Israel and the Palestinians will provide for an 'economy of peace', events during the period of the negotiations have confounded their optimism.[34] Mass unemployment, extended periods of closure either of parts or of the whole West Bank and Gaza Strip, endemic and systemic structural and infrastructural weaknesses, and a wholly unhealthy dependent economic relationship has countered the notion that economic prosperity could allow difficult political decisions to prosper. In essence, the idea that economic activity would so involve, energize and preoccupy the majority of the Palestinian populations, thus buying them off and dissuading them from involvement in political agitation, has not been borne out by the evidence of the past years. As we have said, hungry people, whose hope for their and their childrens' future turns to despair, make for angry people. Many people can cope with a denial of their national aspirations and dreams of a perfect world, as long as their personal circumstances are financially ameliorated in compensation. However when externally imposed economic circumstances are so severe as to be oppressive, people tend to view the political system that sustains their straitened lives with eyes that see succour in radical solutions. The tenet that the denial of rights and the legitimacy of a people's struggle could at least be assuaged by a flourishing economy has, despite the infusion of vast amounts of foreign aid, failed. The Israeli preoccupation with its security fears, with the resultant cost being declining Palestinian living standards, have perversely led to an increase in Israel's vulnerability to further attacks, since the economic conditions necessary to contain Palestinian violence have failed to materialize; this is precisely because Israel's security fears have fuelled actions which have directly led to a worsening of Palestinians' economic conditions.

The Paris Protocol on Economic Relations promised to lay the groundwork for strengthening the Palestinian economic base and extending to the Palestinians autonomy in the economic decision-making process in accordance with its own development plan, and the rights to pursue its own economic priorities.[35] This aspect of the peace process was included because of the acceptance of the principle that 'national sovereignty in economic decision-making is an important prerequisite to political independence.'[36] However, the reality has been continued and compounded dominance of the Palestinian economic sector by the Israeli economy, ensuring that Palestinian ability to determine economic policy is severely limited and that the interdependence of the two economies is balanced most favourably for the Israelis.

Israel has severely reduced Palestinian access, in terms of goods and persons, to the Israeli economy, citing security concerns for their actions. Israel has cut the number of Palestinians working in Israel, resulting in severe Palestinian unemployment. Frequent closures, collective punishments, curfews and security actions have also ensured the underemployment of the workforce and the underdevelopment of the economy. The financial costs of closure alone far outweigh donor assistance. The costs of closure are generally borne by individuals, families and small businesses, whereas donor assistance is disbursed to the PISGA, its institutions, and earmarked projects. Long-term damage done to personal financial circumstances and to small to medium businesses is difficult to assess, but donor assistance is not forthcoming in this area. Closures also ensure structural damage to the economy as a result of reduced foreign and expatriate investments and delays to infrastructural development projects.[37]

Businesses need access to labour and capital, yet restrictions in the free movement of labour even within the occupied territories, in raising venture capital, and in business planning capabilities severely limit the prospects of economic growth. Israel not only prevents Palestinians from freely taking up employment in Israel, it also restricts the free movement of goods and persons between the various PISGA-controlled communities, thus isolating local economies and making the planning and development of an integrated economy almost impossible. This is particularly true with regard to the position of Jerusalem, access to which has been tightly controlled, ensuring that Palestinian labourers, contractors and entrepreneurs are excluded from the Jerusalem market, with the corresponding knock-on effects on small businesses and self-employment opportunities. By restricting employment options, Israel ensures that incomes are overall reduced, meaning that spending power is also reduced, further hurting local businesses. This 'multiplier effect – a cycle of fewer jobs and less income' threatens the very survival of the Palestinian economy.[38] PISGA policy-makers and the international donor community are unable or unwilling to address this political problem which afflicts the Palestinian economy and adversely affects fiscal planning and economic development. When skilled and educated Palestinians are forced to accept employment in jobs which do not utilize their skills and training, then support for the continuation of this particular peace process will be set back. Under-utilized ordinary people, with no meaningful role in a stalled project of national reconstruction, will increasingly find the process of state-building hollow. The 'feeling of abandonment is palpable', according to a recent polls, 68.5 per cent of those describing themselves as 'not well-to-do' responded that they were pessimistic about their future, 29.4 per cent responded that they did not trust any political movement, with 20.5 per cent not trusting any of their leaders.[39] Thus the power Israel exerts in unilaterally destabilizing the extremely fragile, nascent Palestinian economy highlights the structural economic asymmetrical power relationship. Therefore, by any indicators, the relative position of the Palestinian economy post-DoP as opposed to pre-DoP, is undoubtedly worse.

5.6   Mediation

It is clear that the DoP, as a bilateral agreement between two very unequal opponents, is inherently flawed in its structural makeup. The Israeli-Palestinian peace process has no inbuilt mechanism to redress or resolve the asymmetrical nature of the power relationship. Whilst mechanisms and provisions exist within the DoP as channels for dispute resolution, crisis prevention, reconciliation, and conflict deterrence and reduction, the foundation of political institutions to defuse political instability, human rights abuses and economic uncertainty, and to ensure compliance and verification of a mutual security environment, and the implementation of agreed arrangements between the Israelis and Palestinians, there are no mechanisms to provide sustained support and political direction from interested third parties and extra-territorial mediators, such as the UN the US or the EU, to nurture and advance the peace process. There are no procedural mechanisms which allow for third party review of settlement terms, for the raising of grievances to external arbitration, for incorporating adjustments to the settlement as new international realities are created, and to anticipate and monitor potential areas of future conflict. There is no ability to refer disputes to higher authorities such as the UN, and indeed there is not even a dispute-resolution role in the Israeli-Palestinian peace process for the sponsors of, or other interested parties to, the Madrid peace process. The DoP effectively locks out any international, independent action aimed at peace-making, peacekeeping and guaranteeing the Israeli-Palestinian agreements. The DoP represents a unique agreement in that it is the only conflict resolution process where a bilateral asymmetrical agreement made between two totally unequal parties has attempted to deliver a lasting peace without the aid and succour of international guarantees and guarantors. Without built-in mechanisms within the peace process to ensure fairness and justice between two such obviously unequal partners in the construction and delivery of an equitable peace process, the public perception that a process is fair and just and that the intent of either protagonist is also benign, is far more important in the absence of external mediators and international guarantors of either side's *bona fides*. Thus political and public actions and reactions are all the more critical for the survival of such a process, ensuring the process is a highly volatile, uncertain and explosive one.

5.7   Administration

As we have seen, the DoP intended to develop the foundation of political institutions to defuse political instability and human rights abuses, economic uncertainty, to ensure compliance and verification within a mutual security environment and to provide a sustainable preventative security regime with a view to implementing an internationally recognized, binding and agreed legal framework setting out specific commitments and obligations within an enforceable conflict prevention regime. While the DoP deals with the provisions for the administration of a conflict resolution framework, such as the procedures and timetables for the implementation of Israeli military redeployment and Palestinian self-government, it is a living document which seeks to maximize and develop confidence-building measures. The bureaucratic regime that is intended by the DoP to develop a conflict resolution framework needs further agreements to ensure its progress, evolution and promotion. Indeed, the foundations have been laid to promote Palestinian autonomous life, to provide representative government, to establish the requisite institutions for the operation of civil society and to further Israeli-Palestinian security cooperation. However, the peace process provided for by the DoP depends for its continued survival on the fragility and uncertainty of the political arena and in that sense the administrative regime which is intended to conduct, manage, regulate and supervise the institution of the Israeli-Palestinian conflict resolution framework is incomplete and hostage to the fortunes of political imperatives.

5.8 Negotiation

Before the DoP neither side officially recognized each other. The negotiating system and techniques employed by the Israelis and Palestinians, although initially secret, aimed to reach a deal that could be built on and improved. Contentious issues which could not be agreed upon were sidestepped to be dealt with in the future. The DoP was meant as a first important step – to break the barrier of past conflict and ensure mutual recognition.

As we have seen in the preceding chapters, the DoP established a nominal agreement for a cease-fire of hostilities, instituted a mutual recognition pact, transferred specified territorial enclaves of Gaza and Jericho to Palestinian authority, provided for the inauguration of an autonomous self-governing Palestinian entity with the prospect of elections to such an autonomous legislative body combined with the devolution of additional civil powers and responsibilities, arranged for the withdrawal and redeployment of Israeli military forces from specified locations and population centres, founded a framework for the resolution of disputes and Israeli-Palestinian public order and security cooperation and offered a plan for Israeli-Palestinian cooperation in bilateral and regional economic and development programmes. It also prepared for further negotiations on unresolvable issues within the framework of a permanent status arrangement covering Jerusalem, refugees, settlements, security arrangements, borders and foreign relations. A rolling process of considerable substantive negotiations followed from the initial DoP because of the inherent contradictions, ambiguities and material differences in interpretation contained within the limitations of the original document. Subsequent sequential documents had to be negotiated to formulate further interim arrangements ready for implementation in order that the process begun by the DoP could proceed.

The DoP as a document represents an agreement to pursue a living legacy, to undertake a process whose final outcome is not determined in advance. The DoP is not a symmetrical agreement outlining mutual obligations on a *quid pro quo* basis, rather it is an agreement to agree to further the basic interests of both sides. For the Israelis, the DoP provides a reliable, legitimate interlocutor and the ability to transfer responsibility for a large proportion of the Palestinian population, if not of the territory they inhabit. For the Palestinians, the DoP provides for the establishment of a legitimated political and moral authority with the mandate to negotiate on behalf of the Palestinian people to pursue Palestinian national interests. However, differences of interpretation not only separate the principal participants but also underline disagreements within both sides' domestic political and public opinion. Negotiations for concluding a comprehensive and final settlement are still ongoing, so the conflict resolution process is still under construction.

5.9   Further research in the field

Research analysing the implications and the utility of the Israeli-Palestinian DoP for conflict resolution in general and as a comprehensive framework for peace-making is rather limited. Such analytical work that exists in the field tends to focus on certain component aspects or parts of the peace process, such as the role of international mediation, economic interdependency, borders, power and threat perception, and conflict intensity in asymmetric intergroup conflict.

As this study has found, there is no one existing framework which captures the essence of the peace process, as the changing nature of the political realities has forced a constant realignment and re-assessment of the structural configurations. Rather than dismiss the Israeli-Palestinian peace process as a unique and therefore unusable formula for peace-making, one fundamental premise remains: negotiations, however imperfect, are more to be desired than renewed or continued conflict.

The secretly negotiated Israeli-Palestinian peace process broke down, and through, barriers of seemingly intractable conflict. This peace process offered a path to peace which had eluded all previous attempts to find a resolution to the Israeli-Palestinian conflict. The formula of finding common ground and common cause while agreeing to disagree on outstanding fundamental issues allowed a process of peace-building to be nourished and to grow. By seeking out points of agreement and trusting in the dynamics of time the process boldly attempted to initiate and promote an atmosphere of hope and willingness to construct a new relationship, based on cooperation, not conflict.

Considering further research in the field of Israeli-Palestinian peace-making, it is very difficult to know where to begin, precisely because of the highly politicized and unfinished nature of this particular process. The Israeli-Palestinian conflict is about conflicting legitimacy, over claim to the same land, to the same water, to the same air. Making sense of an existential conflict has been, and will continue to be, problematical. As an example of theoretical peace-modelling, the Israeli-Palestinian process has probably more political detractors than intellectual advocates. Prescriptions range from scrapping the entire process as fundamentally flawed to fine-tuning and finessing the progress already made. As a general, transferable, utilitarian model for peace-making, the Israeli-Palestinian peace process provides some genuinely positive and negative standards, and highlights some very interesting and significant features worthy of further examination.

Negatives

The main criticisms include:

(1) The DoP has not resolved the Israeli-Palestinian conflict on a permanent basis.
(2) The DoP has not developed a sustainable preventative security regime involving a reciprocal and cooperative positive peace agreement based on shared goals and principles of justice, economic interdependence, collective security and sense of shared community, and an equitable and lasting settlement which masters inherent asymmetrical power inequalities.
(3) The dynamics forging the peace process need much more work before it can be deemed complete.
(4) The DoP offers no guarantees that the parties would apply it in full or negotiate in good faith when postponed issues were raised.
(5) The DoP is phrased in generalities that leave room for wide interpretations and do not make specific provisions for guidance past the interim phase.
(6) The DoP is, and will remain, inherently imbalanced and unjust because one party, Israel, will always have the unilateral power of veto.
(7) Mass unemployment, extended periods of closure, endemic and systemic economic structural and infrastructural weaknesses, and a wholly unhealthy dependent economic relationship have countered the notion that economic interdependence and integration between Israel and the Palestinians will provide for an 'economy

of peace', and have confounded the optimism that economic prosperity could allow difficult political decisions to prosper.

(8) The DoP, as a bilateral agreement between two very unequal opponents, is inherently flawed in its structural makeup: the peace process has no inbuilt mechanism to redress or resolve the asymmetrical nature of the power relationship; there are no mechanisms to provide sustained support and political direction from interested third parties and extra-territorial mediators, such as the UN the US or the EU, to nurture and advance the peace process; there are no procedural mechanisms which allow for third party review of settlement terms, for the raising of grievances to external arbitration, for incorporating adjustments to the settlement as new international realities are created, and which anticipate and monitor potential areas of future conflict; there is no ability to refer disputes to higher authorities such as the UN, and indeed there is not even a dispute-resolution role in the Israeli-Palestinian peace process for the sponsors of, or other interested parties to, the Madrid peace process; and the DoP effectively locks out any international, independent action aimed at peace-making, peacekeeping and guaranteeing the Israeli-Palestinian agreements.

(9) The bureaucratic regime that is intended, by the DoP, to develop a conflict resolution framework, needs further agreements to ensure its progress, evolution and promotion.

(10) Negotiations for concluding a comprehensive and final settlement are still ongoing, so the conflict resolution process is still under construction.

Positives

The main positives include:

(1) The DoP instituted a mutual recognition pact which afforded the Palestinians and Israelis the opportunity to negotiate their shared futures directly, in light of mutual public acknowledgement of each other's existence.

(2) The DoP provides for the implementation of a recognized, binding and agreed legal framework setting out specific commitments and obligations, within an enforceable conflict prevention regime.

(3) The DoP established a nominal agreement for a cease-fire cessation of hostilities.

(4) The DoP transferred specified territorial enclaves to Palestinian authority.

(5) The DoP provided for the inauguration of an autonomous self-governing Palestinian entity with the prospect of elections to such an autonomous legislative body combined with the devolution of additional civil powers and responsibilities.

(6) The DoP arranged for the withdrawal and redeployment of Israeli military forces from specified locations and population centres, founded a framework for the resolution of disputes and Israeli-Palestinian public order and security cooperation.

(7) The DoP offered a plan for Israeli-Palestinian cooperation in bilateral and regional economic and development programmes.

(8) The DoP prepared for further negotiations on unresolvable issues within the framework of a permanent status arrangement covering Jerusalem, refugees, settlements, security arrangements, borders and foreign relations.

The fundamental flaw of the Israeli-Palestinian particular peace process, as we have seen, is that it has no inbuilt mechanism to redress or resolve the asymmetrical nature of the power relationship. Only with such a flaw remedied, could the Israeli-Palestinian peace-making example be recommended as a conflict resolution model for use in other settings of inter-ethnic, existential conflict.

5.10 The Future of the peace process

Israeli prime minister Netanyahu's years in office were marred by violence, allegations of political corruption and a deterioration in Israel's foreign relations, and in Israeli-Palestinian relations in particular. Netanyahu's government pursued a more inflexible and ideological path with regard to its peace policy, through settlement construction, expropriation of land, closures, and collective security punishments, irrespective of the detrimental impact such actions would have on its principal Arab peace partners, Egypt, Jordan and the Palestinians, or even on Israel's growing economic and political relations with peripheral Arab states, such as Morocco, Tunisia, Qatar and Oman. By undermining relations with the Palestinians, Egypt and Jordan, Netanyahu undermined the very foundations of Israel's peace strategy by discouraging any enthusiasm for compromise with Israel among the moderate advocates of the pursuit of peaceful policies. King Hussein was so incandescent with anger following the ground-breaking at the Jabal Abu Ghneim settlement, that he wrote a public letter of condemnation to Netanyahu, as Jordanian public opinion turned against the Israel-Jordan peace treaty. Egypt became increasingly critical of Israel as Israel's policies in the West Bank undercut President Mubarak's efforts in the peace process. Egypt has been an important and strategic ally in brokering Israeli-Palestinian negotiations. However, Mubarak felt compelled to join with Syria in initiating Arab moves to isolate Israel in the Arab world following the violence sparked by the Jerusalem tunnel incident, and the announcement of the Jabal Abu Ghneim project. Arab-Israeli relations were publicly frosty. Israel's relations with her principal trading partners, the EU, also deteriorated in light of Netanyahu's settlement policy, which the EU views as detrimental to building confidence in the peace process.

Israel's relations with its primary ally, the US, became strained to the extent that the new US Secretary of State, Madeleine Albright, chose not to visit Israel until Netanyahu proved 'more willing to move towards peace', preferring to travel to the Middle East 'only if she could accomplish something substantial.'[40] Albright eventually made her maiden visit to the region on 10 September 1997 in response to deteriorating Israeli-Palestinian relations and to deflect criticism of neglecting the peace process. Albright had intended to visit 'to focus on the broader political initiative' once 'progress on security issues' had been made.[41] However, because no progress at all had been made and both Netanyahu and Arafat descended into mutual distrust and antipathy, unwilling to entertain compromise, handicapped by extremist political constituencies and unable to negotiate in good faith, Albright's visit was deemed necessary by President Clinton to save the peace process and restore confidence in it.[42] Albright had been expected to upbraid Netanyahu and demand he proved Israel's good faith by freezing settlement construction, together with his adherence to the Oslo accords in the form of unblocking tens of millions of dollars in tax revenues owed by Israel to the PA, and softening the policies of closure on the PA areas. However, in light of the July and September suicide attacks, Albright's 50-hour visit was dominated by Israel's determination to fight Islamic terrorism, demanding that Arafat take action against Hamas and Islamic Jihad.[43] Albright blamed both sides for the crisis, describing it as 'neither inevitable nor accidental', and criticized Netanyahu and Arafat for failing to live up to 'their full obligations as partners in peace', however, Netanyahu's director of communications and policy planning, David Bar-Ilan, reiterated Israel's position on settlement activity, stating that 'we cannot freeze settlements any more than we can freeze life.'[44]

Netanyahu had previously responded to US pressure regarding his peace policies in September 1996, saying that:

> regardless of the fact that our relationship with the US is of the first rank of Israel's strategic assets, it is not the supreme asset. The supreme asset is our security, those things that are sacred to us like Jerusalem. If a regime should arise in the US and say 'You must give in on all this in exchange for relations with the US,' I will not give in.[45]

Even Israel's relations with US Jewry have become strained because of Netanyahu's backing for the attempt by the Israeli Orthodox religious establishment to outlaw non-Orthodox conversions to Judaism which has brought conflict between the US Reform and Conservative religious communities.[46]

Israel's 'political isolation is not a natural reaction of the anti-semitic international community but a direct function of Likud policy.'[47] Netanyahu's vision of the peace process was allegedly deliberately leaked to the Israeli press, with Ze'ev Schiff, *Ha'Aretz's* highly respected and well connected military correspondent being the first to print Netanyahu's 'Allon-plus' map. The highlights of the 'Allon-Plus Plan' include:

- Israel will govern areas of the West Bank east of the Green Line up to the crests of the first hills
- The Jordan Valley and its western slopes will remain in Israeli hands for a distance of 15km from the Jordan River, or further south from the Dead Sea westward to the desert
- The Palestinians will control the northwest shore of the Dead Sea, and a corridor from Ramallah to Jericho
- Greater Jerusalem will expand to Ma'ale Adumim and Kfar Adumim on the east towards the Etzion Bloc in the south and towards Bethel in the north
- The corridor connecting Israel's western hills to Jerusalem will be widened from two sides, from the Etzion Bloc in the south up to Beit Horon in the north
- The Jewish settlements near Nablus and Jenin will either remain in the Palestinian zone or be evacuated
- The Palestinians will have a secure passageway from the West Bank to the Gaza Strip, in accordance with the DoP, plus three additional corridors from parts of the West Bank to Tulkarm, Qalqilya and Jericho

- In addition to the existing Jerusalem-Dead Sea road, Israel will have four secure east-west passageways, which will cross the West Bank to the Jordan Valley and the Dead Sea
- In Jerusalem, there will be a 'functional solution' for the holy sites.[48]

After assuming office Netanyahu repeatedly indicated his desire to proceed directly to final status negotiations without completing the obligations of redeployment as laid down in the interim arrangements. The main reasoning seemed to be that the less territory redeployed from in the interim phase, the stronger the Israelis' hand in the bargaining over the permanent settlement. During his visit to the White House on 13 February 1997, Netanyahu presented to President Clinton maps prepared by Israeli military experts, and had two military advisers explain how Israel's security concerns dictated the drawing of the maps. Described as 'Allon-plus', these maps represent Netanyahu's strategic visions of what he hoped to achieve in final status talks. The 'Allon-Plus Plan' divides the approximately 40 per cent of the occupied territories that Israel will cede to Palestinian jurisdiction into five isolated enclaves. According to the 'Allon-plus' plan, Netanyahu aimed to conclude a final settlement whilst retaining over 50 per cent of West Bank territory, consisting of Greater Jerusalem and the retention of most of Area C-designated territory. Israel will hand over Area B to complement Area A already concluded, where the majority of the Palestinian population lives. However Israel will retain full control over Area C. The maps do not outline the powers and responsibilities the Palestinians will assume for Area B; this point is subject to further negotiation. The suggestion may be that Israel may offer full sovereignty over Gaza in return for agreement to partial sovereignty in the West Bank.[49] Palestinian officials have rejected the Netanyahu proposals outright, clinging to their hopes of unofficial promises made them by former PM Peres, which envisaged the return of some 90 per cent of the West Bank. Netanyahu's intention to publicize his intentions may be analysed as playing to Israeli domestic, and to international opinion, rather than attempting to recruit the Palestinians, in order to emphasize the difference between the Likud and Labour, and to impress that only Netanyahu's Likud is capable of delivering a settlement which is acceptable to a sceptical Israeli public. This is rather ironic in that, even by outlining the 'Allon-plus' agenda, Likud was adopting the more pragmatic approach to an Israeli-Palestinian political settlement which has traditionally been the preserve of Labour. Indeed even the name of the plan endorsed the 1970s Labour vision of an Israeli-Palestinian compromise, which died when Likud came to power in 1977. As each party has worked to neutralize the peace policies of the other, Netanyahu's acceptance of the Oslo accords may be deemed to be an abandonment of an absolutist programme in favour of a tactical and pragmatic minimalist position, in order to minimize the ideological damage of the DoP – in essence 'Allon-plus means Oslo-minus'.[50] A *Ha'Aretz* editorial argued that this new plan amounted to a repudiation of the Likud's Greater Israel ideology and an acceptance of 'the principle of "Land for Peace" and is working within the framework of Oslo.'[51] However, for the Palestinians, this plan represented the more likely scenario that Israel's political establishment would move more closely together in favour of such a settlement and that sharp ideological differences would dissipate, meaning that the Palestinians would face a more united and determined negotiating partner, domestically strengthened with a less divisive vision of the future. This was all the more likely following the election of Ehud Barak, portrayed as tough on security issues, as Labour party leader on 3 June 1997. The national security-conscious Barak was the only Labour cabinet minister to refrain from voting for the Oslo accords,[52] and he openly admitted on 20 July 1997 that Arafat and the Palestinians represented number three on his list of priorities of regional relations, behind Egypt and Jordan.[53]

On 15 July 1997 a UN Special General Assembly session met to consider Israel's settlement policy. By a vote of 131 to three (Israel, US and Micronesia) the UN increased the pressure of its 'Emergency' session of 25 April 1997, when 134 voted for a resolution that condemned settlement activity as illegal and a hindrance to the peace process. The 25 April binding resolution confirmed the applicability of the Geneva Convention to the occupied territories, reaffirmed the applicability of international law there and demanded that member states comply in the 'cessation of all forms of assistance and support for illegal Israeli activities in the Occupied Palestinian Territory, including Jerusalem, in particular settlement activities'.[54] The 15 July resolution represents the General Assembly's displeasure with Israel's refusal to cooperate with the Secretary-General's special representative, following the representative's report on administrative harassment of Palestinians in East Jerusalem. The resolution also expanded from the 25 April resolution's focus on settlement activity, to call upon Israel to reverse all its illegal actions against

East Jerusalem residents. The resolution further called on member states to halt any support for Israeli settlements by companies or individuals, and asked for a ban on the import of any goods produced in settlements including in Jerusalem. The resolution asked the Secretary-General to host a conference of the High Contracting Parties of the Geneva Convention on the Protection of Civilians on how to enforce the convention. This UN resolution represents an incremental approach consisting of a framework of collective measures, in a continuation from previous actions which allows for further action in the future. With even the EU member states voting in favour of the resolution, Israel and the US found themselves in isolation. However the Israeli political establishment indignantly rejected the resolution and cast 'slurs on the motivation of the world community for harbouring such sentiments' by claiming the UN was 'ignoring wars and suffering, to preoccupy itself with two or three bulldozers preparing housing for young couples'. Israel's leaders preferred to hide behind the immunity offered by the US's continued support at the UN rather than reflect on the reason for the erosion of Israel's international standing.[55]

Thus any signs of US-Israel strains must not be overemphasized. The US still maintains a staunch commitment to Israel in deflecting criticism and calls for international condemnation, particularly at the UN. Immediately prior to the Mahane Yehuda market suicide bombing of 30 July 1997 the US administration attempted to engage both sides in secret negotiations in order to finesse a deal, with President Clinton involving Thomas Pickering, Under Secretary of State for Political Affairs and number three at the State Department, in a meeting with Saeb Erekat and Uzi Arad in Washington in mid-July 1997.[56] However the US was unable to concoct a formula which was mutually favourable. Whilst appearing to be somewhat vague on possible progress in the peace process, and being seen as adopting a rather strong pro-Israel bias, the US has assiduously guarded its position as principal international broker ensuring neither the UN nor the EU has a meaningful political role within the process. US initiatives have been deemed by some critics as amounting to little more than 'interference to contain the situation whenever the Palestinian territories seem to be on the verge of an explosion'.[57]

This situation ensured that Arafat was left internationally isolated and facing mounting domestic discontent. Arafat was reported to have decided that the peace process would remain frozen until new Israeli elections, after having concluded that he could expect no effective support from the Americans, the Europeans or the Arab world, in pressing Israel to abide by its obligations and commitments. Arafat's position was precarious and at times contradictory. On the one hand he had to avoid sacrificing further concessions and internal discontent, whilst on the other he must survive intact until a new Israeli government could be elected. Arafat cannot defend his domestic position without being seen to be embarking on a path of confrontation with the Israelis and the US, but such a confrontation may well bring his downfall as his position is so dependent on Israeli and American acceptance. Arafat's dilemma is that he may be seen to be encouraging and leading Palestinian resistance whilst appearing to be clamping down on violent Palestinian agitators for Israel's benefit. If Arafat disappoints an increasingly disillusioned Palestinian public, he will pave the way for Islamist, Jordanian, or more likely, an increasingly impatient Fatah leadership to cultivate an alternative leadership. Arafat has traditionally used local Fatah cadres, represented by the Fatah Higher Committee, to assert control over the population and channel mass protests. However, Fatah cadres are responding that Arafat can no longer automatically guarantee his command of the Fatah masses whilst corruption within his administration persists and no substantive gains are made in the peace process. Prior to the Mahane Yehuda bombing, Arafat was engaged in an initiative to restore credibility to the flagging peace process. Saeb Erekat was dispatched to Washington where he announced that the US was preparing a new initiative to calm rising Palestinian discontent. The initiative was based on a 'pause, or temporary freeze, on settlement construction at Jabal Abu Ghneim in return for Palestinian agreement to jump-start the final status negotiations'. In return the PA would be required by the US to show 'resolve to prevent violence'. Such a request for 'a pause' in settlement construction was significant for two reasons. Firstly, the initiative undermined the original Palestinian demand for the Jabal Abu Ghneim project to be cancelled. Secondly, the focus on Jabal Abu Ghneim meant that the more ambitious Israeli plans for annexing 12 500 dunams from five Palestinian villages (Abu Dis, Bethany, A-Tour, Anata and Hizme) for the massive Adumim settlement bloc was surprisingly ignored. The 'new master plan for Ma'ale Adumim is much more dangerous than Jabal Abu Ghneim, because it lays the foundations for Greater Jerusalem' which will split the West Bank into two disconnected parts, and 'it totally ignores the Arab nature of East Jerusalem, and thus isolates the neighborhoods inside Greater

Jerusalem, separating them from each other and from the rest of the West Bank.' On completion of this major annexation, Ma'ale Adumim and Jerusalem will probably be united under one administrative authority, ensuring that territorial continuity and political unity will make it inevitable that the entire area will be allocated to Israel in any final agreement. Rabin announced this Labour plan in 1994, and as long as the lands remained confiscated, they may have been recovered during the interim phase; however, once the lands are annexed, they will no longer be subject to the interim phase, as they will be regarded as relating to Ma'ale Adumim settlement, and therefore being a subject of the final status talks. The PA has remained silent over this issue: indeed, it seems to have already reached a secret understanding with Israel on this matter. The PA's outrage over Jabal Abu Ghneim makes little sense if they are prepared to accept the Ma'ale Adumim annexation, for it effectively precludes a Palestinian political presence in East Jerusalem after final status negotiations. Thus, with the suspected construction of a new Legislative Council building in Abu Dis, it seems that the PA has accepted Abu Dis as their alternative capital, despite denials. In light of this master plan which will prevent geographical continuity of any future Palestinian state and which denies Palestinian access to East Jerusalem as a capital, the PA's outrage over Jabal Abu Ghneim seems like 'an attempt to deflect the people's attention from the PA's abject surrender'.[58]

Regarding the future of the peace process, its forward momentum has been effectively stalled for a long time now. Breakdowns in the continuation of the process, and in mutual cooperation and goodwill had been precipitated by renewed Jewish settlement construction, with media attention focused in particular at Jabal Abu Ghneim (Har Homa). The General Security Service warned Netanyahu that a breakdown in Israeli-Palestinian security cooperation, precipitated by the Jerusalem tunnel incident and the Jabal Abu Ghneim settlement crisis, would mean that Israeli internal security could not be guaranteed without Palestinian aid. PA-Hamas relations oscillated between stability and repression in the wake of the February-March 1996 suicide bombings. The PA was obliged to appear to be fighting Hamas 'terrorism' for the Israelis whilst having to negotiate a *modus operandi* within the Palestinian community. On the one hand, the PA conducted raids against Hamas, such as the successful 14 July 1997 raid on a Bayt Sahur Hamas 'bomb factory', in order to increase its 'red lines' profile with the Israelis in fighting terrorism against Israeli targets, whilst appearing to be sustaining Palestinian nationalist aspirations. However Fatah elements were also involved in anti-Israeli armed attacks, a situation which undermined the logic of a PA-Hamas political divide. Hamas recovered its popularity as repressive Israeli measures bit deep, and the PA appeared as willing Israeli helpers. On 19 July 1997 some 20 000 people took to the streets of Hebron in a pro-Hamas demonstration, and on the political front Hamas made important gains in recent union elections. Hamas seemed to be adopting a wait-and-see posture to the collapsing peace process, but the Mahane Yehuda market suicide bombing of 30 July 1997 and the Ben-Yehuda Street suicide bombing of 4 September 1997 propelled Hamas-style rejectionism and militancy back to centre stage.

The Likud-led government's words and deeds since assuming power did little to inspire confidence in their intentions towards the peace process, such as invigorating the settlement-building programme in the occupied territories and clarifying that it would not concede to Palestinian demands over Jerusalem, nor would it countenance a sovereign Palestinian state. Arafat had few weapons or allies with which to oppose Israeli power and unilateral actions. The US, co-sponsor of the Madrid peace process, technically locked out of involvement in the Israeli-Palestinian peace process by the DoP, had however the moral power and authority, if not the will, to exert pressure on Israel to maintain its good faith with regard to furthering the peace process. However the US was almost negligent in this regard, failing to redress the inequitable nature of the Israeli-Palestinian relationship. President Clinton has been one of the most pro-Israel chief executives of recent times and Congress has displayed hawkishly pro-Israel views, such as enacting the unilateral, and provocative, decision to move the US embassy in Israel from Tel Aviv to Jerusalem, despite international condemnation of such a move in advance of a permanent settlement being concluded.[59] With the Mahane Yehuda market and Ben-Yehuda Street suicide bombings, the entire peace process was postponed, until a more propitious future, though at times it looked more as though it had been abandoned.[60] The Likud-led government took the intransigent stance of demanding security before peace while enacting counter-measures against the Palestinian population which created the conditions for undermining the very security Israel craves. Israel made unreasonable and impossible security demands of Arafat whilst imposing a security clampdown and closure policy which ensured a massive breach of trust between the Palestinians and their leaders, and between the Palestinians and the Israelis. Effectively, Israel wanted Arafat to crush his own people without regard to due process of legal norms and observance of basic human rights. The peace process is now worsening peoples lives, not improving them. Israeli-Palestinian political terrorism and acts of appalling violence are a 'ghastly memorial to political blindness'.[61] Violence and terrorism are the inevitable consequences of failed political policies. Peace 'has proved an illusion, largely because, since June 1996, security has been seen as its essential precondition rather than its consequence.'[62] Yet, 'irony of ironies', it was the Netanyahu government which drew the immediate benefits from the Mahane Yehuda bombing, because it needed to 'make no disgraceful concessions to the Palestinians', but instead could harden its own demands, knowing that Arafat could not 'resist the damage to his own position', and it knew that the US had, 'once more, been forced into line' by having to condemn terrorist action. Therefore concessions from Israel, perhaps the only way to revive the peace process, could no longer be required, for countering terrorism must always be the 'greater imperative' than the pursuit of peace.[63]

Yossi Beilin, quoted in the Jerusalem daily *Kol Ha'ir*, reviewed the Israeli-Palestinian peace process following the 1996 Israeli election, thus:

What is Oslo? Oslo amounts to the separation of the intermediate arrangement from the permanent one. For many years the Palestinians said, 'We'll agree to the intermediate stage, on condition that we know in advance what the final result will be. Otherwise you will bog us down in the intermediate.... The Palestinians held to this position until, as a result of weakness ... they finally agreed to what they had always refused before. The result is Oslo. That's all it amounts to. Apart from mutual recognition and so on, it boils down to a separation between the intermediate and the permanent arrangements. And look what's happened. Here's the Likud back in power, and they can tell Arafat,

  'Sorry, that all you get. Yes the intermediate arrangements we'll keep. Anything beyond that is Disneyland. Such is our opinion. What's yours? You want a Palestinian state with Jerusalem as its capital? Fine! Let's sit down and talk for two hundred years'. It's the Shamir system. No preconditions![64]

Thus, if the Israeli-Palestinian DoP was intended to achieve a state in which conflicting parties agree to cease all politically motivated and national-goal oriented hostile acts toward one another, and contract to coexist benignly, with mutual respect, refrain from malevolent acts aimed at the disruption of the internal affairs to the detriment of the other party in the pursuit of national-goals, and allow for the free movement of peoples, goods, services and ideas, within an agreed institutional framework based on justice and respect for human rights, as a means of conflict resolution, then as yet the diagnosis must be in the negative, and the prognosis for achieving such a state is not good.

Writing on the peace process during the term of a Likud-led Israeli administration it is somewhat difficult not to feel pessimistic as regards the long-term health of the Israeli-Palestinian peace process. However, in order that a negative interpretation should not offer too many hostages to fortune as regards predicting the future of Israeli-Palestinian relations and the course of international diplomacy, it is incumbent in terms of balance and breadth that a positive caveat be added regarding important sub-themes and alternative developments which surround the Israeli-Palestinian peace process. Despite the above-noted deficiencies, the DoP has led to some positive changes in the Israeli-Palestinian relationship, and has resulted in a degree of Palestinian autonomy and the creation of significant Palestinian institutions, a situation which could only be reversed by hostilities. Despite the frustrations of the DoP and its incomplete status, the DoP does at least allow for the future by its very existence, and by providing the option for rejuvenating the peace process under a different Israeli administration. No peace process is set in concrete: there will always remain the possibility that reforms of policy by either party and changes in political circumstances will lead to more fruitful efforts at resolving the Israeli-Palestinian conflict. The Israeli-Palestinian peace process is one of many under the umbrella of the Madrid structure. It is therefore possible that progress in other areas may help stimulate progress in a seemingly stalled Israeli-Palestinian process. Furthermore, the international diplomatic context will change, bringing with it new diplomatic efforts and new realities to be defined and dealt with. There are many interested parties to the Israeli-Palestinian peace process who may take a greater interest and more participative position with regard to making constructive and effective contributions than they have to date, such as the European Union and the Arab states. It is in this context that one cannot discount the possibility of alternative developments and of new peace efforts reviving and creatively influencing the Israeli-Palestinian relationship and the wider Middle East peace process. After all, Norway's key role in brokering the Oslo accords was instrumental yet a complete surprise to many analysts. In the final analysis, the DoP offers the only pragmatic and peaceful alternative to violence for Israeli-Palestinian relations.

Notes

Introduction

1 K.N. Waltz, *Man, the State and War: a Theoretical Analysis* (NY: Columbia University Press, 1959); W. Levi, 'On the Causes of War and the Conditions of Peace', *Journal of Conflict Resolution IV* (Dec. 1960).

2 Conflict resolution as an academic discipline was stimulated by various movements, synthesizing the study of industrial relations, mediation and two-track international diplomacy, peacemaking, alternative dispute resolution, and interpersonal and intercultural disputes practices, particularly in the US, and has developed since the 1950s, defined as a multi- and inter-disciplinary field grounded in Western culture and socio-economic traditions. For further reading see: R. Blake, H. Shepard and J. Moulton, *Managing Intergroup Conflict in Industry* (Houston TX: Gulf, 1964); J. Burton, *Conflict and Communication: the Use of Controlled Communication in International Relations* (London: Macmillan, 1969); I.W. Zartman, *The Negotiation Process* (Beverly Hills CA: Sage Press, 1978); H. Saunders, 'An Israeli-Palestinian Peace', *Foreign Affairs,* 61 no. 1 (Fall 1982); A. Curle, *Making Peace* (London: Tavistock, 1971).

3 S.H. Rolef (ed.), *Political Dictionary of the State of Israel* (Jerusalem: The Jerusalem Publishing House, 1993), p. 60.

4 W. Levi, 'On the Causes of War and the Conditions of Peace,' *Journal of Conflict Resolution IV* (Dec. 1960), p. 415.

5 W. Khalidi, 'The Palestine Problem: an Overview', *Journal of Palestine Studies*, Vol. XXI, No. 1 (1991), pp. 5–6.

6 Professor Y. Liebowitz, quoted in the *Independent*, 03/04/92, p. 16. (NB Dates are given in the English abbreviated form: 03/04/92 signifies 3 April 1992.)

7 E. Haetzni, quoted in the *Independent*, 26/01/91.

8 Stegner, 'Psychology of Conflict of Human Beings' in E. McNeil (ed.), *The Nature of Human Conflict* (Englewood Cliffs, NJ: Prentice Hall, 1965), p. 51.

9 Erickson quoted in L. Branson/G. Goethals (eds), *War: Studies from Psychology, Sociology and Anthropology* (New York: Basic Books, 1964), p. 128.

10 E. Said, *The Question of Palestine* (New York: Vintage, 1980), p. 10.

11 Ibid.

12 A. Frangi, *The PLO and Palestine* (London: Zed Books, 1983), p. 15.

13 Golda Meir, quoted in the *Sunday Times*, 15/06/69.

14 I. Deutscher, *The Non-Jewish Jew and Other Essays* (Oxford: OUP, 1968), pp. 136–7.

15 Y. Harkabi, *Israel's Fateful Hour* (New York: Harper and Row, 1988), p. 78.

16 A. Cowell, quoted in G. Leach, *The Africaners: Their Last Great Trek* (London: Routledge, 1989), p. xi.

17   Eretz Yisrael Hashlemah, 'the Integral Land of Israel', refers to the indivisibility of Eretz Yisrael including the territories west of the Jordan River in Israeli hands since 1967. Many in Israel object to the translation, 'Greater Israel', because of the obvious Nazi Germany connotation. S.H. Rolef (ed.), *Political Dictionary of the State of Israel* (Jerusalem: Jerusalem Publishing House, 1993), p. 133.
18   Ministry of Foreign Affairs, *'Declaration of Principles on Interim Self-Government Arrangements'* (Jerusalem, 1993), p. 21. Article I, 'Aim of the Negotiations', ibid, p. 21.

Chapter 1

1   *The Holy Bible* (Revised Standard Version) (Glasgow, Collins, 1971), p. 765.
2   Ministry of Foreign Affairs, *Declaration of Principles on Interim Self-Government Arrangements* (Jerusalem, 1993), p. 21.
3   Y. Bar-Siman-Tov, 'The Arab-Israeli Conflict: Learning Conflict Resolution', *Journal of Peace Research*, Vol. 31 no. 1 (1994), p. 81. See also: E.E. Azar, P. Jureidini and R. McLaurin, 'Protracted Social Conflict: Theory and Practice in the Middle East', *Journal of Palestine Studies*, Vol. VIII no. 1 (Autumn 1978), pp. 41–60.
4   Y. Bar-Siman-Tov, 'The Arab-Israeli Conflict: Learning Conflict Resolution', *Journal of Peace Research*, Vol. 31 no. 1 (1994), p. 81.
5   Ibid, pp. 87–8.
6   Ibid, p. 90.
7   Ibid, pp. 90–1.
8   Ibid, p. 89.
9   Ministry of Foreign Affairs, *Overview of the Middle East Peace Process-May 1996*, http://www.israel-mfa.gov.il.
10   J.S. Murray, 'Using theory in conflict resolution practice' in D.J. Sandole and H. van der Merwe (eds), *Conflict Resolution Theory and Practice: Integration and Application* (Manchester: Manchester University Press, 1993), p. 228. For further reading see: R. Fisher and W. Ury, *International Mediation: a Working Guide for Practitioners* (Boston: International Peace Academy, 1978), pp. 8–11.
11   J.S. Murray, 'Using theory in conflict resolution practice', p. 228.
12   Ibid, pp. 228–9.
13   Ibid, pp. 228–9.
14   D.J. Sandole, 'Paradigms, theories, and metaphors in conflict and conflict resolution: Coherence or confusion?' in D.J. Sandole and H. van der Merwe (eds), *Conflict Resolution Theory and Practice*, p. 4.
15   K.N. Waltz, *Man, the State, and War: a Theoretical Analysis* (NY: Columbia University Press, 1959), p. 232.
16   For further reading, see M. Deutsch, *The Resolution of Conflict: Constructive and Destructive Processes* (New Haven CT: Yale University Press, 1973).
17   D.J. Sandole, 'Paradigms, Theories and Metaphors', p. 5.
18   Ibid, p. 5.
19   Ibid, p. 6.
20   D.J. Sandole, 'Traditional approaches to conflict management: Short-

term gains vs. long-term costs', *Current Research on Peace and Violence*, Vol. 9 (1986), pp. 119–24.

21 Conflict structure-sources of conflict = conflicts of interest. Primary independent variables – conflicts of interest can maintain division, as shared interests can become starting points for resolution based on common cause. Conflicts of understanding – cognitive differences can exacerbate conflict; however shared visions can lead to shared objectives, thereby lessening conflict. Conflicts of ideologies – often contrasting ideological perspectives are unresolvable through bargaining, indeed the main feature of ideological conflict is its intractability. Differences in ideology and perception add a competitive dimension to conflict, making resolution more difficult to achieve, as competing parties view compromised outcomes with dissatisfaction, seeing such compromise as competing for advantage. Ideological imagery can influence conflict immensely, to the size and/or intensity of conflict. See D. Druckman, 'An analytical research agenda for conflict and conflict resolution' in D.J. Sandole and H. van der Merwe (eds), *Conflict Resolution Theory and Practice: Integration and Application* (Manchester: Manchester University Press, 1993), pp. 25–9. See also: K. Zechmeister and D. Druckman, 'Determinants of resolving a conflict of interest: a simulation of political decision making', *Journal of Conflict Resolution*, Vol. 17 (1973), pp. 63–88; J. Thibaut, 'The development of contractual norms in bargaining: Replication and variation', *Journal of Conflict Resolution*, Vol. 12 (1968), pp. 102–12; R. Axelrod, *Conflict of Interest* (Chicago: Markham, 1970); B. Brehmer and K.R. Hammond, 'Cognitive factors in interpersonal conflict', in D. Druckman (ed.), *Negotiations: Social-Psychological Perspectives* (Beverly Hills CA: Sage Publications, 1977); L. Coser, *The Functions of Social Conflict* (Chicago: Free Press, 1956).

22 The two most prominent conflict processes are bargaining and debate, incorporating factors that influence the amount and rate of concessions made by bargainers, and the roles of behaviour and persuasion in negotiation. In a complex process involving expectations, evaluations, and adjustments, such information-processing aspects of bargaining depend on responsiveness, bargainers being acutely aware of comparisons between their and their opponents' concessions, 'a process referred to as the monitoring function in negotiation.' The evaluation of debating systems and the organizational structures employed within a negotiating process provides an insight to the development of the negotiating process, reflecting the substantive complexity of the resolution process. By adding such burdens and pressures as time, external expectation and restricted information-processing, different interpretations can be inferred from differing implications, affecting the influence on intentions, in distinguishing motives and determining strategy, in turn affecting the paths chosen during negotiations. See D. Druckman, 'An analytical research agenda for conflict and conflict resolution' in D.J. Sandole and H. van der Merwe (eds), *Conflict Resolution Theory and Practice*, p. 30. For further reading see S. Siegel and L.E. Fouraker, *Bargaining and Group Decision Making: Experiments in Bilateral Monopoly*

(Westport, CT: Greenwood, 1977); D. Druckman, 'The influence of the situation in interparty conflict', *Journal of Conflict Resolution*, Vol. 15 (1971), pp. 523–54; C. Walcott, P.T. Hopmann, T.D. King, 'The role of debate in negotiation', in D. Druckman (ed.), *Negotiations*; A. Rapoport, *Fights, Games, and Debates* (Ann Arbor MI: University of Michigan Press, 1960).

23 'By "influences on conflict" we refer to the distinction made between person, role, and situational variables. Of all the issues raised by social psychologists, none is more central to the discipline than the relative importance of these factors as determinants of behaviour. Of all the settings in which this issue has been explored, none is more relevant than negotiation. Negotiators are individuals, they usually represent constituencies, and their behaviour is influenced by the negotiating situation.' Whilst culture is an important influence on behaviour, it cannot be categorically stated that culture is the primary or dominant determinant of conflict behaviour, indeed, cultural imperatives can be 'broad constraints within which a wide range of diplomatic behaviors can occur.' 'Negotiating behaviour is sensitive to circumstances and historical time periods that are themselves shaped by traditions, ideologies, and institutions. Many possibilities exist in any culture; which is chosen depends on the situation. Clues to the motives for particular moves are to be found in the interplay between the enduring (cultural) and changing (situational) aspects of diplomacy.' An added and important concept to keep in mind is the 'boundary role conflict', arising out of the 'competing demands made by one's own and other parties as well as the demands on negotiators made by the multiple constituencies and opponents as these align and realign in the context of shifting coalitions in multilateral conferences.' Situational influences, such as pre-negotiation, communication, tactics, incentives, timetables and structural complexity, on the conflict resolution framework can have major impacts not only on the conflict resolution process but also on the final outcomes. See, D. Druckman, 'An analytical research agenda for conflict and conflict resolution' in D.J. Sandole and H. van der Merwe (eds), *Conflict Resolution Theory and Practice*, pp. 32–5. For further reading see B.M. Bass, 'Effects on the subsequent performance of negotiators of studying issues or planning strategies alone or in groups', *Psychological Monographs*, No. 614 (1966); D. Druckman, 'Boundary role conflict: Negotiation as dual responsiveness', *Journal of Conflict Resolution*, Vol. 21 (1977), pp. 639–62; J. G. Stein (ed.), *Getting to the Table* (Baltimore MD: Johns Hopkins University Press, 1989); J. Rothman, 'A pre-negotiation model: Theory and testing', *Policy Studies*, No. 40, the Leonard Davis Institute for International Relations, Hebrew University of Jerusalem (1990).

24 The contextual influences on conflict can be of major importance, from 'broad systemic influences' to 'more immediate interventions', with differences of cooperation, competition and transformation in the negotiating process decreasing or encouraging bargaining flexibility. Systemic influences interact upon and entwine a negotiating process, relating exchanges between domestic, regional and international pol-

itical issues and events with the negotiating process. It is in this context that the resolution of a complex, protracted conflict depends more significantly on the relationship between the negotiating structure and the behaviour of the participants. See, D. Druckman, 'An analytical research agenda for conflict and conflict resolution' in D.J. Sandole and H. van der Merwe (eds), *Conflict Resolution Theory and Practice*, p. 35. For further reading see, D.G. Pruitt, *Negotiating Behavior* (New York: Academic Press, 1981).

25 For further reading see: J.W. Burton, *Conflict: Resolution and Prevention* (London: Macmillan, 1990); J.W. Burton and F. Dukes, *Conflict: Readings in Management and Resolution* (London: Macmillan, 1990); J.W. Burton and F. Dukes, *Conflict: Practices in Management, Settlement and Resolution* (London: Macmillan, 1990).

26 J.W. Burton, 'Conflict resolution as a political philosophy' in D.J. Sandole and H. van der Merwe (eds), *Conflict Resolution Theory and Practice*, p. 55.

27 Ibid, p. 60.

28 Ibid, p. 64.

29 C.R. Mitchell, 'Problem-solving exercises and theories of conflict resolution', in D.J. Sandole and H. van der Merwe (eds), *Conflict Resolution Theory and Practice*, p. 91.

30 J.V. Montville, 'The healing function in political conflict resolution', in D.J. Sandole and H. van der Merwe (eds), *Conflict Resolution Theory and Practice*, p. 112.

31 Ibid, p. 112.

32 Ibid, p. 113.

33 Ibid, p. 115.

34 Ibid, p. 115.

35 Ibid, p. 115.

36 Ibid, p. 117.

37 Ibid, p. 118.

38 Ibid, p. 118.

39 R. Moses, 'Acknowledgement: the balm of narcissistic hurts', *Austin Riggs Centre Review*, 3, (1990), p. 1.

40 For a discussion of views see R. Fisher (ed.), *International Conflict and Behavioral Science* (New York: Harper and Row, 1969).

41 J.W. Burton, 'Resolution and Conflict', *International Studies Quarterly*, Vol. 16 (Mar. 1972), pp. 9–10.

42 Ibid, pp. 10–11.

43 Ibid, p. 20.

44 R. Fisher and W. Ury, *Getting to Yes: Negotiating Agreement Without Giving In* (New York: Houghton Mifflin, 1981), p. 4.

45 Ibid, pp. 6–14.

46 J.W. McDonald, 'International conference diplomacy: Four principles' in D.J. Sandole and H. van der Merwe (eds), *Conflict Resolution Theory and Practice*, p. 248.

47 Ibid, p. 248.

48 Ibid, p. 249.

49 Ibid, p. 250.

50 Ibid, pp. 250–9.

51 Ibid, p. 259.
52 G.F. Kennan, *American Diplomacy 1900–1950* (Chicago: Chicago University Press, 1957), p. 96.
53 G.F. Kennan, *Russia, the Atom and the West* (New York: Greenwood, 1958), p. 27.
54 G.F. Kennan, *The Cloud of Danger: Current Realities of American Foreign Policy* (Boston: Little, Brown, 1977) p. 34.
55 G.F. Kennan, *Realities of American Foreign Policy* (Princeton NJ: Princeton University Press, 1954), pp. 63–4.
56 H.A. Kissinger, *A World Restored – Europe After Napoleon: the Politics of Conservatism in a Revolutionary Age* (Boston: Houghton Mifflin, 1964), p. 1.
57 Ibid, p. 2.
58 Ibid, p. 1.
59 Ibid, p. 1.
60 Ibid, p. 4.
61 H.A. Kissinger, quoted in W. Isaacson, *Kissinger: a Biography* (London: Faber and Faber, 1992), p. 82.
62 For an assessment of H.A. Kissinger as a policy-maker, see S. Brown, *The Crises of Power: Foreign Policy in the Kissinger Years* (New York: Columbia, 1979).
63 H.A. Kissinger, *White House Years* (Boston: Little, Brown, 1979), p. 55.
64 Ibid, p. 232.
65 'when domestic structures – and the concept of legitimacy on which they are based – differ widely, statesmen can still meet, but their ability to persuade has been reduced for they no longer speak the same language'; 'Domestic Structure and Foreign Policy', in H.A. Kissinger, *American Foreign Policy* (3rd ed.) (New York: Norton, 1977), p. 12.
66 'The Nature of the National Dialogue', Address to the Pacem in Terris III Conference, Washington, October 8, 1973, reprinted in ibid, p. 125.
67 P.W. Dickson, *Kissinger and the Meaning of History* (New York: Cambridge University Press, 1978), p. 20.
68 H.C. Kelman, 'International Relations: Psychological Aspects', *International Encyclopaedia of the Social Sciences*, Vol. VIII (NY, 1968), p. 76.
69 G.F. Kennan, *Realities of American Foreign Policy* (Princeton NJ: Princeton University Press, 1954), p. 48.
70 W.T. Fox, 'The Causes of Peace and the Conditions of War', the *Annals (How Wars End)*, 392 (Nov. 1970), pp. 2–3.
71 Ibid, p. 8.
72 Ibid, p. 9.
73 Ibid, p. 11.
74 R. Smoke, *War: Controlling Escalation* (Cambridge, MA: Harvard University Press, 1977), pp. 30–5.
75 For a more detailed explanation of the action-reaction cycle, see ibid, pp. 241–5.
76 Ibid, p. 294–5.
77 'One of the ways in which escalation gets out of control – one that is not always apparent – is a seemingly careful step that activates some nation's previously latent motive or interest.' R. Smoke, *War: Controlling Escalation*, p. 235.

78 O.J. Lissitzyn, 'International Law in a Divided World', *International Conflict*, 542 (Mar. 1963), p. 68.
79 For a discussion on the concepts of war in international law, see: R. Falk, *Legal Order in a Violent World* (Princeton, NJ: Princeton University Press, 1968); K. Knorr and S. Verba (eds), *The International System* (Princeton, NJ: Princeton University Press, 1961); G. Schwarzenberger, *International Law and Order* (London: Oceana Publications, 1971).
80 T.C. Schelling, *The Strategy of Conflict* (Cambridge, MA: Harvard University Press, 1963), p. 15.
81 For further reading see: subjective portrayals – B. Silverstein and K. Flamenbaum, 'Biases in the perception and cognition of actions of enemies', *Journal of Social Issues*, Vol. 45 no. 2 (1989), pp. 51–72; distortions/misperceptions – S.M. Burn and S. Oskamp, 'In-group biases and the US-Soviet conflict', *Journal of Social Issues*, Vol. 45 no. 2 (1989), pp. 73–89; G.N. Sande, G.R. Goethals, L. Ferrari and L. Worth, 'Value-guided attribution: Maintaining the moral self-image and the diabolical enemy-image', *Journal of Social Issues*, Vol. 45 (1989), pp. 51–72; R. Jervis, *Perception and Misperception in International Politics* (Princeton, NJ: Princeton University Press, 1976).
82 N.N. Rouhana and S.T. Fiske, 'Perception of Power, Threat, and Conflict Intensity in Asymmetric Intergroup Conflict-Arab and Jewish Citizens of Israel', *Journal of Conflict Resolution*, Vol. 39 no. 1 (Mar. 1995), pp. 50–1.
83 Ibid.
84 Issac defines social power as 'the capacities to act possessed by social agents in virtue of the enduring relations in which they participate.' J.C. Isaac, 'Beyond the Three Faces of Power: a Realist Critique' in T.E. Wartenberg (ed.), *Rethinking Power* (Albany NY: SUNY Press, 1992), p. 47. Gidden's definition of power is the capability to secure outcomes where the realisation of these outcomes depends on the agency of others. A. Giddens, *Central Problems of Social Theory* (Berkeley CA: University of California Press, 1979), p. 93. Both definitions emphasize the relations of interdependence, which makes the distinction between 'power over' and 'power to'. Similarly Rorty argues that power is both relational and marginal in the sense that whatever group is empowered always and only has power relative to someone else's lack of power and to someone else's complicit cooperation. The attribution of power is typically the attribution of marginal power, 'more power than Y, or even power over Y, to bring it about that he does something.' But even that is not enough, because unless we specify what kind of action is in question – to bring about what – the attribution of power is empty. A.O. Rorty, 'Power and Powers: a Dialogue between Buff and Rebuff' in T. E. Wartenberg (ed.), *Rethinking Power*, p. 6.
85 See J.Z. Rubin and B.R. Brown, *The Social Psychology of Bargaining and Negotiation* (New York: Academic Press, 1975).
86 See B.H. Raven and J.Z. Rubin, *Social Psychology* (New York: Wiley, 1983); and B.H. Raven, 'Political Applications of the Psychology of Interpersonal Influence and Social Power', *Political Psychology*, Vol. 11 no. 3 (1990), pp. 493–520.

87 See: H.H. Kelley and J.W. Thibaut, *Interpersonal Relations: a Theory of Interdependence* (New York: Wiley-Interscience, 1978); L.D. Molm, 'Punishment and Power: a Balancing Process in Power-Dependence Relations', *American Journal of Sociology*, Vol. 96 no. 6 (1989), pp. 1392–418.

88 N.N. Rouhana and S.T. Fiske, 'Perception of Power', pp. 50–74.

89 Ibid.

90 Ibid.

91 Ibid.

92 Ibid.

93 Ibid.

94 Ibid.

95 Ibid.

96 K. Avruch and P.W. Black, 'Conflict Resolution in Intercultural Settings: Problems and Prospects' in D.J. Sandole and H. van der Merwe (eds), *Conflict Resolution Theory and Practice*, p. 140.

97 R. Cohen, *Culture and Conflict in Egyptian-Israeli Relations* (Bloomington IA: University of Indiana Press, 1990), p. 7.

98 J.F. Hamill, *Ethno-Logic: the Anthropology of Human Reasoning* (Urbana IL: University of Illinois Press, 1990), p. 104.

99 For a fuller discussion see, E.A. Nakhleh, 'The Arab world after the Gulf War: Challenges and Prospects' in E. Boulding (ed.) *Building Peace in the Middle East: Challenges for States and Civil Society* (Boulder, CO: Westview Press, 1994), pp. 111–20.

100 Conversations with the author, in Jerusalem, Cairo, Luxor, Aswan, Hurghada, Dahab, Eilat, between 02/08/90–21/08/90.

101 S. Shaker, 'Development and Islamic Values' in E. Boulding (ed.) *Building Peace in the Middle East*, p. 237.

102 For further reading, see L. Rosen, *Bargaining Reality: the Construction of Social Relations in a Muslim Community* (Chicago: University of Chicago Press, 1984).

103 S. Osseiran, 'The Democratization Process in the Arab-Islamic States of the Middle East' in E. Boulding (ed.) *Building Peace in the Middle East*, pp. 79–90.

104 S. Shaker, 'Development and Islamic Values', pp. 238–240. See also: M. Boisard, *Humanism in Islam* (New York: Amer Trust Pubs, 1973); F. Mernissi, *La Peur-modernité: Conflit Islam démocratie* trans. M.J. Lakeland (Reading, MA: Addison Wesley, 1992).

105 C. Amjad-Ali, 'Democratization in the Middle East from an Islamic Perspective' in E. Boulding (ed.) *Building Peace in the Middle East*, pp. 69–77. See also A. Lijphart, *Democracy in Plural Societies: a Comparative Exploration* (New Haven CT: Yale University Press, 1977).

106 C. Satha-Anand, 'Core Values for Peacemaking in Islam: the Prophet's Practice as Paradigm' in E. Boulding (ed.) *Building Peace in the Middle East*, p. 295.

107 B. Lewis, *The Political Language of Islam* (Chicago: University of Chicago Press, 1991), pp. 78–9.

108 C. Satha-Anand, 'Core Values', pp. 295–302.

109 J. Galtung, 'Three Approaches to Peace: Peacekeeping, Peacemaking and Peacebuilding' in J. Galtung, *Peace, War and Defence*, p. 302.

110 B. Woodward, 'Nonviolent Struggle, Nonviolent Defence and Nonviolent Peacemaking' in C.M. Stephenson (ed.), *Alternative Methods for International Security* (Washington DC: University Press of America, 1991), p. 141.
111 Ibid, p. 148.
112 *The Glorious Koran*, trans. A. Yusif Ali (1977) VIII:39, quoted in C. Satha-Anand, 'Core Values', p. 300.
113 R. Falk, 'World Order Conceptions and the Peace Process' in E. Boulding (ed.) *Building Peace in the Middle East*, p. 189. See also: R. Falk, 'Theory, Realism, and World Security' in M.T. Klare and D.C. Thomas (eds), *World Security: Trends and Challenges at Century's End* (New York: St Martin's Press, 1991), pp. 6–24.
114 R. Falk, 'World Order Conceptions and the Peace Process', pp. 190–5.
115 Ibid.
116 Ibid.
117 Ibid.
118 Ibid.
119 See, N. Chomsky, *World Orders: Old and New* (London: Pluto Press, 1994), pp. 4–8.
120 See *The Challenge to the South*, Report of the South Commission (Oxford, 1990).
121 The *Guardian*, 23/03/92.
122 N. Chomsky, *World Orders*, p. 5.
123 W. Churchill, *The Second World War*, Vol. 5 (London: Houghton Mifflin, 1951), p. 382.
124 *New York Times*, 29/01/91.
125 Week in Review, *New York Times*, 02/06/92.
126 N. Chomsky, *World Orders*, p. 271.
127 President Bush said in January 1991 that the US was 'the only nation on this earth that could assemble the forces of peace. This is the burden of leadership.' Quoted in the *Guardian*, 30/01/91, p. 1.
128 President Bush in a speech before Congress, 11/09/90, quoted in *The Economist*, 15/09/90, p. 43.
129 L. Voronkov, 'International Peace and Security: New Challenges to the UN' in D. Bourantonis and J. Weiner (eds), *The UN in the New World Order* (New York: St Martin's Press, 1995), p. 1.
130 'The First Days of Euphoria', the *Guardian*, 25/02/91, p. 22.
131 J. Weiner, 'Leadership, the UN, and the New World Order' in D. Bourantonis and J. Weiner (eds), *The UN in the New World Order*, p. 41.
132 See, J. Nye, *Bound to Lead: the Changing Nature of American Power* (New York: Basic Books, 1991).
133 'When Cold Warriors Quit', *The Economist*, 08/02/92, p. 15.
134 J. Weiner, 'Leadership, the UN, and the New World Order', pp. 41, 42.
135 J. MacGregor-Burns, *Leadership* (New York: Harper and Row, 1978), p. 2.
136 J. Weiner, 'Leadership, the UN, and the New World Order', p. 42.
137 Ibid, pp. 42–3.
138 See: G. Modelski, 'Long Cycles in World Leadership', in W.R. Thompson (ed.), *Contending Approaches to World Systems Analysis* (Beverly Hills CA: Sage Press, 1983), p. 138; G. Modelski, *Long Cycles in World Politics*

(London: University of Washington Press, 1987), p. 17. See also
J. Weiner, 'Leadership, the UN, and the New World Order', p. 43.

139   Ibid, p. 44.
140   J. MacGregor-Burns, *Leadership* (New York: Harper and Row, 1978),
        p. 19.
141   O. Young, 'Political Leadership and Regime Formation: on the Devel-
        opment of Institutions in International Society', *International Organisation*,
        Vol. 45 no. 3 (1991), p. 288.
142   R. Keohane, *After Hegemony: Cooperation and Discord in the World Po-
        litical Economy* (Princeton NJ: Princeton University Press, 1984), pp.
        32–3; R. Gilpin, *The Political Economy of International Relations* (Princeton
        NJ: Princeton University Press, 1987), p. 76.
143   C. Kindleberger, *The World in Depression 1929–1939* (Berkeley: Univer-
        sity of California Press, 1973), pp. 28/305.
144   D. Snidal, 'The Limits of Hegemonic Stability Theory', *International
        Organisation*, Vol. 39 no. 4 (1985), pp. 579–614.
145   J. Weiner, 'Leadership, the UN, and the New World Order', p. 47.
146   Ruggie, 'International Regimes, Transactions and Change' in Krasner
        (ed.), *International Regimes* (Ithaca NY, 1983), p. 196.
147   J.S. Mill, *On Liberty* (London: Hackett Publishers, 1974), p. 68.
148   J. Weiner, 'Leadership . . .', p. 50.
149   US Secretary of State, G. Shulz, 'The UN after 40 Years: Idealism and
        Realism', *State Department Bulletin*, 85, 2101 (Aug. 1985), p. 20.
150   J. Weiner, 'Leadership . . .', p. 50.
151   H.S. Bienen, 'America: the Firsters, the Decliners, and the Searchers
        for a New American Foreign Policy', in R. Leaver and J.L. Richardson
        (eds), *The Post-Cold War Order: Diagnoses and Prognoses* (Australia: Paul
        and Co., 1993), p. 160.
152   'Defining the National Interest: a Process of Trial and Error', *Congres-
        sional Quarterly*, 26/03/94, pp. 750–4.
153   See H.R. Nau, *The Myth of America's Decline: Leading the World Economy
        into the 1990s* (New York: Oxford University Press, 1990).
154   'The Reluctant Sheriff', *The Economist*, 09/06/93, p. 13.
155   E.H. Carr, *The Twenty Years' Crisis* (London: Macmillan, 1939), p. 289.
156   J. Weiner, 'Leadership . . .', p. 53.
157   Senator R. Dole (R-KS) quoted in the *Guardian*, 25/09/93.
158   'Foreign Policy: Is Congress Still Keeping Watch?', *Congressional Quar-
        terly*, 21/08/93, pp. 2267–9.
159   See R.M. Nixon, *Beyond Peace* (New York: Random House, 1994).
160   Clinton/Gore National Security Position Paper, Internet Gopher: go-
        pher marvel.loc.gov, Clinton-speeches.src.
161   S. Zunes, 'The Roots of US Middle East Policy and the Need for Alter-
        natives' in E. Boulding (ed.) *Building Peace in the Middle East*, p. 181.
162   Ibid.
163   Ibid, pp. 180–1.
164   Ibid, pp. 180–1.
165   A.F.K. Organski, *Thirty-Five Billion Dollar Bargain Strategy and Politics in
        US Assistance to Israel* (New York: Columbia University Press, 1990), p. 28.
166   Former IDF Major-General Peled interviewed in S. Zunes, 'The Roots
        of US Middle East Policy', p. 181.

167 I. Leibowitz, quoted in ibid, pp. 180–1.

168 Ibid.

169 Y. Shamir, *Summing up: an Autobiography* (London: Weidenfeld and Nicholson, 1994), pp. 193–4.

170 S. Zunes, 'The Roots of US Middle East Policy', p. 179.

171 H. Kissinger, *Years of Upheaval* (Boston: Little, Brown, 1982), p. 621.

172 S. Zunes, 'The Roots of US Middle East Policy', pp. 183–184.

173 Ibid.

174 For further discussion, see: B. Reich, 'The US and Israel: the Nature of a Special Relationship' in D. Lesch (ed.), *The Middle East and the US: a Historical and Political Reassessment* (Boulder CO: Westview Press, 1996), pp. 233–48; V. Seward, *The Middle East: Internal and External Responses to Change* (London: HMSO, 1993); S.A. Ambrose, *Rise to Globalism* 7th edn. (Harmondsworth: Penguin, 1993).

175 E. Watkins, 'The Unfolding US Policy in the Middle East', *International Affairs*, Vol. 73 no. 1 (January 1997), p. 1.

176 For further discussion, see: Y. Y. Haddad, 'Islamist Perceptions of US Policy in the Middle East' in D. Lesch (ed.), *The Middle East and the US: a Historical and Political Reassessment* (Boulder CO, 1996), pp. 419–37.

177 Since the 1970s, the US has become a net oil importer, and when combined with a projected increase in global demand for oil, particularly from Asia, the consequences for the US-Middle East relationship are important, see 'Middle East Oil – US dependence Grows and Prices are Stable' in *APS Review of Oil Market Trends*, 29/07/96; P. Crow, 'Rising Tide of US Imports Sparks Debate on Energy Security', *Oil and Gas Journal Predicasts PROMT*, 17/06/96.

178 See, 'Middle East Policy: Losing its Balance? Reluctance to Criticise Israel Raises Issue of "Honest Broker"', *International Herald Tribune*, 06/05/96.

179 'Arabs must . . . take warning against over-dependence on the US, especially when its leaders show no respect for principles', *Gulf News* quoted in B. May 'Saudi withholds support for US raids on Iraq', *Reuters*, 04/09/96.

180 R. Fisk, 'Interview with Osama Bin Laden – Why We Reject the West', *Independent*, 10/07/96.

181 Y.Y. Haddad, 'Islamist Perceptions of US Policy', pp. 419–37.

182 I. Kant, *Kant's Political Writings*, 2nd ed. (Cambridge: Cambridge University Press, 1991[1795])

183 M. Doyle, 'Liberalism and World Politics', *American Political Science Review*, Vol. 80 no. 4 (Dec. 1988), p. 1161.

184 J.R. ONeal, F.H. ONeal, Z. Maoz and B. Russett, 'The Liberal Peace: Interdependence, Democracy, and International Conflict, 1950–85', *Journal of Peace Research*, Vol. 33 no. 1 (1996), p. 12.

185 For further reading see: W.K. Domke, *War and the Changing Global System* (New Haven CT: Yale University Press, 1988), pp. 43–51.

186 K.N. Waltz, 'Kant, Liberalism, and War', *American Political Science Review*, Vol. 56 no. 2 (Jun. 1962), p. 333.

187 See, W.J. Dixon, 'Democracy and the Management of International Conflict', *Journal of Conflict Resolution*, Vol. 37 no. 1 (Mar. 1993), pp. 42–68; W.J. Dixon, 'Democracy and the Peaceful Settlement of

International Conflict', *American Political Science Review*, vol. 88 no. 1 (Mar. 1994), pp. 14–32; T.C. Morgan and S.H. Campbell, 'Domestic Structure, Decisional Constraints and War: So Why Kant Democracies Fight?', *Journal of Conflict Resolution*, Vol. 35 no. 2 (Jun. 191), pp. 187–211; T.C. Morgan and V.L. Schwebach, 'Take Two Democracies and Call Me in the Morning: a Prescription for Peace?', *International Interactions*, Vol. 17 no. 4 (May 1992), pp. 305–20; Z. Maoz and B. Russett, 'Normative and Structural Causes of Democratic Peace, 1946–1986', *American Political Science Review*, Vol. 87 no. 3 (Apr. 1993), pp. 624–38.

188   For further reading, for a functionalist perspective, see D. Mitrany, *A Working Peace System* (Chicago: Quadrangle, 1964); and for a pluralist perspective, K.W. Deutsch, S.A. Burrell, R.A. Kann, M. Lee, M. Lichterman, R.E. Lindgren, F.L. Loewenheim and R. Van Wagenen, *Political Community and the North Atlantic Area* (Princeton NJ: Princeton University Press, 1957).

189   W.K. Domke, *War and the Changing Global System* (New Haven CT: Yale University Press, 1988), p. 46; C. Pentland, *International Theory and European Integration* (NY: Free Press, 1973), p. 81; B. Russett, *Grasping the Democratic Peace, Principles for a Post-Cold War World* (Princeton NJ: Princeton University Press, 1993).

190   M. Gasiorowski and S.W. Polachek, 'Conflict and Interdependence: East-West Trade and Linkages in the Era of Detente', *Journal of Conflict Resolution*, Vol. 26 no. 4 (Dec. 1982), pp. 709–29; J.A. Kroll, 'The Complexities of Interdependence', *International Studies Quarterly*, Vol. 37 no. 2 (Jun. 1993), pp. 321–48.

191   T. dos Santos, 'The Structure of Dependence', *American Economic Review*, vol. 60 no. 2 (Mar. 1970), pp. 231–6; I. Wallerstein, 'The Rise and Future Demise of the World Capitalist System', *Comparative Studies in Society and History*, Vol. 16 no. 2 (Apr. 1974), pp. 387–415.

192   For a history of the interdependence tradition in political science, see J. de Wilde, *Saved from Oblivion: Interdependence Theory in the First Half of the 20th Century. A Study of the Causality between War and Complex Interdependence* (Aldershot: Dartmouth, 1991). For a review of dependency, see, M. Blomstrom and B. Hettne, *Development Theory in Transition* (London: Zed Books, 1984).

193   For further reading see: B.J. Cohen, *The Question of Imperialism* (New York: Basic Books, 1973); V.I. Lenin, 'Imperialism, the Highest Stage of Capitalism' in *Collected Works*, 47 Vols (Progress Publishers/London: Laurence and Wishart, [1939] 1990).

194   K. Barbieri, 'Economic Interdependence: a Path to Peace or a Source of Interstate Conflict?', *Journal of Peace Research*, Vol. 33 no. 1 (1996), p. 30.

195   For further reading see: S.W. Polachek, 'Conflict and Trade', *Journal of Conflict Resolution*, Vol. 24 no. 1 (Mar. 1980), pp. 57–78; 'Theories of International Integration, Regionalism, Alliance, and Cohesion' in J.E. Dougherty and R. Pfaltzgraff, *Contending Theories of International Relations*, 3rd ed. (New York: HarperCollins, 1990), pp. 431–67; E.B. Haas, *Beyond the Nation-State* (Stanford CA: Stanford University Press, 1964); D. Mitrany, *A Working Peace System* (Chicago: Quadrangle, 1964).

196 For further reading see: T. Balogh, *Unequal Partners, Volume One: the Theoretical Framework* (Oxford: Blackwell, 1963); R.N. Cooper, *The Economic of Interdependence: Economic Policy in the Atlantic Community* (New York: McGraw Hill, 1968); A. Emmanuel, *Unequal Exchange: a Study of the Imperialism of Trade* (New York: Monthly Review Press, 1972); M. Gasiorowski, 'Economic Interdependence and International Conflict: Some Cross-National Evidence', *International Studies Quarterly*, Vol. 30 no. 1 (Mar. 1986), pp. 23–8; A.O. Hirschman, *National Power and the Structure of Foreign Trade* (Berkeley CA: University of California Press, [1945]1980); K.N. Waltz, *Theory of International Politics* (Reading MA: Addison-Wesley, 1979).

197 K. Barbieri, 'Economic Interdependence', pp. 31–3.

198 Ibid.

199 Ibid.

200 Ibid.

201 Ibid.

202 A. Bendana, 'Conflict Resolution: Empowerment and Disempowerment', *Peace and Change*, Vol. 21 no. 1 (Jan. 1996), pp. 68–70.

203 Ibid.

204 Apologies to Chien-Shiung Wu (1913–1997), who overturned the law of symmetry, previously an irrefutable theorem of physics.

205 A. Bendana, 'Conflict Resolution', pp. 72–73.

206 Ibid, pp. 73–4.

207 Ibid, pp. 74–6.

208 Ibid.

209 M. Abu-Nimer, 'Conflict Resolution in an Islamic Context: Some Conceptual Questions', *Peace and Change*, Vol. 21 no. 1 (Jan. 1996), pp. 25–7.

210 Ibid, pp. 29–31.

211 Ibid, pp. 32–6.

212 For further reading see: J. Esposito, *The Islamic Threat: Myth or Reality* (New York: Oxford University Press, 1992); P.H. Gulliver, *Disputes and Negotiation: a Cross Cultural Perspective* (New York: Academic Press, 1979); L. Rosen, *The Anthropology of Justice, Law as Culture in Islamic Society* (New York: Cambridge University Press, 1989); A. Yosuf-Ahmad, *Arab-Arab Conflicts 1945–1981* (Beirut: Center for the Studies of Arab Union, 1988); K. Avruch, P. Black and J. Scimecca (eds), *Conflict Resolution: Cross Cultural Perspectives* (Westport CT: Greenwood Press, 1991).

213 S.E. Ibrahim, 'Future Visions of the Arab Middle East', *Security Dialogue*, Vol. 27 no. 4, p. 425.

214 For further reading, see: D. Fromkin, *A Peace to End all Peace: Creating the Modern Middle East 1914–1922* (London: Penguin, 1989); N. Chomsky, *The Fateful Triangle: the US, Israel and the Palestinians* (London: Pluto Press, 1983); S. Peres, *The New Middle East* (New York: Henry Holt, 1993); E.W. Said, *The Question of Palestine* (Reading: Vintage, 1992); J. Dumbrell, *The Making of US Foreign Policy* (Manchester: Manchester University Press, 1990).

215 S.E. Ibrahim, 'Future Visions', pp. 428–30.

216 For further reading, see: M. E. Selim, *Mediterraneanism: a New Dimension in Egypt's Foreign Policy*, Al-Ahram Strategic Papers, no. 27 (Cairo,

March 1995); M. Harbottle, 'Collective Security Under Subregional Arrangements: a Cooperative Approach' in E. Boulding (ed.), *Building Peace in the Middle East*, pp. 213–21.

217 World Bank, *Claiming the Future: Choosing Prosperity in the Middle East and North Africa* (Washington DC, 1995), pp. 15–31.

218 Egyptian President Mubarak, quoted in S.E. Ibrahim, 'Future Visions', p. 430.

219 Ibid, pp. 430–1.

220 For further reading see: A. Hourani, *A History of the Arab Peoples* (New York: Warner Books, 1991), pp. 353–415; M. Feld, *Inside the Arab World* (London: John Murray, 1994); A. Hourani, P.S. Khoury and M.C. Wilson (eds), *The Modern Middle East* (London: I.B. Tauris, 1993); R. Patai, *The Arab Mind* (New York: Charles Schribner's Sons, 1983); A.R. Norton (ed.), *Civil Society in the Middle East* (Leiden: Brill Academic Publishers, 1995).

221 S.E. Ibrahim, 'Future Visions', pp. 425–8.

222 For further reading, see: S.E. Ibrahim, 'Ethnic Conflicts and State Building in the Arab World' in G. Kemp and J.G. Stein (eds), *Powder Keg in the Middle East* (Washington DC: American Association for the Advancement of Science, 1995), pp. 45–64.

223 S.E. Ibrahim, 'Future Visions', pp. 431–3.

224 Ministry of Foreign Affairs, *DoP*, p. 21.

Chapter 2

1 'Censure acquits the raven, but pursues the dove', Juvenal, *Satires* II. 63 quoted in J.M. and M.J. Cohen, *The New Penguin Dictionary of Quotations* (London: Penguin, 1992), p. 227.

2 S.H. Rolef (ed.), *Political Dictionary of the State of Israel* (Jerusalem: Jerusalem Publishing House, 1993), p. 405.

3 Ibid, pp. 403–4.

4 Ibid, pp. 375–6.

5 O. Massalha, *Towards the Long-Promised Peace* (London: Saqi Books, 1994), p. 27.

6 R. Twite and T. Herman, *The Arab-Israeli Negotiations: Political Positions and Conceptual Framework* (Tel Aviv: Papyrus, 1993), pp. 17–25.

7 Ibid, pp. 19–20.

8 O. Massalha, *Towards the Long-Promised Peace*, p. 25.

9 Ibid, p. 28.

10 *Rapport Annuel Mondial sur le Systeme Economique et les Strategies (Ramses) 92, Le Monde et son Evolution* (Paris, Institut Francais des Relations Internationales [IFRI-Dunod], 1991), p. 131.

11 'To jaw-jaw is always better than to war-war.' Winston S. Churchill, Speech at the White House, 26 October 1954, *New York Times*, 27 October.

12 *Newsweek*, 13/09/93, p. 15.

13 A. Shlaim 'Prelude to the Accord: Likud, Labour, and the Palestinians', *Journal of Palestine Studies (JPS)*, Vol XXIII, no. 2 (Winter 1994), pp. 8–9.

14 S. Roy, 'Separation or Integration: Closure and the Economic Future of the Gaza Strip Revisited', *Middle East Journal*, Vol. 48 (Winter 1994), pp 11–30.

15 See: A. Alawnah, 'The Impact of the Intifada on the Palestinian and Israeli Economies', *New Outlook*, 1990, p. 23; B'tselem, *The System of Taxation in the West Bank and Gaza Strip as an Instrument for the Enforcement of Authority During the Uprising* (Jerusalem: B'tselem, 1990), pp. 7–40; M. Sela, 'By Bread and Olives Alone', *Jerusalem Post*, 17/02/89; for ID cards see *New York Times*, 15/05/88; J. Hiltermann, 'Israel's Strategy to Break the Intifada', *Journal of Palestine Studies*, Vol. XIX No. 2 (Winter 1990), pp. 88–9; see also S. Mishal and R. Aharoni, *Speaking Stones: Communiqués from the Intifada Underground* (Syracuse NY: Syracuse University Press, 1994).

16 Between 12/87 and 12/89, Gulf remittances fell from $250m to $75m p.a. a trend that continued; S. Roy, *Gaza Strip: the Political Economy of De-development* (Washington DC: Institute for Palestine Studies, 1995), p. 295.

17 S. Roy, 'The Political Economy of Despair: Changing Political and Economic Realities in the Gaza Strip', *Journal of Palestine Studies*, Vol XX No. 3 (Spring 1991), p. 61.

18 For example, Palestinians withdrew c.$250 000 from Jordanian banks in 1988 & 1989, J. Stork, 'The Gulf War and the Arab World', *World Policy Journal*, Vol. VIII No. 2 (Spring 1991), p. 369.

19 *Jerusalem Post*, 17/02/89.

20 S. Roy,'From Hardship to Hunger: the Economic Impact of the Intifada on the Gaza Strip', *American-Arab Affairs*, No. 34 (Fall 1990), p. 117.

21 See, S. Roy, *Gaza Strip: the Political Economy of De-development* (Washington DC, 1995).

22 Ibid, p. 304.

23 For conditions during the war see: UNRWA, *Situation of Palestinian Civilians under Israeli Occupation: Gaza Strip, March–May 1991* (Vienna: UNRWA 1991), p. 1. On 16–17/01/91 US-led multinational force began their air offensive against Iraqi forces, *New York Times*, 17/01/91.

24 UNRWA, *The Continuing Emergency in the Occupied Territory and Lebanon and Structural Socio-Economic Problems* (Vienna: UNRWA, 1993), pp. 2–3.

25 F. Collins,'The Rescue of the Palestinian Economy', *Al-Fajr*, 03/06/91. For a fuller discussion see: S. Roy, 'Separation or Integration: Closure and the Economic Future of the Gasa Strip Revisited', *Middle East Journal*, Vol. 48 No. 1 (Winter 1994), pp. 11– 29; B. Bahbah, 'The Economic Consequences on Palestinians', *The Palestinians and the War in the Gulf* (Washington DC: Center for Policy Analysis on Palestine, 1991) pp. 17–21; T. Farer, 'Israel's Unlawful Occupation', *Foreign Policy*, No. 82 (Spring 1991) pp. 37–58; C. Maynes, 'Dateline Washington: a Necessary War?', *Foreign Policy*, No. 82 (Spring 1991) pp. 159–77.

26 See B. Bahbah, 'The Economic Consequences on Palestinians', pp. 17–21.

27 *New York Times*, 15/03/91.

28 *New York Times*, 14/08/90.

29 For a fuller discussion on PLO funding, structure and Palestinian social

and welfare structures, see particularly, K. Nakhleh, *Indigenous Organisations in Palestine: Towards a Purposeful Societal Development* (Jerusalem: Arab Thought Forum, 1991); The Health Development Information Project (in cooperation with WHO), *Infrastructure and Health Services in the West Bank: Guidelines for Health Care Planning – the West Bank Rural PHC Survey* (Ramallah: Health Development Information Project, 1993); G. Ovensen, *Responding to Change: Trends in Palestinian Household Economy* (Oslo: FAFO, 1994); M. Heiberg and G. Ovensen, *Palestinian Society: in Gaza, West Bank and Arab Jerusalem – a Survey of Living Conditions* (Oslo: FAFO, 1993); S. Mussalam, *The PLO: its Function and Structure* (Brattleboro VT: Amana Books, 1990); J. Hiltermann, *Behind the Intifada: Labour and Women's Movements in the Occupied Territories* (Princeton NJ: Princeton University Press, 1991).

30   UNRWA, *The Continuing Emergency in the Occupied Territory and Lebanon*, p. 3.
31   Ibid, p. 6.
32   *Jerusalem Post International Edition*, 16/02/91, p. 24.
33   Ibid, p. 24.
34   Ibid, p. 24.
35   For the PLO's cash crisis, see: *Middle East International*, 05/93/93, 11/06/93, 28/08/93; *The Economist*, 28/09/91; *Glasgow Herald*, 19/07/91; *Le Monde* 25/07/93; *Scotsman* 27/07/93; *Independent*, 16/08/93, 26/08/93, 28/08/93.
36   For Palestinians living in Kuwait see *Middle East International*, 17/08/90, pp. 19–20, 30; 14/09/90, pp. 2, 16, 19; 28/09/90, pp. 8–9, 08/03/91, p. 9; 22/03/91, p. 15; 05/04/91, pp. 7, 21–2.
37   For Palestinian responses to the Iraqi invasion see: *Middle East International*, 17/08/90, 3, 12, 14–5, 19, 24–5, 30–1; 14/09/90, 10, 16; 28/09/90, pp. 8–9, 22; 26/10/90, p. 12; 24/11/90, p. 5; 07/12/90, pp. 6–7; 21/12/90, pp. 3, 17–18; 11/01/91, pp. 15–6; 25/01/91, p. 9; 22/02/91, pp. 9–10; 08/03/91, pp. 17, 21, 05/04/91, pp. 21–2.
38   S.H. Rolef (ed.), *Political Dictionary of the State of Israel*, p. 370.
39   A.A. Said, 'Introduction', in *Mawaqif 2*, (Jan.–Feb. 1969): 3–4.
40   *Middle East International*, 29/05/92, p. 17.
41   *Jerusalem Post*, 04/09/93.
42   *Jerusalem Post*, 17/07/93.
43   S.H. Rolef, *Political Dictionary of the State of Israel*, p. 355.
44   O. Massalha, *Towards the Long-Promised Peace*, p. 91.
45   For profiles on Baker see: J. Newhouse, 'The Tactician', *New Yorker*, 07/05/90, pp. 50–82; M. Dowd and T. Friedman, 'The Fabulous Bush and Baker Boys', *New York Times Magazine*, 06/05/90, pp. 34–67; M. Kramer, 'Playing for the Edge', *Time*, 13/02/89, pp. 26–33.
46   Washington Institute for Near East Policy, Building for Peace: an American Strategy for the Middle East (Washington DC, 1988).
47   J. Broder, 'The Bush League', *Jerusalem Post*, 22/10/92, pp. 16–18.
48   W. Quandt, *Peace Process* (Washington DC: Brookings Institute, 1993), 417f.
49   *New York Times*, 27/12/88.
50   *New York Times*, 27/12/88.
51   N. Chomsky, *Deterring Democracy* (London: Verso Books, 1991), pp. 29–30.

52 N. Chomsky, *World Orders: Old and New* (London: Pluto Press, 1994), p. 190.
53 D. Painter, *Oil and the American Century* (Baltimore MD: Johns Hopkins University Press, 1986), 208f.
54 Editorial, *New York Times*, 31/08/93.
55 See: *Middle East International*, 21/01/89, p. 8; 18/02/89, p. 10; 31/03/89, pp. 5–6; 13/05/89, p. 9; 27/05/89, pp. 6–7.
56 For US-Israeli relations during this period see *Jerusalem Report*, 22/10/92, pp. 16–18
57 For 'Five-Point Framework for an Israeli-Palestinian Dialogue' see *Middle East International*, 03/11/89, pp. 2, 5–7; 17/11/89, pp. 7–8, 10, 16–7; 01/12/89, pp. 16–7; 15/12/89, pp. 4–6.
58 O. Massalha, *Towards the Long-Promised Peace*, pp. 41–42.
59 Palestinians in conversation with the author in the Old City in Jerusalem on 02/08/90.
60 Egyptians in conversation with the author during the marches in the centre of Cairo on 10/08/90.
61 *Al-Ahram*, 11–18/08/90.
62 *Jerusalem Post*, 05/08/90.
63 O. Massalha, 'Pour en Finir avec les Abiguites', *L'Humanité*, 26/03/91, p. 15.
64 *Rapport Annuel Mondial sur le Système Economique et les Strategies (Ramses) 92, Le Monde et son Evolution* (Paris, Institut Francais des Relations Internationales [IFRI-Dunod], 1991), p. 127.
65 O. Massalha, *Towards the Long-Promised Peace*, pp. 44–67.
66 Ibid, p. 44.
67 *Washington Post*, 07/03/91.
68 *Le Monde*, 13/04/91, p. 3.
69 'Proche-Orient: De la Guerre à la Paix?', *Le Monde* (Numero Special, Nov. 1991), p. 108.
70 Reported in *Le Monde*, 01/11/91, p. 4.
71 A. Margalit, 'The Violent life of Yitzhak Shamir', *NY Review of Books*, 14 May 1992, p. 24.
72 D. Makovsky, *Making Peace with the PLO: the Rabin Government's Road to the Oslo Accords* (Boulder CO: Westview Press, 1996), pp. 13–14.
73 Ibid, p. 17.
74 Ibid, p. 17.
75 Ibid, p. 15.
76 Speech by FM Holst on 28/09/93, in *Middle East Insight*, Sept./Oct., 1993.
77 D. Makovsky, *Making Peace with the PLO*, p. 15.
78 Interview, 22/03/95, with J. Alpher, quoted in D. Makovsky, *Making Peace with the PLO*, p. 18.
79 H. Ashrawi, *This Side of Peace* (New York: Simon and Schuster, 1995), p. 220.
80 Interview with Hirschfeld, 20/06/94 quoted in D. Makovsky, *Making Peace with the PLO*, p. 19.
81 J. Corbin, *Gaza First: the Secret Channel to Peace between Israel and the PLO* (London: Bloomsbury, 1994), p. 38.
82 D. Makovsky, *Making Peace with the PLO*, pp. 19–20.

83   J. Corbin, *Gaza First*, p. 46.
84   Ibid, pp. 51–63.
85   Interview with Rabin, 04/1093, quoted in D. Makovsky, *Making Peace with the PLO*, p. 23.
86   Ibid.
87   Ibid.
88   Ibid.
89   See, S. Peres, *Battling for Peace* (London: Random House, 1995).
90   D. Makovsky, *Making Peace with the PLO*, p. 26.
91   *Jerusalem Post*, 11/11/94.
92   D. Makovsky, *Making Peace with the PLO*, p. 29, note 24.
93   *New York Times*, 13/03/94.
94   Interview, 22/06/94, quoted in D. Makovsky, *Making Peace with the PLO*, p. 29, note 23.
95   Ibid, p. 29.
96   J. Corbin, *Gaza First*, p. 62.
97   See, 'The Oslo Agreement: An Interview with Nabil Shaath', *Journal of Palestine Studies*, Vol. XXIII, No. 1 (Autumn 1993), p. 7.
98   D. Makovsky, *Making Peace with the PLO*, p. 32.
99   'I preferred to offer Jericho as a sign of our intent to continue nego-tiations, even if "Gaza First" would be the main policy. There were no Jewish settlements in the immediate Jericho area, therefore there would be no need to discuss their fate. We proposed an administra-tive centre to be set up in Jericho to take pressure off Jerusalem, especially since Jericho is not far from Jerusalem. Its proximity to the Jordan River opened a preferred solution in my eyes for the future, a confed-eration between Jordanians and Palestinians.' S. Peres, *The New Middle East* (New York: Henry Holt, 1993), p. 23.
100 Yigal Allon had been Rabin's mentor. Allon interview, *Davar*, 30/08/94. See also Eban interview, *Yediot Aharanot*, 29/07/94.
101 D. Makovsky, *Making Peace with the PLO*, pp. 34–5.
102 Ibid, p. 37.
103 S. Peres, *Battling For Peace* (London: Random House, 1995), p. 331.
104 Interview with Peres, 18/08/94, quoted in D. Makovsky, *Making Peace with the PLO*, p. 37.
105 Interview with Peres, 31/12/93, quoted in Makovsky, p. 38.
106 Ibid, pp. 36–8.
107 Interview, Haim Ramon, 15/11/93, quoted in Makovsky, p. 39.
108 Ibid, p. 39.
109 Ibid.
110 Ibid, pp. 39–41.
111 Ibid.
112 Sayigh was a PNC member, and Israel refused public contact with PNC members, because of their association as PLO officials.
113 S. Peres, *Battling for Peace*, p. 284.
114 D. Makovsky, *Making Peace with the PLO*, pp. 42–43.
115 Interview, Hirschfeld, 20/06/94; Interview, Larsen, 23/11/93, quoted in Makovsky, p. 42.
116 J. Corbin, *Gaza First*, p. 76.

117 D. Makovsky, *Making Peace with the PLO*, p. 46.

118 Interview with Savir and Qurai, 05/01/94, quoted in Makovsky, p. 47.

119 Ibid.

120 'Savir added an unofficial note calling for Israel to assent to mutual recognition with the PLO, arguing that recognition would lead the PLO to renounce terrorism and temper its other demands.' D. Makovsky, *Making Peace with the PLO*, p. 49.

121 J. Corbin, *Gaza First*, p. 93.

122 Ibid, p. 94.

123 Ibid, p. 100.

124 S. Peres, *Battling for Peace*, p. 330.

125 Interview, 08/12/94, quoted in Makovsky, p. 51.

126 Interview, Singer, 19/06/94, quoted in Makovsky, p. 51.

127 Interview, Rabin, 04/10/93, quoted in Makovsky, p. 51.

128 J. Corbin, *Gaza First*, p. 109.

129 D. Makovsky, *Making Peace with the PLO*, p. 53; J. Corbin, *Gaza First*, pp. 104–5.

130 Makovsky, pp. 53–4.

131 Interview, Singer, 19/06/94, quoted in Makovsky, p. 55.

132 S. Peres, *Battling for Peace*, p. 62.

133 Ibid, p. 339.

134 D. Makovsky, *Making Peace with the PLO*, p. 58.

135 J. Corbin, *Gaza First*, pp. 110–3.

136 Rabin had added demands on security of the settlements; the borders of the areas from which the IDF would withdraw; and the security of Israelis travelling through Palestinian entities. Ibid, p. 115.

137 There were 25 according to Corbin (p. 116); 26 according to Makovsky (p. 59).

138 J. Corbin, *Gaza First*, p. 116.

139 D. Makovsky, *Making Peace with the PLO*, pp. 59–60.

140 J. Corbin, *Gaza First*, p. 117.

141 Interview with Singer, 30/12/94, quoted in Makovsky, pp. 59–60.

142 Interview, Juul, 08/10/94, quoted in Makovsky, p. 61.

143 Interview, Peres, 31/12/93 quoted in Makovsky, pp. 62–3.

144 Ibid, p. 62.

145 Interview, Peres, 19/06/94, quoted in Makovsky, p. 63.

146 J. Corbin, *Gaza First*, p. 136.

147 Ibid, p. 134.

148 D. Makovsky, *Making Peace with the PLO*, p. 64.

149 Ibid, p. 64.

150 Ibid, p. 114.

151 Interview, Peres 31/12/93, quoted in Makovsky, p. 115.

152 Ibid, p. 115.

153 Ibid, p. 115.

154 Interview, Rabin, 04/10/93, quoted in Makovsky, p. 116.

155 Interview, Peres, 31/12/93, quoted in Makovsky, p. 116.

156 S. Peres, *Battling for Peace*, p. 343.

157 H. Ashrawi, *This Side of Peace*, p. 255; pp. 257–9.

158 Interview, Singer, 15/01/95 quoted in Makovsky, p. 66.

159 Interview, Rabin, 04/10/93, quoted in Makovsky, p. 66.
160 Ibid, pp. 66–7.
161 Ibid, p. 67.
162 Interview, Tibi, 22/11/93, quoted in Makovsky, p. 67.
163 Ibid, p. 68.
164 Hirschfeld said the new PLO position paper included 'just two or three' contentious issues relating to security and PLO institutions in Jerusalem, down from the previous month's 26. Interview, Hirschfeld, 22/06/94, quoted in Makovsky, p. 68.
165 Ibid, p. 69.
166 J. Corbin, *Gaza First*, pp. 148–60.
167 D. Makovsky, *Making Peace with the PLO*, p. 71.
168 For the letter's full text see Makovsky, Appendix XIX.
169 Annexe II, Agreed Minutes, Ministry of Foreign Affairs, *Declaration of Principles on Interim Self-Government Arrangements* (*DoP*) (Jerusalem, 1993), p. 37.
170 Ibid, pp. 35–6.
171 See, 'Excerpts from Speeches at the Secret Oslo Signing Ceremony, 20/08/93' in D. Makovsky, *Making Peace with the PLO*, Appendix XV.
172 Savir addressing Conference of Presidents of Major American Jewish Organizations; 27/02/94, quoted in Makovsky, pp. 69–70.
173 Ibid. p. 70.
174 J. Corbin, *Gaza First*, p. 179.
175 Interview, Neriah, 14/06/94, quoted in Makovsky, p. 73.
176 J. Corbin, *Gaza First*, p. 173/p. 197.
177 H. Ashrawi, *This Side of Peace*, p. 261.
178 J. Corbin, *Gaza First*, pp. 172–7.
179 D. Makovsky, *Making Peace with the PLO*, pp. 76–7.
180 Ibid, p. 75.
181 Ministry of Foreign Affairs, *DoP*, p. 21.
182 J. Corbin, *Gaza First*, p. 182.
183 D. Makovsky, *Making Peace with the PLO*, pp. 79–81; and J. Corbin, *Gaza First*, pp. 180–202.
184 Ibid, p. 185. Ministry of Foreign Affairs, *DoP*, p. 38.
185 Rabin's letter stated that Israel recognized 'the PLO as the representative of the Palestinian people'. *DoP*, p. 39.
186 Interview, Singer, 19/06/94, quoted in Makovsky, p. 79.
187 *DoP*, p. 38.
188 Ibid, p. 38. J. Corbin, *Gaza First*, pp. 188–90.
189 *DoP*, p. 40. J. Corbin, *Gaza First*, pp. 189–90.
190 J. Corbin, *Gaza First*, p. 192.
191 *DoP*, p. 40.
192 J. Corbin, *Gaza First*, p. 198; D. Makovsky, *Making Peace with the PLO*, p. 80.
193 *DoP*, p. 21. Also see J. Corbin, *Gaza First*, pp. 200–1.
194 J. Corbin, *Gaza First*, p. 202.
195 S.H. Rolef, *Political Dictionary of the State of Israel*, pp. 309–10. (Political upheaval refers to the change in government in 1977 following the elections to the 9th Knesset.)

196 B. Reich, N. Dropkin and M. Wurmser, 'Soviet Jewish Immigration and the 1992 Israeli Knesset Elections', *Middle East Journal*, 48, no. 2 (Spring 1993), p. 470.

197 L. Hader, 'The 1992 Electoral Earthquake and the Fall of the "Second Israeli Republic",' *Middle East Journal*, 46, no. 4 (Autumn 1992), p. 616.

198 M. Aronoff, *Power and Ritual in the Israel Labour Party* (Armonk NY: M.E. Sharpe, 1993), p. 229.

199 M.J. Aronoff, 'Labor in the Second Rabin Era: the First Year of Leadership' in R.O. Freedman (ed.), *Israel Under Rabin* (Boulder CO: Westview Press, 1995), p. 129.

200 Green Line is Israel's pre-5th June 1967 eastern border delineated in the armistice agreements with Syria and Jordan and its southern border with the Gaza Strip in the armistice agreement with Egypt in the aftermath of the 1948 War of Independence. The border line was coloured green on the original maps drawn up at Rhodes. Only Israel's borders with Lebanon since 1948 and with Egypt since 1982 are referred to as 'International Boundaries'. S.H. Rolef (ed.), *Political Dictionary*, p. 133.

201 Interview with Joseph Harif in *Ma'ariv* 26/06/92, quoted in *Time*, 06/07/92, p. 11.

202 Ibid, p. 14.

203 'PLO Central Council, Statement on the Peace Process, Tunis 10/05/92.', broadcast on 11 May 1992 over Sana'a Voice of Palestine in Arabic, translated in FBIS on 13/05/92.

204 C. Mansour, 'The Palestinian–Israeli Peace Negotiations: an Overview and Assessment', *Journal of Palestine Studies*, Vol. XXII, No. 3 (Spring 1993), p. 18.

205 Institute for Palestine Studies, *The Palestinian-Israeli Peace Agreement: a Documentary Record* (Washington DC: Institute for Palestine Studies, 1993), pp. 27–8.

206 According to IDF statistics, roughly 120 000 Palestinians served time in Israeli prisons and detentions centres. D. Makovsky, *Making Peace with the PLO*, p. 95.

207 *Jerusalem Post*, 30/04/94.

208 A. Shlaim, 'Prelude to the Accord: Likud, Labour, and the Palestinians', *Journal of Palestine Studies*, Vol XXIII, no. 2 (Winter 1994), p. 6.

209 A. Margalit, 'The General's Main Chance', *NY Review of Books* (11/6/92), p. 12.

210 A. Shlaim, 'Prelude to the Accord', p. 11.

211 Ibid, p. 13.

212 Ibid, p. 14.

213 *Le Monde*, 28/01/93, p. 26.

214 *Le Monde*, 29/01/93, p. 5.

215 *Agence France Presse*, 12/02/93.

216 'The United States must not waver . . . in its financial, security and moral commitments to Israel.' Clinton also stated his opposition to the creation of an independent Palestinian state in address to B'nai B'rith Convention, Washington DC 09/09/92 (Transcript – Reference Centre, US Information Agency, US Embassy, London).

217 Nabil Sha'ath interview in *Journal of Palestine Studies,* Vol. XXIII, No. 1 (Autumn 1993), p. 6.

218 A. Shlaim, 'Prelude to the Accord', pp. 15–18.

219 T. Friedgut, 'Israel's Turn Toward Peace', in R. Friedman (ed.), p. 71.

220 Ibid, pp. 71–2. Ben-Gurion's views and their influence on the building of the State can be found in S. Teveth, *Ben Gurion and the Palestinian Arabs: From Peace to War* (Oxford: Oxford University Press, 1985). On the perception of 'dangers of Levantinization,' with respect to absorption of immigrants from Middle Eastern countries, see S. Swirski, *Israel: The Oriental Majority* (London: Zed Books, 1989).

221 T. Friedgut, 'Israel's Turn Toward Peace', p. 72.

222 *Time*, 29/04/96, p. 25.

223 For discussions of influences on Israeli society into accepting negotiations with the PLO, see, Y. Beilin, 'Welcome to the Peace Plan', *Midstream*, Nov. 1993, pp. 3–4; M. Oren, *Special Report: Israel-Palestinian Peace* (Jerusalem: American Jewish Committee 1993); F. Ajami, 'The Other Side of a Dream', *US News and World Report*, 13/09/93, pp. 10–11; 'Survey of Israel', *The Economist*, 22/01/94, p. 4.

224 *New York Times*, 03/08/93, p. A10.

225 *New York Times*, 02/06/93, p. A3, and see also, L. Mylroie, 'Israel in the Middle East', in G. Mahler (ed.), *Israel after Begin* (Albany NY: SUNY Press, 1990), pp. 137–54.

226 For a fuller discussion on PLO-Tunis/PLO West Bank relations; PLO-Tunis/Hamas relations, see Z. Schiff and E. Ya'ari, *Intifada: the Palestinian Uprising – Israel's Third Front* (New York: Simon and Schuster, 1991).

227 *New York Times*, 14/07/92, *Washington Post*, 14/07/92.

228 Government Press Office, *'Basic Policy Guidelines of the Rabin Government'*, Jerusalem, 15/07/92.

229 Ministry of Foreign Affairs, Information Dept., *Excerpts from Rabin Speech*, Jerusalem, 21/09/93.

230 See also J. Mendilow, 'The Israeli Election Campaign: Valence and Position Dimensions' in A. Arian and M. Shamir (eds), *The Elections in Israel – 1992* (Albany NY: SUNY Press, 1994), p. 23.

231 *New York Times*, 10/01/94.

232 For a discussion of the Soviet *aliya* of 1990–1, see S. Della Pergola, 'The Demographic Context of the Soviet Aliya,' *Jews and Jewish Topics in the Soviet Union and Eastern Europe*, 16, no. 3 (Winter 1991), pp. 41–56, particularly p. 55.

233 For summaries and discussions of the migration balance in the West Bank territories after 1967, see M. Benvenisti, *1986 Report: Demographic, Economic, Legal, Social, and Political Development* (Jerusalem: West Bank Data Base Project, 1986), p. 1.

234 F. Gottheil, 'Demographic and Economic Forces Underlying Likud's Perspective of the West Bank,' in B. Reich and G.R. Kieval (eds), *Israeli Politics in the 1990s* (Westport CT: Greenwood Press, 1991), Table 8.2, p. 137.

235 See G. Doron, 'Labour's Return to Power in Israel', *Current History*, No. 1 (Jan. 1993); C. Haberman, 'Cabinet in Israel Backs Autonomy for Palestinians', *New York Times*, 31/08/93; *JTA Bulletin*, New York, 13/09/93.

236 H. Cobban, 'Israel and the Palestinians: From Madrid to Oslo and Beyond' in R.O. Freedman (ed.), p. 107.

237 J.J. Holst, 'Reflections on the Makings of a Tenuous Peace', *Middle
East Insight* (Sept.–Oct. 1993), p. 31.

238 *Jerusalem Post*, 17/04/92.

239 D. Makovsky, *Making Peace with the PLO*, p. 86.

240 Ibid, p. 88.

241 Ibid, p. 89.

242 Ibid, pp. 90–1.

243 Interview, Haber, 19/10/93, quoted in Makovsky, p. 87.

244 Ibid, pp. 92–4.

245 Ibid, pp. 92–4.

246 Ibid, pp. 94–7.

247 Interview with Tsur, 05/12/93, quoted in Makovsky, p. 97.

248 Ibid, pp. 97–9.

249 Ibid, p. 101.

250 *Yediot Aharanot*, September 1992.

251 *US News and World Report*, 26/12/94.

252 D. Makovsky, *Making Peace with the PLO*, p. 101.

253 Interviewed by Carson Tveit, Norwegian TV, 11/09/94, quoted in
Makovsky, p. 101.

254 Speech at Tel Aviv University, 16/11/92, quoted in Makovsky, p. 110.

255 Speech delivered at Tel Aviv University, May, 1991, excerpted in
A. Klieman (ed.), *Middle East Deterrence: the Convergence of Theory and
Practice* (Tel Aviv: Tel Aviv University/*Jerusalem Post*/Westview Press, 1994).

256 Speech at the International Centre for Peace in the Middle East, Jerusalem, 17/12/92, quoted in Makovsky, p. 112.

257 *New York Times*, 14/07/92.

258 Speech at Tel Aviv University, 16/11/92, quoted in Makovsky, p. 112.

259 *New York Times*, 21/01/93.

Chapter 3

1 Avot d'R Nathan, quoted in C. Shindler, *Ploughshares into Swords? Israelis and Jews in the Shadow of the Intifada* (London: I.B. Tauris, 1991),
flyleaf.

2 E. Said, *The Politics of Dispossession* (London: Chatto and Windus, 1994),
p. 413.

3 Ministry of Foreign Affairs, *'Declaration of Principles on Interim Self-
Government Arrangements' (DoP)* (Jerusalem, 1993), p. 21.

4 Published in the *MidEast Mirror* 09/12/93.

5 Shimon Peres, FM of Israel, to Johan Jorgen Holst, FM of Norway on
Palestinian institutions in Jerusalem, dated Jerusalem, 11/10/93.

> Dear Minister Holst, I wish to confirm that the Palestinian institu-
> tions of East Jerusalem and the interests and well-being of the
> Palestinians of East Jerusalem are of great importance and will be
> preserved. Therefore all the Palestinian institutions of East Jerusa-
> lem, including the economic, social, educational, and cultural, and
> the holy Christian and Moslem places, are performing an essential

task for the Palestinian population. Needless to say, we will not hamper their activity; on the contrary, the fulfillment of this important mission is to be encouraged. Sincerely, Shimon Peres Foreign Minister of Israel.

PLO Chairman Arafat first mentioned an Israeli 'letter of assurances' on the question of Jerusalem in Johannesburg on 10/05/94, but the Israeli government repeatedly denied the existence of any secret agreements or unpublished documents (PM Rabin stated as much to the Knesset on 12/05/94). When the full text of the letter was made public following continued rumours and leaks and was published by the Israeli media on 07/06/94, the opposition accused the government of deception. Disclosure of the letter was particularly embarassing for the Israeli government given its threats, in the wake of Arafat's Johannesburg speech, to close down or curb Palestinian offices in Jerusalem, including Orient House, Palestinian delegation headquarters. FM Peres, speaking on Qol Yisrael on 07/06/94 stressed that the letter did not constitute a document, that it was written to FM Holst not Arafat explaining that the negotiations would not have continued if he had not made the commitments regarding Palestinian institutions in East Jerusalem, that he was not in the habit of publishing every letter he writes to FMs, and that the letter contained no promises for the future and that if the Palestinians conducted autonomy activities from Orient House it would be closed down. For the full text see, 'Israel's Secret Letter', *Palestine Report*, 12/06/94, p. 4; *MidEast Mirror*, 07/06/94; and see also US Assistant Secretary Pelletreau's testimony before the Europe and Middle East Subcommittee of the House Foreign Affairs Committee, 'Asst. Secretary of State Robert Pelletreau, Remarks on Jerusalem and the occupied territories, Washington DC 14/06/94', *Journal of Palestine Studies*, Vol. XXIV, No. 1 (Autumn 1994), pp. 149–151.

6   J. Singer, 'The Declaration of Principles on Interim Self-Government Arrangements – Some Legal Aspects', *Justice*, no. 1 (Winter 1994), p. 5.
7   B. Dajani, 'The September 1993 Israeli-PLO Documents: a Textual Analysis', *Journal of Palestine Studies*, Vol. XXIII, No. 3 (Spring 1994), p. 5.
8   *DoP*, p. 39.
9   B. Dajani, 'The September 1993 Israeli-PLO Documents', pp. 6–9.
10 *DoP*, p. 38.
11 J. Corbin: *Gaza First: the Secret Norway Channel to Peace Between Israel and the PLO* (London: Bloomsbury, 1994), p. 185.
12 B. Dajani, 'The September 1993 Israeli-PLO Documents', p. 6.
13 *DoP*, p. 38.
14 Ibid, p. 40.
15 B. Dajani, 'The September 1993 Israeli-PLO Documents', p. 7.
16 Institute for Palestine Studies, *The Palestinian-Israeli Peace Agreement: a Documentary Record* (Washington DC: Institute for Palestine Studies, 1993), p. 13.
17 B. Dajani, 'The September 1993 Israeli-PLO Documents', p. 7.
18 Institute for Palestine Studies, *The Palestinian-Israeli Peace Agreement*, p. 12.

19 Ibid, p. 13.
20 *DoP*, p. 38.
21 Ibid, p. 39.
22 B. Dajani, 'The September 1993 Israeli-PLO Documents', p. 8.
23 Ibid, pp. 8–9.
24 'The Oslo Agreement: an Interview with Nabil Shaath', *Journal of Palestine Studies*, Vol. XXIII, No. 1 (Autumn 1993), p. 6.
25 B. Dajani, 'The September 1993 Israeli-PLO Documents', p. 9.
26 'An Interview with Nabil Shaath', p. 9.
27 *Newsweek*, 27/09/93, pp. 18–19.
28 *Agence France Presse*, 23/05/94.
29 *Newsweek*, 27/09/93, pp. 18–19.
30 *DoP*, p. 21.
31 J. Singer, 'The Declaration of Principles', p. 4.
32 *DoP*, p. 24.
33 *Time*, 20/09/93, p. 42.
34 B. Dajani, 'The September 1993 Israeli-PLO Documents', pp. 13–17.
35 *DoP*, p. 22.
36 Institute for Palestine Studies, *The Palestinian-Israeli Peace Agreement*, p. 5.
37 B. Dajani, 'The September 1993 Israeli-PLO Documents', pp. 14–15.
38 J. Singer, 'The Declaration of Principles', pp. 5–6.
39 W. Quandt, 'Democracy', *Foreign Affairs*, Vol. 73 No. 4 (Jul./Aug. 1994), p. 2.
40 E. Said, *The Politics of Dispossession*, pp. xlii–xliv.
41 *Newsweek*, 27/09/93, p. 19.
42 J. Singer, 'The Declaration of Principles', p. 6.
43 Ibid, p. 6.
44 *DoP*, p. 22.
45 Ibid, p. 23.
46 B. Dajani, 'The September 1993 Israeli-PLO Documents', pp. 9–10.
47 Institute for Palestine Studies, *The Palestinian-Israeli Peace Agreement*, p. 2.
48 Ibid, p. 10.
49 J. Singer, 'The Declaration of Principles', pp. 6–7.
50 *DoP*, p. 22.
51 J. Singer, 'The Declaration of Principles', pp. 6–7.
52 Ibid, p. 7.
53 *DoP*, p. 22.
54 Ibid, p. 35.
55 J. Singer, 'The Declaration of Principles', p. 7.
56 Institute for Palestine Studies, *The Palestinian-Israeli Peace Agreement*, pp. 2–10.
57 *DoP*, p. 36.
58 J. Singer, 'The Declaration of Principles', pp. 7–8.
59 *DoP*, pp. 23–36.
60 Institute for Palestine Studies, *The Palestinian-Israeli Peace Agreement*, pp. 3–4.
61 J. Singer, 'The Declaration of Principles', pp. 8–9.

62 Institute for Palestine Studies, *The Palestinian-Israeli Peace Agreement*, p. 4.
63 *DoP*, p. 25.
64 Institute for Palestine Studies, *The Palestinian-Israeli Peace Agreement*, p. 3.
65 *Jerusalem Post*, 11/09/93, p. 6.
66 *Newsweek*, 20/09/93, p. 13.
67 *DoP*, p. 36.
68 Ibid, p. 25.
69 Ibid, p. 25.
70 J. Singer, 'The Declaration of Principles', pp. 8–9.
71 Ibid, pp. 8–10.
72 *DoP*, pp. 3–11.
73 Ibid, pp. 26–27.
74 Ibid, p. 26.
75 J. Singer, 'The Declaration of Principles', p. 10.
76 *Kol Israel* 30/08/93, translated in *Foreign Broadcast Information Service* (FBIS), 31/08/93, pp. 30–2.
77 Arafat speech in al-Dustur[Amman] 20/09/93 as translated in (FBIS), *Daily Report: Near East and South Asia*, 21/09/93, pp. 1–4.
78 *DoP*, p. 26.
79 J. Singer, 'The Declaration of Principles', p. 10.
80 *Jordanian Times*, 05/11/91.
81 Institute for Palestine Studies, *The Palestinian-Israeli Peace Agreement*, pp. 4–5.
82 *DoP*, pp. 21–40.
83 Institute for Palestine Studies, *The Palestinian-Israeli Peace Agreement*, pp. 1–13.
84 B. Dajani, 'The September 1993 Israeli-PLO Documents', p. 12.
85 *DoP*, pp. 29–31.
86 J. Singer, 'The Declaration of Principles', p. 11.
87 *DoP*, pp. 27–31.
88 Ibid, p. 37.
89 Ibid, p. 26.
90 J. Singer, 'The Declaration of Principles', p. 11.
91 Institute for Palestine Studies, *The Palestinian-Israeli Peace Agreement*, pp. 6–7.
92 B. Dajani, 'The September 1993 Israeli-PLO Documents', pp. 13–17.
93 Ibid, p. 15.
94 J. Singer, 'The Declaration of Principles', pp. 11–12.
95 Institute for Palestine Studies, *The Palestinian-Israeli Peace Agreement*, pp. 10–11.
96 *DoP*, pp. 29–31.
97 B. Dajani, 'The September 1993 Israeli-PLO Documents', pp. 15–16.
98 Institute for Palestine Studies, *The Palestinian-Israeli Peace Agreement*, pp. 6–7.
99 *DoP*, pp. 29–31.
100 J. Singer, 'The Declaration of Principles', p. 12.
101 Institute for Palestine Studies, *The Palestinian-Israeli Peace Agreement*, pp. 6–7.

102 *DoP*, p. 23.

103 Ibid, p. 22.

104 Institute for Palestine Studies, *The Palestinian-Israeli Peace Agreement*, pp. 6–7.

105 J. Singer, 'The Declaration of Principles', pp. 12–13.

106 *DoP*, pp. 23–4.

107 S. Avineri, 'Sidestepping Dependency', *Foreign Affairs*, Vol. 73 No. 4 (Jul./Aug. 1994), pp 12–15.

108 *DoP*, p. 30.

109 *Middle East Research and Information Project*, No. 184 (Sep./Oct. 1993).

110 E. Said, 'The *Politics of Dispossession*', p. xxxix.

111 B. Dajani, 'The September 1993 Israeli-PLO Documents', p. 10.

112 S. Avineri, 'Sidestepping Dependency', p. 13.

113 Ibid, p. 13.

114 E. Said, *The Politics of Dispossession*, p. xl.

115 S. Avineri, 'Sidestepping Dependency', p. 14.

116 *DoP*, pp. 24–32.

117 B. Dajani, 'The September 1993 Israeli-PLO Documents', p. 16.

118 *DoP*, pp. 35–36.

119 B. Dajani, 'The September 1993 Israeli-PLO Documents', p. 17.

120 *Newsweek*, 20/09/93, p. 38.

121 Ibid.

122 Ibid., p. 15.

123 *Time*, 20/09/93, p. 38.

124 *DoP*, p. 23.

125 Ibid, p. 23.

126 J. Singer, 'The Declaration of Principles', p. 13.

127 *DoP*, p. 21.

128 Institute for Palestine Studies, *The Palestinian-Israeli Peace Agreement*, p. 5.

129 B. Dajani, 'The September 1993 Israeli-PLO Documents', pp. 18–23.

130 Institute for Palestine Studies, *The Palestinian-Israeli Peace Agreement*, p. 2.

131 W. Laqueur and B. Rubin (eds), *The Israeli-Arab Reader, a Documentary History of the Middle East Conflict* (New York: Penguin, 1984), p. 365.

132 Institute for Palestine Studies, *The Palestinian-Israeli Peace Agreement*, p. 2.

133 B. Dajani, 'The September 1993 Israeli-PLO Documents', pp. 18–23.

134 *Newsweek*, 20/09/93, p. 12.

135 A. Shlaim, 'The Oslo Accord', *Journal of Palestine Studies*, Vol. XXIII, No. 3, (Spring 1994), pp. 24–40.

136 E. Said, *The Politics of Dispossession*, p. 415.

137 See W. Laqueur and B. Rubin (eds), *The Israeli-Arab Reader*, pp. 609–15; S. Touval, *The Peace Brokers, Mediators in the Arab-Israeli Conflict, 1948–1979* (Princeton NJ: Princeton University Press, 1982), pp. 284–320; and UN Security Council Resolution 242, 22/11/67 and UN Security Council Resolution 338, 21–22/10/73 in D. Peretz, *The West Bank: History, Politics, Society and Economy* (Boulder CO: Westview Press, 1986), pp. 148–50.

138 *Time*, 20/09/93, p. 40.
139 Institute for Palestine Studies, *The Palestinian-Israeli Peace Agreement*, p. 12. For PLO Charter Articles: 2 (territory); 6 (Jews), 7, 8, 9, 10, 15, 21, 25, 26, 29 and 30 (armed struggle); 19, 20, 22 and 23 (renunciation of Israel); and 28 (rejection of compromise of aims) see J. Becker, *The Rise and Fall of the PLO* (New York: St. Martin's Press, 1984), pp. 230–4.
140 *Jerusalem Post*, 11/09/93.
141 *Jerusalem Post*, 24/07/93.
142 J. Corbin, *Gaza First*, p. 39.
143 'An Interview with Nabil Shaath', p. 6.
144 J. Corbin, *Gaza First*, pp. 135–6.
145 Ibid, p. 39.
146 *Independent*, 01/09/93.
147 *International Herald Tribune*, 01/09/93.
148 E. Said, *The Politics of Dispossession*, p. xxviii.
149 Ibid, p. xxxvi.
150 Ibid, p. 416.
151 *Vanity Fair* (May 1994), p. 72.
152 *Kol Israel*, Jerusalem, 13/09/93 text of live broadcast 1555 GMT. *BBC Summary of World Broadcasts*.
153 *Jordanian TV*, text of live broadcast from the White House 13/09/93. 1605 GMT. *BBC Summary of World Broadcasts*.
154 Yasser Arafat address to US Palestinians, *MidEast Mirror*, 13/09/93.
155 *Kol Israel*, Jerusalem, 0908 GMT, 21/09/93, address to the Knesset.
156 *Yediot Aharonot*, reporting Rabin's speech to the Labour Party, 03/09/93.
157 Interview with D. Makovsky, *Jerusalem Post*, 16/10/93, p. 9.
158 *Time*, 20/09/93, p. 33.
159 *Scotland on Sunday*, 19/09/93.
160 *Time*, 13/09/93, p. 40.
161 *Time*, 20/09/93, p. 38.
162 *European Wireless File-News Alert*, USIS Information Centre, US Embassy, London, 01/09/93.
163 *Time*, 20/09/93, p. 43.
164 *Time*, 20/09/93, p. 43.
165 *Time*, 20/09/93, p. 36.
166 *International Herald Tribune*, 01/09/93.
167 *Newsweek*, 20/09/93, p. 13.
168 *Newsweek*, 20/09/93, p. 18.
168 *Newsweek*, 27/09/93, p. 14.
170 *Jerusalem Post*, 18/12/93, p. 9.
171 *Jerusalem Post*, 20/09/93, p. 6.
172 *Jerusalem Post*, 18/09/93, p. 3.
173 *Jerusalem Post*, 10/09/93, p. 2.
174 *Newsweek*, 13/09/93, p. 13.
175 Netanyahu, speech to Knesset, 20/09/93, http://www.israel-mfa.gov.il.
176 *Newsweek*, 13/09/93, p. 14.
177 *Jerusalem Post*, 18/09/93, p. 4.
178 *Jerusalem Post*, 18/09/93, p. 4.

179 *Independent on Sunday*, 19/09/93.
180 *Agence France Presse*, 04/05/94.
181 *Newsweek*, 13/09/93, p. 13.
182 *Jerusalem Post*, 18/09/93, p. 6.
183 *Guardian*, 23/09/93.
184 *Newsweek*, 13/09/93, p. 13.
185 *Jerusalem Post*, 11/09/93, p. 2.
186 J. Corbin, *Gaza First* p. 210.
187 S. Roy, 'The Seed of Chaos, and of Night: the Gaza Strip After the Agreement', *Journal of Palestine Studies*, Vol. XXIII, No. 3 (Spring 1994), p. 85.
188 *Independent*, 09/10/93.
189 *Newsweek*, 13/09/93, p. 14.
190 *MidEast Mirror*, 13/09/93.
191 'The land of Palestine will never be a product of trade.' *Le Monde*, 01/09/93.
192 *Newsweek*, 20/09/93, p. 13.
193 For discussion over discrepancy see, J. and J. Wallach, *Arafat: in the Eyes of the Beholder* (London: W.H. Allen, 1991), pp. 28–9 and A. Hart, *Arafat: a Political Biography* (Bloomington IA: Indiana University Press, 1989), p. 67.
194 *Al-Quds*, 26/09/93.
195 *Time*, 23/07/90, p. 24.
196 *Jerusalem Post*, 11/09/93, p. 2.
197 E. Said, *The Politics of Dispossession*, p. xxxiii.
198 Ibid, p. xviii.
199 Ibid, p. xxiii.
200 Ibid, p. xxvii.
201 Ibid, p. xvii.
202 Ibid, p. xxxiv.
203 Ibid, p. xxxv.
204 A. Shlaim, 'The Oslo Accord', *Journal of Palestine Studies*, Vol. XXIII, no. 3 (Spring 1994), p. 35.
205 E. Said, *The Nation* (NY), 20/09/93.
206 E. Said, *The Politics of Dispossession* (London, 1994), p. xxxv.
207 Ibid, p. xxxviii.
208 Y. Ben Efrat, 'A Deal, Not Peace', *Challenge*, Vol. IV, no. 5 (Sep.–Oct. 1993), pp. 9–10.
209 Ibid, pp. 9–10.
210 B. Dajani, 'The September 1993 Israeli-PLO Documents', pp. 22.
211 Haydar 'Abd Al-Shafi, interview, *Journal of Palestine Studies*, Vol. XXIII, no. 1 (Autumn 1993), pp. 4–15.
212 Ibid, pp. 4–15.
213 Ibid, pp. 4–15.
214 Ibid, pp. 4–15.
215 *Kol Israel*, Jerusalem, 0908 GMT, 21/09/93, *BBC Summary of World Broadcasts*.
216 *DoP*, p. 21.

Chapter 4

1   S. Leonard, *Mediation: the Book* (Evanston IL: Evanston Publishers, 1994), p. viii.

2   R. Shehadeh, 'Questions of Jurisdiction: a Legal Analysis of the Gaza-Jericho Agreement', *Journal of Palestine Studies*, Vol. XXIII, No. 4 (Summer 1994), pp. 18–25.

3   Ministry of Foreign Affairs, *'Declaration of Principles on Interim Self-Government Arrangements'* (Jerusalem, 1993), p. 24.

4   Annexe I, 'The Protocol Concerning Withdrawal of Israeli Military Forces and Security Arrangements', Ministry of Foreign Affairs, *'Agreement on the Gaza Strip and the Jericho Area'* (Jerusalem, 1994), numbered separately, pp. 1–40.

5   Article II.3 states that 'this redeployment shall constitute full implementation of Article XIII of the Declaration of Principles with regard to the Gaza Strip and the Jericho Area only.' Article XIII.1 of the DoP states that 'After the entry into force of this Declaration of Principles, and not later than the eve of elections for the Council, a redeployment of Israeli military forces in the West Bank and the Gaza Strip will take place, in addition to withdrawal of Israeli forces carried out in accordance with Article XIV.' Article XIV refers the Israeli withdrawal to Annex II, in which, Annex II.1 and 2 are the relevant sections detailing the withdrawal timetable envisaged, namely,
    1. 'The two sides will conclude and sign within two months from the date of entry into force of this Declaration of Principles, an agreement on the withdrawal of Israeli military forces from the Gaza Strip and Jericho Area,'
    2. 'Israel will implement an accelerated and scheduled withdrawal of Israeli military forces from the Gaza Strip and Jericho Area, beginning immediately with the signing of the agreement on the Gaza Strip and Jericho Area and to be completed within a period not exceeding four months after the signing of this agreement.'
    Ministry of Foreign Affairs, *'Agreement on the Gaza Strip and the Jericho Area'*, p. 3. For Article XIII, see Ministry of Foreign Affairs, *DoP*, pp. 26–30.

6   Annex IV Protocol on Economic Relations in, Ministry of Foreign Affairs, *'Agreement'*.

7   Ibid, p. 9.

8   Proclamation 2, section 3, 7 June 1967 quoted in M. Benvenisti, *The West Bank Data Project: a Survey of Israel's Policies*, (Washington DC: American Enterprise Institute, 1984), p. 37.

9   Y. Blum, 'The Missing Revisioner: Reflections on the Status of Judea and Samaria', *Israel Law Review* 3 1968, p. 292–3.

10   M. Shamgar, 'The Observance of International Law in the Administered Territories', *Israel Year Book of Human Rights*, Vol. 1 (Tel Aviv, 1971), p. 266.

11   M. Shamgar, *Military Government in the Territories*, (Jerusalem: Hebrew University, 1982), pp. 44–5.

12   The Hague, 18/10/07, the Israeli High Court confirmed the applicabil-

ity of the Hague Regulations most notably ruling in the 1979 Elon Moreh case. *Izat Mohammad Mustafa Dwaikat and Others v. Government of Israel and Others*, HCJ 390/79 (1980, 34 P.D. (1) 1), and for a fuller discussion see I. Lustick 'Israel and the West Bank after Elon Moreh: the Mechanics of *De Facto* Annexation', *Middle East Journal* (Autumn 1981), p. 557.

13 R. Shehadeh, *Occupiers' Law: Israel and the West Bank*, (Washington DC: Institute for Palestine Studies, 1985), pp. 76–7.

14 Ministry of Defence, *Orders, Proclamations and Appointments*, Vol. 19 (Israeli Government Printing Office).

15 For a further discussion of the Israeli military court system see P. Hunt, *Justice? The Military Court System in the Israeli-Occupied Territories* (Ramallah: Omar El Muktar, 1987).

16 *DoP*, p. 35.

17 See Annex III Protocol Concerning Legal Matters in Ministry of Foreign Affairs, *Agreement*, pp. 1–3.

18 For a fuller discussion of the legal order, see: W. Mallison, 'The United Nations and the National Rights of the People of Palestine'; S. Mallison, 'The Application of International Law to the Israeli Settlements in Occupied Territory'; M. Adams, 'The Universal Declaration of Human Rights and the Israeli Occupation of the West Bank and Gaza'; R. Shehadeh, 'An Analysis of the Legal Structure of Israeli Settlements in the West Bank', all in I. Abu-Lughod (ed.), *Palestinian Rights: Affirmation and Denial* (Wilmette IL: Medina Press, 1982).

19 Annex III Protocol Concerning Legal Matters in, Ministry of Foreign Affairs, *Agreement*, pp. 9–10.

20 *MidEast Mirror*, 20/04/94.

21 See Annex II Protocol Concerning Civil Affairs in, Ministry of Foreign Affairs, *Agreement*, pp. 11–12; p. 22.

22 Annex II Protocol Concerning Civil Affairs, Article II.B.22.; Article II.B.32.a.b.c.d.e. in, Ministry of Foreign Affairs, *Agreement*, pp. 11–12; 22.

23 Ministry of Foreign Affairs, *Agreement*, pp. 5–6.

24 Decree reinstating pre-1967 laws in West Bank and Gaza Strip, Tunis 20/05/94, published in *al-Quds*, 24/05/94.

25 Article VII, Ministry of Foreign Affairs, *Agreement*, p. 9.

26 *Ha'Aretz*, 23/05/94.

27 *Report Pursuant of Title VIII of Public Law 101–246 Foreign Relations Authorisation Act and Written Policy Justification Required by Section 583.b.1 of the Middle East Peace Facilitation Act of 1994, Part E of Title V of Public Law 103–236.*

28 Article IV, *DoP*, p. 22.

29 Ministry of Foreign Affairs, *Agreement*, pp. 18–19.

30 See N. Aruri, 'A New Palestinian Charter', *Journal of Palestine Studies*, Vol. XXIII, No. 4 (Summer 1994), pp. 5–17.

31 J. Singer, 'The Declaration of Principles on Interim Self-Government Arrangements – Some Legal Aspects', *Justice*, no. 1, (Winter 1994), p. 6.

32 See, PLO, 'Draft Basic Law for the National Authority in the Transitional Period', Tunis Apr. 94 in *Journal of Palestine Studies*, Vol. XXIII, No. 4 (Summer 1994), pp. 137–45.

33   See N. Aruri, 'A New Palestinian Charter', pp. 5–17.
34   Ministry of Foreign Affairs, *Agreement*, pp. 8–9.
35   Article 103 in 'Draft Basic Law for the National Authority in the Transitional Period,' Tunis April 1994, *Journal of Palestine Studies*, Vol. XXIII, No. 4 (Summer 1994), p. 145.
36   *Yediot Aharanot*, 07/09/93.
37   See Annex II.3b, *DoP*, p. 30, and Article V.1b and VI.2a and 2b in Ministry of Foreign Affairs, *Agreement*, pp. 5–7 and Article 103 in 'Draft Basic Law', p. 145.
38   See Article IX, *DoP*, p. 25, and Article VII, Ministry of Foreign Affairs, *Agreement*, pp. 8–9.
39   Article 103, 'Draft Basic Law' op. cit., p. 145.
40   Preamble, Annex IV Protocol on Economic Relations, in Ministry of Foreign Affairs, *Agreement*.
41   Article I in Annex IV Protocol on Economic Relations, ibid.
42   Article II.1, 2 and 4 in Annex IV Protocol on Economic Relations, ibid.
43   See World Bank, *Developing the Occupied Territories: an Investment in Peace*, Vol. 2: '*The Economy*' (Washington DC, 1993), p. 26.
44   *Jerusalem Post*, 23/11/88.
45   For a fuller discussion on Palestinian economic issues, see: S. Roy, *Gaza Strip: the Political Economy of De-development* (Washington DC: Institute for Palestine Studies, 1995); M. Benvenisti, *The West Bank Data Project: a Survey of Israel's Policies* (Washington DC: American Enterprise Institute, 1984); F. Gharaibeh, *The Economies of the West Bank and Gaza Strip* (Boulder CO: Westview Press, 1985); G. Abed, *The Palestinian Economy: Studies in Development under Prolonged Occupation* (London: Routledge and Chapman-Hall, 1988); G. Abed, *The Economic Viability of a Palestinian State* (Washington DC: Institute for Palestine Studies, 1990).
46   G. Aronson, *Israel, Palestinians and the Intifada: Creating Facts on the West Bank*, (Washington DC: Institute for Palestine Studies/London: Keegan Paul, 1987,1990), pp. 332–3.
47   S. Mishal and R. Aharoni, *Speaking Stones: Communiqués From the Intifada Underground* (Syracuse NY: Syracuse University Press, 1994), pp. 46–7.
48   E. Murphy, 'PNA (Economic Aspects of Oslo-Paris Protocol-Cairo Agreement)', *Middle East Report*, (May–Jun./Jul.–Aug.), pp. 35–8.
49   For a fuller discussion see *Prospects for Sustained Development of the Palestinian Economy in the West Bank and Gaza Strip*, UNCTAD, Geneva UNCTAD/DSD/SEU/2, 27/09/93.
50   IBRD/World Bank, *Emergency Assistance*, p. 17.
51   *Financial Times*, 21/10/93.
52   For a fuller discussion see Y. Aharoni, *The Israeli Economy: Dreams and Realities* (London: Routledge, 1991), especially Chapter 5, 'The Role of the Government in the Different Economic Branches of the Israeli Economy'.
53   Ministry of Foreign Affairs, *Agreement, Agence France Presse*, 28/04/94. See also E. Murphy, 'PNA', pp. 35–8.
54   *Independent*, 05/01/95; *The Economist*, 21/01/95.

55 *AFP*, 28/04/94.
56 Annex IV Protocol on Economic Relations, in Ministry of Foreign Affairs, *Agreement*.
57 Ibid.
58 Ibid.
59 *Arab Press Service*, 11/04/94, 09/04/94, and 16/04/94.
60 *Financial Times*, 11/11/94.
61 E. Murphy, 'PNA', p. 38.
62 Palestinian economist and PLO adviser in telephone conversation with the author, Jericho, 13/06/94.
63 See S. Elmusa, 'Power and Trade: the Israeli-Palestinian Economic Protocol', *Journal of Palestine Studies*, Vol. XXIV, No. 2 (Winter 1995), pp. 14–32.
64 Article III.2b in Annex IV Protocol on Economic Relations, in Ministry of Foreign Affairs, *Agreement*.
65 Article III.2a(1) and (2); 4. in Annex IV Protocol on Economic Relations, ibid.
66 Appendices I, II and III to Annex IV Protocol on Economic Relations, ibid.
67 Article III.2b in Annex IV Protocol on Economic Relations, ibid.
68 Article III.8a(i), (ii) and (iii) in Annex IV Protocol on Economic Relations, ibid.
69 Israeli Central Bureau of Statistics, *Statistical Abstract 1993* (State of Israel, 1993).
70 Article III.7 in Annex IV Protocol on Economic Relations, in Ministry of Foreign Affairs, *Agreement*.
71 See World Bank, *Developing the Occupied Territories: an Investment in Peace*, Vol. 2: 'The Economy', p. 33.
72 K. Nashashibi and O. Kanaan, 'Which Trade Arrangements for the West Bank and Gaza?' *Finance and Development*, Vol. 31, No. 3 (1994), pp. 10–13.
73 Articles VIII.11 and IX.6 in Annex IV Protocol on Economic Relations, in Ministry of Foreign Affairs, *Agreement*.
74 For a fuller discussion see: K. Nashashibi and O. Kanaan, 'Which Trade Arrangements for the West Bank and Gaza?', pp. 10–13; M. El-Jaafari, 'Non-Tariff Trade Barriers: the Case of the West Bank and Gaza Strip Agricultural Exports', *Journal of World Trade*, Vol. 5 No. 3 (1991), pp. 15–32; O. Hamad and R. Shaban, 'One-Sided Customs and Monetary Union: the Case of the West Bank and Gaza Strip under Israeli Occupation', in S. Fischer, *et al.*, (eds), *The Economics of the Middle East* (Cambridge MA, 1993), pp. 117–48.
75 See Article III, items 8–14 in Annex IV Protocol on Economic Relations, in Ministry of Foreign Affairs, *Agreement*.
76 The International Bank for Reconstruction and Development/The World Bank, *Emergency Assistance Programme for the Occupied Territories* (Washington DC, 1994); *Associated Press*, 01/05/94, 02/05/94, 03/05/94.
77 European Investment Bank, 'European Investment Bank Proposed Financing in Gaza and the West Bank' (Luxembourg 06/04/95), Facsimile Transmission-Information and Communications Department.

78   R. Brynen, 'International Aid to the West Bank and Gaza: a Primer', *Journal of Palestine Studies*, Vol. XXV, no. 2 (Winter 1996), pp. 47–8.

79   See 'Can Aid Buy Palestinian Peace?', *Financial Times*, 14/06/94, p. 23; 'PECDAR Statement', *Palestine Report*, 12/06/94, p. 10; 'No $ for Education', *Palestine Report*, 12/06/94, p. 10; 'Money for Police', *Palestine Report*, 12/06/94, p. 10; 'Officers Get Salaries', *Palestine Report*, 12/06/94, p. 7. Regarding the evolution of the aid programme see R. Brynen, 'Buying Peace? A critical assessment of international aid to the West Bank and Gaza', *Journal of Palestine Studies*, Vol. XXV, no. 3 (Spring 1996), pp. 79–92.

80   Sectoral Working Groups, spheres, shepherds and secretariats:
   • Agriculture – Spain, UNDP
   • Education – France, UNICEF
   • Employment Generation, Public Works, Sweden/UNDP, ILO
   • Environment – Netherlands/UNRWA, UNSCO
   • Health – Italy, WHO
   • Infrastructure and Housing, Germany/World Bank, UNSCO
   • Institution/Capacity Building, EU/World Bank, UNSCO
   • Police, Norway, UNSCO
   • Private Sector and Trade, US/World Bank, UNDP
   • Public Finance, US/World Bank, IMF
   • Tourism, Spain, UNDP
   • Transportation and Communications, France/UNDP, ILO.

81   'Israel, PLO, AHLC, "Tripartite Action Plan for the Palestinian Authority", Paris 02/04/95', *Journal of Palestine Studies*, Vol. XXIV, No. 4 (Summer 1995), pp. 143–6.

82   Ibid, pp. 143–6.

83   See IBRD/World Bank, *Developing the Occupied Territories: an Investment in Peace*, Vols. 1–6.

84   Donor countries and amounts pledged: Austria $1.6m; Canada $1.1m; Denmark $1.5m; European Union $2.4m; Finland $1m; Israel $2.5m; Italy $3m; Japan $5m; Netherlands $1m; Norway $2m; Sweden $1.5m; Britain $2m; USA $5m. IBRD/The World Bank, *Emergency Assistance Programme for the Occupied Territories*, p. 6.

85   Ibid, p. 6.

86   *Palestine Report*, 05/06/94, p. 16.

87   R. Brynen, 'International Aid', pp. 51–3.

88   Ibid, pp. 51–3.

89   R. Brynen, 'International Aid', pp. 51–3.

90   Nabil Sha'ath in *Reuters World Report*, 05/06/94; Yasir Arafat in *Reuters World Report*, 15/11/94.

91   See 'International Bank for Reconstruction and Development, Donor Assistance to Palestine, 1994–5, Washington DC 1995', published in *Palestine Economic Pulse* – January 1996, printed in *Journal of Palestine Studies*, Vol. XXV, no. 3 (Spring 1996), pp. 141–2.

92   R. Brynen, 'Buying Peace? A Critical Assessment of International Aid to the West Bank and Gaza', *Journal of Palestine Studies*, Vol. XXV, no. 3 (Spring 1996), pp. 79–92.

93   *New York Times*, 12/06/95; see also PLO Commitments Compliance

Act of 1993 (Public Law 101–246) and the Middle East Peace Facilitation Act of 1994 (Public Law 103–246).

94 UNDP, *1993 Compendium of External Assistance to the Occupied Palestinian Territories* (Jerusalem: R. Brynen, 1993); R. Brynen, 'Buying Peace?', pp. 80–1.

95 *Reuters World Report*, 11/09/95; *Building Blocks 1*, No. 4 (Oct./Dec. 1995).

96 R. Brynen, 'Buying Peace?', pp. 82–3.

97 UNSCO had a $3.1m budget for FY 1995, and a staff of over 30. As of July 1995, these included 14 international staff (7 professionals) and 17 local staff. It reports directly to the Secretary-General.

98 See the 'Tripartite Action Plan for the Palestinian Authority', *Journal of Palestine Studies*, Vol. XXIV, No. 4 (Summer 1995), p. 145.

99 January 1996 figures.

100 Ambassador M.K. Albright, *Letter to Ambassadors to the UN* (New York: UN Press Office, 08/08/94).

101 Article II.1. in, 'Agreement on Preparatory Transfer of Powers and Responsibilities', Erez Checkpoint Gaza, 29/08/94, in *Journal of Palestine Studies*, Vol. XXIV, No. 2 (Winter 1995), p. 110.

102 See R. Shehadeh, 'Israel stands on its legal position', *Middle East International*, 23/09/94, pp. 18–19.

103 Article VI.5 of 'Agreement on Preparatory Transfer', p. 111.

104 Article VI.3; Article VI.4; Annex II.5; Annex II.8; Annex II.9; ibid, pp. 109–26.

105 Article VIII.4; Annex II.4; ibid, p. 111; p. 116.

106 Article VII.1; .6 and .7 in ibid, p. 111. The Joint Israeli-Palestinian Liaison Committee was established under Article X of the DoP, p. 25.

107 Article IX in 'Agreement on Preparatory Transfer', pp. 112–13.

108 See also Article IX.1.a. in ibid, pp. 112.

109 See R. Shehadeh, 'Transfers and Powers: the August Agreement and the Jordanian Option', *Middle East Report* (May–June/July–August 1995), pp. 29–32.

110 Annex V.1; .3.a; 1; .3.b; .8; .3, in 'Agreement on Preparatory Transfer', pp. 120–3.

111 Annex V Appendix B, ibid, pp. 122–3.

112 Ibid, p. 113.

113 *New York Times*, 11/09/95 and 13/09/95; *Washington Post*, 11/09/95; J. Roemer, 'The Battle for Hebron', *Challenge* (Nov.–Dec. 1995 No. 34), pp. 10–11.

114 See N. Parry, 'Plea for Gazan Students', *Middle East International*, 06/10/95, pp. 19–20.

115 S. Peres, speech at the DoP signing, 13/09/93, in *DoP*, pp. 9–10.

116 Y. Rabin, speech at the DoP signing, 13/09/93, ibid, pp. 16–17.

117 'Agreement on Preparatory Transfer', p. 114.

118 *al-Hamishmar*, 15/07/94.

119 See 'Interview with Usama Halabi' in *Middle East Report*, (May–Jun./Jul.–Aug. 1995), pp. 33–4.

120 See Article VII.1. and .9; Article VIII.4; Article III.2 and 3, in 'Agreement on Preparatory Transfer', pp. 109–26.

121   See, Ministry of Foreign Affairs, *Israeli-Palestinian Interim Agreement on the West Bank and the Gaza Strip*, Washington DC 28/09/95 (Jerusalem, 1995).
122   Article XI 'Land', Items 1 and 2, ibid, p. 14.
123   See Maps 1,3,4,7, in 'Consolidated Map of the West Bank', ibid.
124   Article VII 'Guidelines for Hebron' in Annex I 'Protocol Concerning Redeployment and Security Arrangements', ibid, pp. 51–3.
125   See Article VII.3 and .4.a and 'Hebron Map No. 9'; and Article VII 'Guidelines for Hebron' in Annex I 'Protocol Concerning Redeployment and Security Arrangements', ibid, pp. 51–3.
126   See Article XIII.1, ibid, p. 16.
127   See Maps 1,3,4,7, in 'Consolidated Map of the West Bank', ibid.
128   Article XI.2.a.b, ibid, pp. 14–15.
129   See Article XIII.2.a, ibid, p. 16.
130   Article XI.2.c, ibid, p. 15.
131   Article XIII.2.b(8), ibid, p. 18.
132   Preamble, ibid, p. 6.
133   Article XXXI.5, ibid, p. 25.
134   Article III.3; .4 and Article IV, ibid, p. 10. Elections to the Palestinian Council were held on 20/01/96.
135   Article IX.1; .2; .4 and .6, ibid, pp. 12–13.
136   Ibid, p. 16.
137   Ibid, pp. 129–30.
138   Ibid, pp. 19–20.
139   Ibid, p. 8.
140   Ibid, pp. 119–20.
141   Ibid, p. 9.
142   Ibid, p. 21.
143   'Summary of the Oslo II or Taba Agreement, Washington DC, 28/09/95', Source: Israeli Embassy, Washington DC, published in 'Documentation', *Middle East Policy*, Vol. IV, No. 3 (Mar. 1996), p. 208.
144   Ministry of Foreign Affairs, *Israeli-Palestinian Interim Agreement*, p. 33.
145   Annex I, Article II.1.a, 1.b, 1.d; 3.b, 3.c, 3.d, ibid, p. 33.
146   See, R. Brynen, 'International Aid to the West Bank and Gaza: a Primer', *Journal of Palestine Studies*, Vol. XXV, No. 2 (Winter 1996), pp. 46–53; K. Shikaki, 'The Peace Process, National Reconstruction, and the Transition to Democracy in Palestine', *Journal of Palestine Studies*, Vol. XXV, No. 2 (Winter 1996), pp. 5–20.
147   For a full outline see Department of State, Conference to Support Middle East Peace, Co-Sponsors' Summary, Washington DC 01/10/93, *Journal of Palestine Studies*, Vol. XXIII, No. 2 (Winter 1994), pp 128–9.
148   Ministry of Foreign Affairs, *Israeli-Palestinian Interim Agreement*, pp. 51–3.
149   Article XXXI.6. 'Final Clauses', in Ministry of Foreign Affairs, *Israeli-Palestinian Interim Agreement*, p. 27.
150   'The Hebron Protocol in the Context of the Peace Process, 15/01/97', http://www.israel-mfa.gov.il.
151   'Guidelines of the Government of Israel, June 1996', http://www.israel-mfa.gov.il.
152   '*1996 Likud Party Platform*', http://www.israel-mfa.gov.il.

153 *'Guidelines of the Government of Israel, 16/06/96'*, http://www.israel-mfa.gov.il.
154 *New York Times*, 17/06/96; *Washington Post*, 17/06/96, 18/06/96; *Washington Times*, 17/06/96, 18/06/96; 20/06/96.
155 *MidEast Mirror*, 12/07/96.
156 *New York Times*, 03/06/96.
157 *Middle East International*, 02/08/96.
158 *MidEast Mirror*, 28/06/96; *Middle East International*, 05/07/96.
159 *New York Times*, 17/06/96; *Washington Post*, 17/07/96.
160 *New York Times*, 24/07/96; *Middle East International*, 02/08/96.
161 *Washington Post*, 10/08/96; *Middle East International*, 16/08/96.
162 *New York Times*, 30/08/96.
163 *Washington Times*, 08/06/96.
164 *New York Times*, 20/07/96.
165 *Kol Israel*, 06/06/96, 17/07/96; *Ma'ariv*, 18/07/96; *New York Times*, 06/08/96.
166 *Kol Israel*, 10/06/96,16/07/96; *New York Times*, 30/07/96, 16/08/96; *Washington Times*, 13/08/96.
167 *Palestine Report*, 23/08/96.
168 *New York Times*, 03/08/96.
169 *Middle East International*, 02/08/96.
170 *Washington Times*, 14/08/96, 15/08/96.
171 *New York Times*, 16/08/96.
172 *MidEast Mirror*, 03/06/96, 18/06/96; *New York Times*, 17/06/96; *Middle East International*, 05/07/96; *Christian Science Monitor*, 03/07/96; *MidEast Mirror*, 02/07/96.
173 Ministry of Foreign Affairs, *Israeli-Palestinian Interim Agreement*, pp. 44–5.
174 Ibid, p. 51.
175 'Agreement on the Temporary International Presence in the City of Hebron, 21/01/97', http://www.israel-mfa.gov.il; see also Ministry of Foreign Affairs, *Israeli-Palestinian Interim Agreement*, pp. 51–3.
176 *Washington Post*, 19/05/96; *MidEast Mirror*, 20/05/96.
177 *Washington Post*, 04/06/96; *Washington Times*, 04/06/96.
178 *Kol Israel*, 16/06/96.
179 Al-Haq, *Punishing a Nation: Israeli Human Rights Violations During the Palestinian Uprising Dec. 1987–Dec. 1988* (Boston MA: South End Press, 1990), p. 154.
180 Ibid, p. 156.
181 J.S. Pictet (ed.), Commentary: IV Geneva Conventions Relative to the Protection of Civilian Persons in Time of War (Geneva: ICRC, 1958), p. 333.
182 B'Tselem, 'Limitations on the Right to Demonstrate and Protest in the Territories: Information Sheet, Jan. 1992', p. 4.
183 *DoP*, p. 25.
184 Ministry of Foreign Affairs, *Israeli-Palestinian Interim Agreement*. Quotes from Annex I, Article I.3,4,6.
185 *New York Times*, 02/08/96, *Middle East International*, 16/08/96.
186 *MidEast Mirror*, 15/05/96; *Jerusalem Post International Edition*, 08/06/96; *New York Times*, 02/08/96.

187 *Kol Israel*, 16/05/96; *Washington Times*, 22/07/96; *Middle East International*, 02/08/96.

188 *Jerusalem Post International Edition*, 08/06/96.

189 *Washington Post*, 26/07/96, 27/07/96, 29/07/96; *New York Times*, 27/07/96.

190 *Kol Israel*, 25/07/96, 28/07/96.

191 *Kol Israel*, 12/08/96.

192 *New York Times*, 17/06/96; *Kol Israel*, 01/07/96.

193 *MidEast Mirror*, 11/07/96, 15/07/96; *Washington Times*, 11/07/96.

194 *New York Times*, 20/07/96.

195 *Journal of Palestine Studies*, Vol. XXVI, no. 1 (Autumn 1997), p. 118.

196 *Kol Israel*, 01/07/96.

197 *New York Times*, 02/09/96; *Washington Post*, 02/09/96.

198 *Washington Times*, 04/09/96, 05/09/96; *Middle East International*, 06/09/96.

199 *MidEast Mirror*, 09/09/96.

200 *MidEast Mirror*, 04/09/96, 05/09/96, 06/09/96, 09/09/96, 10/09/96; *Middle East International*, 20/09/96.

201 *Scotsman*, 25/09/96.

202 *New York Times*, 26/09/96, *Scotsman*, 26/09/96.

203 *Guardian*, 27/09/96; *Scotsman*, 27/09/96.

204 *The Times*, 27/09/96.

205 *Yediot Aharanot*, 27/09/96.

206 *New York Times*, 27/09/96; *Washington Post*, 27/09/96.

207 *Washington Post*, 28/09/96; *Middle East International*, 04/10/96.

208 *New York Times*, 28/09/96; *Guardian*, 28/09/96.

209 *Washington Post*, 27/09/96.

210 *Scotsman*, 28/09/96.

211 *Guardian*, 28/09/96; *New York Times*, 28/09/96; *Washington Post*, 28/09/96.

212 *Scotsman*, 30/09/96.

213 *New York Times*, 30/09/96, 01/10/96; *Middle East International*, 04/10/96.

214 *Washington Post*, 01/10/96, 02/10/96; *MidEast Mirror*, 02/10/96; *New York Times*, 02/20/96, 11/10/96; *Independent*, 03/10/96; *Middle East International*, 25/10/96.

215 *Washington Post*, 03/10/96; *Washington Times*, 03/10/96; *New York Times*, 03/10/96.

216 *Yediot Aharanot*, 05/09/96 in *http://www.israel-mfa.gov.il.gopher://israel-info.gov.il*

217 *MidEast Mirror*, 19/09/96.

218 *New York Times*, 07/10/96, 08/10/96, 17/10/96.

219 *Yediot Aharanot*, 25/10/96 in *http://www.israel-mfa.gov.il.gopher://israel-info.gov.il.*

220 *New York Times*, 07/10/96, 08/10/96.

221 *Washington Post*, 09/10/96; *New York Times*, 09/10/96; *Middle East International*, 18/10/96.

222 *Washington Times*, 16/11/96, 21/11/96.

223 *Washington Times*, 08/10/96, 09/10/96, 16/10/96.

224 *New York Times*, 16/10/96; *Washington Times*, 16/10/96.

225 *Washington Times*, 19/10/96, 22/10/96, 23/10/96; *New York Times* 22/10/96, 23/10/96.
226 *New York Times*, 24/10/96.
227 *Washington Times*, 26/10/96.
228 http://www.israel-mfa.gov.il.gopher://israel-info.gov.il.
229 *New York Times*, 29/20/96; *Washington Post*, 29/10/96; *Washington Times*, 29/10/96.
230 http://www.israel-mfa.gov.il.gopher://israel-info.gov.il.
231 *New York Times*, 08/11/96.
232 *MidEast Mirror*, 12/11/96, 13/11/96.
233 *MidEast Mirror*, 14/11/96, 15/11/96; *New York Times*, 14/11/96; *Washington Post*, 14/11/96.
234 *Washington Post*, 05/11/96, 19/11/96; *MidEast Mirror*, 04/11/96, 05/11/96.
235 *Washington Times*, 17/10/96, 18/10/96.
236 *Jerusalem Post International Edition*, 23/11/96.
237 *MidEast Mirror*, 19/11/96.
238 *Washington Times*, 19/12/96.
239 *Ma'ariv*, 22/11/96, http://www.israel-mfa.gov.il.
240 *Middle East International*, 06/12/96; *New York Times*, 26/11/96.
241 *New York Times*, 27/11/96.
242 *MidEast Mirror*, 27/11/96, 28/11/96, 29/11/96.
243 *Journal of Palestine Studies*, Vol. XXVI, no. 3 (Spring 1997), p. 170.
244 Ibid, p. 170.
245 *Washington Times*, 01/12/96, 02/12/96, 04/12/96; *New York Times*, 02/12/96; *Washington Post*, 02/12/96.
246 *Ma'ariv*, 05/12/96, http://www.israel-mfa.gov.il; *Washington Times*, 04/12/96.
247 *Kol Israel*, 26/12/96; *Jerusalem Post International Edition*, 04/01/97.
248 *Washington Post*, 06/12/96; *MidEast Mirror*, 05/12/96.
249 *Jerusalem Post International Edition*, 14/12/96.
250 *Journal of Palestine Studies*, Vol. XXVI, no. 3 (Spring 1997), p. 172.
251 *New York Times*, 12/12/96; *Middle East International*, 20/12/96, 10/01/97.
252 *New York Times*, 13/12/96; *Washington Post*, 13/12/96; *Middle East International*, 10/01/97.
253 *New York Times*, 14/12/96, 16/12/96; *Middle East International*, 20/12/96.
254 *New York Times*, 14/12/96, 16/12/96; *Middle East International*, 20/12/96.
255 *New York Times*, 16/12/96; *Middle East International*, 20/12/96; *MidEast Mirror*, 16/12/96, 17/12/96.
256 *New York Times*, 17/12/96; *Washington Post* 17/12/96; *Washington Times*, 15/12/96, 17/12/96; *MidEast Mirror*, 19/12/96.
257 *Washington Post*, 16/12/96, 17/12/96.
258 *MidEast Mirror*, 17/12/96, 18/12/96; *Washington Post*, 18/12/96.
259 *Yediot Aharanot*, 19/12/96, http://www.israel-mfa.gov.il.
260 *New York Times*, 20/12/96.
261 *Ma'ariv*, 20/12/96, http://www.israel-mfa.gov.il.
262 *Jerusalem Post International Edition*, 28/12/96.
263 *Journal of Palestine Studies*, Vol. XXVI, no. 3 (Spring 1997), p. 175.
264 *New York Times*, 22/12/96.
265 *New York Times*, 23/12/96.

266 *Washington Post*, 23/12/96; *Washington Times*, 23/12/96.
267 *Washington Times*, 24/12/96.
268 *New York Times*, 25/12/96; *Washington Times*, 25/12/96, 27/12/96; *Washington Post*, 25/12/96.
269 *New York Times*, 26/12/96; *Middle East International*, 10/01/97.
270 *Washington Times*, 28/12/96.
271 *New York Times*, 31/12/96, 01/01/97; *Washington Post*, 01/01/97.
272 *New York Times*, 02/01/97.
273 *New York Times*, 01/01/97; *Washington Post*, 01/01/97.
274 *New York Times*, 02/01/97; *Washington Post*, 02/01/97; *Middle East International*, 10/01/97.
275 *New York Times*, 03/01/97; 04/01/97; *Middle East International*, 10/01/97.
276 *New York Times*, 04/01/97.
277 *Washington Post*, 06/01/97; *Middle East International*, 10/01/97.
278 *Washington Post*, 07/01/97, 09/01/97; *New York Times*, 01/07/97.
279 *Washington Times*, 09/01/97; *Palestine Report*, 17/01/97.
280 *Washington Post*, 09/01/97, 11/01/97.
281 *Kol Israel*, 09/01/97; *New York Times*, 10/01/97.
282 *New York Times*, 12/01/97, *Washington Post*, 12/01/97.
283 *MidEast Mirror*, 13/01/97, 14/01/97; *New York Times*, 13/01/97; *Middle East International*, 24/01/97.
284 *New York Times*, 14/01/97; *Washington Post*, 14/10/97.
285 *New York Times*, 15/01/97, 17/01/97; *Middle East International*, 24/01/97.
286 *Palestine Report*, 31/01/97.
287 *Washington Post*, 15/01/97.
288 *New York Times*, 15/01/96; *Middle East International*, 07/03/97.
289 *Journal of Palestine Studies*, Vol. XXVI, no. 3 (Spring 1997), pp. 111–22.
290 'Protocol Concerning the Redeployment in Hebron, 17/01/97', http://www.israel-mfa.gov.il.
291 Christopher's letter to Arafat remains unpublished.
292 'Note for the Record', http://www.israel-mfa.gov.il.
293 *New York Times*, 17/01/97.
294 *Jerusalem Post International Edition*, 10/02/97.
295 *Journal of Palestine Studies*, Vol. XXVI, no. 3 (Spring 1997), p. 113.
296 'Protocol Concerning the Redeployment in Hebron, Main Points, 17/01/97', http://www.israel-mfa.gov.il.
297 'Protocol Concerning the Redeployment in Hebron, 17/01/97', http://www.israel-mfa.gov.il.
298 Ibid.
299 *New York Times*, 16/01/97; *Washington Post*, 16/01/97.
300 *Christian Science Monitor*, 16/01/96.
301 *Ha'Aretz*, 16/01/97, http://www.israel-mfa.gov.il.
302 *Christian Science Monitor*, 16/01/96.
303 *Near East Report*, 27/01/97.
304 The vote was 87–17, with 1 abstention and 15 absent. *New York Times*, 16/01/97, 17/01/97; *Washington Post*, 16/01/97, 17/01/97; *MidEast Mirror*, 16/01/97; *Middle East International*, 24/01/97.
305 *New York Times*, 15/01/97, 16/01/97; *Middle East International*, 24/01/97, 07/02/97.

306 *New York Times*, 04/02/97, *Washington Post*, 14/02/97.
307 L. Andoni, 'Redefining Oslo: Negotiating the Hebron Protocol', *Journal of Palestine Studies*, Vol. XXVI, no. 3 (Spring 1997), pp. 17–30.
308 *Reuters*, 15/01/97, quoted in ibid, pp. 29–30.
309 Ibid, pp. 20–1.
310 Ministry of Foreign Affairs, *Israeli-Palestinian Interim Agreement*, p. 6.
311 'Statement to the Knesset by PM Netanyahu on the Protocol Concerning Redeployment in Hebron, Jerusalem, 16/01/97', http://www.israel-mfa.gov.il.
312 See, US Special Middle East Coordinator Ross, 'Statement on Further Redeployments', Jerusalem, 15/01/97; US State Dept. Spokesman Burns, 'Statement on Further Redeployments', Washington DC, 15/01/97; Dennis Ross, 'On-the-Record Briefing on the Hebron Agreements', Washington DC, 17/01/97; *Journal of Palestine Studies*, Vol. XXVI, no. 3 (Spring 1997), pp. 140–5.
313 'Note for the Record', http://www.israel-mfa.gov.il.
314 Secretary Christopher, 'Letter of Assurance to PM Netanyahu', Washington DC, 15/01/97, http://www.israel-mfa.gov.il.
315 'Statement to the Knesset by PM Netanyahu on the Protocol Concerning Redeployment in Hebron, Jerusalem, 16/01/97', http://www.israel-mfa.gov.il.
316 'Note for the Record', http://www.israel-mfa.gov.il; Secretary Christopher, 'Letter of Assurance to PM Netanyahu', Washington DC, 15/01/97, http://www.israel-mfa.gov.il.
317 'Further Redeployments: the Next Stage of the Israeli-Palestinian Interim Agreement, Legal Aspects', 19/01/97, http://www.israel-mfa.gov.il.
318 L. Andoni, 'Redefining Oslo: Negotiating the Hebron Protocol', *Journal of Palestine Studies*, Vol. XXVI, no. 3 (Spring 1997), pp. 26–7.
319 Interview with Joel Singer, *Kol Israel*, 11/03/97, http://www.israel-mfa.gov.il.
320 'Statement to the Knesset by PM Netanyahu on the Protocol Concerning Redeployment in Hebron, Jerusalem, 16/01/97', http://www.israel-mfa.gov.il.
321 E. Said, 'The Real Meaning of the Hebron Agreement', *Journal of Palestine Studies*, Vol. XXVI, no. 3 (Spring 1997), pp. 33–5.
322 Ibid, p. 34.
323 'Interview with Azmi Bishari', *Journal of Palestine Studies*, Vol. XXVI, no. 3 (Spring 1997), p. 74.
324 Ibid, p. 67.
325 Ibid, p. 71.
326 E. Said, 'The Real Meaning', p. 36.
327 *Journal of Palestine Studies*, Vol. XXVI, no. 3 (Spring 1997), p. 113. See also Chapter 6, between notes 303 and 304.
328 *MidEast Mirror*, 23/01/97.
329 Labour and Likud Knesset Members, 'National Agreement Regarding the Negotiations on the Permanent Settlement with the Palestinians', Tel Aviv, 22/01/97, *Journal of Palestine Studies*, Vol. XXVI, no. 3 (Spring 1997), pp. 160–2.

330 *New York Times*, 26/01/97; *Washington Post*, 27/01/97; *Near East Report*, 10/02/97.

331 *Ha'Aretz*, 22/02/96; *Ofra Nequda*, July 1996; *Kol Israel*, 31/07/96, reprinted in *Journal of Palestine Studies*, Vol. XXVI, no. 1 (Autumn 1996), pp. 148–152.

332 Foundation for Middle East Peace, G. Aronson, 'A Labour-Likud Consensus on the Future of Palestine?', in *Report on Israeli Settlement in the Occupied Territories*, March 1997.

333 Foundation for Middle East Peace, G. Aronson, 'Israel's Plans for "Further redeployments"', *Report on Israeli Settlement in the Occupied Territories*, March 1997.

334 *Washington Times*, 16/01/97; *Journal of Palestine Studies*, Vol. XXVI, no. 3 (Spring 1997), p. 113.

335 *Journal of Palestine Studies*, Vol. XXVI, no. 3 (Spring 1997), p. 113.

336 S. Avineri, 'Sidestepping Dependency', *Foreign Affairs*, vol. 73, no. 4 (Jul.–Aug. 1994), pp. 12–15.

337 Preamble of the 'Protocol on Economic Relations', Annexe IV of the, Ministry of Foreign Affairs, *Agreement on the Gaza Strip and Jericho Area, Cairo, 04/05/94*.

338 J. Olmstead, 'Thwarting Palestinian Development', *Middle East Report* (Oct.–Dec. 1996), p. 11.

339 Ibid, p. 12.

340 S. Roy, 'Economic Deterioration in the Gaza Strip', *Middle East Report*, July–Sept. 1996, pp. 36–39; Local Aid Coordination Committee, *Partners in Peace*, (UN/World Bank, July 1996), p. 80.

341 M. Rabbani, 'Palestinian Authority, Israeli Rule: From Transitional to Permanent Arrangement', *Middle East Report*, Oct.–Dec. 1996, p. 22.

342 J. Olmstead, 'Thwarting Palestinian Development', p. 13.

343 M. Rabbani, 'Palestinian Authority, Israeli Rule', p. 6; *Palestine Report* 2/13, 30/08/96, p. 20/22; *Palestine Report* 2/14, 06/09/96, pp. 10–11.

Conclusion

1 *Qu'ran*: Sura 8, Al-Anfal, verses 53–61, in *The Koran*, translated by N. Dawood (London: Penguin, 1990), p. 131.

2 Ministry of Foreign Affairs, *Declaration of Principles on Interim Self-Government Arrangements* (Jerusalem, 1993), p. 21.

3 F.O. Hampson, *Nurturing Peace: Why Peace Settlements Succeed or Fail* (Washington DC: US Institute of Peace Press, 1996), p. 9.

4 Ibid, p. 9.

5 K.J. Holsti, *Peace and War, Armed Conflicts and International Order, 1648–1989* (Cambridge: Cambridge University Press, 1991), pp. 337–9.

6 Ministry of Foreign Affairs, *DoP*, p. 21.

7 M.H. Ellis, 'The Future of Israel/Palestine: Embracing the Broken Middle', *Journal of Palestine Studies*, Vol. XXVI, no. 3 (Spring 1997), p. 57.

8 M. Singer and M. Eichenwald, *Making Oslo Work* (Ramat Gan: BESA/ Jaffee Center, 1997), pp. 14–15.

9 Ibid, pp. 14–15.

10 *Middle East International*, 19/01/96, pp. 16–17.

11 *Middle East International*, 29/08/97, p. 7.

12 *Middle East International*, 19/07/96, p. 16.

13 B. Dajani, 'An Alternative to Oslo?', *Journal of Palestine Studies*, XXV, No. 4 (Summer 1996), p. 13.

14 *DoP*, p. 22.

15 *Middle East International*, 05/07/96, pp. 19–20.

16 *DoP*, p. 23.

17 Article XXIII.5. Ministry of Foreign Affairs, '*Agreement on the Gaza Strip and the Jericho Area*' (Jerusalem, 1994), p. 18 and Article XXXI.6. Ministry of Foreign Affairs, '*Israeli-Palestinian Interim Agreement on the West Bank and the Gaza Strip*' (Jerusalem, 1995), p. 27.

18 On 24/07/22; whilst Britain assumed, under the League of Nations, responsibility for Palestine, which included the territories of western Palestine and Transjordan, and the Balfour Declaration was included in the text of the mandate, however Britain was under no obligation to extend or apply the promises made in the Balfour Declaration to Transjordan. See S.H. Rolef (ed.), *Political Dictionary of the State of Israel* (Jerusalem: Jerusalem Publishing House, 1993), pp. 208–12.

19 M. Rabbani, 'Palestinian Authority, Israeli Rule: From Transitional to Permanent Arrangement', *Middle East Report* (Oct.–Dec. 1996), p. 4.

20 Ibid, p. 5.

21 See, 'Palestinian anger at corruption', *Scotsman*, 14/06/97, p. 12; and 'Rampant corruption among Palestinian officials alleged', *Scotsman*, 30/07/97, p. 11.

22 E. Said, *The Politics of Dispossession* (London: Chatto and Windus, 1994), p. 413.

23 Published in the *MidEast Mirror*, 09/12/93.

24 B. Dajani, 'An Alternative to Oslo?', p. 22.

25 Ministry of Foreign Affairs, *Declaration of Principles*, p. 21.

26 *New York Times*, 14/07/92.

27 Speech at Tel Aviv University, 16/11/92, quoted in D. Makovsky, *Making Peace with the PLO: the Rabin Government's Road to the Oslo Accords* (Boulder CO: Westview Press, 1996), p. 112.

28 *New York Times*, 21/01/93.

29 Haydar 'Abd Al-Shafi interview in *Journal of Palestine Studies*, Vol. XXIII, no. 1 (Autumn 1993), pp. 4–15.

30 Ibid, pp. 4–15.

31 Ibid, pp. 4–15.

32 Ibid, pp. 4–15.

33 *Kol Israel*, Jerusalem, 0908 GMT, 21/09/93, *BBC Summary of World Broadcasts*.

34 S. Avineri, 'Sidestepping Dependency', *Foreign Affairs*, vol. 73, no. 4 (Jul.–Aug. 1994), pp. 12–15.

35 Preamble of the 'Protocol on Economic Relations', Annex IV of the Ministry of Foreign Affairs, *Agreement on the Gaza Strip and Jericho Area*.

36 J. Olmstead, 'Thwarting Palestinian Development', *Middle East Report* (Oct.–Dec. 1996), p. 11.

37 M. Rabbani, 'Palestinian Authority, Israeli Rule', p. 22.

38 J. Olmstead, 'Thwarting Palestinian Development', p. 13.
39 M. Rabbani, 'Palestinian Authority, Israeli Rule', p. 6; *Palestine Report* 2/13, 30/08/96, p. 20/22; *Palestine Report* 2/14, 06/09/96, pp. 10–11.
40 *Time*, 15/09/97, p. 72.
41 Ibid.
42 *Scotsman*, 11/09/97, p. 14.
43 *Middle East International*, 29/08/97, p. 7.
44 *Scotsman*, 12/09/97, p. 16.
45 *Journal of Palestine Studies*, Vol. XXVI, no. 2 (Winter 1997), p. 132.
46 R.O. Freedman, 'Netanyahu's year of failure', *Middle East International*, 25/07/97, p. 18.
47 Ibid.
48 *Ha'Aretz*, 29/05/97.
49 *MidEast Mirror*, 13/02/97, 14/02/97, 17/02/97; *Washington Post*, 14/02/97, 15/02/97; *New York Times*, 14/02/97.
50 'Bibi's New Algebra: Allon plus=Oslo minus', *Challenge*, Vol. VIII, no. 4 (Jul.–Aug.), pp. 2–3.
51 *Ha'Aretz*, 30/05/97.
52 *Middle East International*, 13/06/97, p. 7.
53 Ibid, 25/07/97, p. 8.
54 Ibid, 02/05/97, p. 10.
55 Ibid, 25/07/97, pp. 6–7.
56 Ibid, 25/07/97, p. 4.
57 Ibid, 25/07/97, p. 5.
58 M. Schwartz, 'The New Jerusalem: Final Cut', *Challenge*, Vol. VIII, no. 4 (Jul.–Aug.), pp. 8–9, p. 19.
59 Senator R. Dole (Republican, Kansas) submitted the following bill to relocate the US embassy to Jerusalem by 31/05/99, with the groundbreaking to begin on 31/12/96. Rep. N. Gingrich (Republican, Georgia) submitted an identical bill (HR 1595) to the House the same day. See Senate of the United States, 104th Congress, First Session, S.770, 'Jerusalem Embassy Relocation Implementation Act of 1995', 09/05/95.
60 Suicide attacks numbers 19 and 20.
61 *Scotsman*, 31/07/97, p. 11.
62 Ibid.
63 Ibid.
64 *Challenge*, Vol. VIII, no. 4 (Jul.–Aug.), p. 22. Yitzhak Shamir, interviewed just after the election of 1992 by Ma'ariv's Yosef Harif, stated that had his party won re-election, 'I would have conducted negotiations on autonomy for ten years, and in the meantime we would have reached half a million people in Judea and Samaria.' R. Slater, *Rabin of Israel: Warrior for Peace* (New York: Harper Paperbacks, 1996), p. 505.

Index